Lappland &
the Far North
p290

Östersund &
the Bothnian Coast
p264

Uppsala &
Central Sweden
p107

Stockholm &
Around p50

Göteborg &
the Southwest
p144

The Southeast
& Gotland p221

Malmö & the
South p183

PAGE
339
SURVIVAL
GUIDE

VITAL PRACTICAL INFORMATION TO
HELP YOU HAVE A SMOOTH TRIP

Language

3 1336 09262 9600

THIS EDITION WRITTEN AND RESEARCHED BY

Becky Ohlsen,

Anna Kaminski, K Lundgren

welcome to Sweden

Swedish Style

In some ways, visiting Sweden feels like walking right into a fashion or home-decor magazine. There are no boring outfits on the streets of Stockholm, and the care with which houses and cottages and cafes and public spaces are decorated and kept up throughout the country is truly inspiring. But Swedish style is never too showy; form and function are tightly linked in this society known for valuing moderation, practicality, order, simple lines and clever designs. Whether you decide to shop for your own versions or just enjoy the scenery around you, it's hard not to fall for the cool aesthetics of this place.

Landscape

Truth be told, the best thing about Sweden is its natural beauty. But to really appreciate this country's charms, you have to leave the city behind. Whether that means sailing across an archipelago to visit an island or two, or trekking along a kingly trail through the northern wilderness, just depends on your preferences – why not try both? Hiking, camping, cycling, skiing, boating, fishing and foraging for mushrooms and berries are all major Swedish pastimes, and it's easy to get in on the action from just about any place in the country.

Frozen wastelands, cosy cottages, virgin forest, rocky islands, reindeer herders and Viking lore – Sweden has all that and mad style, too.

(left) Wood cabin in birch and aspen forest, Åre (p269)
(below) Prästgatan, Gamla Stan, Stockholm (p55)

The Sami

The northern part of Sweden is home to the indigenous Sami people, whose traditionally nomadic lifestyle is built around reindeer herding. Sami culture, including handicraft, homes and villages, methods of transport and style of cooking, is one of the many things a visitor can become immersed in while spending time in Lappland. Don't miss the chance to learn about this unique group of people: spend a night or two in a Sami reindeer camp or take a dogsledding tour. If you're on a more limited schedule, have a meal in a Sami restaurant or pick up some handmade Sami woodwork or leather goods to take home as souvenirs.

Vikings & History

Ancient rune stones poke up out of the grass in parks all over Sweden; huge stone ship settings and unobtrusive burial mounds are almost as common. Walled medieval cities and seaside fortresses are regular stops on the travellers' circuit. Viking ruins and the stories surrounding them are very much a part of the modern Swedish landscape, and it's easy to feel as if you're walking through history. In fact, you are.

Sweden

Top Experiences

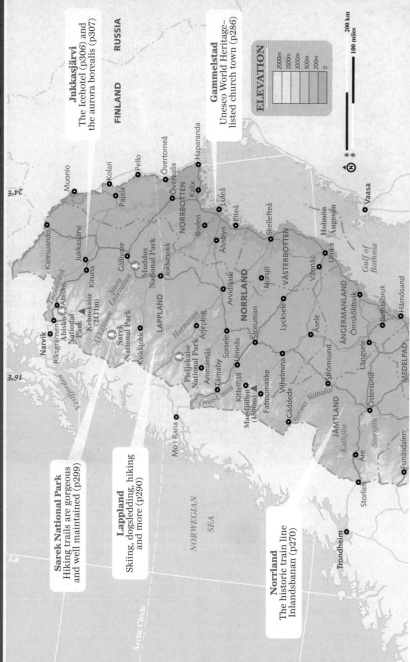

Jukkasjärvi
The Icehotel (p306) and the aurora borealis (p307)

Gammelstad
Unesco World Heritage–listed church town (p286)

Sarek National Park
Hiking trails are gorgeous and well maintained (p299)

Lappland
Skiing, dogsledding, hiking and more (p290)

Norrland
The historic train line Inlandsbanan (p270)

ELEVATION

| 2000m |
| 1500m |
| 1000m |
| 500m |
| 200m |
| 0 |

200 km
100 miles

FINLAND
RUSSIA
NORWEGIAN SEA
Gulf of Bothnia

Muonio
Kolari
Pajala
Pello
Övertorneå
Överkalix
Karesuando
Jukkasjärvi
Kiruna
Gällivare
Jokkmokk
Kalix
Haparanda
Luleå
Boden
Piteå
Narvik
Rikisgränsen
Abisko
National Park
Kebnekaise
(2111m)
Sarek
National Park
Kvikkjokk
Muddus
National Park
Stora Luleälven
Torneträsk
Akkajaure
LAPPLAND
Hornavan
Älvsbyn
Skellefteå
Arvidsjaur
Pieljekaise
National Park
Arjeplog
Ammarnäs
Tärnaby
Sorsele
Umnäs
Storuman
NORRLAND
Lycksele
Norsjö
Vännäs
VÄSTERBOTTEN
Umeå
Holmön
Ängesön
Vaasa
Mo i Rana
Kittelfjäll
Marsfjället
(1590m)
Fatmomakke
Vilhelmina
Åsele
ÅNGERMANLAND
Örnsköldsvik
Gäddede
Ströms Vattudal
Strömsund
Långsele
Gåxsjö
Bollstabruk
Härnösand
MEDELPAD
JÄMTLAND
Storsjön
Kallsjön
Östersund
Åre
Storlien
Funäsdalen
Trondheim

Arctic Circle
68°N
64°N
8°E
16°E
24°E

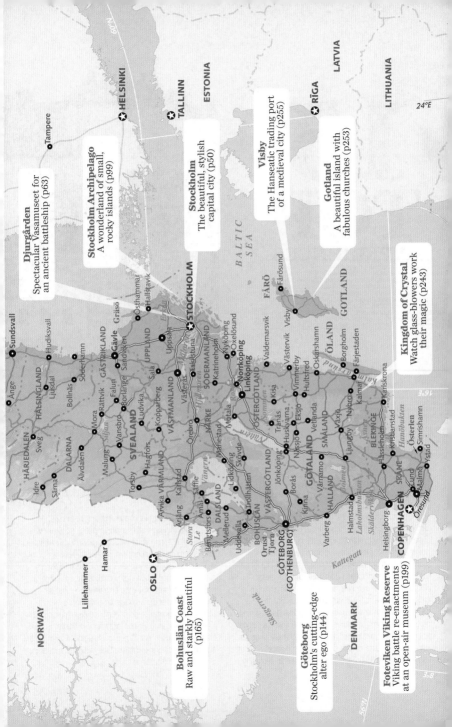

Djurgården
Spectacular Vasamuseet for an ancient battleship (p63)

Stockholm Archipelago
A wonderland of small, rocky islands (p99)

Stockholm
The beautiful, stylish capital city (p50)

Visby
The Hanseatic trading port of a medieval city (p255)

Gotland
A beautiful island with fabulous churches (p253)

Kingdom of Crystal
Watch glass-blowers work their magic (p243)

Bohuslän Coast
Raw and starkly beautiful (p165)

Göteborg
Stockholm's cutting-edge alter ego (p144)

Foteviken Viking Reserve
Viking battle re-enactments at an open-air museum (p199)

NORWAY

DENMARK

ESTONIA

LATVIA

LITHUANIA

BALTIC SEA

Kattegatt

Skagerrak

HELSINKI

TALLINN

RĪGA

OSLO

STOCKHOLM

COPENHAGEN

GÖTEBORG (GOTHENBURG)

Tampere

Hamar

Lillehammer

Sundsvall

Ånge

Hudiksvall

Ljusdal

Sveg

Idre

Särna

Älvdalen

Mora

Malung

Torsby

Arvika

Årjäng

Bengtsfors

Mellerud

Uddevalla

Orust

Tjörn

Trollhättan

Lidköping

Skövde

Kinna

Borås

Varberg

Halmstad

Helsingborg

Lund

Malmö

Ystad

Simrishamn

Kristianstad

Hässleholm

Ljungby

Växjö

Nybro

Kalmar

Karlskrona

Värnamo

Jönköping

Nässjö

Eksjö

Vetlanda

Tranås

Vimmerby

Hultsfred

Oskarshamn

Västervik

Valdemarsvik

Borgholm

Färjestaden

Huskvarna

Kisa

Linköping

Norrköping

Motala

Katrineholm

Oxelösund

Nyköping

Eskilstuna

Västerås

Sala

Örebro

Karlstad

Säffle

Åmål

Kristinehamn

Filipstad

Hagfors

Ludvika

Kopparberg

Borlänge

Falun

Rättvik

Vansbro

Sveg

Ljusdal

Bollnäs

Söderhamn

Gävle

Sandviken

Uppsala

Östhammar

Hallstavik

Södertälje

Griisö

FÅRÖ

FÅRÖ

Fårösund

Visby

GOTLAND

ÖLAND

Öresund

Hanöbukten

Kalmarsund

Laholmsbukten

Skälderviken

Österlen

SKÅNE

BLEKINGE

HALLAND

SMÅLAND

GÖTALAND

ÖSTERGÖTLAND

VÄSTERGÖTLAND

BOHUSLÄN

DALSLAND

VÄRMLAND

DALARNA

HÄRJEDALEN

HÄLSINGLAND

SVEALAND

VÄSTMANLAND

NÄRKE

SÖDERMANLAND

UPPLAND

GÄSTRIKLAND

Vänern

Vättern

Mälaren

Dalälven

Siljan

Stora Le

Klarälven

Göta

Kattegatt

Sommen

15
TOP
EXPERIENCES

Stockholm

1 The nation's capital city (p50) calls itself 'beauty on water', and it certainly doesn't disappoint in the looks department. Stockholm's many glittering waterways reflect slanted northern light onto spice-hued buildings, and the crooked cobblestone streets of Gamla Stan are magic to wander through. Besides its aesthetic virtues, Stockholm also has top-notch museums, first-class dining and all the shopping anyone could ask for. Its clean and efficient public transport, and multilingual locals, make the city a cinch to navigate, and at the end of the day you can collapse in a cushy designer hotel.

Hiking

2 Particularly in the northern reaches, Sweden has some absolutely gorgeous hiking trails, most of which are well maintained and supplied with conveniently located mountain huts along the way. The season is relatively short, but it's worth a bit of extra planning to get out into the wilderness: its natural landscape is one of Sweden's best assets. Good places to venture out to include Kungsleden and Padjelantaleden trails, Sarek National Park, and Tyresta National Park, just southeast of Stockholm. See p37 for more.
Stenshuvud National Park

Northern Delights

3 The twin phenomena that have made the north of Sweden so famous – one natural, one artificial – are both found beyond the Arctic Circle. No other natural spectacle compares to the aurora borealis (p307) – the shape-shifting lights that dance across the night sky during the Arctic winter (October to March). The Icehotel (p306), humble igloo turned ice palace, takes its inspiration from the changeable nature of the northern lights, and is re-created in a slightly different form every winter. Aurora borealis (northern lights) over Kiruna

Medieval Cities

4 It's hard to overstate the beauty of the Hanseatic port town of Visby (p255), in itself justification for making the quick ferry trip to Gotland. Inside its thick medieval walls are twisting cobblestone streets, fairy-tale cottages draped in flowers and gorgeous ruins atop hills with stunning Baltic views. The city walls, with 40-plus towers and the spectacular church ruins within, are a travel photographer's dream, and make an ideal scenic stroll. The city is also a food-lover's heaven, packed with top-notch restaurants accustomed to impressing discriminating diners.

TOP PHOTO CORPORATION/TOP PHOTO/CORBIS ©

CHRISTIAN ÅSLUND / LONELY PLANET IMAGES ©

CHRISTER FREDRIKSSON / LONELY PLANET IMAGES ©

ANDERS BLOMQVIST / LONELY PLANET IMAGES ©

Local Cuisine

5 Traditionally, basic Swedish cuisine is a humble, healthy enterprise based around fish, potatoes and preserved meat. But in recent years the country's top chefs have pushed the boundaries so that alongside classic everyday dishes such as fried herring or meatballs, or even more exotic northern fare like arctic char or reindeer with wild berries, you'll also find innovative, experimental dishes that are fiercely global in influence and ambition. Dining out in Sweden can be an adventure and an experience; see p31.
Smörgåsbord

Göteborg

6 The edgy alter ego to Stockholm's confident polish, Göteborg (p146) is a city of contrasts, with slick museums, raw industrial landscapes, pleasant parks, can-do designers and cutting-edge food. Try delectable shrimp and fish – straight off the boat or at one of the city's five Michelin-rated restaurants. There's the thrill-packed chaos of Sweden's largest theme park, the cultured quiet of its many museums, and you can't leave without window-shopping in Haga and Linné. For a unique way of getting there, jump on a boat and wander the 190km-length of the Göta Canal.

7

JONATHAN SMITH / LONELY PLANET IMAGES ©

8

GRAEME CORNWALLIS / LONELY PLANET IMAGES ©

Kingdom of Crystal

7 In the Glasriket (Kingdom of Crystal; p243) a rich mix of skill and brawn combine to produce stunning (and often practical) works of art. Watch local glass-blowers spin bubbles of molten crystal into fantastic creatures, bowls, vases and sculptures. Choose something for the mantelpiece or try blowing for yourself at the well-stocked centres in Kosta and Orrefors. For history on the 500-year-old industry there's Småland Museums (p237) in Vaxjo, and for the ultimate finish enjoy a cocktail at Kjell Engman's cobalt-blue bar at the Kosta Boda Art Hotel.

Gotland & Fårö

8 Merchants in the 12th and 13th centuries dotted the beautiful island of Gotland with fabulous churches. Today, Gotland's lovely ruins, remote beaches, idyllic bike- and horse-riding paths, peculiar rock formations, excellent restaurants and rousing summer nightlife attract visitors from all over the world. The event of the season is Medieval Week, which brings Visby's old town alive with costumes, re-enactments and markets. Film buffs and nature lovers will want to head north to visit Ingmar Bergman's stomping ground of Fårö (p261). Limestone formations, Fårö

HOLGER LEUE / LONELY PLANET IMAGES ©

ANDERS BLOMQVIST / LONELY PLANET IMAGES ©

Islands of Stockholm's Archipelago

9 Scattered between the city and the open Baltic Sea, this archipelago (p99) is a mesmerising wonderland of small rocky isles, some no more than seagull launch-pads, others studded with deep forests and fields of wildflowers. All are within easy striking distance of the city, with regular ferry services and a number of organised tours for easy island-hopping. Hostels, camping grounds and more upmarket slumber options make over-nighting a good option, as does the growing number of excellent restaurants.

Bohuslän Coast

10 Caught between sky and sea, the coast of Bohuslän (p165) is raw and starkly beautiful, its skerries thick with birds and its villages brightly painted specks among the rocks. Choose from myriad quaint seaside bolt-holes. Film star Ingrid Bergman loved pretty Fjällbacka, the bargain-hunting Norwegians flock to Strömstad, and every sailor knows Tjörn is the place to be in August for the round-island regatta. For a real taste of Swedish summer, spread your beach blanket on a smooth rock and tuck into a bag of peel-and-eat shrimp. Fjällbacka

Vikings

11 There are still real, live Vikings, and you can visit them at one of Sweden's most absorbing attractions. An evocative 'living' reconstruction of a late–Viking Age village, Foteviken Viking Reserve (p199) was built on the coast near the site of the Battle of Foteviken (1134) and contains some 22 reed-roofed houses. You can tour all of these, check out the great meeting hall, see a war catapult and buy Viking-made handicrafts. It's all admirably legit, too – the reserve's residents hold to old traditions, laws and religions. Traditional Viking boat

Winter Sports

12 Winter sports in Lappland (p290) are a major draw. To go cross-country skiing, just grab a pair of skis and step outside; for downhill sports, be it heliskiing or snowboarding, Åre (p269) is your best bet. Few pastimes are as enjoyable as rushing across the Arctic wasteland pulled by a team of dogs, the sled crunching through crisp snow – but if you want something with a motor, you can test your driving (and racing) skills on the frozen lakes instead.

ANDERS BLOMQVIST / LONELY PLANET IMAGES ©

CONTA330 / DREAMSTIME ©

COLOURIA MEDIA / ALAMY ©

GRAEME CORNWALLIS / LONELY PLANET IMAGES ©

ANDERS BLOMQVIST / LONELY PLANET IMAGES ©

Inlandsbanan

13 Take a journey through the middle of Norrland along this historic train line (summer only; p270), which passes by small mining towns, deep green forests, herds of reindeer and, if you're lucky, the occasional moose along the way. Built during the 1930s and rendered obsolete by 1992, the line has more than enough charm and historical appeal to make up for its lack of speed – you'll have plenty of time to contemplate the landscape of central Norrland, in other words. It's a beautiful, oddball means of transport, best suited to those for whom adventure trumps efficiency.

World Heritage Sweden

14 Sweden is home to an abundance of Unesco World Heritage–recognised treasures. Whether you're keen on untamed nature or humankind's mark upon it, you'll find plenty to explore here. A fine example is Gammelstad church town (p286) near Luleå – the largest in Sweden, and the medieval centre of northern Sweden. Features of the town include the stone Nederluleå church (built in 1492), which has a reredos worthy of a cathedral and choir stalls for a whole consistory, and the 424 wooden houses where the rural pioneers stayed overnight on their weekend pilgrimages.

Unesco-listed town wall, Visby

Vasamuseet

15 Sweden is filled with great museums, but Vasamuseet in Stockholm (p63) is unique: a purpose-built preservation and display case for an ancient sunken battleship. The ship was the pride of the Swedish Crown when it set out in August 1628, but pride quickly turned to embarrassment when the top-heavy ship tipped and sank to the bottom of Saltsjön, where it would wait 300 years for rescue. The museum explains – in fascinating multimedia – how it was found, retrieved and restored, why it sank in the first place, and what it all means to the Swedish people.

need to know

Currency
» Kronor (Skr)

Language
» Swedish
» Finnish
» Sami dialects

When to Go

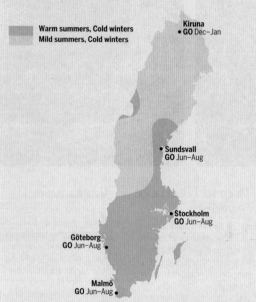

Warm summers, Cold winters
Mild summers, Cold winters

Kiruna
• GO Dec–Jan

• **Sundsvall**
GO Jun–Aug

•**Stockholm**
GO Jun–Aug

Göteborg
GO Jun–Aug •

Malmö
GO Jun–Aug •

High Season
(mid-Jun–Aug)

» Season starts at Midsummer; expect warm weather and most sights and accommodation to be open.

» Some restaurants and shops close in August as Swedes take their own holidays.

Shoulder
(Sep–Oct)

» Weather is still good, even if there's no one around to enjoy it.

» Many tourist spots are closed, but you'll have the rest all to yourself.

» Hotel rates return to normal but drop at weekends.

Low Season
(Nov–May)

» This season's many charms include outdoor adventures, the northern lights and holiday markets.

» Book accommodation and winter activities in advance.

» Many campsites and hostels close for the winter.

Your Daily Budget

Budget less than
Skr800

» Dorm bed: Skr175-250

» Great food halls and markets for self-catering

» Most museums offer student discounts plus an afternoon of free admission

Midrange
Skr800–1600

» Double in midrange hotel: Skr800-1600

» Top-end hotel prices drop in summer

» Meal at a midrange restaurant: Skr75-185

» Discount cards for large city attractions from tourist offices

Top end over
Skr1600

» Double in top-end hotel: Skr1600-2600

» Three-course dinner at a fine restaurant: Skr350-600

Money

» ATMs widely available. Credit cards accepted in most hotels and restaurants.

Visas

» Americans don't need a visa to enter Sweden; some nationalities will need a Schengen visa, good for 90 days.

Mobile Phones

» Most mobile phones work in Sweden, though often with hefty roaming fees. Pre-paid local SIM cards work in some phones.

Transport

» Traffic rules are similar to mainland Europe (drive on the right, steering wheel on the left). Buses and trains are plentiful and efficient.

Websites

» **Visit Sweden** (www. visitsweden.com) Official tourist-bureau website.

» **Swedish Institute** (www.si.se/English) Scholarly info on Swedish culture.

» **The Local** (www. thelocal.se) News from Sweden in English.

» **Smorgasbord** (www.sverigeturism. se/smorgasbord) A searchable info database.

» **Lonely Planet** (www. lonelyplanet.com/ sweden) Great for trip planning.

Exchange Rates

Australia	$1	Skr6.64
Canada	$1	Skr6.54
Europe	€1	Skr9.14
Japan	¥100	Skr8.90
UK	£1	Skr10.49
US	$1	Skr6.80

For current exchange rates see www.xe.com.

Important Numbers

Country code	☑46
International access code	☑00
International directory assistance	☑118 119
Directory assistance within Sweden	☑118 118
Emergency	☑112

Arriving in Sweden

» **Stockholm-Arlanda Airport**

» **Arlanda Express train** – every 10 to 15 minutes from 5am to 12.30am

» **Flygbuss airport shuttle** – every 10 to 15 minutes

» **Taxis** – Skr495; 30 to 45 minutes

Cheap Eats

One strategy for getting the most for your dining dollar in Sweden is to do as the locals do, and make lunch your big meal. Most restaurants, including some very exclusive, expensive places, have a daily lunch deal that's an excellent bargain and a chance to try some really nice food for less money.

Look for *dagens lunch* or *dagens rätt*; it's usually served from 11.30am to 2pm. The price typically includes a main dish, bread, salad, a beverage and coffee.

first time

Everyone needs a helping hand when they visit a country for the first time. There are phrases to learn, customs to get used to and etiquette to understand. The following section will help demystify Sweden so your first trip goes as smoothly as your fifth.

Language

Visiting Sweden is comparatively easy – even for the inexperienced – partly because most Swedes speak excellent English. Some may be reluctant to stretch their language skills, but it's usually possible to communicate the basics in English – even in remote villages.

Booking Ahead

It's a good idea to book accommodation in advance in large cities; you'll rest easier and probably also get a discounted rate. Outside of peak season (mid-June through to August) it's not necessary to book in most parts of the country, though Stockholm is an exception.

Hello.	*Hej.*	hey
I would like to book ...	*Jag skulle vilja boka ...*	yaa sku·le vil·ya boh·ka ...
a single room	*ett enkeltrum*	et en·kelt·rum
a double room	*ett dubbeltrum*	et du·belt·rum
My name is ...	*Jag heter ...*	yaa hey·ter ...
from ... to ... (date)	*från ... till ...*	frawn ... til ...
How much is it ...?	*Hur mycket kostar det ...?*	hoor mew·ket kos·tar de ...
per night	*per nat*	peyr nat
per person	*per person*	peyr peyr·shohn
Thank you (very much).	*Tack (så mycket).*	tak (saw mew·ke)

What to Pack

» Credit card and ATM card

» Drivers license

» Map to first night's accommodation

» Hat, scarf, sunglasses

» Travel plug adaptor

» Student ID if you have one (for discounts)

» Plastic utensils for impromptu picnics

What to Wear

Stockholm is a ludicrously fashionable city, as are Malmö and Göteborg. Casual dress is OK, but you'll be conspicuous at nightclubs or top-end restaurants if you don't snazz it up. From September to May, bring a hat, gloves and scarf for nights out. Many clubs enforce a coat-check; be prepared to hand over your top layer.

Outside major cities, dress for the weather. If hiking, wear waterproof shoes – the ground stays marshy well after the snow melts. Warm clothing and rain gear are crucial for outdoor activities year-round. In summer, bring a bathing suit; there are ample opportunities to take a plunge. Don't forget sunglasses and sunscreen, even in winter.

Checklist

» Check that your passport is valid

» Check airline baggage restrictions

» Decide if you need travel or car-hire insurance

» Make any necessary bookings

» Inform your credit/ debit card companies

Etiquette

Sweden is a polite society but not a casually chatty one – strangers typically won't make idle conversation while waiting in queues or riding buses, and attempts to do so may be greeted with confusion. Once the ice is broken, Swedes are helpful and happy to show off their English. You'll be asked your thoughts on their country and about current events in your own; don't be surprised if they're better-informed than you.

» Thanks
The most commonly uttered word in Swedish is *tack* – it means thanks, but also please, and it's applied liberally in all situations. When in doubt, throw it out there.

» Excuse Me
To get someone's attention, say *ursäkta mig* (excuse me). If you step on their foot, say *förlåt* (forgive me) instead.

» Greetings
The catch-all greeting is *hej*. For someone you know well, say *tjena (sheh-na)*.

Tipping

» When to Tip
Tipping is rare and usually reserved for great service.

» Restaurants & Bars
Tipping is not expected except with an evening meal – service is figured into the bill, but a small gratuity (10 to 15%) for good service at dinner is customary.

» Taxis
Tipping is optional, but most people round up the bill to the nearest Skr10.

» Hotels
Service is figured into the bill, but a small tip (around Skr10 a day) for housekeeping is appreciated.

Money

In large cities, credit and debit cards can be used almost everywhere, and ATMs can be found every few blocks. Visa and MasterCard work everywhere, while American Express and Discover are less widely accepted. The default system uses cards with microchips; if your card has no chip or pin, ask the clerk to swipe it.

In small towns and rural areas, shops, restaurants, hostels and campgrounds are more likely to be cash-only. Changing cash is convenient but relatively expensive, depending on the amount you change.

Keep a Skr5 coin with you, as many public restrooms charge a Skr5 fee (even in petrol stations and department stores).

if you like...

Hiking

Sweden is an awesome place to hike, with its springy, well-kept trails, and its excellent network of huts and campgrounds. The season is short but the list of options is long, from barren wastelands to mountain treks, deep forests to placid fields.

Kungsleden The royal trail, a popular, accessible northern route (p308)

Höga Kusten Leden Awesome views from high coastal cliffs (p282)

Sarek National Park Challenging terrain for expert hikers (p299)

Skåneleden Lush path along Sweden's southern coast (p207)

Arctic Trail An 800km joint development of Sweden, Norway and Finland, entirely above the Arctic Circle (p37)

Kebnekaise Sweden's tallest peak is a highlight of hiking in Norrland (p305)

European long distance paths E1 and E6 run from Varberg to Grövelsjön (1200km) and from Malmö to Norrtälje (1400km) (p37)

Finnskogleden A 240km-long route along the border between Norway and the Värmland region in Sweden (p37)

Alpine Adventures

Norrland in winter is home to all manner of exciting cold-weather activities, from cross-country and downhill skiing to dogsledding to hanging out with herds of reindeer.

Åre A fabulous ski resort in a chic little town (p269)

Riksgränsen Primarily for expert skiers, this resort nestles right up against the Norwegian border (p308)

Tärnaby A fun town at the edge of a gorgeous lake, with a growing ski resort that's more laid-back than its neighbour at Hemavan (p293)

Båtsuoj Sami Camp If you've never had a chance to meet a reindeer before... (p296)

Jokkmokk Winter Market Apart from great shopping and street theatre, this huge market also features reindeer races (p298)

Abisko At this well-equipped national park you can go hiking, snowmobiling, dogsledding, or just kick back and gaze at the northern lights (p306)

Small Villages

The country is dotted with tiny masterpieces: little red cottages, cobblestoned town squares or windswept fishing huts clinging to the coastline. Discover your own, or hightail it to any of these.

Eksjö One of Sweden's best-preserved wooden towns (p236)

Vadstena A rewarding end for pilgrims visiting St Birgitta (p230)

Skanör Idyllic summer beach town (p200)

Höga Kusten The tiny fishing villages along the High Coast are to die for (p280)

Tällberg A lovely collection of red-painted wooden buildings set along a twisty scenic road (p137)

Trosa An easily accessible, completely adorable harbour town (p67)

Nora Not only gorgeous, but also filled with no shortage of ice cream (p123)

Sigtuna Within easy reach of Stockholm and Uppsala, this adorable village boasts numerous church ruins and Sweden's oldest main street (p103)

Vaxholm A photogenic harbour and famous fortress entice flocks of visitors to this archipelago town (p98)

GRAEME CORNWALLIS / LONELY PLANET IMAGES ©

» View of Lapporten from Abisko National Park (p306)

Cycling

Sweden is very friendly to the two-wheeled set. Not only are there well marked bicycle lanes, but most towns have a place where visitors can rent or borrow a bicycle to ride around. Plus, not only is cycling a greener mode of transport, it forces you to slow the pace and really take in your surroundings.

Gotland Wide bike paths and sea views make for lovely cycling (p253)

Öland Cycle between farmers markets and nature reserves on this peaceful island (p249)

Göta Canal Cycle alongside the locks en route to Vättern (p235)

Örebro Everyone in this college town rides a bicycle (p124)

Stockholm Sure, car traffic can be hectic here, but the shared bike program and lots of new bike paths make it cycle-friendly (p50)

Åre The bike park here delivers an amped-up cycling experience (p269)

Boat Trips

Don't forget, this is the land of 100,000 lakes (maybe even a few more). You haven't really done Sweden until you've gone out onto the water. Whether you hire a canoe yourself or book a tour, go ahead and get your feet wet.

Stockholm Archipelago This is what Stockholmers wish they had time to do on holiday (p99)

Göta Canal Float between locks and lakes on a tour of this peaceful canal (p235)

Bohuslän Ferries Hop from ferry to ferry in Bohuslän (p165)

Luleå Archipelago The northern archipelago is well worth exploration (p286)

Tiveden National Park Hire a canoe at any number of places here and explore the wilderness (p127)

Under the Bridges of Stockholm Strömma Kanalbolaget (www.stromma.se) offers a number of good tours of Stockholm's waterways, including this two-hour canal tour (p98)

Fine Dining

Sweden has its act together foodwise. Given the number of superstar chefs in the media, the focus on organic and sustainably procured ingredients, and a devotion to great atmosphere, it's no surprise there are some fantastic places to fill up.

Mathias Dahlgren The celebrated chef's double-Michelin restaurant fits right in at the uber-classy Grand Hôtel (p82)

Kungsholmen Another celebrity chef, Melker Andersson, runs this hip waterside joint (p86)

Wasa Allé Tuck into gourmet Swedish slow cuisine (p157)

Fond Sample one of Göteborg's five Michelin-rated restaurants (p157)

Krakas Krog Delicate local food on picture-perfect Gotland (p261)

Sånninggården A foodie beacon serving game in classic Lappland style (p294)

Länsmansgården A historic building near Sunne that appears in Selma Lagerlöf's *Gösta Berling's Saga*, and a picturesque place for a fine traditionally Swedish lunch (p131)

If you like...dogsledding, Kiruna, Abisko and Jokkmokk in Norrland are great places to try this rugged, thrilling method of transportation.

Swedish Design

Gorge yourself on the sleek and spartan, the rounded corner, the clever tool, the vividly printed fabric and the inventive glasswork that define Swedish design – from established artists now part of the design canon to new talents making a name for themselves.

Nationalmuseusm An object lesson, literally, in the evolution of Swedish design – a permanent exhibit shows key examples of innovatively designed items arranged in chronological order (p60)

Svenskt Tenn Home of Josef Frank's signature fabrics and other iconic pieces (p91)

DesignTorget Great selection of clever gadgets and decor from up-and-coming designers (p91)

Velour Chic jeans, knits and jumpsuits from a savvy Göteborg designer (p160)

Kosta Outlets Stock up on gorgeous glass in the heart of the Glasriket (p243)

Shopping

Shopping in Sweden is easy to do – almost too easy. Look for glass and crystal, authentic handicrafts marked with the *slöjd* (handicraft) sticker, fine linens, chic designer clothing and funky gadgets Ikea doesn't have yet.

Stockholm's shopping streets The pedestrian thoroughfares of Biblioteksgatan, Drottninggatan and Västarlånggatan are retail heaven (p90)

Svensk Slöjd Authentic handicrafts and high-quality gifts made by Swedish handicraft artists who are part of a strictly regulated crafts guild (p91)

DEM Collective Scandi-cool combined with free-trade materials (p160)

Prickig Katt Retro hats and vintage frocks at a hipster Göteborg boutique (p160)

Kvinnfolki Gotland's woollens, truffles and stones reshaped with loving artistry (p259)

Formargruppen Cooperative designer shop and gallery in Malmö (p194)

Sami Duodji Gallery and shop with authentic Sami handicraft (p297)

Sami Culture

The Sami, Sweden's indigenous population, have a rich, often embattled culture that fascinates visitors and locals alike. There are many opportunities to learn more, be it a visit to an absorbing museum or an overnight (or longer) stay in a traditional Sami reindeer camp.

Ájtte Museum A stellar museum presenting the history and current status of the Sami people in Sweden (p297)

Båtsuoj Sami Camp Stay overnight with traditional reindeer herders at this forest camp (p296)

Visit Sápmi A gateway for visitors interested in learning about Sami culture (p300)

Arjeplog Silvermuseet This museum in a former nomad school has a stunning collection of Sami silver objects (p296)

Nutti Sami Siida Take a reindeer-sled excursion with this ecotourism expert (p302)

month by month

January

This is the peak of winter in Sweden, with freezing temperatures and snow in most regions. Winter sports activities draw the crowds.

Kiruna Snow Festival

Based around a snow-sculpting competition, this annual fest (www.kirunalapland.se) began in 1985 to celebrate a rocket launch and now draws artists from all over to carve ever more elaborate and beautiful shapes out of the snow. It also features reindeer-sled racing, with Sami traditions emphasised.

Göteborg International Film Festival

Sweden's 'second city' hosts an annual film festival that draws some 200,000 visitors each year, with short films, documentaries and features, plus seminars and parties.

February

It's still peak winter weather, with snow sports being the main draw.

Jokkmokk Winter Market

A large annual gathering of Sami people from across Scandinavia, this festival (www.jokkmokksmarknad.se) includes a market, meetings, craft shows, performances and more.

Vasaloppet

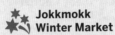

This huge annual ski race (www.vasaloppet.se) between Sälen and Mora, started in 1922, commemorates Gustav Vasa's history-making flight on skis in 1521; it has grown into a week-long ski fest and celebration with several different races: short, gruelling or just for fun.

March

The winter season begins to wind down in the southern half of the country, though winter sports are still going strong in Norrland.

House of Metal

An annual hardcore music festival (www.house-ofmetal.se) in Umeå, at Folkets Hus. House of Metal features big-name artists as well as local bands.

Liljevalchs Spring Salon

The Djurgården gallery's annual springtime launch of the new year in art brings to the fore up-and-coming artists as well as new work from established names.

April

The weather's still cold in April but the days are longer and brighter.

Walpurgis Night

This public holiday, a pagan holdover that's partly to celebrate the arrival of spring, involves lighting huge bonfires, singing songs and forming parades; parties are biggest in the student towns, such as Uppsala.

May

Spring tourism starts to pick up as the days get longer and warmer; summer-only hostels and campgrounds start to open for the season.

May Day

Traditionally a workers' marching day in

industrial towns and cities, it's observed with labour-movement events, brass bands and marches.

June

Midway through June is the official peak of summer. Weather is perfect, hotel rates are low and travelling is effortless.

 ### Sweden Rock Festival

This large annual three-day summer rock festival is held in Sölvesborg (www.swedenrock.com) and features huge metal and hard-rock bands like Whitesnake, Joan Jett & the Blackhearts, Judas Priest and Ozzy Osbourne, with camping available on site.

 ### Swedish National Day

Known merely as Swedish Flag Day until 1983, the public holiday (6 June) commemorates the crowning in 1523 of King Gustav Vasa and Sweden's independence from the Danish-led Kalmar Union.

 ### Smaka På Stockholm

Taste samples from some of Stockholm's top kitchens in manageable quantities, and watch cooking duels at this week-long annual food fest (www.smakapastockholm. se) in Kungsträdgården.

 ### Midsummer

Arguably the most important Swedish holiday, Midsummer starts on the first Friday after 21 June with the raising of the maypole, followed by lots of singing, dancing, drinking

and the mass consumption of pickled herring with potatoes and sour cream. The next day is primarily spent recovering from the long night. Whenever possible, the holiday stretches out into at least a three-day weekend; be aware that many tourist facilities (museums, boat tours) are closed, along with several restaurants and shops.

 ### Öjeby Church Market

This market near Piteå (www.pitea.se) attracts some 20,000 visitors each year.

July

July is peak summer tourism season: the weather is fine, attractions are open and everyone is cheerful.

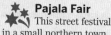 ### Piteå Dansar

One of Sweden's biggest street festivals, the PDOL (www.pdol.se) draws some 120,000 visitors for music, dance, crafts, food and a carnival.

 ### Pajala Fair

This street festival in a small northern town (www.pajala.se) in early July draws 40,000 people for crafts, food, folk music and more.

 ### Stockholm Jazz Festival

Held on the island of Skeppsholmen, this internationally known jazz fest (www.stockholmjazz. com) brings artists from all over, including big names like Van Morrison and Mary J Blige; evening jam sessions at famed

Stockholm jazz club Fasching are a highlight.

 ### Musik vid Siljan

A midsummer music festival (www. musikvidsiljan.se), it takes place in the towns around Lake Siljan, and includes chamber, jazz and folk music; tourist offices for Mora, Leksand and Rättvik will have up-to-date schedules.

 ### Rättvik Folklore Festival

An annual celebration of international folk dance (www.folklore.se) on the shores of Lake Siljan.

 ### Storsjöyran

Östersjön hosts this annual three-day music festival (www.storsjoyran. se), which features international artists and crowds of up to 55,000 people.

August

The weather is as nice as in July, but many Swedes (especially Stockholmers) are out of town on their own holidays, and some restaurants are closed for most of August.

 ### Classic Car Week

Rättvik hosts this gathering of motorheads and the objects of their devotion (www.classiccarweek.com, in Swedish); there are monster truck battles, drive-in movies, laid-back cruising and lots of chrome.

 ### Visby Medieval Week

Find yourself an actual knight in shining armour

at this immensely popular annual fest (www.medel-tidsveckan.se), which puts Gotland's medieval city to great use with a market, games, costumes and a huge banquet. Be sure to reserve accommodation and transport to the island in advance.

Dalhalla

The stunning Dalhalla venue in Rättvik hosts an opera festival (www.dalhalla.se) with the awesome acoustics of the venue allowing for mostly unamplified performances.

Stockholm Pride

This annual parade and festival (www.stockholm-pride.org/en) is dedicated to creating an atmosphere of freedom and support for gay, lesbian, bisexual and transgender people.

Way Out West

Göteborg hosts this music fest (www.way-outwest.se) has featured the likes of Robyn, Prince, Kanye West, Fleet Foxes, the Hives and Empire of the Sun.

Kräftskivor (Crayfish Parties)

Swedes celebrate the end of summer by wearing bibs and party hats while eating lots of crayfish and drinking *snaps* (usually aquavit). In the north, parallel parties take place but with *surströmming* (strong-smelling fermented Baltic herring), while in the south similar gatherings in September feast on eels and *snaps*.

(above) Stockholm Pride (p74)
(below) Raising a Midsummer maypole at the Hembygdsgård Gammelgård open-air museum in Rättvik (p139)

September

Days begin to grow shorter and cooler, and many seasonal tourist facilities (campgrounds, some hostels, outdoor cafes) close for the season, but the weather can still be gorgeous.

Tjejmilen
Sweden's biggest sporting event for women (www.tjejmilen.se) features 24,000 runners of all ages in a race that begins from Gärdet in Stockholm.

Göteborg International Book Fair
Scandinavia's biggest book fair, this event (www.bok-bibliotek.se) brings together authors, readers, publishers, agents, teachers, librarians and the media.

Öland's Harvest Festival
This celebration of the local harvest (www.skordefest.nu) takes place each autumn in Borgholm, Öland.

Lidingöloppet
Enshrined in the *Guinness World Records* as the world's largest terrain race, this annual event (www.lidingoloppet.se) takes place on Lidingö, just northeast of Stockholm.

October

Though the travel infrastructure can feel largely abandoned, autumn is a lovely time of year in Sweden, and you'll essentially have the place to yourself.

Stockholm Open
A huge event among the international tennis crowd, this annual tournament (www.ifstockholmopen.se) draws its share of top-100 male players from all over the world.

Hem & Villa
This is the country's largest interior decor and design fair, drawing more than 60,000 visitors eager to check out new furniture trends, textiles, lighting schemes, and arts and crafts. The event (www.hemmassan.se), held in Stockholm, includes displays, lectures and – of course – shopping.

Uppsala Short Film Festival
For the past 30 years, this annual film festival (www.shortfilmfestival.com) has screened more than 300 short films a year at four cinemas in central Uppsala.

Umeå International Jazz Festival
International jazz musicians have filled Umeå's stages for this annual event (www.umeajazzfestival.se) for more than 40 years running.

November

Grey winter is here, but the holiday season has yet to begin;w November can be a little tough unless you're a film nerd or a winter-sports enthusiast. In which case, you're golden.

Stockholm International Film Festival
Screenings of new international and independent films, director talks and discussion panels draw cinephiles to this important annual festival (www.stockholmfilmfestival.se); tickets go quickly, so book early if you're interested.

Stockholm International Horse Show
This annual horse show (www.stockholmhorseshow.com) advertises itself as the largest indoor equestrian event in the world. It takes place in the Globe in southern Stockholm.

Gamla Stan Christmas Market
Usually opening in mid-November, this adorable, softly glowing market (www.stortorgetsjulmarknad.com) in Gamla Stan's main square (Stortorget) can almost singlehandedly lift the spirits on a cold winter night. Shop for handicrafts and delicacies, or just wander with a mug of cocoa and a saffron bun.

St Martin's Day
In Sweden, the 10th of November is St Martin's Eve, and, regardless of how the tradition originally began, these days the holiday is all about the goose. Ideally that is the traditional dinner of roasted goose, on your plate.

December

The month in which Sweden cheerfully rages against the dying of the light, aided by hot spiced wine, delicious seasonal treats and loads of candles everywhere.

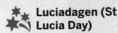

Luciadagen (St Lucia Day)

On 13 December, wearing a crown of lit candles, 'Lucia' leads a white-clad choir in traditional singing in a celebration that seems to merge the folk tradition of the longest night and the story of St Lucia of Syracuse.

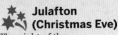

Julafton (Christmas Eve)

The night of the smörgåsbord and the arrival of *jultomten* (the Christmas gnome), carrying a sack of gifts, this is the biggest celebration at Christmas time.

itineraries

Whether you've got six days or 60, these itineraries provide a starting point for the trip of a lifetime. Want more inspiration? Head online to lonelyplanet. com/thorntree to chat with other travellers.

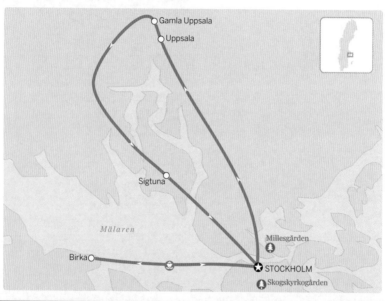

One Week
Stockholm & its Surrounds

Start in **Stockholm**, where mandatory attractions include the Kungliga Slottet (Royal Palace), Gamla Stan (the lovely Old Town) and Skansen (a family-friendly open-air museum that is basically Sweden in miniature). You can cover those in a couple of days, which leaves an evening for enjoying some of the capital city's nightlife in Södermalm – try the clubs and bars in the SoFo district. On day three, take a boat tour to the ancient settlement on **Birka**; it's an all-day affair that gets you both history and scenery.

The next day, check out the spectacular cathedral and palace at **Uppsala** and delve into early Swedish history via the burial mounds and museum at **Gamla Uppsala**. On the way back, explore the village of **Sigtuna**, with its old-fashioned buildings and atmospheric church ruins. The following day, visit the sculpture museum at **Millesgården**, or make a pilgrimage to Greta Garbo's memorial at the Unesco-recognised cemetery **Skogskyrkogården**. Finally, take an hour-long boat tour of Stockholm's canals for a cool new perspective on the city, then tick off any of the city's museums you've been meaning to get to.

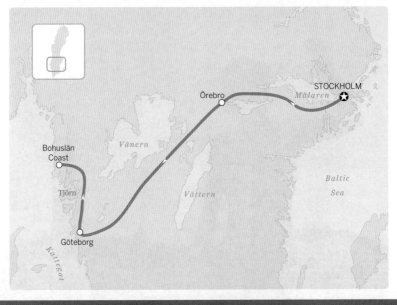

Two Weeks
Stockholm & Göteborg

You can see a good stretch of Sweden in the space of two weeks. To get a sense of the things that make Sweden so quintessentially Swedish, we suggest spending the first week of your trip as outlined in the Stockholm and its Surrounds itinerary, exploring the sights in and around the stylish capital city, **Stockholm**. Then, make your way west toward Göteborg, Sweden's so-called 'second city', a worthy destination in its own right. Take your time getting there – you'll want to stop along the way to visit the lively college town of **Örebro**, tour its moat-protected castle and wander through the nearby Stadsparken, one of Sweden's most beautiful city parks.

Continue heading southwest, between the huge inland lakes Vänern and Vättern, and into **Göteborg**. This engaging city is easily worth a few days of exploration – visit its theme park and museums, notably the art and design collection at Röhsska Museet, but more importantly, do some Michelin-star dining and trend-focused shopping, perhaps in the attractive and well-preserved Haga district, Göteborg's oldest suburb. Take the whole clan along for the rides at the huge amusement park that is Liseberg, one of Sweden's most visited tourist attractions. Pick up some picnic supplies at Feskekörka, a fish market shaped like a church, or settle in for some locally sourced, gourmet 'slow food' at chef Mats Nordström's Wasa Allé. And don't miss the cool, retrofitted art space at Röda Sten, a gritty power-station-turned-gallery that exhibits some of the edgiest artwork around and has a wild range of evening events to boot.

Spend the rest of week two exploring the craggy coastline and rickety fishing villages of the **Bohuslän Coast**. Check out the Bronze Age rock carvings on the Tanum plain, then have a go at making sense of them with the help of the Vitlycke Museum. Cross the bridge from Stenungsund (on the Swedish mainland) to the island of **Tjörn**, a favourite of landscape artists and sailors alike. Wander the tiny villages admiring sailboats, have a summer barbecue on the deck of a youth hostel, or make a meal of smoked fish from Åstols Rökeri.

JEAN-PIERRE LESCOURRET / LONELY PLANET IMAGES ©

KRIS DAVIDSON / LONELY PLANET IMAGES ©

» (above) Statue near Stadshuset, Stockholm (p61)
» (left) Reindeer migrating to Lappland mountains

Legend:
- Stockholm to Kiruna
- Stockholm to Malmö

Jukkasjärvi
Kiruna
Gällivare
Jokkmokk
Arvidsjaur
Luleå
Umeå
Höga Kusten
Sundsvall
Mora
Rättvik
Lake Siljan
Leksand
STOCKHOLM
Marstrand
Brännö   Göteborg
Varberg
Lund
Malmö
ATLANTIC OCEAN
NORWAY
FINLAND
RUSSIA
ESTONIA
Fårö
LATVIA
Öland
LITHUANIA
BELARUS
RUSSIA
POLAND
UNITED KINGDOM
NORTH SEA
DENMARK
GERMANY

Two Weeks
Stockholm to Malmö

> Start your journey in **Stockholm**. The wonderful capital city will hold your attention for as many days as you can devote to it. (See the previous Stockholm itinerary for some ideas.) When it's time to move on, head toward dynamic **Göteborg**, and its surrounding coastline, whose charms include pretty fishing villages and spectacular, otherworldly light. Make your way south along the coast, stopping to dodge mopeds in beachy **Brännö** and enjoy the eye candy in upscale **Marstrand**.

Further south, stop in at **Varberg** and see the preserved body of Bocksten Man displayed in its medieval fortress. Continue south to the brainy and beautiful university town of **Lund**, Sweden's second-oldest town, with a striking cathedral and the great cafe culture that goes along with a large student population. Just south of here is **Malmö**, a diverse and lively city that sometimes feels more a part of neighbouring Denmark – no surprise really, as Copenhagen is only a bridge away. If you have extra time in Malmö, stop by the Foteviken Viking Reserve, a living reconstruction of a Viking-era village.

Two Weeks
Stockholm to Kiruna

> The journey from **Stockholm** to the northernmost city in Sweden actually merits the term epic. You'll cross vast stretches that seem to be populated by nothing but reindeer. You'll also see the fertile, forested breadbasket of the country. Start out heading toward the lovely **Lake Siljan** region, home to the carved wooden Dala horses and filled with red-painted huts and hobbitlike villages. You can easily spend a couple of days here hopping between **Mora**, **Rättvik** and **Leksand**.

Continue northeast toward **Sundsvall** and **Höga Kusten** region for glorious scenery and cliffside hiking. From there, it's quite an easy gulf-side journey up to the cool urban centres of Norrland: **Umeå** and **Luleå**, each with its own charm. From Luleå, jag inland to **Arvidsjaur**, where you can choose from a range of outdoor adventures, and then on to **Jokkmokk**, whose Sami museum, Ájtte, mustn't be missed. (If your trip coincides with the Jokkmokk Winter Market, be sure to allow time for exploring it.) From Jokkmokk, you can either bus northward or catch the historic Inlandsbanan railway to **Gällivare**, its northern terminus. Continue to **Kiruna**, last outpost of the north, and its neighbour **Jukkasjärvi**, home of the famed Icehotel.

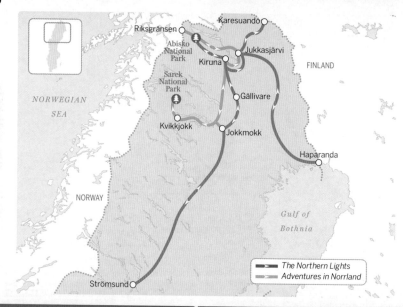

The Northern Lights
Adventures in Norrland

Five to Seven Days
The Northern Lights

Start at the top: fly into **Kiruna**. This northern outpost is a great base for taking in some of the world's last truly wild landscapes. Start with a hike in the easily accessible but vast and untamed **Abisko National Park**, just a short train ride from Kiruna. In Abisko you can also take a chairlift to a viewing station and see the northern lights (aurora borealis), roughly between October and March depending on weather. (In parts of Lappland from late May to July you can see the midnight sun.) If you're here during summer, take a scenic ride on the Inlandsbanan railway from **Gällivare** toward **Strömsund** and back. You'll cross the Arctic Circle around **Jokkmokk**, which is a Sami cultural centre and home to the inspiring Ájtte Museum.

Returning to the Kiruna area, zip over to **Jukkasjärvi** for a look at the famed Icehotel and a chance to visit a Sami reindeer camp. Shoppers and golfers might take a side trip to **Haparanda**, which excels at both pursuits. And completists might opt for a visit to **Karesuando**, the northernmost village in Sweden.

Two Weeks
Adventures in Norrland

Spend some time in **Kiruna**, stocking up on supplies and getting accustomed to the pace of life in the far north. Don't leave town without making your way to nearby **Jukkasjärvi** to see the oldest church in Lappland and tour a Sami reindeer yard. When you're ready, hop the train toward Norway to reach **Abisko National Park**. There's fantastic, easily accessible hiking here, plus a luxurious STF mountain lodge where you can stay and replenish your supplies. This is also a good place to try dogsledding, an ace way to get around in the northern winters. Cross-country skiers can start here to glide along the Kungsleden trail – which doubles as one of Sweden's best places for long treks in summer. A little further north is **Riksgränsen**, where Alpine skiers will find a large resort with plenty of expert-only runs (and outdoor hot tubs).

For more hiking, head to **Kvikkjokk**, gateway to the rugged and challenging **Sarek National Park**. If you're hooked on dogsledding and want more of that, head to **Jokkmokk**, where you can book a tour from an hour or two to a whole week.

Eat & Drink Like a Local

Foodie Gems

If you're interested in the best of Swedish food, you shouldn't miss the following places:

Mathias Dahlgren (p82) Does obscenely fine things to local produce at what has become Stockholm's new epicurean mecca.

Grands Veranda (p82) Another Dahlgren creation, and the place to go for a traditional Swedish smörgåsbord year-round.

Sånninggården (p294) North of Hemavan, this rustic barn in the middle of nowhere draws Sweden's gourmets to feast on local delicacies such as reindeer steak, Arctic char, and pheasant fillet with chanterelle pie.

Fond (p157) Michelin-rated Fond is where renowned chef Stefan Karlsson dishes up delectable modern Swedish cuisine in a chic, minimalist dining room.

Salt & Brygga (p192) Malmö's stylish slow-food restaurant presents updated, all-organic Swedish cuisine made with seasonal ingredients, in an allergy-free space with minimal environmental impact.

Sweden has come a long, long way from the days of all-beige fish and potato platters. Not only has immigration and membership in the European Union introduced new flavours to the Swedish menu, a new wave of bold young chefs has been experimenting with traditional Swedish fare and melding it with various other influences. The result is an exciting dining scene on a par with some of the best food cities in Europe.

Classic Cuisine

Traditional Swedish cuisine is based on simple, everyday ingredients known generally as *husmanskost*, or basic home cooking. The most famous example of this, naturally, is Swedish meatballs. Other classic *husmanskost* dishes, largely based around fish and potatoes, include various forms of pickled and fried herring, cured salmon, and *pytt i panna*, a potato hash served with sliced beets and a fried egg on top that may be the ultimate comfort food. Of course, the most thorough introduction to all the staples of Swedish cooking is the smörgåsbord, commonly available during the winter holidays.

One specialty food that not many visitors (and not all that many Swedes, either) take to immediately is *surströmming*. It's a canned, fermented Baltic herring opened and consumed ritually once a year, during late August and early September. It's usually wrapped in *tunnbröd* (soft, thin, unleavened bread like a tortilla) with boiled potato, onions and other condiments, all washed down with ample amounts of

FOODIE FESTIVALS

Eat your heart out during Sweden's brief but abundant summers, when festivals celebrate (with food) the traditional patterns of seasonal change.

Smaka på Stockholm Browse an array of teaser plates from some of Stockholm's top kitchens at this week-long annual fest in Kungsträdgården (www.smakapastockholm.se), usually held in early June.

Midsummer's Eve Not technically a 'foodie' holiday, Midsummer's Eve nevertheless relies heavily on the consumption of traditional food and drink. It starts on the first Friday after June 21 with the raising of the maypole, followed by lots of singing, dancing, drinking and the massive consumption of pickled herring with potatoes and sour cream. The next day, Midsummer, is primarily spent recovering from the long night.

Kräftskivor (crayfish parties) Swedes celebrate the end of summer by wearing bibs and party hats while eating crayfish and drinking *snaps*. Similar parties take place in parts of the country with *surströmming* (strong-smelling fermented Baltic herring) or eels – but the *snaps* element remains consistent.

snaps (a distilled alcoholic beverage, such as vodka or aquavit). *Surströmming* may be an acquired taste, but it has a legion of hardcore fans, mostly in northern Sweden. It even boasts its own festival in the village of Alfta. Cans of it make excellent souvenirs, as long as you wrap them well to avoid the truly nightmarish possibility of a leak into your suitcase.

The prevalence of preserved grub harks back to a time when Swedes had little choice but to store their spring and summer harvests for the long, icy winter. The landscape similarly influences menus in various parts of the country; you'll find regional specialties wherever you travel, from Västerbotten pie to saffron pancakes.

Wild game forms a large part of Swedish cuisine, particularly in the northern part of the country. Traditional Sami cooking relies heavily on reindeer, whether cured, dried, roasted or preserved as sausage. Elk and moose are also fairly common. Other northern specialities include *ripa* (ptarmigan) and Arctic char, a cousin of salmon and trout. Particularly in Sami cooking, game is often served with rich sauces that incorporate wild berries.

Speaking of berries, another uniquely Scandinavian taste is that of the *hjortron*, or cloudberry. These grow in the marshes of Norrland and look a bit like pale raspberries, but their flavour is almost otherworldly, and Swedes consider them a delicacy. They're often served as a warm sauce over ice cream.

Other traditional foods worth trying include *toast skagen* (toast with bleak roe, crème fraiche and chopped red onion), the classic *köttbullar och potatis* (meatballs and potatoes, usually served with lingonberry jam, known as *lingonsylt*), and *nässelsoppa* (nettle soup, traditionally served with hard-boiled eggs). Pea soup and pancakes are traditionally served on Thursdays. Seafood staples include caviar, gravadlax or gravlax (cured salmon), the ubiquitous *sill* (herring), eaten smoked, fried or pickled and often accompanied by Scandi trimmings like capers, mustard and onion.

Swedes are devoted to their daily coffee ritual, *fika*, which inevitably also includes a pastry – often *kanelbullar* (cinnamon buns) or *kardemummabullar* (cardamom rolls). (Since the late '90s there's even been an annual official celebration of *kanelbullar*: Cinnamon Bun Day on October 4.) Almond paste (marzipan) is a common ingredient in pastries, such as the princess torte, a delicate cake with a lime-green marzipan shell commonly available at bakeries. Gourmet *konditori* (old-fashioned bakery-cafes) and cafes offer their own variations on all the standard cakes and cookies – best to sample several and choose a favourite.

Contemporary Tendencies

Essentially, contemporary Swedish cuisine melds global influences with local produce and innovation: think baked wood-pigeon with potato-and-apple hash or cauliflower 'cornet' with white chocolate and caviar. Locals have rediscovered the virtues of their own pantry. The result is an intense passion for seasonal, home-grown ingredients,

CHRISTIAN ASLUND / LONELY PLANET IMAGES ©

ANDERS BLOMQVIST / LONELY PLANET IMAGES ©

» (above) Traditional Swedish crayfish party (p32)
» (left) Smoked mackerel fillets

whether apples from Kivik or bleak roe from Kalix. Equally important is the seasonality of food; expect succulent berries in spring, artichokes and crayfish in summer, and hearty truffles and root vegetables in the colder months.

Another growing obsession is a predilection for sustainable farming, small-scale producers and organic produce. Increasingly, restaurants and cafes pride themselves on serving clean, organically grown grub, as well as actively supporting ethical, ecofriendly agricultural practices. Practically all the coffee served in big chain hotels is certified organic, for example, as is most of what you'll find alongside it on the breakfast buffet.

Not surprisingly, this newfound culinary savvy has affected the tourist trade. Gastro-themed itineraries and activities are on the rise, with everything from Gotland truffle hunts to west-coast lobster safaris, while numerous tourist boards stock culinary guides to their respective regions.

Festive Flavours

Around Christmas, many restaurants start offering a *julbord,* a particularly gluttonous version of Sweden's world-famous smörgåsbord buffet. Among the usual delicacies of herring, gravlax, meatballs, short ribs and *blodpudding* (blood pudding) are seasonal gems like baked ham with mustard sauce and *Janssons frestelse,* a hearty casserole of sweet cream, potato, onion and anchovy. *Julmust,* a sweet dark-brown soft drink that foams like a beer when poured, and *glögg,* warm spiced wine, are also Yuletide staples. The best accompaniment to a warm cup of *glögg,* available at kiosks everywhere in winter,

is a *pepparkaka* (gingerbread biscuit) or a *lussekatt* (saffron bun).

During Sweden's short, intense summers, many people hit the countryside for lazy holidays and alfresco noshing. Summer lunch favourites include various *inlagd sill* (pickled herring) with *knäckebröd* (crispbread), strong cheese like the crumbly *Västerbottens ost,* boiled potatoes, diced chives and cream, strawberries, plus a finger or two of *snaps* and some light beer 'to help the fish swim down to the stomach'. Towards the end of summer, Swedes celebrate (or commiserate) its passing with *kräftskivor* (crayfish parties) where people wearing bibs and party hats get together to eat *kräftor* boiled with dill, drink *snaps* and sing *snapsvisor* (drinking songs).

For sweet-tooths, the lead-up to Lent means one thing: the *semla* bun. A wickedly decadent concoction of a wheat-flour bun crammed with whipped cream and almond paste, it was traditionally eaten on *fettis-dagen* (Fat Tuesday). These days, it under-mines diets as early as January.

Drinks

In the early days, when Stockholm was a rough port town full of stumbling sailors, alcohol taxes were levied according to where you happened to be when you fell down drunk or threw up. (These days, the same method can be used to decide which bars to frequent – or avoid.) Liquor laws and cus-toms have changed a bit since those days, motivated not least by Sweden's need to conform more closely to European Union (EU) standards. But there are still a few guidelines to navigate when pursuing adult beverages in Sweden.

Öl (beer) is ranked by alcohol content; the stronger the beer, the higher its price and,

ETIQUETTE

For the most part, table manners in Sweden are the same as those in the rest of Europe. On very formal occasions, wait for the host to welcome you to the table before beginning to eat or drink. Aside from a proper *skål,* don't clink glasses (it's considered vulgar), and refrain from sipping your wine outside of toasts until the host has declared that everyone may drink freely. Don some decent socks when dining in someone's home, as you'll generally be expected to take off your shoes in the foyer. (It's not uncommon to bring along a pair of house shoes to change into.) Swedes are typically quite punctual, so make an effort to arrive at the agreed-upon time rather than 'fashionably late'. And don't go empty-handed; a bottle of wine or flowers will make the right impression.

RESOURCES

» Culinary Skåne (www.skanskama-tupplevelser.com) is a network of restaurants and growers that produce a regional guide to produce, cuisine and epicurean events.

» Swedish Institute (www.sweden.se) provides a detailed discussion of Swedish food; follow the 'Lifestyle' tab.

» Äkta Sylt (www.aktasylt.se) is a website devoted to lingonberry jam, its preservation and marketing; in Swedish.

» *Hembakat är Bäst* is Ikea's Swedish cookbook (available in English); it presents deconstructed photos of classic recipes.

» *Vår Kokbok* is a classic swedish cookbook from the '50s, akin to Betty Crocker in the US.

generally speaking, the more flavour it has. Light beers (*lättöl;* less than 2.25%) and 'folk' beers (*folköl;* 2.25% to 3.5%) account for about two-thirds of all beer sold in Sweden; these can be bought in supermarkets. Medium-strength beer (*mellanöl;* 3.5% to 4.5%) and strong beer (*starköl;* over 4.5%) can be bought only at outlets of the state-owned alcohol store, Systembolaget, or in bars and restaurants. 'Systemet', as it's often called, is also the only place (other than bars and restaurants) to buy hard liquor or wine.

Much like North American domestic brews, the everyday Swedish beer produced by mass breweries like Falcon, Åbro, Pripps and Spendrups is notable only for its complete lack of distinctive flavour. There are a few good microbrews available in taverns (look for Jämtlands brewery's very good Fallen Angel bitter; Tärnö's Nils Oscar range is good, too, as are the Gotland brewery's line from Visby), and imports from the rest of Europe are much easier to find than in pre-EU days. In bars and restaurants, domestic brews such as Spendrups, Pripps or Falcon cost anywhere from Skr40 to Skr58 a pint, and imported beer or mixed drinks can be twice that. Ultra-sweet pear and apple ciders are also common, frequently in light-alcohol or alcohol-free versions.

Wines and spirits can be bought only in bars and restaurants and at Systembolaget. Sweden's trademark spirit is *brännvin*, of which Absolut Vodka is the most recognisable example. One subsection of *brännvin*, called aquavit and drunk as *snaps*, is a fiery and strongly flavoured drink that's usually distilled from potatoes and spiced with herbs. (A small shot of aquavit is sometimes called a *nubbe*, and it's often accompanied by raucous drinking songs, or *snapsvisor*, when used to wash down pickled herring or crayfish.)

The legal drinking age in Sweden is 18 years; this applies to buying beer in grocery stores and any kind of alcohol in bars and restaurants. The minimum age to buy alcohol at a Systembolaget store is 20 years. Many bars and restaurants impose higher age limits for admission.

Of course, the beverage you're most likely to encounter in Sweden isn't even alcoholic. Coffee is the unofficial national drink, with an ever-increasing number of cafes ditching the percolated stuff for Italian-style espresso. The daily ritual of coffee and a pastry *(fika)* is an easy and rewarding one to adopt during your visit. (Tea is also readily available.) And *saft* is cordial commonly made from lingonberries, blueberries and elderflowers, though the word can refer to ordinary apple or orange juice as well.

Practical Info
Where to Eat

Hotels and hostels offer *frukost* (breakfast) buffets that typically include yoghurt and cereal, several types of bread, pastries, crispbread and/or rolls, with *pålägg* (toppings) including butter, sliced cheese, boiled eggs, sliced meat, liver pâté, Kalles caviar (an iconic caviar spread), pickled herring, sliced cucumber and marmalade. Several coffee chains (Wayne's Coffee, Espresso House) now dot the landscape, offering reliably decent cappuccinos and lattes along with breakfast pastries.

A hearty lunch has long been a mainstay of the workforce, with cafes and restaurants usually serving a weekday lunch special (or a choice of several) called *dagens rätt* at a fixed price (typically Skr65 to Skr95) between 11.30am and 2pm Monday to Friday. It's a practice originally supported and subsidised by the Swedish government with the goal of keeping workers happy and efficient, and it's still one of the most economical ways

WORKING THE SYSTEM

Visiting the once-draconian state-run liquor store chain Systembolaget, with its iconic green-and-yellow sign, has become a much more pleasant experience in recent years. Gone are the days of timidly handing your modest order to a stern clerk on the other side of a glass pane and waiting to see if it would be filled, and with what level of disapproval.

Today, with liquor laws having relaxed considerably to be more in line with the European community, Systembolaget shops are actually enjoyable places. Browsing is encouraged, and the selection of wine and spirits in most locations is excellent. Booze is never cheap in Sweden, but prices are nowhere near as forbidding as they once were. And expanded opening hours (most locations are now open on Saturdays) make the idea of, say, picking up a bottle of Shiraz for dinner seem almost inviting.

For a full list of Systembolaget outlets and a look at what's on offer, visit www.systembolaget.se. You'll also find information on the origins of 'Systemet' and its public-health policies. Product catalogs, available online or in-store, offer suggestions on food and wine pairings, as well as handy flavour descriptions (though only in Swedish).

to sample top-quality Swedish cooking. The *dagens rätt* usually includes a main course, salad, beverage, bread and butter, and coffee.

For a lighter lunch, head to a small cafe or *konditori*, where staples include substantial pastries and the delectable *smörgås* (open sandwich), an artfully arranged creation usually topped with greens, shrimp or salmon, roe, boiled egg and mustard-dill sauce. Most cafes and coffee shops these days serve hearty, great-value salads that include grains or pasta with lettuce and veggies, plus various other exotic goodies in an enormous bowl (typically costing Skr70 to Skr80).

Cheap Eats

Street snacks are the cheapest, quickest way to fill up in Sweden, particularly in cities but also on beaches, along motorways and in campgrounds. A snack kiosk with a grill is known as a *gatukök* – literally, street kitchen. In the world of Swedish street food, hot dogs reign supreme – the basic model is called a *grillad korv med bröd*, grilled sausage with bread (hot dog in a bun), although you can also ask for it boiled *(kokt)*. Adventurous souls can do a mind-boggling variety of things to the *korv*, chiefly involving rolling it up in flatbread with any number of accompaniments, from shrimp salad, mashed potatoes or coleslaw to fried onions. Kebab stands and fast-food windows run a close second for quick and cheap eats.

Opening Times

Restaurants generally open from 11.30am to 2pm for lunch, and from 5pm until 10pm for dinner. Cafes, bakeries and coffee shops are likely to be open all day, from 7am or 8am in the morning until 6pm.

Tipping

Tipping is not common in Sweden. A service cost is figured into the bill. If you've had excellent service, a 10% to 15% tip is a suitable compliment.

Self-Catering

Easily found in Swedish towns and villages, the main supermarket chains are ICA, Konsum and Hemköp (the last often found inside Åhléns department stores). Plastic carrier bags usually cost Skr2 to Skr5 at the cashier.

Supermarkets across Sweden have pre-prepared foods for quick snacks, but making your own meals is easy enough if you're hostelling or staying in camping grounds. Produce in standard supermarkets is often uninspiring, but fresh, seasonal fruits and vegetables are readily available at market squares such as Hötorget in Stockholm as well as at rural farm shops and roadside stands.

Vegetarians & Vegans

Vegetarian and vegan restaurants are common; excellent veggie buffets are easy to find in major cities, and even in rural areas restaurants generally have a herbivorous main-course option. For this reason we haven't created a separate category for vegetarian listings in this book.

Outdoor Adventures

Top Winter Sports

Skiing
Dogsledding
Snowmobiling

Best for Hiking

Abisko in the north
Sarek in the north
Padjelanteleden in the north
Kungsleden in the north

Best for Cycling

Örebro in central Sweden
Skåne in the south
Gotland in the southeast

Safety Guidelines

Be aware of local laws, regulations and etiquette about wildlife and the environment.
Pay any fees and possess any permits required by local authorities.
Obtain reliable information about physical and environmental conditions along your intended route (eg from park authorities).
Walk only in regions and on trails within your realm of experience.
Be sure you are healthy and feel comfortable walking for a sustained period.
Even if you're visiting in winter, bring a good pair of sunglasses to protect your eyes from glare of snowy surfaces.

Sweden is ideal for outdoor activities: it has thousands of square kilometres of forest with hiking and cycling tracks, vast numbers of lakes connected by mighty rivers, and a range of alpine mountains. Much of the information available on the internet is in Swedish. If you can't read the language, contact the national organisations (listed under individual activities in this section) for the sport you're interested in. Regional and local tourist offices and staff at outdoor stores can also point you in the right direction.

Hiking

Swedes love their hiking, and there are many thousands of kilometres of marked trails that make most of the country a trekker's dream.

European Long Distance Footpaths E1 and E6 run from Varberg to Grövelsjön (1200km) and from Malmö to Norrtälje (1400km), respectively. But Kungsleden (p308), in Lappland, is the best-known and most user-friendly trail in Sweden. Finnskogleden (p133) is a 240km-long route along the border between Norway and the Värmland region in Sweden. The Arctic Trail (800km) is a joint development of Sweden, Norway and Finland and is entirely above the Arctic Circle; it begins near Kautokeino in Norway and ends in Abisko, Sweden. The 139km Padjelantaleden (p298) is a generally easy route, with long sections of duckboards and bridged rivers. The mountainous part of western Jämtland is also one of Sweden's most popular hiking areas.

Mountain trails in Sweden are marked with cairns, wooden signposts or paint on rocks and trees. Marked trails have bridges across all but the smallest streams, and wet or fragile areas are crossed on duckboards. Overnight huts and lodges along these trails are maintained by Svenska Turistföreningen (STF).

The best hiking time is between late June and mid-September, when trails are mostly snow-free. After early August the mosquitoes have gone.

Equipment

Hikers should be well-equipped and prepared for snow in the mountains, even in summer. Prolonged bad weather in the northwest isn't uncommon – Sarek and Sylarna are the most notorious areas. In summer you'll need good boots, waterproof jacket and trousers, several layers of warm clothing (including spare dry clothes), warm hat, sun hat, mosquito repellent (a mosquito head-net is also highly advisable), water bottle, maps, compass and sleeping bag. Basic supplies are often available at huts, and most lodges serve meals (but check first, especially outside of high season). If you're going off the main routes you should obviously take full camping equipment.

Information

The best source for hiking information is the youth-hostel organisation **Svenska Turist-föreningen** (Swedish Touring Association; STF; ☑08-463 21 00; www.svenskaturistforeningen.se), one of Sweden's largest tour operators. Most of its publications are Swedish-only, but STF staff will answer questions and provide information in English by phone or email.

STF lodges sell up-to-date maps, but it's a good idea to buy them in advance. Fjäll-kartan (Skr127 each) is the best series for hikes. Try **Kartbutiken** (☑08-20 23 03; www.kartbutiken.se; Kungsgatan 74, Stockholm).

Mountaineering & Rock Climbing

Mountaineers head for Sylarna, Helags-fjället, Sarek National Park and the Kebnekaise region.

The complete traverse of Sylarna involves rock climbing up to grade 3. The ridge traverse of Sarektjåhkkå (2089m) in Sarek, the second-highest mountain in Sweden,

is about grade 4. There are lots of other glacier and rock routes in Sarek. The Keb-nekaise area has many fine climbing routes (grades 2 to 6), including the north wall of Kaskasapakte (2043m), and the steep ridges of Knivkammen (1878m) and Vaktposten (1852m).

For qualified guides, contact **Svenska Bergsguideorganisation** (Swedish Mountain Guide Association; ☑098-01 26 56; www.utsidan.se/sbo). The website is in Swedish, but under *medlemmar* there's a list of guides and their contact details.

Rock climbers can practise on the cliffs around Stockholm and Göteborg – there are 34 climbing areas with 1000 routes around Göteborg, and some 200 cliffs around the capital. For further information, try the helpful **Svenska Klätterförbundet** (Swedish Climbing Federation; ☑08-618 82 70; www.klatterforbundet.se).

Cycling

Sweden is perfect for cycling, particularly in Skåne and Gotland. It's an excellent way to look for prehistoric sites, rune stones and quiet spots for free camping. The cycling season is from May to September in the south, and July and August in the north.

You can cycle on all roads except motorways (green sign with two lanes and a bridge on it) and roads for motor vehicles only (green sign with a car symbol). Highways often have a hard shoulder, which keeps cyclists well clear of motor vehicles. Secondary roads are mostly quiet and safe by European standards.

You can take a bicycle on some regional trains and buses. Long-distance buses usually don't accept bicycles; Sveriges Järnväg (SJ) allows them on trains June through October (Skr249). Bikes are transported free on some ferries.

You can hire bicycles from campsites, hostels, bike workshops and sports shops for about Skr100 a day or Skr500 a week.

Some country areas, towns and cities have special cycle routes – contact local tourist offices for information and maps. Kustlinjen (591km) runs from Öregrund (Uppland) southwards along the Baltic coast to Västervik, and Skånespåret (800km) is a fine network of cycle routes. The well-signposted 2600km-long Sverigeleden extends from Helsingborg in the south to Karesuando in the north, and links points of

RESPONSIBLE HIKING

Rubbish

Carry out all your rubbish, and make an effort to carry out rubbish left by others. Never bury your rubbish. Sanitary napkins, tampons, condoms and toilet paper should be carried out despite the inconvenience, as they burn and decompose poorly.

Human Waste Disposal

Contamination of water sources by human faeces can lead to the transmission of all sorts of nasties. Where there is a toilet, please use it. Where there is no toilet, bury your waste. Dig a small hole 15cm (6in) deep and at least 100m (320ft) from any watercourse. Cover the waste with soil and a rock. In snow, dig down to the soil.

Washing

Don't use detergents or toothpaste in or near watercourses, even if they are biodegradable. For personal washing, use biodegradable soap and a water container (or even a lightweight, portable basin) at least 50m (160ft) away from the watercourse. Wash cooking utensils at a similar distance using a scourer, sand or snow instead of detergent.

Erosion

Hillsides and mountain slopes, especially at high altitudes, are prone to erosion. Stick to existing trails and avoid short cuts.

Fires & Low-Impact Cooking

Don't depend on open fires for cooking or warmth. The cutting of wood for fires in popular trekking areas can cause rapid deforestation. Cook on a light-weight kerosene, alcohol or Shellite (white gas) stove and avoid those powered by disposable butane gas canisters.

Wildlife Conservation

Hunting and fishing anywhere in Sweden requires a permit specific to that area; ask locally at the tourist office to find out the seasons and rules in that area.Don't attempt to exterminate animals in huts. In wild places, they are likely to be protected native animals.

Environmental Organisations

The best source of information on conservation is the Swedish environmental protection agency, Naturvårdsverket (www.naturvardsverket.se).

interest with suitable roads (mostly with an asphalt surface) and bicycle paths.

Brochures and maps are available from **Svenska Cykelsällskapet** (Swedish Cycling Association; ☎08-751 6204; www.svenska-cykel sallskapet.se).

Boating & Sailing

Boating and sailing are hugely popular in Sweden. The 7000km-long coastline, with its 60,000 islands, is a sailor's paradise, but look out for the few restricted military areas off the east coast.

Inland, lakes and canals offer pleasant sailing in spring and summer. The main canals are the Göta Canal, the Kinda Canal and the Dalsland Canal. Various companies offer short canal cruises; contact local tourist offices for details.

Those with private boats will have to pay lock fees and guest harbour fees (around Skr150 per night, although some small places are free). A useful guide is the free, annual *Gästhamnsguiden*, which is published in Swedish by **Svenska Kryssarklubben** (Swedish Cruising Club; ☎08-448 28 80; info@sxk. se). It contains comprehensive details of 500 guest harbours throughout the country and is available from tourist offices.

» (above) Sailboat and houses on the Bohuslän coast (p165)
» (left) Husky-sledding, Arvidsjaur (p295)

Canoeing & Kayaking

Sweden is a real paradise for canoeists and kayakers. The national canoeing body is **Svenska Kanotförbundet** (Swedish Canoe Federation; ☎0155-20 90 80; www.kanot.com). It provides general advice and lists approved canoe centres that hire out canoes (per day/week for around Skr350/1500).

Fishing

There are national and local restrictions on fishing in many of Sweden's inland waters, especially for salmon, trout and eel. Before dropping a line, check with local tourist offices or councils.

Local permits (*fiskkort*) can be bought from tourist offices, sports or camping shops and typically cost Skr60 to Skr120 per day, depending on season and location.

Summer is the best fishing time with bait or flies for most species, but trout and pike fishing in southern Sweden is better in spring or autumn and salmon fishing is best in late summer. Ice fishing is popular in winter.

An excellent web resource for fishing in Sweden is www.cinclusc.com/spfguide (in Swedish), or contact **Sportfiskeförbundet** (Angling Federation; ☎08-704 44 80; info@sport-fiskarna.se).

Skiing

Large ski resorts cater mainly to downhill (alpine and telemark) skiing and snowboarding, but there's also scope for cross-country touring. For cross-country (nordic) skiing, the northwest usually has plenty of snow from December to April. Kungsleden and other long-distance tracks provide great skiing. Most towns have illuminated skiing tracks.

Take the usual precautions: don't leave marked routes without emergency food, a good map, local advice and proper equipment including a bivouac bag. Temperatures of -30°C or lower (including wind-chill factor) are possible, so check the daily forecasts. Police and tourist offices have information on local warnings. In mountain ski resorts, where there's a risk of avalanche (*lavin*), susceptible areas are marked by yellow, multilingual signs and buried-skier symbols. Make sure your travel insurance covers skiing.

Skating

When the Baltic Sea freezes (once or twice every 10 years), fantastic tours of Stockholm's archipelago are possible. The skating season usually lasts from December to March. Less ambitiously, there's skating all winter on many city parks and ponds,

THE RIGHT OF PUBLIC ACCESS

Allemansrätten, the right of public access to the countryside, is not a legal right but a common-law privilege. It includes national parks and nature reserves, although special rules may apply. Full details in English can be found on the website www.allemansratten.se.

You're allowed to walk, ski, boat or swim on private land as long as you stay at least 70m from houses and keep out of gardens, fenced areas and cultivated land. You can pick berries and mushrooms, provided they're not protected species. Generally you should move on after one or two nights' camping.

Don't leave rubbish or take live wood, bark, leaves, bushes or nuts. Fires fuelled with fallen wood are allowed where safe, but not on bare rocks (which can crack from the heat). Use a bucket of water to douse a campfire even if you think that it's completely out. Cars and motorcycles may not be driven across open land or on private roads; look out for the sign *ej motorfordon* (no motor vehicles). Dogs must be kept on leads between 1 March and 20 August. Close all farm gates and don't disturb farm animals or reindeer. Off-limits areas where birds are nesting are marked with a yellow or red-and-yellow sign containing the words *fågelskydd – tillträde förbjudet*.

If you have a car or bicycle, look for free camping sites around unsealed forest tracks leading from secondary country roads. Make sure your spot is at least 50m from the track and not visible from any house, building or sealed road. Bring drinking water and food, and don't pollute any water sources with soap or food waste.

Above all, remember the mantra: 'Do not disturb, do not destroy.'

including Kungsträdgården in Stockholm, with skate-rental booths nearby.

Dogsledding

Sweden's Sami have readily adopted dog-sledding as a means of winter transport, following in the footsteps of the indigenous people of Siberia, and excursions are available in most northern towns. Apart from being the most ecofriendly means of exploring the Arctic wastes, it's also one of the most enjoyable ways of getting around, allowing you to bond with your own husky team and to slow down and appreciate the surrounding wilds as the mood takes you. Most operators offer anything between a two-hour taster to fairly demanding multiday expeditions, staying overnight in rustic forest cabins or Sami winter tents. Some good places to start:

» **Abisko** (p307) Short rides and day packages on offer, as well as weekend multi-activity stays.

» **Kiruna** (p302) Dogsled rides under the northern lights, and there's even an airport pickup by dogsled.

» **Arvidsjaur** (p295) One of the largest Siberian husky kennels in Lappland.

» **Jokkmokk** (p297) Hour-long tasters to seven-day expeditions, including special sleighs for disabled guests.

Snowmobile Safaris

While some may argue that snowmobiles are noisy and not terribly ecofriendly, they are the Arctic equivalent of an all-terrain vehicle and essential for travel within isolated areas, not to mention for rounding up reindeer. Travelling by snowmobile allows you to access difficult terrain and cover more ground than by dog- or reindeer-sled. Snowmobile safaris (including night rides to see the northern lights) are offered by operators in all major northern towns. It's cheaper to ride as a passenger behind an experienced driver, though snowmobiles are available for hire to those with a valid driver's license (get a snowmobile permit from the nearest tourist office). Trails are marked with red crosses on poles.

» **Kiruna** (p302) Day and night trips, as well as three-day wilderness excursions, complete with camping and ice fishing.

» **Arvidsjaur** (p295) Over 600km of snowmobile tracks in and around the area.

ADRENALINE JUNKIES

One of the fastest-growing activities for summer is downhill mountain biking. The sport takes over ski resorts after the snow melts; fully armoured, riders carry their sturdy little bikes up the hill on chair lifts, then barrel down along rough mountain trails at dizzying speeds. **Åre Bike Park** (www.arebikepark.com; lift day-pass Skr240, bike rentals per day from Skr650; ⊙mid-Jun–Oct) is the mother lode, with 35km of slopes, 17 trails and a potential vertical drop of almost 900m. Multiday packages are available.

» **Abisko** (p306) The marked snowmobile track in Abisko National Park allows you to drive along the first section of the Kungsleden.

Golf

Sweden has over 400 golf courses, open to everyone, and many hotel chains offer golf packages. Björkliden, near Abisko, is a golf course 240km above the Arctic Circle, and at the Green Line golf course at Haparanda, playing a round means crossing the Swedish-Finnish border four times. Green fees are around Skr400 (higher near metro areas); for more information, contact **Svenska Golfförbundet** (Swedish Golf Federation; ☑08-622 15 00; sgf.golf.se).

Birdwatching

There are many keen ornithologists in Sweden, and there are birdwatchers' towers and nature reserves everywhere. For further information, contact **Sveriges Ornitologiska Förening** (Swedish Ornithological Society; ☑08-612 25 30; www.sofnet.org, in Swedish).

Horse Riding

Sweden's multitude of tracks, trails, forests, shorelines and mountains make for some fantastically varied riding. Everything from short hacks to full-on treks are on offer (two hours/half day/full day around Skr350/550/850) on Swedish or Icelandic horses. Trips can be arranged through local tourist offices.

Travel with Children

Best Regions for Kids

Stockholm & Around

Museums, a petting zoo and an amusement park make the capital city a delight for kids.

Uppsala & Central Sweden

A great waterpark, family-friendly ski slopes and tons of camping.

Göteborg & the Southwest

The country's biggest amusement park, plus great museums and public parks.

Malmö & the South

One of Sweden's best open-air museums, plus a rad skatepark.

The Southeast & Gotland

Take the family on an easy, island-round bicycle trip on Gotland, or visit Astrid Lindgrens Värld in Vimmerby.

Östersund & the Bothnian Coast

A legendary sea monster, a great zoo, an open-air museum and several kid-friendly hostels.

Lappland & the Far North

Hit the ski slopes or take the kids on a dogsledding adventure in winter, or a good long hike in summer.

Sweden for Kids

If you've got kids, you're guaranteed an easy ride in Sweden. As a general tip, get the kids involved in your travel plans – if they've helped to work out where you're going, chances are they'll still be interested when you arrive! Remember, don't try to cram too much in. Lonely Planet's *Travel with Children*, by Cathy Lanigan, is a useful source of information.

Swedes treat children very well, and domestic tourism is largely organised around children's interests. Many museums have a kids' section with toys, hands-on displays and activities, and there are numerous public parks for kids, plus theme parks, water parks and so on. Most attractions allow free admission for young children – up to about seven years of age – and half-price (or substantially discounted) admission for those up to about 16. Family tickets are often available.

High chairs and cots (cribs) are standard in most restaurants and hotels. Menus usually feature at least a couple of children's meals at a reasonable price. (These are generally along the lines of Swedish meatballs or pancakes with lingonberries and cream – a fairly easy sell even for fussy eaters.) Swedish supermarkets offer a relatively wide choice of baby food, infant formulas, soy and cow's milk, disposable nappies (diapers) etc. There are nappy-changing facilities in most toilets (men's and women's), and breastfeeding in public is not an issue.

Children's Highlights

Theme Parks

» **Liseberg** Sweden's most popular tourist attraction, for good reason

» **Gröna Lund Tivoli** Fun rides and concerts in the heart of Stockholm, with awesome views of the capital from the more gravity-defying rides

» **Junibacken** Pretend you're Pippi Longstocking at this book-based theme park

Open-Air Museums

» **Skansen** A miniature Sweden

» **Himmelsberga** A farm village with quaint cottages

» **Kulturen** A vast museum with buildings from all points in history, in many styles

» **Fredriksdals Friluftsmuseum** An old manor house, a farm, lovely gardens and a French baroque theater

» **Vallby Friluftsmuseum** A farmyard and several craft workshops

» **Jamtli** The north's answer to Skansen, a traditional Sweden in miniature

» **Friluftsmuseet Murberget** More than 80 buildings, including a traditional shop, smithy, church and school, all in typical Norrland style

Museums

» **Tekniska Museet** Thrill tiny nerds with all the science and gadgetry they can handle

» **Naturhistoriska Museet** The forest comes to life in this diorama-filled museum

» **Medeltidsmuseet** Go back in time and underneath Stockholm for the gripping story of the city's foundations

» **Värmlands Museum** Everything you might want to know about the region, past and present, plus some great contemporary art

» **Ájtte Museum** Sami culture gets the attention it deserves, with beautiful multimedia presentations

Rainy-Day Activities

» Crafts in Stockholm's **Kulturhuset**

» **Science Fiction Bookshop** in Stockholm's Gamla Stan

» Catch a Hollywood blockbuster film

Planning

When to Go

Parents will find that travel in the summer tourist season (mid-June through to August) is easier than outside those times, simply because more visitor facilities, sights and activities are up and running then.

If your family is interested in outdoor activities, winter is also a great time to visit Sweden; several ski hills (including the world-class Åre) have family-friendly facilities, bunny slopes, ski schools, day care and so on.

What to Pack

In terms of what to bring with you vs what you can buy there, it's best to relax – if you forget or run out of anything, you'll be able to find it easily in Swedish shops or at hotels. Sweden is at least as well supplied as the US or UK when it comes to baby accoutrements.

Accommodation

Campgrounds have excellent facilities and are overrun with ecstatic, energetic children. They get very busy in summer, so book tent sites or cabins well in advance.

Hotels and other accommodation options often have 'family rooms' that sleep up to two adults and two children for little more than the price of a regular double. Cots for young children are available in most hotels and hostels, usually either free of charge or for a nominal fee.

Hotel staff are accustomed to serving families and should be able to help you with anything you need, from heating bottles to finding a babysitter for a parents' night out.

Transport

Car-rental companies will hire out children's safety seats at a nominal cost, but it's essential that you book them in advance. Long-distance ferries and trains, hotels and some restaurants may even have play areas for children.

Ask about free rides on public transport for young children; this is offered at certain times of day in many cities (for instance, kids under 12 ride free at weekends in Stockholm). Buses are nicely set up for strollers/prams, and most of the time you'll be swarmed by locals trying to help you get the stroller on and off the bus.

regions at a glance

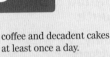

Stockholm & Around

Food ✓✓✓
Museums ✓✓✓
Shopping ✓✓✓

Foodie Central

Travellers will be pleased to know that the days of potatoes and pickled fish for every meal are long gone. Stockholm is a world-class foodie destination, with multiple Michelin stars to its name and a number of celebrity chefs known for transcending expectations with their bold takes on locally sourced, traditionally rooted dishes. You can eat as well here as in most any European capital. It's also a dessert lover's dream city, with a cafe culture that embraces sitting down for coffee and decadent cakes at least once a day.

Best of Museums

There's no chance you'll be bored in a Swedish museum – this country knows how to do them right, and the capital city has several prime examples. Stockholm's museums present the best of the country's art and historical treasures in the most inviting, enchanting atmosphere. Exhibition rooms are as well-planned and well-lit as the rest of the city's stylish spaces, making each museum visit an enthralling multimedia ride.

Ready, Set, Shop

Shopping is practically a sport in the uberchic capital. From tucked-away thrift stores to big-name retail boutiques, fine linens and handicrafts to cleverly designed kitchen gadgets, nearly every type of shopper will find plenty to pick through here. Actual bargains are few and far between, but you can find things here you'll never see elsewhere.

Uppsala & Central Sweden

History ✓✓✓
Industry ✓✓
Museums ✓✓

Historical Sweden

Uppsala and its surrounds are a treat for history buffs: from pre-Viking grave mounds to a hillside castle whose pink walls concealed decades of royal intrigue. Add to that a stash of treasures in its museums, from art and artefacts to ancient manuscripts, and the odd runestone poking up out of the grass here and there.

Remnants of Industry

Central Sweden is the country's industrial workhorse, plying the rich landscape for iron, copper and silver. Many of these places have been transformed into quaint and atmospheric historical sites well worth a visit.

Famous Museums

A major university town, Uppsala has its share of stellar museums. But others are spread throughout the region, from Örebro's fantastic castle and regional art museum, to the ambitious Värmlands Museum in Karlstad, to the homes of beloved Swedish artists Carl Larsson and Anders Zorn and author Selma Lagerlöf.

p50

Göteborg & the Southwest

Coastline ✓✓✓
Food ✓✓✓
Culture ✓✓

Southwest Shore
From kite-surfing in Halland to island-hopping in Bohuslän, there are unlimited options for ocean-lovers in the southwest. Spend the night on one of the coast's remote skerries or join the crowds to watch summertime round-island regattas.

Fresh Seafood
Local chefs boast that seafood arrives first in Göteborg and second in Stockholm, so if you want to experience truly fresh prawns, oysters, lobster or cod, look no further. Select your own dockside, or savour flavour-packed morsels at the region's top-tier restaurants.

Urban Edge
Göteborg's industrial roots make its artists practical – less talk, more action – and there is a gritty refinement to design, music and art across the region. Distinct venues abound: restored power stations, basement boutiques and castle lawns.

p144

Malmö & the South

Variety ✓✓✓
Outdoors ✓✓
Mystery ✓✓

A Bit of Everything
A thorough experience of southern Sweden may include sailing on a restored Viking ship, taking in avant-garde architecture, climbing fortress steps and finishing up with a 5am falafel after a night out in Malmö. The best option is to try it all.

Outdoor Activities
Whether it's with apple picking, gorgeous beaches or some especially nice coastal hikes, southern Sweden is perfect for taking advantage of the great outdoors. More offbeat options include seal safaris, scuba diving and pony trekking.

Secrets of the South
Ancient and present-day mysteries thrive in southern Sweden. Come face-to-face with (hopefully fictional) crime scenes and body parts in Kurt Wallander's Ystad or puzzle over Bronze Age graves and ancient stone ships (or celestial timepieces) at Kivik and Ales Stenar.

p183

The Southeast & Gotland

Activities ✓✓✓
World Heritage ✓✓✓
History ✓✓

Outdoor Activities
The southeast is paradise for the outdoorsy person, with grand ports for sailors, quiet lakeside roads for cyclists and miles of glorious woodland trails. In between, try glassblowing or dip your toe into Astrid Lindgren's cheerful imaginary world.

World's Best
A wander through Visby's cobblestone streets, past fairy-tale cottages and haunting church ruins, and the gasp-inducing view of sky, sea and rock at Öland's southernmost point will make it clear why both have earned Unesco distinction.

Grand History
Steeped in tales of industry and migration, boasting the engineering triumph of the Göta Canal and with some seriously impressive castles, the southeast has plenty of history to share. Not to mention its ecclesiastical past, embodied by Gotland's stunning churches and the pilgrim's route to St Birgitta's abbey.

p221

Östersund & the Bothnian Coast

Wildlife ✓✓
Activities ✓✓✓
Islands ✓✓✓

Mammals & Monsters

Quite apart from the musk oxen, elk and reindeer that you may meet in the wild (or pet at Järvzoo), the waters of Lake Storsjön hide the most elusive creature of all – Östersund's answer to the Loch Ness Monster.

Year-Round Adventure

Åre is adventure central, where you can try your hand at hillcarting, heli-skiing, zorbing and mountain biking. The mountains west of Östersund and the Bothnian Coast offer varied terrain for some superb hiking in summer and skiing in winter.

Jagged Coast

The waters of the Gulf of Bothnia are dotted with myriad forested islands. While some allow you to play out your Robinson Crusoe fantasies, others introduce you to traditional fishing culture and that devil of a delicacy, surströmming.

p264

Lappland & the Far North

Wildlife ✓✓✓
Hiking ✓✓✓
Sami Culture ✓✓✓

Unique Wildlife

There are few places in the world where it's easier to see reindeer, elk and foxes. If you're lucky, you may even spot a brown bear, lynx or wolverine, though they are nocturnal and shy.

Top Trails

The Kungsleden is the most celebrated hiking trail, although Padjelanta and Stora Sjöfjallet offer trails that are no less picturesque. The ascent of Kebnekaise provides exceptional views, while Sarek National Park will challenge even the most experienced of hikers.

Sami Way of Life

Explore the past and present of Europe's only indigenous people: admire Sami silver jewellery through the ages at Áttje Museum or the Silvermuseet, stay with Sami reindeer herdsmen at Båtsuoj Sami Camp and visit the Jokkmokk Winter Market.

p290

> Every listing is recommended by our authors, and their favourite places are listed first

> Look out for these icons:

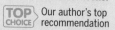 Our author's top recommendation

 A green or sustainable option

 No payment required

See the Index for a full list of destinations covered in this book.

On the Road

Stockholm & Around

Best Places to Eat

» Grands Veranda (p82)

» Rosendals Trädgårdskafe (p83)

» Operakällaren (p81)

» Chokladkoppen (p81)

» Vurma (p85)

Best Places to Stay

» Grand Hôtel Stockholm (p76)

» Rival Hotel (p79)

» Hotel Hellsten (p76)

» Columbus Hotell (p79)

» Zinkensdamm Hotell & Vandrarhem (p79)

Why Go?

Stockholm's good looks and mad style could almost be intimidating. But this city is an accessible beauty, as easy to explore as it is rewarding. Its layout, spread across 14 islands connected by 57 bridges, sounds complicated, but it is compact and easily walkable. Each neighbourhood has a distinct character, yet they're close enough together that you can spend time in several of them on a single day.

The old town, Gamla Stan, is one of Europe's most arresting historic hubs: a concoction of storybook buildings, imposing palaces and razor-thin cobblestone streets.

Meanwhile, just a few metres from this time capsule, the modern city centre shines like a fashion magazine come to life. Downtown is a catwalk, showroom and test kitchen all in one. Everything here is the very latest thing.

And it's all surrounded by pristine forests and an archipelago. What's not to love?

When to Go
Stockholm

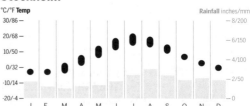

| **Mid-Jun–mid-Aug** Stockholm's long days, uncannily pretty light and mild weather are dreamy. | **Dec–Feb** The city is a frosted cake, with holiday markets and mugs of *glögg* around every corner. | **Sep–Oct** Less-reliable weather, but minimal crowds and beautiful fall colours. |

It's the Water

You'll see signs in many of Stockholm's hotels boasting that the city's tap water is among the cleanest on earth and perfectly good to drink. This is no exaggeration. There's virtually no excuse for buying bottled water in Sweden. Stockholm's tap water comes from Lake Mälaren in the middle of the city, itself clean enough that locals swim in it all summer and fish from it year-round.

Such close ties to the water may help explain Stockholmers' early and thorough embrace of 'green' environmental practices: when people walk past their water source every day on their way to work, it's difficult to ignore the importance of keeping it pure.

Water quality in and around the city is monitored by the Swedish National Food Administration; to learn more, visit www.stockholmvatten.se/en. Meanwhile, carry your own refillable water bottle and don't hesitate to fill it up right from the tap.

DON'T MISS

Museums in Stockholm aren't cheap, but they're excellent value – this city knows how to enthral. A handful you should investigate include the crowd-pleasing **Vasamuseet**, which tells the story of a sunken ship; the **Moderna Museet** for modern-art fans; the **Nationalmuseum** for students of any kind of art or design; and the **Historiska Museet** to get a solid grasp of Swedish history.

Regional Tours

From Stockholm it's easy to arrange various day or half-day tours, whether your interests run toward ancient history, royal palaces or seaside picnics. For something more ambitious, book a multiday journey along the **Göta Canal** (www.stromma. se; 4 days from Skr9775; ☺May–early Sep) from coast to coast.

In just under two hours, the **Archipelago 'Race'** (www. stromma.se; tours Skr290; ☺ tours at 11.15am, 1.15pm & 3.15pm mid-Jun–Aug) whips you along on a guided tour among the islands nearest the city. Boats leave from Strömkajen outside the Grand Hôtel.

Just 25 minutes away by boat, **Fjäderholmarna** (Feather Islands; www.fjaderholmslinjen.se; adult/child round-trip Skr110/55; ☺hourly 10am-midnight May–early Sep) make for an easy escape from the city and are a favourite swimming spot for locals. Boats depart from Slussen.

Other options include an atmospheric all-day trip from Stockholm to the Unesco World Heritage Site of Birka (p103) on the island of Björkö; and a romantic jaunt to Drottningholm (p95) via turn-of-the-century steam ship. Both boat trips depart from Stadshusbron.

TOP TIP

Stockholm is not a crack-of-dawn city. If you want a museum to yourself, arrive right when it opens. But if you're after clubbing crowds, consider a disco nap; chic places don't start hopping before 10pm and stay packed until 4am.

Fast Facts

» Population: 847,073 (city proper)
» Area: 216 sq km
» Telephone area code: 08

Planning Your Trip

Book ahead for accommodation, car hire and big-ticket entertainment (touring exhibitions, film festivals, popular bands). Top-end restaurants require reservations, but usually only a day or so in advance. Do book if you're planning an excursion during summer (to Gotland, for example), especially if you're bringing a vehicle.

Resources

» Official visitor guide: www. visitstockholm.com/en
» Official Sweden blog portal: blogs.sweden.se
» Aftonbladet newspaper guide: www.alltomstock holm.se
» Swedish Film Institute: www.sfi.se
» Lonely Planet: www.lonely planet.com/sweden

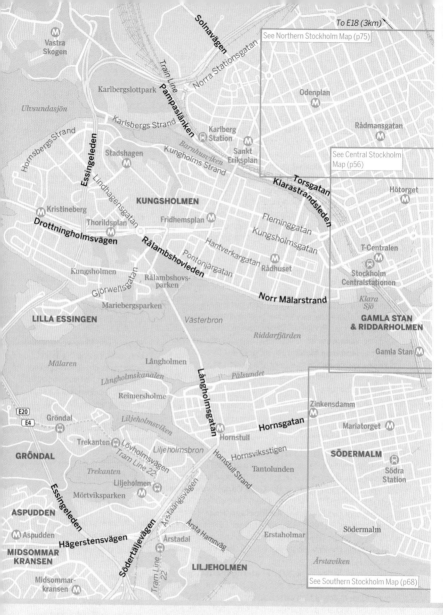

To E18 (3km)

See Northern Stockholm Map (p75)

See Central Stockholm Map (p56)

See Southern Stockholm Map (p68)

Stockholm & Around Highlights

1 Study a shipwreck – and Swedish history – at the **Vasamuseet** (p63)

2 Wander atmospheric **Gamla Stan** (p55) and the Royal Palace

3 Visit Sweden in miniature at **Skansen** open-air museum (p62)

4 Explore the history of Swedish art and design at the **Nationalmuseum** (p60)

5 See cutting-edge international artwork at **Moderna Museet** (p66)

6 Go shopping at big-name boutiques along **Biblioteksgatan** (p90)

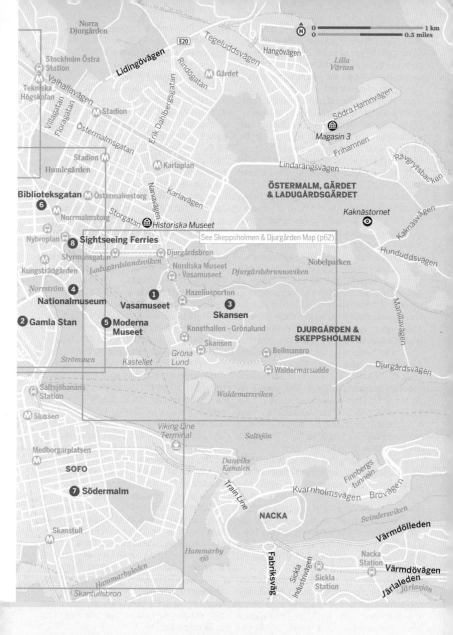

7 Bar-hop bohemian style in **Södermalm** (p67)

8 Sail out into the archipelago on one of many **sightseeing ferries** (p72) for a taste of Stockholm's surroundings

History

Rising land drove Stockholm's early destiny, forcing the centre of Swedish Viking political power to move from northern Lake Mälaren to the lake's outlet for better trade routes. The town charter dates from 1250; that same year, the city's leaders signed a trade treaty with the Hanseatic port of Lübeck.

Stockholm's official founder, Birger Jarl, commissioned the original royal castle Tre Kronor in 1252. The city's name ('tree-trunk islet') appears to have been inspired by locks built from wooden stumps on either side of Stadsholmen.

Difficult times followed. The Black Death of 1350 wiped out around a third of Sweden's population, most of which was concentrated in Stockholm; then Danish Queen Margrethe Valdemarsdotter added insult to injury by besieging the city from 1391 to 1395, amalgamating the crowns of Sweden, Norway and Denmark under the unpopular Union of Kalmar in 1397. Stockholm was a key piece in control of the lands covered by the Kalmar Union, and from 1397 to the early 1500s it was constantly embattled as various Danish and Swedish factions struggled for power.

In what became known as the Stockholm Bloodbath of 1520, Danish King Christian II tricked, trapped and beheaded 82 rebellious Swedish burghers, bishops and nobles on Stortorget in Gamla Stan. One of the victims had a son, Gustav Ericsson Vasa, who led a successful resistance to Danish rule and became Sweden's first king on 6 June 1523, now Sweden's national day.

Vasa's sons, King Erik XIV, King Johan III and King Karl IX, continued their father's nation-building, transforming Stockholm into a major military hub during the Thirty Years War. By the end of the 16th century, Stockholm's population was 9000, and the city had spread from the original old town onto Norrmalm and Södermalm. Stockholm was officially proclaimed the capital of Sweden in 1634.

By 1650 the city boasted a thriving artistic and intellectual culture and a grand new look, courtesy of father-and-son architects the Tessins, who built Drottningholms Slott and several other iconic Stockholm buildings.

The following decades weren't so kind to the capital. A devastating famine brought starving hordes to the city in 1696, and the beloved Tre Kronor went up in flames the following year. Russian military victories shrunk the Swedish empire, another plague engulfed the city in 1711, and King Karl XII was assassinated in Norway in 1718.

A now-fragile Stockholm traded state-building for character-building. Botanist Carl von Linné (1707–78) developed the template for the classification of plants and animals, Anders Celsius (1701–44) came up with the centigrade temperature scale, and royal palace Kungliga Slottet rose from the ashes of Tre Kroner. Swedish science, architecture and arts blossomed during the reign of Francophile King Gustav III (1771–92), but the theatre buff's tyrannical tendencies saw him assassinated by parliament member Jacob Johan Anckarström at a masked ball in the Opera House in 1792. The murder formed the basis of Giuseppe Verdi's opera *A Masked Ball*.

When Sweden's northern and southern train lines were connected via Stockholm's Centralstationen and Riddarholmen in 1871, an industrial boom kicked in. The city's population reached 245,000 in 1890 (an increase of 77,000 in 10 years), and new districts like Östermalm expanded the city limits.

Stockholm hosted the 1912 summer Olympics, but the resulting elation quickly dissipated when Sweden refused to uphold a blockade against Germany during WWI. Britain attacked the country's supply lines, causing starving Stockholmers to riot in Gustav Adolfs torg. During WWII Sweden's official neutrality made it a hot spot for Jewish, Scandinavian and Baltic refugees, the first of many successive waves of migrants.

The city's postwar economic boom saw the advent of Eastern Bloc–style suburban expansion. Along with growth and modernisation came increased violence, notably the still-unsolved murder of Prime Minister Olof Palme on Sveavägen in 1986, and the stabbing death of foreign minister Anna Lindh at the NK department store in 2003.

The worldwide collapse of the IT economy during the 1990s hit tech-dependent Stockholm particularly hard, although the industry later recovered. These days, the capital is part of a major European biotechnology region, as well as a rising star in food and fashion.

◉ Sights

Stockholm is strewn across 14 islands connected by more than 50 bridges. It's a compact, easily walkable city, but the layout – more pinwheel than grid, with water on all

STOCKHOLM IN...

Two Days

Beat the crowds to the labyrinthine streets of **Gamla Stan**, the city's historic old town. Watch St George wrestle the dragon inside **Storkyrkan**, the old-town cathedral, and join a tour of the royal palace, **Kungliga Slottet**. Then trek to **Södermalm** for dizzying views from the top of the public elevator **Katarinahissen**. If the weather's nice, party on the terrace at **Mosebacke Etablissement** or **Debaser**. Spend the next day exploring the outdoor Sweden-in-miniature museum **Skansen**, before dinner and drinks at **Sturehof**.

Four Days

On day three take a **guided boat tour** of Stockholm's waterways. Visit the impressive **Vasamuseet**, then stroll up to **Hötorgshallen** for a big bowl of fish soup and some boutique food shopping. The next day, bus out to beautiful **Millesgården** for sculptures in a dreamy setting, then spend the afternoon doing what Stockholmers do best: shopping. Start with pedestrianised **Biblioteksgatan** off Stureplan, then transition to **Drottninggatan** for souvenirs.

A Week

A week in Stockholm gives you enough time to explore the beautiful surrounds, whether historic villages like **Sigtuna**, pristine palaces like **Skokloster Slott**, or the rugged little islands in the **Stockholm archipelago**. Many of the nearby highlights can be seen in a day trip, but an overnight stay allows for a less frenzied pace.

sides – can be disorienting. Neighbourhoods are closer together than they seem; it's often quicker to walk from one attraction to another than it would be to catch a bus or navigate the tunnelbana system. In other words, the best approach is to allow for a bit of meandering, since you never know when you'll stumble across a delightful surprise.

GAMLA STAN

The old town is Stockholm's historic and geographic heart. Here, cobblestone streets wriggle past Renaissance churches, baroque palaces and medieval squares. Sorbet-coloured merchants' houses sag like wizened old men, and narrow lanes harbour everything from dusty toy shops to candlelit cafes and restaurants.

Västerlånggatan is the quarter's nerve centre, a bustling thoroughfare lined with galleries, eateries and souvenir shops. Step off the main drag and into the tinier alleyways for a surprisingly quiet chance to explore.

Kungliga Slottet   CASTLE
(Royal Palace; Map p56; www.kungahuset.se; Slottsbacken; adult/child Skr100/50; ☺10am-5pm mid-May–mid-Sep, noon-4pm Tue-Sun rest of year, guided tour 2pm) The not-to-be-missed Kungliga Slottet was built on the ruins of the original royal castle, Tre Kronor, which burned

down in 1697. The north wing survived and was incorporated into the new palace, but its medieval designs are now concealed by a baroque exterior. The palace, designed by the court architect Nicodemus Tessin the Younger, took 57 years to complete. With 608 rooms, it's the world's largest royal castle still used for its original purpose.

The sumptuous **state apartments**, including the Hall of State and the Apartments of the Royal Orders of Chivalry, are both open to the public (except during state functions, most of which happen in September; closures are noted on the website), with two floors of royal pomp, 18th- and 19th-century furnishings, and portraits of pale princes and princesses. Look for Queen Kristina's silver throne in the Hall of State and for the decadent Karl XI Gallery, inspired by Versailles' Hall of Mirrors and considered the finest example of Swedish late baroque.

A combination ticket (adult/child Skr140/70) gets you into the palace as well as the **Royal Treasury** and the basement **Museum Tre Kronor**, where you can see the foundations of 13th-century defensive walls and exhibits rescued from the medieval castle during the fire of 1697. From mid-May through September the combination ticket also includes **Gustav III's Antikmuseum**, featuring mainly sculptures collected by the

Central Stockholm

N

200 m
0.1 miles

ÖSTERMALM, GÄRDET & LADUGÅRDSGÄRDET

NORRMALM & VASASTAN

ÖSTRA JÄRNVÄGSGATAN

Birger Jarlsgatan

Vasagatan

Olof Palmes Gata

To Crystal Plaza
Hotel (150m)

See Northern Stockholm Map (p75)

Storgatan
Artillerigatan
Riddargatan
Kaptensgatan
Östermalmstorg
Kommendörsgatan
Linnégatan
Strandvägen
Sibyllegatan
Östermalmstorg
Nybrogatan
Visit Skärgården
Cinderella
Båtarna
Humlegårdsgatan
Grev Turegatan
Nybroplan
Strömma
Kanalbolaget
Humlegården
Sturegatan
Sturegallerian
Shopping
Centre
Berzelii
Park
Näckströmsgatan
Sture-
plan
Biblioteksgatan
Kungsträdgårdsgatan
Norrlandsgatan
Jakobsbergsgatan
Smålandsgatan
Norrmalmstorg
Hamngatan
Kungsträd-
gården
Brunnsgatan
Kungsgatan
Lästmakargatan
Master Samuelsgatan
Västra
Trädgårdsgatan
Eriksbergsgatan
Oxtorget
Regeringsgatan
Johannes
kyrka
Oxtorgsgatan
Malmskillnadsgatan
Sveavägen
Olofsgatan
Hötorget
Hötorget
Sergelgatan
Kulturhuset
T-Centralen
Sergels
Torg
Drottninggatan
Klara Östra
Kyrkogatan
Adolf
Fredriks
Kyrka
Slöjdgatan
Master Samuelsgatan
Klara Västra
Kyrkogatan
Drottninggatan
Apelbergsgatan
Bryggargatan
Klarabergsgatan
Kammakargatan
Barnhusgatan
Målargatan
Klara Norra
Kyrkogatan
Klara Västra
Kyrkogatan
Wallingatan
Kungsgatan
Gamla Brogatan
Vasaplan
Viking Line
Office
Tegnérlunden
Upplandsgatan
Norra
Bantorget
Cityterminalen
Tegnérlunden

16
1
78
43
62
70
59
79
52
49
72
67
46
65
23
74
44
69
61
36
20
63
41
76
31
73
48
60
27
28
54
68
75
55
39
13
15
29
57
18
19
17
50
4
5

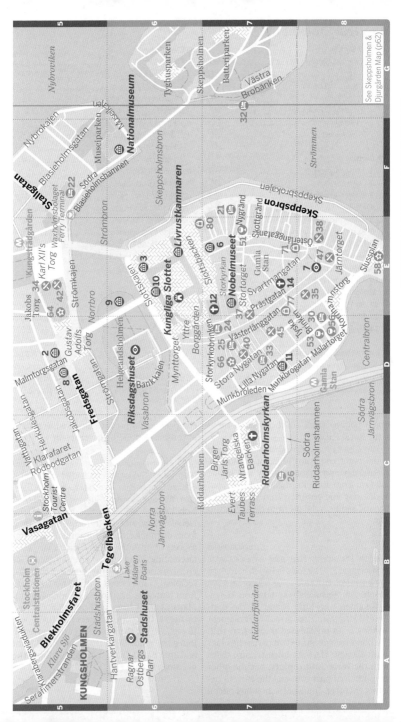

Central Stockholm

king. Opening hours are the same as those of the Royal Palace.

The Changing of the Guard takes place in the outer courtyard at 12.15pm Monday to Saturday and 1.15pm Sunday and public holidays from June to August, and 12.15pm Wednesday and Saturday and 1.15pm Sunday and public holidays from September to May.

FREE Riksdagshuset   CULTURAL BUILDING
(Swedish Parliament; Map p56; www.riksdagen. se; Mynttorget 2; ☺1hr tours in English noon, 1pm, 2pm & 3pm Mon-Fri mid-Jun–Aug, 1.30pm Sat & Sun Oct–mid-Jun) Technically situated on Helgeandsholmen, the little island in the middle of Norrström, the Swedish Parliament building is an unexpected pleasure to visit. The building consists of two parts: the older front section (facing downstream) dates from the early 20th century, but the other more modern part contains the current debating chamber. Tours of the building offer a compelling glimpse into the Swedish system of consensus-building government.

TOP CHOICE Nobelmuseet   MUSEUM
(Map p56; Stortorget; adult/child Skr70/free; ☺10am-6pm, to 8pm Tue mid-May–mid-Sep, 11am-5pm Wed-Sun, to 8pm Tue mid-Sep–mid-May) Nobelmuseet presents the history of the Nobel Prizes and their recipients, with a focus on intellectual history and the cultural aspects of invention. It is a slick space with fascinating short films on the theme of creativity, symbolic gifts donated by prize recipients, interviews with and readings from laureates like Ernest Hemingway and Martin Luther King, and cafe chairs signed by the visiting prize winners (flip them over to see!). To get the most out of the museum, join a free guided tour (in English at 11.15am and 3pm daily). In the Börsen building – the old Stock Exchange.

STOCKHOLM & AROUND STOCKHOLM

Livrustkammaren
MUSEUM

(Royal Armoury; Map p56; www.livrustkammaren.se; Slottsbacken 3; adult/child Skr75/free; ⊙11am-5pm May & Jun, 10am-6pm Jul & Aug, 11am-5pm Tue-Sun, to 8pm Thu Sep-Apr) Livrustkammaren is part of the palace complex, but can be visited separately. It's a family attic of sorts, crammed with engrossing memorabilia spanning more than 500 years of royal childhoods, coronations, weddings and murders. Meet Gustav II Adolf's stuffed battle steed, Streiff; see the masquerade costume worn by Gustav III on the night he was shot; or let the kids try on a suit of armour in the playroom. There's a fairy-tale collection of coronation coaches in the basement, including the outrageously rococo number used for the crowning of Adolf Fredrik and Ulrika Eleonora in 1751. Free guided tours at 2pm; children's tours 1pm.

Riddarholmskyrkan
CHURCH

(Map p56; adult/child Skr30/15; ⊙10am-5pm mid-May–late Sep) The strikingly beautiful Riddarholmskyrkan, on the equally pretty and under-visited islet of Riddarholmen, was built by Franciscan monks in the late 13th century. It has been the royal necropolis since the burial of Magnus Ladulås in 1290, and is home to the armorial glory of the Seraphim knightly order. Look for the marble sarcophagus of Gustav II, Sweden's mightiest monarch, and massed wall plates displaying the coats of arms of the knights. There's a guided tour in English at 2pm, and occasional concerts throughout the year. Riddarholmen is easy to reach by footbridge from the Gamla Stan tunnelbana station.

Storkyrkan
CHURCH

(Map p56; adult/child Skr25/free; ⊙9am-6pm mid-May–Oct, to 4pm rest of year) The one-time venue for royal weddings and coronations, Storkyrkan is both Stockholm's oldest building (consecrated in 1306) and its cathedral. Behind a baroque facade, the Gothic-cum-baroque interior includes extravagant royal-box pews designed by

PENNY-PINCHING PACKAGES

Depending on your plans and energy levels, getting your money's worth out of a visit to Stockholm can be easier with a discount package. The Stockholm Card is available from tourist offices, Storstockholms Lokaltrafik (SL) information centres, some museums, and some hotels and hostels, or online at www.stockholmtown.com. It gives you entry to 80 museums and attractions, travel on SL's public transport network, sightseeing by boat, and various other discounts. It is valid for one, two, three or five days and costs Skr425/550/650/895 (or Skr195/225/245/285 for accompanying children, maximum two children per adult).

Students and seniors get discounted admission to most museums and sights without the card, so you'll need to work out if it's cheaper for you to just get a transport pass and pay admission charges separately. The one-day pass demands an athletic level of sightseeing energy; you may be better off paying admission at a couple of sights and walking between them. To get maximum value out of the multiday cards, plan ahead and be sure to note opening hours; for example, Skansen remains open until late, whereas royal palaces are only open until 3pm or 4pm.

Stockholm à la Carte (from Skr505) is a cut-price package that includes a hotel room. Available weekends year-round and throughout the summer (mid-June to mid-August), its cost depends on the standard of accommodation (prices for central hotels start at around Skr925 per person). Travel agents in other Scandinavian capitals or major Swedish cities can help with arrangements; otherwise contact Destination Stockholm (www.destination-stockholm.com). The website has lots of good information and details of the 51 hotels involved in the scheme.

Nicodemus Tessin the Younger, as well as German Berndt Notke's dramatic sculpture *St George and the Dragon,* commissioned by Sten Sture the Elder to commemorate his victory over the Danes in 1471. Keep an eye out for posters and handbills advertising music performances here.

FREE **Medeltidsmuseet**　　　　MUSEUM
(Medieval Museum; Map p56; www.medeltidsmuseet.stockholm.se; Strömparterren; ⊙noon-5pm Tue-Sun, to 7pm Wed; ⊡) Tucked away beneath Norrbro, the bridge that links Gamla Stan to Helgeandsholmen and Norrmalm, this child-friendly museum has recently been renovated. It was initially established when construction workers preparing to build a car park here in the late 1970s unearthed foundations dating from the 1530s. The ancient walls were preserved as found and, instead of a parking lot, a museum was built around them. The museum's circular plan leads visitors through faithful reconstructions of typical homes, markets and workshops from medieval Stockholm, with plenty of hands-on and multimedia elements to keep the yawns at bay. Also in the museum is the well-preserved 1520s-era ship *Riddarsholm.*

Kungliga Myntkabinettet　　　　MUSEUM
(Royal Coin Cabinet; Map p56; Slottsbacken 6; adult/child Skr60/free, Mon free; ⊙10am-4pm) Across the plaza from the Royal Palace, Kungliga Myntkabinettet gleams with a priceless collection of currency spanning 2600 years. Treasures include Viking silver, the world's oldest coin (from 625 BC), the world's largest coin (a Swedish copper plate weighing 19.7kg) and the planet's first banknote (issued in Sweden in 1661).

Postmuseum　　　　MUSEUM
(Map p56; Lilla Nygatan 5; adult/child Skr50/free; ⊙11am-4pm Tue-Sun) Examining almost four centuries of Swedish postal history, the Postmuseum is not as mind-numbing as it sounds. It's actually rather evocative, featuring old mail carriages, kitsch postcards and a cute children's post office for budding postal workers. There's also a great cafe and a philatelic library with 51,000 books on stamps and postal history.

CENTRAL STOCKHOLM

Some of the city's best museums are smack in the middle of town, within easy walking distance of each other.

Nationalmuseum　　　　MUSEUM
(Map p56; www.nationalmuseum.se; Södra Blasieholmshamnen; adult/child Skr100/free, special

exhibits Skr120; ⊘11am-5pm Wed-Sun, to 8pm Tue Jun-Aug; 11am-5pm Wed-Sun, to 8pm Tue & Thu Sep-May) Sweden's largest art museum, Nationalmuseum houses the nation's collection of painting, sculpture, drawings, decorative arts and graphics, dating from the Middle Ages to the present. Some of the art became state property on the death of Gustav III in 1792, making this one of the earliest public museums in the world. Around 16,000 paintings and sculptures are on display, including magnificent works by the likes of Rembrandt, Rubens and Cézanne, as well as masterpieces by local greats like Anders Zorn, CG Pilo and Carl Larsson. Around 30,000 items make up the decorative-arts collection, including porcelain, furniture, glassware, silverware and late-medieval tapestries. Design aficionados will drool over the *Den moderna formen 1900–2000* exhibition, which follows the evolution of Scandi design and features iconic pieces like Gösta Thames' Cobra telephone and Jonas Bohlin's Concrete chair. There's also an excellent museum shop and a light-filled terrace cafe.

Historiska Museet   MUSEUM
(www.historiska.se; Narvavägen 13; adult/child Skr60/free, 4-8pm Thu Oct-Apr free; ⊘11am-5pm Tue-Sun, to 8pm Thu Oct-Apr, 10am-5pm May-Sep) The national historical collection awaits at this enthralling museum. From Iron Age skates and a Viking boat to medieval textiles and Renaissance triptychs, it spans over 10,000 years of Swedish history and culture. The undisputed highlight is the subterranean Gold Room, a brooding chamber gleaming with Viking bling and rare treasures, including the jewel-encrusted, millennium-old Reliquary for St Elisabeth. The most astonishing artefact, however, is the 5th-century seven-ringed gold collar with 458 carved figures, weighing 823g. Discovered in Västergötland in the 19th century, it was probably used by pagan priests in ritualistic ceremonies. Bring ID to use the museum's free audio guides.

Stadshuset   CULTURAL BUILDING
(Town Hall; Map p56; Hantverkargatan 1; admission by tour only, adult/child Skr90/40 Apr-Oct, Skr60/20 Nov, Dec & Jan-Mar; ⊘tours in English hourly 10am-3pm) A mighty mass of brown bricks (eight million in total), Stadshuset dominates Stockholm's architecture. Topping its hulking square tower is a golden spire and the symbol of Swedish power: the three royal crowns. (It's no coincidence that the tower is one whole metre taller than Copenhagen's equivalent.) Punctured by two courtyards, the building's interior includes the glittering, mosaic-lined Gyllene salen (Golden Hall), Prins Eugen's own fresco recreation of the lake view from the gallery, and the very hall used for the annual Nobel Prize banquet. Part of the tour involves walking down the same stairs you'd use if you'd won the big prize. Entry is by tour only, and these may be interrupted from time to time by preparations for special events. The tower (adult/child Skr40/free; ⊘9am-5pm Jun-Aug, 9am-4pm May & Sep) offers stellar views and a great thigh workout.

Armémuseum   MUSEUM
(Map p56; www.armemuseum.se; Riddargatan 13; adult/child Skr80/free; ⊘11am-8pm Tue, to 5pm Wed-Sun) Delve into the darker side of human nature at Armémuseum, where three levels of engrossing exhibitions explore the horrors of war through art, weaponry and life-size reconstructions of charging horsemen, forlorn barracks and starving civilians. You can even hop on a replica saw horse for a taste of medieval torture.

Hallwylska Museet   MUSEUM
(Hallwyl Collection; Map p56; www.hallwylskamuseet.se; Hamngatan 4; adult/child Skr50/free; ⊘10am-4pm Tue-Sun Jul & Aug, noon-4pm Tue & Thu-Sun, noon-7pm Wed Sep-Jun) A private palace completed in 1898, Hallwylska Museet was once home to compulsive hoarder Wilhelmina von Hallwyl, who collected items as diverse as kitchen utensils, Chinese pottery, 17th-century paintings, silverware, sculpture and her children's teeth. In 1920 she and her husband donated the mansion and its contents to the state. The faux-baroque drawing room is particularly impressive, complete with a rare, playable grand piano. Guided tours (Skr90, including admission) in English take place at 12.30pm daily in July and August; the rest of the year they're only at 1.30pm on Sunday (although you can join one of the more regular tours in Swedish). The museum is not wheelchair-accessible.

Medelhavsmuseet   MUSEUM
(Museum of Mediterranean Antiquities; Map p56; www.medelhavsmuseet.se; Fredsgatan 2; adult/child Skr80/free; ⊘noon-8pm Tue-Fri, to 5pm Sat & Sun, to 5pm Fri Jun-Aug) Housed in an elegant Italianate building, Medelhavsmuseet lures history buffs with its Egyptian, Greek, Cypriot, Roman and Etruscan artefacts. Swoon

Skeppsholmen & Djurgården

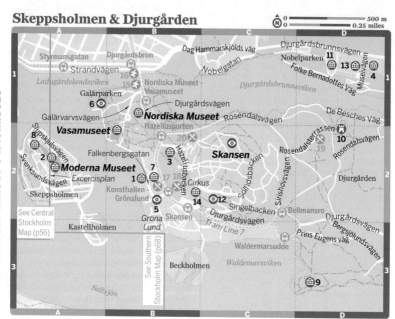

over sumptuous Islamic art and check out the gleaming gold room, home to a 4th-century-BC olive wreath made of gold.

Strindbergsmuseet
MUSEUM

(Map p56; Drottninggatan 85; adult/child Skr50/free; ⊙10am-4pm Jul & Aug, noon-4pm Tue-Sun Sep-Jun) The small but evocative Strindbergsmuseet in the Blue Tower is the well-preserved apartment where writer and painter August Strindberg (1849–1912) spent his final four years. Peep into his closet, scan his study and library (containing some 3000 volumes), do a round of the dining room, and take in the often absorbing temporary exhibits.

Dansmuseet
MUSEUM

(Map p56; www.dansmuseet.nu; Gustav Adolfs Torg 22-24; admission free, special exhibitions adult/child Skr40/free; ⊙11am-4pm Tue-Fri, noon-4pm Sat & Sun) The Dansmuseet focuses on the intersections between dance, art and theatre. Collection highlights include traditional dance masks from Africa, India and Tibet, avant-garde costumes from the Russian ballet, Chinese and Japanese theatre puppets and one of the finest collections of early-20th-century Ballets Russes costumes.

Kulturhuset
LIBRARY

(Map p56; www.kulturhuset.stockholm.se; Sergels Torg; ⊙Tue-Sun) An arts hub; has a reading room with international periodicals, newspapers and books, plus an unusually good selection of graphic novels in many languages, as well as internet access.

Stadsbiblioteket
LIBRARY

(Map p75; Sveavägen 73; ⊙9am-9pm Mon-Thu, to 7pm Fri, noon-4pm Sat & Sun, shorter hours in summer) The main city library is just north of the city centre. Designed by architect Erik Gunnar Asplund and sporting a curvaceous, Technicolor reading room, it's the finest example of Stockholm's 1920s neoclassicist style.

DJURGÅRDEN

This parklike island is a museum-goer's dream. Not only are many of Stockholm's top museums gathered here, but the setting is sublime: gardens, greenery, a lazy river, cycle paths, picnic places, and all of it just one footbridge away from the centre of town.

Skansen
MUSEUM

(Map p62; www.skansen.se; adult/child Skr120/50; ⊙from 10am, check website for current schedule) The world's first open-air museum, Skansen was founded in 1891 by Artur Hazelius to

Skeppsholmen & Djurgården

STOCKHOLM & AROUND STOCKHOLM

give visitors an insight into how Swedes lived once upon a time. You could easily spend a day here and still not see it all (note that prices and closing times vary according to the time of year). Around 150 traditional houses and other exhibits from across the country dot the hilltop – it's meant to be 'Sweden in miniature', complete with villages, nature, commerce and industry. The glass-blowers' cottage is a popular stop; watching the intricate forms emerge from glowing blobs of liquid glass is transfixing. The Nordic Zoo, with elk, reindeer, wolverines and other native wildlife, is a highlight, especially in spring when baby critters scamper around. The formerly summer-only petting zoo has been renovated and is now open year-round.

Buildings in the open-air museum represent various trades and areas of the country. Most are inhabited by staff in period costume, often creating handicrafts, playing music or churning butter while cheerfully answering questions about the folk whose lives they're recreating. Part of the pharmacy was moved here from Drottningholm castle; two little garden huts came from Tantolunden in Södermalm.

There's a bakery (still operational, serving coffee and lunch), a bank/post office, a machine shop, botanical gardens and Hazelius' mansion. There are also 46 buildings from rural areas around Sweden, including a Sami camp, farmsteads representing several regions, a manor house and a school. A map and an excellent booklet in English are available to guide you around. It's also worth noting that the closing times

for each workshop can vary, so check times online to avoid disappointment.

There are cafes, restaurants and hot-dog stands throughout the park. Carrying water isn't a bad idea in summer, and it's not cheating to take the escalator to the top of the hill and meander down from there.

Daily activities take place on Skansen's stages, including folk dancing in summer and an enormous public festival at Midsummer's Eve. If you're in Stockholm for any of the country's other major celebrations, such as Walpurgis Night, St Lucia Day and Christmas, it's a great (if crowded) place to watch Swedes celebrate.

Tobaks & Tändsticksmuseum MUSEUM
(Tobacco & Matchstick Museum; Map p62; www.tobaksochtandsticksmuseum.se; admission incl with Skansen tickets; ⊙from 11am, closing times vary by season, closed Mon Oct-Apr) Skansen incorporates a few other museums, including the Tobaks & Tändsticksmuseum, which traces the history and culture of smoking and the manufacture of iconic Swedish matches.

Skansen Aquarium AQUARIUM
(Map p62; www.skansen.se; adult/child Skr100/50; ⊙from 10am, closing times vary by season) The Skansen Aquarium is worth a wander, its residents including piranhas, lemurs and pygmy marmosets (the smallest monkeys in the world). Intrepid visitors are allowed into the cages of some of the animals.

Vasamuseet MUSEUM
(Map p62; www.vasamuseet.se; Galärvarvsvägen 14; adult/child Skr110/free; ⊙8.30am-6pm Jun-Aug,

10am-5pm Thu-Tue & 10am-8pm Wed Sep-May) A good-humoured glorification of some dodgy calculations, Vasamuseet is the custom-built home of the massive warship *Vasa* and a consistent favourite among visitors. The ship, a whopping 69m long and 48.8m tall, was the pride of the Swedish crown when it set off on its maiden voyage on 10 August 1628. Within minutes, the top-heavy vessel tipped and sank to the bottom of Saltsjön, along with many of the people on board. Tour guides explain the extraordinary and controversial 300-year story of its death and resurrection, which saw the ship painstakingly raised in 1961 and reassembled like a giant 14,000-piece jigsaw. Almost all of what you see today is original.

On the entrance level is a model of the ship at scale 1:10 and a cinema screening a 25-minute film covering topics not included in the exhibitions (in English at 9.30am and 1.30pm daily in summer). There are four other levels of exhibits covering artefacts salvaged from the *Vasa,* life on-board, naval warfare, and 17th-century sailing and navigation, plus sculptures and temporary exhibitions. The bottom-floor exhibition is particularly fascinating, using modern forensic science to recreate the faces and life stories of several of the ill-fated passengers.

The bookshop is worth a browse and there's a restaurant for a well-earned pit stop. Guided tours are in English every 30 minutes in summer, and at least twice daily the rest of the year.

Give yourself a couple of hours to really absorb the place.

Nordiska Museet MUSEUM

(National Museum of Cultural History; Map p62; www.nordiskamuseet.se; Djurgårdsvägen 6-16; adult/child Skr80/free, 5-8pm Wed Sep-May free; ⊙10am-5pm daily Jun-Aug, 10am-4pm Mon-Fri, to 8pm Wed, 11am-5pm Sat & Sun Sep-May) The epic Nordiska Museet is Sweden's largest cultural-history museum and its second-largest indoor space. The building itself is an eclectic, Renaissance-style castle designed by Isak Gustav Clason, who also drew up Östermalms Saluhall (p85). Inside you'll find a sprawling collection of all things Swedish, from sacred Sami objects to fashion, shoes, home interiors and even table settings. The museum boasts the world's largest collection of paintings by August Strindberg, as well as a number of his personal possessions. In all, there are over 1.5 million items dating from 1520 to the present day. Topping it off are the

often dynamic temporary exhibitions. The insightful audio guide (Skr20) offers several hours of English commentary.

Junibacken THEME PARK

(Map p62; www.junibacken.se; adult Skr125-145, child Skr110-125; ⊙10am-6pm Jul–mid-Aug, to 5pm mid-Aug–Jun) Junibacken whimsically recreates the fantasy scenes of Astrid Lindgren's books for children. Catch the flying Story Train over Stockholm, shrink to the size of a sugar cube, and end up at Villekulla cottage where kids can shout, squeal and dress up like Pippi Longstocking. The bookshop is a treasure trove of children's books, as well as a great place to pick up anything from cheeky Karlsson dolls to cute little art cards with storybook themes.

Prins Eugens Waldemarsudde MUSEUM

(Map p62; www.waldemarsudde.com; Prins Eugens väg 6; adult/child Skr100/free; ⊙11am-5pm Tue-Sun, to 8pm Thu) Prins Eugens Waldemarsudde, at the southern tip of Djurgården, is a soulperking combo of water views and art. The palace once belonged to the painter prince, who favoured art over typical royal pleasures. In addition to Eugen's own work, it holds his impressive collection of Nordic paintings and sculptures, including works by Anders Zorn and Carl Larsson. The buildings and galleries, connected by tunnels, are surrounded by soothing gardens and an old windmill.

Thielska Galleriet GALLERY

(Sjötullsbacken; adult/under 18yr Skr80/free; ⊙noon-4pm) Thielska Galleriet, found at the east end of Djurgården, is a must for Nordic art fans, with a savvy collection of late-19th- and early-20th-century works from Scandinavian greats like Carl Larsson, Anders Zorn, Ernst Josephson and Bruno Liljefors, plus a series of Edvard Munch's etchings of vampiric women and several paintings from a bridge you'll recognise from *The Scream*. There's also a plaster cast of Nietzsche's death mask, if you're into that sort of thing. The building is on the small, worn-in side; it feels more like walking through a home than a museum. Take bus 69 from Centralstationen.

Gröna Lund Tivoli AMUSEMENT PARK

(Map p62; www.gronalund.com; adult/under 7yr Skr90/free; ⊙noon-10pm Mon-Sat, to 8pm Sun Jun, 11am-10pm Sun-Thu, to 11pm Fri & Sat Jul-early Aug, hours vary May & early Aug–mid-Sep) Crowded Gröna Lund Tivoli has some 30

STOCKHOLM FOR CHILDREN

Stockholm is well set up for travelling with children. There are baby-changing tables in almost every public bathroom. Even top-end restaurants have high chairs and children's menus available. Hotel and hostel staff are fully accustomed to catering to families and small children. Public transport is no problem: your fellow passengers might elbow each other out of the way to help you lift your stroller onto the bus. Speaking of strollers, they trundle along in huge numbers, which means the sidewalks and paths are adapted to handle them. Stairs usually have a stroller lane, so you can wheel Junior up or down without jarring. Public playgrounds are numerous and well-maintained.

In terms of entertainment, many of Stockholm's best attractions are targeted specifically at children and families. Junibacken (p64) draws young readers into Swedish author Astrid Lindgren's fantastic world, home to Pippi Longstocking and her friends. Naturhistoriska Riksmuseet (p71) offers a child's-eye view of the natural world, with an entire section for hands-on science experiments. Medeltidsmuseet (p60) is entirely kid-oriented, with multimedia displays that transport visitors back in time to the city's earliest days. The Postmuseet (p60) includes a miniature post office for children who want to see how it all works. For slightly older kids and teens, Gröna Lund Tivoli (p64) offers hours of carnival-ride entertainment. Tekniska Museet (p66) will entertain inquisitive brains. And Skansen (p62) is essentially a children's paradise, with dozens of mini-exhibits to explore, snacks everywhere, a petting zoo, singalongs, and staffers in old-timey costumes.

Even if they aren't particularly geared towards children, most of the city's museums have family playrooms available. Nobelmuseet, for instance, has a 'children's club' ('Barnens Nobelklubb') where kids aged between seven and 10 years can share ideas and be creative; other museums have rooms set aside for kid-friendly hands-on learning activities, such as painting, clay-modelling or costume-making.

rides, ranging from the tame (a German circus carousel) to the terrifying (the Free Fall, where you drop from a height of 80m in six seconds after glimpsing a lovely, if brief, view over Stockholm). There are countless places to eat and drink in the park, but whether you'll keep it down is another matter entirely. The Åkband day pass (Skr299) gives unlimited rides, or individual rides range from Skr20 to Skr60. Big-name concerts are often staged here in summer. Gröna Lund is a stop on the Slussen–Djurgården ferry (Skr40).

Rosendals Slott CASTLE
(Map p62; Rosendalsvägen; adult/child Skr70/35; ⊗tours hourly noon-3pm Tue-Sun Jun-Aug) On the northern side of Djurgården, Rosendals Slott was built as a palace for Karl XIV Johan in the 1820s. One of Sweden's finest examples of the Empire style, it sparkles with sumptuous royal furnishings. Admission is by guided tour only. While you're out this way don't miss the wonderful cafe – set among lush gardens and greenhouses and serving tasty organic grub.

Vin & Sprithistoriska Museet MUSEUM
(Wine & Spirits Museum; Map p75; Galärskjulen; adult/child Skr50/free; ⊗10am-7pm Tue, to 4pm Wed-Fri, noon-4pm Sat & Sun) Vin & Sprithistoriska Museet looks at history through a *snaps* (distilled alcoholic beverage such as vodka or aquavit) glass, exploring the often turbulent relationship between Swedes and their beloved *brännvin* (aquavit) and *punsch,* a Swedish alcoholic beverage made with arrack liqueur. It's in the process of moving to a new building on Djurgården, which will include a gallery for its *Absolut Art* collection, a cache of some 800 works by the likes of Damien Hirst and Keith Haring. Until the new building opens, the museum is temporarily closed; check online for updates.

Biologiska museet MUSEUM
(Museum of Biology; Map p62; Hazeliusporten; adult/child Skr45/10; ⊗11am-4pm Apr-Sep, noon-3pm Tue-Fri & 10am-3pm Sat & Sun Oct-Mar) As notable for its creaky wooden building as for its collection of critters, the 1893 Biologiska museet charms visitors with two circular floors of stuffed wildlife in nature dioramas.

Aquaria Vattenmuseum ▪ MUSEUM
(Map p62; Falkenbergsgatan 2; adult/child Skr90/50; ⊗10am-6pm Jul & Aug, 10am-4.30pm Tue-Sun Sep-Jun) A conservation-themed

aquarium complete with steamy tropical jungle, sharks and electric-blue surgeon fish.

Liljevalchs Konsthall `GALLERY`
(Map p62; www.liljevalchs.se; Djurgårdsvägen 60; adult/child Skr80/free; ⊙11am-5pm Tue-Sun, to 8pm Tue & Thu) Has at least four major exhibitions a year of contemporary Swedish and international art, including the popular Spring Salon.

SKEPPSHOLMEN
This small island is home to a couple of major museums. To get here, take the small footbridge from the city centre or hop on the Djurgården ferry from Slussen.

Moderna Museet `MUSEUM`
(Modern Museum; Map p62; www.modernamuseet. se; Exercisplan 4; adult/child Skr100/free, combination ticket with Arkitekturmuseet Skr140; ⊙10am-8pm Tue, to 6pm Wed-Sun) Moderna Museet is Stockholm's modern-art maverick, its booty ranging from paintings and sculptures to photography, video art and installations. Permanent fixtures include work by Pablo Picasso, Salvador Dalí, Robert Rauschenberg, Yinka Shonibare and Paul McCarthy, complemented by top-notch temporary shows. Andy Warhol's first international retrospective was held here in 1968 and it was here that the world first heard his famously misquoted line: 'In the future everybody will be world famous for 15 minutes.' Ponder the quote at the slinky foyer espresso bar, or take in the water views from the fabulous 1st-floor restaurant. Bibliophiles and design fans will adore the well-stocked gift shop.

Arkitekturmuseet `MUSEUM`
(Museum of Architecture; Map p62; Exercisplan 4; www.arkitekturmuseet.se; adult/child Skr60/ free, 4-6pm Fri free, combination ticket with Moderna Museet Skr140; ⊙10am-8pm Tue, to 6pm Wed-Sun) Adjoining Moderna Museet and housed in a converted navy drill hall is Arkitekturmuseet. Focusing on the built environment, it has a permanent exhibition spanning 1000 years of Swedish architecture and an archive of 2.5 million documents, photographs, plans, drawings and models. Temporary exhibitions also cover international names and work. The museum organises occasional themed architectural tours of Stockholm; check the website or ask at the information desk.

Östasiatiska Museet `MUSEUM`
(Museum of Far Eastern Antiquities; Map p62; Tyghusplan 2; adult/child Skr60/free; ⊙11am-8pm Tue, to 5pm Wed-Sun) Houses Asian decorative arts, including one of the world's finest collections of Chinese stoneware and porcelain from the Sing, Ming and Qing dynasties. The often refreshing temporary exhibitions cover a wide range of themes, with past shows including comic-book manga and Chinese video art.

LADUGÅRDSGÄRDET
This wide-open, parklike area is a former military training ground. From the small pink pavilion on the hillside, Borgen, the royalty could enjoy leisurely banquets while watching the troops perform their exercises. It hasn't been used as a training ground since the 1860s; these days the smooth fields of Ladugårdsgärdet are popular for strolls and trail runs, volleyball games, football matches and hot-air balloon rides.

Ladugårdsgärdet is part of the 27-sq-km Ekoparken, the world's first national park within a city. An impressive 14km long, its combo of forest and open fields stretches far into the capital's northern suburbs. This section of it, reached by bus 69 from Centralstationen or Sergels Torg, boasts three fine museums, an art gallery and one of Stockholm's loftiest views.

Tekniska Museet `MUSEUM`
(Museum of Science & Technology; Map p62; www. tekniskamuseet.se; Museivägen 7; adult/child/ under 6yr Skr160/95/free, family Skr450; ⊙10am-6pm, to 8pm Wed) A sprawling wonderland of interactive science and technology exhibits. One of its biggest drawcards is Cino4 (adult/child Skr70/40), Sweden's first 4D, multisensory cinema. There's also a huge model railroad, a survey of inventions by women, and a climate-change game, among many other things.

Etnografiska Museet `MUSEUM`
(National Museum of Ethnography; Map p62; Djurgårdsbrunnsvägen 34; admission free, special exhibitions Skr80; ⊙10am-5pm Mon-Fri, to 8pm Wed, 11am-5pm Sat & Sun) Presents evocative displays on various aspects of non-European cultures, including dynamic temporary exhibitions and frequent live performances. The cafe is a treat, with great music, imported sweets and beverages, and authentic global dishes.

WORTH A TRIP

TROSA

The area around Stockholm has no shortage of adorable seaside towns, the kind of place where the entire point of visiting is to stroll around with an ice-cream cone and marvel at how cute everything is. One of the nicest of these, and among the easiest to reach from the capital, is Trosa. About an hour south of Stockholm, it's well set up for tourism without being obnoxiously overdone. A visit here is a very efficient way to revel in tasteful seaside charm: every little red cottage has perfect white trim, flower boxes are overflowing, the main shopping street (pedestrians only, of course) meanders gently between wooden antique shops and courtyard cafes. There's a marina, a tiny lighthouse, a murky canal to walk beside, and even one of those miniature tourist trains you can hop onto if your feet get tired.

To get here from Stockholm, take the tunnelbana red line to Liljeholmen (Skr36, 10 minutes), then cross the tracks to the bus stop and hop onto the Trosabus (Skr100, one hour). You can buy Trosabus tickets at the Stockholm tourist office or with a credit card once you're on the bus. (If you're using your own wheels, ask at the tourist office for the free brochure on roadside attractions between Trosa and Järna.) Return buses leave from Trosa harbour at 4.15pm and 5pm, with additional trips at 6.30pm Saturday and 4.30 and 8pm Sunday.

Stop in at the tourist office for a brochure about Trosa's 'Heritage Trail', a self-guided walk that takes you past the Town Hall (originally built in 1711 but burned down and re-built in 1883), several bridges, an old schoolhouse, and down to the harbour. You'll pass by Punschgränd, an alley once home to the production of Trosa Punsch, a dangerously potent liquor that came in three colours: yellow, green and blue.

For coffee and pastries, head to **Tre Små Rum** (Östra Långgatan 8; pastries/sandwiches from Skr35/55; ⊘9am-5pm Tue-Fri, to 4pm Sat, 10am-3pm Sun), a pretty bakery-cafe in an 18th-century wooden house with a shady courtyard off the main drag. (If you fall in love with the place, you can stay the night; singles/doubles start at Skr750/1250.)

There's also a hostel across the canal, **Vandrarhemmet Snipan** (☑156-12 142; www. vandrarhemmetsnipan.com; Västra Långgatan 1; s/d/tr/f Skr280/400/500/540), just 500m from the main square. It has two shared guest kitchens, several family rooms, a four-bedroom apartment and cabins available.

From Trosa harbour you can arrange a speedboat tour of the surrounding archipelago with **Trosa Rederi** (☑709-58 66 98; www.trosarederi.se). Ask about tickets at the tourist office in either Stockholm or Trosa.

For more information, contact **Trosa Turism** (☑156-522 22; www.trosa.se).

Sjöhistoriska Museet
MUSEUM

(National Maritime Museum; Map p62; Djurgårdsbrunnsvägen 24; adult/child Skr50/free; ⊘10am-5pm Tue-Sun) A must for fans of model ships (there are over 1500 mini vessels in the collection). The museum's exhibits also explore Swedish shipbuilding, sailors and life on deck.

Kaknästornet
TOWER

(Kaknäs TV tower; adult/child Skr45/20; ⊘9am-10pm Jun-Aug, 10am-9pm Sep-Dec, 10am-9pm Mon-Sat, 10am-6pm Sun Jan-May) About 500m from the museums is the 155m-tall Kaknästornet, the automatic operations centre for radio and TV broadcasting in Sweden. Opened in 1967, it's still the city's tallest building. There's a small visitor centre on the ground floor and an observation deck

and cafe near the top, both providing stellar city and archipelago views.

Magasin 3
GALLERY

(www.magasin3.com; Elevator 4, Magasin 3 Bldg, Frihamnen; adult/child Skr40/free; ⊘11am-7pm Thu, to 5pm Fri-Sun, closed Jun-Aug & Christmas holidays) Magasin 3 is one of Stockholm's best contemporary-art galleries. Located in a dockside warehouse northwest of Kaknästornet, its six to eight annual shows often feature specially commissioned, site-specific work from the likes of American provocateur Paul McCarthy. Take bus 1 or 76 from the city centre.

SÖDERMALM

Stockholm's southern island is known as the edgy, bohemian part of town. It's here that

Southern Stockholm

See Central Stockholm Map (p56)

Riddarfjärden

Söder Mälarstrand

Centralbron

Saltsjöbanans Station

Skinnarviksparken

Mariaberget

Guldgränd

6

14

20

Södermalmstorg

Stockholms Stadsmuseum

7 Slussen

Brännkyrkagatan

26 22

Mariagränd

30

Hornsgatan

Zinkensdamm

Krukmakargatan

Mariatorget

8

Sankt Paulsgatan

Söderledstunneln

Repslagargatan

Götgatan

11

32

Mariatorget

24

Swedenborgsgatan

Björngårdsgatan

Medborgarplatsen

Ringvägen

Wollmar Yxkullsgatan

18

Rosenlundsgatan

Maria Prästgårdsgata

Medborgarplatsen

Maria Skölgata

Högbergsgatan

Maria Bangata

Fatbursgatan

Fatbursparken

Ånghästparken

Södra Station

Folkungagatan

Tantolunden

Sköldgatan

Fatburskvarngatan

Västgötagatan

Södermalmsallén

Magnus Ladulåsgatan

Åsötorget

Rosenlundsparken

Tidelius gatan

Ringvägen

Tjurbergsgatan

Hallandsgatan

Sjukhusbacken

Jägargatan

Helgalunden

Blekingegatan

Allhelgonagatan

Sachsgatan

Tjurberget

SÖDERMALM

Vickergatan

Eriksdalsgatan

Årstaviken

Eriksdalslunden

Hammarby Slussväg

you'll find the coolest secondhand shops, art galleries, bars and espresso labs. The hills at the island's northern edge provide stunning views across Gamla Stan and the rest of the central city. Plus there are a couple of museum heavyweights to seek out.

Fotografiska   MUSEUM

(Map p68; fotografiska.eu; Stadsgårdshamnen 22; adult/child Skr110/free; ⊙10am-9pm) A chic, upmarket photography museum has taken over Stora Tullhuset (the building once earmarked for the long-awaited ABBA mu-

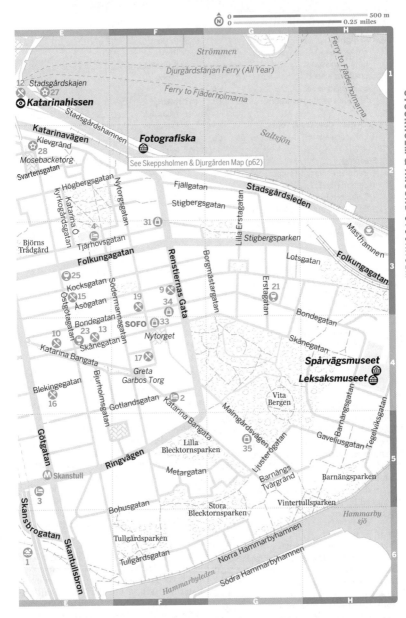

N 0 ————— 500 m
0 ————— 0.25 miles

Strömmen

Djurgårdsfärjan Ferry (All Year)

Ferry to Fjäderholmarna

Ferry to Fjäderholmarna

Saltsjön

12 Stadsgårdskajen
🟢 ✡27
◎ **Katarinahissen**

Stadsgårdshamnen

Katarinavägen
Klevgränd
✡ 28
Mosebacketorg

Svartensgatan

Fotografiska
🏛

See Skeppsholmen & Djurgården Map (p62)

Högbergsgatan

Nytorgsgatan

Fjällgatan

Stigbergsgatan

Stadsgårdsleden

Katarina Ö
Kyrkogårdsgatan

Björns
Trädgård

Tjärhovsgatan

4

31 🔒

Lilla Erstagatan

Stigbergsparken

Masthamnen

Folkungagatan

Stigbergsgatan

Lotsgatan

Folkungagatan

🟢25

Kocksgatan

Renstiernas Gata

Borgmästargatan

Erstagatan

21

🟢15

Östgötagatan

Åsögatan

Södermannagatan

19

🟢9 ✕

34
🔒

Bondegatan

10

23 13

Bondegatan

SOFO 🔒33

Nytorget

Skånegatan

Katarina Bangata

17 ✕

Greta
Garbos Torg

Skånegatan

Spårvägsmuseet

Leksaksmuseet 🏛

Blekingegatan

16

Bjurholmsgatan

Gotlandsgatan

Katarina Bangata

2

Vita
Bergen

Barnängsgatan

Tegelviksgatan

Götgatan

Ringvägen

Lilla
Blecktornsparken

35

Malmgårdsvägen

Ljusterögatan

Gaveliusgatan

Ⓜ Skanstull

Metargatan

Barnängs
Tvärgränd

Barnängsparken

🟢
3

Skånsbrogatan

Bohusgatan

Stora
Blecktornsparken

Vintertullsparken

Hammarby
sjö

Skantullsbron

Tullgårdsparken

Tullgårdsgatan

Norra Hammarbyhamnen

🟢
1

Hammarbyleden

Södra Hammarbyhamnen

---

seum) and it's a good fit. The temporary exhibitions are huge, interestingly chosen and well presented; recent examples include a Robert Mapplethorpe retrospective of about 200 prints and a collection of portraits by indie filmmaker Gus Van Sant.

There's also a strong permanent collection of photos from international and Swedish photographers. Follow signs from the Slussen tunnelbana stop to reach the museum.

Southern Stockholm

FREE **Stockholms Stadsmuseum** MUSEUM
(City Museum; Map p68; Slussen; ⊙11am-5pm Tue-Sun, to 8pm Thu) Evocative exhibits cover Stockholm's development from fortified port to modern metropolis via plague, fire and good old-fashioned scandal. The temporary exhibitions are often fresh and eclectic. Housed in the late-17th-century palace designed by Nicodemus Tessin the Elder in Ryssgården.

Spårvägsmuseet MUSEUM
(Transport Museum; Map p68; www.sparvags museet.sl.se; Tegelviksgatan 22; adult/child Skr40/20; ⊙10am-5pm Mon-Fri, 11am-4pm Sat & Sun) In a former bus depot near the Viking Line terminal, Spårvägsmuseet is Stockholm's transport museum and an atmospheric spot to spend a rainy afternoon. An impressive collection of around 40 vehicles includes horse-drawn carriages, vintage trams and buses, and a retro tunnelbana carriage (complete with original advertisements). Take bus 2 or 66.

Leksaksmuseet MUSEUM
(Toy Museum; Map p68; www.leksaksmuseet.se; Tegelviksgatan 22; admission with Spårvägsmuseet ticket; ⊙10am-5pm Mon-Fri, 11am-4pm Sat & Sun) Sharing an entrance with Spårvägsmuseet, Leksaksmuseet is packed with everything you probably ever wanted as a child (and may still be hankering for as an adult). Get nostalgic over lovingly worn teddy bears, vintage Barbies, model railways, planes and cars, or battle it out with a video game.

Katarinahissen LIFT
(Map p68; Slussen; adult/child Skr10/5; ⊙8am-10pm mid-May–Aug, 10am-6pm Sep–mid-May) You'll get great views from the balcony of Katarinahissen, a lift that dates from the 1930s which takes you 38m up to the heights of Slussen. If you prefer, zigzagging wooden stairs also lead up the cliffs to the balcony. From here you can follow the small footpath, Fjällgatan, for a scenic walk among the vintage wooden houses along the ridge.

SUBURBS

It's well worth venturing beyond the city centre. In the surrounding suburbs you'll find some of Stockholm's most inviting attractions, from museums to parks to castles and even a cemetery. Thanks to a smooth-as-butter transit system, all of these places are easy to reach.

TOP CHOICE Millesgården   MUSEUM
(Map p96; www.millesgarden.se; Herserudsvägen 32, Lidingö; adult/child Skr95/free; ⊙11am-5pm, closed Mon Oct–mid-May) Beautiful Millesgården was the home and studio of sculptor Carl Milles, whose delicate water sprites and other whimsical sculptures dot the city landscape. The grounds include a crisp modern gallery for changing exhibitions of contemporary art, Milles' elaborately Pompeiian house and an exquisite outdoor sculpture garden where items from ancient Greece, Rome, medieval times and the Renaissance intermingle with Milles' own creations. There's also a museum shop and a cafe. Take the tunnelbana to Ropsten, then bus 207.

FREE Skogskyrkogården   CEMETERY
(Woodland Cemetery; Map p96; www.skogskyrkogarden.se; Söckenvagen; ⊙24hr) One of Stockholm's more unusual attractions, Skogskyrkogården is an arrestingly beautiful cemetery set in soothing pine woodland. Designed by the great Erik Gunnar Asplund and Sigurd Lewerentz, it's on the Unesco World Heritage list and famed for its functionalist buildings. Famous residents include Stockholm screen goddess Greta Garbo. A visitor guide is available on the website in several languages. To get here, take the tunnelbana to T-Skogskyrkogården.

Naturhistoriska Riksmuseet   MUSEUM
(National Museum of Natural History; Map p96; www.nrm.se; Frescativägen 40; adult/child Skr80/free; ⊙10am-6pm Tue-Fri, from 6pm Sat & Sun) Sweden's largest museum, Naturhistoriska Riksmuseet was founded by Carl von Linné in 1739. There are hands-on displays about nature and the human body, as well as whole forests' worth of taxidermied wildlife, dinosaurs, marine life and the hardy fauna of the polar regions. The museum is located 300m north of T-Universitetet tunnelbana stop.

Cosmonova   PLANETARIUM, CINEMA
(Map p96; ☑519 551 30; adult/child Skr90/50, no child under 5yr admitted) Adjoining

Naturhistoriska Riksmuseet is Cosmonova, a combined planetarium and IMAX theatre with themes ranging from mummies and dinosaurs to the deep sea and prehistoric sea 'monsters'. Films are screened on the hour, and reservations by phone are recommended. Combination tickets are available, covering both Naturhistoriska Riksmuseet and Cosmonova (adult Skr115 to Skr135, child Skr40 to Skr50).

FREE Hagaparken   PARK
(Map p96; ⊙dawn-dusk) Crowning a hilltop at Haga Park is the peculiar Koppartälten (Copper Tent), built in 1787 as a stable and barracks for Gustav III's personal guard. It now contains a cafe and a restaurant, as well as Haga Parkmuseum, with displays about the park, its pavilions and the royal palace, Haga slott (not open to the public).

Also in the park, **Gustav III's Paviljong** (Gustav III's Pavilion; entry by guided tour only adult/child Skr70/35; ⊙tours hourly noon-3pm Tue-Sun Jun-Aug) is a superb example of late-neoclassical style; the furnishings and decor reflect Gustav III's interest in all things Roman after his Italian tour in 1782.

The steamy **Fjärilshuset** (Butterfly House; www.fjarilshuset.se; adult/child Skr95/50; ⊙10am-5pm Apr-Sep; to 4pm Oct-Mar) recreates a tropical environment, complete with free-flying birds and butterflies and some very friendly fish. It's a fascinating and lovely place any time of year, but it's an especially delightful retreat on a cold winter day.

To reach Hagaparken, take bus 515 from Odenplan to Haga Norra.

Ulriksdals Slott   CASTLE
(Map p96; Ulriksdals Park; guided tours adult/child Skr70/35; ⊙tours hourly noon-3pm Tue-Sun Jun-Aug) North of Hagaparken, 17th-century royal pad Ulriksdals Slott was home to King Gustaf VI Adolf and his family until 1973. Several of their exquisite apartments, including the drawing room, dating from 1923, are open to the public. The stables house Queen Kristina's magnificent 17th-century coronation carriage (officially open to group tours only, but it's worth asking), while the **Orangery** (admission included with castle tour; ⊙noon-4pm Tue-Sun Jun-Aug) contains Swedish sculpture and Mediterranean flora. Head to T-Bergshamra tunnelbana stop, then take bus 503.

🏃 Activities

One thing visitors will notice about Stockholm, particularly during summer months, is how fit and active the majority of locals are. Outdoor activity is a well-integrated part of the city's healthy lifestyle, and there are numerous ways in which a visitor can get in on the action.

CYCLING

Stockholm is a very bicycle-friendly city. Cycling is best in the parks and away from the busy central streets and arterial roads, but even busy streets usually have dedicated cycle lanes (often shared with pedestrians). There's also a separate network of paved walking and cycling paths that make it easy to reach most parts of the city; these smaller paths can be quite beautiful, taking you through green fields and peaceful forested areas. Tourist offices carry maps of cycle routes.

Stockholm City Bikes   BICYCLE RENTAL
(www.citybikes.se; 3-day/season card Skr165/300, season card purchased online Skr250; ☺6am-10pm) City Bikes has around 90 self-service bicycle-hire stands across the city. Bikes can be borrowed for three-hour stretches and returned at any City Bikes stand. You'll need to purchase a bike card online or from the tourist office (see p93), a Storstockholms Lokaltrafik (SL) centre, or one of several hotels and hostels (see website for list). Rechargeable season cards are valid from April through October.

Sjöcafé   BICYCLE RENTAL
(Map p62; bicycles per hr/day Skr80/275; ☺9am-9pm) This cottage at the base of Djurgårdsbrun rents cruiser-style bicycles from a handy location.

SAILING & BOATING

Water surrounds and permeates the city, and it's hard not to want to get out there if you're walking around on a warm, sunny day. Fortunately, getting out there is easy to do. The city canals are mostly gentle and easily navigable, even for novices; if you're unsure, discuss your level of experience with staff before you rent equipment. Some places also offer guides.

Sjöcafé   CANOEING
(Map p62; canoes per 1st hr/next hr/day Skr80/75/350; ☺9am-9pm Apr-Sep) From Sjöcafé, by the bridge leading to Djurgården, you can rent canoes as well as in-line skates, kayaks, row boats and pedal boats.

Strandbryggan   YACHTING
(Map p62; www.strandbryggan.se; Strandvägskajen 27, Strandvägen; ☺10am-close) Across the water from Sjöcafé, floating restaurant-bar Strandbryggan offers yachts for charter for up to 12 passengers from April to September. Prices start at around Skr2000 per hour (minimum three hours), and you can add catering from the restaurant.

SWIMMING

Swimming is permitted just about anywhere people can scramble their way to the water. Popular spots include the rocks around Riddarfjärden and the leafy island of Långholmen, the latter also sporting a popular gay beach.

Eriksdalsbadet   SWIMMING
(Map p68; www.eriksdalsbadet.se; Hammarby Slussväg 8; adult/child Skr90/40; ☺6.30am-9pm Mon-Thu, to 8pm Fri, 9am-5pm Sat, 9am-6pm Sun) At the southern edge of Södermalm is this sprawling complex, with both indoor and outdoor pools (with all the trimmings).

Centralbadet   SWIMMING, SPA
(Map p56; www.centralbadet.se; Drottninggatan 88; admission Skr180, Fri-Sun Skr220; ☺7am-9pm Mon-Fri, 9am-9pm Sat, 9am-6pm Sun, closed Sun May–mid-Sep) For more-atmospheric splashing about, head to art-nouveau Centralbadet, where entry includes pool, sauna and gym access. Treatments available for an additional fee include massage, facials and body wraps; these are best booked two weeks ahead. You can also hire towels (Skr30) and robes (Skr50).

WALKING & CLIMBING

Stockholm is laced with parks that offer some good walks; the most obvious place to find them is on Djurgården. Climbers have better options, with around 150 cliffs within 40 minutes' drive of the city.

Klätterverket   INDOOR CLIMBING
(Marcusplatsen 17, Nacka; adult/child Skr90/70; ☺noon-10pm Mon-Fri, 10am-8pm Sat & Sun mid-Jun–Aug, 10am-10pm Mon-Fri, to 8pm Sat & Sun rest of year) One of Sweden's largest indoor climbing centres, with around 1000 sq m of artificial climbing. Next to the J-train Sickla stop.

Tours

Taking a tour can be an efficient way of getting a handle on the city's highlights. For a

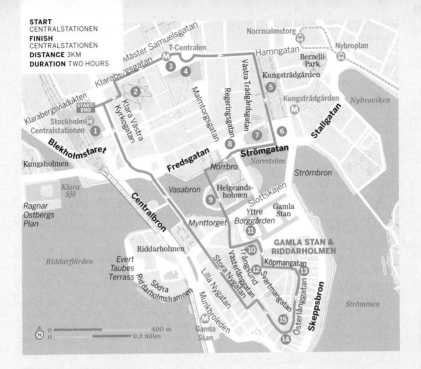

Walking Tour
Central Stockholm

❭ Starting at ❶ **Centralstationen**, cross Vasagatan and enter side street Klara Vattugränd. Turn left onto Klara Västra Kyrkogatan, past the church ❷ **Klara kyrka**. Follow Klarabergsgatan to ❸ **Sergels Torg**, home to frenzied commuters, casual shoppers and the odd demonstration. Pop into arts hub ❹ **Kulturhuset**, with its exhibitions, theatres, cafes and creative spaces.

Continue a short way along Hamngatan before turning right into the grand ❺ **Kungsträdgården**. Originally the kitchen garden for the Royal Palace, this park is now a popular spot for sun-soaking in the warmer months and ice skating in the colder ones.

At ❻ **Karl XII's Torg** there's a statue of the warmongering King Karl XII. On your right is ❼ **Operan**, the Royal Opera House (opened in 1896), and across the road you'll see the narrow strait Norrström, the freshwater outflow from Lake Mälaren. Continue along the waterfront, past ❽ **Gustav Adolfs Torg**, then turn left and cross the Riksbron bridge. Continue across the islet ❾ **Helgeandsholmen**, between the two parts of Sweden's parliament building, Riksdagshuset. Cross Stallbron bridge to arrive on Stadsholmen, Stockholm's medieval core.

Cross Mynttorget and, and follow Västerlånggatan for a block, then turn left (east) into Storkyrkobrinken to reach the city's oldest building, ❿ **Storkyrkan**. Facing the cathedral across the cobblestone square is ⓫ **Kungliga Slottet**. Källargränd leads southward to ⓬ **Stortorget**, the cobblestone square where the Stockholm Bloodbath took place in 1520.

Head east along Köpmangatan to small square ⓭ **Köpmantorget** and the oft-photographed statue of St George and the Dragon. Turn right into Österlånggatan and follow it past antique shops and art galleries until you reach ⓮ **Järntorget**, where metals were bought and sold in days long past. From there, keep right and turn into Västerlånggatan, looking out for ⓯ **Mårten Trotzigs Gränd** by No 81 (Stockholm's narrowest lane).

Turn left (northwest) into Stora Nygatan before crossing over Vasabron to head back to Centralstationen.

unique perspective, try seeing the city from the water or from up in the air.

Strömma Kanalbolaget
BOAT

(www.stromma.se) Tours large and small, from a 50-minute cruise around Djurgården (Skr150) to a three-hour 'brunch cruise' including a decadent buffet (Skr440). There are also hop-on hop-off tours by bus (from Skr220) and boat (Skr100). Best bet: 'Under the Bridges of Stockholm', a two-hour canal tour, running daily 10am to 7pm (Skr200).

Millennium Tour
WALKING

(www.stadsmuseum.stockholm.se; tours Skr120; ⊙tours 11.30am Sat, 6pm Wed) Fans of Stieg Larsson's madly popular crime novels (*The Girl with the Dragon Tattoo* etc) will enjoy this walking tour pointing out key locations from the books and films. Buy tickets or a self-guided tour map (Skr40) at the Stadsmuseum gift shop.

Stockholm Metro Art Tours
ART

(www.sl.se/art; tours free; ⊙tours in English 3pm Tue, Thu & Sat Jun-Aug) The stations of Stockholm's tunnelbana system are famous for their art installations, often featuring big-name artists like Siri Derkert, whose work on the Östermalm station in 1965 spurred this project. Guides provide background on the artists and how each theme came about. To join the one-hour tour, meet at the main ticket office in Sergels torg near Centralstationen. (Tours in Swedish depart at 1.30pm on the same days.)

ABBA City Walk
WALKING

(www.stadsmuseum.stockholm.se; tours Skr120; ⊙tours 4pm Fri & Sat Jul-Sep) Discover the places where Sweden's greatest pop band lived and worked in the 1970s. Tickets or a self-guided tour map (Skr40) are available at the Stadsmuseum gift shop.

Stockholm Ghost Walk
GHOST

(www.stockholmghostwalk.com; adult/child Skr200/100; ⊙tours 4pm Fri & Sat Jul-Sep) This 90-minute walking tour features tales of murder, mayhem, hauntings and executions, narrated with gusto by multilingual costumed guides. The walk starts at Järntorget in Gamla Stan. Dinner packages available.

Far & Flyg
HOT-AIR BALLOON

(www.farochflyg.se; flights Skr1995; ⊙flights late May–mid-Sep, weather-dependent) Float over Stockholm in a hot-air balloon for up to an hour and see the city from a rare vantage point.

✨ Festivals & Events

There's a bounty of festivals, concerts and other happenings on Sergels Torg and Kungsträdgården throughout the summer, and the major museums exhibit temporary exhibitions on a grand scale. *What's On Stockholm* (available at the tourist office) lists daily events.

Stockholm Marathon
SPORT

(www.stockholmmarathon.se) A marathon run in early June, with about 21,000 runners.

Smaka På Stockholm
FOOD

(www.smakapastockholm.se) This six-day celebration of Stockholm's food scene is held in late May/early June. The program includes gourmet food stalls and entertainment on Kungsträdgården.

Stockholm Jazz Festival
MUSIC

(www.stockholmjazz.com) One of Europe's premier jazz festivals; usually held in mid-June.

Stockholm Pride
GAY & LESBIAN

(www.stockholmpride.org) In late July/early August Stockholm goes pink with a week of parties and cultural events plus a pride parade.

Stockholms Kulturfestival
CULTURAL

(www.kulturfestivalen.stockholm.se) In August; one week of everything (and anything) from sidewalk opera to street theatre and dance gigs, with most of the 600-odd cultural events free.

Lidingöloppet
SPORT

(www.lidingoloppet.se) The world's largest cross-country foot race, with 30,000 participants, is held in late September in Lidingö, on Stockholm's outskirts.

Stockholm Open
SPORT

(www.stockholmopen.se) Over a week of international tennis and courtside celebrity-spotting, held in October.

Stockholm International Film Festival
FILM

(www.stockholmfilmfestival.se) In November; a major celebration of local and international cinema with guest speakers who are often top actors and directors.

🛏 Sleeping

Whether you slumber in youth hostels, B&Bs, boutique digs or big-name chains, you can expect high-quality accommodation in Stockholm. The trade-off is that it can be an expensive city to sleep in, but deals

Northern Stockholm

Northern Stockholm

◎ Top Sights
Vin & Sprithistoriska Museet A1

◎ Sights
1 Stadsbiblioteket.................................C2

🛏 Sleeping
2 Birger Jarl Hotel.................................C1
3 Hostel Bed & Breakfast......................C2
4 Hotel Hellsten....................................C2
5 Rex Hotel...C2

✗ Eating
6 Caffé Nero..C2
7 ICA Baronen C2
8 Lao Wai..C2
9 Republik C2
10 Sibiriens Soppkök.............................C1
11 Storstad...C2
12 Tranan...B2
13 Vurma...A2

🍸 Drinking
14 Olssons...C2

do exist! Major hotel chains are invariably cheaper booked online and in advance, and most hotels offer discounted rates on weekends (Friday and Saturday night) and in summer (from Midsummer to mid-August), sometimes up to 50% off the listed price.

Hotel prices typically include a large buffet breakfast. Wireless internet is nearly always available, but frequently for an extra charge. We've noted below (with the @ symbol) when there's a computer available for guest use.

A number of agencies, including **Bed & Breakfast Service** (☏660 55 65; www.bed breakfast.se) and **Bed & Breakfast Agency** (☏643 80 28; www.bba.nu), can arrange apartment or B&B accommodation from around Skr400 per person per night.

Stockholm's Svenska Turistföreningen (STF) hostels are affiliated with Hostelling International (HI), and a membership card yields a Skr50 discount. At SVIF (Sveriges vandrarhem i förening) hostels and independent hostels, no membership cards are required. Many have options for single, double or family rooms. Generally, you'll pay extra to use the hostel's linen; bring your own sleeping sheet to save around Skr50 per night. Many hostels have breakfast available, usually for an additional Skr65 to Skr90.

Hostels tend to fill up during the late afternoon in peak summer season, so arrive early or book in advance. They can also be busy in May, when Swedish school groups typically visit the capital. It's also worth noting that many hostels have limited reception-desk hours; you should call to make arrangements if arriving outside of those hours.

The following options are organised by neighbourhood.

GAMLA STAN

Ideal for romantics, though admittedly pricier than other parts of the city, Stockholm's medieval nexus has several atmospheric slumber spots that put you in easy reach of other thriving city neighbourhoods.

Rica Hotel Gamla Stan   HOTEL €€

(Map p56; www.rica.se; Lilla Nygatan 25; s/d Skr1195/1495; @) If you fancy classic Swedish interiors, rush to Rica, where the smallish rooms feature everything from powder-blue wallpaper and dainty furniture to vintage chandeliers. The revamped bathrooms add a modern edge to the 17th-century building, and the location is perfect for soaking up Gamla Stan's history.

Lord Nelson Hotel   HOTEL €€€

(Map p56; www.lordnelsonhotel.se; Västerlånggatan 22; s/d Skr1450/1790; @) Yo-ho-ho, me scurvy barnacles! It's a tight squeeze but this pink-painted, glass-fronted building feels like a creaky old ship loaded with character. At just 5m wide, the 17th-century building is Sweden's narrowest hotel. Its nautical theme extends to brass and mahogany furnishings, antique sea-captain trappings and a model ship in each of the small rooms. Some are in need of a little TLC, but all are comfy and clean, and we adore the little rooftop sun deck.

Mälardrottningen   HOTEL €€

(Map p56; www.malardrottningen.se; Riddarholmen; cabin s/d from Skr850/1125) At one time the world's largest motor yacht, this stylish, cosy option features well-appointed cabins, each with a bathroom. The vessel was launched in 1924, and was once owned by American heiress Barbara Hutton (a modest gift from her father for her 18th birthday). Upperdeck, seaside rooms offer the best views, and three rooms come with queen-size beds for spacious slumber.

Lady Hamilton Hotel   HOTEL €€€

(Map p56; www.ladyhamiltonhotel.se; Storkyrkobrinken 5; s/d Skr1390/2090) Expect old-style luxury (with more-modern touches where it counts, such as in the bathrooms). The building dates back to the 1470s, and is packed with antiques and portraits of Lady Hamilton herself. If you're not a fan of church bells, request a room away from Storkyrkobrinken.

First Hotel Reisen   HOTEL €€€

(Map p56; www.firsthotels.com; Skeppsbron 12; s/d Skr1495/1995, ste from Skr3195; @) Stockholm's oldest hotel once hummed with sailors. These days it's pulling a trendier crowd with its sexy black foyer and slinky restaurant-bar. Cool gives way to classic in the clean, comfortable (though slightly tired-looking) rooms. Suites come with jacuzzis and a sea view. The real highlight is the candlelit basement plunge pool and spa, complete with 16th-century, barrel-vaulted ceiling.

Victory Hotel   HOTEL €€€

(Map p56; www.victoryhotel.se; Lilla Nygatan 5; s/d Skr1490/1990, apt Skr1600-2300; @) Nautical antiques, art and model ships define the wonderfully quirky Victory. Most rooms are fairly small (though perfectly comfy), while the museumlike suites are larger. There are also four apartments available for long-term rentals (three nights or more).

CENTRAL STOCKHOLM

The handiest area for Centralstationen and Cityterminalen, Stockholm's bustling, 'downtown' Norrmalm district is awash with shops and an easy walk to several major sights. Just to the north, trendy Vasastan harbours some top-notch eating and drinking spots.

TOP CHOICE Grand Hôtel Stockholm   HOTEL €€€

(Map p56; www.grandhotel.se; Södra Blasieholmshamnen 8; s/d from Skr1950/2550; @) This is where the literati, glitterati and nobility call it a night. A waterfront landmark, with several exclusive restaurants and a see-and-be-seen piano bar, it remains Stockholm's most sumptuous lodgings. Room styles span royal Gustavian to contemporary chic. Room 701 (the Flag Suite) has a unique tower with a 360-degree view; room 702 is the astounding Nobel Room, where the literature prizewinner slumbers overnight.

TOP CHOICE Hotel Hellsten   HOTEL €€

(Map p75; www.hellsten.se; Luntmakargatan 68; s/d Skr1190/1490; @) Hip Hellsten is owned by anthropologist Per Hellsten, whose slick slumber number features objects from his travels and life, including Congan tribal masks and his grandmother's chandelier. Rooms are supremely comfortable and individually styled, with themes ranging from rustic Swedish to Indian exotica; some even feature original tile stoves. The sleek bathrooms sport phones and hand-cut Greek slate. Hotel extras include a sauna and a small fitness room, as well as live jazz in the lounge on Thursday evening.

Nordic Sea Hotel
HOTEL €€

(Map p56; www.nordicseahotel.com; Vasaplan 4; s/d from Skr910/1250; @) A fantastic deal if you time it right and book ahead, this sister hotel to the slightly more upmarket Nordic Light has smallish but sleek rooms, great service and a cool lobby lounge area with an impressive 9000L aquarium in the foyer. The breakfast buffet is enormous. Most notably, one of the two hotel bars is the famous Absolut Icebar (p87; hotel guests get a small discount on the exorbitant admission price). In addition to the standard rooms, there are even cheaper Express Rooms, windowless micro-bunks with all the mod cons, starting at Skr570. The Arlanda Express is just steps from the lobby.

Nordic Light Hotel
HOTEL €€€

(Map p56; www.nordiclighthotel.com; Vasaplan 7; r from Skr1870; @) Another design option, the Nordic Light is a minimalist Scandi statement, with slick, well-equipped rooms. The signature 'mood rooms' ditch conventional artwork for custom-designed light exhibits, which guests can adjust to suit their temperament. Additional hotel perks include mini gym, saunas and chic lobby bar.

Berns Hotel
HOTEL €€€

(Map p56; www.berns.se; Näckströmsgatan 8; s/d from Skr1650/1850; @) Popular with rock stars, the rooms at forever-hip Berns come equipped with CD players and styles ranging from 19th-century classical to contemporary sleek. Some rooms are more impressive than others (the balcony rooms get our vote); Room 431 was once a dressing room used by the likes of Marlene Dietrich and Ella Fitzgerald. Part of a historical entertainment complex, with buzzing restaurants, bars and live acts, it's a sparkly choice for the party crew.

Clarion Hotel Sign
HOTEL €€€

(Map p56; www.clarionsign.com; Östra Järnvägsgatan 35; r Skr1000-4000; P@≋) Stockholm's largest hotel is also among its newest design options. Behind the striking granite-and-glass facade, trendsetters lounge on Arne Jacobsen Egg chairs, nosh at New York chef Marcus Samuelsson's ultra-hip bar-restaurant Aquavit, and recharge at the rooftop spa, complete with 35°C plunge pool. The seriously slick rooms showcase design objects from across Scandinavia, with each floor dedicated to a particular Nordic nation's designers.

Rex Hotel
HOTEL €€

(Map p75; www.rexhotel.se; Luntmakargatan 73; s/d Skr1090/1390; @) While a little less luxe than its sibling Hotel Hellsten across the street, Rex's small but stylish rooms still deliver the same flat-screen TVs, rich colour schemes and Greek-stone bathrooms. Rooms in an additional building feature urbane concrete walls, walnut furniture and lush velvet textiles. Other positives include a fab glassed-in breakfast space, a Viking-worthy brick-and-stone curved staircase and fascinating travel photography by the affable owner.

Rica Hotel Kungsgatan
HOTEL €€

(Map p56; www.rica.se; Kungsgatan 47; s/d Skr1195/1495; @) Shopaholics will appreciate the direct elevator link to fashion hot-spot PUB (p92) at this temptingly central option. Refurbished rooms sport black wallpaper and lacquered wall panels, red lamps and flat-screen TVs, while the ecofriendly bath products are a civilised touch. A recent revamp added a dose of up-to-the-minute style and bold, bright-coloured artwork to the sleek lobby bar.

Hostel Bed & Breakfast
HOSTEL €

(Map p75; ☎15 28 38; info@hostelbedandbreakfast.com; Rehnsgatan 21; dm from Skr290, s/d/tr incl breakfast Skr500/680/990; @) Located only a few steps from T-Rådmansgatan tunnelbana station, in a quiet, off-the-beaten-track neighbourhood just north of the city centre, this pleasant, informal basement hostel has modern bathrooms, vivid wallpaper, a tidy guest kitchen and a laundry for guests (Skr50 including detergent).

City Backpackers
HOSTEL €€

(Map p56; ☎20 69 20; www.citybackpackers.org; Upplandsgatan 2A; dm Skr190-280, s/d with bath Skr600/890, with shared bath Skr500/650; @) The closest hostel to Centralstationen has clean rooms, friendly staff, free bike hire and excellent facilities, including a sauna, a laundry and kitchen (with a free stash of pasta). Private rooms, most dorms and the bathrooms have recently been renovated. Bonus for female guests: there are four- and eight-bed female-only dorms if you prefer, and you can borrow a hairdryer from reception.

Queen's Hotel
HOTEL €€

(Map p56; www.queenshotel.se; Drottninggatan 71A; s/d from Skr950/1150; @) A marble staircase and antique lift lead you up to this homely hotel, located in an early-20th-century building on a central pedestrian mall. Rooms are simple, white and soothing, with classic furniture, wood floors and the odd chandelier.

SKEPPSHOLMEN

Connected to the city centre by bridge and to Djurgården by ferry, this leafy island is home to some marvellous museums and views.

TOP CHOICE Vandrarhem af Chapman & Skeppsholmen
HOSTEL €

(Map p56; ☑463 22 66; www.svenskaturistforeningen.se/afchapman; adult/child in dm from Skr260/130, s/d Skr560/590; @) The legendary *af Chapman* is a storied vessel that has done plenty of travelling of its own. It's now well anchored in a superb, quiet location, swaying gently off Skeppsholmen. Bunks in dorms below deck have an unsurprisingly nautical ambience. Staff are friendly and knowledgeable about the city and surrounding areas. Apart from showers and toilets, all facilities are on dry land in the Skepps-holmen hostel, where you'll find a good kitchen with a laid-back common room and a separate TV lounge. Laundry facilities and 24-hour internet access are available.

ÖSTERMALM

Ostentatious Östermalm melds A-league boutiques, restaurants and nightclubs with some outstanding museums. There's a good range of accommodation options, too, from friendly hostels to top-of-the-line design hotels.

Hotel Stureplan
HOTEL €€

(Map p56; www.hotelstureplan.se; Birger Jarlsgatan 24; s/d Skr1250/1450, loft s/d Skr1295/1495, windowless s/d Skr995/1295; @) A chic, ideally situated boutique, Stureplan offers individually designed rooms with pared-back Gustavian decor (think high ceilings, spangly chandeliers and antique tile stoves) with high-tech touches like flat-screen TVs. Some rooms face the inner courtyard, others the busy Birger Jarlsgatan, so request the former if you're a light sleeper. (And if you

really want it quiet, ask for one of the cosy, yacht-inspired windowless rooms.) There are also super-modern loft rooms and lovely, airy suites in varying degrees of luxury.

STF Vandrarhem Gärdet
HOSTEL €

(☑463 22 99; gardet@stfturist.se; Sandhamnsgatan 59; s/d/tr Skr475/720/985; @) Surrounded by forested trails and open fields in quiet Gärdet, this efficient hostel works more like a no-frills hotel. Everything is sleek and modern with an office feel, though the lobby has some designer touches: red pin chairs, sheepskins, flat-screen TVs. There are no dorms, just private rooms of varying configurations (some lack windows, some have sofa beds, most have refrigerators). Rooms are tiny but well planned, and all have their own bathroom and TV. Towels and sheets are included in the price; breakfast can be had for an extra fee, and there's a good guest kitchen. Take bus 1 from Centralstationen to Östhammarsgatan bus stop, or catch it outside Gärdet tunnelbana station.

A&Be Hotell
HOTEL €€

(Map p56; www.abehotel.com; Grev Turegatan 50; s Skr540-840, d Skr690-990) Staying in this pretty and intimate old-fashioned hotel is like crashing with an elderly aunt – antique rugs and chandeliers, anonymous portraits of the aristocracy, potted plants and lampshades galore. Run by a warm Polish family, its quietest rooms are those facing the garden. Breakfast is an extra Skr50.

Crystal Plaza Hotel
HOTEL €€

(off Map p56; www.crystalplazahotel.se; Birger Jarlsgatan 35; s/d Skr1030/1150; @) Housed in an 1895 building, flaunting an eight-storey tower and neoclassical columns, this friendly hotel offers wonderfully cosy (albeit smallish) rooms. There's also a sauna, gym and tiny lobby bar. Rates are cheapest when booked early.

Birger Jarl Hotel
HOTEL €€€

(Map p75; www.birgerjarl.se; Tulegatan 8; standard s/d Skr1490/1690, design r from Skr2490; @) One of Stockholm's original design hotels, the Birger Jarl was undergoing renovations when we visited; it was business as usual except for shifting the entrance to Birger Jarlsgatan 61A (around the back of the building). Plans include a redo of the lobby, addition of a verandah, and some 30 new rooms and suites. Currently, standard rooms are on the small and tired side, with a vague '70s vibe, but the designer rooms, each put together by a different Swedish designer, are an immersive experience. There's a gym and sauna to boot.

LÅNGHOLMEN

Långholmen Hotell & Vandrarhem HOSTEL €
(☎668 05 10; www.langholmen.com; dm Skr210, 2-/4-bed cells Skr490/840, private cell with bathroom from Skr500; @) Guests at this hotel-hostel, in a former prison on Långholmen island, sleep on bunks in a cell. (The friendly, efficient staff assure you they will not lock you in.) The kitchen and laundry facilities are good, the restaurant serves meals all day, and weekend and summer discounts are available. Långholmen's popular summertime bathing spots are a towel flick away. There are also hotel-standard rooms, also in cells but spruced up with textured wall coverings and mod fixtures (singles/doubles including breakfast Skr1070/1535).

SÖDERMALM

The Södermalm district is only a 15-minute walk or quick subway ride from the Viking Line boats and Centralstationen and your best bet for interesting budget or midrange accommodation. At the other end of the spectrum, it's also home to the design-literate Clarion.

Bed & Breakfast 4 Trappor APARTMENT €€
(Map p68; ☎642 3104, 0735-69 38 64; www.4trappor.se; Gotlandsgatan 78; 1/2 guests Skr775/950, incl breakfast Skr850/1100) For elegant slumming, you can't beat this sassy, urbane apartment, complete with a cosy, polished-floorboard bedroom (maximum two guests), a modern bathroom and a well-equipped kitchen (with its own espresso machine). Breakfast is served in the wonderful owners' next-door apartment, and the chic SoFo address means easy access to Stockholm's coolest shops and hang-outs. There's a two-night minimum stay and a discounted rate for stays of more than five nights. It's a huge hit, so book months ahead.

TOP CHOICE Rival Hotel HOTEL €€
(Map p68; www.rival.se; Mariatorget 3; s/d from Skr1495/1595; @) Owned by ABBA's Benny Andersson and overlooking leafy Mariatorget, this ravishing design hotel is a chic retro gem, complete with vintage 1940s movie theatre and over-the-top art-deco cocktail bar. The super-comfy rooms feature posters from great Swedish films and a teddy bear to make you feel at home.

All rooms boast flat-screen TVs and good-sized bathrooms, and there's a scrumptious designer bakery-cafe beside the foyer.

TOP CHOICE Columbus Hotell HOTEL €€
(Map p68; www.columbus.se; Tjärhovsgatan 11; s/d from Skr995/1395; @) Family owned and highly recommended, Columbus is nestled in a quiet part of Södermalm, near T-Medborgarplatsen station, and set around a cobblestone courtyard by a pretty park. The decor is classic homestyle Swedish, with linens and light-wood floors and spare, elegant furnishings. In addition to the basic rooms (which have TVs, phones and shared bathroom facilities), there are wonderfully homey hotel-standard rooms and a couple of big suites (from Skr1995).

TOP CHOICE Zinkensdamm Hotell & Vandrarhem HOSTEL €
(☎616 81 00; www.zinkensdamm.com; Zinkens väg 20; dm/s Skr235/440, d with/without bathroom Skr780/600; @) With a foyer that looks like one of those old Main St facade recreations you find in cheesy museums, the Zinkensdamm STF is unabashedly fun. It's attractive and well equipped – complete with an ubersleek guest kitchen and personal lockers in each room – and caters for families with kids as well as pub-going backpackers. It can be crowded and noisy, but that's the trade-off for an upbeat vibe. The hostel breakfast buffet isn't spectacular, but the cafe in the lobby sells good coffee and pastries as well as other meals throughout the day.

Den Röda Båten – Mälaren/Ran HOSTEL €
(Map p68; ☎644 43 85; www.theredboat.com; Söder Malärstrand, Kajplats 6; dm Skr260-310, hostel s/d Skr520/650, hotel s/d from Skr900/1200; @) The 'Red Boat' is a hotel and hostel on two vessels, *Mälaren* and *Ran*. The hostel section is the cosiest of Stockholm's floating accommodations, thanks to lots of dark wood, nautical memorabilia and friendly staff. Linens are included in the price. Hotel-standard rooms are roomier, with blond wood, maritime paintings and breakfast; sea-view rooms cost about Skr200 more but are worth it.

Hotel Anno 1647 HOTEL €€€
(Map p68; www.anno1647.se; Mariagränd 3; budget s/d Skr1140/1390, standard Skr1990/2440; P @) Just off buzzing Götgatan, this historical slumber spot has labyrinthine hallways,

affable staff, and both budget and standard rooms. The latter are the winners, with old floorboards, rococo wallpaper and the odd chandelier. Economy rooms are simple but clean, with shared bathrooms and noise from the street at night.

Clarion Hotel
HOTEL €€

(Map p68; www.clarionstockholm.com; Ringvägen 98; s/d from Skr1170/1370; P@) This designer darling feels like a modern-art museum, its wide ramp leading into the foyer dotted with ubercool furniture and modelled on the Tate Modern. The foyer features a huge wall mural and sculptures by Kirsten Ortwed, and there's a fetching lounge-bar for a stylish sip. Rooms are an uncluttered combo of sleek lounges, huge beds with designer sheets and massive windows for urban gazing.

Hilton Stockholm Slussen
HOTEL €€€

(Map p68; www.hilton.com; Guldgränd 8; r from Skr1690; @) Perched between the chaotic Slussen interchange and Södermalm's underground highway, Stockholm's unmissable Hilton sports modern, comfortable rooms with swirly marble bathrooms and everything you'd expect in a top-notch business hotel. Several rooms have stunning city views. There's a hugely popular bar with an outdoor terrace in good weather, and the vast lobby and other public areas are well suited to meeting up with friends before a night exploring Söder.

KUNGSHOLMEN

This mostly residential island has one large and high-quality sleeping option, which is well placed for Kungsholmen's cast of first-class restaurants.

First Hotel Amaranten
HOTEL €€

(www.firsthotels.com/amaranten; Kungsholmsgatan 31; s/d from Skr1360/1560; @) Evoking an upmarket furniture showroom, this chain hotel boasts a plunge pool and stylish spa centre. Retox in the swanky bar or retreat to your mod-Scandi room, where the wi-fi is free.

OUTLYING AREAS

If things get desperate in town, there are more than 20 hostels around the county easily reached by SL buses, trains or archipelago boats within an hour or so. There are also numerous summer campsites, many offering cheap cabin accommodation. More options are mentioned in the Around Stockholm section (see p95).

Hotel J
HOTEL €€€

(www.hotelj.com; Ellensviksvägen 1, Nacka Strand; s/d from Skr1525/1890; @P) This newly expanded hotel with a breezy Hamptons vibe is a popular weekend getaway for Stockholmers. The chic summer house, built in 1912, is named after the boats used in the America's Cup. The scent of nonchalant wealth wafts unmistakably through the air here. Rooms are decorated with comfortable furniture and fine linens; several have balconies. To get here, take the tunnelbana to T-Slussen then bus 404 or 443.

Bredängs Vandrarhem & Camping
HOSTEL, CAMPGROUND €

(☏97 62 00; www.bredangvandrarhem.se; Stora Sällskapsväg 51; sites Skr265, dm Skr220, hostel s/d Skr400/580, cabins Skr1400; ☺campsite early Apr-early Oct) This is a lakeside option 10km southwest of central Stockholm. It's well equipped, with a hostel and modern cabins. Just a 700m walk from T-Bredäng station; if you're driving, it's well signposted from the E4/E20 motorway.

Hotel Formule 1
HOTEL €

(www.hotelformule1.com; Mikrofonvägen 30, Hägersten; r from Skr520) Just about the cheapest hotel option has small, uninspiring rooms that accommodate up to three people; facilities are shared. It's 4km southwest of town (take the tunnelbana to T-Telefonplan).

✗ Eating

Stockholmers like to think of themselves as consummate foodies. In a relatively small city with more than half a dozen Michelin-starred restaurants, it's understandable. Top chefs are veritable celebrities, and getting a table at the restaurant of the moment can take some wrangling. Admittedly, Stockholm's epicurean highlights don't come cheap, but it's a world-class food scene, and you can eat as well here as in any major European city.

Of course, most visitors won't plan on five-star dining every day. Stockholm's many small cafes and coffee shops offer a good range of standard lunch fare, from enormous salads made with pasta or quinoa to quiches and freshly made baguettes.

Most of the top eating spots offer trendy takes on humble *husmanskost* (classic Swedish home cooking). There's also an ever-growing number of ethnic eateries; it's no longer any trouble to find Ethiopian, Thai, Tex-Mex or Japanese food in Stockholm. A quick way to explore a range of flavours is to hit up one of Stockholm's market halls, filled with boutique grocery shops as well as interesting little eateries. And the many vegetarian buffets strewn across the city might just be the best way to snag a bargain.

In terms of street food, Stockholm has a few reliable options. For a quick, inexpensive snack, it's hard to beat a *grillad korv med bröd* – your basic grilled hot dog on a bun – available for between Skr15 and Skr30 from carts all over town. Options for decorating your dog include shrimp salad and curried potatoes, and the adventurous can opt for a *korv* roll with the lot. For something that feels a little more classically Swedish, there are also a couple of fried-herring carts downtown.

Between meals, take time to investigate Stockholm's vibrant cafe culture. Just about every Stockholmer takes part in a daily coffee-and-cakes ritual, usually midafternoon but often late into the evening. Look for signs saying *konditori*, and feast your eyes on the always-amazing display cases of cakes and pastries.

GAMLA STAN

TOP CHOICE Chokladkoppen
CAFE €

(Map p56; Stortorget; cakes & snacks Skr35-75) Arguably Stockholm's best-loved cafe, hole-in-the-wall Chokladkoppen sits slap bang on the old town's enchanting main square. It's a gay-friendly spot, with cute waiters, a look-at-me summer terrace and yummy grub like broccoli-and-blue-cheese pie and scrumptious cakes.

Den Gyldene Freden
SWEDISH €€€

(Map p56; Österlånggatan 51; lunch Skr165-265, dinner Skr175-425; ⊙closed Sun) Simmering since 1722, this venerable barrel-vaulted restaurant is run by the Swedish Academy, where (rumour has it) its members meet to decide the winners of the Nobel Prize. Personally, we think it should go to the chefs, whose sublime offerings include civilised *husmanskost* dishes like quail stuffed with duck liver, celeriac purée, Gotland truffles and *rôti jus*.

Hermitage
VEGETARIAN €€

(Map p56; Stora Nygatan 11; buffets Skr110; 🖉) Don't let the '80s-style coffee-shop decor put you off; herbivores love Hermitage for its simple, tasty, vegetarian nosh. Salad, home-made bread, tea and coffee are included in the price.

Café Art
CAFE €

(Map p56; Västerlånggatan 60; lunch Skr69-75) This atmospheric, barrel-vaulted cellar cranks up the cosy factor with its candlelit tables, snug nooks and art-slung walls. A perfect spot for *fika* (daily coffee and cake ritual), it also makes a mean baguette and great shrimp salads.

Sundbergs Konditori
CAFE €

(Map p56; Järntorget 83; bagels & ciabattas Skr55-65) Dating from 1785, this is Stockholm's oldest bakery-cafe, complete with chintzy chandeliers, regal oil paintings and a copper samovar full of self-serve coffee. Mix and match with gleaming pastries and a soothing selection of bagels, ciabattas, pies and omelettes.

Cafe Järntorget
ICE CREAM €

(Map p56; Västerlånggatan 81; waffle cones Skr25-47) If you make no other snack stops in Gamla Stan, make it this ice-cream shop. It's the one place in town that reliably offers such outlandishly Swedish flavours as black licorice (*lakrits*), cloudberry (*hjörtron*), and the ambrosia that is saffron-and-honey ice cream.

Siam Thai
THAI €€

(Map p56; Stora Nygatan 25; mains Skr165-205; ⊙lunch Mon-Sat, dinner Mon-Sun) Thai food is no longer even remotely exotic in Stockholm, but this long-standing bamboo-lined hole in the wall has long since traded novelty for comfortable reliability anyway. There's outdoor seating in summer, but indoor tables are a nice respite from the Gamla Stan crowds. Food is keyed to Scandi palates, so if you like yours spicy, be sure to ask; service is friendly and accommodating. *Dagens rätt* (daily lunchtime special) available from Skr80.

CENTRAL STOCKHOLM

TOP CHOICE Operakällaren
FRENCH, SWEDISH €€€

(Map p56; ☑676 58 00; www.operakallaren.se; Karl XII's Torg 10; starters Skr230-300, mains Skr310-515, tasting menus Skr1450; ⊙6-10pm Tue-Sat) Inside Stockholm's show-off Opera House, the century-old Operakällaren is a major gastronomic event. Decadent chandeliers, golden mirrors and exquisitely carved ceilings set the scene for French-meets-fusion adventures like seared scallops with caramel, cauliflower purée, *pata negra* ham and brown butter emulsion. Book at least two weeks ahead.

Grands Veranda
SWEDISH €€€

(Map p56; grandhotel.se; Grand Hôtel Stockholm, Södra Blasieholmshamnen 8; breakfast buffets Skr270, smörgåsbord Skr475, mains Skr195-370; ⊙7-11pm, smörgåsbord 1-4pm & 6-10pm Sat & Sun Feb, 6-10pm Mon-Fri, 1-4pm & 6-10pm Sat & Sun Mar, Apr & Sep-Nov, noon-3pm & 6-10pm Mon-Fri, 1-4pm & 6-10pm Sat & Sun May-Aug, Christmas buffet Dec) Head here, inside the Grand Hôtel, for the famous breakfast buffet or the gluttonous smörgåsbord. Get in early for a window seat and tuck into both hot and cold Swedish staples, including gravadlax with almond potatoes, herring, meatballs and lingonberry jam. It's like a belt-busting crash course in classic Nordic flavours.

Tranan
SWEDISH €€€

(Map p75; www.tranan.se; Karlbergsvägen 14; starters Skr55-125, mains Skr155-295; ⊙11.30am-midnight Mon-Thu, 11.30am-1am Fri, 5pm-1am Sat, to 11pm Sun, 6pm-midnight Mon-Sun late Jun-Aug) Locals pack this comfy but classy neighbourhood bistro, with its seafood-heavy menu and red-checked tablecloths. Food combines Swedish *husmanskost* with savvy Gallic touches; don't miss the fried herring. On the weekend, DJs hit the decks in the pumping, 30-something basement bar (except in summer, when the bar is closed).

Sibiriens Soppkök
SOUP €€

(Map p75; Roslagsgatan 25; lunch Skr80-90, soups Skr100-145; ⊙10am-10pm Mon-Fri, noon-10pm Sat) With a room as warm and inviting as a bowl of soup, Siberiens is dreamy on a chilly day. Chalkboard menus, potted plants and candlesticks crowd the tiny space; head in early for a good seat. At the top of the class is the seafood soup (Skr145), a luscious blend of tomato, saffron, orange, wine, salmon, prawns and mussels. The ever-changing daily menu also includes tapas, pasta and Mediterranean wines.

Bakfickan
SWEDISH €€€

(Map p56; mains Skr135-275; ⊙11.30am-11pm Mon-Fri, noon-10pm Sat) Calling the Opera House home, the 'back pocket' of fine-dining darling Operakällaren is crammed with opera photographs and deco-style lampshades. Dexterous old-school waiters serve comforting Swedish *husmanskost*, and the counter seats make it a perfect spot for solo dining. Late at night, rumour has it, this is where the opera singers hang out.

Storstad
FRENCH €€

(Map p75; www.storstad.se; Odengatan 41; starters Skr95-225, fish Skr185-255, mains Skr165-295; ⊙4pm-1am Mon-Wed, to 3am Fri, 6pm-3am Sat, closed Sun) This attractive bistro near Oden-plan, which shares a corner (and owners) with Olssons bar, serves Scandi classics like *toast skagen* or Swedish meatballs alongside traditional French favourites like *moules frites* and tarte Tatin. It transforms into a lively cocktail bar later in the evening.

Republik
EUROPEAN €€€

(Map p75; www.restaurant-republik.com; Tulegatan 17; lunch Skr90-145, bar menus Skr135-285; ⊙lunch Mon-Fri, dinner until midnight Tue-Sat) Republik's buzzing bar was voted Stockholm's best a few years ago, yet the ultimate indulgence here is the restaurant. Set lunches change by day of the week and are heavy on the fish and seafood; there are also meaty mains (entrecôte, veal) and a bar menu that features lighter fare such as a fennel salad, a burger and an artful take on the classic shrimp sandwich.

Lao Wai
VEGETARIAN €€

(Map p75; Luntmakargatan 74; lunch Skr90, dinner Skr145-195; ⊙lunch 11am-2pm Mon-Fri, dinner 5.30-10pm Tue-Sat; ⊘) Tiny, herbivorous Lao Wai does sinfully good things to tofu and vegetable combos, hence the faithful regulars. Nosh virtuously on dishes like Sichuan-style smoked tofu with shitake, chillies, garlic shoots, snow peas and black beans.

Mathias Dahlgren
SWEDISH €€€

(Map p56; ✆679 35 84; Grand Hôtel Stockholm, Södra Blasieholmshamnen 6; Matbaren mains Skr250-395, Matsalen 5-/8-course menus Skr1350/1650; ⊙Matbaren noon-2pm Mon-Fri, 6pm-midnight Mon-Sat, Matsalen 7pm-midnight) Celebrity chef Matthias Dahlgren has settled in at the Grand Hôtel with a two-sided restaurant: there's the formal, elegant Matsalen ('Dining Room'), which has been awarded two Michelin stars, and the more casual Matbaren ('Food Bar'), boasting a Michelin star of its own. Both sides focus on seasonal ingredients, so menus change daily according to what's freshest. In the dining room you can choose from two set menus with five or eight courses (wine pairings extra). Reservations are recommended, although it's possible to drop in at the Food Bar.

Vetekatten
CAFE €

(Map p56; Kungsgatan 55; snacks from Skr25, salads Skr69-75; ⊙7.30am-8pm Mon-Fri, 9.30am-

5pm Sat, noon-5pm Sun) A cardamom-scented labyrinth of cosy nooks, antique furnishings and oil paintings, Vetekatten is not so much a cafe as an institution. Wish back the old days over filling sandwiches, heavenly scrolls and warming cups of tea.

Caffé Nero
CAFE €

(Map p75; Roslagsgatan 4; coffee & pastries from Skr25, lunch from Skr70; ☺7am-10pm Mon-Fri, 8am-10pm Sat, 8am-6pm Sun) Architect Tadao Ando would approve of the brutal (and brutally hip) concrete interiors at this Vasastan hang-out. Local hipsters down mighty coffee, grappa shots, panini and Italian home cooking, from sublime veal meatballs to tiramisu.

Pontus!
SWEDISH €€€

(Map p56; Brunnsgatan 1; bar menus Skr95-270, mains Skr185-420; ☺breakfast & lunch Mon-Fri, dinner Mon-Sat) This Östermalm favourite has remodelled and expanded in a lot of interesting ways; though, thankfully, the beloved library wallpaper remains. There's a redone dining room, a new bar space, a seafood bar, and a cute, tiny, white-tiled deli that offers breakfast.

Grill
INTERNATIONAL €€€

(Map p56; www.grill.se; Drottninggatan 89; starters Skr130-225, mains Skr190-450; ☺11.15am-2pm & 5pm-1am Mon-Fri, 4pm-1am Sat, 3pm-midnight Sun; ⏍) Kick-started by culinary stars Melker Andersson and Danyel Couet, this outrageous restaurant-bar features themed spaces, from Miami art deco to Astroturf garden party. The menu is a global affair, innovatively arranged by grill type. A separate vegetarian menu includes options such as a quorn burger (Skr195) and caprese salad (Skr135).

ÖSTERMALM

Café Saturnus
CAFE €

(Map p56; Eriksbergsgatan 6; baguettes/pastries Skr55/25; ☺7am-8pm Mon-Fri, 9am-7pm Sat & Sun) For velvety caffè latte, Gallic-inspired baguettes and perfect pastries, saunter into this casually chic bakery-cafe. Sporting a stunning mosaic floor, silky striped wallpaper and a few outdoor tables, it's a fabulous spot to flick through the paper while devouring Stockholm's finest cinnamon bun.

Örtagården
VEGETARIAN €€

(Map p56; Nybrogatan 31, 1st fl, Östermalms Saluhall Bldg; lunch/dinner buffets Skr95/129; ☺10.30am-10pm Mon-Fri, 11am-10pm Sat, 11am-9pm Sun; ⏍) Perched above Östermalms Saluhall, this popular, casual buffet is a great place to fill

up on your veggies. You may need to elbow your way to a table, but you'll be rewarded with a vast selection of inventive salads and filling sides. The buffet is no longer strictly vegetarian, but that's what the chefs are best at; the meat-based dishes can be underwhelming. Be sure to save room for the ice-cream bar.

Sturehof
SEAFOOD €€€

(Map p56; www.sturehof.com; Stureplan 2; mains Skr135-485; ☺11am-2am Mon-Fri, noon-2am Sat, 1pm-2am Sun) Superb for late-night sipping and supping, this convivial brasserie sparkles with gracious staff, celebrity regulars and fabulous seafood-centric dishes (the bouillabaisse is brilliant). Both the front and back bars are a hit with the eye-candy brigade and perfect for a post-meal flirt.

Brasserie Elverket
EUROPEAN €€€

(www.brasserieelverket.se; Linnégatan 69; lunch Skr79-225, dinner Skr165-265, 3-course theatre menus Skr395-595; ☺lunch Mon-Fri, brunch Sat & Sun, dinner Mon-Sat) In an old electricity plant reborn as an experimental theatre, this slick, dimly lit restaurant-bar peddles bold, adventurous grub like melon and vanilla consommé served with cardamom pannacotta and a pineapple-sage salsa. Starters are a pick-and-mix tapas-style affair, and the weekend brunch buffet (Skr199) is one of Stockholm's best. Once fed, kick back in the slinky lounge with an absinthe-laced Belgian Bastard.

DJURGÅRDEN

Rosendals Trädgårdskafe
CAFE €€

(Map p62; www.rosendalstradgard.se; Rosendalsterrassen 12; cakes Skr35-55, soups Skr85, mains Skr135-145; ☺11am-5pm Mon-Fri, to 6pm Sat & Sun May-Sep, shorter hours rest of year, closed Jan) Set among the greenhouses of a pretty botanical garden, Rosendals is an idyllic spot for heavenly carrot cake and an organic wine (Skr75 per glass) in the summer or a warm cup of *glögg* (spicy mulled wine) and a *lussekatt* (saffron roll) in winter. Lunch includes a brief menu of organic soups, sandwiches (such as ground-lamb burger with chanterelles) and gorgeous salads. Much of the produce is biodynamic and grown on site, and the cafe-shop (closed January) sells everything from preserved lemons and freshly baked bread to Rosendals' very own cookbook. Take bus 47; it's a 15-minute walk from Djurgårdsbron.

SELF-CATERING

Supermarkets in Stockholm are plentiful and easy to find; here are a few handy ones, but you'll see branches in most every neighbourhood. Don't forget you'll need to purchase a plastic grocery bag (Skr5) if you haven't brought along your own.

Hemköp (Map p56; Klarabergsgatan 50; ⊙7am-9pm Mon-Fri, from 10am Sat & Sun)The handiest central supermarket, located in the basement of Åhléns department store.

Coop Konsum (Map p68; Katarinavägen 3-7; ⊙7am-9pm Mon-Fri, from 9am Sat & Sun)

ICA Baronen (Map p75; Odengatan 40; ⊙8am-10pm)

Vivo T-Jarlen (Map p56; ⊙7am-9pm Mon-Fri, 10am-7pm Sat, 11am-7pm Sun) Inside Östermalmstorg tunnelbana station; enter from Grev Turegatan.

Blå Porten
SWEDISH €€

(Map p62; www.blaporten.com; Djurgårdsvägen 64; pastries from Skr25, mains Skr85-175; ⊙lunch & dinner) Blissful on sunny days, when you can linger over lunch or *fika* in a garden reminiscent of a Monet painting, this cafe next to Liljevalchs Konsthall boasts an obscenely tempting display of baked goods, as well as lip-smacking Scandi and global meals. Mercifully, many of Djurgården's museums are within rolling distance.

Restaurang Hasselbacken
SWEDISH €€€

(Map p62; www.restauranghasselbacken.com; Hazeliusbacken 20; mains Skr185-285, 2-/3-course menus Skr355/455; ⊙breakfast, lunch & dinner) Slip into this vintage jewel-box dining room for modern Scandi fare, such as white asparagus with rhubarb glaze, black morel and parmesan foam. In between swoons, take in the superb coffered ceiling. The restaurant is part of Scandic Hotel Hasselbacken.

Wärdshuset Ulla Winbladh
SWEDISH €€€

(Map p62; ✆534 89 701; www.ullawinbladh .se; Rosendalsvägen 8; starters Skr115-265, mains Skr195-445) Named after one of Carl Michael Bellman's lovers, this villa was built as a steam bakery for the Stockholm World's Fair (1897) and now serves fine food in intimate rooms and a blissful garden setting. Sup on skilfully prepared dishes such as lake Hjälmaren pikeperch fried with mustard, creamy barley and crayfish, or opt for simple Scandi favourites such as herring with Kvibille cheese and homemade crispbread. Roxette fans should ask the staff to point out the artwork of singer Marie Fredriksson. We recommend booking a week ahead in summer.

SÖDERMALM

Nystekt Strömming
SWEDISH €

(Map p68; Södermalmstorg; half/full meals Skr50/70; ⊙hours vary, generally 11am-8pm Mon-Fri, 11am-6pm Sat & Sun) The best place to get a quick snack of freshly fried herring in Stockholm is this humble cart outside the tunnelbana station at Slussen. Large or small combo plates come with big slabs of the fish and a selection of sides and condiments, from mashed potato and red onion to salads and hardbread; more portable wraps and the delicious herring burger go for Skr45.

Gondolen
SWEDISH €€€

(Map p68; www.eriks.se; Stadsgården 6; mains Skr195-295, 3-course menus Skr495; ⊙lunch Mon-Fri, dinner Mon-Sat, dinner only Jun-Aug) Perched atop the iconic Katarinahissen (the vintage Slussen elevator), Gondolen combines killer city views with contemporary Nordic brilliance from chef Erik Lallerstedt. Play 'spot the landmark' while carving into gems like thyme-roasted halibut with lobster sauce and root-vegetable cake.

Pelikan
SWEDISH €€€

(Map p68; Blekingegatan 40; mains Skr135-235; ⊙dinner daily, lunch Sat & Sun) Lofty ceilings, wood panelling and no-nonsense waiters in waistcoats set the scene for classic *husmanskost* at this century-old beer hall. The herring options are particularly good and there's usually a vegetarian special to boot. Minimum age is 23 years.

Chutney
VEGETARIAN €

(Map p68; chutney.se; Katarina Bangata 19; pastries Skr35, mains Skr65-75; ⊙lunch & dinner; ✎) Sitting among a string of three inviting cafes along this block, Chutney is one of Stockholm's earliest vegetarian restaurants. Huddle on the pillowed benches and sample the vaguely Middle Eastern- and Asian-themed veggie delights, or just hang out with a beer and watch the Söder crowds filter by.

String
CAFE €

(Map p68; cafestring.com; Nytorgsgatan 38; coffees Skr20, sandwiches Skr50-55, salads & mains Skr65-75; ☺9.30am-9pm Mon-Thu, to 7.30pm Fri, 10.30am-7pm Sat & Sun) This retro-funky SoFo cafe does a bargain weekend brunch buffet (Skr70; 10.30am to 1pm). Load your plate with everything from cereals, yoghurt and fresh fruit to pancakes, toast and amazing homemade hummus. Fancy that '70s chair you're plonked on? Take it home; almost everything you see is for sale.

Gildas Rum
CAFE €

(Map p68; Skånegatan 79; coffee & pastries from Skr20; ☺8am-11pm Mon-Thu, to 8pm Fri, 9am-8pm Sat, 9am-9pm Sun) This sweet cafe has a bit of a Parisian-boudoir-meets-library feel, with its bookish decor, rich wallpaper and velvet sofas. Get a mismatched mug of foamy latte and a pastry, and settle in among the stylish Söder crowd.

Crêperie Fyra Knop
CAFE €€

(Map p68; Svartensgatan 4; crêpes from Skr50, mains Skr80-98; ☺dinner Mon-Fri, lunch & dinner Sat & Sun) Head here for perfect crêpes in an intimate setting, plus a hint of shanty-town chic – think reggae tunes and old tin billboards for Stella Artois. A good place for a quiet tête-à-tête before you hit the clubs down the street.

Östgöta Källaren
SWEDISH €€

(Map p68; Östgötagatan 41; lunch Skr68-98, mains Skr115-189; ☺to 1am, kitchen closes 11.30pm) The regulars at this soulful pub-cum-restaurant range from multipierced rockers to blue-rinse grandmas, all smitten with the dimly lit romantic atmosphere, amiable vibe and hearty Swedish, Eastern European and French-Mediterranean grub. It shares an entrance with the underworldy Vampire Lounge (p86).

Koh Phangan
THAI €€€

(Map p68; ☎642 50 40; www.kohphangan.nu; Skånegatan 57; starters Skr85-95, mains Skr169-195; ☺11am-midnight Mon-Tue, to 1am Wed-Fri, 1pm-1am Sat & Sun) Best at night, this outrageously kitsch Thai restaurant has to be seen to be believed. Tuck into your *kao pat gai* (chicken fried rice) in a real *tuk-tuk* to the accompanying racket of crickets and tropical thunder, or kick back with beers in a bamboo hut. DJs occasionally hit the decks and it's best to book ahead.

Bröd & Salt
BAKERY €

(Map p68; Renstiernas Gata 28; small/large cappuccinos Skr30/35, breakfast Skr49-65; ☺breakfast & lunch) For high-quality organic baked goods and real espresso drinks made with care, try this cool white-tiled hole in the wall, with a rough-hewn wooden bar, black-and-white photos, picture windows and a huge mural of the bakery. Self-caterers should grab a loaf of fresh bread to go.

Söderhallarna
FOOD HALL €

(Map p68; Medborgarplatsen 3; ☺10am-6pm Mon-Wed, to 7pm Thu & Fri, to 4pm Sat; ☒) This food hall on Medborgarplatsen contains a cinema as well as shops selling everything from cheese and smallgoods to decent vegetarian grub.

KUNGSHOLMEN

⬛TOP CHOICE Vurma
CAFE €

(www.vurma.se; Polhemsgatan 15; sandwiches Skr35-69, salads Skr65-75, ☺10am-6pm, kitchen closes 5.30pm) Squeeze in among the chattering punters, fluff up the cushions and eavesdrop over a vegan latte at this kitsch-hip cafe-bakery. The scrumptious sandwiches and salads are inspired; try the salad with chèvre, marinated chicken, tomato, cucumber, walnuts, apple and mustard. You'll find other branches in Vasastan (Gästrikegatan 2, Map p75) and Södermalm (Bergsunds Strand 31).

Östermalms Saluhall
FOOD HALL €€

(Map p56; Östermalmstorg; ☺9.30am-6pm Mon-Thu, to 6.30pm Fri, to 4pm Sat) Stockholm's historic, gourmet food market spoils taste buds with fresh fish, seafood and meat, as well as fruits, vegetables and hard-to-find cheeses. The building itself is a Stockholm landmark, designed as a Romanesque cathedral of food in 1885. For a quick lunch, belly up to the bar at Sushi Baren; for a real treat, grab a table at Lisa Elmqvist (meals Skr140 to Skr350), one of the city's top seafood eateries (trust staff recommendations). There's a clean, free, well-hidden toilet in the far corner opposite the market entrance.

Hötorgshallen
FOOD HALL €

(Map p56; Hötorget; ☺10am-6pm Mon-Fri, to 3pm Sat Jun & Jul, 10am-6pm Mon-Thu, to 6.30pm Fri, to 4pm Sat rest of year) Located below Filmstaden cinema, Hötorgshallen is Stockholm at its multicultural best, with stalls selling everything from fresh Nordic seafood to fluffy hummus and fragrant teas. Ready-to-eat options include Lebanese spinach parcels, kebabs and vegetarian burgers. For the ultimate feed, squeeze into galley-themed dining nook Kajsas Fiskrestaurang for soulful *fisksoppa* (fish stew) with mussels and aioli (Skr85).

Kungsholmen SWEDISH €€€

(☎505 24 450; www.kungsholmen.com; Norr Mälarstrand, Kajplats 464; soups Skr95-230, sushi 140-325, grills Skr225-375; ☺5pm-1am Mon-Sun) Owned by celebrity chef Melker Andersson, this hip 'food court' features six open kitchens cooking up different specialities, including soups, sushi, bistro grub, bread and ice cream. Add in a sleek, cocktail-savvy bar, weekend DJ sessions and a waterside location, and you'll understand why it's best to book.

 Drinking
================

Stockholm is a stylish place to drink, whether you're after cocktails or coffee. (Most coffee shops also do great food, however, so we've reviewed them in the Eating section; after all, it's the rare Swede who sips a cup of coffee without a little something to nibble on.) In fact, just about the only kind of place you'll have trouble finding here is a dive bar with bad lighting, frumpy regulars and cheap swill on tap.

The coolest and most casual drinking holes are on Södermalm, the bohemian island in the south part of town. (And if you *are* looking for a cheap dive, this would be a good place to start; try near the corner of Tjärhovsgatan and Östgötagatan.) For a moneyed, glamorous scene, head to Östermalm's late-night clubs. Beautiful old-fashioned beer halls like Pelikan (p84) offer a publike atmosphere with a dose of classic Swedish elegance. Even the hotel bars are surprisingly decent, often drawing the ultra-chic cocktail crowd.

Note that many places charge a mandatory Skr20 to Skr50 coat-check fee.

Locals often save money by meeting for drinks at home before they go out. To do the same, hit up a Systembolaget, the state-owned alcohol monopoly, to buy booze to take away. (Supermarkets also sell low-alcohol beer, up to 3.5%.)

Pet Sounds Bar BAR

(Map p68; www.petsoundsbar.se; Skånegatan 80; speciality cocktails Skr100-116; ☺from 5pm Mon-

Sat) A SoFo favourite, this jamming bar pulls in music journos, indie culture vultures and the odd goth rocker. While the restaurant serves decent Italian-French grub, the real fun happens in the basement. Head down for a mixed bag of live bands, release parties and DJ sets.

Snotty's BAR

(Map p68; Skånegatan 90; pints around Skr52; ☺4pm-1am) This mellow hang-out down the street from the Pet Sounds Bar, friendly and free of attitude, is one of the most comfortable places to drink in Stockholm. It has a vaguely retro vibe, a smooth wooden bar and record covers all over the walls.

Akkurat BAR

(Map p68; www.akkurat.se; Hornsgatan 18; beers around Skr72; half/full order mussels Skr145/205; ☺to midnight Mon, to 1am Tue-Sun) Valhalla for beer fiends, Akkurat boasts a huge selection of Belgian ales as well as a good range of Swedish-made microbrews, including Nynäshamn's Ångbryggeri. Extras include a vast wall of whisky, and mussels on the menu.

Vampire Lounge BAR

(Map p68; Östgötagatan 41; ☺from 5pm) The name says it all: this dark basement bar is bloodsucker-themed all the way through. There are perspex 'windows' in the floor showing buried caches of anti-vamp supplies such as holy water, crosses and garlic – just in case. It shares an entrance with Östgöta Källaren restaurant (p85).

Soldaten Svejk PUB

(Map p68; Östgötagatan 35) This crowded, wood-floored, amber-windowed pub, decorated with heraldic shields, specialises in great Czech beer on tap, including the massively popular Staropramen. Line your stomach with simple, solid Czech meals (Skr97 to Skr135); the smoked cheese is

---

TOP FIVE HOTEL BARS

» **Cadier Bar** (p76) At the Grand Hôtel Stockholm.

» **Absolut Icebar** (p77) At the Nordic Sea Hotel.

» **Eken Bar** (p80) At the Hilton Stockholm Slussen.

» **Rival Hotel** (p79)

» **Clarion Hotel Sign** (p77)

sublime. Head in early or prepare to queue for a table.

Marie Laveau BAR

(Map p68; www.marielaveau.se; Hornsgatan 66; ☺5pm-midnight Tue & Wed, to 3am Thu-Sat) In an old sausage factory, this kicking Söder playpen draws a boho-chic crowd. The designer-grunge bar (think chequered floor and subway-style tiled columns) serves killer cocktails and contemporary nosh (Skr85 to Skr215), while the sweaty basement hosts club nights on the weekend.

Berns Salonger BAR

(Map p56; www.berns.se; Berzelii Park; ☺bistro 11.30am-midnight Mon-Fri, noon-midnight Sat, 1-11pm Sun, nightclub 11pm-4am Thu-Sat, also Wed & Sun occasionally, midnight-5am Thu-Sat) A Stockholm institution since 1862, this glitzy entertainment palace remains one of the city's hottest party spots. While the gorgeous ballroom hosts some brilliant live-music gigs, the best of Berns' bars is the intimate basement bar, packed with cool creative types, top-notch DJs and projected art-house images. Check the website for a schedule of events; some require advance ticket purchase.

Le Rouge BAR

(Map p56; Österlånggatan 17; ☺11.30am-2pm & 5pm-1am Mon-Fri, 5pm-1am Sat) Fin-de-siècle Paris is the inspiration for this decadent lounge in Gamla Stan, a melange of rich red velvet, tasselled lampshades, inspired cocktails and French bistro grub. (The adjoining restaurant is run by two of Stockholm's hottest chefs, Danyel Couet and Melker Andersson.) DJs hit the decks Thursday to Saturday.

Olssons BAR

(Map p75; Odengatan 41; ☺9pm-3am Wed-Sat, opens earlier in summer) The blue neon sign outside this bar tips you off to its former life as a shoe store. These days, it serves as the back bar to Storstad (p82), forming a busy corner of activity along this neighbourhoody street. It's best in warm weather, when outdoor tables fill up with the early evening crowd.

Mälarpaviljongen CAFE, BAR

(www.malarpaviljongen.se; Norr Mälarstrand 63; ☺from 11am summer only) When the sun's out, few places beat this alfresco waterside spot for some Nordic dolce vita. A hit with both gay and straight punters, its cosy, glassed-in gazebo is only upstaged by the ubercool floating pontoon, where sexy crowds and lakeside views make for a fabulous evening guzzle. Opening times are at the weather's mercy.

El Mundo BAR

(Map p68; www.matkultur.nu, in Swedish; Erstagatan 21; ☺5pm-midnight Mon-Sat, from 4pm Fri) Backgammon boards, Mexicana film posters and a bar made from pressed olive-oil tins give this intimate hang-out a sultry Latin vibe. Out the back there's a closet-size art gallery and out the front a convivial 30-something crowd.

Lilla Baren at Riche BAR

(Map p56; Birger Jarlsgatan 4; ☺5pm-2am Tue-Sat) A darling of Östermalm's hip parade, this pretty, glassed-in bar mixes smooth bar staff, skilled DJs and a packed crowd of fashion-literate media types; head in by 9pm to score a seat. The adjoining restaurant does upmarket Scandi-meets-French-Mediterranean cuisine.

Absolut Icebar BAR

(Map p56; www.nordic hotels.se; Nordic Sea Hotel, Vasaplan 4; admission booked online/drop-in Skr180/195; ☺drop-in 9.15pm-1am Fri & Sat, also Thu Jun–mid-Sep, reservations recommended all other times) It's touristy. Downright gimmicky! And you're utterly intrigued, admit it: a bar built entirely out of ice, where you drink from glasses carved of ice on tables made of ice. The admission price gets you warm booties, mittens, a parka and one drink. Refill drinks cost Skr95.

Systembolaget LIQUOR STORE

(Map p56; www.systembolaget.se; Klarabergsgatan (Klarabergsgatan 62; ☺10am-8pm Mon-Fri, to 3pm Sat); Lilla Nygatan (Lilla Nygatan 11; ☺10am-6pm Mon-Wed, to 7pm Thu & Fri, to 3pm Sat); Regeringsgatan (Regeringsgatan 44; ☺10am-7pm Mon-Fri, to 3pm Sat)

☆ Entertainment

Stockholm has an active club scene, especially Thursday to Sunday. Many clubs charge for admission (around Skr150), and several have age limits, usually with no under-25s allowed. Even in the middle of winter locals dress to the nines to go out clubbing, so if you hope to make it past a stern doorperson, you're advised to do the same.

For most concerts and events, the tourist office can sell you tickets or tell you where to get them. (Call ☏508 28 508 to check.)

GAY & LESBIAN STOCKHOLM

Stockholm is a dazzling spot for queer travellers. Sweden's legendary open-mindedness makes homophobic attitudes rare, and party-goers of all persuasions are welcome in any bar or club. As a result, Stockholm doesn't really have a gay district, although you'll find most of the queer-centric venues in Södermalm and Gamla Stan. For club listings and events, pick up a free copy of street-press magazine *QX*, found at many clubs, shops and cafes around town. Its website (www.qx.se) is more frequently updated and has listings in English. *QX* also produces a free, handy *Gay Stockholm Map*, available at the tourist office.

Good bars and clubs include the following:

Lady Patricia (Map p68; www.patricia.st; Stadsgårdskajen 152; ☺6pm-3am Sun) This is a perennial Sunday-night favourite with its superb seafood restaurant, two crowded dance floors, drag shows and Schlager-loving crowd. It's all aboard a docked old royal yacht.

RFSL (www.rfsl.se/stockholm; Sveavägen 59) The national organisation for gay and lesbian rights is a good source of information, with a library and cafe to boot.

Roxy (Map p68; www.roxysofo.se; Nytorget 6; brunch Skr115, burgers Skr210; ☺dinner Mon-Fri, lunch & dinner Sat & Sun) A chic restaurant-bar in Södermalm, it's popular with the creative set, all of whom nibble on brilliant modern-Mediterranean nosh to sultry tango tunes.

Side Track (Map p68; www.sidetrack.nu; Wollmar Yxkullsgatan 7; ☺Wed-Sat) This establishment is a particular hit with down-to-earth guys, with a low-key, publike ambience and decent grub for peckish punters on the prowl.

Torget (Map p56; www.torgetbaren.com; Mälartorget 13) In Gamla Stan, this is Stockholm's premier gay bar-restaurant, with mock-baroque touches and a civilised salon vibe.

For an up-to-date calendar visit www.visit stockholm.com, or pick up the free monthly *What's On Stockholm* guide (at the tourist office, Centralstationen and most hotels). Another good source if you can navigate a little Swedish is the Friday 'På Stan' section of *Dagens Nyheter* newspaper (www.dn.se). **Ticnet** (www.ticnet.se) is a frequently used on-line ticket outlet for big concerts and sporting events.

Nightclubs

Stockholm is home to some mighty clubs, with DJ royalty regularly on the decks. You'll find the slickest spots in Östermalm, especially on and around Stureplan. Expect an entry charge of Skr150 to Skr200 at the trendiest venues, and plan on dressing up if you want to get in. Södermalm offers a more varied scene, with club nights spanning local indie to salsa, and a more denim-friendly crowd.

Café Opera CLUB
(Map p56; www.cafeopera.se; Operahuset, Karl XXI's Torg; admission Skr185; ☺10pm-3am Wed-Sun) Rock stars need a suitably excessive place to schmooze, booze and groove, one with bulbous chandeliers, haughty ceiling frescoes and a jet-set vibe. This bar-club combo fits the bill, but it's also welcoming enough to make regular folk *feel* like rock stars. If you only have time to hit one primo club during your visit, this is a good choice.

Sturecompagniet CLUB
(Map p56; www.sturecompagniet.se; Sturegatan 4; admission from Skr150; ☺10pm-3am Thu-Sat) Swedish soap stars, flowing champagne and look-at-me attitude set a decadent scene at this glitzy, multilevel playpen. Dress to impress and flaunt your wares to commercial house. Big-name guest DJs come through frequently.

Grodan CLUB
(Map p56; www.grodannattklubb.se; Grev Turegatan 16; admission Skr150; ☺10pm-3am Fri & Sat) At street level there's a packed bar and mock-baroque restaurant serving great mod-nosh. In the cellar, A-list DJ talent from Stockholm, London and beyond spins the vinyl, pumping out house and electro tracks for sweat-soaked clubbers.

Spy Bar CLUB
(Map p56; www.thespybar.com; Birger Jarlsgatan 20; admission Skr160; ☺10pm-5am Wed-Sat) No longer the super-hip star of the scene it once was, the Spy Bar (aka 'the Puke' because *spy*

means vomit in Swedish) is still a landmark and fun to check out if you're making the Östermalm rounds. It covers three levels in a turn-of-the-century flat (spot the tile stoves). If it's packed or obnoxious, try the ground-level bar Laroy, which tends to be a little more relaxed and grown-up.

Live Music

Stockholm's music scene is active and varied. On any one night you can catch emerging indie acts, edgy rock, blues and Balkan pop. Jazz and blues have a particularly strong presence, with several legendary venues saxing it up and an annual jazz festival held in mid-July.

All of the following clubs have admission charges most nights; typical prices range from Skr125 to Skr350, but they'll vary widely depending on who's performing.

Debaser   LIVE MUSIC
(Map p56; www.debaser.se; Karl Johanstorg 1, Slussen; ☺7pm-1am Sun-Thu, 8pm-3am Fri & Sat) The king of rock clubs hides away under the Slussen interchange. Emerging or bigger-name acts play most nights, while the killer club nights span anything from rock-steady to punk and electronica.

Mosebacke Etablissement   LIVE MUSIC
(Map p68; www.mosebacke.se; Mosebacketorg 3; tickets up to Skr250; ☺to 11pm Mon & Tue, to 1am Wed & Sun, to 2am Thu-Sat) Eclectic theatre and club nights aside, this historic culture palace hosts a mixed line-up of live music. Tunes span anything from home-grown pop to antipodean rock. The outdoor terrace (featured in the opening scene of August Strindberg's novel *The Red Room*) combines dazzling city views with a thumping summertime bar.

Glenn Miller Café   JAZZ, BLUES
(Map p56; Brunnsgatan 21A; ☺5pm-1am Mon-Thu, to 2am Fri & Sat) Simply loaded with character, this tiny jazz-and-blues bar draws a faithful, fun-loving crowd. It also serves excellent, affordable French-style classics like mussels with white wine sauce.

Fasching   JAZZ
(Map p56; www.fasching.se; Kungsgatan 63; tickets Skr115-300; ☺to midnight Mon-Thu, to 4am Fri & Sat) Music club Fasching is the pick of Stockholm's jazz clubs, with live music most nights. DJs take over with either Afrobeat, Latin, neo-soul or R&B on Friday night

and retro-soul, disco and rare grooves on Saturday.

Stampen   JAZZ
(Map p56; www.stampen.se; Stora Nygatan 5; admission free Mon-Thu, from Skr125 Fri & Sat; ☺8pm-1am Mon-Wed, to 2am Thu-Sat) Once a pawn shop, Stampen is better known as one of Stockholm's music-club stalwarts, swinging to live jazz and blues every night. The free blues jam, at 2pm on Saturday, pulls everyone from local noodlers to the odd music legend.

Concerts, Theatre & Dance

Stockholm delivers outstanding dance, opera and music performances; for an overview, pick up the free *What's On Stockholm* guide from the tourist office. Most ticket sales are handled by the tourist office as well. Alternatively, you can buy tickets direct from Ticnet (☑0771-70 70 70; www.ticnet.se).

Tickets generally aren't cheap and often sell out, especially for Saturday shows, but you can occasionally get good-value last-minute deals. Operas are usually performed in their original language, while theatre performances are invariably in Swedish.

Konserthuset   CLASSICAL MUSIC
(Map p56; ☑50 66 77 88; www.konserthuset.se; Hötorget; tickets Skr80-325) Head here for classical concerts and other musical marvels, including the Royal Philharmonic Orchestra.

Operan   OPERA
(Map p56; ☑791 44 00; www.operan.se; Operahuset, Gustav Adolfs Torg; tickets Skr50-800) The Royal Opera is the place to go for thunderous tenors, sparkling sopranos and classical ballet. It also has some bargain tickets in seats with poor views, and occasional lunchtime concerts for less than Skr200 (including light lunch).

Folkoperan   THEATRE
(Map p68; ☑616 07 50; www.folkoperan.se; Hornsgatan 72; tickets Skr265-450) Folkoperan gives opera a thoroughly modern overhaul with its intimate, cutting-edge and sometimes controversial productions. The under-26s enjoy half-price tickets.

Dramaten   THEATRE
(Map p56; ☑667 06 80; www.dramaten.se; Nybroplan; tickets Skr190-320) The Royal Theatre stages a range of plays in a sublime art-nouveau environment. Dramaten's experimental stage Elverket at Linnégatan 69 (same contact details), pushes the

boundaries with edgier offerings performed in a converted power station.

Stockholms Stadsteatern
THEATRE

(Map p56; ☑50 62 02 00; Kulturhuset, Sergels Torg; tickets around Skr250, under 26yr around Skr100) Regular performances are staged at this theatre, as well as guest appearances by foreign theatre companies.

Dansens Hus
DANCE

(Map p56; ☑50 89 90 90; www.dansenshus.se; Barnhusgatan 12-14; tickets up to Skr300) The stomping ground of Mats Ek's Cullberg Ballet, this place is an absolute must for contemporary dance fans. Guest artists have included everyone from British choreographer Akram Khan to Canadian innovator Daniel Léveillé.

Globen
STADIUM

(☑0771-31 00 00; www.globearenas.se; Globentorget 2) This huge white spherical building (it looks like a giant golf ball) just south of Södermalm hosts regular big-name pop and rock concerts, as well as sporting events and trade fairs. Even if nothing's going on inside, you can take a ride up and over the building inside SkyView, a mini-globe whose glass walls offer great views across town. Take the tunnelbana to T-Globen.

Sport

Bandy matches, a uniquely Scandinavian phenomenon, take place all winter at Stockholm's ice arenas.

For the ultimate Scandi sport experience, head to an ice hockey game. Contact

Globen (☑50 83 53 00; www.globearenas.se; Arenavägen, Johanneshov; tickets Skr150-250) for details; matches take place here up to three times a week from October to April. There are regular football fixtures, too. Purchase tickets through **Ticnet** (☑0771-31 00 00; www.ticnet.se).

Impromptu public ice-skating areas spring up during the winter at Kungsträdgården in Norrmalm and at Medborgarplatsen in Södermalm. Skate-rental booths next to the rinks hire out equipment (per hour adult/child Skr40/25).

Zinkensdamms Idrottsplats
BANDY

(Map p68; Ringvägen 16) Watching a bandy match is great fun. The sport, a precursor to ice hockey but with more players (11 to a side) and less fighting, has grown massively popular since the rise of the Hammarby team in the late '90s. There's a round vinyl ball instead of a puck, and the rules are similar to football, except that you hit the ball with a stick instead of kicking it. The season lasts from November to March, so make sure you bring your own thermos of *kaffekask* – a warming mix of coffee and booze. For the low-down on upcoming matches, check out www.svenskbandy.se/stockholm (in Swedish). Tickets (around Skr125) can be purchased at the arena gate.

🛍 Shopping

Stockholm is a seasoned shopper's paradise. It's practically a sport here. Clothing retailer H&M, the Ikea of fashion, was founded

---

ANNO SUPERSTAR

Anno Superstar is, among many other things, a Stockholm shopper extraordinaire with a rabid Twitter following – in large part because of the dressing-room photos she posts of herself trying on recent purchases. She's from Luleå but has lived in Stockholm for the past nine years and is a notorious shoe hound.

What are some of your favourite places to shop in Stockholm? I love the Science Fiction Bookshop in the old town. Lisa Larsson in Söder has some really amazing '60s dresses. Another cool place – Sivletto, a rockabilly heaven with both '50s clothes and hairdressers!

Do you have a favourite place to go out for a drink? There's a really great place called Vampire Lounge (p86). It's famous for its ice-cream drinks. You can have no more than two. And the vampire theme goes through the whole place, even into the bathrooms.

What else do you love about living in Stockholm? I like that it's a big city but still feels small. You can walk everywhere. I love all the water. And the communal bikes program (p94) – that's awesome. I rented a bike for the first time last year. And I think we're getting even more bike lanes soon.

SWEDISH DESIGN

Now that Ingvar Kamprad's unmistakably huge blue-and-yellow Ikea stores are sprouting up all over the world, Swedish design may have lost some of its exotic appeal. But that just means more people can know the sleek, utilitarian joy of invisible drawers, paper chandeliers and round squares.

Most of the clever designs Ikea brings to the masses originated among Stockholm's relentlessly inventive designers, and you can see these artifacts in their undiluted form all over the city in museums, shops, and shops that are so exclusive they may as well be museums.

Functional elegance defines Swedish design, although in recent decades a refreshing tendency towards the whimsical has lightened the mood. Stockholm's Nationalmuseum (p60) tells the story through chronologically arranged objects. You can also find examples of both historic and contemporary design at upmarket shops like Svenskt Tenn, home to floral fabrics by design legend Josef Frank, and Nordiska Galleriet, with its dizzying array of neat things to look at.

Södermalm's main drag Götgatan is home to democratically priced DesignTorget as well as the iconic **10 Swedish Designers** (Map p68; Götgatan 25). Known in Swedish as Tiogruppen, 10 Swedish Designers started in 1970 when a band of young textile designers (notably Tom Hedqvist) introduced unapologetically bold, geometric patterns. These days, their eye-catching graphics cover tote bags, wallets, cushions, plates and napkins.

here and has outlets all over the city. For big-name Swedish and international retail outlets like Diesel, Urban Outfitters, Whyred and Face Stockholm, hit the pedestrianised **Biblioteksgatan** from Östermalm to Norrmalmstorg, as well as the smaller streets that branch off it. Östermalm is generally good for browsing at high-dollar boutiques. For the slightly funkier and artier stores and galleries, head to Södermalm. And for souvenirs and postcards, Gamla Stan has the most stores per square inch, but pedestrian thoroughfare Drottninggatan offers super-cheap Viking hats and Absolut Swede T-shirts in mass quantities.

Svenskt Tenn
DESIGN

(Map p56; www.svenskttenn.se; Nybrogatan 15) As much a museum of design as an actual shop, this iconic store is home to the signature fabrics and furniture of Josef Frank and his contemporaries. Browsing here is a great way to get a quick handle on what people mean by 'classic Swedish design'.

Svensk Slöjd
DESIGN

(Map p56; Nybrogatan 23) If you like the traditional Swedish wooden horses but want one that looks a little unique (or maybe you'd prefer a traditional wooden chicken instead?), check out this shop. It's crammed with quirky hand-carved knick-knacks as well as luxurious woven textiles, handmade candles, ironwork, knitted clothing, and other high-quality gifts.

Iris Hantverk
DESIGN

(Map p56; Kungsgatan 55; ⊙10am-8pm Mon-Fri, to 3pm Sat) Similar to the handicraft standby Svensk Slöjd and equally worth exploring, this shop has impeccably made woodwork, linens, textiles, candlesticks, handmade soaps, glassware and crafting books.

DesignTorget
DESIGN

Götgatan (Map p68; Götgatan 31, Södermalm); Sergels Torg (Map p56; Basement, Kulturhuset, Sergels Torg); Östermalm (Map p56; Nybrogatan 11) If you love good design but don't own a Gold Amex, head to this chain, which sells the work of emerging designers alongside established denizens.

Ekovaruhuset
FAIR TRADE

(Map p56; Österlånggatan 28) With a sister shop in Manhattan, this enlightened concept store stocks fair-trade organic products, from cosmetics and chocolates to trendy threads and too-cute babywear. Expect anything from Edun T-shirts from Peru to in-the-know labels like Zion and Misericordia.

Chokladfabriken
FOOD, DRINK

(Map p68; Renstiernas Gata 12; ⊙closed Sun) For an edible souvenir, head straight to this savvy chocolate-peddler, where seasonal Nordic ingredients are used to make heavenly cocoa treats. There's a cafe for an on-the-spot fix, and smaller branches in

Norrmalm (Map p56; Regeringsgatan 58) and Östermalm (Grevgatan 37).

Lisa Larsson Second Hand VINTAGE

(Map p68; Bondegatan 48; ⊙1-6pm Tue-Fri, 11am-3pm Sat, closed Sun-Mon) The pick of Södermalm's stylish thrift shops, this small space is packed with treasures dating from the '30s to the '70s. Look for leather jackets, handbags, shoes and vintage dresses.

Sivletto VINTAGE

(Map p68; www.sivletto.com; Malmgårdsvägen 16-18; ⊙noon-6pm Mon-Fri, until 8pm Thu, 11.30am-4.30pm Sat, closed Sun) Illustrating Sweden's fascination for 1950s America, this retro shop sells all kinds of clothes, accessories, furniture and home decor. Inside, there's a pinball machine and even a hair salon.

Science Fiction Bookshop BOOKS

(Map p56; www.sfbok.se; Västerlånggatan 48; ⊙10am-7pm Mon-Fri, to 5pm Sat, noon-5pm Sun) In some ways, this seems an unlikely location for a science fiction-fantasy-comic bookshop, but in other ways it makes perfect sense. Regardless, this is the place to come for comics and graphic novels both mainstream and obscure (in English and Swedish), as well as books, games, toys and posters.

Hedengrens BOOKS

(Map p56; Sturegallerian Shopping Centre) Inside the upmarket Östermalm shopping mall is this great bookstore, with a huge selection of new fiction and nonfiction books in English (including a cylindrical sci-fi and fantasy section).

Sweden Bookshop BOOKS

(Map p56; Slottsbacken 10) The official source for Swedish literature in translation, this shop tends to have the latest novels before they're widely available. There are also books about Swedish culture and history in several languages, as well as a great children's-book section.

Naturkompaniet OUTDOOR EQUIPMENT

(Map p56; Kungsgatan 4) Find everything you might need for an excursion into the Swedish wilderness here, from backpacks and sleeping bags to woolly socks, headlamps, cooking stoves and compasses.

PUB DEPARTMENT STORE

(Map p56; Drottninggatan 72-6; ⊙10am-7pm Mon-Fri, to 6pm Sat, 11am-5pm Sun) Historic department store PUB is best known as the former workplace of Greta Garbo, and advertisements still work that angle pretty strongly. A major revamp has since turned it into Stockholm's hottest new fashion and lifestyle hub. Bag yourself fresh Nordic labels like Stray Boys, House of Dagmar and Baum & Pferdgarten, refuel at the slinky cafe-bar or check out the edgy art space.

Åhléns DEPARTMENT STORE

(Map p56; Klarabergsgatan 50) For your all-in-one retail therapy, scour department-store giant Åhléns.

NK DEPARTMENT STORE

(Map p56; Hamngatan 12-18) The upmarket rival of Åhléns.

Information

Emergency

24-hour medical advice (☎32 01 00)
24-hour police stations Kungsholmen (☎401 00 00; Kungsholmsgatan 37, Kungsholmen); Södermalm (☎401 03 00; Torkel Knutssonsgatan 20, Södermalm)
AutoAssistans (☎020-53 65 36) Roadside assistance for vehicle breakdowns.
Emergency (☎112) Toll-free access to the fire service, police and ambulance.

Internet Access

Nearly all hostels and most hotels have a computer or two with internet access for guests, and most offer wi-fi access in rooms (though often with a fee). There are also wi-fi hubs in Centralstationen (requiring an account), and most coffee shops offer free wi-fi access to customers. Those without their own computer have fewer options, but most public libararies offer internet service if you sign up for a free membership card. Computers in the tourist office let you buy internet time with a credit card (Skr29 for two hours), although it's a fairly hectic environment.

Sidewalk Express (www.sidewalkexpress.se; per hr Skr29) Cityterminalen (City Bus Terminalen); Kungsgatan (Kungsgatan 44); Slussen (Götgatan 25); Vasastaden (Odenplan 22) Rows of computer monitors and tall red ticket machines mark out these self-service internet stations scattered across the city. There are also several banks of them at Stockholm-Arlanda Airport.

Media

Dagens Nyheter (www.dn.se) Daily paper with a great culture section and a weekend event listing ('På Stan'). The website (in Swedish) is a good place to look for bar and restaurant news.
Nöjesguiden (www.nojesguiden.se) Entertainment and pop-culture news and event listings.

Svenska Dagbladet (www.svd.se) Daily news, in Swedish.

Medical Services
Apoteket CW Scheele (☑454 81 30; Klarabergsgatan 64; ☺24hr pharmacy)
CityAkuten (☑412 29 00; Apelbergsgatan 48; ☺8am-8pm) Emergency health and dental care.
Södersjukhuset (☑616 10 00; Ringvägen 52) The most central hospital.

Money

ATMs are plentiful, with several at Centralstationen and all the airports; expect queues on Friday and Saturday evenings in the downtown area.

The exchange company Forex has over a dozen branches in the capital and charges Skr15 per travellers cheque; the following are two handy locations:
Forex-Vasagatan (Vasagatan 16; ☺5.30am-10pm Sun-Fri, to 6pm Sat) Near the tourist office and Centralstationen.
Stockholm-Arlanda Airport (Terminal 2; ☺5.30am-10pm Sun-Fri, to 6pm Sat)

Post

You can buy stamps and send letters at a number of city locations, including newsagents and supermarkets – keep an eye out for the Swedish postal symbol (yellow on a blue background). There's a convenient outlet next to the Hemköp supermarket in the basement of central department store **Åhléns** (Map p56; Klarabergsgatan 50).

Telephone

Coin-operated phones are virtually nonexistent; most payphones are operated with phonecards purchased from any Pressbyrån newsagency location (or with a credit card, although this is ludicrously expensive). Ask for a *telefon kort* for Skr50 or Skr120, which roughly equate to 50 minutes and 120 minutes of local talk time, respectively. (Be sure to specify you're using the card on a payphone, not refilling a cellphone.) For mobile phones, check with your service provider to ensure your network is compatible with Sweden's. For longer visits, it may be worthwhile buying a cheap mobile phone you can load with prepaid minutes and use as needed.

Tourist Information
Stockholm Tourist Centre (Map p56; ☑508 28 508; www.visitstockholm.com; Vasagatan 14; ☺9am-6pm Mon-Fri, 10am-5pm Sat, 10am-4pm Sun) Directly across the street (Vasagatan) from Centralstationen.

PAY TO PEE

Most public toilets charge Skr5 or Skr10, payable with Skr5 or Skr10 coins, so keep a few handy. Note that coin-pay public toilets are being phased out in favour of pay-by-text-message.

❶ Getting There & Away

Air

Stockholm's main airport, **Stockholm-Arlanda** (☑797 60 00; www.arlanda.se, www.lfv.se), is 45km north of the city centre and can be reached from central Stockholm by both bus and express train.

Bromma Airport (☑797 68 00) is 8km west of Stockholm and is used for some domestic flights. **Skavsta Airport** (☑0155-28 04 00), 100km south of Stockholm, near Nyköping, is mostly used by low-cost carriers like Ryanair and Wizz Air.

Boat

Both **Silja Line** (Map p56; ☑22 21 40; www.tallinksilja.com; Silja & Tallink Customer Service Office, Cityterminalen) and **Viking Line** (Map p56; ☑452 40 00; www.vikingline.fi; Cityterminalen) run ferries to Turku and Helsinki. **Tallink** (Map p56; ☑22 21 40; www.tallinksilja.com; Silja & Tallink Customer Service Office, Cityterminalen) ferries head to Tallinn (Estonia) and Riga (Latvia).

Bus

Most long-distance buses arrive and depart from **Cityterminalen** (Map p56; www.cityterminalen.com), which is connected to Centralstationen. The **main counter** (☺7am-6pm) sells tickets for several bus companies, including Flygbussarna (airport coaches), Swebus Express, Svenska Buss, Eurolines and Y-Buss.

Car & Motorcycle

The E4 motorway passes through the city, just west of the centre, on its way from Helsingborg to Haparanda. The E20 motorway from Stockholm to Göteborg via Örebro follows the E4 as far as Södertälje. The E18 from Kapellskär to Oslo runs from east to west and passes just north of central Stockholm.

Train

Stockholm is the hub for national train services run by **Sveriges Järnväg** (SJ; ☑0771-75 75 75; www.sj.se).

ⓘ Getting Around

To/From the Airport

The **Arlanda Express** (☑020-22 22 24; www.
arlandaexpress.com; one-way Skr260, student
Skr130) train service from Centralstationen takes
20 minutes to reach Arlanda; trains run every
10 to 15 minutes from about 5am to 12.30am. In
peak summer season (mid-June to August), two
adults can travel together for Skr280.

The same trip in a taxi costs around Skr495,
but agree on the fare first and don't use taxis
without a contact telephone number displayed.
Taxi Stockholm (☑15 00 00) is one reputable
operator. **Airport Cab** (☑25 25 25; www.air
portcab.se) goes from Stockholm to Arlanda for
a flat fee of Skr365 to Skr390, and the opposite
direction for Skr475.

A cheaper option is the **Flygbuss** (www.flygbus
sarna.se) service between Stockholm-Arlanda
and Cityterminalen. Buses leave every 10 or 15
minutes (Skr110, 40 minutes). Tickets can be
purchased online, at Cityterminalen or on arrival
at the Flygbuss counter at the airport's main
terminal. If you have plenty of time, it's also possible to buy a ticket for Stockholm's regular public
bus 592 to Märsta, then change to the local train
(pendeltåg) to reach Centralstationen (Skr72).
(The bus will also eventually get there, but it takes
much longer and costs the same.)

Bicycle

Bicycles can be carried free on SL local trains,
except during peak hour (6am to 9am and 3pm
to 6pm weekdays). They're not allowed in Centralstationen or on the tunnelbana, although
you'll occasionally see some daring souls.

Stockholm City Bikes (www.citybikes.se;
3-day/season card Skr165/300, season card
purchased online Skr250; ☺6am-10pm) There
are around 90 self-service bicycle-hire stands
across the city. Bikes can be borrowed for three-
hour stretches and returned at any City Bikes
stand. Purchase a bike card online or from the
tourist office. Rechargeable season cards are
valid April to October.

Boat

Djurgårdsfärjan city ferry services connect
Gröna Lund Tivoli on Djurgården Nybroplan
(summer only) and Slussen (year-round) as frequently as every 10 minutes in summer (and less
frequently at other times); a single trip costs
Skr36 (free with an SL transport pass).

Car & Motorcycle

Driving in central Stockholm is not
recommended. Skinny one-way streets,
congested bridges and limited parking all
present problems; note that Djurgårdsvägen
is closed near Skansen at night, on summer
weekends and some holidays. Don't attempt

driving through the narrow streets of Gamla
Stan.

Parking is a major problem, but there are
P-hus (parking stations) throughout the city;
they charge up to Skr60 per hour, though the
fixed evening rate is usually more reasonable. If
you do have a car, one of the best options is to
stay on the outskirts of town and catch public
transport into the centre.

Public Transport

Storstockholms Lokaltrafik (SL; www.sl.se)
runs all tunnelbana (T or T-bana) trains, local
trains and buses within the entire Stockholm
county. There is an SL information office at
Centralstationen (basement concourse;
☺6.30am-11.15pm Mon-Sat, 7am-11.15pm Sun)
and another near the **Sergels Torg entrance**
(☺7am-6.30pm Mon-Fri, 10am-5pm Sat & Sun),
which issues timetables and sells the SL Tourist Card and Stockholm Card. (There are other
offices at stations Fridhemsplan, Gullmarsplan,
and Tekniska Högskolan, open 7am to 6.30pm
Monday to Friday and 10am to 5pm Saturday.)
You can also call ☑600 10 00 for schedule and
travel information.

The Stockholm Card (see p60) covers travel
on all SL trains and buses in greater Stockholm.
International rail passes (eg Scanrail, Interrail)
aren't valid on SL trains. SL offers several kinds
of tickets and passes for bus and tunnelbana
travel: individual ticket for one/two/three
zones Skr36/54/72; pre-paid strip of 16 tickets
Skr200; unlimited travel cards 24/72 hours
Skr115/230; seven-day pass Skr300; 30-day
pass Skr790.

Coupons, tickets and passes can be bought
at tunnelbana stations, Pressbyrån kiosks,
some central bus stops, SL railway stations
and SL information offices. Tickets cannot be
bought on buses. You can, however, pay by text
message if you're travelling with a mobile phone.
Instructions are posted at bus stops; essentially,
you text the number of zones you're crossing
to ☑72150, and you'll receive a ticket by return
message, which you then show the driver when
you board. Travelling without a valid ticket can
lead to a fine of Skr1200.

BUS While the bus timetables and route maps
are complicated, they're worth studying as there
are some useful connections to suburban
attractions. Ask **SL** (☑600 10 00) or any tourist
office for the handy inner-city route map Inners-
tadsbussar. It's also available online (www.sl.se).

Inner-city buses radiate from Sergels Torg,
Odenplan, Fridhemsplan (on Kungsholmen)
and Slussen. Bus 47 runs from Sergels Torg
to Djurgården, and bus 69 from Centralstationen and Sergels Torg to the Ladugårdsgärdet
museums and Kaknästornet. Useful buses for
hostellers include bus 65 (Centralstationen to

Skeppsholmen) and bus 43 (Regeringsgatan to Södermalm).

Inner-city night buses run from 1am to 5pm on a few routes. Most leave from Centralstationen, Sergels Torg, Slussen, Odenplan and Fridhemsplan to the suburbs.

Check where the regional bus hub is for each outlying area. Islands of the Ekerö municipality (including Drottningholm palace) are served by buses with numbers 301 to 323 from T-Brommaplan. Buses to Vaxholm (the 670) and the Åland ferries (the 637 to Grisslehamn and 631 to Kapellskär) depart from T-Tekniska Högskolan. Odenplan is the hub for buses to the northern suburbs, including Hagaparken.

TRAIN Local trains *(pendeltåg)* are most useful for connections to Nynäshamn (for ferries to Gotland), to Märsta (for buses to Sigtuna and the short hop to Stockholm-Arlanda Airport) and to Södertälje. There are also services to Nockeby from T-Alvik; Lidingö from T-Ropsten; Kårsta, Österskär and Näsbypark from T-Tekniska Högskolan; and to Saltsjöbaden from T-Slussen. SL coupons and SL travel passes are valid on all of these trains, and should be bought before boarding.

TRAM The historic No 7 tram runs between Norrmalmstorg and Skansen, passing most attractions on Djurgården. Both the Stockholm Card and SL Tourist Card are valid on board, as well as regular SL tickets.

METRO (TUNNELBANA) The most useful mode of transport in Stockholm, run by SL. Its lines converge on T-Centralen, connected by an underground walkway to Centralstationen. There are three main lines with branches. The blue line has a comprehensive collection of modern art decorating the underground stations, and several stations along other lines are decorated as well, often by famous artists.

Taxi

Taxis are readily available but expensive, so check for a meter or arrange the fare first. The flag fall is around Skr45, then Skr10 to Skr13 per kilometre. (A 10km ride that takes 15 minutes should cost around Skr230 to Skr250.) At night, women travelling alone should ask about *tjejtaxa*, a discount rate offered by some operators. Use one of the established, reputable firms, such as **Taxi Stockholm** (☑15 00 00), **Taxi 020** (☑020-20 20 20) and **Taxi Kurir** (☑30 00 00).

AROUND STOCKHOLM

With royal palaces, vintage villages and Viking traces, the greater Stockholm county is certainly worth a venture or three. Handily, the SL Tourist Card or travel passes allow unlimited travel on all buses and local trains

in the area. Free timetables are available from the SL office in Centralstationen, the SL terminals at Slussen or Östrastationen and the SL website.

Just to the east of Stockholm, the magical islands of the Stockholm archipelago have inspired the likes of writer August Strindberg and artist Anders Zorn. Ferry services aren't expensive and there's a travel pass available if you fancy a spot of island-hopping.

Drottningholm

The royal residence and parks of Drottningholm on Lovön are justifiably popular attractions and easy to visit from the capital.

It's a good idea to use the Stockholm Card here, otherwise seeing everything on the grounds can get expensive.

◎ Sights

Drottningholms Slott CASTLE
(Map p96; www.royalcourt.se; adult/child Skr80/40, combined ticket incl Chinese Pavilion Skr120/60; ⊙10am-4.30pm daily May-Aug, noon-3.30pm daily Sep, noon-3.30pm Sat & Sun Oct-Apr, closed mid-Dec–early Jan) Still the royal family pad for part of the year, the Renaissance-inspired main **palace**, with its geometric baroque gardens, was designed by architectural great Nicodemus Tessin the Elder and begun in 1662, about the same time as Versailles. You can either walk around the wings open to the public on your own or take a one-hour guided tour (no additional charge; English tours at 10am, noon, 2pm and 4pm daily from June to August, reduced schedule rest of the year). Tours are recommended, especially for an insight into the cultural milieu that influenced some of the decorations.

The **Lower North Corps de Garde** was originally a guard room, but it's now replete with gilt-leather wall hangings, which used to feature in many palace rooms during the 17th century. The **Karl X Gustav Gallery**, in baroque style, depicts this monarch's militaristic exploits, though the ceiling shows classical battle scenes. The highly ornamented **State Bedchamber of Hedvig Eleonora** is Sweden's most expensive baroque interior, decorated with paintings that feature the childhood of Karl XI. The painted ceiling shows Karl X and his queen, Hedvig Eleonora. Although Lovisa Ulrika's collection of more than 2000 books has been moved to the Royal Library in

STOCKHOLM & AROUND DROTTNINGHOLM

STOCKHOLM & AROUND AROUND STOCKHOLM

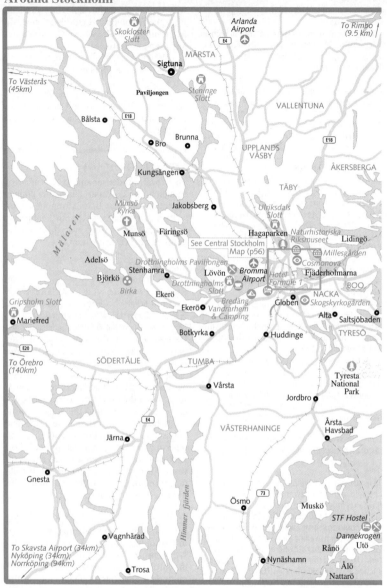

Stockholm, her library here is still a bright and impressive room, complete with most of its original 18th-century fittings. The elaborate staircase, with statues at every turn, was the work of both Nicodemus Tessin the Elder and the Younger. Circular

Drottningholms Slottskyrka (admission free), the palace chapel, wasn't completed until the late 1720s.

Drottningholms Slottsteater & Teatermuseum

MUSEUM

(Court Theatre and Museum; www.dtm.se; entry by tour adult/child Skr90/70; ☉tours hourly noon-

ropes, pulleys, wagons and wind machines. Scenes can be changed in less than seven seconds!

Illusion was the order of the day here, and accordingly the theatre makes use of fake marble, fake curtains and papier-mâché viewing boxes. Even the stage was designed to create illusions regarding size.

The fascinating guided tour takes you into other rooms in the building, where highlights include hand-painted 18th-century wallpaper and an Italianate room *(salon de déjeuner)* with fake three-dimensional wall effects and a ceiling that looks like the sky.

Kina Slott CASTLE

(adult/child Skr70/35, combined ticket incl royal palace Skr120/60; ⊙11am-4.30pm May-Aug, noon-3.30pm Sep) At the far end of the royal gardens is Kina Slott, a lavishly decorated Chinese pavilion built by King Adolf Fredrik as a birthday surprise for Queen Lovisa Ulrika in 1753. Restored between 1989 and 1996, it boasts one of the finest rococo chinoiserie interiors in Europe. There's a cafe on the premises serving good waffles, and the admission price includes guided tours, which run at 11am, 1pm and 3pm daily from June to August (the schedule is reduced in May and September).

On the slope below Kina Slott, the carnivalesque **Guards' Tent** (admission free; ⊙11am-4.30pm mid-Jun–mid-Aug) was erected in 1781 as quarters for the dragoons of Gustav III, but it's not really a tent at all. The building now has displays about the gardens and Drottningholm's Royal Guard.

✖ Eating

Bring a picnic with you and enjoy lunch out in the gardens, or munch away at one of the two restaurants by the palace. There's also a small kiosk by the driveway entrance.

Drottningholms Paviljongen CAFE €€

(Map p96; light meals Skr65-110, mains Skr155-225) Close to the boat dock, this cafe peddles light meals like sandwiches and heartier mains, as well as coffee and cakes. Outdoor seating lends the place a garden-party vibe.

Drottningholms Wärdshus SWEDISH €€

(Malmbacken 8; mains Skr160-265) Opposite the palace grounds, this more upmarket option has a predilection for meaty mains, from roast lamb to seared cod.

4pm May, 11am-4pm Jun-Aug, 1-3pm Sep) Slottsteater was completed in 1766 on the instructions of Queen Lovisa Ulrika. Remarkably untouched from the time of Gustav III's death (1792) until 1922, it's now the oldest theatre in the world still in its original state; performances are held here in summer using 18th-century machinery, including

☆ Entertainment

Drottningholms Slottsteater　　THEATRE
(www.dtm.se; tickets Skr275-895) The royal palace's whimsical 18th-century theatre stages
(mostly opera) productions in summer that
are well worth an encore.

ℹ️ Getting There & Away

If you're not short of time you can cycle out to
the palace. Otherwise, take the tunnelbana to
T-Brommaplan and change to any bus numbered
between 301 and 323. If you're driving, there are
few road signs for Drottningholm, so get hold of
a decent map. The car park is second on the left
after crossing Drottningholmsbron.

　　Strömma Kanalbolaget (Map p56; ☎1200
40 00; www.stromma.se) will take you to the
palace by boat. Frequent services depart from
Stadshusbron (Stockholm) daily between May
and mid-September, with less frequent daily
departures mid- to late September, and weekend-only services in October (one-way/return
Skr120/165). A *kombibiljett* (combined ticket;
Skr280) includes return travel and admission to
the palace and Chinese pavilion.

Vaxholm

Despite the summer hordes, Vaxholm
redeems itself with its easy accessibility,
charming side streets and storybook
summer houses. The latter were a hit with
fashionable 19th-century urbanites, who
flocked here for some seaside R&R. An easy
35km northeast of the city, the settlement
itself was founded in 1647, with the oldest
buildings in Norrhamn, a few minutes' walk
north of the town hall. Equally photogenic
is Hamngatan, awash with interesting
architecture, galleries, boutiques and
souvenir shops. Vaxholm's most famous
local, however, is its hulking fortress. It's
also the gateway to the archipelago's central
and northern reaches.

◉ Sights

Vaxholm Kastell　　HISTORIC SITE
(Citadel; adult/child Skr50/free; ⊘11am-4pm daily
Jun, to 5pm Jul & Aug, 11am-5pm 1st & 2nd weekends
Sep) The construction of Vaxholm Kastell, a
fortress on an islet just east of the town, was
originally ordered by Gustav Vasa in 1544,
but most of the current structure dates from
1863. The fortress was attacked by the Danes
in 1612 and the Russian navy in 1719. Nowadays, it's home to the National Museum of
Coastal Defence and a restaurant and con-

ference centre. The ferry across to the island
departs regularly from Söderhamn (the bustling harbour) and costs Skr45 return.

FREE **Hembygdsgård**　　MUSEUM
(Trädgårdsgatan 19; ⊘11am-4pm Sat & Sun May-
Aug) The Hembygdsgård preserves the finest
old houses in Norrhamn. The **fiskarebos-
tad** is an excellent example of a late-19th-
century fisherman's house, complete with
typical Swedish fireplace. The cafe here is
open daily from mid-May to mid-September.

🛏️ Sleeping & Eating

**Vaxholm/Bogesunds
Slottsvandrarhem**　　HOSTEL €
(☎54 17 50 60; www.bogesundsslottsvandrarhem.
se; dm/s from Skr195/295; 🅿️@) By a castle
5km southwest of Vaxholm, this is a pleasant, well-equipped STF hostel, complete
with summertime cafe and a blissfully bucolic setting. Bus 681 stops on the main road
about 500m from the hostel.

Waxholms Hotell　　HOTEL €€
(www.waxholmshotell.se; Hamngatan 2; s/d
Skr1100/1225; @) Just opposite the harbour
front, Waxholms combines art-nouveau and
modern detailing. Discounted rooms with
half and full board are available here in July,
and on weekends year-round. This grand
place is in the centre of the action, and there
are restaurants on the premises, including
Kabyssen, a summer-only pub with a popular outdoor terrace.

Melanders Fisk　　SEAFOOD €€
(Hamngatan 2; mains from Skr89; ⊘lunch & dinner
daily Jun-Aug, 10am-6pm Fri, 10am-3pm Sat rest of
year) On the waterfront, Melanders Fisk is a
seafood market that includes a cafe serving
quality grub. If there's a fish stew on the
day's menu don't miss it, but any seafood
dish here is bound to be satisfying.

ℹ️ Information

Tourist office (☎54 13 14 80; www.vaxholm.se;
⊘10am-6pm Mon-Fri, to 4pm Sat & Sun Jun-
Aug, 10am-3pm Mon-Fri, to 2pm Sat & Sun Sep-
May) Located inside the *rådhus* (town hall), off
Hamngatan; look for the onion dome, a product
of the *rådhus* rebuilding in 1925. Also on Hamngatan: a bank, supermarkets and other services.

ℹ️ Getting There & Away

Bus 670 from T-Tekniska Högskolan tunnelbana
station runs regularly to the town.

Waxholmsbolaget (☑679 58 30; www.wax holmsbolaget.se) boats sail frequently between Vaxholm and Strömkajen in Stockholm (about 40 minutes). **Strömma Kanalbolaget** (☑12 00 40 00; www.stromma.se) sails between Strandvägen and Vaxholm three times daily from mid-June to mid-August (Skr220); once daily Tuesday to Sunday from early May to mid-June and mid-August to early October; once daily Thursday to Sunday early February to early May and early October to late November; and once daily Saturday and Sunday late November to late December and mid-January to early February (no services late December to mid-January).

Stockholm Archipelago

Mention the archipelago to Stockholmers and prepare for gushing adulation. Buffering the city from the open Baltic Sea, it's a mesmerising wonderland of buffed isles studded with deep forests and fields of wildflowers. Exactly how many islands there are is debatable, with headcounts ranging from 14,000 to 100,000 (the general consensus is 24,000). Whatever the number, it's an unmissable area and much closer to the city than many visitors imagine, with regular ferry services and a number of organised tours for easy island-hopping. Hostels, campsites and more-upmarket slumber options make longer stays an inviting option, as does the growing number of smashing restaurants. And while the archipelago is an obvious summer playground, don't underestimate its wintertime appeal – when silent, snow-laced landscapes make for a soothing sojourn.

🏃 Activities

Waxholmsbolaget BOAT TOUR
(Map p56; ☑679 58 30; www.waxholmsbolaget.se)
The biggest boat operator in the archipelago. Timetables and information are available from its offices outside the Grand Hôtel Stockholm on Strömkajen, at the harbour in Vaxholm, and online. The company divides the archipelago into three areas: Norra Skärgården is the northern section (north from Ljusterö to Arholma); Mellersta Skärgården is the middle section, taking in Vaxholm, Ingmarsö, Stora Kalholmen, Finnhamn, Möja and Sandhamn; and Södra Skärgården is the southern section, with boats south to Nämdö, Ornö and Utö.

STOCKHOLM & AROUND STOCKHOLM ARCHIPELAGO

IDIOSYNCRATIC ISLANDS

If you're after an offbeat island jaunt, consider catching a boat across Åland, which is popular with local day trippers. Technically Finnish but officially autonomous, the Åland islands (population 25,400) sport their own flag and culture. It all goes back to a League of Nations decision made in 1921 to quash a Swedish-Finnish spat over sovereignty. Åland took its own flag in 1954, and has been issuing its own stamps (prized by collectors) since 1984. Both the euro and Swedish krona are legal tender here. A number of Swedish dialects are spoken, while a few Ålanders speak Finnish.

Although Åland joined the EU along with Finland in 1995, it was granted a number of exemptions, including duty-free tax laws, which allowed the essential ferry services between the islands and mainland Finland and Sweden to continue operating profitably.

The islands are a hit for summer cycling and camping holidays; there are medieval churches, ruins and fishing villages to explore. The capital (and only town) of Åland is Mariehamn. In summer it heaves with tourists but still manages to retain its village flavour, and the marinas at the harbours are a picture-perfect sight when loaded up with gleaming sailing boats. The main pedestrian street, Torggatan, is a colourful and crowded hive of activity, and there are some fine museums – enough for a leisurely day's exploration. Åland's most striking attraction is the medieval castle, Kastelholm, in Sund, 20km northeast of Mariehamn. You can only visit on guided tours, which run frequently (in English) from June to August.

For more information, check out www.visitaland.com (which also has a newly updated timetable of all ferry and air traffic to Åland from both Sweden and Finland) or contact the main companies operating between Sweden and Åland. Of these, Viking Line (www.vikingline.aland.fi) and Silja Line (www.silja.com) continue on to Finland, while Eckerö Linjen (www.eckerolinjen.fi) and Birka Cruises (www.birkacruises.com) operate only between the islands and Sweden. Once on the islands, you can happily pedal almost anywhere thanks to the bridges and handy network ferries.

WORTH A TRIP

EKERÖ & MUNSÖ

These long and narrow islands in Lake Mälaren are joined together and have a main road running most of their length. The free car ferry to Adelsö departs from the northern end of Munsö.

The two churches of Ekerö and Munsö both date from the 12th century. **Munsö kyrka** is a particularly fetching structure with a round tower and narrow steeple.

Buses 311 and 312 frequently run out here from T-Brommaplan in Stockholm.

Waxholmsbolaget's Båtluffarkortet (Boat Hiking Pass) gives unlimited rides on its services (Skr420 for five days) plus a handy archipelago map with suggested itineraries.

Stromma Kanalbolaget BOAT TOUR
(Map p56; ☑12 00 40 00; www.stromma.se; Nybrokajen) If time is short, consider taking the Thousand Island Cruise offered by Stromma Kanalbolaget, running daily between late June and early August. The full-day tour departs from Stockholm's Nybrokajen at 9.30am and returns at 8.30pm; the cost of Skr1075 includes lunch, dinner, drinks and guided tours ashore. The tour includes three island stops and swimming opportunities.

ARHOLMA

Arholma is one of the most interesting islands in the archipelago's far north. Everything was burnt down during a Russian invasion in 1719; the landmark lighthouse was rebuilt in the 19th century. A popular resort in the early 20th century, it's noted for its traditional village and chapel, as well as its fine sandy beaches and rocky bathing spots.

Arholma has a summer cafe, a shop, a simple campsite, and bike and kayak rental. **Vandrarhem Arholma** (☑0176-560 18; dm/s Skr150/180) is a pleasant STF hostel in a renovated barn; booking in advance is essential.

You can take bus 676 from Stockholm Tekniska Högskolan to Norrtälje, then 636 to Simpnäs (three to six daily), followed by a 20-minute ferry crossing to the island (Skr36).

SIARÖFORTET

The tiny island of Kyrkogårdsön, in the important sea lane just north of Ljusterö (40km due northeast of Stockholm), may be only 400m long but it's one of the archipelago's most fascinating islands.

After the outbreak of WWI, military authorities decided that the Vaxholm Kastell just didn't cut it, so construction of a new fort began on Kyrkogårdsön in 1916. Dubbed Siaröfortet, it's now a fascinating **museum** (Map p96; admission Skr50), where you can check out the officers' mess, kitchen, sleeping quarters and tunnels, plus two impressive 15.2cm cannons (they're trained on passing Viking Line ferries!). There are no fixed opening times; contact the STF hostel to arrange a tour.

STF Vandrarhem Siaröfortet (Map p96; ☑24 30 90; dm/s Skr200/375; ⊙late Apr–mid-Oct) is an excellent STF hostel in the old soldiers' barracks. Canoe hire and breakfast are available; advance booking is recommended.

Blidösundsbolaget (☑24 30 90; www.blidosundsbolaget.se) ferries to Siaröfortet depart from Strömkajen in Stockholm and sail to Siaröfortet via Vaxholm around three times daily in the peak summer season (mid-June to mid-August), with greatly reduced services the rest of the year. The journey takes one hour and 45 minutes from Stockholm (Skr100) and 50 minutes from Vaxholm (Skr50).

FINNHAMN

This 900m-long island, northeast of Stockholm, combines lush woods and meadows with sheltered coves, rocky cliffs and visiting eagle owls. While it's a popular summertime spot, there are enough quiet corners to indulge your inner hermit.

Vandrarhem Finnhamn (☑54 24 62 12; info@finnhamn.nu; dm/s Skr275/450; @) is an STF hostel in a large wooden villa, with boat hire available. It's the largest hostel in the archipelago; advance booking is essential. The **Finnhamns Café & Krog** (☑54 24 64 04) boasts good meals and a sterling view.

Waxholmsbolaget (Map p56; ☑679 58 30) sails from Strömkajen to Finnhamn, via Vaxholm, around twice daily (Skr130, 2½ hours). **Cinderella Båtarna** (Map p56; ☑12 00 40 00) also sails here daily from early May to mid-September, with reduced services mid-April to early May. Boats depart from Strandvägen in Stockholm (Skr140, one hour and 10 minutes).

SANDÖN

A manageable 2.5km long, Sandön is the archipelago's summertime party hot spot. Stockholm status-slaves sail in on 12-footers for Midsummer schmoozing and boozing, while serious sailors flock here for regattas like the Gotland Rund each July – so the place is rather expensive and best visited as a day trip. Camping is prohibited. Sandön's hub is the northern settlement of Sandhamn. Here, narrow alleys, rust-red cottages and the Royal Swedish Yacht Club's Hamptons-style clubhouse keep the cameras clicking. For the best beaches head to Trovill, near the island's southern tip.

Dykarbaren (✆57-15 35 54; lunch Skr155-175, dinner Skr195-335; ☺May-Oct) is a popular restaurant-bar just 50m from the quay, with lunch specials from Skr85.

The historic **Sandhamns Värdshus** (✆57-15 30 51; mains Skr115-235) serves a lip-smacking fish-and-shellfish casserole.

Leader of the island's culinary pack is **Seglarrestaurangen** (✆57 45 04 21; mains Skr195-365), considered one of the archipelago's best restaurants. You'll find it inside the upmarket **Seglarhotellet** (www.sandhamn.com; d with/without balcony Skr2590/2390), whose spa centre's combo of indoor pool, Jacuzzi, sauna and gym is open to nonguests.

Waxholmsbolaget (✆679 58 30) sails from Strömkajen to Sandhamn, via Vaxholm, once daily (Skr130, three hours). **Cinderella Båtarna** (✆12 00 40 00) does the same run from mid-April to mid-September; boats leave from Strandvägen (Skr130).

A quicker option is to take bus 433 or 434 from Slussen to Stavsnäs (Skr36, 50 minutes) and catch a ferry from there (Skr75, 40 to 60 minutes). Check ferry times at www.waxholmsbolaget.se before catching the bus, to avoid a long wait at Stavsnäs.

Strömma Kanalbolaget (✆12 00 40 00) runs tours from Nybroplan to Sandhamn daily between early June and mid-August (Skr300), departing at 9.45am and returning at 5.45pm (with two hours at Sandhamn). The price includes a one-hour guided walk.

SVARTSÖ

Rugged Svartsö (Black Island) is another mid-archipelago gem. At just over 5km wide and 2km long, its resident population of 77 booms to 2500 in summer, when fans step ashore for low-fuss rural bliss. Thick with tall trees, old farmers' fields and five lakes, its relatively flat landscape makes it perfect for a day's lazy cycling. It's also a good spot for birdwatching in spring and autumn.

At its southernmost point sits tiny Alsvik, one of two ferry stops on Svartsö (the other is at Skälvik). Here you'll find a waterside cafe in the summer, as well as five tiny, basic **cabins** (✆54 24 71 10; Skr550) for rent. Accommodation is of the bunk-bed variety, with a handy cooker in each cabin. There are no bathroom facilities; there's a bathing spot 100m away for back-to-nature grooming.

Also at the harbour, handy **Svartsö Lanthandel** (Map p96; ✆54 24 73 25; www.svartsolanthandel.se) is a grocery store, pharmacy and post office in one (check website for current opening hours). You can order alcohol (delivered to the island twice a week), withdraw money and hire bicycles (Skr50/125 per hour/day). Nearby, restaurant-bar **Svartsö Krog** (Map p96; ✆54 24 72 55; mains Skr175-250; ☺lunch & dinner Apr-Dec) serves tasty Swedish grub in a rustic-chic setting. The bar mural honours old locals.

Waxholmsbolaget (✆679 58 30) sails from Strömkajen in Stockholm to Alsvik and Skälvik, via Vaxholm, twice daily (one-way Skr110, two hours). Around four daily ferries head to Svartsö from Boda.

To reach Boda, take bus 438 from Slussen in Stockholm, but check the ferry schedule at www.waxholmsbolaget.se beforehand to avoid long connection times.

From early May to mid-September, **Cinderella Båtarna** (✆12 00 40 00) runs several times daily to Svartsö (Skr135, 1½ hours), via Vaxholm, from Strandvägen. Reduced services operate between mid-April and early May.

UTÖ

Star of the archipelago's southern section, Utö has it all: sublime sandy beaches, lush fairy-tale forests, sleepy farms, abundant bird life and a highly rated restaurant. At 13km long and up to 4km wide, its network of roads and tracks make for heavenly cycling sessions.

◉ Sights & Activities

Most of the sights are at the northern end of the island, near Gruvbryggan.

Iron Mine   MINE

The most unusual of its sights is Sweden's oldest iron mine, which opened in 1150 but closed in 1879. The three pits are now flooded – the deepest is Nyköp ingsgruvan (215m).

The mining museum (opposite the *värdshus* or inn) keeps variable hours, so check locally. The well-preserved, 18th-century miners' houses on Lurgatan are worth a peek, while the Dutch-style windmill (⊘11am-3pm mid-Jun–mid-Aug) has beautiful coastal views.

Stora Sand
BEACH

The best sandy beach is Stora Sand on the south coast; it's a gorgeous 40-minute bike ride from the *värdshus*. Routes to the beach are occasionally closed due to military training exercises; ask at the tourist office for updates.

Glaciated Rock Slabs
SCENERY

To eye the glaciated rock slabs on the east coast, walk for about 20 minutes through the forest towards Rävstavik.

🛏 Sleeping & Eating

TF hostel
HOSTEL €

(☑50 42 03 15; receptionen@utovardshus.se; Gruvbyggan; dm Skr350; ⊘May-Sep) This hostel, associated with the nearby *värdshus*, is in a former summer house. Reception and meals are at the *värdshus*.

Dannekrogen
EUROPEAN €€

(Map p96; ☑50 15 70 79; mains Skr150-250; ⊘May-Sep) Near the Gruvbryggan harbour, lively Dannekrogen has a young, casual vibe, with grub ranging from hearty fish stew to polenta. The adjoining bakery peddles scrumptious treats, including some delicious carrot-cake cupcakes.

ℹ Information

Destination Stockholms Skärgård (☑54 24 81 00; www.dess.se; Lillström, 18497 Ljusterö) For information on cabin and chalet rental in the archipelago.

Skärgårdsstiftelsen (www.skargardsstif telsen.se) For excellent archipelago information in English and other languages.

Tourist office (☑50 15 74 10; ⊘10am-4pm May-Sep) You can get a reasonable sketch-map of the island from the tourist office, found in a small cabin by the guest harbour at Gruvbryggan, also known as Gruvbyn (the northernmost village). When the tourist office is closed, ask at the *värdshus*, just up the hill.

Visit Skärgården (Map p56; ☑10 02 22; www. visitskargarden.se; Kajplats 18, Strandvägen; ⊘9am-5pm Mon-Fri, 10am-4pm Sat, 11am-4pm Sun) This new waterside information centre can advise on (and book) various types of archipelago accommodation and tours, as well as give you ideas on what to see and do.

ℹ Getting There & Around

From Stockholm, Waxholmsbolaget sails once daily to Utö (Skr130, 3½ hours). A quicker way to reach the island is to take the *pendeltåg* from Stockholm Centralstationen to Västerhaninge, then bus 846 to Årsta brygga. From there, Waxholmsbolaget ferries leave up to eight times a day in summer (less frequently the rest of the year) for Utö (Skr80, 45 minutes), but make sure you know whether your boat stops at Spränga or Gruvbryggan first. Ask at the **guest harbour** (☑50 15 74 10) about bike hire (Skr100 per day).

Kapellskär

Kapellskär is so tiny it can't really even be described as a village – there's little to it except for a campsite, hostel and large ferry terminal. The coastline, however, is spectacular, dotted with small, still-working fishing villages, and the surrounding countryside is delightfully pastoral. Most people come here for ferry connections to Finland and Estonia; see p353 for details.

There's also a small memorial for the 852 passengers killed in the Estonia ferry disaster of September 1994; it's up the hill across the main road from the ferry terminal.

An STF hostel (☑0176-441 69; Riddersholm; dm/s Skr200/300) sits off the E18, 2km west of the ferry terminal; book in advance outside of the peak summer season (mid-June to mid-August). There's no restaurant, so bring provisions.

Viking Line's direct bus from Stockholm Cityterminalen to meet the ferries costs Skr65, but if you have an SL pass take bus 676 from T-Tekniska Högskolan to Norrtälje and change to bus 631, which runs every two hours or so weekdays (three times Saturday and once Sunday).

Tyresta National Park

Some of the best hiking and wilderness scenery can be found in the 4900-hectare Tyresta National Park, only 20km southeast of Stockholm. Established in 1993, the park is noted for its two-billion-year-old rocks and virgin forest, which includes 300-year-old pine trees. It's a beautiful area, with rocky outcrops, small lakes, marshes and a wide variety of bird life.

At the southwestern edge of the park is Nationalparkernas Hus (National Parks Visitor Centre; ☑08-745 33 94; admission free; ⊘9am-4pm Tue-Fri, 10am-5pm Sat & Sun Mar-

DON'T MISS

A VIKING VISIT IN BIRKA

The historic Viking trading centre of Birka (Map p96; www.stromma.se; round-trip cruises adult/child Skr310/155; ⊙9.30am, 10am, 10.05am, 10.15am, 11am, 11.15am Mon-Fri, 10am, 10.30am, 10.35am, 10.45am, 11.30am, noon Sat & Sun May–mid-Sep), on Björkö in Lake Mälaren, makes a fantastic day trip. A Unesco World Heritage Site, it was founded as a village around AD 760 with the intention of expanding and controlling trade in the region.

The village attracted merchants and craft workers, and the population quickly grew to about 700. A large defensive fort with thick dry-stone ramparts was constructed next to the village. In 830 the Benedictine monk Ansgar was sent to Birka by the Holy Roman Emperor to convert the heathen Vikings to Christianity; he hung around for 18 months. Birka was abandoned in the late 10th century when Sigtuna took over the role of commercial centre.

The village site is surrounded by the largest Viking-age cemetery in Scandinavia, with around 3000 graves. Most people were cremated, then mounds of earth were piled over the remains, but some Christian coffins and chambered tombs have been found. The fort and harbour have also been excavated. A cross to the memory of St Ansgar can be seen on top of a nearby hill.

Exhibits at the brilliant Birka Museum (⊙11am-6.30pm daily late Jun–mid-Aug, to 3pm May–late Jun & mid-Aug–early Sep) include finds from the excavations, copies of the most magnificent objects, and an interesting model of the village in Viking times.

Round-trip cruises to Birka on Strömma Kanalbolaget's *Victoria* from Stadshusbron in central Stockholm make for a full day's outing. The cruise price includes a visit to the Birka Museum and a guided tour in English of the settlement's burial mounds and fortifications. Ferries do not run during the Midsummer holidays.

Oct, to 4pm Sat & Sun Nov-Feb). Here you can discover all of Sweden's 28 national parks through exhibitions and slide shows. Be sure to check out the centre itself: it's built in the shape of Sweden, complete with all 41 corners! There are even 'lakes' on the floor, indicated by different stones.

Ask for the national park leaflet in English and the *Tyresta Nationalpark och Naturreservat* leaflet in Swedish, which includes an excellent topographical map at 1:25,000 scale. From the visitor centre there are various trails into the park. *Sörmlandsleden* track cuts across 6km of the park on its way to central Stockholm.

Access to the park is easy. Take the *pendeltåg* to Haninge centrum (also called Handen station) on the Nynäshamn line, then change to bus 834. Some buses run all the way to the park, while others stop at Svartbäcken (2km west of Tyresta village).

Sigtuna

Just 40km northwest of Stockholm, Sigtuna is one of the cutest, most historically relevant villages in the area. Founded around AD 980, it's the oldest surviving town in Sweden, and the main drag, Stora gatan, is very likely Sweden's oldest main street.

Around the year 1000, Olof Skötkonung ordered the minting of Sweden's first coins in the town, and ancient church ruins and rune stones are scattered everywhere. Indeed, there are about 150 runic inscriptions in the area, most dating from the early 11th century and typically flanking ancient roads.

Most of Sigtuna's original buildings went up in flames in devastating late-medieval fires, but the main church survived and many of the quaint streets and wooden abodes still follow the medieval town plan.

◎ Sights

Mariakyrkan   CHURCH
(⊙9am-4pm daily Sep-May, to 8pm Jun-Aug) During medieval times, Sigtuna boasted seven stone-built churches, though most have since crumbled. Mariakyrkan is the oldest brick building in the area – it was a Dominican monastery church from around 1250, but became the parish church in 1529 after the monastery was demolished by Gustav Vasa. Pop in for restored medieval paintings and free weekly concerts in summer. The adjacent St Olof church was built in the early 12th century, but by the 17th century it was a

ruin. Nearby, the ruins of **St Per** and **St Lars** can be seen off Prästgatan.

Sigtuna Museum
MUSEUM

(☑59 12 66 70; Stora gatan 55; adult/child Skr25/free; ⊙noon-4pm Tue-Sun Sep-May, noon-4pm daily Jun-Aug) This museum looks after several attractions in the town, all of them on Stora gatan and near the tourist office.

Lundströmska gården
MUSEUM

(adult/child Skr10/5; ⊙noon-4pm daily mid-Jun–mid-Aug, noon-4pm Sat & Sun Sep) Lundströmska gården is an early-20th-century, middle-class home and general store, complete with period furnishings and goods.

FREE **Sigtuna rådhus**
HISTORIC BUILDING

(⊙noon-4pm daily Jun-Aug, noon-4pm Sat & Sun Sep) The smallest town hall in Scandinavia, Sigtuna *rådhus* dates from 1744 and was designed by the mayor himself. It's on the town square opposite the tourist office. The main museum building has displays of gold jewellery, runes, coins and loot brought home from abroad.

Steninge Slott
CASTLE

(Map p96; ☑59 25 95 00; www.steningeslott.se) The magnificent private palace Steninge Slott, 7km east of Sigtuna, dates from 1705 and was designed by Nicodemus Tessin the Younger. At the time of research it was closed for renovation; check the website for updates and a schedule of guided tours. In the beautiful grounds there is also the excellent **Slottsgalleria** (gallery tours Skr80; ⊙11am-6pm Mon-Fri, 10am-5pm Sat & Sun), complete with art gallery, glassworks, candle-making area, cafe and restaurant. Exhibitions change frequently; check the website to see what's on.

Rosersbergs Slott
CASTLE

(☑59 03 50 39; guided tours adult/child Skr70/35; ⊙tours hourly 11am-4pm Jun-Aug) Another palace, Rosersbergs Slott is on Lake Mälaren about 9km southeast of Sigtuna. Built in the 1630s, it was used as a royal residence from 1762 to 1860; the interior boasts exquisite furnishings from the Empire period (1790–1820). Highlights include the lavishly draped State Bedchamber and Queen Hedvig Elisabeth Charlotta's conversation room. The palace cafe serves delicious light meals and cakes in regal surrounds.

Skokloster Slott
CASTLE

(Map p96; ☑402 30 60; www.skoklostersslott.se; adult/child Skr70/free; ⊙11.30am-4.30pm Sat & Sun Apr & Oct, 11.30am-4.30pm Tue-Sun May, 11.30am-5.30pm Tue-Sun Jun, 10.30am-5.30pm daily Jul & Aug, 12.30-4.30pm Tue-Fri, 11.30am-4.30pm Sat & Sun Sep) Skokloster Slott, around 11km due northwest of Sigtuna (26km by road), is a whitewashed baroque palace with a fragile beauty unusual in Sweden. It was built between 1654 and 1671 and has impressive stucco ceilings and collections of furniture, textiles, art and arms. There's also a small cafe. Guided tours run daily from April to October (Skr40); it's a good idea to call in advance to check times, as the schedule can change.

🍴 Sleeping & Eating

Stora Brännbo
HOTEL €€

(www.storabrannbo.se; Stora Brännbovägen 2-6; s/d Skr550/890; P@) Just north of central Sigtuna, this large hotel and conference centre offers small, contemporary rooms in soothing neutral hues with flat-screen TVs and fluffy bathrobes. There's a sauna, Jacuzzi and gym for guests, and the bountiful breakfast includes waffles and freshly squeezed orange juice.

Sigtunastiftelsens Gästhem
HOTEL €€€

(www.sigtunastiftelsen.se; Manfred Björkquists allé 2-4; s/d Skr1995/3500) This attractive, imposing place is run by a Christian foundation. It might look like a cross between a cloister and a medieval fortress, but its 62 unique rooms – each named for a historical figure and decorated accordingly – are much cosier than you'd think.

Sigtuna Stadshotell
HOTEL €€€

(info@sigtunastadshotell.se; Stora Nygatan 3; s/d Skr1790/2290; @) The pick of Sigtuna's lodgings, this historic white-on-white hotel features sleek and uberstylish interiors, spa treatments and a clued-up restaurant hailed as a rising star.

Rosersbergs Hotell & Konferens
HOTEL €€

(☑12 20 20 00; www.rosersbergsslott.se; r & board from Skr1995; P@) Housed in a palace wing once used to accommodate royal family guests. Rooms are simple yet impeccably stylish, with old wooden floorboards, Gustavian-style furnishings, the odd tile stove and views of either the palace courtyard or gardens. All rooms have basins, though facilities are shared.

Tant Brunn Kaffestuga
CAFE €

(☑59 25 09 34; Laurentii gränd; coffees & cakes from Skr35) In a small alley off Storagatan, this delightful 17th-century cafe is set around a pretty courtyard. It's well worth seeking out for its home-baked bread and pastries (the apple pie is divine); just watch your head as you walk in, as the roof beams sag precariously.

Farbror Blå Café & Kök   CAFE €€
(☑59 25 60 50; Stora torget 14; mains Skr195-225) Adjacent to the town hall, this cosy nosh spot is the 'uncle' *(farbror)* to the 'aunt' of Tant Brunn; both names are taken from a popular children's story. Head in for bistro-style meals like veal cutlet with honey-roasted potatoes, tomato-basil cream cheese and black pepper sauce.

ⓘ Information

Stora gatan is also home to banks and supermarkets.
Tourist office (☑59 48 06 50; info@sigtu naturism.se; Storagatan 33; ⊙10am-6pm Mon-Sat, 11am-5pm Sun Jun-Aug, 10am-5pm Mon-Fri, 11am-4pm Sat & Sun Sep, 10am-5pm Mon-Fri, 11am-4pm Sat, noon-4pm Sun Oct-May) Inhabits an 18th-century wooden house, Drakegården.

ⓘ Getting There & Around

Travel connections from Stockholm are easy. Take a local train to Märsta, from where there are frequent buses to Sigtuna (570 or 575, Skr72). To get to Rosersbergs Slott, take the SL *pendeltåg* train to Rosersberg, then walk the final 2km to the palace (signposted). For Skokloster, take a half-hourly SJ train to Bålsta, then bus 311 (ask the driver to let you off at the stop for Skokloster).

Mariefred

Tiny, lakeside Mariefred is a pretty little village that pulls in the crowds with its grand castle, Gripsholm Slott.

◉ Sights

Gripsholm Slott   CASTLE
(www.gripsholmslott.se; adult/child Skr80/40; ⊙10am-4pm mid-May–mid-Sep) Gripsholm Slott is the epitome of castles, with its round towers, spires, drawbridge and creaky wooden halls. It contains some of the state portrait collection, which dates from the 16th century.

Originally built in the 1370s, it passed into crown hands by the early 15th century. In 1526 Gustav Vasa took over and ordered the demolition of the adjacent monastery.

A new castle with walls up to 5m thick was built using materials from the monastery, but extensions, conversions and repairs continued for years. The oldest 'untouched' room is Karl IX's bedchamber, dating from the 1570s. The castle was abandoned in 1715, but renovated and extended during the reign of Gustav III (especially between 1773 and 1785). The moat was filled in and, in 1730 and later in 1827, two 11th-century rune stones were found. These stones stand by the access road and are well worth a look; one has a Christian cross, while the other describes an expedition against the Saracens. Gripsholm Slott was restored again in the 1890s, the moat was cleared and the drawbridge rebuilt.

Grafikens Hus   MUSEUM
(www.grafikenshus.se; adult/child Skr85/free; ⊙11am-5pm daily May-Sep, 11am-5pm Sat & Sun Oct-Apr) Another worthy pit stop is nearby Grafikens Hus, a centre for contemporary graphic art and printmaking.

🛏 Sleeping & Eating

Gripsholmsviken Hotell & Konferens   HOTEL €€
(www.gripsholmsviken.se; r from Skr1295; ⊙mid-Jun–mid-Aug) In what was once a royal distillery commissioned by Gustav III in the late 18th century, this revamped option offers hostel and hotel lodgings. The in-house restaurant is a slinky affair, there's a cafe on the leafy grounds, and the castle is a mere 500m to the east.

Gripsholms Värdshus & Hotell   HOTEL €€€
(www.gripsholms-vardshus.se; Kyrkogatan 1; s/d Skr1300/2290; @) Opened in 1609, Gripsholms is Sweden's oldest inn and Mariefred's slumber darling. Charming and elegant, its 45 individually furnished rooms are full of antiques, many also having great views of the castle. There's also a beautiful, highly regarded restaurant (mains Skr175 to Skr300) on site.

Broccoli   CAFE €
(☑132 00; meals Skr75-175; ⊙11am-5pm daily May-Aug, noon-4pm Thu-Sun Sep-Apr) Sharing an entrance with Grafikens Hus, this tasty cafe is a better option than the overpriced, underwhelming Gripsholms Slottcafé near the castle. There's an emphasis on local produce, with edibles ranging from focaccias and salads to ditch-the-diet cakes.

❶ Information

Tourist office (☏297 90; www.mariefred.se; ⏰10am-6pm Mon-Fri, 11am-5pm Sat Jun-Aug, 11am-5pm Sun Jul & early–mid-Sep, 10am-3pm Mon-Sat early–mid-Sep, 11am-3pm Sat mid-Apr–May) Offers a map and notes (in English) for a self-guided walking tour of the idyllic village centre, filled with cobblestone streets and 18th-century buildings.

❶ Getting There & Away

Mariefred isn't on the main railway line – the nearest station is at Läggesta, 3km to the west, with trains from Stockholm every two hours in summer. A **museum railway** (☏210 06; www.oslj.nu; one-way/return from Skr60/80) from Läggesta to Mariefred runs on weekends from early May to late September (daily from Midsummer to mid-August), roughly every hour during the day; call to check the schedule. Bus 303 runs hourly from Läggesta to Mariefred.

The steamship **S/S Mariefred** (☏08-669 88 50; www.mariefred.info) departs from Stadshusbron in Stockholm for Mariefred from Tuesday to Sunday mid-June to mid-August, and weekends only from late May to mid-June and from mid-August to early September (Skr260 return). A ticket from Stockholm, including an SJ train, the museum railway and S/S Mariefred, costs around Skr275 one-way and is available at the tourist office in Stockholm.

Uppsala & Central Sweden

Includes »

Best Places to Eat

» Kopparhatten Café & Restaurang (p135)

» Magnussons Krog (p113)

» Kalle på Spangen (p121)

» Nora Glass (p124)

» Hälls Konditori Stallbacken (p126)

Best Places to Stay

» Hotell Hackspett (p119)

» Behrn Hotell (p126)

» STF Vandrarhem Leksand (p137)

» Moraparken (p140)

» STF Nora Tåghem (p124)

Why Go?

A compact wonderland of painted wooden horses marching across green hills dotted with little red cabins, central Sweden is such a perfect distillation of all the Swedish highlights it could almost be one of those Las Vegas theme parks. It's an easily explored area right in the middle of the country, so travellers on a tight schedule can see a lot of what makes Sweden so Swedish.

The Lake Siljan area, with its idyllic villages and evergreen forest, represents the country's heartland. Further north, the landscape gets wilder and more rugged, a teaser offering hints of Lappland and the far north. In between lies Sweden's industrial core – perhaps not glamorous, but illuminating and important.

Uppsala and Örebro are lively cultural centres with well-preserved historical buildings and great museums, dining, shopping and nightlife. Outdoorsy types will have plenty to do too, from skiing and hiking to birdwatching and canoeing.

When to Go
Uppsala

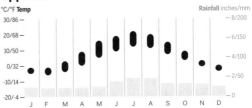

Mid-Jun–Aug The weather's fine, accommodation prices are low and attractions are open.

Sep–Oct Many sights are closed, but the weather's fair and autumn leaves mean gorgeous scenery.

Dec–Feb Winter means bundling up, but central Sweden during the Christmas holidays is lovely.

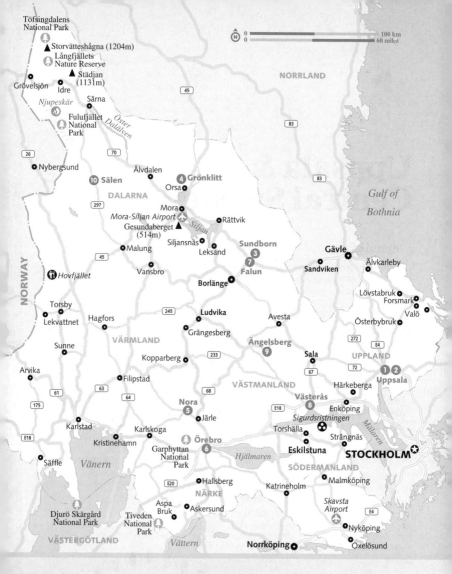

Uppsala & Central Sweden Highlights

1 Ponder the ancient burial mounds at **Gamla Uppsala** (p109)

2 Soak up science and artefacts at Uppsala's **Museum Gustavianum** (p111)

3 Visit Carl Larsson's inspiring family home in **Sundborn** (p134)

4 Watch roly-poly bears at play in **Grönklitt** (p142)

5 Stop for ice cream in **Nora** (p123)

6 Wander the lovely city park and historic Wadköping village in **Örebro** (p124)

7 See regional art and history in Dalarnas Museum, **Falun** (p135)

8 Sleep underwater, or in a treehouse, in **Västerås** (p119)

9 Explore an atmospheric old mine at **Ängelsberg** (p123)

10 Hit the ski slopes at **Sälen** (p142)

UPPLAND

Uppsala

📀 018 / POP 198,000

Drenched in history but never stifled by the past, Uppsala has the party vibe of a university town to balance out its large number of important buildings and general atmosphere of weighty cultural significance. It's a terrific combination, and one that makes the town both fun and functional, not to mention very rewarding for the interested traveller.

On the city's edge is Gamla (Old) Uppsala, the original site of the town – once a flourishing 6th-century religious centre where human sacrifices were made to the Norse gods, and home to an ancient burial ground.

On 30 April, students dressed in white gather to celebrate the Walpurgis Festival. Traditionally, this includes a student boat race on the river at 10am and a run down Carolinabacken at 3pm, as well as various processions and singing.

◎ Sights

Gamla Uppsala   ARCHAEOLOGICAL SITE

The seat of Western culture, according to Olof Rudbeck's 1679 book *Atlantica*, was Sweden: specifically, Gamla Uppsala. Rudbeck (1630–1702), a scientist, writer and all-around colourful character, amassed copious evidence proving that Gamla Uppsala was, in fact, the mythical lost city of Atlantis.

In retrospect, this seems unlikely. But the spot, 4km north of the modern city, is a fascinating attraction nevertheless. One of Sweden's largest and most important burial sites, Gamla Uppsala contains around 300 mounds from the 6th to 12th centuries. The earliest and most impressive are three huge grave mounds (admission free; ◎24hr). Legend has it they contain the pre-Viking kings Aun, Egil and Adils, who appear in *Beowulf* and Icelandic historian Snorre Sturlason's *Ynglingsaga*. More recent evidence, however, suggests that the occupant of Östhögen (East Mound) was a woman, probably a female regent in her twenties or thirties.

Speculation has surrounded the burial site from the beginning. Early press reports include that of medieval chronicler Adam of Bremen – who never actually visited – describing a vast golden temple in Gamla Uppsala in the 10th century.

Allegedly, animal and human sacrifices were strung up in a sacred grove outside.

When Christianity arrived around 1090, Thor, Odin and the other Viking gods began to fade. From 1164, the archbishop of Uppsala had his seat in a cathedral on the site of the present church (admission free; ◎9am-6pm May-Aug, 9am-4pm Sep-Apr).

If you feel like a wander, Eriksleden is a 6km 'pilgrims path' between the cathedral in Uppsala and the church in Gamla Uppsala. Its namesake, Erik the Holy, was king of Sweden from around 1150 until the Danes beheaded him 10 years later. The story is that his head rolled down the hill, and where it stopped a spring came up. The main trail also provides access to a ridged wilderness area called Tunåsen, with a panoramic viewpoint (follow signs along Eriksleden just south of Gamla Uppsala to 'utsiktsleden').

Buses 2, 110 and 115 run to Gamla Uppsala daily and are very frequent (between them there's one every 10 minutes Monday to Friday, and every 40 minutes at weekends).

Gamla Uppsala Museum   MUSEUM

(www.raa.se/gamlauppsala; adult/student/child Skr60/40/free; ◎10am-4pm daily, guided tours in English 11am May-Aug, noon-3pm Wed, Sat & Sun Sep–mid-Dec & Jan-Apr) Gamla Uppsala Museum contains finds from the cremation mounds, a poignant mix of charred and melted beads, bones and buckles. More intact pieces come from various boat graves in and around the site. The museum is arranged as a timeline – useful for re-creating the history of the area.

Follow signs from the grave mounds to Disagården (admission free, guided tours adult/student/child Skr30/15/free; ◎10am-5pm Jun-Aug, tours 1pm, children's tours 2pm in Swedish), a 19th-century farming village turned open-air museum consisting of 26 timber buildings and a platform stage that serves as the focal point for Uppsala's Midsummer celebrations.

Next to the unexcavated flat-topped mound Tingshögen (Court Mound), is Odinsborg (www.odinsborg.nu; lunch buffet adult/child Skr165/85; ◎noon-6pm), a restaurant known for its horns of mead and Viking feasts (although daintier refreshments are offered at the summer cafe downstairs).

Uppsala Slott   CASTLE

(Map p110; www.uppsalaslott.se; admission by guided tour only, adult/child Skr80/15, includes admis-

Uppsala

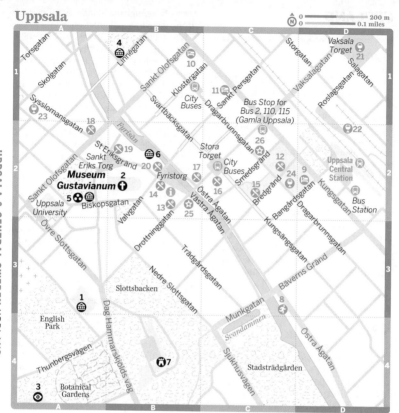

sion to art museum; ☺tours in English 1pm & 3pm Tue-Sun late Jun-Sep) Pink and ponderous, Uppsala Slott was built by Gustav Vasa in the 1550s. It contains the state hall where kings were enthroned and Queen Kristina abdicated. It was also the scene of a brutal murder in 1567, when King Erik XIV and his guards killed Nils Sture and his two sons, Erik and Svante, after accusing them of high treason. The castle burned down in 1702, but was rebuilt and took on its present form in 1757.

At the castle entrance marked E, the **Uppsala Art Museum** (www.uppsala.se/konstmuseum; adult/child Skr40/free, free 4-8pm Wed; ☺noon-4.30pm Tue-Fri, 11am-5pm Sat & Sun Jun-Aug) displays Swedish and international contemporary art and ceramics as well as the art-study collection of Uppsala University.

FREE **Domkyrkan**   CHURCH
(Cathedral; Map p110; www.uppsaladomkyrka.se; ☺8am-6pm daily May-Sep, 10am-6pm Sat Oct-Apr) The Gothic Domkyrka dominates the city, just as some of those buried here, including St Erik, Gustav Vasa and the scientist Carl von Linné, dominated their country. Tours are available in English at 11am and 2pm Monday to Saturday in July and August.

Gustav's funerary sword, silver crown and shiny golden buttons are kept in the **treasury** (adult/child Skr40/free; ☺10am-5pm Mon-Sat, 12.30-5pm Sun May-Sep, limited hours Oct-Apr) in the cathedral's north tower, along with a great display of medieval textiles. Particularly fine are the clothes worn by the three noblemen who were murdered in the castle: they're the only example of 16th-century Swedish high fashion still in existence. Tours in English run from Monday to Saturday in July and August, starting at 3pm.

Uppsala

Botanical Gardens

GARDENS

(www.botan.uu.se; Villavägen 6-8; admission free; ⊘7am-9pm May-Sep, 7am-7pm Oct-Apr) The Botanical Gardens, below the castle hill, show off more than 10,000 different species and are pleasant to wander through. Attractions include the 200-year-old **Linnaeum Orangery** (Map p110; ⊘9am-3pm Mon-Fri May-Sep, 9am-2pm Mon-Fri Oct-Apr) and a tropical **greenhouse** (Skr40).

⎡TOP CHOICE⎤ Museum Gustavianum

MUSEUM

(www.gustavianum.uu.se; Akademigatan 3; adult/child Skr50/free; ⊘11am-4pm Tue-Sun,

from 10am Jul & Aug) A wondercabinet of wondercabinets, the Museum Gustavianum rewards appreciation of the weird and well-organised. The shelves in the pleasantly musty building hold case after case of obsolete tools and preserved oddities: stuffed birds, astrolabes, alligator mummies, exotic stones and dried sea creatures. A highlight is the fascinating 17th-century **Augsburg Art Cabinet** and its thousand ingenious trinkets. Don't miss Olof Rudbeck's vertiginous **anatomical theatre**, where executed criminals were dissected.

Carolina Rediviva

LIBRARY

(Map p110; Dag Hammarskjölds väg 1; adult/under 12yr Skr20/free; ⊘9am-6.30pm Mon-Thu, 9am-5.30pm Fri, 10am-5pm Sat, 11am-4pm Sun May–mid-Sep, 9am-8pm Mon-Fri, 10am-5pm Sat mid-Aug–mid-Jun) Rare-book and map fiends should go directly to Carolina Rediviva, the university library. In a small, dark display room, glass cases hold precious maps and manuscripts, including some illuminated Ethiopian texts and the first book ever printed in Sweden. Occupying its own glowing VIP nook is the surviving half of the *Codex Argentus* (AD 520), aka the Silver Bible, written in gold and silver ink on purple vellum; aside from being pretty, it's also linguistically important as the most complete existing document written in the Gothic language.

⎡FREE⎤ Upplandsmuseet

MUSEUM

(Map p110; www.upplandsmuseet.se; Sankt Eriks Torg 10; ⊘noon-5pm Tue-Sun) Upplandsmuseet, in an 18th-century watermill, houses county collections of folk art, music and the history of Uppsala from the Middle Ages onwards, as well as more modern displays. (Temporary installations have included photographs from the life of author Astrid Lindgren.) In particular, kids will find the inventive dioramas and reconstructions engrossing.

Linnémuseet

MUSEUM

(Map p110; www.linnaeus.se; Svartbäcksgatan 27; adult/child Skr60/free; ⊘11am-5pm Tue-Sun May-Sep, tours in English 2.30pm daily) No matter how many times the brochures refer to 0 'sexual system' of classification, the excitement to be had at Linnémuseet is primarily intellectual; still, botanists and vegetarians will enjoy a visit to the pioneering scientist's home and workshop. The adjoining **Linnéträdgården** (adult/child Skr60/free, admission free with Linnémuseet ticket;

shop & exhibit 11am-5pm Tue-Sun May-Sep, park 11am-8pm Tue-Sun May-Sep) is a reconstructed version of Sweden's oldest botanical garden – Linné's playground – with more than 1300 species arranged according to the system he invented.

Bror Hjorth's House　　　　　　GALLERY
(www.brorhjorthshus.se; Norbyvägen 26; adult/child Skr40/free, Fri free; noon-4pm Thu-Sun, also Tue & Wed in summer) Bror Hjorth's House, the studio of beloved local artist Bror Hjorth (1894–1968), is jam-packed with Hjorth's charming paintings and sculptures, and hosts temporary exhibitions.

Rune Stones　　　　　　RUINS
(Map p110) In the grassy, sloping park between Domkyrkan and the main Uppsala University building are nine typical Uppland rune stones.

Activities

Lennakatten　　　　　　STEAM TRAIN
(www.lennakatten.se; all-day ticket adult/child Skr180/90; 9am-5pm Wed-Thu & Sat Jul–mid-Aug, Sun Jun-Sep) You can ride the narrow-gauge steam train 33km into the Uppland countryside. Schedules vary, so check online for updates. The trains depart from the Uppsala Östra museum station, in Bergsbrunnaparken, about 1km east of Uppsala Central Station.

M/S Kung Carl Gustaf　　　　　　BOAT TOUR
(Map p110; 070-293 81 61; www.mskungcarlgustaf.se; Islandsbron bridge) Slow down the pace with a boat cruise to the baroque castle of Skokloster. M/S *Kung Carl Gustaf*, a 19th-century ex-steamship, sails Tuesday to Sunday from mid-May to mid-August. Tours (round-trip Skr200, one-way Skr50, over 85 years free) leave Islandsbron at 11am and return at 4.15pm, allowing about two hours at Skokloster. There are also evening river cruises at 7pm Tuesday to Saturday from mid-May to mid-September; the cruise plus buffet and entertainment costs Skr400 per person. Cash only.

Fyrishov　　　　　　WATER PARK
(www.fyrishov.se; Idrottsgatan 2; adult/child Skr90/70; 6am-9.30pm Mon-Fri, 7.30am-9pm Sat & Sun) Families with water-loving children should head for Fyrishov, one of Sweden's largest water parks. It features the full complement of slides, jacuzzis, waterfalls and wave machines.

Sleeping

Best Western Hotel Svava　　　　　　HOTEL €€
(www.bestwestern.se; Bangårdsgatan 24; s/d Skr750/1150; P) Named after one of Odin's Valkyrie maidens, Hotel Svava, right opposite the train station, is a very comfortable top-end business-style hotel with summer and weekend discounts that make it a smashing deal.

Hotel Uppsala　　　　　　HOTEL €€
(hoteluppsala@profilhotels.se; Kungsgatan 27; s/d Skr799/850; P) Uppsala's largest hotel, Hotel Uppsala has all the standard business-hotel amenities plus Hästens beds, birchwood floors, and microwaves and fridges in many rooms. There's also a Scottish-style pub attached to the hotel. Be aware that rates zoom upward outside of the peak summer months, making it a less-enticing option.

Samariterhemmets Gästhem　　　　　　GUESTHOUSE €
(www.samariterhemmet.se; Samaritergränd 2; s/d incl breakfast Skr450/650) Run by a Christian charity, this clean, central and inviting guesthouse shares a building with a church. Old-style rooms with separate bathrooms are decorated in cool creams and antique furniture.

STF Uppsala St Persgatan　　　　　　HOSTEL €
(Map p110; 10 00 08; bokning@uppsalacityhostel.se; Sankt Persgatan 16; dm/s/d from Skr170/350/400;) STF Uppsala St Persgatan is recommended for its sheer convenience – you really can't stay anywhere more central for these prices. Rooms, all named after famous Uppsala landmarks, are small but decent (although dorms suffer from traffic and level-crossing noise). There's wi-fi access in parts of the hostel. No breakfast is served, but a kitchen is available.

STF Vandrarhem
Sunnersta Herrgård　　　　　　HOSTEL €
(32 42 20; www.sunnerstaherrgard.se; Sunnerstavägen 24; dm Skr235, s/d from Skr385/550; Jan–mid-Dec; P) In a historic manor house about 6km south of the city centre, this hostel has a parklike setting at water's edge and a good restaurant on site. You can rent bikes (Skr50/200 per day/week) or borrow a boat, and there's free wi-fi. Hotel-standard rooms are available (single/double Skr620/740). Take bus 20.

Uppsala Vandrarhem & Hotell　　　　　　HOSTEL €
(24 20 08; www.uppsalavandrarhem.se; Kvarntorget 3; dm Skr190, s/d hostel Skr445/550, s/d

hotel Skr750/895; P) This hostel, with hotel-grade rooms also available, is located in a sort of mini-mall away from the action but easily walkable from Uppsala Central Station. Rooms on two levels face an enclosed courtyard that works as a breakfast room. (Late sleepers should ask for an upstairs room.) Access to the kitchen and a grocery store on the corner make self-catering convenient. Breakfast is included in the hotel prices and Skr69 extra for hostellers.

Fyrishov Camping   CAMPGROUND €

(www.fyrishov.se; ldrottsgatan 2; sites Skr130, 4-bed cabins from Skr895) This campsite, 2km north of the city, is great for families with water babies: it's attached to water park Fyrishov, with discounted swim-and-stay packages (from Skr995 for cabins). Take bus 1 from Dragarbrunnsgatan.

✗ Eating

TOP CHOICE Magnussons Krog   SWEDISH €€

(Map p110; www.magnussonskrog.se; Drottninggatan 1; pub meals Skr159-219, mains Skr209-335; ⊘lunch & dinner) Try the house-favourite Bookmaker steak sandwich, or any of the specials on the chalkboard; a recent cured-salmon plate with potatoes and dill was outstanding, and easily large enough to share if you could be made to part with any of it. Late-night bar snacks (Skr109 to Skr129) help soak up delicious cocktails, which you can enjoy at outdoor tables on a busy riverside corner in fair weather, or propped on pillows in a cosy nook indoors.

Ofvandahls   CAFE €

(Map p110; Sysslomansgatan 3-5; cakes & snacks around Skr55) Something of an Uppsala institution, this classy *konditori* (bakery-cafe) dates back to the 19th century and is a cut above your average coffee-and-bun shop. It's endorsed by no less a personage than the king, and radiates old-world charm – somehow those faded red-striped awnings just get cuter every year.

Eko Caféet   CAFE €€

(Map p110; Drottninggatan 5; mains Skr65-95; ⊘lunch & dinner Mon-Sat; ⍾) This funky little place with retro and mismatched furniture serves some of the best coffee in town, alongside a creative menu of fresh and healthy salads, soups and seafood, including plenty of vegan and vegetarian options. It frequently hosts live jazz and folk, as well as changing art exhibits and general studenty

goings-on. Things quiet down somewhat in the summer, when it just opens for lunch Monday to Friday.

Hambergs Fisk   SEAFOOD €€€

(Map p110; Fyristorg 8; lunch from Skr85, dinner Skr145-275; ⊘11.30am-10pm Tue-Sat) No need to ask at the tourist office about where to eat: if you're there, you'll be close enough to smell the aromas of dill and seafood tempting you into this excellent fish restaurant. Self-caterers should check out the fresh fish counter inside.

Tzatziki   GREEK €€€

(Map p110; Fyristorg 4; starters Skr59-99, mains Skr139-249) Tzatziki will supply all your moussaka and souvlaki needs. There's cosy seating in the 16th-century interior, and in summer the outside tables by the riverside thrum with diners. Service is fast, the food tasty and there are several veggie options.

Amazing Thai   THAI €€

(Map p110; Bredgränd 14; starters Skr55, mains Skr129-155, dinner buffet adult/child Skr149/89; ⊘lunch & dinner) This small, family-friendly spot inside a shopping centre is popular for lunch thanks to its good-value buffet and welcoming atmosphere. The evening menu features a good selection of fragrant stir-fries, noodle dishes and curries.

Jalla   FAST FOOD €

(Map p110; Stora Torget 1; salad bar Skr75, meals Skr60-99; ⊘10am-9pm) Get your fix of cheap and (relatively) healthful felafel, kebabs and meze platters at this efficient fast-food joint right on the main square; it's packed with young people at all hours.

Saluhallen   FOOD HALL €€

(Map p110; Sankt Eriks Torg; ⊘10am-6pm Mon-Thu, to 7pm Fri, to 4pm Sat, restaurants also open 11am-4pm Sun) Stock up on meat, fish, cheese and fancy chocolate at this indoor market, or hit one of the restaurant corners for a bite; a couple stay open late for dinner, with pleasant terrace bars available in summer.

Hemköp   SUPERMARKET

(Map p110; Stora Torget; ⊘to 10pm) Find groceries at the central Hemköp supermarket.

☕ Drinking & Entertainment

In the evenings, local students converge on the university bars on Sankt Olofsgatan (hard to get into if you're not an Uppsala student, but worth a go). Just follow the crowds to find out which ones are currently primo.

Concert Hall
BAR

(Map p110; Vaksala Torget 1; ⊙5-8pm Tue-Sat & during evening events) For a cool view over the city, head to the 6th-floor bar inside the huge, blocky Concert Hall.

Katalin & All That Jazz
BAR

(Map p110; Godsmagasinet, Östra Station) Katalin, in a former warehouse behind the train station, hosts regular live jazz and blues, with occasional rock and pop bands. There's a good restaurant too, and in summer the sun-splashed back patio is jammed with great-looking people acting like they're not checking each other out.

O'Connor's
PUB

(Map p110; Stora Torget 1) Upstairs on the main square is this friendly Irish pub and restaurant, with live music six nights a week and a selection of over 70 beers from around the world.

Svenssons Taverna
BAR

(Map p110; Sysslomansgatan 14) This cool tavern has a winning combination of vaguely mariner-themed interior and shady outdoor seating area.

Systembolaget
LIQUOR STORE

(Map p110; Dragarbrunnsgatan 50) For alcohol, Systembolaget is inside the Svava shopping centre.

Royal Cinema
CINEMA

(Map p110; Dragarbrunnsgatan 44) New releases play here.

Filmstaden
CINEMA

(Map p110; www.sf.se, in Swedish; Drottninggatan 3) Hollywood blockbusters play here.

❶ Information

Emergency
Police (☑114 14; www.polisen.se/english; Svartbäcksgatan 49)

Internet Access
Library (Svartbäcksgatan 17; ⊙noon-6pm Mon-Fri, 11am-2pm Sat late Jun–mid-Aug, 9am-8pm Mon-Thu, 9-6pm Fri, 11am-4pm Sat & Sun mid-Aug–late Jun) Free internet access; bring ID and expect longish waits.

Sidewalk Express (per hr from Skr29) Inside the train station. To log on, buy vouchers from the coin-operated machines.

Medical Services
Apoteket Kronan (Svartbäcksgatan 8; ⊙10am-7pm Mon-Fri, to 3pm Sat) Pharmacy chain; one of five city centre locations.

Uppsala University Hospital (Akademiska sjukhuset; ☑611 22 97; Uppsala Care, Entrance 61, Sjukhusvägen) Has an urgent-care facility for foreign visitors, as well as an after-hours pharmacy.

Money
Head over to Stora Torget to find banks and ATMs. Next door to the tourist office is a **Forex** (☑10 30 00; Fyristorg 8; ⊙9am-7pm Mon-Fri, to 3pm Sat), offering currency-exchange services.

Post
You can buy stamps at the tourist office, most supermarkets and Pressbyrån shops. There are mailboxes at Stora Torget and Uppsala Central Station.

Tourist Information
Tourist office (☑727 48 00; www.uppsalatourism.se; Fyristorg 8; ⊙10am-6pm Mon-Fri, to 3pm Sat year-round, plus noon-4pm Sun mid-Jun–mid-Aug) Pick up the *Walking Tour of Uppsala* leaflet, and *What's On Uppsala* for event listings.

❶ Getting There & Away

The Flygbuss (bus 801) departs at least twice an hour around the clock for nearby Arlanda Airport (45 minutes, adult/child Skr110/65); it leaves from outside the Uppsala train station.

Swebus Express (☑0200-21 82 18; www.swebusexpress.se) runs regular direct services to Stockholm (Skr59, one hour, at least hourly), Västerås (from Skr139, 3½ hours, six daily), Örebro (from Skr189, 4½ hours, four to seven daily) and Falun (from Skr239, 5½ hours, two daily).

There are frequent SJ trains to/from Stockholm (Skr39-69, 40 minutes one-way), Gävle (from Skr135, 50 minutes, at least seven daily), Östersund (from Skr309, five hours, at least two daily) and Mora (from Skr224, 3¼ hours, two daily).

For car hire, seek out **Statoil** (☑20 91 00; Gamla Uppsalagatan 48), next to the Scandic Uppsala Nord hotel. There are three petrol stations with car hire, 1.5km along Vaksalagatan: **OKQ8** (☑29 04 96; Årstagatan 5-7) often has some good deals.

❶ Getting Around

Upplands Lokaltrafik (☑0771-14 14 14; www.ul.se) runs public transport within the city and county. City buses depart from Stora Torget and the nearby streets. Tickets for 90 minutes of unlimited bus travel can be purchased for Skr30/18 per adult/child.

Northern Uppland

Once a centre of industry, this region is now mainly a series of picturesque relics ideal for picnicking, lazing on the grass, taking photos and generally idling about. The landscape consists of buttery green hills dotted with small red cottages and postcard villages linked by winding roads, birch trees and ultralush vegetation. The main sights of interest are the centuries-old ironworks and mines scattered around the countryside. From vast gorges ripped into the ground to spick-and-span forge workers' cottages, they make fascinating visual history lessons.

The word *bruk*, which is part of many local place names, means an industrial village that processed raw materials, such as iron ore. Most appeared in the 17th century and were owned, run and staffed by Dutch and Walloon (Belgian) immigrants. The profits were used to build fine mansions, surrounded by humble workers' homes.

To learn more about the area's industrial heritage, ask at tourist offices for the free booklet *Vallonbruk in Uppland*, or check out www.svetur.se/vallonbruken.

ÖSTERBYBRUK
0295

You'd never guess from its placid air, but Österbybruk and its ironworks were founded solely to make munitions for Gustav Vasa's interminable wars. Today the village is a sleepy place, but it does contain most basic facilities (bank, bakery, supermarket, pizzeria and so on) and a summer **tourist office** (214 92; 11am-5pm Jun-Aug) amid the ironworks milieu.

The pleasant ironworks area includes the mansion **Österbybruk Herrgård**, which has **summer art exhibitions** (noon-4pm Sat & Sun May-Sep, daily Jun-Aug), **workers' homes** and the world's best-preserved 17th-century **Walloon forge**. The forge here mainly produced bar iron that was exported to Sheffield: it bore a stamp of two linked Os. In winter, the stacks of iron were taken to the port by sled. Tours of the grounds take place daily in summer (noon, 2pm and 3.30pm mid-June to mid-August; adult/child Skr40/free).

The impressive 15th-century castle **Örbyhus Slott** (214 06; www.orbyhus-slott.com; adult/child Skr60/25; 1pm Sat & Sun mid-May–mid-Sep, 1pm & 3pm Jul–mid-Aug), 10km further west, is where King Erik XIV was imprisoned by his brother Johann, before being murdered with a bowl of pea soup laced with arsenic.

A diminutive hostel with 20 beds, **Dannemora Vandrarhem** (215 70; Storrymningsvägen 4; dm Skr175; May-Oct; P) is near the Dannemora mine and based in old workers' houses. Reception is only open from 5.30pm to 7pm, so be sure to plan ahead.

Part of the ironworks estate, **Wärdshuset Gammel Tammen** (212 00; info@gammeltammen.se; s/d Skr995/1400) is a lovely old inn in one wing of Österbybruk Herrgård. The noted wildlife artist Bruno Liljefors lived here from 1917 to 1932. Its 26 rooms are cosy and peaceful – some have views out over the duck pond – and there's a recommended **restaurant** (dagens rätt; lunch Skr95, mains Skr150; noon-10pm Jun-Aug).

Just uphill from the Gammel Tammen, in a former stable, **Karins Stallcafé** (coffee Skr15, pastries from Skr20; 11am-5pm May-Jul, 11am-4pm Aug) is a summer cafe and twee crafts shop that serves lunches and snacks, accompanied by chunks of homemade bread, on outdoor picnic tables.

Bus 823 runs from Uppsala to Österbybruk (Skr75, one hour, at least 10 daily).

LÖVSTABRUK
0294

Tiny Lövstabruk (Leufsta Bruk), 24km due north of Österbybruk, is a great example of a mansion with associated factories. In 1627 the Dutchman Louis de Geer came to Lövstabruk, and the mansion was built for his grandson, Charles de Geer, around 1700. Workers mostly came from Walloonia in Belgium; hence the local name for the forges, *wallonbruk*. The house and its factories were destroyed by a Russian attack in 1719, but everything was rebuilt and iron production continued until 1926.

The **tourist office** (310 70; 11am-5pm mid-Jun–mid-Aug, noon-4pm Sat & Sun mid-Aug–mid-Jun) has moved into the Stora Magasinet building, next to the Wärdshus. Buy tickets here for various one-hour guided tours (adult/child Skr60/40) – the mansion (1pm and 4pm), the mansion and park (2.30pm), and the factory (11.30am). There's also a themed tour, the subject of which changes every year. Tours run daily from mid-June to August, and on Saturday and Sunday from mid-May to mid-June.

B&B Läkarvillan (310 04; www.lovstabruk.se; s/d Skr650/900) is a well-preserved house on the ironworks grounds that has whitewashed rooms decorated with pretty antiques. There's also a fine restaurant (mains Skr165 to Skr185) serving everything from coffee and cakes to a full à la carte menu.

To reach Lövstabruk, take bus 811 from Uppsala to Östhammar (1¼ hours, every 30 minutes Monday to Friday, hourly at weekends), then change to bus 835 (55 minutes, four to eight daily). The total cost of the journey is Skr80.

FORSMARK
☑ 0173

The surroundings of the **Forsmarksbruk** ironworks are ideal for photographers; its bone-white church, manor house, workshops and English gardens, set around a central pond, are starkly beautiful. The **statue of Neptune** in the middle of the pond dates from 1792. The seasonal **tourist office** (**☑** 500 15; ☺ 9am-4pm Jul–mid-Aug) is staffed until 4pm, but open until 9pm for brochures. These days the main employer in the area is the nearby nuclear power station, which is infamous for leaking radioactive waste into the Baltic Sea in June 2005.

The **bruksmuseum** (admission free; ☺ 11am-5pm Mon-Fri, 11am-3pm Sat & Sun mid-Jun–mid-Aug), full of old carriages, rusty tools, sleeping quarters and a factory office, is definitely worth a look, although its opening times are erratic outside the peak summer season. There's also a kid-friendly science-experiment room with a downhill-ski simulation machine and an electric scooter you can take for a spin.

Friendly staff at **Forsmark Wärdshus** (**☑** 173-501 00; www.forsmarkswardshus.se; ☺ summer only) cope admirably with the hungry coach parties at this lovely old inn. As well as devouring lunch (Skr80), you can stay in one of the charming rooms (single/double including breakfast Skr650/950) overlooking the English park, and rent bicycles (Skr100 per day).

To reach Forsmark, take bus 811 from Uppsala to Östhammar (1¼ hours, every 30 minutes Monday to Friday, hourly at weekends), then change to bus 835 (45 minutes, four to eight daily). The total cost of the journey is Skr80.

SÖDERMANLAND

Nyköping
☑ 0155 / POP 51,644

Once the setting for one of Swedish royalty's greatest feuds, Nyköping these days is a pretty, mellow town where the big activities include strolling along the river and sitting by the harbour.

⊙ Sights & Activities

By Stora Torget, there's the old **rådhus** (town hall) and **St Nicolai Kyrka**, with a splendid pulpit; free guided tours of the church run at 3pm Monday to Friday, and at 2pm Sunday. Two rune stones and 700 Bronze Age rock carvings decorate **Släbroparken**, about 2.5km northwest of town.

Take a walk along the river: 'Sweden's longest museum', or so the publicity goes. For longer hikes, the 1000km-long **Sörmlandsleden** (**☑** 355 64; www.sormlandsleden.se) passes through town on its way around the county. In summer you can also explore the nearby **archipelago**; enquire at the tourist office, or via Trosa Rederi (www.trosarederi.se).

FREE **Nyköpingshus**　　　CASTLE

(☺ 24hr) The ruined castle Nyköpingshus hosted some violent times in the Swedish monarchy. The bickering among King Birger and his two brothers, Erik and Valdemar, peaked in 1317 when Birger invited his brothers to a 'peace banquet'. When they arrived at the castle, he hurled them into the dungeon and threw the keys in the river, letting them starve to death. (It didn't do Birger much good, as he was driven to exile in Denmark the following year.) This cheerful episode is recreated each summer as *The Nyköping Banquet*, a traditional play; ask for a schedule at Sörmlands Museum.

Inside the castle grounds, **Sörmlands Museum** (www.sormlandsmuseum.se; ☺ 11am-7pm Jun-Aug, 11am-5pm Sun & with scheduled programs rest of year) includes **Kungstornet** (King's Tower), a whitewashed four-storey castle tower that now holds the museum shop; **Gamla Residenset**, the old governor's residence; and the neighbouring **Konsthallen**, with a series of varying exhibitions and performances. Guided tours of Kungstornet take place in English at 2pm Saturday and Sunday year-round, and daily in summer.

🛏 Sleeping & Eating

Clarion Hotel Kompaniet　　HOTEL **€€**
(cc.kompaniet@choice.se; Folkungavägen 1; r from Skr1090; **P**@**☒**) This enormous structure near the harbour features stylish modern rooms – not huge, but intelligently arranged, and many with nice views – in a building that was once home to a furniture factory.

Prices vary seasonally, but all include breakfast and a dinner buffet (or a sandwich for those who arrive late).

Nyköpings Vandrarhem HOSTEL €
(⌂070-679 56 08; Brunnsgatan 4; dm/s/d Skr185/310/430; ℗) So close to the castle that you'd feel threatened if there were a siege, this SVIF hostel is homely and casual. The kitchen is great, there are picnic tables in the yard, and the folks in charge are accommodating and helpful. The riverside location is hard to beat.

Strandstuviken Camping CAMPGROUND €
(⌂978 10; strandstuviken@hotmail.com; sites Skr150, 4-/5-bed cabin Skr375/425; ⊙May-Sep) The nearest camping ground is this beachside family-friendly place, just off the Sörmlandsleden walking trail. Has 10 cabins, some tent sites and dorms; there's also a sauna, minigolf, and canoe and bicycle hire. It's a good 9km southwest of town, though, with no public transport.

Café Hellmans CAFE €
(Västra Trädgårdsgatan 24; mains Skr75-95; ⊙8am-6pm Mon-Fri, 9am-5pm Sat, 11am-4pm Sun) A charming cafe with a boutique shop attached, Hellmans is a nice spot for lunch, with expansive buffets as well as bagels and subs from Skr35. Also has good coffee and excellent cakes to enjoy in the summer courtyard.

Aktersnurran CAFE €
(Skeppsbron; ice cream 1/2/3 scoops Skr18/24/34, sandwiches Skr32-66) Aktersnurran is one of several casual bar-restaurants along the harbour; the crowds shift from one terrace to the other according to time of day and availability of live music. This is the simplest in the line-up, with basic meals like pizza, meatballs and burgers, as well as sweet-smelling waffle cones.

ℹ Information

Banks, supermarkets and other services can be found on Västra Storgatan, running west from Stora Torget.

Tourist office (⌂24 82 00; turism@nykoping. se; Stadshuset, Stora Torget; ⊙8am-6pm Mon-Fri, 10am-4pm Sat & Sun) Located inside the town hall on the main square.

ℹ Getting There & Around

Nyköping's **Skavsta Airport** (⌂28 04 00; www. skavsta-air.se), 8km northwest of town, has flights to/from the UK and the European

continent with Ryanair (see p349). Airport buses meet most flights and run to/from Stockholm (Skr119, 80 minutes). Local buses 515 and 715 run every 10 minutes from Nyköping to Skavsta (Skr25, 20 minutes); alternatively, a **taxi** (⌂21 75 00) costs about Skr150.

The bus and train stations are roughly 800m apart on the western side of the central grid. Nyköping is on the regular **Swebus Express** (⌂0200-21 82 18; www.swebusexpress. se) routes, including Stockholm-Norrköping-Jönköping-Göteborg/Malmö, and Stockholm-Norrköping-Kalmar. To get to Eskilstuna, take local bus 701 or 801. SJ trains run every hour or two to Norrköping (Skr75, 40 minutes), Linköping (Skr145, 1¼ hours) and Stockholm (Skr100, one hour). Most X2000 services don't stop in Nyköping.

The tourist office has bikes for rent (day/week Skr40/200).

Eskilstuna
⌂016 / POP 96,311

Although its suburban ordinariness doesn't exactly scream 'tourist destination', Eskilstuna has some family-friendly sights, primarily its famous zoo, and just northeast of town is one of the most extraordinary rock carvings in Sweden. The small old town is also an attractive shopping district.

⊙ Sights & Activities

Parken Zoo ZOO
(www.parkenzoo.se; adult/child Skr170/120; ⊙10am-6pm daily Jul–mid-Aug, 10am-4pm Mon-Fri, 10am-6pm Sat & Sun May-Jun & mid-Aug–early Sep) Parken Zoo is one of central Sweden's most popular family attractions. Animals on show include monkeys, komodo dragons and some beautiful white tigers that were successfully bred here. It's not a cheap day out: additional charges are levied for **parking** (Skr40); the **amusement park** (day ticket Skr175; ⊙as for the zoo but opens at noon), which has kiddies' rides and some larger whizzy things; and the **swimming pool** (adult/child Skr50/35; ⊙10am-7pm Jun-Aug).

Parken Zoo is 1.5km west of the town centre. Bus 1 (Skr21, 25 minutes) leaves frequently from the train and bus stations.

FREE Sigurd Carving ARCHAEOLOGICAL SITE
(⊙24hr) The vivid, 3m-long Viking Age rock carving Sigurdsristningen illustrates the story of Sigurd the Dragon Slayer, a hero whose adventures are described in *Beowulf* and the Icelandic sagas. The story inspired Wagner's

Ring Cycle, and The Hobbit and Lord of the Rings also borrow from it.

Carved into the bedrock around AD 1000, the carving shows Sigurd roasting the heart of the dragon Fafnir over a fire. Sigurd's stepfather Regin persuaded him to kill Fafnir for the dragon's golden treasure. Sigurd touches the heart to see if it's cooked, then sucks his finger, and voila – he tastes the dragon's blood and suddenly understands the language of birds. They warn him that Regin is plotting to kill him and keep the treasure, so Sigurd attacks first, chopping off his stepfather's head; the unfortunate fellow is shown in the left corner of the carving, among his scattered tools. Also depicted is Sigurd's horse Grani, a gift from Odin, tied to the tree where the birds perch.

The runes in the dragon's body, unrelated to the legend, explain that a woman named Sigrid raised a nearby bridge (the abutments can still be seen) in memory of her husband Holmger. A walking path along the river starts from the parking lot; ask at the tourist office about raft trips.

The carving is situated near Sundby-holms Slott and Mälaren lake, 12km north-east of Eskilstuna. To get there, take bus 225.

FREE Rademachersmedjorna MUSEUM

(Rademacher Forges; Rademachergatan; ☺10am-4pm Mon-Fri year-round, plus some weekends in summer) The Rademachersmedjorna contain the carefully preserved 17th-century remnants of Eskilstuna's ironworking past. Visitors can see workshops where the tradition continues: iron-, silver- and goldsmiths all still work here. Stay alert for sightings of 'Sundin of the Gab', a local craftsman who produced masterworks.

FREE Eskilstuna Konstmuseum MUSEUM

(Portgatan 2, Munktellstaden; ☺11am-4pm Tue, Wed & Fri, to 8pm Thu, noon-4pm Sat & Sun) Eskilstuna Konstmuseum has an ambitious and very cool art collection in a beautiful space in the Munktell area. A chic little restaurant is attached.

FREE Ebelingmuseet MUSEUM

(Eskilstunavägen 5; ☺noon-4pm Wed-Sun) Hosts bizarre steel sculptures by Allan Ebeling and paintings by his daughter Marianne, plus various temporary exhibitions. The old wooden houses and pretty riverside areas in Torshälla are also worth a look. Take bus 2 or 15 from Eskilstuna to Torshälla (Skr21, 40 minutes).

🛏 Sleeping & Eating

STF Hostel Eskilstuna HOSTEL €

(✆51 30 80; www.vilstasporthotell.se; dm Skr160, s/d hostel from Skr300/420; P) Lying in the Vilsta nature reserve 2km south of town, this hostel is well provided for – all rooms have TV and en-suite bathroom. It's part of the Vilsta sport complex, with gym, jacuzzi and sports facilities on hand. Hotel rooms are also available; room rates include breakfast. Take bus 12 from Fristadstorget.

City Hotell Eskilstuna HOTEL €€

(www.cityhotell.se; Järnvägsplan 1; s/d Skr715/995, f Skr1195-1595) Right opposite the train station, this is among the better hotels. Rooms are spacious and comfortable, and some have balconies or cylindrical Swedish stoves, giving them a hint of the 19th century.

Restaurang Tingsgården SWEDISH €€€

(✆51 66 20; Rådhustorget 2; starters Skr59-110, mains Skr185-239; ☺11am-11pm Mon-Fri, noon-11pm Sat, noon-10pm Sun) This intimate restaurant, inside a wonderful wooden 18th-century house in the old town, is a treat. Its menu is heavy on the meat and fish, from lamb and goose to mountain trout, with a dessert menu of Swedish favourites. The massive annual julbord (a particularly gluttonous version of Sweden's smörgåsbord) runs from late November until Christmas (Skr399 to Skr499). In summer, you can sit out on a large deck overlooking the twinkling river.

Café Kaka CAFE €

(www.cafekaka.se; Kyrkogatan 6; sandwiches Skr40-50, wraps/salads Skr75/85; ☺11am-6pm) Kaka is a funky, upbeat cafe and meeting place, serving up sandwiches, wraps, and big, filling salads, with the occasional live DJ.

ℹ Information

The **tourist office** (✆710 23 75; www.eskilstuna.se; Nygatan 15; ☺10am-6pm Mon-Fri, 10am-2pm Sat year-round, plus 10am-2pm Sun May-Aug) dispenses helpful information. You'll find most services around Fristadstorget and the pedestrianised part of Kungsgatan. The central **public library** (✆10 13 51; Kriebsensgatan 4; ☺9am-8pm Mon-Thu, 9am-6pm Fri, 10am-3pm Sat) has free internet access.

ⓘ Getting There & Around

The bus station is located 500m east of the train station, beside the river. Local bus 701 goes roughly hourly to Nyköping (Skr96, 1¾ hours). **Swebus Express** (⌨0200-21 82 18; www.swebusexpress.se) operates up to six buses daily on its Stockholm–Eskilstuna–Örebro route, but trains are best for destinations such as Örebro (Skr100, one hour, every two hours), Västerås (Skr40, 30 minutes, hourly) and Stockholm (Skr95, one hour, hourly).

VÄSTMANLAND

Västerås

⌨021 / POP 137,207

With its cobbled streets, higgledy-piggledy houses and flourishing flower gardens, Västerås' old town is an utter delight. But Sweden's sixth-largest city is a place of two halves: head southeast and you'll find modern shopping centres, large industries and sprawling suburbs that bear no resemblance to the teeny lanes and crafts shops you've left behind.

Västerås is also a handy base for exploring Mälaren lake and important pagan sites nearby.

◉ Sights

FREE Konstmuseum   MUSEUM
(Map p120; Fiskartorget 2; ⊙11am-4pm Tue-Fri, noon-4pm Sat & Sun Jun-Aug, 10am-5pm Tue-Fri, noon-5pm Sat & Sun Sep-May) The art museum, based in the stately town hall, is devoted to exhibiting contemporary Swedish painters.

The permanent collections, with works by artists such as Ivan Aguéli and Bror Hjorth, also get an occasional airing.

FREE Vallby Friluftsmuseum   MUSEUM
(off Map p120; www.vallbyfriluftsmuseum.se; ⊙10am-5pm) Vallby Friluftsmuseum, off Vallbyleden near the E18 interchange, 2km northwest of the city, is home to an extensive open-air collection. Among the 40-odd buildings, there's an interesting farmyard and craft workshops. Take bus 10 or 12.

FREE Västmanlands Länsmuseum   MUSEUM
(Map p120; www.vastmanlandslansmuseum. se; Karlsgatan 2; ⊙10am-5pm Tue, Wed & Fri, to 8pm Thu, noon-4pm Sat & Sun) Västmanlands Länsmuseum is a cultural centre that stages exhibitions of contemporary art, photography and sculpture, as well as hosting speakers and presentations; look for a current schedule of events at the tourist office or online.

FREE Domkyrkan   CHURCH
(Cathedral; Biskopsgatan; ⊙8am-5pm Mon-Fri, 9.30am-5pm Sat & Sun) The fine brick-built Domkyrka was begun in the 12th century, although most of what you see today is late-14th-century work. It contains carved floor slabs, six altar pieces and the marble sarcophagus of King Erik XIV.

Behind the cathedral is the quaint old-town area **Kyrkbacken**. Once the student district and now a well-preserved portion of pre-18th-century Västerås, it's studded with artisans' workshops.

ARTY ALTERNATIVE LODGINGS

In addition to Västerås' normal, run-of-the-mill hotels, there are two unique accommodation possibilities in and around town. Both created by local artist Mikael Genberg, they are well worth investigating if you like your lodgings with a twist.

The **Hotell Hackspett** (Woodpecker Hotel; Map p120) is a fabulous tree house in the middle of Vasaparken. The cabin is 13m above the ground in an old oak tree; guests (and breakfast) are hoisted up and down in a basket. The second of Genberg's fascinating creations is the **Utter Inn** (Otter Inn): a small, red floating cabin in the middle of Mälaren lake, accessible only by boat. The bedroom is downstairs – 3m below the surface – and is complete with glass viewing panels to watch the marine life outside. There's room for two people, and a canoe is provided.

Accommodation in the tree house or lake cabin costs Skr1100 per person per night if you bring your own food and bed linen; the 'deluxe package' (linen is supplied, and food delivered in the evening and morning) is Skr1500 per person. Both places can be booked through the Västerås tourist office (p121). Genberg also has a website (www.mikaelgen-berg.com); it's in Swedish, but the photographs will give you an idea of his creations.

Västerås

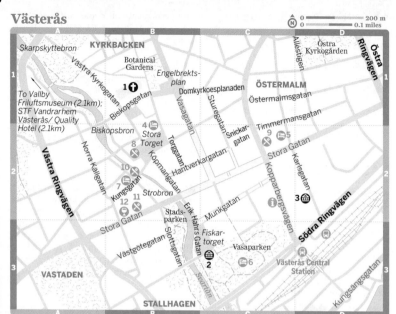

FREE **Anundshög** ARCHAEOLOGICAL SITE

(⊙24hr) The city is surrounded by ancient pre-Christian sites. The most interesting and extensive is Anundshög, the biggest *tumulus* (burial ground) in Sweden, 6km northeast of the city. It has a full complement of prehistoric curiosities, such as mounds, stone ship settings and a large 11th-century rune stone. The two main stone ship settings date from around the 1st century. The area is part of the Badelunda Ridge, which includes the 13th-century **Badelunda Church** (1km north) and the 16m-wide **Tibble Labyrinth** (1km south). Ask at the tourist office for the handy map *Badelunda Forntids Bygd*. Take bus 12 to the Bjurhovda terminus, then walk 2km east.

🛏 Sleeping

Västerås Mälarcamping CAMPGROUND €

(www.nordiccamping.se; Johannisbergsvägen; sites/cabins from Skr150/450; @) The closest campsite is this place, 5km southwest of the city near Mälaren lake. It has recently been renovated and renamed (from Johannisbergs Camping), with up-to-date facilities including wireless internet access. To get there, take bus 25.

STF Vandrarhem Västerås/Quality Hotel HOSTEL €

(off Map p120; ☑30 38 00; info.vasteras@quality.choicehotels.se; Svalgången 1, Vallby; s/d Skr430/580; **P**☒) A couple of kilometres out of town, this hotel offers hostel accommodation through STF (Svenska Turistföreningen; Swedish Touring Association) in about a dozen of its regular hotel rooms. The building is a crazy suburban-industrial colossus with exterior and common areas painted entirely in varying shades of white. Glass roofs over some of the rooms let in the long summer nights (if you want them to). There's a bar and restaurant in the lobby, as well as a pool table, sauna and swimming pool.

Klipper Hotel HOTEL €

(Map p120; www.klipperhotel.com; Kungsgatan 4; s/d incl breakfast Skr595/695; **P**) The attractive, family-run Klipper has one of the best locations in the city, near the river in the old town and 700m from the bus and train stations. The comfortable (if smallish) rooms are simple and fresh. Budget rooms are available for Skr395 (no breakfast, and you make your own bed).

Västerås

First Hotel Plaza HOTEL €€
(Map p120; reservations.plaza@firsthotels.se; Karlsgatan 9A; s/d Skr850/1250; P❄@) Bang in the centre of the modern city, this 25-storey skyscraper was built for gravity-defying lounge lizards: it boasts the highest cocktail bar in Sweden. Some rooms have views over Mälaren lake, and there's a spa with masseurs, sauna and gym, and a Mediterranean-inspired restaurant.

Elite Stadshotellet HOTEL €€
(Map p120; info@vasteras.elite.se; Stora Torget; s/d Skr1250/1500; P@) Many of the rooms at the Elite, in a lovely art-nouveau building, have prime views over the main square – request one if you like people-watching. The decor is tasteful (pale walls, leafy bedspreads and mahogany timber), the staff are obliging and there's a highly regarded restaurant and English-style pub attached.

🍴 Eating & Drinking

Kalle på Spangen CAFE €
(Map p120; www.kallepaspangen.se; Kungsgatan 2; lunch Skr65) This great cafe, right by the river in the old part of town, has several cosy, creaky-floored rooms filled with mismatched furniture and gilt-edged grandfather clocks. Lunch specials, such as the lasagne, are hefty and include salad, beverage, bread and coffee.

La Tapita SPANISH €
(Map p120; www.latapita.nu; Stora Gatan 46; tapas Skr26-66, lunch Skr70; ⊙11am-11pm Mon-Fri, 5-11pm Sat) This Spanish-themed tapas bar and restaurant has a mellow atmosphere, enhanced by Latin music and piles of southern Mediterranean grub. Nibble an array of tapas, tuck into pasta, fish and meat mains, or share a paella Valenciana with a friend.

Bill & Bobs SWEDISH €€
(Map p120; www.billobob.se; Stora Torget 5; mains Skr145-279) A diverse crowd settles down at this casual spot to drink and chatter at the outdoor tables on the square. Caesar salad and hamburger with bacon and bearnaise sauce are among Bill & Bobs' popular 'classic' dishes.

ICA SUPERMARKET
(Map p120; Kopparbergsvägen 15) Around the corner from the First Hotel Plaza.

Systembolaget LIQUOR STORE
(Map p120; Stora Gatan 48) For alcohol.

ⓘ Information

The **tourist office** (☑39 01 00; www.vasteras malarstaden.se; Kopparbergsvägen 8; ⊙10am-6pm Mon-Fri, 10am-3pm Sat) can help with visitor enquiries for the town and region.

There's a **Forex** (☑18 00 80; Stora Gatan 18; ⊙9am-7pm Mon-Fri, 9am-3pm Sat) currency-exchange office, banks, ATMs and most other services visitors will require along Stora Gatan.

ⓘ Getting There & Around

Västerås airport (☑80 56 00; www.vasteras flygplats.se) is 6km east of the city centre, and is connected by bus L941. Budget carrier Ryanair flies here daily from the UK, and other budget airlines reach a variety of destinations, including Crete and Turkey (weekly). Check the airport website for an updated schedule.

The bus and train stations are adjacent, on the southern edge of Västerås. Regional buses 65 and 69 run to Sala (Skr64, 45 minutes, up to eight weekdays, two Saturday and Sunday) as do trains (Skr45, 25 minutes, three daily). **Swebus Express** (☑0200-21 82 18; www.swebus press.se) runs to Uppsala (Skr157, three hours, five daily), Stockholm (Skr105, 1½ hours, six daily) and Örebro (Skr105, 1¼ hours, eight daily).

Västerås is accessible by hourly trains from Stockholm (Skr115, one hour). Trains to Örebro

(Skr100, one hour), Uppsala (Skr115, 1½ hours) and Eskilstuna (Skr65, 30 minutes) are also frequent.

For taxis, call **Taxi Västerås** (☏18 50 00).

Sala

☏0224 / POP 21,535

The source of tiny Sala's parklike charm is distinctly unfrivolous. The local silver mine made Sweden rich in the 16th and 17th centuries, and its creation changed the face of the town: those small rivers, ponds and canals that weave so prettily through and around the neighbourhood were actually built to power the mines.

◉ Sights & Activities

Sala Silvergruva   MINE, MUSEUM
(☏0224-677 260; www.salasilvergruva.se; ☺10am-5pm May-Sep, 11am-4pm Oct-Apr) Even if you're reluctant to take the plunge, the above-ground parts of Sala Silvergruva, a mine about 2km south of the town centre, are nice to walk around. Bring a camera – the weird landscape of mysterious, purpose-built structures occasionally sprouts chimneys or falls away into deep holes. The mine closed in 1908. The 30-odd buildings in the museum village contain artists' workshops, a cafe, a mine museum and even a small **police museum** (adult/child Skr20/10; ☺noon-4pm Jun-Aug), full of rusty knuckledusters.

Beneath the surface are 20km of galleries, caverns and shafts, which you can explore on one of two mine tours. The more frequent tour is the informative one-hour **60 Metersturen** (adult/child Skr140/70). The 90-minute tour, **150 Metersturen** (Skr200/100), goes down to 150m. Tours begin every half-hour or so between 11am and 3.30pm between June and August. To be sure of catching a tour in English, book ahead.

Both village and mine are off the Västerås road. It's a pretty walk along the **Gröna Gången** (Green Walk), which takes you southwest via the parks and the **Mellandammen** pond at Sofielund. Public transport connections aren't good; take the Silverlinjen bus from Sala train station to Styrars, then walk the remaining 500m.

Väsby Kungsgård   MUSEUM
(www.vasbykungsgard.se; Museigatan 2; adult/child Skr25/free; ☺1-4pm Mon-Fri) In the main park in town is Väsby Kungsgård, a 16th-century royal farm where Gustav II Adolf

(possibly) met his mistress. Excitement for the traveller is confined to the beautifully preserved interiors and 17th-century weapons collection.

FREE **Aguélimuseet**   MUSEUM
(www.sala.se/turism/aguelimuseet; Vasagatan 17; ☺11am-4pm Wed-Sun) Aguélimuseet exhibits the largest display of oils and watercolours by local artist Ivan Aguéli (1869–1917) in Sweden, as well as work by some of his contemporaries. Aguéli was a pioneering Swedish modernist whose motto was 'One can never be too precise, too simple or too deep.' In summer there are also temporary exhibitions. Entry is via the town library.

FREE **Norrmanska Gården**   HISTORIC BUILDING
(Brunnsgatan 26) The houses and courtyard called Norrmanska Gården were built in 1736; the area is now home to shops and a cafe.

🛏 Sleeping & Eating

STF Vandrarhem & Camping Sala   HOSTEL €
(☏127 30; sites from Skr50, dm Skr140, s/d from Skr210/280; ☷) This haven of tranquillity is in the woods near the Mellandammen pond, 2km southwest of the town centre. It's a pet-friendly complex with camping, minigolf and a homely cafe (open June to August). Walk along Gröna Gången from the bus station, or take the Silverlinjen bus to the water tower and walk the rest of the way. Reservations are necessary from September to mid-May.

Hotell Svea   HOTEL €
(www.hotellsvea.com; Väsby gatan 19; s/d Skr495/595) Friendly 10-roomed Svea puts the emphasis on its personal service. Rooms are old-fashioned, with shared baths, but it's clean and comfortable – and exceptionally handy for the train and bus stations.

Lilla Gömman Kök & Bar   CAFE €€
(Brunnsgatan 26; lunch from Skr70, dinner Skr85-175; ☺11am-2pm Mon & Tue, 11am-10pm Wed & Thu, noon-1am Fri & Sat) This restaurant, inside the rustic 18th-century wooden courtyard of Norrmanska Gården, has a great outdoor patio and includes a cute pub. On the lunch menu, you'll find meals such as pasta, panini, baked potatoes and salads. It's a popular evening spot, too, with a decent dinner menu.

DON'T MISS

ÄNGELSBERG

Looking more like a collection of gingerbread houses than an industrial relic, **Engelsberg Bruk** (✆131 00), a Unesco World Heritage Site in the tiny village of Ängelsberg, was one of the most important early-industrial ironworks in Europe. During the 17th and 18th centuries, its rare timber-clad **blast furnace** and **forge** (still in working order) were state-of-the-art technology, and a whole town sprang up around them. Today you can wander the perfectly preserved estate, made up of a mansion and park, workers' homes and industrial buildings. **Guided tours** (Skr50) run daily from mid-June to mid-August, and less frequently from May to mid-June and mid-August to mid-September; call for details or pop into the tourist information hut located near the parking area.

Nya Servering (⊙11am-8pm) is not far from Ängelsberg train station and serves fast food, coffee and simple sandwiches. There's a good view from here across to the island Barrön on Åmänningen lake, where the world's oldest-surviving **oil refinery** is located – it was opened in 1875 and closed in 1902.

Ängelsberg is around 60km northwest of Västerås, from where regional trains run every hour or two (from Skr85, 45 minutes); from Ängelsberg train station it's a 1.5km walk north to the Engelsberg Bruk site. If you have your own wheels, it's a gorgeous drive from pretty much any direction.

ℹ Information

The **tourist office** (✆552 02; www.sala.se/turism; Stora Torget; ⊙8am-5pm Mon-Fri year-round, plus 10am-2pm Sat May-Sep) inside the town hall faces the main square; it doesn't always stick to posted hours, but brochures are also available at the **library** (✆555 01; Norra Esplanaden 5). Internet access is available at both the tourist office and library. The free town map is useful if you want to use the walking paths.

ℹ Getting There & Around

For transport to and from Västerås, see p121. Going to or from Uppsala, take regional bus 848 (1¼ hours, hourly Monday to Friday, nine buses Saturday and Sunday). Sala is on the main Stockholm-Mora rail line (via Uppsala), with daily trains every two hours (Skr145, 1¾ hours).

Ask about bike hire at the tourist office.

Nora

✆0587 / POP 10,447

One of Sweden's most seductive old wooden towns, Nora sits snugly on the shores of a little lake, clearly confident in its ability to charm the pants off anyone. Slow your pace and take the time to succumb to its captivating features, such as quaint cobbled streets, old-world steam trains, mellow boat rides and decadent ice cream.

◉ Sights & Activities

TOP CHOICE **Kvarteret Bryggeriet**   GALLERY
(www.norart.se; admission free; ⊙11am-5pm Jun-Aug) At the end of Prästgatan is a collection of buildings that once housed a brewery, now adapted to contain several art galleries and studios. A collective of locals puts on a knockout gallery show in the main building each summer, including work by established and rising Swedish artists. The building itself is a work of art, restored just enough to be functional without losing any of its charm. Check online or ask at the main gallery for openings and evening events.

Pershyttan   RAILWAY
(return/one-way Skr90/60; ⊙mid-Jun–mid-Aug) Trips on the museum railway were temporarily on hold at the time of our visit, but ordinarily the train takes you 10km southeast to Järle or 2.5km southwest to the excellent old mining village at Pershyttan, where there's a guided tour at 3pm daily from July to August, and 3pm Saturday and Sunday from May to June and September. Check at the tourist office to see if they've resumed.

Göthlinska Gården   HISTORIC BUILDING
(tour adult/child Skr70/free; ⊙1pm Sat & Sun May-Jun, daily Jul & Aug) The manor house, Göthlinska Gården, just off the main square, was built in 1739 and is now a museum featuring furniture, decor and accoutrements from

the 17th century onward; entrance is by guided tour only.

Alntorps Island   ISLAND
(ticket Skr20; ⊙10am-6pm daily Jul & Aug, 10am-6pm Sat & Sun mid-May–Jun & early Sep; ⊕) Though it's technically a youngsters' activity, you don't need to be a child to appreciate the entertaining boat trips to Alntorps island. Boats depart roughly every half hour from the little jetty near the STF hostel. A walk around the island takes about an hour, and there are swimming spots and a cafe. Camping and cabins can be booked in advance through the tourist office (but if you plan to stay, do bring supplies).

🛏 Sleeping & Eating
Self-caterers will find supermarkets on Prästgatan and near Nora Glass at the end of Storgatan.

STF Nora Tåghem   HOSTEL €
(⌨146 76; info@norataghem.se; dm/d Skr190/280; ⊙May–mid-Sep) Outdoing its home town in the cuteness department, this hostel lets you sleep in the tiny but adorable antique bunks of 1930s railway carriages. All compartments have great views over the lake, and there's a cafe that does breakfast, plus sandwiches and snacks in summer.

Trängbo Camping   CAMPGROUND €
(⌨123 61; www.trangbocamping.se; sites Skr190, cabins from Skr300; ⊙May-Sep) This small campsite is by the lake 1.5km north of Nora (a lakeshore walking path leads from the train station/tourist office). Amenities are fine, if basic, and there's a place for swimming and beach volleyball. Guests can hire boats and canoes (per hour/day Skr40/250).

Nora Stadshotell   HOTEL €€
(www.norastadshotell.se; Rådstugugatan 21; s/d Skr765/1140) You can't miss this elegant building, planted smack on the main square, although the white-furnitured rooms don't quite live up to the exterior's promise. However, there are good-value lunch deals (Skr85) at the restaurant, which can be eaten on the airy summer terrace, along with à la carte evening mains from Skr129 and a comfortable pub.

⌜TOP⌟ Nora Glass   ICE CREAM €
⌞CHOICE⌟
(Storgatan 11; ice creams Skr25-65; ⊙10.30am-6.30pm May-Aug) Nora is renowned for its incredible ice cream, made here for more than 80 years. You never know what flavours will

be available – three or four different ones are churned out freshly each day – but you do know that they're worth queuing for. If hazelnut is among the day's selections, don't pass it up.

Strandstugan   CAFE €
(Storgatan 1; mains Skr65; ⊙summer only) Down by the lake is this delightful red wooden house, set in a flower-filled garden, where you can get coffee, sandwiches, quiches, desserts and other home-baked goodies, as well as Nora Glass ice cream creations. Try the local specialty, *Bergslags paj*, a quiche made with venison, chanterelles and juniper berries.

ℹ Information
At the train station by the lake, the **tourist office** (⌨811 20; Stationshuset; ⊙10am-6pm Mon-Sat, 10.30am-4pm Sun Jun & Aug, 9am-7pm Mon-Sat, 10.30am-4pm Sun Jul, 9am-noon & 1-4pm Mon-Fri Sep-May) books various guided tours (from June to August), including a **town walk** (adult/child Skr60/30) available in English. Alternatively, buy a brochure (Skr10) for self-guided walks.

ℹ Getting There & Around
Länstrafiken Örebro buses run every hour or two to Örebro (Skr52, 40 minutes) and other regional destinations.

Ask at the tourist office about bike rental.

NÄRKE

Örebro
⌨019 / POP 135,460
A substantial, culturally rich city, Örebro buzzes around its central feature: the huge and romantic castle surrounded by a moat filled with water lilies. The city originally sprung up as a product of the textile industry, but it's now decidedly a university town – students on bicycles fill the streets, and other relaxed folk gather on restaurant patios and in parks. It's an ideal spot to indulge in standard holiday activities, like nursing a beer in a terrace cafe or shopping unhurriedly along a cobbled street.

⦿ Sights & Activities

Slottet   CASTLE
(Map p125; www.orebroslott.se; guided tours adult/child Skr65/25; ⊙tours 1pm Sat & Sun mid-Jun–

Örebro

mid-Aug, performances daily mid-Jun–mid-Aug)
The magnificent Slottet now serves as the
county governor's headquarters. While the
castle was originally constructed in the late
13th century, most of what you see today
is from 300 years later. The outside is far
more dramatic than the interior (where
the castle's conference business is all too
evident). Parts of the interior are open for
exhibits, but to really explore you'll need
to take a tour; there's a historical one at
4.30pm (in Swedish or English, depending
on numbers) or 'Secrets of the Vasa Fortress'
at 2.30pm (in English), which is a slightly
toe-curling piece of costumed clowning
around. Book either one through the tourist
office. The northwest tower holds a small
history exhibition (admission free; ☺10am-
5pm daily May-Aug, noon-4pm Tue-Sun Sep-Apr).

Stadsparken PARK
(Map p125; 🚼) East of the castle, Örebro is
blessed with the Stadsparken, an idyllic and
kid-friendly park once voted Sweden's most
beautiful. It stretches alongside Svartån
(the Black River) and merges into the
Wadköping museum village. The village,
named after what the author Hjalmar
Bergman called his hometown in his novels,
is a cobblestone maze of workshops, cafes,
a bakery and period buildings – including

Örebro

Kungsstugan (the King's Lodgings; a
medieval house with 16th-century ceiling
paintings) and Cajsa Warg's house (home

of an 18th-century celebrity chef). You can wander the village at any time, but the shops, cafe, displays and museums are open roughly 11am to 4pm (sometimes 5pm) Tuesday to Sunday year-round; there are guided tours at 1pm and 3pm June to August (Skr20). Most information is posted in Swedish, but there's a small tourist office with brochures in English.

TOP
CHOICE **Länsmuseum & Konsthall** MUSEUM
(Map p125; www.orebrolansmuseum.se; Engelbrektsgatan 3; admission free; ⊙11am-5pm Tue & Thu-Sun, to 9pm Wed) The Länsmuseum & Konsthall has strong and topical temporary exhibits – a recent one featured protest posters from the '60s, and a consideration of the era's clothing and home furnishings as cultural indicators. It's also home to a permanent collection of artwork grouped by theme, and historical displays about the region (mostly in Swedish). The surrounding grounds are often dotted with wacky sculptures.

Biologiska Museet MUSEUM
(Map p125; Fredsgatan; adult/child Skr25/10; ⊙11am-2pm Mon-Fri mid-Jun–mid-Aug) Many Swedish schools once had private natural history collections, but most were binned in the 1960s. Örebro's Biologiska Museet, in Karolinska Skolan, is a survivor; it's well worth a glance for its tier upon tier of stuffed birds.

St Nikolai Kyrka CHURCH
(Map p125; Kyrkogatan 8; ⊙10am-5pm Mon-Fri, 11am-3pm Sat) The 13th-century St Nikolai Kyrka has some historical interest: it's where Jean Baptiste Bernadotte (Napoleon's marshal) was chosen to take the Swedish throne. Just opposite, on Drottninggatan, is the Rådhus (town hall; Map p125); if you're around at the right time, stop to hear the chimes (⊙12.05pm & 6.05pm year-round, plus 9pm Jun-Sep), when sculptures representing the city's past, present and future come wheeling out of a high arched window.

FREE **Svampen** TOWER
(www.svampen.nu; Dalbygatan 4; ⊙11am-4pm Sat & Sun, daily May-Aug) The first of Sweden's modern 'mushroom' water towers, Svampen was built in 1958 and now functions as a lookout tower. There are good views of lake Hjälmaren and a cafe at the top (daily specials Skr95). Take bus 11.

Arboga Rederi CRUISE
(Map p125; ☎107 191; www.lagerbjelke.com) Offers a number of cruises. The evening trips on Hjälmaren (adult/child Skr260/free; 7pm Wednesday to Friday mid-May to September, plus Saturday in July) include an onboard shrimp supper. Order tickets by phone or online.

🛏 Sleeping

TOP
CHOICE **Behrn Hotell** HOTEL €€
(Map p125; www.behrnhotell.se; Stortorget 12; s/d Skr910/1050; [P][❄][@]) Excellently situated on the main square, the Behrn Hotell goes the extra mile with individually decorated rooms – ranging from strictly business to farmhouse or edgy modern Scandinavian. Do it right and get a room with a balcony or a suite with old wooden beams, chandeliers and a jacuzzi. There's also a spa, and a restaurant that serves dinner Tuesday to Friday.

Gustavsvik Camping CAMPGROUND, CABIN €€
(www.gustavsvik.se; Sommarrovägen; sites/cabins Skr305/1035; ⊙mid-Apr–early Nov; [P][≋]) This camping facility is 2km south of the city centre, and it's attached to a family-oriented waterpark that can be a bit of a madhouse in summer. There are various swimming and soaking pools, minigolf, a cafe, a gym, a restaurant-pub and bike rental (Skr60 per day). Cabins have full kitchens, TV and wireless internet. Book ahead in summer. Take bus 11.

🍴 Eating

Cheap eat options such as pizza and kebabs abound. For self-caterers there's a supermarket in the Kompassen Centre on Stortorget.

TOP
CHOICE **Hälls Konditori Stallbacken** BAKERY-CAFE €
(Map p125; Engelbrektsgatan 12; coffee Skr20, pastries Skr17, mains Skr35-85) One of two locations of this bakery-cafe (the other's in Järntorget), Hälls is a classic old-style *konditori* and a favourite hangout for locals. Go for *fika* (coffee and cake) or more substantial salads, quiche and sandwiches.

Mera Coffeehouse CAFE €
(Map p125; Stortorget 6; espresso Skr20, baguettes Skr49) This sleek space on the main square is a handy lunch or coffee stop; it peddles hearty sandwiches and a decent range of

UPPSALA & CENTRAL SWEDEN NÄRKE

espresso drinks. Window seats make for good people-watching.

Creperiet
CAFE €

(Map p125; Nikolaigatan; lunch special, salads & crepes Skr79, ciabatta Skr59; ☺11am-7pm Mon-Fri, to 5pm Sat; ⟨⟩) This large underground space is extremely kid-friendly; a play area occupies about a third of the room. But it's no frumpy parental refuge: the long, low room is neatly designed, with subdued colours and well-chosen lighting. There are also tables outdoors on a terrace. The menu is mostly healthy salads and crepes filled with fresh veggies.

Pacos
TEX-MEX €€

(Map p125; Olaigatan 13A; lunch Skr69-85, dinner Skr98-169; ☺11am-11pm Mon-Thu, 11am-midnight Fri & Sat, noon-5pm Sun) OK, maybe Tex-Mex isn't exactly what you expected to be eating in the middle of Sweden, but the fun decor and chirpy music at Pacos make for a nice change of pace, and the lunch specials are good value, especially the pizza-pasta-salad buffet (Skr79).

Drinking & Entertainment

To buy your own alcohol to-go, head to Systembolaget (Map p125; Stortorget 10).

Bishops Arms
PUB

(Map p125; Drottninggatan 1; ☺until at least midnight) Whether or not you're convinced by the 'authentic English pub' schtick, the bar's outdoor drinking area, with super castle views, is a swinging spot on a summer evening. There are also pub meals available for under Skr100.

Harrys
PUB

(Map p125; Hamnplan; beer from Skr50, pub meals Skr119-259; ☺from 5pm) Though it's part of a sort of blah chain, Harrys has a good location in a cool old brick factory building by the river. It's popular and has a comprehensive menu of pub meals, live music on a Thursday, and a nightclub on Friday and Saturday.

ⓘ Information

Banks can be found along Drottninggatan, south of the castle.

Library (☎21 10 00; Näbbtorgsgatan) Has internet access.

Tourist office (☎21 21 21; www.orebro.se/turism; ☺10am-6pm Mon-Fri, 10am-2pm Sat & Sun Sep-May, 10am-6pm Mon-Fri, 10am-4pm Sat & Sun Jun-Aug) Inside the castle.

ⓘ Getting There & Away

Long-distance buses leave from opposite the train station and run almost everywhere in southern Sweden. **Swebus Express** (☎0200-21 82 18; www.swebusexpress.se) has connections to Norrköping, Karlstad and Oslo (Norway); Mariestad and Göteborg; Västerås and Uppsala; and Eskilstuna and Stockholm.

Train connections are also good. Direct SJ trains run to/from Stockholm (Skr210, two hours) every hour with some via Västerås (Skr100, one hour) and Göteborg (Skr250, 2¾ hours). Other trains run daily to Gävle (Skr290, three to four hours) and Borlänge (Skr180, 2¼ hours), where you can change for Falun and Mora.

ⓘ Getting Around

Town buses leave from Järntorget and cost Skr20/10 per adult/child.

Cykeluthyrning (☎21 19 09), at the Hamnplan boat terminal, rents bikes from May to September from Skr90 per day.

For a cab, call **Taxi Kurir** (☎12 30 30).

Askersund & Around

☎0583 / POP 11,278

There's not much to Askersund beyond a cute harbour and cobblestone square (which doubles as a parking lot), but it's a nice place to relax or to stock up for a visit to the nearby Tiveden National Park. It's also one of Närke's oldest inhabited places; Vikings started a burial ground here around AD 900.

◉ Sights & Activities

Tiveden National Park
PARK

Carved by glaciers, this trolls' home and former highwaymen's haunt about 33km south of Askersund makes for wonderful wild walking. The park is noted for its ancient virgin forests, which are very rare in southern Sweden, and has lots of dramatic bare bedrock, extensive boulderfields and a scattering of lakes.

Several self-guided walks, including the 6km Trollkyrka ('troll church') trail, start from the visitor centre (☺10am-4pm May-Sep, 11am-4pm Sat & Sun Apr & Oct) in the southeastern part of the park, 5km north of Rd 49 (turn-off at Bocksjö). You can pick up brochures and maps, and there's a small shop.

A few kilometres north along Rd 49 is the turn-off to Fagertärn, a pretty lake that fills with blood-red water lilies in July. Legend says a fisherman called Fager traded his daughter to the fearsome water spirit Näcken in exchange for a good catch. On their wedding day, the daughter rowed out onto the lake alone and drove a knife into her heart, and the lilies have been stained red ever since.

The park is a bit out of the way, and there's no public transport, but if you have your own wheels it's worth a stop, especially for hikers.

The area is also good for cycling (Sverigeleden passes nearby), canoeing (☑0584-47 40 83), fishing, cross-country skiing and horse riding (☑070-654 91 59). The tourist office in Askersund can help make arrangements.

Stjernsund Manor HISTORIC BUILDING

(☑100 04; admission by tour only, adult/under 12yr Skr60/free; ☺11am, noon, 2pm, 3pm & 4pm mid-May–Aug) Home to Prince Gustav, 'the Singing Prince', in the 1850s, Stjernsund Manor contains one of the best-preserved 19th-century interiors in Sweden, with elegant furniture and gilt, glass and velvet fixtures and fittings. There's also an appealing cafe in the nearby estate-manager's old house. The manor is 5km south of Askersund; the best way to get there is via a day cruise on the M/S *Wettervik*.

M/S Wettervik CRUISE

(☑0709-77 02 63; www.wettervik.se) In July and early August, the M/S *Wettervik* makes various trips from the harbour, including an excursion to Stjernsund Manor (adult/under 12yr Skr195/free), which departs Askersund at 1pm and returns at 4.30pm. The price includes boat tour, castle tour and light refreshments. Book at the tourist office or online.

FREE Hembygdsgård MUSEUM

(Hagavägen; ☺noon-3pm Mon-Fri mid-Jun–mid-Aug) Hembygdsgård is a collection of old wooden farm buildings, and a children's zoo with rabbits, sheep and ducks.

🛏 Sleeping & Eating

Aspa Herrgård HOTEL €€€

(www.aspaherrgard.se; s/d Skr1680/2210; P@) For a true treat, try this luxurious boutique hotel, based in a 17th-century manor house in a comely country setting (17km south of town on Rd 49). With its draped beds, flowery cushions and graceful Greek statues, it's the perfect place for a romantic weekend (look online for package deals). There's an exclusive restaurant (nonguests should reserve) and a tiny Bellman museum.

Café Garvaregården B&B €

(www.cafegarvaregarden.com; Sundsgatan; r incl breakfast Skr700) This desperately lovely B&B in the centre of town is a real find. It offers simple but charming accommodation in an 18th-century house, around a flower-filled courtyard. There's an inviting cafe downstairs (open 10am to 5pm daily; weekends only in winter). Unusually for Sweden, prices drop in winter (s/d Skr500/600).

STF Tivedstorp Vandrarhem HOSTEL €

(☑0584-47 20 90; www.tivedstorp.se; dm Skr150, s/d Skr350/500; ☺Apr-Oct) This STF complex has hostel accommodation in cute red grass-roofed cabins, plus a cafe (open 10am to 7pm daily June to August, and 10am to 4pm Saturday and Sunday May and September) and activity centre. It's about 3km north of the Tiveden National Park visitor centre; you'll need your own transport to get here.

Husabergsudde Camping CAMPGROUND €

(www.husabergsudde.se; sites Skr50-170, 2-/4-bed cabins Skr330/440; ☺May-Aug) This is a large, lakeside campsite with top amenities, 1.5km south of town on Hwy 50. You can rent canoes and rowing boats (per hour/day Skr35/180) and bicycles (per hour/day Skr15/75). There's no public transport to the site, and reception closes at 3pm on Sunday.

Café Tutingen SWEDISH, ITALIAN €

(Storgatan; pastries Skr35, sandwiches Skr50-75; ☺9am-6pm Mon-Sat, 11am-5pm Sun) Built in 1784, this charming cafe across the square from the tourist office has low ceilings, warped old floorboards and mismatched but shapely seating. It does good sandwiches and excellent pastries, all baked on the premises. Best of all is the garden, filled with roses and daisies, and containing the perfect balance of sun and shade.

ℹ Information

Tourist office (☑810 88; turistbyran@askersund.se; Lilla Bergsgatan 12A; ☺10am-7pm mid-Jun–mid-Aug, 10am-12.30pm & 1-4pm Mon-Fri mid-Aug–mid-Jun) Located on the main square. Ask for information on walking and cycling routes around the lake, as well as canoe and kayak rental (per hour/day Skr75/250).

ℹ Getting There & Around

Länstrafiken buses 708 and 841 each run four times on weekdays to Örebro (841 doesn't run

OUTDOOR ACTIVITIES

Getting out into nature is one of the most rewarding things to do in this part of Sweden. And it's easy. Outdoors enthusiasts have a number of options within easy reach, for all types of weather.

Skiers are spoiled for excellent choices, as sleepy little **Sälen** (p142) transforms itself in winter into a major destination for skiers of all abilities . There's also good skiing at the smaller, slightly more remote **Grönklitt** (p142) and at the bustling, snowboard-friendly **Sunne** (p131). At **Hovfjället** (p133) you can opt for downhill or cross-country skiing, or choose something more unusual, like snowshoeing, dogsledding or wolf-watching.

Torsby and its surrounds are also a good base for warm-weather activities like hiking and cycling. **Finnskogleden** (p133) is a well-marked 240km trekking path that roughly follows the Norwegian border. Dalarna has **Siljansleden** (p136), a 300km network of walking and cycling paths surrounding the scenic Lake Siljan. And near Sälen it's easy to hop onto the southern section of **Kungsleden** (p308), the popular walking trail through Norrland. Walking trails are also plentiful in and around **Tiveden National Park** (p127), which is a good place to enquire about fishing as well.

For a good summary of fishing in this part of Sweden, visit www.sportfiskeguide.se; the website has information on where to go, what's required, where to stay, and how to find a guide, in Swedish and English. Fishing generally requires you to purchase a Fiskekort, which must be bought locally where you intend to fish. Anglers will find some great fishing in and around **Grövelsjön** (p143), along with excellent skiing, hiking, rock climbing, river paddling, and most other outdoor activities. The village is inside a nature reserve.

---

in July). Bus 704 runs frequently to the mainline train station at Hallsberg.

Husabergsudde Camping does bike and boat hire.

VÄRMLAND

Karlstad

☑ 054 / POP 85,753

A pleasant and compact town centre wrapped in layers of perpetually snarled traffic, Karlstad makes itself useful as a base for travellers pursuing outdoor activities in Värmland. There are several sights worth seeing in town, and a large student population means it has a decent restaurant and bar scene.

◉ Sights & Activities

TOP CHOICE **Värmlands Museum**   MUSEUM

(www.varmlandsmuseum.se; adult/child Skr60/ free; ◷10am-6pm Mon-Tue & Thu-Fri, to 8pm Wed, 11am-5pm Sat & Sun) The award-winning and imaginative Värmlands Museum is on Sandgrundsudden (now converted into a very pleasant park) near the library. Its sensory displays cover local history and culture from the Stone Age to current times, including

music, the river, forests and textiles. Some components of the museum are open-air, activity-based displays about local industry and working life, including a log-driving museum and a mineral mine, just outside of town; pick up brochures at the museum or tourist office.

FREE **Mariebergsskogen**   PARK

(www.mariebergsskogen.se; Stadspark; ◷7am-10pm) For green spaces and picnic spots, seek out Mariebergsskogen, a combined leisure park, open-air museum and animal park in the southwestern part of town (about 1km from the centre). Also here is Naturum Värmland with a cafe and shop, perched over Lake Vänern. Take bus 1 or 31.

Domkyrka   CHURCH

(◷10am-7pm Mon-Fri, to 4pm Sat, to 6pm Sun Jun-Aug, 10am-4pm daily Sep-May) It's worth peeking into the 18th-century *domkyrka*, a soothing space with chandeliers and votive ships.

FREE **Old Town Prison**   MUSEUM

(Karlbergsgatan 3; ◷10am-5pm) You can visit the small and creepy old town prison in the basement of Clarion Hotel Bilan, with original cells and prisoners' letters.

Gamla Stenbron BRIDGE

On the eastern river branch, find Gamla Stenbron – at 168m, it's one of Sweden's longest stone bridges.

Boat Cruises CRUISE

(21 99 43; www.karlstad.se; adult/child Skr80/50) From Tuesday to Saturday late June to mid-August, there are regular two-hour boat cruises on Vänern lake, leaving from the harbour behind the train station. A cheaper option (Tuesday to Sunday, summer only) is the 'boat bus' – city 'buses' No 91-97 circle Karlstad on the water, and you can use your regular city bus ticket (Skr23, or Skr30 if purchased onboard).

🛏 Sleeping

Clarion Hotel Bilan HOTEL €€

(cc.bilan@choice.se; Karlbergsgatan 3; s/d from Skr890/1090; P) The town's old jail cells have been converted into large, bright and cleverly decorated rooms with exposed-wood ceiling beams and funky shapes – and a display in the basement letting you in on the building's history. There's a guest sauna, and complimentary afternoon tea.

Skutbergets Camping CAMPGROUND €

(www.camping.se/s10; sites Skr170, cabins from Skr430) This big friendly lakeside campsite, 7km west of town off the E18 motorway, is part of a large sports recreation area, with beach volleyball, a driving range, minigolf, exercise tracks and a mountain-bike course. There are also sandy and rocky beaches nearby. Take bus 18.

Hotell Freden HOTEL €

(www.fredenhotel.com; Fredsgatan 1; hostel s Skr370, hotel s/d Skr480/580) One of a number of central hotels opposite the train station, Freden is a simple budget hotel with comfortable single, double and hostel-standard rooms with shared bathrooms.

STF Vandrarhem Karlstad HOSTEL €

(56 68 40; karlstad.vandrarhem@swipnet.se; dm Skr200, s/d from Skr350/600; P) The hostel, in an impressive, renovated military building on a hillside, is off the E18 at Kasernhöjden, 1km southwest of Karlstad's centre, and has good facilities. Reception hours are limited (8am to 10am & 4pm to 7.30pm), so call ahead. Take bus 100.

🍴 Eating & Drinking

Make tracks to the main square, Stora Torget, and its surrounds for good eating and drinking options – most have outdoor summer seating.

Valfrids Krog TAPAS €€

(Östra Torggatan; mixed grill Skr190, tapas plates Skr135) This is a relaxed spot for a drink or meal, with light, tapas-style snacks (such as mini-chorizo, chicken drumsticks and asparagus), mixed grills of meat or seafood, and good Swedish and international mains catering to most tastes.

Kebab House FAST FOOD €€

(Västra Torggatan 9; pizza Skr72-112, kebabs Skr89, mains Skr90-250) Don't be fooled by the name – the Kebab House is a cut above regular fast-food places and serves good-value pizza, kebabs, pasta and salads. In summer, battle your way to one of the popular outdoor tables, in the middle of the busy pedestrianised street.

Källaren Munken SWEDISH €€€

(restaurang@munken.nu; Västra Torggatan 17; starters Skr89-115, mains Skr155-268; closed Sun) Inspired gourmet meals, like roasted stag in lingonberry-chanterelle sauce, are served up in this elegant but cosy 17th-century vaulted cellar, the oldest building in town.

Båten FLOATING RESTAURANT

(Magasin 1, Inre Hamn; Jun-Aug) The huge Båten ('the boat'), on a boat moored at the harbour, is a highly rated open-air restaurant and a very popular summer drinking (and eating) spot.

Hemköp SUPERMARKET

(Fredsgatan 4) Inside Åhléns.

Systembolaget LIQUOR STORE

(Drottninggatan 26) Near the Hemköp supermarket.

ℹ Information

Sharing the same building as the library at the edge of the town centre, the **tourist office** (29 84 00; www.karlstad.se; Bibliotekshuset, Västra Torggatan 26; 9am-7pm Mon-Fri, 10am-6pm Sat, 10am-3pm Sun mid-Jun–late Aug; 9am-6pm Mon-Thu, 9am-5pm Fri, 10am-3pm Sat late Aug–mid-Jun) has lots of info on both town and county (including fresh-air escapes in the region's forests) and its rivers and lakes. Internet access is available in the library. Banks and ATMs line Storgatan.

ℹ Getting There & Around

Karlstad is the major transport hub for western central Sweden. The long-distance bus terminal is at Drottninggatan 43, 600m west of the train station.

Swebus Express (📞0200-21 82 18; www.swebusexpress.se) has daily services on a number of routes, including Karlstad-Falun-Gävle, Karlstad-Göteborg, Stockholm-Örebro-Karlstad-Oslo and Karlstad-Mariestad-Jönköping.

Intercity trains to Stockholm (Skr365, 3¼ hours) run frequently. There are also several daily services to Göteborg (Sk210, three to four hours) and express services to Oslo (Skr275, three hours).

Värmlandstrafik (📞020-22 55 80) runs regional buses. Bus 302 travels to Sunne (Skr80, 1¼ hours, one to five daily) and Torsby (Skr95, two hours, one to three daily). Local trains also operate on this route – prices are the same as for buses.

Free bikes are available from the city's two **Solacykeln booths**: Stora Torget (📞29 50 29; ⊙7.30am-7pm Mon-Fri, 10am-3.30pm Sat May-Sep) and outer harbour (⊙9.30am-5.30pm Mon-Fri, 10am-3.30pm Sat Jun-Aug). All you need is a valid ID.

Sunne

📞0565 / POP 13,255

Sunne has the largest ski resort in southern Sweden. In summer, it's a quiet spot with a number of cultural attractions. It also has a proud literary heritage, as the hometown of both Selma Lagerlöf and Göran Tunström. (The latter lived at Ekebyvägen 56 and is buried near the east gable of Sunne Church.)

◎ Sights & Activities

Mårbacka   MUSEUM
(www.marbacka.s.se; adult/child Skr70/35; ⊙10am-4pm daily Jun-Aug, 11am-3pm Sat & Sun May & Sep, 11am-2pm Sat Oct-Dec & Feb-Apr, closed Jan) The most interesting place in the area is the house at Mårbacka, where Swedish novelist Selma Lagerlöf (1858–1940) was born. She was the first woman to receive the Nobel Prize for Literature, and many of her tales are based in the local area. Admission is by guided tour only (45 minutes), which leave on the hour – a tour in English is given daily in July at 2pm. Mårbacka is 9km southeast of Sunne; enquire at the tourist office about buses.

Sundsbergs Gård   MUSEUM
(adult/child Skr50/free; ⊙noon-4pm Tue-Thu, Sat & Sun late Jun–mid-Aug) Sundsbergs Gård, opposite the tourist office, featured in Lagerlöf's *Gösta Berling's Saga* and now contains a forestry museum, furniture and textiles

collection, art exhibition, cafe and manor house.

Rottneros Park   PARK
(www.rottnerospark.se; adult/child Skr110/40; ⊙10am-4pm May-Jun & Sep, 10am-6pm Jul & Aug; ♿) Known as 'Ekeby' in *Gösta Berling's Saga,* Rottneros Park, 6km south of Sunne, soothes travel-weary adults with flower gardens, a tropical greenhouse and an arboretum. There's lots for kids, including the rope-swinging delights of Sweden's largest climbing forest. The attached warehouse has temporary exhibitions. Rottneros has its own train station. Take bus 302.

Freya af Fryken   BOAT TOUR
(www.frejaaffryken.se; short tours adult/child Skr100/50, with fika Skr190/100; ⊙Jul–mid-Aug) The steamship *Freya af Fryken* sank in 1896, but it was raised and lovingly restored in 1994. Now you can sail along the lakes north and south of Sunne; departures are several times weekly in summer. Lunch and dinner cruises are also on the program.

Ski Sunne   SNOW SPORTS
(📞602 80; www.skisunne.se; day pass adult/child Skr270/220) Ski Sunne, the town's ski resort, has nine different descents, a snowboarding area and a cross-country skiing stadium. In summer the resort becomes a mountain-bike park.

🛏 Sleeping & Eating

Sunne SweCamp Kolsnäs   CAMPGROUND €
(www.kolsnas.se; sites/2-/4-bed cabins Skr190/450/560; ♿♿) This is a large, family-oriented campsite at the southern edge of town, with minigolf, a restaurant, a beach and assorted summer activities, plus bikes, boats and canoes for rent. There's a good restaurant attached.

STF Vandrarhem Sunne   HOSTEL €
(📞107 88; www.sunnevandrarhem.se; Hembygdsvägen 7; dm Skr170) Part of a little homestead museum just north of town, this well-equipped hostel has beds in sunny wooden cabins. There's a futuristic kitchen, antique dining room and outside tables and chairs for alfresco meals. Breakfast is available (Skr50) and bikes can be rented (Skr60 per day).

Länsmansgården   CAFE, INN €€
(info@lansman.com; Ulfsby; buffet lunch noon-3pm Skr99; s/d from Skr895/1190) This historic 'sheriff's house' also features in Lagerlöf's *Gösta Berling's Saga*. It's a picturesque

place for a fine lunch or restful evening in one of the romantic bedrooms, named after the book's characters. The restaurant (*dagens* lunch Skr85; evening buffet Skr150) specialises in Swedish cuisine, made using fresh local ingredients including pike, salmon, beef, reindeer and lamb. The mansion is 4km north of Sunne centre, by Rd 45 (toward Torsby).

Saffran & Vitlök   CAFE €
(Storgatan 27; www.saffranvitlok.se; salads Skr65; ⊙11am-6pm Mon-Fri, to 3pm Sat) A haven of calm beside a busy intersection, this cafe serves giant bowls of hefty salads to take away or dine in, as well as excellent coffee, sandwiches, pastries and hot dishes. It lives up to the name (*vitlök* is garlic), so just follow your nose and you'll find it.

Strandcaféet   CAFE €€
(Strandpromenaden; daily lunch special Skr99, mains Skr79-199; ⊙lunch & dinner May-Sep) In the park is this appealing beach cafe, with outdoor seating over the water and live music on some summer evenings. Look for dinner specials (like pig roast or all-you-can-eat lobster) midweek.

ⓘ Information
Banks, supermarkets and most other tourist facilities are on Storgatan.

Tourist office (☑164 00; www.sunneturism.se; Kolsnäsvägen 4; ⊙9am-9.30pm daily mid-Jun–mid-Aug, 9am-4.30pm Mon-Fri, 9am-2pm Sat & Sun mid-Aug–mid-Sep, 9am-4.30pm Mon-Fri rest of year) Located at the campsite reception building and offers internet access (Skr10 for 15 minutes).

ⓘ Getting There & Around
Värmlandstrafik Bus 302 runs to Torsby (Skr55, 45 minutes, one to three daily) and Karlstad (Skr80, 1¼ hours, one to five daily). Regional trains to Torsby and Karlstad (one to three daily) are faster than the bus, but cost the same.

Torsby
☑0560 / POP 12,414
Sleepy Torsby, deep in the forests of Värmland, is only 38km from Norway. It's the home town of Sven-Göran Eriksson, the former manager of England's national football team. The area's history and sights are linked to emigrants from Finland, who settled in western parts of Sweden in

the mid-16th century and built their own distinctive farms and villages in the forests.

⊙ Sights

TOP CHOICE Ritamäki Finngård   MUSEUM
(☑501 76; admission free; ⊙11am-6pm Jun-Aug) Known for its characteristic smokehouse, Ritamäki Finngård, 32km west of Torsby and 5km from Lekvattnet, is one of the best-preserved Finnish homesteads in the area. It was probably built in the late 17th century and was inhabited until 1964, making it the last permanently inhabited Finnish homestead in Sweden. It's surrounded by a nature reserve. Bus 310 goes to Lekvattnet but there is no public transport to Ritamäki.

Torsby
Finnkulturcentrum   CULTURAL CENTRE
(www.finnkulturcentrum.com; Rd 45; admission Skr20; ⊙11am-5pm mid-Jun–mid-Aug, 10am-4pm Tue-Fri, 10am-2pm Sat mid-Aug–mid-Jun) Torsby Finnkulturcentrum is just beyond the Info-centre towards town, and has displays describing the 17th-century Finnish settlement of the area, covering smokehouses, hunting, music and witchcraft. There's also a terrace cafe, with seats overlooking a calm lake.

Fordonsmuseum   MUSEUM
(Gräsmarksvägen 8; adult/child Skr40/free; ⊙10am-5pm Mon-Fri, noon-5pm Sat & Sun May-Sep) Next door to the Finnkulturcentrum, the Fordonsmuseum will appeal to motorheads with its collection of vintage cars, motorcycles and fire engines.

Hembygdsgården Kollsberg   MUSEUM
(☑718 61; Levgrensvägen 36; adult/child Skr20/free, guided tours Skr40; ⊙noon-5pm Jun-Aug) Hembygdsgården Kollsberg, down beside Fryken lake, is a dinky homestead museum with several old houses, including a Finnish cabin. A cafe serves coffee and waffles (Skr40) and the traditional local dish *motti med fläsk* (oat porridge with pork, Skr80).

🏃 Activities
There are a number of summer activities and tours in the area, including fishing, canoeing, white-water rafting, rock climbing, mountain biking, and beaver and elk safaris. Contact the tourist office for information.

You can also catch boat trips on the *Freya af Fryken* (p131) from Torsby.

Finnskogleden
HIKING

An easy and well-marked long-distance path that roughly follows the Norwegian border for 240km, from near Charlottenberg to Søre Osen in Norway (it passes the old Finnish homestead Ritamäki Finngård). A guide book (Skr125, from tourist offices) has text in Swedish only but all the topographical maps you'll need. The best section, Øyermoen to Röjden (or vice versa), requires one or two overnight stops. Bus 311 runs from Torsby to near the border at Röjdåfors (twice daily on weekdays), and bus 310 runs to Vittjärn (twice daily on weekdays), 6km from the border on Rd 239.

Fortum Ski Tunnel
SKIING

(www.skitunnel.se; Vasserudsvägen 11, Valberget; adult/child rental packet Skr200/130, 1hr pass Skr160/120; ⊘noon-7pm Tue-Fri, 10am-5pm Sat & Sun Jun, Jul & Dec–mid-Jan, 9am-8pm Mon-Sat, 9am-5pm Sun Aug-Nov, 3-7pm Thu & Fri, 10am-3pm Sat & Sun mid-Jan–Feb) Looking like something you might use to smash atoms is Sweden's first ski tunnel (1.3km); controlled conditions and a gentle incline make it a great workout or equipment-testing track. It also contains the world's only indoor biathlon shooting range.

Hovfjället
SKIING

(www.hovfjallet.se; day pass adult/child from Skr270/220, alpine ski hire Skr245/200; ⊘Dec–mid-Apr) For skiing outdoors, check out Hovfjället, 20km north of Torsby. There are several ski lifts and a variety of runs. The resort also offers dogsledding on weekends, plus other activities such as snowshoeing, mountain biking and wolf-viewing trips.

🛏 Sleeping & Eating

Vägsjöfors Herrgård
B&B €

(www.vagsjoforsherrgard.com; sites Skr180, dm Skr205, r per person from Skr585) This large manor house is 20km north of Torsby, by a stunning lake. Rooms are individually decorated and the decor is genteel; there are hostel beds and campsites too. Order lunch or use the guest kitchen.

Hotell Örnen
HOTEL €€

(hotell-ornen@telia.com; Östmarksvägen 4; s/d Skr740/890) Cosy Örnen is a pretty lemon-coloured place set behind a white picket fence smack-bang in the town centre. Bright white Swedish-style rooms practically vibrate with wholesomeness and folky charm.

Torsby Camping
CAMPGROUND €

(www.torsbycamping.se; Bredviken; sites Skr160, cabins from Skr400; ⊘May–mid-Sep) With its child-friendly beach, playgrounds and minigolf, this large, well-equipped lakeside campsite (5km south of town along Rd 45) is a popular family spot. There's a variety of huts and chalets for rent, including a cool 'studio' cottage with a lake-facing picture window (Skr1150).

Heidruns Bok- & Bildcafé
CAFE €

(🗹421 26; www.heidruns.se; Fensbol 39; fika from Skr28; ⊘noon-6pm mid-Jun–Aug) In summer there's live music, poetry and other entertainment at this charming cafe, run by local poet Bengt Berg; Sundays are the big day for entertainment. You can feast on books and artwork, or on excellent home-baked cakes. Heidruns is 10km north of Torsby, at Fensbol on E45.

Faktoriet
SWEDISH €

(Båthamnen; mains Skr85-125, drinks from Skr69; ⊘4-11pm Wed-Thu, 4pm-2am Fri & Sat) By far the most appealing eatery in Torsby is down at the harbour (at the far end of Sjögatan). With a patio deck over the water, this is a cool restaurant with light meals (pasta, baked potatoes, fajitas) and a popular bar.

Wienerkonditoriet
CAFE €

(Järnvägsgatan 6; coffee Skr20, pastries from Skr17; ⊘9am-6pm) This homey cafe on the main drag feels like an auntie's living room, complete with family portraits on the walls.

ℹ Information

Tourist office (🗹105 50; www.torsby.se, in Swedish; Gräsmarksvägen 12; ⊘9am-6pm Mon-Fri, 10am-3pm Sat & Sun Jun–Aug; 9am-4pm Mon-Fri Sep–mid-Jun) is in the large, grass-roofed Torsby Infocentre a couple of kilometres west of town, on Rd 45.

ℹ Getting There & Around

See p132 for travel information. There are a few buses that run north of Torsby, but generally on weekdays only.

DALARNA

Falun

🗹 023 / POP 56,044

An unlikely combination of industrial and adorable, Falun is home to the region's most important copper mine and, as a consequence, the source of the deep-red paint that renders Swedish country houses so uniformly cute. It's the main city of Dalarna, putting it within easy striking distance of some of Sweden's best attractions, and the town itself is a pretty place to roam. Falu Kopparbergsgruva (Copper Mountain Mine) is unique enough to appear on Unesco's World Heritage List. Even more compelling is the home of painter Carl Larsson, a work of art in itself and absolutely unmissable.

⊙ Sights & Activities

The Unesco World Heritage listing actually encompasses a much larger area than just the Kopparbergsgruva. The free brochure *Discover the Falun World Heritage Site* places Falun in historical context and pinpoints all the smelteries, slag heaps and mine estates within a 10km radius of the town.

Falu Kopparbergsgruva   MUSEUM

Falun's copper mine was the world's most important by the 17th century and drove many of Sweden's international aspirations during that period. These days it makes for a fascinating day out.

Tradition says a goat called Kåre first drew attention to the copper reserves, when he rolled in the earth and pranced back to the village with red horns. The first historical mention is in a document from 1288, when the Bishop of Västerås bought shares in the company. As a by-product, the mine produced the red paint that became a characteristic of Swedish houses – Falu Red is still used today. The mine finally closed in 1992.

You can go on a one-hour tour of the mine; be sure to bring warm clothing. Prices include museum entry and in high season you shouldn't have to wait more than an hour for an English tour. Between October and April, tours must be booked in advance.

If you're getting peckish, the pretty cafe **Gjuthuset**, serving coffee, sandwiches and cake, teeters on the edge of the Great Pit. Opposite the main reception is **Geschwornergården Värdshus** (lunch Skr75), which is a more stately affair and does excellent hot lunch specials.

Mining Complex   MINE

(✆78 20 30; www.falugruva.se; tours adult/child Skr190/70; ⊙noon Mon-Fri, noon & 2pm Sat & Sun) The mining complex, to the west of town at the top end of Gruvgatan, contains various sights. Most dramatic is the **Stora Stöten**

(Great Pit), a vast hole caused by a major mine collapse in the 17th century. By some miracle, the miners were on holiday that day and no one was harmed. There are lookouts around the crater edge, and numerous **mine buildings** including a 15m waterwheel and shaft-head machinery. Opening hours are complicated – check the website for details. Take bus 709.

Mine Museum   MUSEUM

(adult/child Skr50/free; ⊙10am-6pm) The mine museum contains everything you could possibly want to know about the history, administration, engineering, geology and copper production of the mine, as well as the sad story of Fat Mats the miner.

Carl Larsson-gården   MUSEUM

(www.carllarsson.se; Sundborn; admission by guided tour only, adult/child Skr120/60; ⊙10am-5pm May-Sep, 11am-5pm Mon-Fri Oct-Apr) Whatever you do, don't miss Carl Larsson-gården, home of artist Carl Larsson and his wife, Karin, in the picturesque village of Sundborn. After the couple's deaths, their early-20th-century home was preserved in its entirety by their children, but it's no gloomy memorial. Lilla Hyttnäs is a work of art, full of brightness, humour and love.

Superb colour schemes and furniture fill the house: Carl's portraits of his wife and children are everywhere, and Karin's tapestries and embroidery reveal she was as skilled an artist as her husband. Even today, the modern styles throughout the house (especially the dining room) will inspire interior decorators, and the way the family lived, suffused in art and learning, will inspire practically everyone.

Tours (45 minutes) run hourly; call in advance for the times of English tours (alternatively, borrow an English handbook and follow a Swedish tour).

If you like Larsson's work, you can see more at the **Carl Larssons Porträttsamling** (Kyrkvägen 18, Sundborn; adult/under 12yr Skr25/free, free with ticket stub from Carl Larsson-gården; ⊙11am-5pm mid-Jun–mid-Aug), where there are 12 portraits of local worthies. You might also ask at the ticket counter about temporary exhibitions in nearby galleries, which change frequently but are usually interesting.

Bus 64 (Skr36) runs frequently from Falun to Sundborn village (13km).

FREE Dalarnas Museum   MUSEUM
(www.dalarnasmuseum.se; Stigaregatan 2-4;
☺10am-6pm Tue-Fri, 10am-4pm Sat, noon-4pm
Sun & Mon May-Aug, noon-5pm Sat-Mon, 10am-
5pm Tue-Fri Sep-Apr) Dalarnas Museum is a
super introduction to Swedish folk art, music and costumes. Selma Lagerlöf's study is
preserved here, and there are ever-changing
art and craft exhibitions, including a great
regional collection of textiles.

Kristine Kyrka   CHURCH
(Stora Torget; ☺10am-6pm Jun-Aug, 10am-4pm
Sep-May) A sea of baroque blue-and-gold hits
you at Kristine Kyrka, which shows off the
riches brought to town by the 17th-century
copper trade.

Stora Kopparbergs Kyrka   CHURCH
(Kyrkbacksvägen 8; ☺10am-6pm Mon-Sat, 9am-
6pm Sun) Falun's oldest building is Stora Kopparbergs Kyrka, dating from the late 14th
century, with brick vaulting and folk-art
flowers running round the walls.

Hopptornen   TOWER
(☺10am-6pm Sun-Thu, to 11pm Fri & Sat mid-
May–mid-Aug) Hopptornen, the tower and ski
jump in the hills behind the town, has great
views; you can either walk or take a lift to
the top (Skr20).

🛌 Sleeping

Falu Fängelse Vandrarhem   HOSTEL €
(♪79 55 75; www.falufangelse.se; Villavägen 17;
dm/s Skr210/300; @) This hostel really feels
like what it is – a former prison. Dorm beds
are in cells, with heavy iron doors and thick
walls, concrete floors and steel lockers for
closets. The place is extremely friendly,
though, and common areas are spacious and
full of well-worn, denlike furniture. There's
a back deck in summer. The shower and
toilet facilities are somewhat limited, so it's
worth asking if a room with a bathroom is
available.

Scandic Hotel Lugnet Falun   HOTEL €€
(falun@scandic-hotels.com; Svärdsjögatan 51; s/d
from Skr790/940; P@☒) This large, modern
building stands out a mile with its ski-jump
design. It has heaps of facilities, including a
restaurant, a bar and even a bowling hall in
the basement. Steep summer and weekend
discounts make it a smoking deal. The hotel
is just east of the centre on Rd 80, close to
Lugnet.

Hotel Falun   HOTEL €
(Trotzgatan 16; s/d with shared shower Skr600/700;
P@) There are some good hotel choices
near the tourist office, including this place,
which has comfortable modern rooms
(cheaper rooms have private toilet, but
shared showers).

Lugnets Camping & Stugby   CAMPGROUND €
(lugnet-anl@falun.se; sites Skr185, simple 2-bed
huts Skr320, cabins Skr895; ☒) This long, thin
campsite is 2km northeast of town, in the
ski and sports area. Amenities are good: crazy golf, boules and a nearby outdoor swimming pool will keep kids amused. Take bus
705 or 713.

🍴 Eating & Drinking

TOP CHOICE Kopparhatten Café
& Restaurang   CAFE €
(Stigaregatan 2-4; kopparhatten.se; coffee Skr25,
sandwiches from Skr40, lunch buffet Skr79, mains
Skr75-150; ☺lunch & dinner) An excellent
choice is this funky, arty cafe-restaurant below Dalarnas Museum. Choose from sandwiches, soup or a good vegetarian buffet
for lunch; and light veggie, fish and meat
evening mains. There's an outside terrace
overlooking the river, and live music on Friday nights in summer.

Banken Bar & Brasserie   SWEDISH €€€
(www.bankenfalun.se; Åsgatan 41; lunch Skr175,
3-course menu Skr450; ☺lunch & dinner Mon-Sat,
until 1am Fri & Sat) Based in a former bank,
classy Banken has a splendid interior and
matching service. The menu includes a *gott
& enkelt* ('good and simple') category – featuring the likes of burgers and pasta – plus
more upmarket 'world cuisine' options, set
menus and daily lunch specials.

Bryggcaféet   CAFE €
(Fisktorget; fika Skr35; ☺10am-6pm) This fab
cafe is in a dinky little brick building that
was once the fire station. It serves good coffee and cakes, and has a large deck by the
river.

ICA   SUPERMARKET
(Falugatan 1) This place is recommended for
self-caterers, and it's centrally located.

Systembolaget   LIQUOR STORE
(Åsgatan 19) For alcohol.

ℹ Information

Most services (such as banks and supermarkets) are on or just off Stora Torget.

Library (☑833 35; Kristinegatan 15; ⊙10am-7pm Mon-Thu, to 6pm Fri, 11am-3pm Sat) Free internet access.

Tourist office (☑830 50; www.visitfalun.se; Trotzgatan 10-12; ⊙9am-7pm Mon-Fri, to 5pm Sat, 11am-4pm Sun mid-Jun–mid-Aug, 10am-6pm Mon-Fri, to 2pm Sat mid-Aug–mid-Jun) Staff can help with visitor information.

ℹ Getting There & Around

Falun isn't on the main train lines – change at Borlänge when coming from Stockholm or Mora – but there are direct trains to and from Gävle (Skr130, 1¼ hours, every two hours), or regional buses (Skr100, two hours) equally often.

Swebus Express (☑0200-21 82 18; www.swebusexpress.se) has buses on the Göteborg-Karlstad-Falun-Gävle route, and connections to buses on the Stockholm-Borlänge-Mora route.

Regional transport is run by **Dalatrafik** (☑0771-95 95 95; www.dalatrafik.se, in Swedish), which covers all corners of the county of Dalarna. Tickets cost Skr20 for trips within a zone, and Skr15 extra for each new zone. A 31-day *länskort* (county pass) costs Skr1000 and allows you to travel throughout the county; cards in smaller increments are also available. Regional bus 70 goes hourly to Rättvik (Skr50, one hour) and Mora (Skr80, 1¾ hours).

Lake Siljan Region

Typically, when you ask Swedes where in Sweden they would most like to go on holiday, they get melty-eyed and talk about Lake Siljan. It's understandable – the area combines lush green landscapes, outdoor activities, a rich tradition of arts and crafts, and some of the prettiest villages in the country.

It's the picture of tranquillity now, but 360 million years ago Lake Siljan felt Europe's largest meteor impact. Crashing through the Earth's atmosphere, the giant lump of rock hit with the force of 500 million atomic bombs, obliterating all life and creating a 75km ring-shaped crater.

The area is a very popular summer destination, with numerous outdoor festivals and attractions. Maps of Siljansleden, an excellent network of walking and cycling paths extending for more than 300km around Lake Siljan, are available from tourist offices for Skr20. Another way to enjoy the lake is by boat: in summer, M/S

Gustaf Wasa (☑070-542 10 25; www.wasanet.nu; Skr85-275) runs a complex range of lunch, dinner and sightseeing cruises from the towns of Mora, Rättvik and Leksand. Ask at any tourist office or go online for a schedule.

The big Midsummer festival Musik vid Siljan (www.musikvidsiljan.se) is held in venues around the lakeside towns in early July; look for schedules at tourist offices.

Check out the Siljan area website (www.siljan.se) for lots of good information.

LEKSAND
☑0247 / POP 15,289

Leksand's main claim to fame is its Midsummer Festival, the most popular in Sweden, in which around 20,000 spectators fill the bowl-shaped green park on the first Friday evening after 21 June to sing songs and watch costumed dancers circle the maypole. (It's also the namesake of a popular brand of hardbread.) Norsgatan is the main pedestrian mall, with shops and cafes.

◎ Sights & Activities

Look for the unusual belltower near the bridge between Norsgatan and Kyrkallén.

Munthe's Hildasholm HISTORIC BUILDING
(www.hildasholm.org; Klockaregatan 5; admission by guided tour only, tour Skr100, garden only Skr30; ⊙11am-5pm daily mid-Jun–mid-Aug, Sat & Sun mid-Aug–mid-Sep) Built by Axel Munthe (1857–1949), who served as the Swedish royal physician and wrote the best-selling memoir *The Story of San Michele*, Munthe's Hildasholm is a sumptuously decorated National Romantic–style mansion, set in beautiful gardens by the lake. Munthe built it for his second wife, an English aristocrat, in 1910–11; Munthe himself rarely visited the mansion as he spent most of his time attending to the Swedish Queen Viktoria on the island of Capri. Tours run on the hour; book ahead for tours in English.

Leksands Kyrka CHURCH
(Kyrkallén; ⊙10am-6pm Jun–mid-Aug, 10am-3.30pm rest of year) Leksands Kyrka, with its distinctive onion dome, dates from the early 13th century, but has been extensively renovated and enlarged. The church contains extravagant baroque furnishings; check the posted schedules for evening concerts in summer. Guided tours run mid-June to mid-August at 10am and 1pm Monday to Friday, 10am Saturday and 1pm Sunday.

Siljansnäs Naturum   NATURE RESERVE

(221 05; Siljansnäs, on Björkberget; www.naturumdalarna.se; admission free; 10am-4pm Tue-Sun, longer hours in summer;) Siljansnäs Naturum, 14km northwest of Leksand, has information about the meteor and local flora and fauna, with a slightly moth-eaten collection of 50 stuffed animals. Two-hour English-language guided tours of the nature reserve take place at 11am Monday and Friday. There are activities for toddlers, nature walks and films; kids can even paint their own wooden horse. The highlight is the 22m-high **viewing tower**, with stunning 360-degree views around the lake. Bus 84 runs from Leksand to Siljansnäs, then it's a 300m walk to Naturum.

Sleeping & Eating

Quick eats surround the main square, where you'll also find branches of all the main supermarket chains.

STF Vandrarhem Leksand   HOSTEL €
TOP CHOICE

(152 50; info@vandrar hemleksand.se; Parkgården, Källberet; dm Skr180, s/d Skr220/360;) It's a little out of the way (2km south of town), but this is a lovely wee hostel and Dalarna's oldest, with ultracute wooden huts built around a flowery courtyard. Bikes are available for rent (Skr70 per day). Reserve early, as it's popular with groups.

Hotell Leksand   HOTEL €€

(0247-145 70; www.hotelleksand.com; Leksandsvägen 7; s/d Skr1090/1190;) This is a small, modern and conveniently situated hotel in the heart of town. The rooms are mostly nondescript, but the people here are friendly and it's not a bad place to lay your head. Phone ahead, as the reception keeps short hours.

Siljans Konditori   BAKERY €

(Sparbanksgatan 5; sandwiches Skr39-79, buffet Skr65-85, ice cream Skr25-39; 8am-7pm Mon-Fri, 9am-5pm Sat, 11am-5pm Sun) This large and inviting bakery-cafe serves good sandwiches (on its own fresh bread) from a busy corner of Stora Torget.

Leksands Gårdcafeet   CAFE €€

(Norsgatan 19; dagens lunch Skr85, salads Skr99, foccaccia Skr80) A cute old wooden house with a front patio and back garden seating, this busy but friendly cafe serves tempting coffee and pastries as well as enormous, filling pasta salads. Order at the counter and you get a buzzer that goes off when your food is ready.

Bygatan 16   SWEDISH €€

(Bygatan 16; mains Skr125-225; dinner Mon-Sat) Bygatan is a smart place with a menu of light and main meals, including creative pasta, beef and fish dishes. The restaurant is closely linked to the local hockey team, and has a special 'hockey menu' during the playing season.

Shopping

Leksands Hemslöjd   CRAFT

(Kyrkallén 1; www.leksandshemslojd.se; 10am-6pm Mon-Sat) This shop across from the tourist information office sells high-quality textiles, knitted cloths, ceramics, and other local crafts including Dalahäst, candleholders, linens, yarn and wooden knives.

Information

Banks and supermarkets line Sparbankgatan.

Library (802 45; Kulturhuset, Kyrkallén) Across the street from the tourist office, has internet access (including wireless), regional information and art exhibitions.

Tourist office (79 61 30; leksand@siljan.se; Kyrkallén 8; 9am-7pm Mon-Fri, 10am-5pm Sat & Sun mid-Jun–mid-Aug, 10am-5pm Mon-Fri mid-Aug–mid-Jun) In the huge historic building that formerly housed the art museum.

Getting There & Around

There are a couple of direct intercity trains running every day from Stockholm to Leksand (Skr240, three hours). Bus 58 regularly connects Leksand with Tällberg (Skr35, 20 minutes), and bus 258 goes to Rättvik (Skr50, 20 to 50 minutes).

TÄLLBERG

0247 / POP 200

The main reason to visit Tällberg is that it's adorable: a whole village of precious little gingerbread houses, mostly painted Falu Red, sprinkled over a green hillside sloping toward a lake.

It knows it's cute, too – the town of 200 residents supports eight upmarket hotels and several chic boutiques. It's a tourist hot spot and an appealing place for lunch and a walk, but unless you're after a romantic countryside escape, it's perhaps better to stay in Rättvik or Leksand and visit for the afternoon.

Charm personified, **Klockargården** (www.klockargarden.com; Siljansvägen 6; s/d/ste from Skr745/845/1245;) is a collection of old

DON'T MISS

VIKING BURIAL MOUNDS AT SOLLERÖN

Just 15km from Mora is the small island settlement of Sollerön, where you'll find the largest and best-preserved Viking burial ground in Dalarna. The site includes grave fields from the Iron Age with an estimated 50 to 140 graves, plus other evidence of habitation from the Stone Age (and, naturally, a cafe serving coffee and sandwiches).

Grab a pamphlet for a self-guided tour and follow the 3km walking trail (most of it wheelchair-accessible) among the burial mounds and other features. Points of interest include the Sacrificial Well, where ancient Vikings allegedly made sacrifices to the likes of Odin and Thor. Rumour has it that the well never runs dry in summer or freezes in winter.

Though it's well off the main drag now, and about as quiet as they come, this northern section of Lake Siljan was once an important part of the iron industry and home to a vibrant farming community. Initially, everyone assumed the grave mounds were leftover from the island's days as farming country. But in 1928 a grave was discovered in one of the mounds, leading to another 10 graves being excavated, at which point locals understood the significance of their lumpy fields. Three of the swords found in the graves are now preserved at Stockholm's Museum of National Antiquities.

It's a scenic area even if you're not all that jazzed about ancient burial grounds: the cafe occupies one building in the old homestead museum, alongside a wooden Viking longship and some antique farm equipment. To get here, take bus 107 from Mora bus station (Skr25, 25 minutes, frequent departures Monday to Saturday).

timber buildings set around a grassy green courtyard, plus a newer wing built in 2004. Each unique room is decorated in a tasteful country style, all the suites have jacuzzis, and several rooms have balconies. Frequent summer craft fairs and folk concerts take place on the grounds. The restaurant has a daily lunch buffet for around Skr100; à la carte mains cost Skr145 to Skr245. Weekend and holiday packages are available.

Tällberg's oldest hotel, **Åkerblads** (www.akerblads.se; Sjögattu 2; s/d from Skr850/1630; P❄) is an elegant affair, arranged inside a beautiful collection of buildings dating from the 15th century onwards. There's a relaxation suite and a whole menu of spa treatments, garden tennis and ping-pong for entertainment. The hotel restaurant is considered one of the region's finest, with a lunch buffet and à la carte main courses nightly (*dagens* lunch Skr145, salmon and herring buffet Skr175, mains Skr195 to Skr345).

Bus 58 between Rättvik and Leksand stops in the village regularly (two to six times daily). Tällberg is also on the train line that travels around Lake Siljan; the train station is about 2km below the village proper.

RÄTTVIK
♪ 0248 / POP 10,811

Rättvik is a totally unpretentious town in an area that sometimes borders on the precious. Nonetheless, it's a very pretty place, stretching up a hillside and along the shores of Lake Siljan. There are things to do year-round, for kids and adults alike, whether you like skiing, cycling, hiking or lolling on beaches.

A full program of special events in summer includes a **folklore festival** (www.folklore.se) in late July and **Classic Car Week** (www.classiccarweek.com) in late July or early August.

⊙ Sights & Activities

Scandinavia's longest wooden pier, the impressive 628m **Långbryggan**, runs out into the lake from just behind the train station. The 13th-century church has 87 well-preserved **church stables**, the oldest dating from 1470. The pseudo-rune **memorial** beside the church commemorates the 1520s uprising of Gustav Vasa's band against the Danes – the rebellion that created modern Sweden.

Vidablick Utsiktstorn　　　　　　　　TOWER
(adult/child Skr30/5; ⊙10am-6pm Jun-Aug) An enterprising 17-year-old built Vidablick Utsiktstorn, a viewing tower about 5km southeast of town, from where there are great panoramas of the lake, a good cafe and a summer-only youth hostel (dorm beds Skr150). On your way up the tower, check out the miniature reconstruction of the village as it was at the turn of the century, made by a local carpenter in the 1930s.

FREE Hembygdsgård
Gammelgård   MUSEUM
(⊙11am-5pm mid-Jun–mid-Aug) You can get
your open-air-museum fix at Hembygdsgård
Gammelgård, 500m north of the church –
it's a 1909 collection of buildings that were
moved here during the '20s from villages
around Rättvik parish. There's a good collection of furniture painted in the local style.
The grounds are always open for exploring,
but the cafe and building interiors are open
summer-only.

FREE Kulturhuset   CULTURAL CENTRE
(Storgatan 2; ⊙11am-7pm Mon-Thu, to 3pm Fri, to
2pm Sat, 1-5pm Sun) Central Kulturhuset houses the public library, art exhibitions and a
display describing the Siljan meteor impact.
The helpful staff go above and beyond to
answer any questions you might have about
the area.

SommarRodel   EXTREME SPORTS
(www.rattviksbacken.se; 1/3 rides Skr60/150;
⊙11am-6pm or 7pm Jun-Aug, closed when rain-
ing) The 725m-long SommarRodel, a sort of
snowless bobsled chute, is lots of fun. You
hurtle down a ski hill at 56km/h, which feels
very fast so close to the ground. Now with
paintball!

Ski Slopes   SKIING
(www.rattviksbacken.se; day pass adult/child
Skr260/210) The easy ski slopes are excellent;
there are four lifts.

🛏 Sleeping
Summer accommodation in Rättvik disap-
pears fast, so it's worth booking ahead –
even for campsites. Central places to stay
are few and far between, but the STF hostel
is tops.

TOP CHOICE STF Vandrarhem   HOSTEL €
(⊉105 66; Centralgatan; s/d Skr490/560; ℗ @) A
comfortable hostel with cozy rooms in three
wooden buildings clustered around a grassy
courtyard. A quiet place with good facilities,
including a nice kitchen with a large dining/
TV room in the main building, and picnic
tables on the lawn for alfresco dining. Reception is at the Enåbadet campsite office.

Stiftsgården Rättvik   HOTEL €€
(www.stiftsgarden.org; Kyrkvägen 2; s/d from
Skr495/870) This picturesque, church-run
place is by the lake, away from the hustle
and bustle of town but is still within easy

walking distance and near footpaths and
outdoor activities. Rooms are simple but
pleasant; breakfast is included, and lunch
(Skr85) and dinner (Skr100) are available.
Canoes and cycles can be hired.

Enåbadet   CAMPGROUND €
(⊉0248-561 00; www.enabadet.se; Furudalsvägen
1; sites Skr200, cabins from Skr500) A large, bustling campsite by the river off Centralgatan
(1km from the train station), behind the STF
hostel, this area includes a *fäbod* (summer
livestock farm) and is built to echo the traditional, rustic look of old farmhouse buildings. The walking trail Siljansleden passes
through the site.

Siljansbadet Camping   CAMPGROUND €
(⊉0248-561 18; www.siljansbadet.com; sites
Skr200, 4-bed cabins from Skr450; ⊙May-Oct)
Near the train station, this shady, woodsy
campsite is on the lake shore and boasts its
own Blue Flag beach.

Hotell Vidablick   HOTEL €€
(vidablick@hantverksbyn.se; Faluvägen; s/d from
Skr650/1100, 4-6 bed condo Skr900) Vidablick is
an excellent choice, with rustic hotel accommodation in grass-roofed huts, some with
lake views. The hotel is behind the OKQ8
petrol station on the road to Leksand, about
3km south of town. The attached restaurant
(open May to August; *dagens* lunch Skr80;
coffee and cakes Skr35) has free wi-fi, a great
view from its outdoor tables, and dance
nights on Thursday.

Jöns-Andersgården   B&B €€€
(www.jonsandersgarden.se; Bygatan 4; d with
shared/private bathroom Skr1150/1435, ste
Skr1850; ⊙mid-Apr–mid-Oct; ℗) Beds here are
in traditional wooden huts dating from the
15th century, way up on the hill with superb
views. Rooms are all in tip-top shape with
modern interiors, and there's one suite that
has its own sauna. If you don't have transport the owners will pick you up from the
train station by arrangement, and breakfast
is included in the price. Take bus 74.

🍴 Eating & Drinking
Fricks Konditori   CAFE €
(Stora Torget; fika Skr30, sandwiches from Skr35)
An old-fashioned bakery-cafe with a casual,
neighbourhoody feel, Fricks offers sandwiches, quiches and salads but specialises
in decadent cakes and pastries. It's opposite the train station and is a local gossip
hang-out.

Jöns-Andersgården
SWEDISH, ITALIAN €€

(www.jonsandersgarden.se; Bygatan 4; mains Skr155-229; ☺Thu-Sun May-Sep) If you can stir your stumps and make it up the hill, you'll find this rather sweet restaurant tucked at the top, attached to the hotel of the same. Dishes such as lemony chicken with gremolata potatoes, and tagliatelle with truffle oil, bring a taste of Italy to this very Swedish establishment. Take bus 74.

Systembolaget
LIQUOR STORE

(Storgatan) There's a Systembolaget on the main drag.

☆ Entertainment

Dalhalla
CONCERT VENUE

(☏79 79 50; www.dalhalla.se) Dalhalla, an old limestone quarry 7km north of Rättvik, is used as an open-air theatre and concert venue in summer; the acoustics are incredible and the setting is stunning. Check online for a schedule of shows and ticket information.

❶ Information

Rättvik's facilities include banks and supermarkets on Storgatan.

Library (☏701 95; Storgatan 2) Offers internet access.

Tourist office (☏79 72 10; rattvik@siljan.se; Riksvägen 40; ☺10am-7pm Mon-Fri, to 5pm Sat & Sun mid-Jun–mid-Aug, 10am-5pm Mon-Fri mid-Aug–mid-Jun) Located at the train station, it has info for the entire Siljan region.

❶ Getting There & Around

Buses depart from outside the train station. Dalatrafik's bus 70 runs regularly between Falun, Rättvik and Mora. A couple of direct intercity trains per day from Stockholm (Skr265, 3½ hours) stop at Rättvik (otherwise you have to change at Borlänge). There are local trains every couple of hours between Rättvik and Mora (Skr55, 25 minutes).

MORA

☏0250 / POP 20,153

Mora is spliced with Sweden's historic soul. Legend has it that in 1520 Gustav Vasa arrived here in a last-ditch attempt to start a rebellion against the Danish regime. The people of Mora weren't interested, and Gustav was forced to put on his skis and flee for the border. After he left, the town reconsidered and two yeomen, Engelbrekt and Lars, volunteered to follow Gustav's tracks, finally overtaking him in Sälen and changing Swedish history.

Today the world's biggest cross-country ski race, Vasaloppet, which ends in Mora, commemorates this epic chase, and involves 90km of gruelling Nordic skiing. Around 15,000 people take part on the first Sunday in March. In summer, you can walk the route on the 90km Vasaloppsleden.

◉ Sights & Activities

Vasaloppsmuseet
MUSEUM

(www.vasaloppet.se; Vasagatan; adult/child Skr40/15; ☺10am-5pm daily mid-Jun–mid-Sep, 10am-5pm Mon-Fri mid-Sep–mid-Jun) Even if you have no interest in skiing, you may be pleasantly surprised by the excellent Vasaloppsmuseet, which really communicates the passion behind the world's largest cross-country skiing event. There's some fantastic crackly black-and-white film of the first race, a display about nine-times winner and hardy old boy Nils 'Mora-Nisse' Karlsson, and an exhibit of prizes. Outside the museum is the race finish line, a favourite place for holiday snaps.

Zornmuseet
MUSEUM

(www.zorn.se; Vasagatan 36; adult/child Skr60/free; ☺9am-5pm Mon-Sat, 11am-5pm Sun mid-May–mid-Sep, noon-5pm Mon-Sat, 1-5pm Sun mid-Sep–mid-May) Zornmuseet displays many of the best-loved portraits and characteristic nudes of the Mora painter Anders Zorn (1860–1920), one of Sweden's most renowned artists. His naturalistic depictions of Swedish life and countryside are shown here, as is the Zorn family silver collection.

Zorngården
MUSEUM

(Vasagatan 36; admission by tour adult/child Skr90/20; ☺10am-4pm Mon-Sat, 11am-4pm Sun mid-May–mid-Sep, noon-3pm Mon-Sat, 1-4pm Sun mid-Sep–mid-May) Next door, the Zorn family house Zorngården is an excellent example of a wealthy artist's house and reflects Zorn's National Romantic aspirations (check out the Viking-influenced hall and entryway). Access to the house is by guided tour (every 15 minutes in summer; phone ahead for English tours).

🛌 Sleeping

TOP CHOICE / Moraparken
CAMPGROUND, HOTEL €€

(moraparken@mora.se; tent Skr120, 2-/4-bed cabins from Skr330/600, hotel s/d Skr995/1295; **P @**) This extra-fancy campsite and hotel are combined in a great waterside spot, 400m northwest of the church. There's a swimming beach, laundry, kitchen, minigolf and more. A hodgepodge of camping cabins are well-equipped and full of rustic

THE DALA HORSE

What do Bill Clinton, Elvis Presley and Bob Hope have in common? They've all received a Swedish Dalahäst as a gift. These iconic, carved wooden horses, painted in bright colours and decorated with folk-art flowers, represent to many people the essence of Sweden.

The first written reference to a Dalahäst comes from the 17th century, when the bishop of Västerås denounced such horrors as 'decks of cards, dice, flutes, dolls, wooden horses, lovers' ballads, impudent paintings', but it's quite likely they were being carved much earlier. Sitting by the fireside and whittling wood was a common pastime, and the horse was a natural subject – a workmate, friend and symbol of strength. The painted form that is so common today appeared at the World Exhibition in New York in 1939 and has been a favourite souvenir for travellers to Sweden ever since.

The best-known Dala horses come from Nusnäs, about 10km southeast of Mora. The two biggest workshops are Nils Olsson Hemslöjd (372 00; www.nohemslojd.se; 8am-6pm Mon-Fri, 9am-5pm Sat & Sun mid-Jun–mid-Aug; 8am-5pm Mon-Fri, 10am-2pm Sat mid-Aug-mid-Jun) and Grannas A Olsson Hemslöjd (372 50; www.grannas.com; 9am-6pm Mon-Fri, 9am-4pm Sat & Sun mid-Jun–mid-Aug; 9am-5pm Mon-Fri, 10am-1pm Sat mid-Aug–mid-Jun), where you can watch the carving and painting, then buy up big at the souvenir outlets. Wooden horse sizes stretch from 3cm high (Skr70) to 50cm high (around Skr3300).

Public transport to Nusnäs isn't great: bus 108 runs frequently from Mora but only Monday to Friday.

charm. The hotel rooms (all ground floor in the main building) have wooden floors and a sleek, modern look. The Vasaloppet track and Siljansleden pass through the grounds, and you can hire canoes to splash about on the pond.

Målkull Ann's B&B & Vandrarhem
HOSTEL, B&B €€

(381 96; www.maalkullann.se; Vasagatan 19; hostel dm Skr170, s/d Skr320/500, B&B s/d Skr600/960, pensionat r from Skr720; P@) Housed in several buildings near the Vasaloppsmuseet, this comfortable place has a good range of options. There are cosy B&B rooms with cheerful countrified decor (tariffs include breakfast) and there's the STF youth hostel (at Fredsgatan 6) for just the basics. There's also one suite with a view over the finish line of the Vasaloppet path (Skr960). Guests can book time in the sauna, there are bikes for hire (Skr70 per day), and there's a computer with internet access (Skr20). Reservations are recommended.

Mora Hotell & Spa
HOTEL €€

(www.morahotell.se; Strandgatan 12; s/d from Skr1028/1248; P@) There's been a hotel here since 1830, although the current version is as modern as it gets, with all the facilities you'd expect from a big chain – plus personality. Rooms combine clean lines, wooden floors and earthy tones with bright folk-art accents. Head to the spa for steam rooms, jacuzzis, massage and body treatments.

✕ Eating

For eats, head to Kyrkogatan, the pedestrianised shopping street in the town centre; there aren't a wealth of options to be found, but between bar snacks and substantial cafe fare you're sure to find something. For self-caterers there are also several supermarkets here.

Mora Kaffestuga
CAFE €

(Kyrkogatan 8; meals Skr35-85) For a quick lunch – such as your basic salads, quiches and sandwiches – this popular, stylish little coffee shop has a grassy garden out back.

Helmers Konditori
CAFE €

(Kyrkogatan 10; meals Skr35-75) Right next door to Mora Kaffestuga is another recommended bakery-cafe, drawing a slightly less fashion-forward crowd with plenty of homemade bread, sandwiches and cakes.

ℹ Information

Library (267 79; Köpmangatan) Free internet access.

Tourist office (59 20 20; Strandgatan 14; mora@siljan.se; 10am-5pm Mon-Fri, 10am-2pm Sat year-round, closed Mon mid-Sep–mid-Nov) The tourist office is located in the large yellow house off E-45 near the lakeside.

ℹ Getting There & Around

The Mora-Siljan Airport is 6km southwest of town on the Malung road. **Nextjet** (www.nextjet. se) has two to three flights to Stockholm-Arlanda on weekdays and one on Sunday (50 minutes).

All Dalatrafik buses use the bus station at Moragatan 23. Bus 70 runs to Rättvik and Falun, and buses 103, 104, 105 and 245 run to Orsa. Once or twice daily, bus 170 goes to Älvdalen, Särna, Idre and Grövelsjön, near the Norwegian border.

Mora is the terminus for **SJ** (☎0771-75 75 75; www.sj.se) trains and the southern terminus of Inlandsbanan (Inland Railway), which runs north to Gällivare (mid-June to mid-August). The main train station is about 1km east of town. The more central Mora Strand is a platform station in town, but not all trains stop there, so check the timetable. When travelling to Östersund, you can choose between Inlandsbanan (Skr395, 6¼ hours, one daily, mid-June to August only) or bus 45 (Skr250, 5¼ hours, four daily). For more information on the Inlandsbanan, see p270.

Hire a car in Mora to see the best of the region, especially northwest Dalarna; for smaller budget models try **OKQ8** (☎139 58; Vasagatan 1). You can rent bikes at **Intersport** (☎59 39 39; Kyrkogatan 7).

GRÖNKLITT BJÖRNPARK

Fat-bottomed roly-poly bear cubs are the star attraction at **Grönklitt Björnpark** (www.orsagronklitt.se; family/ adult/child Skr560/210/140; ⊙10am-6pm mid-Jun-Aug, 10am-3pm Sep–mid-Jun), a wildlife reserve 16km from Orsa. Even if there are no cubs around during your visit, there's plenty to see: lynx, wolves, red foxes, wolverines, and a new snow leopard. The animals have a lot of space and natural surroundings, which is ideal for them, but it means there's plenty of room to hide, so you may not see the more skittish creatures. For the closest views, follow the posted feeding schedule. Summer activities such as fishing, canoeing and elk or beaver safaris can also be booked at the park, and on certain mornings you can do yoga on 'tiger hill' (check online for schedules). Plans are underway to expand the park to nearly twice its current size. Bus 118 runs from Mora to Grönklitt, via Orsa (twice daily weekdays, once on Sunday).

ORSA & GRÖNKLITT

☎0250 / POP 7000

Orsa, 16km north of Mora, is a natural stopping point on the way to the area's biggest attraction, the humongous bear park further north in Grönklitt. In winter there's a **ski area** (day ski pass adult/child Skr285/235; ⊙Dec-Mar) at Grönklitt.

Orsa Camping (☎462 00; www.orsagronklitt. se; Orsa; sites from Skr150, cabins per week from Skr5400;) is a big campsite beautifully situated on the shores of the lake in Orsa. Rates vary depending on length of stay. It's particularly suitable for families, with several playgrounds, a waterslide, canoe hire, minigolf and a beach to keep the kids happy.

There's a **tourist office** (☎55 25 50; orsa@ siljan.se; Dalagatan 1; ⊙10am-4pm Mon-Fri, to 2pm Sat mid-Jun–mid-Aug; to 5pm Mon-Fri mid-Aug– mid-Jun) in Orsa, with a bank about three blocks down Dalagatan and a grocery and Systembolaget both nearby.

Buses 103 and 104 run regularly between Mora and Orsa.

Sälen & Around

☎0280 / POP 400

A split-personality village, Sälen transforms itself completely from a quiet fishing paradise in summer into one of Sweden's largest and poshest ski resorts in winter. It's a tiny spot in the wilds of Dalarna, and in addition to its seven ski areas it's a good base for all kinds of outdoor activities, including canoeing, horse riding and wildlife safaris (ask at the tourist office).

🏃 Activities

The **ski areas**, with chalets, pubs and nightclubs, are strung out for 20km along the road running through the steep-flanked mountains west of Sälen. There are over 100 lifts, pistes of all degrees and guaranteed snow from 15 November to mid-April. For details visit www.skistar.com. About 45km north of Sälen, cheaper and quieter skiing is available at **Näsfjället**.

In summer, the ski hills convert to **mountain-bike parks**; the ski area at **Lindvallen** (☎0771-84 00 00) has a whole summer season built around the sport, and you can rent helmets and gear at the lift or via the tourist office. The bike park is open Thursday to Sunday from mid-June through August.

There's some good **hiking** in summer, mainly north of the road. Buy map (Skr20) of the southern section of Kungsleden (p308) at the tourist office.

🛏 Sleeping & Eating

Winter visitors should contact their travel agent or the tourist office for accommodation, or **SkiStar** (📞0771-84 00 00; www.skistar .com) for packages.

Kläppen HOTEL €€
(📞96 200; 6-bed condo in summer from Skr485) Some of the area's most luxurious resorts become very affordable in the summer; condos at Kläppen, for instance, are a smoking deal in July and August, when the price of an average hostel room fetches you a fully equipped apartment with kitchenette, patio, jacuzzi and pool access. Most resorts can also book guided canoe tours (adult/child from Skr280/220) and other activities in the area.

STF Vandrarhem Sälens HOSTEL €
(📞820 40; info@salensvandrarhem.se; Gräsheden; dm/s Skr170/290) This rustic hostel 27km north of Sälen is a fantastic hideaway. It's based in a peaceful nature reserve at Gräsheden (near Näsfjället), with some great walks nearby and the southern section of Kungsleden passing 2km from the hostel. Breakfast is available for Skr55 (order in advance).

Bullans CAFE €
(Centrumhuset; coffee Skr22, dagens rätt Skr85; ⊗8am-6pm Mon-Fri, 9am-3pm Sat & Sun) This surprisingly chic cafe is located inside the shopping centre (which also doubles as the town centre).

ℹ Information

Head first to the Centrumhuset complex, where you'll find a bank, doctor, pharmacy, Systembolaget and most other facilities, including the **tourist office** (📞187 00; info@salen.se; Centrumhuset; ⊗9am-6pm Mon-Thu, 10am-6pm Fri, 9am-3pm Sat & Sun Jun-Aug & Dec-Apr; 9am-6pm Mon-Fri, 10am-2pm Sat May & Sep-Nov). Opposite the complex are supermarkets and stores where you can rent ski gear during winter, and inline skates, boats and canoes in summer.

ℹ Getting There & Around

Bus 95 runs all the way from the ski area to Mora via Sälen, once daily in the ski season (otherwise you have to change buses at Lima). In winter, jump on the ski bus, which tours around the ski area.

Idre & Grövelsjön
📞0253

Though part of the Swedish heartland, Idre and its surrounding wilderness feel utterly remote – the rugged landscape looks nothing like the rest of Dalarna. The skiing and hiking here are excellent.

Idre Fjäll ski centre (📞410 00; www.idrefjall. se; day lift passes adult/child Skr365/295; ⊗Nov-Apr), 9km east of Idre, has three chairlifts, 29 ski-tows and 42 downhill runs – including 11 black runs and 60km of prepared cross-country tracks.

The **tourist office** (📞200 00; info@idreturism .se; Framgårdsvägen 1; ⊗10am-6pm daily mid-Jun-Aug, 8am-5pm Mon-Fri Sep-May) has brochures, hiking advice and internet access (Skr20 for 15 minutes). Staff can book accommodation and arrange activities such as dogsledding, skiing, hiking, canyoning, rock climbing, boat trips, elk and beaver safaris, horse riding, rafting and canoeing.

Grövelsjön, 38km northwest of Idre and close to the Norwegian border, lies on the edge of the wild 690-sq-km **Långfjällets Nature Reserve**, noted for its lichen-covered heaths, moraine heaps and ancient forests. Reindeer from Sweden's southernmost Sami community wander throughout the area.

Sörälvens Fiske Camping (www.soralven-camping.com; Västanå 519; sites/ cabins Skr190/550) has good fishing-themed shared facilities with well-maintained four-bed cabins in a riverside setting. It's just out of Idre, 2.5km towards Grövelsjön, and well signposted.

Excellent **STF Fjällstation Grövelsjön** (📞59 68 80; grovelsjon@stfturist.se; 2-/4-bed r Skr590/1160; ⊗Feb-Apr & mid-Jun–Sep) in Grövelsjön has lots of facilities, including a kitchen, a spa, a shop and outdoor gear hire. The restaurant serves breakfast, lunch and dinner; ask about half and full board.

At the north edge of town on the main drag is the appealing **Restaurang Njalla** (Byvägen 30; mains Skr85-265; ⊗10am-3pm Mon-Sat), serving traditional Sami cuisine. Fill up on a hearty reindeer burger or try the *renskavspanna*, a plate of sliced reindeer meat with crispy fried potatoes and lingonberry jam. Or opt for a three-meat sampler (Skr95).

Dalatrafik bus 170 travels on a route between Mora, Idre and Grövelsjön (2¼ hours from Mora to Idre, 3¾ hours to Grövelsjön). There are three services to Grövelsjön on weekdays, and one or two on weekends.

Göteborg & the Southwest

Includes »

Best Places to Eat

» Magnus & Magnus (p156)

» Fond (p157)

» Feskekörka (p158)

» Magasinet Härön (p166)

» Restaurang Sjöboden (p177)

Best Places to Stay

» Utpost Hållö (p169)

» Vanilj Hotell (p154)

» Hotel Flora (p155)

» Hotell Gästis (p182)

» Salt & Sill floating hotel (p166)

Why Go?

It's not surprising that Sweden's southwest, with its five different *landskap* (regions), has a knack for diversity.

Heading the cast is Sweden's 'second city' of Göteborg and its kicking bars, cafes, museums and theme-park thrills. Just south, the Halland coast is home to sandy Blue Flag beaches and Sweden's top windsurfing. The Västergötland region is low-key and eclectic: don't miss Trollhättan, Sweden's film-production capital, or the fairy-tale Läckö Slott. Threading its way across it all is the peaceful Göta Canal.

North of Göteborg lies the beautiful Bohuslän coastline, a marvel of electric blue waters, granite islands and sparkling red-and-white fishing villages. Behind it, cocoa-coloured cliffs frame luridly green valleys, while mysterious Bronze Age rock carvings intensify the region's enigmatic air.

Further inland, Dalsland evokes a Swedish Twin Peaks with its brooding, watery landscape of silent lakes and thick, dark forests. Europe's third-largest lake, Vänern, is a canoeist's paradise.

When to Go

Göteborg

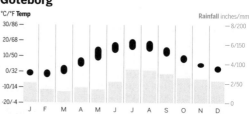

Jul & Aug Sailboat-loving Swedes beeline to Bohuslän. Gote-börg festivals run back to back.

May & Sep Ideal time for avoiding summer crowds. Pack a raincoat or windcheater.

Dec & Jan Inland lakes and canals freeze over, perfect skating and ice-fishing conditions.

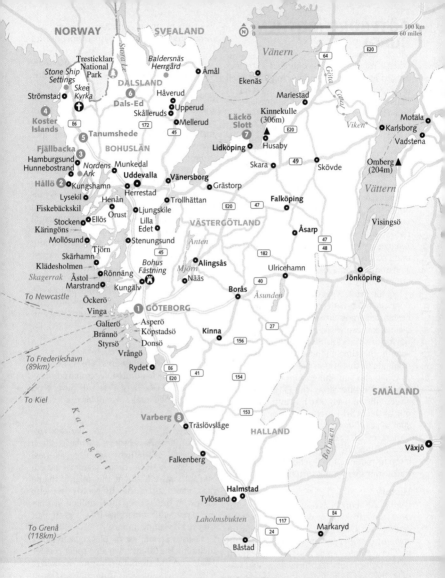

Göteborg & the Southwest Highlights

① Plummet down scary roller coasters, take in counterculture art and be surprised by cutting-edge Swedish home cooking in **Göteborg** (p146)

② Feast on shrimp and archipelago views on the tiny island of **Hållö** (p168), a short ferry trip from Smögen (p168)

③ Be charmed by **Fjällbacka** (p169), Ingrid Bergman's favourite summer haunt

④ Pedal (or splash) your way around the dazzling **Koster Islands** (p171)

⑤ Decode mystic Bronze Age artwork at the Unesco World Heritage Site in **Tanumshede** (p165), Bohuslän

⑥ Glide across silent lakes and international borders from secluded **Dals-Ed** (p172)

⑦ Listen to opera staged on the broad lawns of **Läckö Slott** (p176), north of Lidköping

⑧ Surf at Apelviken and relax in a vintage Russian bathhouse in **Varberg** (p181)

GÖTEBORG (GOTHEN-BURG)

♪031 / POP 500.085

Often caught in Stockholm's shadow, gregarious Göteborg socks a mighty punch of its own. Some of the country's finest talent hails from its streets, including music icons José González and Soundtrack of Our Lives. Ornate architecture lines its tram-rattled streets, grit-hip cafes hum with bonhomie, and must-sees include Scandinavia's amusement park heavyweight, Liseberg.

From the Centralstationen at the northern end of town, shop-lined Östra Hamngatan leads southeast across one of Göteborg's few 17th-century canals, through a verdant green Kungsparken (King's Park) to the city's 'Champs Élysées'. The shop-lined 'Avenyn' culminates at the dramatic (and once scandalising) Poseidon fountain and Konstmuseet, one of many fine museums around town.

To the west, Vasastan, Haga and Linné districts buzz with creativity. Fashionistas design fair-trade threads, artists collaborate over mean espressos and street artists sex up forlorn facades. Stockholm may represent the 'big time', but many of the best ideas originate in this grassroots town.

When the sun shines, hop on a boat for a blissful cruise along the Göta älv (Göta river). Alternatively, catch a tram and head out to the nearby archipelago for a mellow spot of island-hopping.

Best of all, Göteborg is comparatively cheaper than its east-coast rival, making it a top introduction to Sweden that shouldn't make your piggy bank turn up its trotters.

History

Gamla Älvsborg fortress, standing guard over the river 3km downstream of the centre, is Göteborg's oldest significant structure, with portions dating back to medieval times. It was a key strategic point in the 17th-century territorial wars, and was held by Denmark for seven years before being yielded to Sweden in 1619. Two years later the Swedes founded Göteborg.

The Dutch played an important part in shaping the fledgling city. Still fearful of Danish attack, the Swedes employed Dutch experts to construct a defensive canal system in the centre. The workers lived in what is now the revitalised Haga area: around a fifth of the original buildings are still standing. Most of Göteborg's oldest wooden buildings

went up in smoke long ago – the city was devastated by no fewer than nine major fires between 1669 and 1804.

Once Sweden had annexed Skåne in 1658, Göteborg expanded as a trading centre. Boom-time came in the 18th century, when merchant companies like the Swedish East India Company made huge amounts of wealth. Look around and you'll notice the many grandiose buildings built using that period's profits.

From the 19th century, shipbuilding was a major part of the city's economy, until the industry totally collapsed in the 1980s. The former shipyards and much of the heavy industry (including Volvo) are on the northern island of Hisingen across the monumental bridge Älvsborgsbron, southwest of the city. Volvo's first car wheeled out of Göteborg in 1927. It's now one of Sweden's largest companies (although it was taken over by Ford in 1999), and it's estimated that a quarter of the city relies on the company in some way. Today Göteborg is Sweden's most important industrial and commercial city and Scandinavia's busiest port.

◎ Sights

After Liseberg, museums are Göteborg's strongest asset: admission to most is covered by the Göteborg Pass. All have good cafes attached and several have specialist shops.

Liseberg AMUSEMENT PARK
(☑40 01 00; www.liseberg.se; adult/under 110cm Skr90/free; ⊗11am-11pm most days Jun–mid-Aug, 3-9pm or 10pm during Christmas period) Scream yourself silly at this mighty theme park, southeast of the city centre. Sweden's largest, it draws over three million visitors every year, and sometimes it feels as though they're all visiting at once!

There's a number of blockbuster rides, including the 90km/h wooden roller coaster Balder or the stomach-churning Kanonen, where you're blasted from 0 to 75km/h in under two seconds. Most recently, the Liseberg Tower has been transformed into the mind-numbing AtmosFear, Europe's tallest free-fall attraction. Enjoy the views during the 90-second ride to the top, and wish you hadn't during the three-second, 116m free fall back down. Softer options include carousels and fairy-tale castles, as well as summertime shows and concerts.

Each ride costs between one and four coupons (Skr20 each) per go, but it probably makes sense to buy a pass (one/two days Skr310/430). The Göteborg Pass gets you into the park for free, but you'll still need coupons for the rides and games. Opening hours are complex – check the website. To get there, take tram 4 or 5, and enter from Örgrytevägen or Getebergsled.

Stadsmuseum   MUSEUM

(www.stadsmuseum.goteborg.se; Östindiska huset, Norra Hamngatan 12; adult/under 25yr Skr40/ free; ☉10am-5pm Tue-Sun, to 8pm Wed) You'll find the remains of the *Äskekärrkeppet*, Sweden's only original Viking vessel, at Stadsmuseum, alongside silver treasure troves, weaponry and bling from the same period. Other highlights include exhibits on Göteborg's history and an impressive booty of East Indian porcelain (the museum is located in the 18th-century former HQ of the Swedish East India Company).

Röda Sten   ARTS CENTRE

(www.rodasten.com; Röda Sten 1; adult/under 21yr Skr40/free; ☉noon-5pm Tue-Sun, to 7pm Wed) Occupying a defunct, graffitied power station beside the giant Älvsborgsbron, Röda Sten is one of Sweden's coolest art centres. Its four gritty floors are home to any number of temporary exhibitions, ranging from edgy Swedish photography to New York sound installations. There's an indie-style cafe with summertime riverside seating, weekly live music and club nights, as well as offbeat one-offs like punk bike races, boxing matches and stand-up comedy. To get there, take tram 3 or 9 to Vagnhallen Majorna, walk towards Klippan (p153), continue under Älvsborgsbron and look for the brown-brick building.

Beside Röda Sten, check out work-in-progress the Thing, a communal 'sculpture' in the vein of Lars Vilks' *Nimis* (p215). On weekends, families head here with hammers and nails to further its evolution.

Konstmuseet   MUSEUM

(www.konstmuseum.goteborg.se; Götaplatsen; adult/under 25yr Skr40/free; ☉11am-6pm Tue & Thu, to 9pm Wed, to 5pm Fri-Sun) Göteborg's premier art collection awaits at Konstmuseet, with works by the French Impressionists, Rubens, Van Gogh, Rembrandt and Picasso, as well as Scandinavian masters such as Bruno Liljefors, Edvard Munch, Anders Zorn and Carl Larsson.

Other highlights include a superb sculpture hall, the Hasselblad Center photographic collection, and temporary exhibitions showcasing next-gen Nordic art.

ℹ GÖTEBORG PASS

The brilliant Göteborg Pass discount card is well worth bagging, even if all you're planning to do is park in Göteborg (home to Sweden's priciest street parking and most dedicated traffic wardens). Other perks include free or reduced admission to a bundle of attractions (including Liseberg and the museums), plus free city sightseeing tours and travel by public transport within the region.

The card costs Skr285/175 per adult/child for 24 hours or Skr395/275 for 48 hours. It's available at tourist offices, hotels, Pressbyrån newsagencies and online (usually at a discount) at www.goteborg.com.

Göteborgspaketet is an accommodation package offered at various hotels, with prices starting at Skr645 per person per night in a double room. It includes the Göteborg Pass for the number of nights you stay. You can book the package in advance over the internet or telephone the tourist office on ☎60 66 96. More expensive packages include theatre or concert tickets, casino passes, spa visits etc.

Outside, Götaplatsen is dominated by the bronze Poseidon fountain, infamous for scandalising locals upon its unveiling in 1931. This 7m-high colossus originally had private parts most men could only wish for. Alas it was all too much for Göteborg's strait-laced citizens, who forced poor Poseidon to undergo drastic reduction surgery.

Feskekörka   MARKET

(Fish Church; www.feskekörka.se; Rosenlundsgatan; ☉9am-5pm Tue-Thu, to 6pm Fri, 10am-3pm Sat) The tummy-rumbling Feskekörka is a curious-looking fish market shaped like a church. It is actually consecrated as one as well, so you may catch a bride and groom posing alongside the shellfish.

Maritiman   MUSEUM

(www.maritiman.se; Packhusplatsen 12; adult/5-15yr Skr90/50; ☉11am-6pm May-Sep, to 4pm Apr & Oct) Near the opera house, the world's largest floating ship museum is made up of 20 historical crafts, including fishing boats, a light vessel and a firefighter, all linked by walkways. Shinny down into the 69m-long

Göteborg

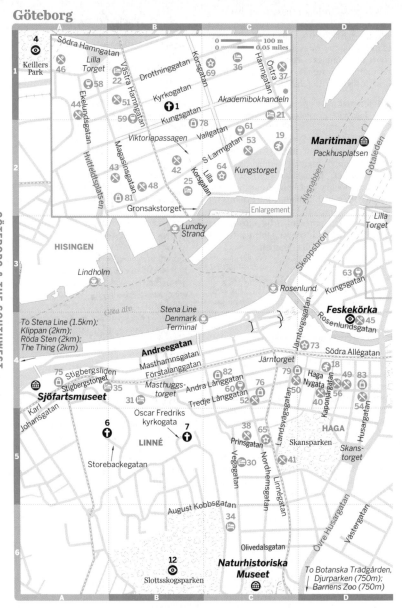

Maritiman
Packhusplatsen

Lilla Torget

Feskekörka

Sjöfartsmuseet

HISINGEN

Lindholm

Lundby Strand

Rosenlund

Stena Line Denmark Terminal

To Stena Line (1.5km); Klippan (2km); Röda Sten (2km); The Thing (2km)

Andreegatan

Masthamnsgatan
Förstalanggatan

Stigbergsliden
Stigbergstorget

Masthuggs-torget

Andra Långgatan
Tredje Långgatan

Järntorget

Haga Nygata

HAGA

Skansparken

Skanstorget

Oscar Fredriks kyrkogata

LINNÉ

Storebackegatan

Prinsgatan

August Kobbsgatan

Olivedalsgatan

Naturhistoriska Museet

Slottsskogsparken

To Botanska Trädgården, Djurparken (750m); Barnens Zoo (750m)

submarine *Nordkaparen* for a throat-tightening glimpse into underwater warfare. Another highlight is the labyrinthine 121m-long destroyer *Småland,* which saw service from 1952 to 1979. Inside, hunched figures listen to crackling radio messages, and the bunks look just-slept-in – you half expect to meet uniformed sailors in the dim, twisting passages...

Allow a couple of hours to explore.

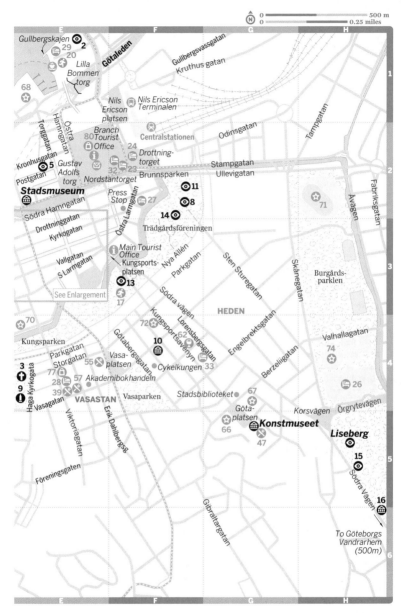

Sjöfartsmuseet MUSEUM

(www.sjofartsmuseum.goteborg.se; Karl Johansgatan 1-3; adult/under 25yr Skr40/free; ⊙10am-5pm Tue-Sun, to 8pm Wed) The main museum of maritime history is Sjöfartsmuseet, by Stigbergstorget about 2km west of the city centre. Tram 3, 9 or 11 will get you there. The collection includes model ships, cannons, a ship's medical room and a large collection of figureheads, such as the vicious-looking Vinthunden from the frigate with the same name. The attached **aquarium** (included in

Göteborg

the entry fee) wriggles with Nordic marine life. Outside, the **Sjömanstornet** (Mariner's Tower), topped by a statue of a grieving woman, commemorates Swedish sailors killed in WWI.

Naturhistoriska Museet MUSEUM

(www.gnm.se; Slottsskogsparken; adult/under 25yr Skr40/free; ⊙11am-5pm Tue-Sun) The Natural History Museum contains the world's only stuffed blue whale. In the lead-up to Christmas, visitors are occasionally allowed to step inside its mouth for that Jonah feeling. If slightly dated, this is an impressive natural-history museum, with an overall collection spanning 10 million specimens of wildlife from around the world. To get there, take tram 1 or 6.

Universeum MUSEUM

(www.universeum.se; Södra Vägen 50; adult/3-16yr/ family Skr160/99/475; ⊙10am-8pm late Jun–Aug, to 6pm Sep–late Jun) The spectacular Universeum is a top spot for families and nature fiends. A funicular takes you to the top of an indoor mountain, from where you follow the course of a Scandinavian stream down through rivers and lakes to the sea – shark tunnel ahoy! Things take a tropical turn in the absorbing rainforest: birds and butterflies flitter, while more-gruesome denizens dwell in Piranha River, Caiman Creek, Anaconda Swamp and Stingray Lagoon. When you're done, go button crazy with the fantastically fun, hands-on science exhibitions, where themes range from nanotechnology and space travel to mixing music.

Röhsska Museet MUSEUM

(www.designmuseum.se; Vasagatan 37-39; adult/ under 25yr Skr40/free; ⊙noon-8pm Tue, noon-5pm Wed-Fri, 11am-5pm Sat & Sun) Refreshing Röhsska Museet is Sweden's only art and design museum. Exhibitions cleverly contrast the classic and the cutting edge, whether it's Josef Frank and Bruno Mathsson furniture or 18th-century porcelain and Scandi-cool coat-stands. Eastern treasures include Chinese sculptures and Japanese theatre masks, while the museum's burgeoning fashion collection spans haute couture to '80s politicised T-shirts. Temporary exhibitions often favour the offbeat – cocktail gowns and accessories or 'conversation pieces'.

Varldskulturmuseet   MUSEUM

(Museum of World Culture; www.varldskulturmuseet.se; Södra Vägen 54; adult/under 21yr Skr40/free; ☺noon-5pm Tue & Fri-Sun, to 9pm Wed & Thu) In a striking building by London-based architects Cécile Brisac and Edgar Gonzalez, the enlightened Varldskulturmuseet sees ethnography, art and global politics collide in immersive multimedia exhibitions. Recent themes have included exhibits on threats to human existence and what makes people travel.

Nya Älvsborgs Fästning   CASTLE

At the mouth of the Göta älv, squat red **Elfsborgs Fortress** has had a gripping history. Built in the 17th century to defend the young city from Danish attack, it saw action again in the early 18th century during the Great Nordic War. Visitors can see the church built for Karl XII's troops, and the dungeons for when they misbehaved.

The fortress lies about 8km downstream from Göteborg. **Strömma** (www.stromma.se) runs boat trips and **guided tours** (adult/6-11yr/family Skr160/80/465) three to four times daily from early May to mid-August. Tours depart from Lilla Bommen harbour, north of the train station. Several are free for Göteborg Pass holders.

Volvo Museum   MUSEUM

(☏66 48 14; Hisingen; adult/6-12yr Skr50/20; ☺10am-5pm Tue-Fri, to 6pm Wed, 11am-4pm Sat & Sun) Pay homage to one of Sweden's enduring icons at the Volvo Museum, which contains everything from the company's debut vehicle to the most cutting-edge experimental designs – including the first jet engine used by the Swedish Air Force.

The museum is about 8km west of the city centre at Arendal. Fittingly, it's tricky to get to without a car. Take tram 5 or 10 to Eketrä-gatan, then bus 32 to Arendal Skans.

Trädgårdsföreningen
GARDENS

(City Park; www.tradgardsforeningen.se; Nya Allén; adult/child Skr20/free; ⊙7am-8pm, from 9am Sat & Sun) Laid out in 1842 and recently restored to better reflect its original plan, the lush Trädgårdsföreningen is a large protected area off Nya Allén. Full of flowers and tiny cafes, it's popular for lunchtime escapes and is home to Europe's largest **rosarium**, with around 2500 varieties. The gracious 19th-century **Palmhuset** (admission free; ⊙10am-6pm) is a bite-size version of Crystal Palace in London, with five differently heated halls: look out for the impressive camellia collection and the 2m-wide tropical lily pads.

Botaniska Trädgården
GARDENS

(www.gotbot.se; Carl Skottsbergsgatan 22A; voluntary Skr20 admission; ⊙gardens 9am-sunset, greenhouses 10am-5pm May-Aug, to 4pm Sep-Apr) More botanical bliss awaits at the Botaniska Trädgården. Sweden's largest botanical garden, it breathes easy with around 16,000 plant species.

Slottsskogsparken
PARK

(admission free; ⊙24hr) Just across Dag Hammarskjöldsleden, Slottsskogsparken is superb for a stroll. The Naturhistoriska Museet is perched on a hill in the park, with other attractions including **Barnens Zoo** (Children's Zoo; admission free; ⊙daily May-Aug) and **Djurgårdarna** (admission free), an animal park with farm animals, elk, deer and other furry and feathered Swedish creatures. Feeding time at the seal pond is 2pm daily and penguins nosh a half-hour later.

Keillers Park
PARK

(Hisingen) The rocky heights of Ramberget (87m) in Keillers Park give the best view of the city. Get there on the city bus tour (p154) or take a tram to Ramsbergsvallen and walk the rest of the way up.

Domkyrkan
CHURCH

(Gustavi Cathedral; Kyrkogatan 28; ⊙8am-6pm Mon-Fri, 10am-4pm Sat & Sun) The elegant Domkyrkan was consecrated in 1815, the two previous cathedrals on this site having both been destroyed by town fires. Although many of the cathedral's contents are relatively modern, seasoned features include an 18th-century clock and reredos.

Hagakyrkan
CHURCH

(Haga Kyrkoplan; ⊙11am-3pm Mon-Thu, to 1pm Sat) The park behind the beautiful 19th-century Hagakyrkan is home to a simple yet moving **monument** to Swedish hero Raoul Wallenberg. A Nordic Schindler of sorts, Wallenberg is credited with saving the lives of around 15,000 Hungarian Jews during WWII. Wallenberg himself was arrested by the Russian government in 1945 and executed two years later.

Masthuggskyrkan
CHURCH

(Storebackegatan; ⊙9am-6pm daily Jun-Aug, 9am-4pm Mon-Fri rest of year) One of Göteborg's most distinctive buildings, this is a welcome landmark for sailors and is a smashing viewpoint over the western half of the city. Completed in 1914, its interior resembles an upturned boat.

Haga district
NEIGHBOURHOOD

The Haga district is Göteborg's oldest suburb, dating back to 1648. A hardcore hippie hang-out in the 1960s and '70s, its cobbled streets and vintage buildings are now a gentrified blend of cafes, op shops and boutiques. During some summer weekends and at Christmas, store owners set up stalls along Haga Nygata, turning the neighbourhood into one big market.

Linné district
NEIGHBOURHOOD

A short walk west of the Haga district, the Linné district holds fast to its grungy roots, especially along the Långgatan streets. Here, uberhip cafes, junk shops and street-smart boutiques mix it with seedy sex shops and eclectic locals. It's a magnet for creative types and home to the kicking **Andra Långdagen block party**, a wild, one-day street bash on Andra Långgatan organised by the street's traders and fans. Held annually between April and June (check the Andra Långgatan group on Facebook for dates), it's a thumping concoction of curbside DJ sets, film screenings, barbecues, clothes swaps and backyard B-boy battles. Looking out over the 'hood is the spindly, neo-Gothic **Oscar Fredriks kyrka** (Oscar Fredriks Kyrkogatan; ⊙9am-4pm Mon-Fri), another 19th-century ecclesial creation.

Göteborgs-Utkiken
BUILDING

(Lilla Bommen torg 1; admission Skr30; ⊙11am-4pm daily Jul & Aug, 11am-3pm Mon-Fri Sep-Jun) Across town, the red-and-white 'skyscraper' Göteborgs-Utkiken, nicknamed 'The Lipstick' for obvious reasons, has killer views of the harbour from the top.

CREATIVE OUTSKIRTS

The tiny, creative hub of Kvarnbyn, a district of Mölndal 8km south of Göteborg, has long attracted architects, designers and artists looking to escape the high rents and pressures of the city. Here, a brooding landscape of roaring rapids gripped by grain mills and historic factories (Mölndal means valley of the mills) has been transformed into a dynamic yet low-key cultural centre.

The district's nexus is the smart, interactive **Mölndals Museum** (www.museum.mol ndal.se; Kvarnbygatan 12; admission free; ☉noon-4pm Tue-Sun). Located in an old police station, the museum is like a vast warehouse with a 10,000-strong booty of local nostalgia spanning a 17th-century clog to kitchen kitsch and a re-created 1930s worker's cottage. With a focus on memories and feelings, it's an evocative place where you can plunge into racks of vintage clothes, pull out hidden treasures and learn more about individual items on the digital catalogue. One particular highlight is the eclectic collection of chairs, including beautifully crafted pieces from the nearby village of Lindome, one of Sweden's most historic furniture-making areas. The temporary exhibitions are clever (a circus exhibit will skip from art to brain research and finish up with a bit of history) and the in-house cafe boasts summertime seating right by the rapids. The museum also hires out a brilliant, hand-held computer guide (in Swedish), which leads you through Kvarnbyn's industrial landscape using a lively mix of historical anecdotes, animation and soundscapes.

The town also hosts some noteworthy cultural events. On a Saturday in mid- to late April, **Kvarnbydagen** (Kvarnbyn Day; www.kvarnbydagen.se) sees local artists and designers open their studios to the public. In September **Kulturnatt** (Culture Night) is a starlit spectacle of open studios and art installations, as well as dance and music performances; the district's website www.molndal.se (in Swedish) has details under Kultur & Fritid. To reach Kvarnbyn from Göteborg, catch a Kungsbacka-bound train to Mölndal station, then bus 756 or 752 to Mölndals Museum.

Klippan precinct   HISTORIC SITE

Once a bustle of industry (with glassworks, foundries, breweries and salting houses) the Klippan precinct has been revamped into a rather fetching heritage centre. It includes 18th-century sailors' cottages, the remains of Gamla Älvsborg fort (ransomed from the Danes in 1619), a brewery opened by the Scot David Carnegie (now a hotel) and St Birgittas kapell. Klippan is just off Oscarsleden, about 400m east of Älvsborgsbron – take tram 3 or 9 to Vagnhallen Majorna.

Kronhuset   HISTORIC BUILDING

Lying between Postgatan and Kronhusgatan, Kronhuset is the city's oldest secular building, a former arsenal built in Dutch style between 1642 and 1654. It was here that Karl X held the disastrous *riksdag* (parliament) in 1660 – he died while it was in session. **Kronhusbodarna**, across the courtyard from Kronhuset, houses several workshops making and selling pottery, silverware, glass and textiles. It's also home to the wicked **Göteborgs Choklad & Karamellfabrik** (www. goteborgschoklad.se; ☉11am-6pm Mon-Fri, to 4pm Sat), a candy factory-cum-shop where the sticky treats include *skumklubba* (marsh-mallows on a stick, dipped in dark chocolate and desiccated coconut).

⚡ Activities

Cycling

The tourist office has the free map *Cykelkarta Göteborg*, covering the best routes. See p162 for longer-term bicycle-hire details.

Styr & Ställ   CYCLING

(www.goteborgbikes.se; 1/2hr Skr10/70) Göteborg's handy city-bike system, was launched in 2011. A three-day bike subscription (Skr10) can be purchased directly from docking stations around the city. The first half-hour is free, making it ideal for quick trips.

Swimming

Hagabadet   SWIMMING

(www.hagabadet.se; Södra Allégatan 3; ☉6.30am-9pm Mon-Thu, to 8pm Fri, 9am-7pm Sat, 10am-7pm Sun) For a vintage splash, head to the magnificent indoor swimming pool Hagabadet. For Skr399 you can swim all day and use the attached sauna, gym and aerobics facilities; between 6.30am and 9am a dip in the pool costs Skr115. There's also a luxe choice of spa treatments and a bookable Roman bath (Skr350 per person for two hours).

Delsjön lake
SWIMMING

Outdoor swimming is best in Delsjön lake, 6km east of the centre (take tram 5 to Töpelsgatan). The 3km-long lake is also a good place for a ramble through the woods, canoeing, or fishing for pike or perch. Anglers should ask the tourist office for tackle shop details as a permit is required.

Boating

Näsets Paddlarklubb
BOATING

(📞40 22 37; www.npku.nu, in Swedish; 2/3hr Skr100/150; ⊙10am-8pm Jun-Aug, 11am-6pm Apr-May, Sep-Oct) The local boating club rents out canoes for paddling around Delsjön lake.

Walking

Bohusleden is an easy walking trail that runs for 360km through Bohuslän, from Lindome (south of Göteborg) to Strömstad, passing just east of the city. Purchase guides to the north and south routes from the tourist offices (Skr50).

For perfect island-hopping, take tram 11 southwest to Saltholmen and you'll have at least 15 different islands to explore – see p163.

Rock Climbing

There's some good rock climbing around Göteborg. Trams 6, 7 and 11 go to Kviberg, close to some of the best climbing, at Utby. Contact Göteborgs Klätterklubb (📞68 88 99; www.gbgkk.nu, in Swedish) for information.

🧭 Tours

Paddan City Boat Tour
BOAT

(www.stromma.se; adult/6-11yr/family Skr145/72.50/390; ⊙tours Apr-Oct) Strömma runs 50-minute city tours on its Paddan boats from Kungsportsplatsen, right across from the tourist office. They're an information-packed way to get your bearings and are free with the Göteborg Pass. Strömma also runs dancing and dinner tours from Lilla Bommen torg to the island of Brännö (p163) and a four-hour trip around the island of Hisingen (adult Skr180; ⊙tours May-Sep), among others. Check the website for updated timetables and prices.

City Sightseeing
BUS

(adult/6-11yr/family Skr145/half-price/375) Strömma also runs City Sightseeing bus tours that depart Stora Teatern three to six times daily from mid-May to early September (once daily at other times).

Strömma Cruises
BOAT

(adult/6-11yr/family Skr160/80/465) The tour to Nya Älvsborgs Fästning departs Lilla Bommen torg daily from early May through August. Free with the Göteborg Pass.

✨ Festivals & Events

Göteborg International Film Festival
FILM

(www.filmfestival.org) One of Scandinavia's major film festivals, with flicks spanning all continents and genres. It's usually held in late January.

Clandestino Festival
MUSIC

(www.clandestinofestival.org) A hip-shaking line-up of world music, held in June.

Way Out West
MUSIC

(www.wayoutwest.se) In early August, Way Out West is a mighty three-day music festival pulling in big guns like Kanye West, Sonic Youth, the Hives and José González.

🛏 Sleeping

Göteborg has several high-quality hostels near the city centre. Most hotels offer decent discounts at weekends and in summer. Check the tourist-office website (www.goteborg.com) for hotel, breakfast and Göteborg Pass package deals (from Skr645).

Most hostels are clustered in the central southwestern area, in apartment buildings that sometimes inspire little confidence from the outside, but inside offer accommodation of a very high standard. All are open year-round.

TOP CHOICE / Vanilj Hotel
HOTEL €€

(📞711 62 20; www.hotelvanilj.se; Kyrkogatan 38; s/d incl breakfast from Skr795/995; 🅿 @) On a quiet, central street, this petite slumber spot has the cosy, welcoming feeling of a Swedish home. Rooms are pleasantly light and decorated in sparing Scandinavian style, with wood floors and furniture, crisp sheets and immaculate bathrooms. Breakfast is served in the buzzing cafe downstairs. Get there early for one of the five parking spaces.

Avalon
HOTEL €€

(📞751 02 00; www.avalonhotel.se; Kungstorget 9; s/d from Skr1048/1312; @ ☀) Design-conscious Avalon is steps away from the main tourist office. Rooms are packed with eye-popping Nordic design, bright colours, curvaceous furniture, flat-screen TVs and heavenly pillows. Some rooms feature a mini-spa or their own gym equipment, and the hip resto-bar is an after-work hot spot. The ultimate highlight is the rooftop pool (open May to September), which leans out over the edge for a dizzying dip. Book online for the best rates.

Hotel Flora   HOTEL €€
(☑13 86 16; www.hotelflora.se; Grönsakstorget 2; s/d Skr1150/1395; @) An extreme makeover has turned Flora from frumpy to fabulous, its uberslick rooms now flaunt black, white and a dash-of-bright-colour interiors, designer chairs, flat-screen TVs and sparkling bathrooms. Each has a theme: the royal suite is all done up in flag-worthy blue and yellow. The top-floor rooms have air-con, several rooms offer river views and the chic split-level courtyard is perfect for sophisticated chilling.

STF Vandrarhem Stigbergsliden   HOSTEL €
(☑24 16 20; www.hostel-gothenburg.com; Stigbergsliden 10; dm/d Skr225/550; @) Rooms at Stigbergsliden have a certain monastic simplicity to them, in keeping with the hostel's history as a 19th-century seaman's institute. Staff are especially helpful and besides the usual stuff (big kitchen, laundry, TV room) there is a pleasant sheltered garden. To get there take tram 3, 9 or 11 to Stigbergstorget.

Elite Plaza Hotel   HOTEL €€
(☑720 40 00; www.elite.se; Västra Hamngatan 3; s/d incl breakfast Skr1050/1450; P@) With stucco ceilings and lovely mosaic floors, the Elite Plaza is a grand, old-world establishment with all the modern trimmings. Rooms are spacious, breakfast ample and there's a nice bar. The location is good if you're keen to avoid Avenyn or station hustle-bustle and still want to be within a short walk of shops and a stone's throw from some of the city's best restaurants.

Hotel Royal   HOTEL €€
(☑700 11 70; www.hotelroyal.nu; Drottninggatan 67; s/d incl breakfast from Skr1295/1495; @) Göteborg's oldest hotel (1852) has aged enviably. The grand entrance has been retained, complete with a flowery, art-nouveau painted ceiling and sweeping staircase, and the elegant, airy rooms make necessary 21st-century concessions such as flat-screen TVs and renovated bathrooms. There's also homemade cake for guests, and an excellent breakfast. Check the website for special offers.

Hotell Barken Viking   HISTORIC HOTEL €€
(☑63 58 00; www.liseberg.se; Gullbergskajen; s/d Skr1200/1500; @) *Barken Viking* is an elegant four-masted sailing ship, converted into a stylish hotel and restaurant and moored near Lilla Bommen harbour. Rooms are smart and suitably nautical, with handsome blue carpet, Hamptons-style linen and warm wood panelling. There are discounted package deals, which include entry to Liseberg (double, from Skr1295).

Grand Hotel Opera   HOTEL €€
(☑80 50 80; www.grandhotelopera.se; Norra Hamngatan 38; budget s/d incl breakfast Skr795/995, standard Skr1295/1395; @≋) The sparkling lobby, bar and restaurant of this conveniently located hotel (directly across from the train station and bus terminal) generally bustles with business types. Service is efficient, breakfast excellent, and there's a gym and small pool. Budget rooms in the older part of the hotel are small but adequate, while standard rooms are larger, better decorated and have extras like desks.

Hotel Eggers   HOTEL €€
(☑333 44 40; www.hoteleggers.se; Drottningtorget; s/d from Skr995/1450; P@) Elegant Eggers would make a great set for a period drama. Founded as a railway hotel in 1859, its rooms are a Regency-style treat. A good few have private balconies overlooking the bustling square, and nearby parking spots (Skr120 per 24 hours) can be booked at reception.

Hotel Vasa   HOTEL €€
(☑17 36 30; www.hotelvasa.se; Viktoriagatan 6; s/d from Skr845/995; @) Located in trendy, inner-city Vasastan, family-run Hotel Vasa takes advantage of an attractive 1877 building with high-ceilinged rooms and a pleasant green-and-white breakfast room. Hotel perks include a courtyard garden, jacuzzis in some doubles and coffee and cake in the lobby.

Hotel Gothia Towers   HOTEL €€
(☑750 88 10; www.gothiatowers.com; Mässans Gata 24; budget s/d from Skr895/1095, standard Skr1095/1295; P@) A hop, skip and jump from the entrance to Liseberg is the 23-storey Gothia Towers (take tram 5). Its 704 rooms ooze Nordic cool, especially the 'Design' options: they're all sharp, with clean lines and good bathroom windows for a vista-friendly soak. More bird's-eye views await at Sky bar and restaurant Heaven 23.

GÖTEBORG & THE SOUTHWEST SLEEPING

STF Vandrarhem Slottsskogen   HOSTEL €
(☑42 65 20; www.sov.nu; Vegagatan 21; dm/s/d Skr215/360/500; @) Like a good university dormitory, big, friendly Slottsskogen is a cracking place for meeting people. For a small extra payment there's access to a sauna or sunbed and the buffet breakfast (Skr65) is brilliant. Parking spaces can be booked for Skr70. Take tram 1 or 6 to Olivedalsgatan.

Lisebergs Camping
& Stugbyar Kärralund   CAMPGROUND €
(☑84 02 00; www.liseberg.se; Olbergsgatan 1; sites from Skr165, cottages incl breakfast Skr1495; P @) Liseberg park owns and operates a range of accommodation around Göteborg. Located 4km east of central Göteborg, this family-friendly campsite is the closest one to town (tram 5 to Welandergatan), with 50 camp-sites. Campsites cannot be prebooked.

Göteborgs Vandrarhem   HOSTEL €
(☑40 10 50; www.goteborgsvandrarhem.se; Möl-ndalsvägen 23; dm/s/d Skr220/600/600) This hostel is on a busy four-lane road, but con-venient for getting to Liseberg as early as possible. Extras include a big sunny terrace, tidy rooms and pleasant common spaces. Take tram 4 to Geteebergsäng.

Kvibergs Vandrarhem & Stugby   HOSTEL €
(☑43 50 55; www.vandrarhem.com; Kvibergsvägen 5; hostel/hotel d Skr570/740; P @) This sterling SVIF hostel, a few kilometres northeast of the city centre (tram 6, 7 or 11), boasts super amenities, including flat-screen TVs, wi-fi, sauna, table tennis and a pleasant outdoor area good for barbecuing. Hotel-style rooms and cabins are also available.

Masthuggsterrassens
Vandrarhem   HOSTEL €
(☑42 48 20; www.mastenvandrarhem.com; Masthuggsterrassen 10H; dm/d Skr195/500; @) A handy hostel if you're catching an early ferry to Denmark. It's a clean, quiet, well-run place, if a little out of the way. Take tram 3, 9 or 11 to Masthuggstorget, cross the square diagonally and take the stairs or lift up to Masthuggsterrassen.

Lilleby Havsbad Camping   CAMPGROUND €
(☑56 22 40; www.goteborgscamping.se; Lillebyvä-gen; sites low/high season Skr170/250; ☺Jun-Aug) This agreeable seaside spot lies 20km west of the city centre in Torslanda. Take bus 25 from near Centralstationen to Lillebyvägen, then change to bus 23.

Scandic Hotel Rubinen   HOTEL €€
(☑751 54 00; rubinen@scandichotels.com; Kungsportsavenyn 24; s/d Skr890/1020; @) In the heart of the Avenyn action, with slick, recently renovated rooms and a restaurant-cocktail bar serving Spanish-influenced dishes.

Linné Vandrarhem   HOSTEL €
(☑12 10 60; www.linnehostel.com, in Swedish; Vegagatan 22; dm/s Skr350/550; @) Down the road from Slottsskogen, this SVIF hostel is another central option.

Scandic Hotel Europa   HOTEL €€
(☑751 65 00; europa@scandichotels.com; Köp-mansgatan 38; s/d Skr920/1020; @) Convenient for the train station.

✖ Eating

Göteborg isn't short on great epicurean ex-periences: the city's chefs are at the cutting edge of Sweden's Slow Food movement and there are no fewer than five Michelin-rated restaurants. Happily, there are more casual and less-expensive options for trying the country's best seafood and old-fashioned *husmanskost* (home cooking).

Cool cafes, cheap ethnic gems and foodie favourites abound in the Vasastan, Haga and Linné districts, often with lower prices than their tourist-trap Avenyn rivals. Alas, many places close on Sundays. For something quick, the Nordstan shopping complex has loads of fast-food outlets.

[TOP CHOICE] **Magnus & Magnus**   EUROPEAN €€€
(☑13 30 00; www.magnusmagnus.se; Magasins-gatan 8; 2-/3-course tasting menus Skr395/495; ☺dinner Mon-Sat) Ever-fashionable Magnus & Magnus serves inspired and beautifully presented Modern European dishes in an appropriately chic setting. It's an unpre-tentious place in spite of its popularity, with pleasantly down-to-earth waitstaff. Big windows overlooking Magasinsgatan are ideal for people-watching and there's a courtyard that draws Göteborg's hipsters in summer.

Hemma Hos   TAPAS €€
(☑13 40 90; www.hemmahos.net; Haga Nygata 12; small plates Skr49-99; ☺to midnight) With a smooth black bar and comfortable tables, this Haga restaurant-bar manages to be both urbane and relaxed. Its selection of small plates is decidedly gourmet – moose carpaccio with sharp lingonberry mustard

or suckling pig with potato rösti – and there is a good variety of wine by the glass. Altogether, an ideal pit stop for snacking and people-watching.

Fond
SWEDISH €€€

(☑81 25 80; www.fondrestaurang.com; Götaplatsen; mains Skr255-395, Swedish sampler menus Skr795; ☺lunch & dinner Mon-Sat) Michelin-rated Fond is not only one of Göteborg's best restaurants, its location on Götaplatsen, right under the Konstmuseum, makes it a perfect place for observing the city. Here, renowned chef Stefan Karlsson dishes up delectable, modern Swedish cuisine. The dining room is chic and minimalist, complete with orange lighting, simple furniture and floor-to-ceiling glass windows. The restaurant is closed in summer. Book ahead.

Wasa Allé
SWEDISH €€€

(☑13 13 70; www.wasaalle.se; Vasagatan 24; mains Skr225-295, 3-/7-course menus Skr525/795; ☺lunch Mon-Fri, dinner Sat) At Wasa Allé, the flagship restaurant of Mats Nordström, the goal is to have ingredients come from within four hours of the restaurant, year-round (other than wine of course). The result is an inspiring celebration of local produce. If you're feeling adventurous, opt for the surprise three- to seven-course *stolen* (chair) menu.

Da Matteo
CAFE €

(☑13 06 09; www.damatteo.se; Vallgatan 5; sandwiches & salads Skr40-95; ☺8am-7pm Mon-Fri, 9am-5pm Sat, 10am-5pm Sun) The perfect downtown lunch pit stop and a mecca for coffee snobs, this cafe serves wickedly fine espresso, moreish mini *sfogliatelle* (Neapolitan pastries), sandwiches and great salads. There's a sun-soaked courtyard and a second branch on Viktoriapassagen.

Smaka
SWEDISH €€

(☑13 22 47; Vasaplatsen 3; mains Skr115-225; ☺5pm-1am Sun-Thu, to 2am Fri & Sat) This lively, down-to-earth restaurant-bar cooks up brilliant, old-school, Swedish *husmanskost*, like the speciality meatballs with mashed potato and lingonberries. Mod-Swedish options might include salmon carpaccio with nettle purée or smoked reindeer on rye bread.

Fiskekrogen
SEAFOOD €€€

(☑10 10 05; www.fiskekrogen.se; Lilla Torget 1; mains Skr295-365; ☺dinner Mon-Fri, lunch & dinner Sat) Fiskekrogen serves superlative fish and seafood creations in former Swedish East India Company buildings. Slip into the chic circular dining room, Blåskajsa, choose your drop from the 500-plus wine list, and prepare to toast the chefs. Book ahead.

GÖTEBORG & THE SOUTHWEST EATING

LOCAL KNOWLEDGE

MATS NORDSTRÖM: WASA ALLÉ CHEF & OWNER

Growing up, we had terrible food at home, but then I went to Italy to play handball. I played professionally for one year and I was eating in trattorias each night, so I got interested in food. When I came home I went to cooking school. Back then, it was worse than cleaning the streets to be a chef.

Swedish Slow Food

My goal with Wasa Allé is to create a fine-dining restaurant where everything eaten comes from within four hours of the restaurant. We have one farmer who grows all our vegetables; he tells us what he has and that's what we cook. The only thing we can't do is wine, but 93% of the wine list is organic, natural wine.

Modern Home Cooking

I'm in love with *husmanskost* (home cooking). Our food is very traditional. We use the old flavours with modern techniques and we're not embarrassed by Scandi flavours.

What & Where to Eat in Gothenburg

We get fish 24 hours before Stockholm, so we have the best seafood restaurants in Sweden. You have to eat the herrings from Gothenburg, and langoustines, prawns, cod cheeks, crabs and mackerel in the spring and autumn. Try Kok & Vin, Sjömagasinet or Fiskekrogen.

Björns Bar
TAPAS €€

(✆701 79 79; www.kockvin.se; Viktoriagatan 12; tapas Skr25-165; ⊙6pm-1am Mon-Wed, from 5pm Thu, 4pm-3am Fri & Sat) Underneath Michelin-rated Kock & Vin, Björns draws gourmets late into the night. Select a glass of wine and nibble away at the delectable selection of charcuterie (including air-dried wild goose!) and cheeses.

Hello Monkey
THAI €€

(✆13 04 42; www.hellomonkey.net; Magasinsgatan 26; dim sum Skr89-139, mains Skr 142-275; ⊙5pm-midnight Tue-Fri, 1pm-midnight Sat, 1-10pm Sun) This Thai-inspired bolt-hole on Magasinsga-tan dishes out mouth-tingling salads, noodle dishes and dim sum from a bustling open kitchen. Presentation is picture-perfect, the scene cool-casual and there is an excellent selection of delicious cocktails ranging from mango mojitos to Singapore slings.

Solrosen
VEGETARIAN €

(www.restaurangsolrosen.se; Kaponjärgatan 4; mains Skr60-85; ⊙11.30am-10.30pm Mon-Thu, to 11.30pm Fri, 1-11.30pm Sat, 2-7.30pm Sun, closed Sun Jul & Aug) A 1970s survivor, this laid-back student favourite is a Haga institution (note the photos of passed-on regulars above the counter). Pay tribute over soulful vegetarian dishes and a bountiful salad buffet.

Café Kringlan
CAFE €

(Haga Nygata 13; dish of the day Skr70; ⊙7.30am-7pm) Lunchtime finds tiny Café Kringlan overflowing with customers eager for a rich bowl of soup, salads heaped with shrimps or mouth-watering lemon cake.

En Deli i Haga
DELI €

(Haga Nygata 15; salad buffets Skr60-65; ⊙8am-7pm Mon-Fri, 10am-5pm Sat & Sun) Just next door to Café Kringlan, equally good and just as popular, En Deli dishes out great Medi-terranean-style salads and meze, as well as good soup and sandwiches.

Sjöbaren
SEAFOOD €€

(www.sjobaren.se; Haga Nygata 25; mains Skr99-289; ⊙11am-11pm Mon-Thu, to midnight Fri, noon-midnight Sat, 1-9pm Sun, opens 3pm Sun in sum-mer) In the Haga district, cosy Sjöbaren combines nautical interiors with sublime Swedish seafood. If the weather's on your side, chow down classics like gravlax or fish soup in the gorgeous garden courtyard.

Bar Centro
CAFE €

(Kyrkogatan 31; focaccias Skr30-60; ⊙6pm-6pm Mon-Fri, 7am-5pm Sat, 8am-5pm Sun) Fans of this central, retro espresso bar spill out onto the street, downing smooth espresso and tasty focaccias. The few window seats are perfect for urban voyeurs.

Bar Italia
CAFE €

(Prinsgatan 7; panini Skr30-60; ⊙7.30am-6pm) In the Linné district is this cultish espresso bar, complete with Italian baristi and suspended Vespa. In warm weather watch the hip bri-gade squeeze onto the pavement banquette for perfect caffeine, *cornetti* (croissants), gourmet calzone and gossip. Its gelato is good too.

Alexandras
GREEK

(Kungstorget; soups & stews around Skr40; ⊙1am-6pm Mon-Fri, to 3pm Sat) Located in the central Saluhallen, this famous eatery dishes out excellent hearty soups and stews, and is par-ticularly welcoming on a chilly day.

Crêpe Van
DESSERTS €

(cnr Landsvägsgatan & Prinsgatan; crêpes Skr40-65; ⊙4pm-1.30am Mon-Thu, to 3.30am Fri & Sat) Those with a sweet tooth should head to this unassuming takeaway van, also a favourite of 'flushed and clumsy' patrons late on Fri-day and Saturday.

Le Petit Café
BAKERY €

(Haga Nygata 2; ⊙8.30am-6pm Mon-Fri, 10am-1pm Sat & Sun) Quaint French bakery with an overwhelming selection of cakes, tarts and rolls.

Saluhallen
SELF-CATERING €

(Kungstorget; ⊙9am-6pm Mon-Fri, to 3pm Sat) Göteborg's main central market is jammed with tasty budget eateries and food stalls, and is the perfect place to stock up that pic-nic basket.

Feskekörka
SELF-CATERING €

(www.feskekorka.se; Rosenlundsgatan; ⊙9am-5pm Tue-Thu, to 6pm Fri, 10am-3pm Sat) A market de-voted to fresh fish and squamous things, the 'Fish Church' is heaven (sorry) for seafood fans. Takeaway treats include fresh fish and chips, and yummy shrimp and avocado sal-ads.

Saluhall Briggen
SELF-CATERING €

(Nordhemsgatan 28; ⊙9am-6pm Mon-Fri, to 3pm Sat) It might lack Saluhallen's size and buzz, but this covered market (in an old fire sta-tion) will have you drooling over its bounty of fresh bread, cheeses, quiches, seafood and ethnic treats. It's particularly handy for the hostel district.

Hemköp SUPERMARKET €
(Nordstan shopping complex; ⊙8am-9pm Mon-Fri, 10am-8pm Sat & Sun) Major supermarket in the thick of things.

Ekostore SELF-CATERING €
(Ekelundsgatan 4; ⊙10am-8pm Mon-Fri Aug & Jun, to 7pm rest of year; ⊘) An eco-chic grocery store selling organic and fair-trade products.

🍷 Drinking

Swedish licensing laws mean that bars must have a restaurant section, although in most cases, it's vice versa. While Kungsportsavenyn brims with beer-downing tourists, try the following savvier options.

Lokal COCKTAIL BAR
(www.lokalgbg.se; Kyrkogatan 11; ⊙5pm-1am Mon-Sat) Arguably the best bar in Göteborg, this effortlessly cool hang-out pulls everyone from artists and media types to the odd punk rocker. Drinks are inspired, the nibbles excellent, and music spans soul, jazz and electro.

Bliss LOUNGE
(www.blissresto.com; Magasinsgatan 3; ⊙11.30am-2.30pm Mon-Fri, plus 6pm-1am or 2am Tue-Thu & Sat, 5pm-1am or 2am Fri) Bliss boasts one of the hippest interiors in Göteborg, with low designer seats and slick contemporary tones. It's a long-standing nocturnal favourite: if you're not up to a main meal (they're usually delicious; mains Skr145 to Skr240), simply enjoy a well-shaken cocktail and groove to live DJs until late.

Notting Hill PUB
(www.nottinghill.se; Nordhemsgatan 19A) Another great place for a pint, Notting Hill is a friendly local between the Haga and Linné districts. British pub fare gets a Swedish makeover: the kitchen serves excellent meatballs and raises the bar on bog-standard fish and chips (mains Skr89 to Skr169). It's a cosy place, especially so on quiz nights or during a major football match.

Ölhallen 7:an BEER HALL
(Kungstorget 7) For low-fuss, old-school soul, don't miss this little gem – a well-worn Swedish beer hall that hasn't changed in about 100 years. There's no food, wine or pretension, just beer, and plenty of choices.

Systembolaget LIQUOR STORE
Kungsportsavenyn (Kungsportsavenyn 18); Linnégatan (Linnégatan 28B) Systembolagets are scattered across Göteborg, selling beer, wine and spirits. These are two particularly handy outlets.

⭐ Entertainment
Nightclubs
Clubs have varying minimum-age limits, ranging from 18 to 25, and many may charge admission depending on the night.

Nefertiti LIVE MUSIC
(www.nefertiti.se, in Swedish; Hvitfeldtsplatsen 6; tickets Skr40-220) A Göteborg institution, this effortlessly cool venue is famous for its smooth live jazz, blues and world music, usually followed by kicking club nights spanning everything from techno, deep house and soul to hip hop and funk. Times vary, so check the website.

Pustervik LIVE MUSIC
(www.pusterviksbaren.se, in Swedish; Järntorgsgatan 12) Culture vultures and party people pack this hybrid venue, with its heaving downstairs bar and upstairs club and stage. Gigs range from independent theatre and live music (anything from emerging singer-songwriters to Neneh Cherry) to regular club nights spanning hip hop, soul and rock.

Push CLUB
(www.push.se; Kungsportsavenyn 11; ⊙10pm-3am Fri & Sat) Owned by Stockholm's Sturecompagniet nightclub, white-clad and psychedelically lit Push is a club to see and be seen at. Music ranges from '80s to house. Minimum age is 25.

Greta's GAY
(www.gretas.nu; Drottninggatan 35; ⊙9pm-4am Fri & Sat) The nearest thing in Göteborg to a gay club, Schlager-happy Greta's is kitsch-a-licious fun on Friday and Saturday nights. The minimum age is 20.

Concerts, Theatre & Cinema
Check the local events listings for movies and shows or with the tourist office for what's on where.

Göteborgs Stadsteatern THEATRE
(City Theatre; ☎708 71 00; www.stadsteatern.goteborg.se; Götaplatsen; tickets from Skr120) Stages theatre productions in Swedish.

Göteborgs Konserthuset CLASSICAL MUSIC
(Concert Hall; ☎726 53 10; www.gso.se; Götaplatsen; tickets Skr100-340; ⊙closed summer) Home to the local symphony orchestra, with top international guests and some sterling performances.

LOCAL KNOWLEDGE

ANNIKA AXELSSON: OWNER DEM COLLECTIVE

There really wasn't any organic, fair-trade and fashionable clothing being sold in Göteborg when my partner Karin Stenmar and I started DEM Collective. So in 2004 we set up a factory in Sri Lanka with the idea of producing clothing that would be profitable and benefit the community making it. I think we've proved that it's possible; today women are using our contracts to negotiate better hours and wages. I'm proud of that.

Stockholm versus Göteborg

Stockholmers love to discuss great ideas. In Göteborg, there's less talk, more action. It probably reflects our working-class roots. We've always had a strong student and activist culture here. Göteborg opened its first fair-trade, organic shop in the late 1960s. It took Stockholm until mid-2000 to do that.

On a Sunny Day

Start with breakfast at the water tower in Guldhedstornet. There is a great cafe there and you can just relax and take in the view of Göteborg. Then take the tram to Saltholmen and catch a ferry to Brännö (p163). It's one of the archipelago's most beautiful islands and a lot of artistic people have moved there.

In the Rain

Head to Röhsska Museet (p150). The curator is a progressive thinker, expanding the fashion collection to include recycled clothes and not just haute couture. Varldskulturmuseet (p151) is also fantastic.

GöteborgsOperan
OPERA

(☑13 13 00; www.opera.se, in Swedish; Christina Nilssons Gata; tickets Skr75-640) At Lilla Bommen harbour, this place stages classical and modern ballet and opera and assorted musical performances in a striking contemporary building.

Nya Ullevi
STADIUM

(☑368 45 00; www.ullevi.se; Skånegatan) The city's outdoor stadium hosts rock concerts and sporting events.

Scandinavium
CONCERT VENUE

(☑81 10 20; www.scandinavium.se; Valhallagatan 1) An indoor concert venue near Nya Ullevi.

Biopalatset
CINEMA

(☑17 45 00; Kungstorget) If you're craving celluloid, the multiscreen Biopalatset is a good central option for mainstream films.

Folkets Bio
CINEMA

(☑42 88 10; Linnégatan 21) For independent and art-house offerings.

Sport

Göteborgers are avid sports fans. The city's two biggest stadiums are the outdoor Nya Ullevi for **football** matches, and the indoor Scandinavium for **ice hockey**.

🛍 Shopping

DesignTorget
HOMEWARES

(www.designtorget.se; Vallgatan 14) Cool, affordable design objects from both established and up-and-coming Scandi talent.

Prickig Katt
VINTAGE

(www.prickigkatt.se; Magasinsgatan 19) The outrageous 'Spotted Cat' has retro-clad staff and idiosyncratic fashion from Dutch, Danish and home-grown labels, as well as kitschy wares and out-there handmade millinery and bling.

Velour
CLOTHING

(www.velour.se; Magasinsgatan 19) Local label. Stocks slick, stylish streetwear for guys and girls.

Acne Jeans
CLOTHING

(www.acnestudios.com; Magasinsgatan 19) Stockholm legend, sharing the same address as Prickig Katt and Velour.

DEM Collective
CLOTHING

(www.demcollective.com; Storgatan 11; ⊘Thu-Sat) Head to this bite-size boutique for Scandi-cool fair-trade threads. Completely organic, designs are minimalist, street smart and supremely comfortable. To learn about the founders, see boxed text.

Stiernglans ACCESSORIES
(www.stiernglans.se; Haga Nygata 20) You'll see lovely feathered creations and demure toppers in this brilliant little hat boutique in Haga.

Fanny Michel ACCESSORIES
(⊗Mon-Sat) Viktoriapassagen (Vallgatan 19); Haga (Landsvagsgatan 6) With outlets in Haga and Viktoriapassagen, this shop is awash with lace, hats, scarves and other accessories.

Shelta SHOES
(www.shelta.eu; Andra Långgatan 21) Pimp your style with limited-edition and must-have sneakers and streetwear from big players and lesser-known labels.

Butik Kubik WOMEN'S CLOTHING
(www.butikkubik.se; Tredje Långgatan 8) Run by two young designers, this basement shop is a great place to check out local threads.

Bengans Skivor & Café MUSIC
(www.bengans.se; Stigbergstorget 1) Göteborg's mightiest music store is set in an old cinema, complete with retro signage and indie-cool cafe. Take tram 3, 9 or 11 to Stigbergstorget.

Nordstan shopping complex MALL
(www.nordstan.se; Nordstadstorget) Taking up the same amount of space as 55 football fields, this is one of Europe's largest shopping malls. There are about 180 shops.

ℹ Information

Dangers & Annoyances
Travellers (solo women especially) should take care around the Nordstan shopping complex late at night.

Emergency
Police station (☑114 14; Stampgatan 28)

Internet Access
Sidewalk Express (www.sidewalkexpress.se; per hr Skr19) Sidewalk Express computers are found at Centralstationen and the 7-Eleven shop on Vasaplatsen. To log on, buy vouchers from the coin-operated machines and enter the username and password issued.

Stadsbiblioteket (Götaplatsen; ⊗10am-8pm Mon-Fri, 11am-5pm Sat & Sun, closed Sun Jun-Aug) The city library has free internet access (bring ID).

Medical Services
For 24-hour medical information, phone ☑1177.
Akuttndvården (☑80 78 00; Odinsgatan 10) Emergency dental treatment.

Apotek Hjärtat (☑0771-45 04 50; Nordstan shopping complex; ⊗8am-10pm) Late-night pharmacy.

Östra Sjukhuset (☑343 40 00) Major hospital about 5km northeast of central Göteborg, near the terminus at the end of tram line 1.

Money
Banks with ATMs are readily available, including inside the Nordstan shopping complex and along Kungsportsavenyn.

Forex (www.forex.se) Centralstationen (⊗7am-9pm Mon-Fri, 9am-7pm Sat & Sun); Kungsportsavenyn 22 (⊗9am-7pm Mon-Fri, 10am-4pm Sat); Kungsportsplatsen (⊗9am-7pm Mon-Fri, 10am-3pm Sat); Landvetter Airport (⊗5am-9pm Mon-Fri, to 8pm Sat & Sun); Norstan shopping complex (⊗10am-8pm Mon-Fri, 10am-6pm Sat, 11am-5pm Sun) Foreign-exchange office with numerous branches.

Post
Postal services are now mainly provided by kiosks, newsagents, petrol stations and supermarkets – look for the blue-and-yellow postal symbol.
Post office (Nordstan shopping complex; ⊗7am-7pm Mon-Fri)

Tourist Offices
Branch tourist office (Nordstan shopping complex; ⊗10am-8pm Mon-Fri, 10am-6pm Sat, noon-5pm Sun)
Main tourist office (☑368 42 00; www.goteborg.com; Kungsportsplatsen 2; ⊗9.30am-8pm daily Jul–mid-Aug, to 6pm Jun & end Aug, 9.30am-6pm Mon-Fri, 10am-2pm Sat & Sun May, 9.30am-5pm Mon-Fri, 10am-2pm Sat rest of year) Central and busy, it has a good selection of free brochures and maps.
Västsvenska Turistrådet (www.vastsverige.com) Regional tourist board. Useful for online bookings.

ℹ Getting There & Away
Luggage lockers (small/large up to 24 hours Skr40/50) are available at both Centralstationen and the long-distance bus terminal Nils Ericson Terminalen.

Air
Twenty-five kilometres east of the city, **Göteborg Landvetter Airport** (www.swedavia.se) has as many as 24 direct daily flights to/from Stockholm-Arlanda and Stockholm Bromma Airports (with SAS, Norwegian and Malmö Aviation), as well as daily services to Umeå and several weekly services to Borlänge, Luleå and Sundsvall. It's Sweden's second-biggest international airport.

Direct European routes include Amsterdam (KLM), Brussels (SAS), Copenhagen (SAS and

Norwegian), Frankfurt (Lufthansa), Berlin (Air Berlin), Helsinki (Norwegian and SAS), London (British Airways and easyJet), Manchester (SAS), Munich (Lufthansa), Oslo (Norwegian) and Paris (Air France and SAS).

Göteborg City Airport (www.goteborgairport. se), some 15km north of the city at Säve, is used for budget Ryanair flights to destinations including London Stansted, Glasgow and Frankfurt.

Boat

Göteborg is a major entry point for ferries, with several car/passenger services to Denmark, Germany and Norway; for details see p353.

Nearest to central Göteborg, the **Stena Line** (www.stenaline.se) Denmark terminal near Masthuggstorget (tram 3, 9 or 11) has around eight daily departures for Frederikshavn in peak season. Further west is the Stena Line terminal for the daily car ferry to Kiel (Germany). Take tram 3 or 9 to Chapmans Torg.

For a special view of the region, jump on a boat for an unforgettable journey along the Göta Canal (see p235). Starting in Göteborg you'll pass through Sweden's oldest lock at Lilla Edet, opened in 1607. From there the trip crosses the great lakes Vänern and Vättern through the rolling country of Östergötland and on to Stockholm.

Bus

Västtrafik (www.vasttrafik.se) and **Hallandstrafiken** (www.hlt.se) provide regional transport links. If you're planning to spend some time exploring the southwest counties, it's worth enquiring about discount cards, monthly passes or a *sommarkort*, offering cheaper travel in the peak summer period (from late June to mid-August).

The bus station, Nils Ericson Terminalen, is next to the train station. There's a **Västtrafik information booth** (☉6am-10pm Mon-Fri, 9am-10pm Sat, 9am-7pm Sun) here, providing information and selling tickets for all city and regional public transport within the Göteborg, Bohuslän and Västergötland area.

Swebus Express (www.swebusexpress.com) has an office at the bus terminal and operates frequent buses to most major towns and cities. There are services to Stockholm (Skr439, seven hours) up to nine times daily. Other direct destinations include Halmstad (Skr109, 1¾ hours), Helsingborg (Skr139, three hours), Jönköping (Skr99, 1¾ hours), Malmö (Skr169, three hours) and Örebro (Skr279, four hours).

Prices are generally considerably lower for advanced, nonrefundable bookings, especially for Swebus Express.

Car & Motorcycle

The E6 motorway runs north–south from Oslo to Malmö just east of the city centre and there's also a complex junction where the E20 motorway diverges east for Stockholm.

International car-hire companies **Avis** (☑770 82 00 82; www.avisworld.com), **Europcar** (☑770 77 00 50; www.europcar.com) and **Hertz** (☑771 211 212; www.hertz-europe.com) have desks at Göteborg Landvetter and City Airports.

Train

Centralstationen is Sweden's oldest railway station and now a listed building. It serves **Sveriges Järnväg** (SJ; www.sj.se) and regional trains, with direct trains to Copenhagen (Skr387, four hours) and Malmö (Skr331, 3¼ hours), as well as numerous other destinations in the southern half of Sweden.

Intercity trains to Stockholm depart approximately every one to two hours (Skr511, five hours), with quicker X2000 trains (Skr672, three hours) also approximately every one to two hours.

Overnight trains to the far north of Sweden (via Stockholm) are operated by **Tågkompaniet** (www.tagkompaniet.se).

The main railway lines in the west connect Göteborg to Karlstad, Stockholm, Malmö and Oslo. In the east, the main line runs from Stockholm via Norrköping and Linköping to Malmö. Express buses connect major towns on much the same routes.

① Getting Around

To/From the Airport

Göteborg Landvetter Airport, 25km east of the city, has a frequent **Flygbuss** (☑771 41 43 00; www.flygbussarna.se) service to/from Nils Ericson Terminalen (one-way Skr80, 30 minutes). A taxi from the city centre to the airport will cost Skr345.

Buses from Göteborg City Airport to Nils Ericson Terminalen leave 50 minutes after flight arrivals. For the return journey, they leave the bus terminal around 2½ hours before flight departures (one-way Skr60, 30 minutes). A taxi should cost around Skr260.

Bicycle

For short-term use around the city, try the handy **Styr & Ställ** (www.goteborgbikes.se; 1/2hr Skr10/70) city bikes. A three-day bike subscription (Skr10) can be purchased directly from docking stations around the city. The first half-hour is free.

Proper cycles for longer-term use can be hired at **Cykelkungen** (www.cykelkungen.se; Chalmersgatan 19; 1-day/week Skr150/500; ☉Mon-Sat).

Cyclists should ask the tourist office for the free map *Cykelkarta Göteborg*, covering the best routes.

Public Transport

Buses, trams and ferries run by **Västtrafik** (www.vasttrafik.se) make up the city's public-transport system; there are Västtrafik information booths selling tickets and giving out timetables inside **Nils Ericson Terminalen** (☺6am-10pm Mon-Fri, 9am-10pm Sat, 9am-7pm Sun), in front of the train station on **Drottningtorget** (☺6am-8pm Mon-Fri, 8am-8pm Sat & Sun) and at **Brunnsparken** (☺7am-7pm Mon-Fri, 9am-6pm Sat).

Holders of the Göteborg Pass travel free, including on late-night transport. Otherwise a city transport ticket costs adult/child Skr21/16 (Skr42 on late-night transport). Easy-to-use one- and three-day travel cards (from Västtrafik information booths or Pressbyrån newsagencies) work out much cheaper than buying tickets each time you travel. A 24-hour Dagkort (day pass) for the whole city area costs Skr65, Skr130 for three days.

The easiest way to cover lengthy distances in Göteborg is by tram. Lines, numbered 1 to 13, converge near Brunnsparken (a block from the train station).

Västtrafik has regional passes for 24 hours/ three days (adult Skr240/480) that give un-limited travel on all *länstrafik* (regional) buses, trains and boats within the Göteborg, Bohuslän and Västergötland area.

Taxi

One of the larger companies is **Taxi Göteborg** (☎65 00 00; www.taxigoteborg.se). Taxis can be picked up outside Centralstationen, at Kungsportsplatsen and on Kungsportsavenyn. Women travelling alone at night can expect a fare discount.

AROUND GÖTEBORG

Southern Archipelago

☎031 / POP 4300

A car-free paradise, the southern archipel-ago is a short hop from Göteborg's hustle. Despite the summer crowds, you'll always find a quiet bathing spot or serene pocket of green.

There are nine major islands and numerous smaller ones. The largest island, Styrsö, is less than 3km long. Military restrictions saw most of the area closed to foreigners until 1997; it's now a residential hot spot for cashed-up commuters.

Take tram 11 from central Göteborg to Saltholmen, from where an excellent 16-des-tination passenger-only ferry network runs round the islands. The Göteborg Pass is valid, or you can buy a ticket (adult/child one-way Skr21/16, round-trip Skr42/37) tak-ing you all the way from central Göteborg to Vrångö. Bikes are allowed on the ferries free of charge if there is space, but keep in mind they're not allowed on city trams.

Boats run frequently to Asperö (nine min-utes), Brännö (20 minutes) and Styrsö (30 minutes) from around 5.30am to 1am (less frequently at weekends); services to the oth-er islands are more limited.

The best information about the islands can be found in the English-language booklet *Excursions in the Southern Archipelago,* published by Västtrafik and available from the tourist offices or Västtrafik information booths.

BRÄNNÖ

POP 790

Brännö's beaches and outdoor dance floor are its biggest attractions, although it's hard to take your eyes off the local *lastmoped:* bizarre-looking motorised bikes with large trays attached.

The busiest ferry terminal is Rödsten, in the northeast, but ferries also call at Husvik in the southwest.

From the church in the centre of the island, follow the cycling track through the woods towards the west coast. A 15-minute walk from the end of the track leads to a stone causeway and the island **Galterö** – a strange treeless landscape of rock slabs, ponds, deserted sandy beaches and haunting bird calls. You can watch ships of all sizes and colours heading into or out of Göteborg harbour.

Get away from it all at **Pensionat Bagge** (☎97 38 80; www.baggebranno.se; s/d Skr550/920), a simple, friendly place about a kilometre south of the ferry quay. The same owners operate **Brännö Värdshus** (☎97 04 78; Husviksvägen; mains Skr185-265; ☺11am-11pm daily mid-Jun–mid-Aug, to 9pm Tue-Thu, to 11pm Fri & Sat, to 7pm Sun May & Sep, 11am-7pm Thu & Sun, to 11pm Fri & Sat rest of year), which houses a cosy restaurant, cafe and bakery and serves excellent meals, including the local special-ity *rödtunga* (plaice). It also hosts regular live jazz and folk gigs in summer. There's a grocery shop near the church.

From mid-June to mid-August, **Strömma** (www.stromma.se) runs evening cruises (usually on Thursday) from Lilla Bommen harbour to Husvik's **pier dance floor**, where passengers can groove for a couple of hours before returning to Göteborg. The dinner tour costs Skr545 per adult. Check the website for the latest prices and timetables.

OTHER ISLANDS

Just southeast of Brännö, Köpstadsö is a small island with a quaint village of pretty painted houses and narrow streets. Transport on the island is even more basic than it is on Brännö: locals use individually named wheelbarrows, parked by the quay.

In the central part of the archipelago, Styrsö has two village centres (Bratten and Tängen, both with ferry terminals), a mixture of old and modern houses, and a history of smuggling. There's a cafe, pizzeria and supermarket at Tängen. A bridge crosses from Styrsö to densely populated neighbouring Donsö, with a functioning fishing harbour.

The southern island of Vrångö has a good swimming beach on the west coast, about 10 minutes' walk from the ferry. The northern and southern ends of the island are part of an extensive nature reserve.

Tiny Vinga, 8km west of Galterö, has impressive rock slabs and decent swimming, and has been home to a lighthouse since the 17th century. The writer, composer and painter Evert Taube was born here in 1890 – his father was the lighthouse-keeper. Walona (www.walona.se) runs pleasant three-hour tours (adult/child Skr200/130) from Stenpiren, Skeppsbron (Göteborg) to Vinga (Wednesday to Friday mid-July through August). Check the website for updated times and prices.

MARSTRAND
☑0303 / POP 1300

Looking like a Tommy Hilfiger ad (think crisp white summer houses and moneyed eye candy on gleaming boats), this former spa town and island is a Swedish royal favourite. Boasting the country's most popular *gästhamn* (guest harbour), it's *the* weekend destination for yachting types and a see-and-be-seen summer magnet. If you can tolerate the hiked-up prices, it's a spot worth soaking up.

Looming over the town is doughty Carlstens Fästning (☑602 65, 611 67; www.carlsten.se; adult/7-15yr Skr75/25; ☺11am-6pm daily Jul, to 4pm Jun & Aug, Sat & Sun rest of year, call ahead for hours), a fortress constructed in the 1660s after the Swedish takeover of Bohuslän; later building work was completed by convicts sentenced to hard labour. Its impressive round tower reaches 96m above sea level, and there are smashing archipelago views from the top. Admission includes a guided tour (call ahead for English-language tour times), although you can explore by yourself with an audio guide.

Pick up the English-language *Discover Marstrand* brochure from the tourist office and set off for an hour's walk round the island. Sterling structures include the town hall, which is the oldest stone building in the county, and the 13th-century Maria Kyrka.

Budget accommodation is not Marstrand's forte. The most reasonably priced option is Marstrands Varmbadhus Båtellet (☑600 10; batellet@gmail.com; Kungsplan; 6-bed f per person Skr280; @☎), a private hostel with associated pool and sauna. Turn right after disembarking from the ferry and follow the waterfront for 400m. Only dormitory accommodation is available in the summer.

Located at the northern end of the harbour, the Hotell Nautic (☑610 30; www.hotellnautic.com; Långgatan 6; B&B s/d Skr950/1400; @) has bright, simple rooms decked out for the most part in seaside blues and creams. A couple have balconies with great sea views.

Marstrand's numerous eating options include fast-food stalls along the harbour. Follow your nose to Bergs Konditori (Hamngatan 9; ☺May-Aug), a dockside *konditori* (bakery-patisserie) selling fresh bread, cakes, quiches and sandwiches.

Otto's Kök (www.marstrands.se; Hamngatan 23; lunches around Skr155, dinner mains Skr189-325; ☺lunch daily, dinner Mon-Sat) at the Marstrands Havshotell is one of the island's better dining options and ideal for yacht-spotting.

Opposite the ferry terminal is the tourist office (☑600 87; www.marstrand.se; Hamngatan 33; ☺10am-6pm Mon-Fri, 11am-5pm Sat & Sun Jun-Aug, shorter hours rest of year). There's no ATM or Systembolaget (state-owned liquor store), so bring wealth and wine with you.

From Göteborg you should take the Marstrandsexpressen to Arvidsvik (on Koön) then cross to Marstrand by frequent passenger-only ferry. The complete journey usually only takes about an hour (Skr52).

Bohus Fästning

🔲0303

Survivor of no fewer than 14 sieges, the hulking ruins of Bohus Fästning (www.bo husfastning.se; adult/7-16yr Skr50/25, cash only; ☺10am-7pm daily May-Aug, 11am-3pm daily Sep, 11am-3pm Sat & Sun Oct, 11am-5pm Sat & Sun Apr) stand on an island in the Nordre älv, near Kungälv. Construction of the fortress was ordered in 1308 by the Norwegian king to protect Norway's southern border. The building was enlarged over the centuries, becoming one of Sweden's toys at the Peace of Roskilde in 1658. Its substantial remains include a remarkable round tower. Tourist information for the area is available at the fortress.

Complete with cafe, STF Vandrarhem & Camping Kungälv (🔲189 00; www.va ghals.se; Färjevägen 2, Kungälv; sites from Skr200, s/d Skr450/550; ☺campsite May–mid-Sep; @) boasts a riverside setting directly across the road from the fortress.

Nearby on the river, Kungälvs Båtuthyrning (🔲13 71 19; www.kbu.se, in Swedish; Filaregatan 11) rents small boats (Skr550/850 per three hours/day). Boats must be booked at least one day in advance.

A Västtrafik Grön Express bus runs at least every 30 minutes from Göteborg to Kungälv; get off at the Eriksdal stop and walk the remaining 500m. Journey time is 30 minutes.

BOHUSLÄN

Dramatic, stark and irrepressibly beautiful, the Bohuslän coast is one of Sweden's natural treasures. The landscape here is a grand mix of craggy islands and rickety fishing villages caught between sky and sea. Island-hopping is a must, as is lounging on broad, sun-warmed rocks and gorging on the region's incredible seafood.

Bohuslän Coast

If you're heading north from Göteborg, stop at the tourist office (🔲0303-833 27; www. bastkusten.se; Kulturhuset Fregattan; ☺9am-6pm Mon-Fri, 11am-3pm Sat summer, 9am-5pm Mon-Fri rest of year) in Stenungsund to pick up brochures and maps of the surrounding area.

Transport connections are good – the E6 motorway runs north from Göteborg to Oslo via the larger towns of Stenungsund, Ljungskile, Herrestad, Munkedal and Tanumshede, passing close to Strömstad before crossing the Norwegian border. Local trains run frequently from Göteborg to Strömstad, via much the same towns as the E6 route. Bus connections from these towns to the outlying islands exist, although some aren't terribly regular.

It's an area suited for independent exploration; consider hiring a car or bike in Göteborg and take it in at your own pace.

ROCK CARVINGS 101

Bohuslän's Bronze Age rock carvings (hällristningar) are a prolific sight, a phenomenal 3000-year-old artistic record of religious beliefs, rites and everyday living. Under open skies, the carvings are free to view. The enlightening book The Rock Carving Tour (Skr50), available only from Bohusläns Museum (p170), contains thoughtful interpretations and detailed maps showing you how to find the best Bohuslän sites.

The Tanum plain is particularly rich in carvings, and the entire 45-sq-km area has been placed on the Unesco World Heritage list. Start your odyssey at Vitlycke, within the Tanum area, where you'll find ships, animals, humans and tiny footsteps scattered through the woods. The splendid 22m Vitlycke Rock forms a huge canvas for 500 carvings of 'love, power and magic'. These range from simple cup marks to some of Sweden's most famous rock-art images, including the Lovers, showing a sacred marriage.

If you're bewildered by the long-armed men, sexual imagery and goat-drawn chariots, cross the road to Vitlycke Museum (☺0525-209 50; www.vitlyckemuseum.se; admission free; ☺10am-6pm daily May-Aug, to 4pm Sep, 11am-4pm Oct, open only for booked visits rest of year), which has a determined go at explaining them. There are digital handheld guides, but it's much better to catch the English tour (Skr500), complete with clued-up human being. Call ahead for tour times.

To get to Vitlycke by public transport, take bus 870 or 945 from Tanumshede bus station to Hoghem. From there it's a five- to 10-minute walk. Regional buses on the Göteborg–Uddevalla–Strömstad route stop at Tanumshede.

TJÖRN & AROUND

📞 0304 / POP 14,940

A large bridge swoops from Stenungsund (on the Swedish mainland) to the island of Tjörn (www.sodrabohuslan.com), a magnet for artists thanks to its striking landscapes and stunning watercolour museum. Sailors are equally smitten, with one of Sweden's biggest sailing competitions, the Tjörn Runt, taking place here in August.

Skärhamn and Rönnäng, in the southwest, are the island's main settlements. Their few facilities include a small tourist office (☎60 10 16; turistbyran@tjorn.se; Södra Hamnen; ⊙noon-5pm Mon-Fri, 11am-3pm Sat & Sun Jun-Aug, closed rest of year) at Skärhamn.

Skärhamn is also home to the superb **Nordiska Akvarellmuseet** (Nordic Watercolour Museum; www.akvarellmuseet.org; Södra Hamnen 6; adult/under 25yr Skr70/free; ⊙11am-6pm mid-May–mid-Sep, noon-5pm Tue-Sun rest of year), a sleek waterside building housing world-class exhibits. It also rents out five guest cabins (artists/public Skr500/1000), and the legendary fish dishes at the adjacent gourmet cafe-restaurant **Vatten** (☎67 00 87; www.restaurangvatten.com; lunches Skr125-175, 3-course tasting dinners Skr545; ⊙from noon Jul–mid-Aug, shorter hours rest of year) are a perfect match with the archipelago backdrop.

Rönnängs Vandrarhem (☎67 71 98; www.ronnangsvandrarhem.se, in Swedish; Nyponvägen 5; s/d Skr300/600; P❷), an SVIF hostel in Rönnäng, about 1km from the ferry, is good and spacious, with one sizeable kitchen and a rambling, country-home feel. There's a leafy terrace for lazy summer barbecues.

Magasinet Harön (www.magasinetharon.com; mains Skr149-265; ⊙from noon Jul–mid-Aug), at the northwest end of Tjörn, is the summer home of Göteborg chef Mats Nordström (see p157). His restaurant here, within a stone's throw of the sea in an 1847 fisherman's *magasinet* (depot), becomes a bustling hub in summer. Meals are appropriately seafood intensive and served with all the care of Norström's established Wasa Allé. Take the passenger-only *St Olaf II* ferry from Kyrkesund to get there.

The Tjörnexpressen bus runs up to 10 times weekdays (twice Saturday and Sunday) from Göteborg's bus terminal to Tjörn, calling at Skärhamn, Klädesholmen and Rönnäng. Bus 355 from Stenungsund crosses the island to Rönnäng.

KLÄDESHOLMEN

The 'herring island' of Klädesholmen, to the far south of Tjörn, is one of the west coast's most flawless spots. A mash-up of red and white wooden cottages, its activity is fairly subdued due to the departure of the herring (there were once 30 processing factories here, today reduced to a handful). Find out more at the tiny herring museum (Sillgränd 8; ⊙3-7pm Jul–mid-Aug).

Salt & Sill (☎67 34 80; www.saltosill.se; mains Skr195-325; ⊙May-Sep & Dec, call ahead other times) is a stylish waterside restaurant with an emphasis on local seafood and produce. The herring board is legendary, with herring prepared in six different ways with all the Scandi trimmings. In 2008 the owners opened Sweden's first floating hotel (s/d Skr1790/2190; ❷). The row of slick cubic buildings now houses 23 contemporary rooms, each featuring the hues of its namesake herb or spice.

ÅSTOL

Nearby Åstol looks straight out of a curious dream – think a tiny, barren chunk of rock dotted with rows of gleaming white houses that seem perched on top of each other from the sea. There's not much to do, but it's utterly lovable. Amble round the car-free streets, soak up the views of the other islands, and feast on fish at **Åstols Rökeri** (☎15 34 94; www.astolsrokeri.se; ⊙noon-midnight mid-Jun–mid-Aug, Fri-Sun May–mid-Jun), a fish smokery with summer restaurant attached.

You can reach Åstol by ferry from Rönnäng (once or twice every hour between 5.30am and 11.30pm).

ORUST

📞 0304 / POP 15,370

Sweden's third-biggest island, Orust (www.orust.se) boasts lush woodlands and some breathtakingly pretty fishing villages. It also has a thriving boat-building industry, with over half of Sweden's sailing craft made here. A bridge connects Orust to Tjörn, its southern neighbour.

Orust's tourist office (☎33 44 94; turistbyran@orust.se; Kulturhuset Kajutan, Hamntorget; ⊙noon-4pm Tue-Fri, 10am-2pm Sat) is in the same building as the library in the town of Henån.

There's an outstanding STF hostel, **Tofta gård** (☎503 80; www.toftagard.se, in Swedish; s/d Skr380/560), near Stocken in the island's west, about 5km from the larger village of Ellös. It's located in an old farmhouse and outbuildings in a blissfully bucolic setting, with good walking, swimming and canoeing nearby. There's also a cafe and restaurant here in peak season. Book ahead between October and May.

MOLLÖSUND

Supercute Mollösund, in the island's southwest, is the oldest fishing village on the Bohuslän coast. There's a picture-perfect harbour and several scenic walking paths for a gentle pick-me-up.

Mollösunds Hembygdsmuseum (☑214 69/75; admission free; ⊙4-6pm late Jun–mid-Aug, call to visit at other times) is in an old fisherfolk's house near the water and has exhibits about local life.

Slightly inland from the harbour, **Prästgårdens Pension** (☑210 58; www.prastgardens.se; Kyrkvägen 1; d from Skr1095; [P]) is the most delightful little spot, with high ceilings, vintage wallpaper, antiques, art and a soothing cottage vibe.

Emma's Café, Grill and Vinbar (☑211 75; www.cafeemma.com; lunches Skr45-165; dinner mains Skr129-195; ⊙restaurant 11am-midnight Jun–mid-Aug), another Bohuslän establishment co-owned by Göteborg chef Mats Nordström (see p157), is an excellent place right on the harbour with a small, welcoming hostel (doubles from Skr900). The cosy cafe-restaurant serves hearty dishes created from local and organic ingredients (the fish soup is exceptional). Out of season, book for the hostel and phone to check restaurant hours.

Mollösunds Wärdshus (☑211 08; www.mwhus.se; Kyrkvägen 9; lunches Skr155, mains from Skr265; ⊙restaurant mid-May–Sep, Sat & Sun Apr–mid-May & Oct-Dec) is an upmarket 19th-century inn featuring a slinky, sunny-soaked terrace for lazy wining and dining, and well-turned-out rooms (available from Easter to December; singles/doubles from Skr1045/1245).

There's a supermarket near the harbour.

Bus 375 runs the Uddevalla–Henån–Ellös route and bus 372 goes to Mollösund. The Orustexpressen bus runs several times on weekdays direct from Göteborg to Henån; otherwise change in Stenungsund or Lysekil.

LYSEKIL & AROUND

☑0523 / POP 14,630

With its air of faded grandeur, the former spa resort of Lysekil feels oddly like an English seaside town. It pampers summer visitors less than other Bohuslän towns do, but there's something strangely refreshing about this unfussed attitude.

◉ Sights & Activities

The town of Lysekil harbours some interesting architecture from its 19th-century spa days, such as old bathing huts and **Curmans villor**, the wooden seafront houses built in romantic 'Old Norse' style. Carl Curman was the resort's famous physician, who was able to persuade visitors that Lysekil's sea bathing was a complete cure-all. Crooked street **Gamla Strandgatan** peddles a too-cute collection of painted wooden abodes.

Perched on a hill, the neo-Gothic pink-granite **church** (⊙10am-3pm Mon-Fri, to 1pm Sun, closed Sat) has some superb paintings and stained-glass panes honouring local working life.

Havets Hus   AQUARIUM

(www.havetshus.se; Strandvägen 9; adult/child/13-18yr Skr95/45/70; ⊙10am-4pm daily mid-Feb–Oct, to 6pm mid-Jun–mid-Aug) Havets Hus is an aquarium with sea life from Sweden's only true fjord, which cuts past Lysekil. Wolffish, lumpsuckers, anglerfish...all the cold-water beauties are here.

Stångehuvud Nature Reserve   NATURE RESERVE

Out at the tip of the Stångenäs peninsula, the Stångehuvud Nature Reserve, crammed with coastal rock slab, is worth a stop for its peaceful bathing spots and wooden lookout tower.

Fiskebäckskil   ISLAND

Passenger-only ferries cross the Gullmarn fjord roughly hourly to Fiskebäckskil, where there are cobbled streets, wood-clad houses and lauded seafood restaurant **Brygghuset** (www.brygghuset-krog.com). The interior of the **church** (⊙10am-3pm) recalls an upturned boat, with votive ships and impressive ceiling and wall paintings.

Käringön   ISLAND

Regular ferries are the best way to get to this picture-perfect island, which boasts plenty of good swimming holes and a pretty church. There are also plenty of broad rocks, which make an ideal location for picnicking on a summer's day.

Seal safaris   BOAT TOUR

(☑66 81 61; adult/child/13-18yr Skr180/100/140, combined ticket with Havets Hus Skr250/125/190; ⊙1pm Jul–mid-Aug) Seal safaris lasting 1½ hours leave from near the aquarium; buy tickets at Havets Hus.

GÖTEBORG & THE SOUTHWEST BOHUSLÄN COAST

🍴 Sleeping & Eating

There are a few fast-food places on and around Rosvikstorg and eateries all along the main street.

Strand Vandrarhem & Hotell   HOSTEL €

(☎797 51; www.strandflickorna.se; Strandvägen 1; dm Skr300, s/d hostel Skr750/850, hotel Skr935/1120; P@) The friendly 'beach girls' run a choice of accommodation not far from Havets Hus. Hostel rooms are neat and prettily wallpapered. There are more plush hotel-style rooms on offer too; some have sea views.

Havshotell   HOTEL €€

(☎797 50; www.strandflickorna.se; Turistgatan 13; s/d Skl095/1695; P@) Run by the hostel folk, this more upmarket option is based in a sensitively renovated turn-of-the-20th-century house. The atmospheric rooms feature a seafaring/historical theme.

Siviks Camping   CAMPGROUND €

(☎61 15 28; www.sivikscamping.nu; sites Skr310; ☺end Apr–mid-Sep) Built on large pink-granite slabs by a sandy beach 2km north of town, Siviks is the best campsite in the area, with ample swimming opportunities. Facilities include shop, restaurant, minigolf, dance floor and laundry.

Pråmen   SEAFOOD €€

(www.pramen.nu; Södra Hamnen; mains Skr149-189; ☺noon-late Jul–mid-Aug, Fri & Sat May & Sep) Crabs, mussels, prawns, halibut, salmon: if it swims, scuttles or sticks to rocks in the sea, this popular floating restaurant-bar will have it on the menu.

Café Kungsgatan   CAFE €

(www.cafekungsgatan.se; Kungsgatan 32; lunches Skr80; ☺Mon-Sat) Set back from the seafront, this honest café serves homemade lunches (pasta, quiche, salads, sandwiches, herring pancakes) washed down with all kinds of tea and coffee.

ℹ️ Information

The town is amply serviced, with banks and supermarket.

Public library (Kungsgatan 18; ☺noon-8pm Mon-Thu, to 3pm Fri mid-Jun–mid-Aug, 10am-6pm Mon-Thu, to 4pm Fri, to 1pm Sat rest of year) Has free internet access.

Tourist office (☎130 50; Södra Hamngatan 6; ☺11am-5pm Mon-Fri, to 3pm Sat & Sun Jul–mid-Aug, call for times rest of year) Offers information on various summer boat tours, including island-hopping swimming trips to fishing jaunts.

ℹ️ Getting There & Away

Express buses 840 and 841 run every couple of hours from Göteborg to Lysekil via Uddevalla (Skr128, two hours).

SMÖGEN

☎0523

Another seaside star, Smögen sports a buzzing waterside boardwalk, rickety fishermen's houses, and steep steps leading up into a labyrinth of lovingly restored cottages and pretty summer gardens.

Dubbed **Smögenbryggan**, the boardwalk heaves with bars and shops around the harbour; head in early or out of season if you're seeking solitude. Fishing boats unload their catches of prawns, lobsters and fish at the harbour, where there's a small **fish auction** (www.smogens-fiskauktion.com; Fiskhall; ☺8am Mon-Fri, plus 5pm Thu): the big one happens online these days.

From Smögen harbour, the **Hållö Färjan** (☎312 67, 0706-913 633; www.hallofarjan.se; adult/under 12yr round-trip Skr80/40) leaves every half-hour or so from 9.30am in summer for the nature reserve on the nearby island of **Hållö**. The island's smooth granite boulders, bizarre potholes and deep fissures are the result of thousands of years of glacial carving. Perched on top is a red-and-white 19th-century lighthouse, as well as a small church (ask at the hostel if you want to take a peek inside). Terns and other seabirds nest in the surrounding oat grass, and delicate wild pansies dot the island. It's pristine and remote, an ideal haunt for those keen to capture the true essence of Bohuslän. Utpost Hållö (see boxed text) is the island's gloriously out-of-the-way hostel.

The **Kon-Tiki Dykcenter** (www.kontiki-smogen.se; Madenvägen 3) does boat dives, PADI courses and hires out kayaks (Skr200/350 per three hours/day).

Makrillvikens Vandrarhem (☎315 65; www.makrillviken.se; Makrillgatan; d Skr700-1000; P), in the former spa bathing house with smashing views of the archipelago, is a sterling, hugely popular budget choice – 500m from the boardwalk crowds, and with an old seaside sauna for guest use. There's a small playground, and canoes for hire. Book ahead!

Hotel Smögens Havsbad (☎66 84 50; www.smogenshavsbad.se; Hotellgatan 26; s/d from Skr1045/1490; P@☀) is an architectural haystack, but fortunately it's beautiful on the

CANDLE ON THE WATER

Balanced atop the windswept skerries of Västra Götaland, bright at the country's south-ernmost tip or acting as sturdy wardens of Gotland's sandy shores: the *fyr* (lighthouses) of southern Sweden are as varied as they are beautiful.

There is the red cast-iron skeleton of the Sandhammaren Fyr in Skåne or the sea-worthy Kullagrundet, surrounded by the Baltic 3km south of Smygehuk. For pretty red and white stripes, walk down Citadellsvågen in Malmö, or there is the red-brick, cupola-topped block at Helsingborg that greets visitors coming in on the Scandline ferry from Denmark. Want plain-Jane, tall, thin and white? Look no further than Karlskrona.

Romance and drama aside, lighthouses are also some of the best places to stay for those keen to really experience Sweden's southern coast. Not only are the settings unfailingly pristine and unique, it's a chance to enjoy the ocean, birds and seafood as Swedes do.

Luckily for visitors, there are several lighthouses to choose from, all run as hostels.

At the island of **Stora Karlsö** (☑0498-24 04 50; www.storakarlso.se; s/d Skr 450/900; ☺May-Aug) off the coast of Gotland, you can stay in rooms still decorated with the an-tique furniture left by the lighthouse-keeper. There is a small restaurant if you don't fancy cooking and it's a stunning place to birdwatch. Treeless, rocky Hållö, one of the skerries off the coast of Smögen, feels more remote and raw. The lovely red and white-trimmed cabins of the **Utpost Hållö** (☑0703-53 68 22; www.utpost-hallo.nu; dm from Skr600; ☺mid-May–Aug) are perched on broad granite slabs within 100m of the sea and the lighthouse. It's a great place to take in the ocean, birds and crisp blue skies. There is even a little church. You'll need to take ferries to both islands.

For easy-to-reach, try the shipshape **Smygehuk** (☑0410-245 83, 70 70 14; www.smy gehukhostel.com; s/d Skr300/480; ☺mid-May–mid-Sep) lighthouse in Skåne. It's about an hour out of Malmö and within an easy walk of the town's excellent fish smokehouse.

Fancy just visiting? Scandinavia's strongest lighthouse light, visible from 50km away, is the **Kullens fyr** (☑042-34 70 56; adult/6-12yr Skr20/10; ☺11am-4pm Feb-Nov) on the Kullaberg Peninsula. There has been a light of some kind here for over 1000 years.

---

inside, with light Scandi-style rooms and an excellent seafood restaurant.

There's no shortage of appetising cafes, grill-bars and seafood restaurants all along Smögenbryggan.

Skärets Krog & Konditori (☑323 17; www. skaretskrog.se; Hamnen 1; mains Skr198-355; ☺Sat & Sun May–mid-Jun, daily mid-Jun–mid-Aug), near the Fiskhall, has a ground-floor *konditori* serving light meals and sweet treats and a gourmet upstairs restaurant. Lovingly pre-pared food ranges from hake with lobster foam to homemade pork sausages. The own-ers also run the popular **Coffee Room** (ba-gels & wraps Skr69-89; ☺9am-11pm) around the corner on Sillgatan.

The **tourist office** (☑66 55 50; info@ sostenasturism.se; Bäckeviksorget 5; ☺10am-6pm Mon-Fri, to 5pm Sat & Sun mid-Jun–mid-Aug, 9am-1pm rest of year) is in Kungshamn. During summer there is a second branch in the parking lot of the ICA shopping centre directly over the Smögenbron.

Bus 860 runs regularly from Göteborg to Smögen (Skr152, around 2½ hours) via Uddevalla, Munkedal, Hunnebostrand and Kungshamn. A couple of the services are direct, otherwise you'll have to change in one of the towns en route.

FJÄLLBACKA
☑0525

Film star Ingrid Bergman spent her sum-mer holidays at Fjällbacka (the main square is named after her). Despite the crowds, the tiny town is utterly charming, with its brightly coloured houses squashed between steep cliffs and rolling sea.

The summer-only **tourist office** (☑321 20; www.fjallbacka.com; Ingrid Bergmanstorg; ☺mid-Jun–Aug) can advise on boat trips to the popular, rocky island of Väderöarna. Fjällbacka Båttrafik operates a **Vadero Express** (☑320 01; www.fjbbt.se; adult/under 13yr round-trip Skr 300/150) that runs up to six times daily during the summer from the pier by Ingrid Bergmanstorg to Norra Väderöarna.

After pottering about, eating ice cream and browsing the trinket shops, walk up

DON'T MISS

STORA HOTELLET

This is a whimsical **hotel** (☑310 03; www.storahotellet-fjallbacka.se; Galärbacken; s/d with shared bathroom from Skr1000/1200; **@**) offering a trip 'around the world in 23 rooms'. It was originally owned by a ship's captain who decorated it with exotic souvenirs. He named each room after his favourite port and explorers (and girls!), and each tells its own story. Extras include a restaurant, as well as lobster-fishing packages (from Skr2595 per person) from late September to November.

the **Vetteberget** cliff for unforgettable 360-degree views and mesmerising sunsets. From July to mid-August, Fjällbacka Båttrafik runs 1½-hour **island boat trips** (www.fjbbt.se; adult/8-12yr Skr250/125; ☺10am), including a tour that takes in the local **seal colony** (per person Skr350; ☺3pm). Boats depart from Ingrid Bergmanstorg.

On a teeny little island just off the harbour, **Badholmens Vandrarhem** (☑321 50, 0703-28 79 55; per person Skr200; ☺Apr-Oct) is a low-fuss hostel reached by a causeway. Four plain bunk-bedded huts look out to sea, and there's a cafe, laundry and free sauna for guests nearby.

With its killer waterside location and top-notch grub, laid-back **Bryggan Fjällbacka** (☑310 60; www.brygganfjallbacka.se; Ingrid Bergmanstorg; small plates Skr150, mains Skr260-340; ☺daily Jul-Sep, weekends Apr, Jun & Oct-Dec) is a massive summer hit. Opt for fantastic pub and cafe fare or posh-nosh options. There is an upstairs piano bar and boutique accommodation to boot (dorm/double with shared bathroom Skr590/1590).

The best way to reach Fjällbacka from Göteborg is to take a Strömstad-bound train to Dingle station, then bus 875 to Fjällbacka. The entire journey should cost around Skr152 and take about two hours and 20 minutes, although it's always best to use the Travel Planner option at www.vasttrafik.se to avoid long connection times.

Uddevalla

☑0522 / POP 51,840

You might find yourself in Bohuslän's capital, Uddevalla, while waiting for transport connections. If so, pop into the museum or take a dip in the old spa area at Gustafsberg. Otherwise, it's a mostly modern, industrial place, giving little reason to linger long.

Bohusläns Museum (www.bohuslansmuseum.se; Museigatan 1; admission free; ☺10am-8pm Tue-Thu, to 4pm Fri-Mon), near the bus station, tells the history of the area from the Stone Age onward, with displays on traditional stone, boat-building and fish-preserving industries. There's also an art gallery and restaurant.

Based in an old bathing house, **STF Vandrarhem Gustafsberg/Uddevalla** (☑152 00; www.gustafsberg.se; dm from Skr245; ☺Jun-Aug) enjoys a wonderful waterside location at the old spa of Gustafsberg, 4km from the centre. Bathers have four beaches to choose from if they fancy a dip in the sea or there is a nearby pool. There are recreation areas and a cafe down this way, too. The area can be reached by boat from the jetty across the river from the museum, or by local bus.

The **tourist office** (☑69 84 70; www.uddevalla.com; Södra Hamnen 2; ☺9am-6pm Mon-Fri, to 3pm Sat & Sun mid-Jun–Aug, 11am-4pm Mon-Fri, to 6pm Thu rest of year) can help with information.

Regional buses and trains run daily to Strömstad (Skr104, 1¼ hours) and Göteborg (Skr104, 1¼ hours). **Swebus Express** (www.swebusexpress.com) runs to Oslo (Skr189, three hours) up to seven times daily. Buses drop off and pick up from the bus station on the E6 motorway, rather than in the town centre.

Strömstad

☑0526 / POP 11,929

A sparky resort, fishing harbour and spa town, Strömstad is laced with ornate wooden buildings echoing nearby Norway. Indeed, Norwegians head here en masse in summer to take advantage of Sweden's cheaper prices, lending a particularly lively air to the town's picturesque streets and bars.

There are several fantastic Iron Age remains in the area, and some fine **sandy beaches** at Capri and Seläter. Boat trips run to the Koster Islands, the most westerly in Sweden and popular for cycling.

◉ Sights & Activities

FREE **Stone Ship Settings** ARCHAEOLOGICAL SITE (☺24hr) One of Sweden's largest, most magnificent stone ship settings (an oval of stones, shaped like a boat) lies 6km north-east of Strömstad. Resting in a field full of wildflowers, its lack of visitors makes it a more personal experience than Ales Stenar (p206). There are 49 stones in total, with the stem and stern stones reaching over 3m in height; the site has been dated to AD 400 to 600. Across the road is a huge site containing approximately 40 **Iron Age graves**. Ask at the tourist office or bus station for information on buses out there. Alternatively, there's a gorgeous walking path from the north of town.

Koster Islands
ISLAND
(www.kosteroarna.com) Boat trips (return trip for adult/seven to 19 years Skr120/80) run from Strömstad's north harbour to the beautiful Koster Islands roughly every 30 minutes from July to mid-August and less frequently at other times. North Koster is hilly and has good beaches. South Koster is flatter and better for cycling. There is a **Naturum** (⊙11am-5pm mid-Jun–Aug) on North Koster by Västra Bryggan with information on **Kosterhavets Nationalpark**, Sweden's first marine park.

Skee Kyrka
CHURCH
Open by appointment only (contact the tourist office), the Romanesque stone Skee Kyrka is about 6km east of Strömstad and has a 10th-century nave. There's also a painted wooden ceiling and an unusual 17th-century reredos with 24 sculptured figures. Nearby lie **Iron Age graves**, a curious **bell tower** and a mid-Neolithic **passage tomb** (c 3000 BC).

FREE Strömstads Museum
MUSEUM
(www.stromstadsmuseum.se; Södra Hamngatan 26; ⊙9am-1pm & 2-4pm Mon-Fri, 11am-2pm Sat) In town; housed in an old power station, this museum has been displaying local photography and historical objects since 1981.

Boat Tours
BOAT TOUR
For boats out to **Ursholmen**, Sweden's most westerly lighthouse, seal safaris and mackerel fishing, contact **Selin Charter** (www.selin-charter.se; tours from Skr140; ⊙Jun-Aug). Trips leave from Strömstad's southern harbour.

🛏 Sleeping & Eating

Crusellska Hemmet
HOSTEL €
(✆101 93; www.crusellska.se; Norra Kyrkogatan 12; s/d Skr450/650; ⊙Mar–early Dec; P @) Drifting white curtains, pale decor and wicker

lounges lend this place a boutique vibe. The kitchen is seriously spacious and there's a peaceful garden for alfresco contemplation, as well as a range of pampering spa treatments. Book ahead.

Hotell Krabban
HOTEL €€
(✆142 00; www.hotellkrabban.se; Södra Bergsgatan 15; s/d from Skr790/990; @) 'The Crab' is a small and personal place in the centre of town. Rooms, based in an old wooden building, have nautical undertones. There are cheaper alternatives (around Skr100 less) if you're happy to share a corridor bathroom.

Strömstad Camping
CAMPGROUND €
(✆611 21; www.stromstadcamping.se; Uddevallavägen; sites Skr250, 2-bed cabins from Skr500; ⊙mid-Apr–Aug) In a lovely, large park at the southern edge of town, the campsite also has shady cabins for rent.

🍴 Rökeri is Strömstad
SEAFOOD €€
(dnn.rokerietistromstad.se; Torskholmen; lunches from Skr89, dinner mains Skr129-250; ⊙lunch Tue-Sun, dinner Fri & Sat) This family-run dockside restaurant, fish shop and smokehouse dishes out deep bowls of fish soup, pickled herring and seafood baguettes at lunch. Dinner is similar, if more refined. It's in a perfect location for lazy ocean gazing and the owners take care to source their seafood sustainably.

Restaurang Trädgården
EUROPEAN €€
(www.tradgarden.net; Östra Klevgatan 4; lunches Skr109, dinner mains Skr139-229; ⊙lunch Mon-Sat year-round, dinner Jun-Aug) Chinking glasses and upbeat alfresco supping lure you to this convivial restaurant. In summer, the grilled seafood and meat lunch buffet is a particular hit, while the à la carte menu boasts hearty grills and local classics.

ICA
SUPERMARKET
(Södra Hamngatan 8) Centrally located.

Systembolaget
LIQUOR STORE
(Oslovägen 7) A couple of minutes' walk from the town centre.

ℹ Information

Library (Karlsgatan 17; ⊙11am-7pm Mon & Tue, to 5pm Wed-Fri, closed Sat & Sun) Log on here.

Tourist office (✆623 30; www.stromstad.se; Gamla Tullhuset, Ångbåtskajen 2; ⊙9am-8pm Mon-Sat, 10am-7pm Sun Jun-Aug, 10am-5pm Mon-Fri, 11am-4pm Sep, 11am-4pm Mon-Fri, to

WORTH A TRIP

NORDENS ARK

Snow leopards, wolves and lynx prowl **Nordens Ark** (☑0523-795 90; www.nordensark.se; Åby säteri; adult/5-17yr Skr190/70; ☺10am-7pm daily Jul–mid-Aug, to 5pm May-Jun & late Aug; shorter hours rest of year), a fascinating safari park 12km northeast of Smögen. It shows off animals and plants from countries with a similar climate to Sweden's and has breeding programs for endangered species. If you fancy feeding an Amur leopard, wolverine or red panda, try one of the park's 'Close encounter' tours (about Skr860). Last admission is two hours before closing. Check the website for full opening hours, which vary according to season.

3pm Sat Oct) Located between the two harbours on the main square.

❶ Getting There & Around

Buses and trains both use the train station near the southern harbour. **Västtrafik** (www.vast trafik.se) runs buses 870 and 871 to Göteborg (Skr155, four hours) daily. Strömstad is the northern terminus of the Bohuståg train system, with three or more direct trains running to/from Göteborg (Skr156, three hours).

Ferries run from Strömstad to Sandefjord in Norway (see p352).

For a taxi, call **Taxi Väst** (☑459 000). For car hire, contact **Statoil** (☑121 92; www.statoil.se, in Swedish; Oslovägen 42).

DALSLAND

Northern Dalsland is an introspective mix of long lakes, still forests and silent towns, and the perfect spot to escape the hordes.

To the west, sleepy **Dals-Ed** is sparsely populated – about seven people for every square kilometre – making it ideal for the outdoorsy. You can paddle north from the town of Ed on the fjordlike Stora Le Lake all the way to Norway, passing verdant islands and quiet woodlands. Be sure to enjoy a dip in one of the municipality's 400 or so crystal-clear lakes. Walkers can enjoy miles of quiet trails and, in the later summer, may even be lucky to find mushrooms or berries along the way. Contact **Canodal** (☑618 03; www.canodal.com; Gamla Edsvägen 4, Dals-Ed; 2-person canoes per day/week Skr200/1000) for details. The company also supplies equipment for wilderness camping.

The eastern half of Dalsland is equally watery and peaceful, but with more things to see. The scenic **Dalsland Canal** crosses the region and gets especially interesting (we promise) at Håverud. The canal itself is only 10km long, but it links a series of narrow lakes between Vänern and Stora Le, providing a route 250km long. Not everyone wants to relax on these waterways: a new endurance race, the **Dalsland Kanot Maraton** (www.kanotmaraton.se), sees competitors racing their canoes over a gruelling 55km course here in mid-August.

❶ Getting There & Away

Mellerud is on the main Göteborg–Karlstad train line, and Swebus Express buses between Göteborg and Karlstad stop here once daily (except Saturday) in either direction. Local bus 720 runs a circular route to/from Mellerud via Upperud, Håverud and Skållerud.

Håverud

☑0530

An intriguing triple transport pile-up occurs at tiny Håverud, where a 32m **aqueduct** carries the Dalsland Canal over the river, and a road bridge crosses above them both.

The area around the aqueduct is a chilled-out spot, filled with ambling visitors and the crashing noise of water. Pleasures are simple: visit the Tardis-like **Kanalmuséet** (☑306 24; adult/under 15yr Skr30/free; ☺10am-6pm Jun-Aug), where the history of the canal is told through imaginative displays; sit with a beer and watch boats negotiating the **lock**; or hop on a vessel yourself. Turn-of-the-century canal boat **M/F Storholmen** (☑106 33; www.storhol men.com) runs along the canal to Långbron and Bengtsfors (one-way adult/seven to 12 years Skr275/140) and can be combined with a return trip on the historic **Dalsland-West Värmland Railway** (adult/7-12yr Skr360/180). These mainly run from late June to late August, and can be booked at the tourist office.

The Dalslands Center is the main venue for **Bokdagar i Dalsland** (www.bokdagarid alsland.se, in Swedish), a three-day literature festival held annually in late July or early August, with readings, seminars and book launches focusing on Nordic writers.

The town's **STF hostel** (☑302 75; Museivägen 3; dm Skr225; **P**) overlooks the canal. Rooms are pleasant but can get warm in summer. Outside May to August, book ahead.

Håfveruds Brasseri (☑351 31; Dalslands Centre; ☉daily Jun-Aug, Sat & Sun May & Aug), based in an old paper mill and with shaded lockside tables, serves everything from sandwiches to hearty elk sausages. There's a delicatessen for self-caterers.

The well-stocked **tourist office** (☑189 90; www.dalslandcenter.com, in Swedish; Dalslands Center; ☉10am-7pm Jul–mid-Aug, to 6pm late Aug, to 4pm May, Jun & Sep) can organise fishing licences and canoe hire.

Around Håverud

About 3km south of the aqueduct is **Upperud**, home to the savvy **Dalslands Museum & Konsthall** (www.dalslandsmuseum. se; admission free; ☉11am-6pm daily Jul–mid-Aug, to 5pm Wed-Sun mid-Aug–Oct & Mar-May, 11am-5pm Tue-Sun Jun, to 5pm Sat & Sun Nov–mid-Dec). Pop in for a compact collection of local art, furniture, ceramics, ironware and Åmål silverware, as well as clued-up temporary exhibitions. The small sculpture park in the grounds features some whimsical installations, including a chaotic wooden tower by eccentric artist Lars Vilks. The on-site **Café Bonaparte** (so-called because Napoleon's niece Christine once lived there) combines yummy coffee and snacks with soothing lake views.

Another few kilometres south at **Skållerud** is a beautiful, shiny-red, 17th-century wooden **church** (☉8am-4pm Mon, to 7pm Tue-Fri, 9am-7pm Sat & Sun Apr-Oct, during services Nov-Apr), with well-preserved paintings and biblical sculptures.

Atmospheric **Högsbyn Nature Reserve**, about 8km north of Håverud near Tisselskog, has woodland walks and a shallow bathing spot. Best of all are its impressive Bronze Age **rock carvings** (*hällristningar*): 50 overgrown slabs feature animals, boats, labyrinths, sun signs, and hand and foot marks. The **M/S Dalslandia** (www.dalslandia. com; adult/6-12yr Skr275/140; ☉10.50am Sun Jul–mid-Aug) does a 40-minute stop here on its Sunday trip between Håverud and Bengtsfors. Call ahead to arrange weekday visits.

Baldersnäs Herrgård (☑412 13; www.bald ersnas.eu; admission free), 10km further north past the village of Dals Långed, is a beautiful manor house and grounds, complete with English garden, swimming spots, restaurant and cafe, handicraft stalls and a small Naturum. Quality **accommodation** (s/d from Skr1995) is offered here too, and horse-riding trips can be arranged.

VÄSTERGÖTLAND

Home to Sweden's film-industry hub of Trollhäten, Västergötland is a pleasant mix of stylish manor houses, royal hunting grounds and cultural attractions. Opera lovers flock to Läckö Slott in July, Göta Canal tours abound and the woods are perfect for spotting gangly elk, berry picking or simply strolling.

Vänersborg

☑0521 / POP 37,000

Vänersborg, at the southern outlet of Vänern lake, was once known as 'Little Paris', though it's hard to see why today. The scenic nature reserve and royal hunting grounds outside town are its main attraction, although families may get a kick out of Skräcklen park, with its playgrounds, waffles and splash-happy bathing spots.

◉ Sights & Activities

FREE Vänersborgs Museum   MUSEUM (www.vanersborgsmuseum.se; Östra Plantaget; ☉noon-4pm Tue, Thu, Sat & Sun year-round, plus noon-4pm Wed Jun-Aug) Vänersborgs Museum is the country's oldest provincial museum and has a remarkable southwest African bird collection along with local exhibits and the odd ancient Egyptian artefact.

Hunneberg & Hanneberg Nature Reserve   NATURE RESERVE Described by Linnaeus as an 'earthly paradise', the Hunneberg & Hanneberg Nature Reserve covers two dramatic, craggy plateaus 8km east of town. There are 50km of **walking trails** here that are certainly worth exploring. The deep ravines and primeval forest also make great hiding places for wild elk, and this area has been a favourite royal hunting ground for over 100 years.

GÖTEBORG & THE SOUTHWEST AROUND HÅVERUD

Kungajaktmuseet Älgens Berg MUSEUM
(www.algensberg.com; adult/child Skr60/30; ⏲10am-6pm daily Jun-Aug, 11am-4pm Tue-Sun Sep-Dec & Feb-May, 11am-4pm Tue-Fri Jan) Kungajaktmuseet Älgens Berg, the royal hunting museum, is at Hunneberg and tells you everything you could ever wish to know about elk. There's a great cafe on the grounds, as well as a handicrafts shop. Transport links are tedious – your best bet is to catch the frequent bus 62 from the town square to Vägporten, then walk 2km uphill.

Elk-spotting Safaris TOUR
(☑135 09; adult/5-16yr Skr325/175; ⏲tours Mon-Thu Jul-Aug) The Kungajaktmuseet also runs elk-spotting tours leaving from either the Trollhätten (6.30pm) or Vänersborg (6.45pm) train stations. Tours must be booked in advance through the tourist office or museum.

🛏 Sleeping & Eating

Ronnums Herrgård HOTEL €€
(☑26 00 00; www.ronnums.se; Vargön; s/d from Skr995/1095; P@) Good enough for Nicole Kidman, this luxe mansion is set in gorgeous grounds, out towards Hunneberg. Rooms are seriously elegant, and the oak-floored suites are particularly special. The hotel frequently has special rates and packages: contact it for details. If you feel like a gastronomic treat, the restaurant is one of the region's best.

Hotell 46:an HOTEL €
(☑71 15 61; www.hotell46.com; Kyrkogatan 46; s/d Skr595/850) This small, family-run place, on a quiet residential street near Skräcklen park, offers bright and homey rooms. Reception service is limited, so phone ahead.

Hunnebergs Vandrarhem & Kursgård HOSTEL €
(☑22 03 40; www.hunnebergsgard.se; Bergagårdsvägen 9B, Vargön; dm Skr200; P) In a big old manor house near the cliffs of Hunneberg (7km east of the centre), this is a large, well-equipped SVIF hostel. Take bus 62 from the town square to Vägporten, then walk 500m.

ⓘ Information

Banks and other facilities are mostly along Edsgatan.
Tourist office (☑135 09; www.visittrollhattan vanersborg.se; ⏲9am-6pm Mon-Fri, 10am-4pm Sat & Sun Jul & Aug, 8am-5pm Mon-Fri Sep-Jun) At the train station.

ⓘ Getting There & Away

Trollhättan-Vänersborgs Airport (www.fyrstadsflyget.se) lies midway between the two towns of Trollhättan and Vänersborg. There are around three to four direct flights Monday to Friday (one to two Sunday) to/from Stockholm. Taxis are the only way to access the airport: **Taxi Trollhättan** (☑820 00) charges around Skr200 for the trip from Trollhättan (shared vehicle Skr150), and Skr200 from Vänersborg.

Local buses run from the town square, while long-distance services stop at the train station. Local buses 61, 62 and 65 run roughly half-hourly between Vänersborg and Trollhättan. Express bus 600 runs several times daily to Trollhättan, continuing to Göteborg.

Swebus Express (www.swebusexpress.com) runs up to three times daily to Göteborg (Skr89, 1½ hours) via Trollhättan, and also north to Karlstad (Skr169, 2½ hours).

SJ trains to Göteborg (Skr104, 1½ hours) run about every hour.

Trollhättan
☑0520 / POP 54,300

'Trollywood', as it's colloquially known, is home to Sweden's film industry. A number of local and foreign flicks have been shot in and around the town, including Lebanese-Swedish director Josef Fares' Oscar-nominated *Jalla! Jalla!* (2000) and Danish director Lars von Trier's *Dancer in the Dark* (1999), *Dogville* (2002) and *Manderlay* (2005). Trollhättan itself has the air of a surreal film set: looming warehouses, foggy canals, crashing waterfalls and a futuristic cable car all give it a bizarre and thrilling edge. The town has made the most of its industrial heritage, with red-brick warehouses housing everything from crowd-pleasing museums to the odd art installation. The pièce de résistance is **Waterfall Days** (www.fallensdagar.se), a thumping three-day celebration held in mid-July with live bands, fireworks and some impressive waterworks.

⊙ Sights & Activities

Saab Bilmuseum MUSEUM
(www.saab.com; Åkerssjövägen 10; adult/7-17yr Skr60/30; ⏲9am-5pm mid-Jun–mid-Aug, 11am-4pm rest of year) Saab Bilmuseum is a must for car fanatics and Swedish design buffs. Saab car models span the first (a sensational 1947 prototype) to the futuristic (experimental designs running on biofuel that know if you're drunk!). Electronic handsets (40

minutes' playing time) guide you through the goods.

Innovatum Science Center   MUSEUM

(www.innovatum.se;adult/7-19yr/family Skr75/40/150; ⊙9am-5pm daily mid-Jun–Aug, 11am-4pm Tue-Sun Sep–mid-Jun) Innovatum Science Center, next door to the Saab Bilmuseum, is a fantastic science centre with interactive experiments aimed mainly at children. But don't let that put you off: push the little blighters out of the way and revel in the gyroscopes and whirlpool machines. Why wasn't physics fun like this when we were kids?

Galleri Nohab Smedja   GALLERY

(admission varies; ⊙9am-5pm Mon-Fri Jun-Aug during exhibitions) Innovatum also manages Galleri Nohab Smedja, an old smithy's workshop now used for temporary art exhibitions. The gallery is opposite the museum, just behind the tourist office.

Innovatum Linbana   CABLE CAR

(cable car; ☑289 400; ⊙9am-5pm mid-Jun-Aug, call at other times) In four minutes, the Innovatum Linbana will sweep you over the canal to the hydroelectricity area. Once you're on the far side of the canal, follow the stairs down to the river, where you'll find one of Sweden's most unusual industrial buildings, the potent-looking Olidan power station, which supplied much of the country's electricity in the early 20th century.

Slussområde   PARK

Take a wander southwest to Slussområde, a lovely waterside area of parkland and ancient lock systems. Here you'll find cafes and the Kanalmuseet (Åkersberg; adult/child Skr20/free; ⊙9am-7pm mid-Jun–mid-Aug), which runs through the history of the canal as well as exhibiting over 50 model ships.

Waterfall   WATERFALL

(⊙3pm daily Jul & Aug, 3pm Sat May, Jun & Sep) Northeast near the Hojum power station there are spectacular cascades when the waterfall is unleashed. Normally the water is diverted through the power stations, but at set times the sluice gates are opened and 300,000L per second thunders through. For an even more magnificent sight, wait for the night-time illuminated waterfall (⊙illuminations at 11pm), which usually occurs during the Waterfall Days festival in mid-July.

Tours

Canal tours   BOAT

Two- to three-hour canal tours on the M/S Elfkungen (www.stromkarlen.se; adult/under 15yr Skr200/50; ⊙Jun–mid-Aug) leave at noon from the Slussområde or at 12.30pm from the pier behind the Scandic Swania Hotel (Storgatan 47) in central Trollhätten. Buy tickets on board.

🛏 Sleeping & Eating

Hotell Bele   HOTEL €

(☑125 30; www.hotellbele.se; Kungsgatan 37; s/d Skr695/895; P@) Central, no-frills Bele sits on a pedestrianised street in the heart of town. Its 31 rooms are basic but comfortable, and there's a sauna for pamper-seeking guests.

Gula Villan   HOSTEL €

(☑129 60; trollhattansvandrarhem@telia.com; Tingvallavägen 12; dm Skr185; P) The cheery STF hostel, in a pretty old yellow villa, is about 200m from the train station. Breakfast and bikes are available.

Albert Hotell   SWEDISH €€

(☑129 90; www.alberthotell.se; Strömsberg; 3-course dinners from Skr595; ⊙dinner Mon-Sat, lunch Mon-Fri; P@) This marvellous restaurant hotel combo is based in a splendid 19th-century wooden villa, overlooking the town from a verdant slope just across the river. Superb, modish Nordic dishes might include chocolate fondant with vodka ganache and lingonberries. The hotel itself offers 27 contemporary rooms (single/double from Skr895/1195) in a neighbouring modernist building (request a river-view room), as well as a vintage suite in the main building for hopeless romantics (Skr2900). The place is an easy 10-minute walk across the river from central Trollhätten or a five-minute taxi ride.

Strandgatan   EUROPEAN €€

(☑837 17; www.strandgatan.com; Strandgatan; lunch buffets Skr76; ⊙10am-10pm Sun-Wed, to midnight Thu-Sat) This trendy bistro is one of the best, busiest and cheapest spots in town for a casual feed and chill. In a fantastic location, with canalside seating in summer, it peddles everything from fresh panini, salads and juices to quiche, fish and chips, plump muffins and good coffee.

❶ Information

The **tourist office** (☏135 09; www.visittrollhat-tanvanersborg.se; Åkerssjövägen 10; ☺10am-6pm daily mid-Jun–mid-Aug, 10am-4pm Mon-Fri rest of year) is about 1.5km south of the town centre, near the Innovatum. The tourist office sells a handy Guidebook to Trollhättan's Falls & Locks, which details walking routes in the mazelike industrial areas, as well as a two-day **Sommarkortet** (Skr250), which is the most economic way to see all the attractions.

For internet access, visit the **library** (Kungsgatan 25; ☺10am-7pm Mon-Thu, to 6pm Fri, to 3pm Sat).

❶ Getting There & Around

See p174 for transport details. To reach the attractions in Trollhättan from the train station or the Drottningtorget bus station, walk south along Drottninggatan, then turn right into Åkerssjövägen, or take town bus 21 – it runs most of the way.

Lidköping

☏0510 / POP 38,074

It might be short on wow factor, but cheery Lidköping – set on Vänern lake – is deeply likeable. Its handsome main square, Nya Stadens Torg, is dominated by the curious, squat old courthouse and its tower (it's actually a replica – the original burnt down in 1960). A previous fire in 1849 destroyed most of the town, but the cute 17th-century houses around Limtorget still stand.

Ironically, many of Lidköping's finest attractions (like the enchanting castle, Läckö Slott) lie some distance out of town.

◉ Sights & Activities

Läckö Slott CASTLE
(www.lackoslott.se; adult/under 26yr Skr80/free; ☺10am-6pm daily mid-Jun–Aug, 11am-5pm May–mid-Jun, 11am-3pm Mon-Fri, to 5pm Sat & Sun Sep) An extraordinary example of 17th-century Swedish baroque architecture, with cupolas, towers, paintings and ornate plasterwork, Läckö Slott lies 23km north of Lidköping near Vänern. The first castle on the site was constructed in 1298, but it was improved enormously by Count Magnus Gabriel de la Gardie after he acquired it in 1615. Admission includes a guided tour.

The lakeside castle now boasts 240 rooms, with the most impressive being the **King's Hall**, with 13 angels hanging from the ceiling and nine epic paintings depicting the Thirty Years War.

Guided tours (☺11am-5pm daily May-Aug, to 3pm Mon-Fri, to 4pm Sat & Sun Sep) run on the hour and last 40 minutes, giving you access to the most interesting rooms, including the representative apartments, the count's private chambers and the King's Hall. From mid-June through August there are English-language tours at 11.30am, 1.30pm and 3.30pm daily; call ahead at other times. Otherwise you're free to bumble about in the kitchen, dungeon, armour chamber, chapel and castle gardens. The lower floors contain shops and the atmospheric castle restaurant, **Fataburen** (lunches Skr125; ☺noon-10pm mid-Jun–mid-Aug, to 6pm May–mid-Jun), which uses vegetables and herbs from the castle garden. In the castle grounds, there's a **cafe** (lunches Skr85; ☺10am-6pm mid-Jun–Aug, 11am-4pm May–mid-Jun & Sep) serving snacks.

Classical music and opera events are held in the courtyard several times in July and August; enquire at Lidköping tourist office.

From mid-June to mid-August, bus 133 runs four to eight times a day from Lidköping to the castle (Skr32, one hour). Car parking costs Skr30.

Rörstrand Center HISTORIC BUILDING
(www.rorstrandcenter.se; Fabriksgatan 2-4; ☺10am-5pm Mon-Fri, to 4pm Sat, noon-4pm Sun) Rörstrand Fabriksbod is the second-oldest porcelain factory (still in operation) in Europe. There's a vast shop selling discounted seconds and end-of-line goods, and you can even buy copies of the porcelain used at the Nobel banquets in Stockholm. The **museum** (www.rorstrand-museum.se; admission free) contains everything from 18th-century faience to contemporary creations, and there's a nice cafe.

Vänermuseet MUSEUM
(www.vanermuseet.se; Framnäsvägen 2; adult/under 18yr Skr40/free; ☺10am-5pm Mon-Fri, noon-5pm Sat & Sun Jun-Aug, closed Mon rest of year) Renovated in 2009, Vänermuseet now boasts a 20-cu-metre aquarium, as well as a variety of other exhibits highlighting the nature and culture of Europe's third-largest lake (5650 sq km).

Husaby Kyrka & St Sigfrid's Well CHURCH
Husaby (around 15km east of Lidköping) is inextricably linked to Sweden's history. King Olof Skötkonung, the country's first Christian king, was converted and baptised here by the English missionary Sigfrid in 1008. Olof's royal dunking took place at St Sigfrid's Well, near **Husaby Kyrka** (☺8am-8pm

Mon-Fri, 9am-8pm Sat & Sun May-Aug, 8am-6pm Mon-Fri, 9am-6pm Sat & Sun Sep).

The church dates from the 12th century, but the base of the unusual three-steeple tower may well be that of an earlier wooden structure. Lurking inside are medieval paintings, as well as a 13th-century font and triumphal cross.

Kinnekulle   MOUNTAIN

The 'flowering mountain' Kinnekulle (306m), 18km northeast of Lidköping, is a natural wonderland, with unusually diverse geology and plant life, including mighty ancient oaks. It's also home to rare creatures, including the greater crested newt and short-horned grasshopper. There are numerous short nature trails, or you could explore it on the 45km-long Kinnekulle vandringsled (walking trail), which runs past remainders of the old limestone workings. The tourist office provides a map and the informative *Welcome to Götene and Kinnekulle* brochure. Local trains run to Källby, Råbäck and Hällekis, with access to the trail.

🛏 Sleeping & Eating

Hotel Läckö   HOTEL €€
(☑230 00; www.hotellacko.se; Gamla Stadens Torg 5; s/d incl breakfast Skr750/950) Our favourite in town is this old-school, family-run charmer. The spacious rooms boast high ceilings, solid wooden furniture and crisp linen, while breakfast is served on dainty antique porcelain. There's a cosy little reading room with comfy leather armchairs, and quirky touches like bright bed-curtains and whimsical hanging millinery.

STF Vandrarhem Lidköping   HOSTEL €
(☑664 30; www.lidkopingsvandrarhem.com; Gamla Stadens Torg 4; dm/s/d Skr210/300/460) Just a couple of minutes' walk from the train station, this hostel is in a pretty spot in the old town. Standards are high, and the staff are helpful. They also run a budget hotel on Mellbygatan (single/double Skr495/640).

Krono Camping   CAMPGROUND €
(☑268 04; www.kronocamping.com; Läckögatan; sites Skr330, 2-person cabins Skr500; 🌊) This is a huge, family-oriented lakeside campsite, 1.5km northwest of town beside the road to Läckö Slott, where kids can run wild. There's everything you could possibly need: shop, restaurant, laundry,

minigolf, boules, jacuzzi, sauna, playground and bike hire (day/week Skr100/500).

🔺TOP CHOICE Restaurang Sjöboden   SEAFOOD €€
(www.sjoboden.se; Spikens Fiskehamn; mains Skr173-259; ⊗daily mid-Jun–Aug, Thu-Sun Apr-Dec) Six kilometres south of Läckö Slott, the tiny village of Spiken is home to this unmissable harbourside restaurant where outstanding seasonal creations such as shellfish risotto or hot-smoked salmon keep the foodies swooning. Take bus 132. The same owners run Pirum (☑615 20; www.restaurangpirum.se; Skaragatan 7; mains Skr275; ⊗from 5pm Mon-Sat), a pleasant restaurant and wine bar in Lidköping.

Café Limtorget   CAFE €
(www.limtorget.nu; Mjölnagården, Limtorget 1; ⊗daily) With its rose-filled garden, this cute old wooden cottage is well worth seeking out. It serves sandwiches and ciabatta for around Skr40, plus pastries, waffles (in spring) and other temptations.

Café O Bar   EUROPEAN €€
(www.cafeobar.com; Nya Stadens Torg 4; mains Skr199-239; ⊗Mon-Sat) On the main square, Café O Bar is a fashionable restaurant-bar with a soulful selection of meals ranging from beef bourguignon to halibut with new potatoes.

ℹ Information

Library (Nya Stadens Torg 5; ⊗10am-8pm Mon, to 7pm Tue-Thu, to 6pm Fri, 9am-1pm Sat) Has free internet access.

Tourist office (☑200 20; www.lackokin nekulle.se; Nya Stadens Torg; ⊗10am-6pm Mon-Sat, noon-4pm Sun Jul, 10am-6pm Mon-Fri Aug, 10am-4pm Mon-Fri, 10am-1pm Sat rest of year) Situated in the old courthouse.

ℹ Getting There & Around

Town and regional buses stop on Nya Stadens Torg. Bus 1 runs roughly hourly between Trollhättan, Lidköping and Skara. Västtrafik trains from Lidköping to Hallsberg (Skr180, two hours) or Herrljunga (Skr155, 1½ hours) connect with Stockholm (another Skr250, two hours) and Göteborg services respectively.

Karlsborg

☑0505 / POP 6747

A quiet little town s-t-r-e-t-c-h-e-d alongside Vättern lake, Karlsborg is some 80km east of Lidköping. Amazingly, this peaceful backwater was once intended to be Sweden's capital in times of war, thanks to its beast of a bastion, Karlsborgs Fästning.

Karlsborgs Fästning was one of Europe's largest construction projects. With a circumference of around 5km, this fortress is so huge that it took from 1820 to 1909 to complete; it was out of date even before it was finished and mothballed immediately. Most of the 30-odd buildings inside are original: there's a **military museum** (www.fastningsmuseet.se, in Swedish; adult/7-15yr/family Skr50/20/120; ⊙10am-4pm mid-May–late Jun, to 6pm late Jun–early Aug, to 5pm rest of Aug, to 3pm Mon-Fri rest of year) and a **church**, which has an extraordinary candelabra made from 276 bayonets.

The fortress area is always open. If you're after gun smoke, cannon roar and scuttling rats though, you'll have to book a special-effects **guided tour** (adult/7-12yr Skr110/90; ⊙Jun-Aug) at the fortress's shop.

Karlsborg is the start/end of the western section of the **Göta Canal** (see p235 for details).

Right on the fortress's doorstep, **STF Vandrarhem Karlsborg** (☑446 00; www.karlsborgsvandrarhem.se, in Swedish; Ankarvägen 2; dm/s/d from Skr200/390/460; ⓟ@) is convenient and well kept. There are more sleeping and eating options in town, especially beside the Göta Canal about 2km northwest of the fortress (follow the main road).

The **tourist office** (☑173 50; www.karlsborgsturism.se; Storgatan 65; ⊙9am-noon & 1-4pm Mon-Fri) is on Rödesund off motorway 49 near the *fästning*.

Bus 1 runs every hour or two to Skövde (Skr80, one hour), connecting with SJ trains to Göteborg (Skr155, 1½ hours) or Stockholm (Skr316, two hours).

HALLAND

Sea and sunshine are the name of the game in Halland, with the populations of the most desirable destinations often tripling during the summer months. The long white-sand beaches at Tylösand and Varberg are ideal for lounging, swimming and surfing. If you're heading off the beach, be sure to walk the ramparts and visit the museum of the assertive Varberg fortress.

Halmstad
☑035 / POP 90,000

After roasting themselves on the 6km-long Blue Flag beach at Tylösand (8km west of town), many visitors hit Halmstad's heaving bars and clubs to crank up the party vibe.

Danish until 1645, Halmstad served as an important fortified border town. Its street plan was laid out by the Danish king Christian IV after a huge fire wiped out most of the buildings in 1619. He also awarded Halmstad its coat of arms: you'll see the three crowns and three hearts motif dotted all over the place.

◎ Sights & Activities

In the main square is Carl Milles' sculptural fountain *Europa and the Bull*; Picasso's *(Woman's Head)* is down by the river.

FREE **Halmstads Museum**　　MUSEUM
(www.hallandskonstmuseum.se; Tollsgatan; ⊙noon-4pm Tue-Sun, to 8pm Wed) For a small county gallery, Halmstads Museum churns out some impressive art and design exhibitions. Its modest collection of local treasures is ingeniously displayed, with silver hoards and Viking swords set in cases in the floor for that 'just discovered' feeling.

Medieval Attractions　　CASTLE
Christian IV built **Halmstad Slott** and the town walls. The latter were demolished in the 18th century, although fragments like the north gate **Norre Port** remain. Other medieval attractions include the lovely 14th-century church **St Nikolai Kyrka** (⊙8.30am-6pm Jun-Aug, to 3pm Sep-May), and the half-timbered **Tre Hjärtan** (Three Hearts) building on Stora Torg.

Najaden　　HISTORIC SHIP
The museum ship *Najaden*, berthed outside the castle and built in 1897, was a training ship for the Swedish Royal Navy. At the time of writing, it was undergoing renovations and closed to visitors. Check at the tourist office for new visiting hours and prices.

Mjellby Konstmuseum　　MUSEUM
(www.mjellbykonstmuseum.se; adult/under 20yr Skr60/free; ⊙11am-5pm Tue-Sun Jul-Aug, from noon Sep-Jun) Mjellby Konstmuseum is 5km from town but worth a trip if you're into modern art – the museum includes the permanent Halmstad Group exhibition of surrealist and cubist art.

Halmstad Äventyrsland
AMUSEMENT PARK

(www.aventyrslandet.se; Gamla Tylösandsvägen 1; admission Skr190; ☺10am-7pm Jun-Aug) Halmstad Äventyrsland, lying just out of town on the way to Tylösand, is a theme park for little-ish kids, featuring pirates, fairy-tale characters, dinosaurs, a miniature village, rides and waterslides.

🛏 Sleeping

IN TOWN
Halmstad is a popular town, with a solid smattering of the large hotel chains. The tourist office can arrange private rooms.

Best Western Grand
Hotel Halmstadz
HOTEL €€

(☎280 81 00; www.grandhotel.nu; Stationsgatan 44; s/d Skr850/950; P@) Across from the train station, this hotel has well-kept rooms decorated in traditional style with the odd modern touch. There's a reasonable restaurant and bar.

Scandic Hotel Hallandia
HOTEL €€

(☎295 86 00; hallandia@scandichotels.com; Rådhusgatan 4; s/d r/ste Skr935/1035; P@) On the main square, with modern Scandi-style accommodation; some rooms have balconies overlooking the river.

Kaptenshamn Vandrarhem
HOSTEL €

(☎12 04 00; www.halmstadvandrarhem.se; Stuvaregatan 8; dm from Skr250; P@) This hostel-hotel is in a pleasant brick building about 100m south of the train station and then west on Dillbergsgatan by the river. Rooms are fairly basic, but friendly staff, a leafy back patio and a nearby playground jazz things up.

Hotel Amadeus
HOTEL €€

(☎16 60 00; www.amadeus.nu; Hvitfeldtsgatan 20; s/d Skr850/1095; P@) In spite of the drab exterior, rooms at Hotel Amadeus are comfortably mid-market and clean. There are budget alternatives (up to Skr100 less) for the kronor-conscious.

IN TYLÖSAND

Tylebäck
RESORT €€

(☎19 18 00; www.tyleback.com; Kungsvägen 1; sites Skr230, hostel s/d 700/1000, hotel s/d Skr1000/1400) Accommodation to suit all travellers – camping, hostel, hotel – is offered at Tylebäck, in a stylishly rustic setting.

Hotel Tylösand
RESORT €€

(☎305 00; www.tylosand.se; Tylöhusvägen; d incl breakfast & spa from Skr995; P@☼) Ideal if you're into beaches, clubbing, spa treatments and/or Roxette (it's part-owned by Per Gessle, one half of the Swedish pop duo). It's a large, upmarket complex on the beach, with top-notch sipping and supping options, a shiny spa centre and summer entertainment gigs; check out the glam foyer full of art, and Leifs Lounge nightclub.

First Camp Tylösand
CAMPGROUND €

(☎305 10; www.firstcamp.se/tylosand; Kungsvägen 3; sites/cabins from Skr130/550) A huge and bustling campsite near the beach, with loads of family-friendly facilities. Avoid holidays such as Midsummer, when prices go stratospheric.

🍴 Eating & Drinking
The best dining options in Halmstad are along the pedestrianised Storgatan. On summer nights head to the after-beach parties at Tylösand.

Börje Olssons Skafferi
DELI €

(www.olssonsskafferi.com; Storgatan 23; lunches Skr89 ☺Mon-Sat) One of the better lunch options in town is this well-stocked Mediterranean deli on Storgatan. It has a brilliant lunch buffet with a delectable variety of cold meats, salads, quiches and cheese, as well as outdoor seating.

Skånska
BAKERY €

(Storgatan 40; sandwiches Skr50; ☺Mon-Sat) This is a good old-fashioned bakery with cafe attached. As well as sandwiches, there's a tempting stock of chocolates and cakes to crank up the calories.

Pio & Co
EUROPEAN €€

(Storgatan 37; mains Skr188-298; ☺from 6pm) Award-winning Pio is an upmarket brasserie with an extensive menu of both Swedish and continental favourites – think Halland pork with roasted garlic and potatoes au gratin, and heavenly gnocchi with bok choy.

Hemköp
SUPERMARKET

(Brogatan 14-16) Just off Stora Torg.

Lilla Helfwetet
LOUNGE €

(www.lillahelfwetet.se; Hamngatan 37; ☺Mon-Sat) With its funky dancing devil symbol, you can half guess what awaits you in this great converted warehouse near the river. The supercool restaurant, bar and cocktail lounge transforms into a nightclub on Friday and Saturday nights, when it's party time until 3am.

Halmstad

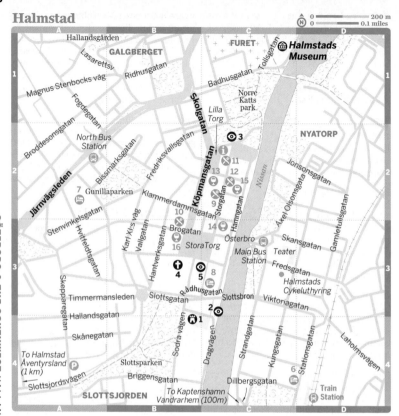

Systembolaget LIQUOR STORE
(Köpmansgatan 5) Just off Stora Torg.

Harrys PUB
(Storgatan 22) Pub complete with a great alfresco terrace.

Bulls Pub PUB
(www.lillahelfwetet.se; Lilla Torg) Equally popular,
in a former fire station.

ⓘ Information

For banks and supermarkets, hit Stora Torg and
Storgatan.
Library (Axel Olsonsgata 1; ⊙10am-8pm Mon-
Thu, to 6pm Fri, to 4pm Sat, noon-4pm Sun)
For free internet access.

Tourist office (⌨12 02 00; www.destination-
halmstad.se; Lilla Torg; ⊙9am-6pm Mon-Fri,
11am-2pm Sat summer, 9am-6pm Mon-Wed &
Fri, 10am-6pm Thu, 10am-1pm Sat rest of year)
Well-stocked office on Lilla Torg near Norre
Port.

ⓘ Getting There & Away

The **airport** (www.halmstadsflygplats.se) is only
2km west of the town centre. Skyways has regular connections to Stockholm-Arlanda Airport
(from Skr500, one hour and 10 minutes).

The train station is in the southeastern corner
of the town centre, and the main bus station is a
few blocks away at Österbro.

Swebus Express (www.swebusexpress.com)
runs buses at least four to five times daily to
Malmö (Skr149, 2¼ hours), Helsingborg (Skr99,
one hour), Göteborg (Skr119, 1¾ hours) and
Lund. It also runs direct services to Jönköping
(Skr229, 2¾ hours) once or twice a week.

Regular trains between Göteborg (Skr182, 1¼
hours) and Malmö (Skr142, two hours) stop in
Halmstad and call in at Helsingborg (Skr105, one
hour) and Varberg (Skr90, 35 minutes).

ⓘ Getting Around

Local **Hallandstrakiken** (www.hallandstrafiken.
se) bus 10 runs half-hourly (hourly in the eve-

Halmstad

nings) to the clubs and beaches at Tylösand (adult/child Skr20/12).

The North Bus Station, located in the north-western corner of central Halmstad, mainly services local buses.

Hire a bike from **Halmstad Cykeluthyrning** (www.halmstadcykeluthyrning.se; Fredsgatan 3; per 24hr/week Skr90/400; ☉9am-6pm daily Jun-Aug). Try **Taxi Halmstad** (🕿21 80 00) for a taxi.

Varberg

🕿0340 / POP 56, 110

Good-looking Varberg lies by the side of a 60km stretch of beautiful white-sand beaches: its population triples in the summer months. The town's darker side includes its fortress, once used as a prison and now home to an impressively preserved bog body.

◉ Sights & Activities

Medieval Fortress CASTLE
(www.lansmuseet.varberg.se; adult/under 20yr Skr70/free; ☉10am-6pm daily Jul-Aug, to 4pm Mon-Fri, noon-4pm Sat & Sun) The medieval fortress, with its superb museum, is Varberg's star attraction. In-house oddities include the poor old Bocksten Man, dug out of a peat bog at Åkulle in 1936. His 14th-century costume is the most perfectly preserved medieval clothing in Europe.

Getterön Nature Reserve NATURE RESERVE
Getterön Nature Reserve is just 2km north of the town and has excellent bird life (mostly waders and geese). The reserve has a **Naturum** (visitors centre; www.getteron.com; Lassavägen 1; ☉10am-4pm daily summer, shorter hours rest of year) with interesting exhibitions.

Varberg Radio Station MUSEUM
(www.alexander.n.se; Grimeton; adult/under 18yr Skr60/free; ☉10am-5pm daily late Jun–Aug, 10am-3pm Sat May & Sep) On the Unesco World Heritage list, Varberg Radio Station lies about 10km east of Varberg. Once part of the interwar transatlantic communication network, it's now the world's only surviving long-wave radio station. There are two English-language **tours** at 1pm and 3pm in June, July and August and one at 1pm in May and September.

Kallbadhuset DAY SPA
(www.kallbadhuset.se; adult/under 15yr Skr60/30; ☉10am-6pm daily, to 8pm Wed mid-Jul–mid-Aug, 10am-5pm daily, to 8pm Wed mid-Jun–mid-Jul & late Aug) Brave the Nordic weather with a dip at Kallbadhuset, a Moorish-style outdoor bathhouse built on stilts above the sea just north of the fort.

Apelviken SURFING
Apelviken, 2km south of Varberg, is Sweden's best spot for windsurfing and kitesurfing. Bring your own kit or rent from **Surfers Center** (🕿67 70 55; www.surferscenter. se, in Swedish; surfboards per hr/day Skr100/300, windsurfing Skr150/500) at the southern end of Apelviken. It also runs courses from June to August: contact the centre for details.

🛏 Sleeping & Eating

Most cheap restaurants line pedestrianised Kungsgatan.

TOP CHOICE/ **Fästningens Vandrarhem** HOSTEL €
(🕿868 28; www.fastningensvandrarhem.se; dm/ s/d from Skr260/360/590) Within the fortress, this SVIF hostel is one of Sweden's finest. Old prison cells – think Sing Sing with bouquets of flowers – make up the single rooms, with larger rooms in surrounding buildings. Either way, rooms are spotless and done up with brightly coloured blankets and pleasing art, making this more B&B than hostel.

DON'T MISS

HOTELL GÄSTIS

Behind a deceptively humdrum exterior awaits a one-of-a-kind hotel (☑180 50; www.hotellgastis.nu; Borgmästaregatan 1; s/d Skr1150/1495; ℗). Quirky details (there are many!) include an elevator shaft covered in pulp-fiction covers and a glimmering basement bath-house modelled on a St Petersburg girl's-school spa, built in 1806 and popular with Lenin when he was in the city. There's a candlelit jacuzzi and after steaming you can relax fireside. Individually styled rooms are cosy, with sparkling bathrooms and nooks full of books. Room prices also include a decent dinner buffet. Best of all, non-guests can also use the bathhouse, but call ahead first.

Getteröns Camping   CAMPGROUND €
(☑168 85; www.getteronscamping.se; sites/cabins from Skr280/890; ☺May–mid-Sep) On a sandy beach on the Getterön peninsula, this well-equipped place has plenty of tent spaces. It does get busy during high season, when most cabins are available only on a weekly basis (from Skr2900).

Vin & Skafferi Hus No. 13   RESTAURANT €€
(☑835 94; www.hus13.se; mains Skr245-315; ☺Jun-Sep) Next door to the fortress hostel, this wine bar and restaurant serves up gourmet dishes – lobster soup, salmon with cauliflower cream, deer fillet – that would have had the prisoners salivating. Dine inside at simple wooden tables or watch tourists stream up to the *fästning* from the pleasant outdoor patio.

ℹ Information

Tourist office (☑868 00; www.visitvarberg.se; Brunnparken; ☺9.30am-7pm Mon-Sat, 1-6pm Sun late Jun–mid-Aug, 10am-6pm Mon-Fri, 10am-2pm Sat Apr–late Jun & mid-Aug–Sep, 10am-5pm Mon-Fri rest of year) Located in the centre of town; most facilities are nearby.

ℹ Getting There & Around

Stena Line ferries operate between Varberg and the Danish town of Grenå (see p351); the ferry dock is next to the town centre.

Buses depart from outside the train station; local buses run to Falkenberg, but regular trains are your best bet for Halmstad (Skr90, 30 minutes), Göteborg (Skr117, 45 minutes) and Malmö (Skr237, 2½ hours).

Bicycle hire at **Cykelhuset Varberg** (www.cykelhusetvarberg.se; Birgirsvenssonsväg 14) costs from Skr95/350 per day/week. For a taxi try **Varbergs Taxi** (☑165 00).

Malmö & the South

Best Places to Eat

» Mrs. Brown (p192)

» Salt & Brygga (p192)

» Flickorna Lundgren (p216)

» Skanörs Fiskrögeri (p200)

» St Jakobs Stenugnsbageri (p198)

Best Places to Stay

» Kivik Strand Logi & Café (p207)

» Mäster Johan Hotel (p191)

» Mormor Anita's Place (p203)

» Sjöbacka Gård (p207)

» STF Vandrarhem Smygehuk (p202)

Why Go?

Artists adore southern Sweden. Here, the light seems softer, the foliage brighter and the shoreline more dazzling. Skåne (Scania) was Danish property until 1658 and still flaunts its differences: the strong dialect (skånska), half-timbered houses and the region's hybrid flag: a Swedish yellow cross on a red Danish background. Copenhagen is a mere bridge away from vibrant Malmö, the region's biggest city.

South of Malmö is a bona fide Viking settlement and some of the country's finest birdwatching. Just to the north, erudite Lund is Sweden's answer to Cambridge. Pottery studios, cultured manors and dramatic cliffs dot Skåne's northwest coast, while its southern shore is home to medieval showpiece Ystad, Bronze Age remains and the apple-orchard landscapes of Österlen.

Northeast of Skåne lies the county of Blekinge, splashed with deep forests and fish-filled lakes, and once seat of Sweden's 17th-century sea power. Topping its crown is the naval city of Karlskrona, a Unesco World Heritage–listed site.

When to Go
Malmö

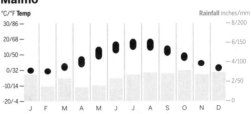

| Jul–Aug Warmest and busiest months; tourists flock to the coast and the Malmö Festival. | May & Sep Cool, clear and peaceful. Autumn weather is ideal for apple harvesting. | Nov–Feb Sweden's mildest winter. Tends to be wet; for snow, head inland. |

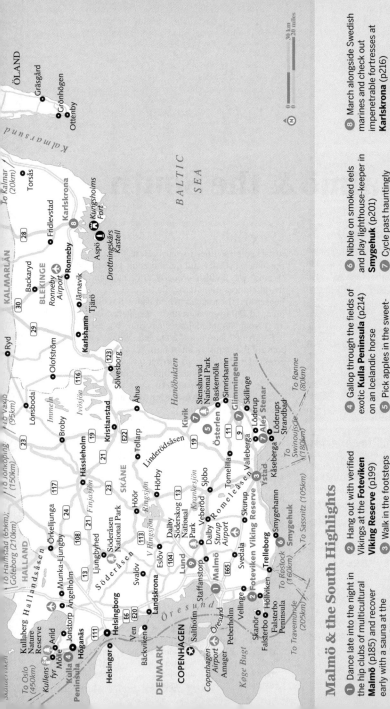

Malmö & the South Highlights

1 Dance late into the night in the hip clubs of multicultural **Malmö** (p185) and recover early with a sauna at the picture-perfect Ribersborgs Kallbadshus

2 Hang out with verified Vikings at the **Foteviken Viking Reserve** (p199)

3 Walk in the footsteps of fictional crime-fighter Inspector Wallander in medieval **Ystad** (p202)

4 Gallop through the fields of exotic **Kulla Peninsula** (p214) on an Icelandic horse

5 Pick apples in the sweet-smelling orchards mellow **Österlen** (p206)

6 Nibble on smoked eels and play lighthouse-keeper in **Smygehuk** (p201)

7 Cycle past hauntingly beautiful stone ships, graves and castles at **Ales Stenar** (p206), **Kivik** (p207) and **Glimmingehus** (p207)

8 March alongside Swedish marines and check out impenetrable fortresses at **Karlskrona** (p216)

9 Listen to the marvellous Domkyrkan clock strike up *In Dulci Jubilo* (p196) in **Lund** (p196)

SKÅNE

Skåne (Scania) is Sweden at its most continental. Connected to Denmark by bridge, its trademark mix of manors, gingerbread-style abodes and delicate, deciduous forests are a constant reminder that central Europe is just beyond the horizon. Dominating the scene is metropolitan Malmö, defined by its melting-pot tendencies and striking, twisting tower. Further out, velvety fields, sandy coastlines and stoic castles create one of Sweden's finest cycling backdrops. Add to this the fact that Skåne is often dubbed Sweden's 'larder' and you have yourself one scrumptious Scandi treat.

Malmö

📞 040 / POP 300,000

Once dismissed as crime-prone and tatty, Sweden's third-largest city has rebranded itself as progressive and downright cool. It's no coincidence that two of Stockholm's hippest icons – rock club Debaser and fashion-forward boutique Tjallamalla – have come to town.

Malmö's second wind blew in with the opening of the mammoth Öresund bridge and tunnel in 2000 (see p186) connecting the city to bigger, cooler Copenhagen and creating a dynamic new urban conglomeration. Such a cosmopolitan outcome seems only natural for what is Sweden's most multicultural metropolis – 150 nationalities make up Malmö's headcount. Here, exotic Middle Eastern street-stalls, urbane Italian coffee culture and hipster skateboard parks counter the town's intrinsic Nordic reserve.

Even the city's lively historic core echoes its multicultural past. The showpiece square of Stortorget evokes Hamburg more than it does Stockholm, while nearby Lilla Torg is a chattering mass of alfresco supping and half-timbered houses that give away the Danish connection.

Gamla Staden (Old Town) is Malmö's heart, encircled by a canal. There are three principal squares here: Stortorget, Lilla Torg and Gustav Adolfs Torg. The castle, Malmöhus Slott, in its park setting, guards the western end of Gamla Staden. Across the canal on the northern side you'll find the bus and train stations as well as the redeveloped harbour precinct. South of the city centre is a complex network of up-and-coming streets with most interest focused on the square

Möllevångstorget. The Öresund bridge is about 8km west of the city centre and is served by a motorway that passes south and east of the city.

History

Malmö really took off in the 14th century with the arrival of the Hanseatic traders, when grand merchants' houses went up, followed by churches and a castle. The greatest medieval expansion occurred under Jörgen Kock, who became the city's mayor in 1524. The town square, Stortorget, was laid out then, and many of the finest 16th-century buildings still stand. After the city capitulated to the Swedes in 1658, Malmö found its groove as an important commercial centre and its castle was bolstered to protect trade.

New-millennium Malmö has traded in its 20th-century heavy industries (car and aircraft manufacture and shipbuilding) for cleaner, greener companies, particularly in the service, financial and IT sectors. The launch of a new university campus in the late 1990s also helped redefine the city, creating a thriving student population (currently around 21,000). In 2010, King Carl XVI Gustaf inaugurated Malmö's ambitious Citytunnel project. The tunnel took five years to build and now connects Centralstationen to the Öresund bridge, giving the city two handy new train stations.

⊙ Sights

Malmöhus Slott   CASTLE

The addition of red-brick, Functionalist buildings in the 1930s might make it look a bit like a factory, but Malmöhus Slott has an intriguing history and houses some of the marvellous Malmö Museer (p186).

Erik of Pomerania built the first fortress here in 1436 to control the growing medieval town and Öresund shipping. This castle was destroyed between 1534 and 1536 during a popular uprising in Skåne. Immediately after the rebellion, King Christian III of Denmark had the castle rebuilt in forbidding late-Gothic and early-Renaissance styles.

Malmöhus Slott's most famous prisoner (from 1567 to 1573) was the Earl of Bothwell. Bothwell married Mary, Queen of Scots, but was forced to flee from Scotland after she was deposed. On reaching Europe, he was detained by the Danes until his death in 1578.

After the Swedish takeover of Skåne in 1648, the Danes made a futile attempt to recapture the castle in 1677. When peace was restored, interest in the castle waned and most of it became derelict by the 19th century. A devastating fire in 1870 left only the main building and two gun towers intact; these sections were revamped in 1930.

Malmö Museer   MUSEUM
(www.malmo.se/museer; Malmöhusvägen; combined entry adult/7-15yr Skr40/10, free with Malmökortet; ⊙10am-4pm daily Jun-Aug, 10am-4pm Mon-Fri, noon-4pm Sat & Sun rest of year) Various museums in and around Malmöhus Slott make up the Malmö Museer. There are cafe-restaurants inside all the museums.

Inside the castle, the intriguing aquarium has a nocturnal hall wriggling with everything from bats to electric eels, and local swimmers like cod and pike. It's associated with the Naturmuseum (Natural History Museum).

The Malmö Konstmuseum boasts a fabulous collection of Swedish furniture and handicrafts as well as Scandinavia's largest collection of 20th-century Nordic art, while the Stadsmuseum (City Museum) combines exhibitions on the region's cultural history with more international themes. Ask for the English-language information sheets at reception or audio guides cost Skr20. The Knight's Hall contains various late-medieval and Renaissance exhibits, such as the regalia of the order of St Knut. The northwest cannon tower is an atmospheric mix of cannons and shiny armour.

A short distance to the west of Malmöhus Slott, the technology and maritime museum Teknikens och Sjöfartens Hus (Malmöhusvägen) is home to aircraft, vehicles, a horse-drawn tram, steam engines, and the amazing 'U3' walk-in submarine, outside the main building. The submarine was launched in Karlskrona in 1943 and decommissioned in 1967. Upstairs, a superb hands-on experiment room will keep kids (as well as you!) engrossed for ages.

The old Kommendanthuset (Commandant's House) arsenal, opposite the castle, hosts photography exhibitions.

Moderna Museet Malmö   MUSEUM
(www.modernamuseet.se; Gasverksgatan 22; adult/under 18yr Skr40/free; ⊙11am-6pm Tue-Sun) Architects Tham & Videgård chose to make the most of the distinct 1901 Rooseum, once a power-generating turbine hall, by adding a contemporary annex, complete with a bright, perforated orange-red facade. Venue aside, the museum has plenty of interesting art that's well worth checking out.

Sankt Petri Kyrka   CHURCH
(Göran Olsgatan; ⊙10am-6pm) This red-brick Gothic beast is Malmö's oldest church, built in the early 14th century. Protestant zealots whitewashed the medieval frescoes in 1555, but the original wall paintings in the Krämarekapellet (inside at the rear of Sankt Petri Kyrka) have been successfully restored. There's a magnificent altarpiece dating from 1611 and a votive ship in the south aisle, dedicated to all who died at sea in WWII. Much of the church has been rebuilt; the 96m tower went up in 1890.

FREE Malmö Konsthall   MUSEUM
(www.konsthall.malmo.se; St Johannesgatan 7; ⊙11am-5pm, to 9pm Wed) Malmö Konsthall, south of central Malmö, is one of Europe's

---

BRIDGING THE GAP

Opened in 2000, the Öresund bridge (www.oresundsbron.com) is the planet's longest cable-tied road and rail bridge, measuring 7.8km from Lernacken (on the Swedish side, near Malmö) to the artificial island of Peberholm (Pepper Island), south of Saltholm (Salt Island). From the island, a further 3km of undersea tunnel finally emerges just north of Copenhagen airport.

Local commuters pay via an electronic transmitter, while tolls for everyone else are payable by credit card, debit card or in euros, Danish or Swedish currency at the Lernacken toll booths. The crossing isn't cheap – for a motorcycle the price is Skr190, private vehicles (up to 6m) pay Skr360 and private vehicles with trailers, vans or minibuses cost Skr720. Discounts are available with the Malmökortet (p187). An alternative option is to catch a commuter train to Copenhagen (Skr105), an easy 35-minute trip from Malmö and a good excuse to explore Denmark's so-hip capital.

If you're travelling between Sweden and Denmark with your own transport, you may want to consider other options (such as ferries between Helsingborg and Helsingør; see p214).

largest contemporary-art spaces, with exhibitions spanning both Swedish and foreign talent. The museum cafe **Smak** (☑50 50 35) serves a brilliant weekend brunch.

FREE **Form/Design Center**   ARTS CENTRE
(www.formdesigncenter.com; Lilla Torg 9; ☺11am-5pm Tue-Sat, noon-4pm Sun) Form/Design Center showcases cutting-edge design, architecture and art against the 16th-century **Hedmanska Gården**. Pour over design magazines in the cafe or bag Scandi-cool design, fabrics and toys in the gallery shop.

The surrounding cobbled streets are restored pockets of the late-medieval town; the half-timbered houses now house galleries and boutiques selling some brilliant arts and crafts.

FREE **Malmö Chokladfabrik**   MUSEUM
(www.malmochokladfabrik.se; Möllevångsgatan 36; ☺10am-6pm Mon-Fri, to 2pm Sat) Watch heavenly cocoa concoctions being made, wander through the mini-museum and devour them at the chocolate-scented cafe.

Galleri PingPong   GALLERY
(www.galleripingpong.se; Rådmansgatan 7; ☺3-6pm Tue-Fri, noon-4pm Sat during exhibitions) Petite local gallery near Malmö Konsthall.

Skånes Konstförening   GALLERY
(www.skaneskonst.se; Bragegatan 15, entrance at Ystadvägen 22; ☺2-6pm Wed-Fri, 1-4pm Sat & Sun during exhibitions) For emerging and lesser-known as well as Scanian artists, check out Skånes Konstförening, about 1km south of Möllevångstorget.

Unusual Buildings   ARCHITECTURE
The northwest harbour redevelopment is home to the **Turning Torso**, a striking skyscraper that twists through 90 degrees from bottom to top. Designed by Spaniard Santiago Calatrava and inaugurated in 2005, the 190m tall building is Sweden's tallest.

For vintage veneers, head for the statue of King Karl X Gustav in the centre of Stortorget and spin around (clockwise from the northwestern corner) to see the following buildings. **Kockska Huset** (1524) is a stately pile that mayor Jörgen Kock had built for himself; it's where Gustav Vasa stayed when he dropped into town. The **County Governor's Residence** is a grand, stuccoed masterpiece built in the 19th century but with a deceptively Ren-

MALMÖKORTET

The discount card Malmökortet offers free bus transport and street parking, entry to several museums, and discounts at other attractions and on sightseeing tours. It's good value at Skr170/200 for one/two days – the price includes one adult and up to two children under 16. Buy it at the tourist office.

aissance style. Next door **Rådhuset** (the city hall) was originally built in 1546, but has since been altered. At the southeastern corner of the square, the city's oldest pharmacy, **Apoteket Lejonet**, flaunts an exquisite art-nouveau interior, with carved wooden shelves, antique medicinal bottles and a glass-plated ceiling. Founded in 1571, the business originally occupied **Rosenvingeskahuset** on Västergatan.

Just off Östergatan, **St Gertrud Quarter** is a cute cluster of 19 buildings from the 16th to 19th centuries, with the mandatory mix of cobbled walkways, restaurants and bars. Across the road, **Thottska Huset** is Malmö's oldest half-timbered house (1558). It's now a restaurant, so peek inside!

Folkets Park   AMUSEMENT PARK
(www.malmofolketspark.se; Norra Parkgatan 2A; ☺park 7am-9pm Mon-Fri, 8am-9pm Sat & Sun, to 10pm May & Sep, to 11pm Jun-Aug, attractions noon-7pm May–mid-Aug) Family-friendly Folkets Park boasts a fairground, pony rides, minigolf and **reptile house** (☑30 52 37; adult/5-14yr Skr80/40).

🏃 Activities

Ask the tourist office for the free cycling map *Cykla i Malmö*. **Rent-a-Bike** (www.travelshop.se; Skeppsbron 10; per 24hr Skr150) near the tourist office or Rundan (p189) both rent bikes.

Aq-va-kul   SWIMMING
(www.aqvakul.se, in Swedish; Regementsgatan 24; adult/2-6yr/7-17yr/family Skr75/30/45/180; ☺9am-8.30pm Mon, Wed & Thu, 7am-8.30pm Tue, 9am-7.30pm Fri, 9am-6pm Sat & Sun) Aq-va-kul is a water park with heated indoor and outdoor pools, a waterslide, wave machine, sauna, solarium and Turkish bath.

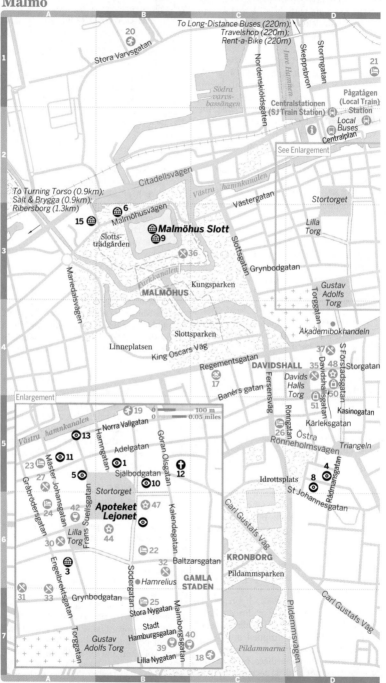

Stora Varvsgatan

20

To Long-Distance Buses (220m);
Travelshop (220m);
Rent-a-Bike (220m)

Nordenskiöldsgatan

Inre Hamnen

Skeppsbron

Stormgatan

21

Södra
varvs-
bassängen

Centralstationen
(SJ Train Station)

Pågatågen
(Local Train)
Station

Local
Buses
Centralplan

See Enlargement

Citadellsvägen

Västra hamnkanalen

Västergatan

Stortorget

To Turning Torso (0.9km);
Salt & Brygga (0.9km);
Ribersborg (1.3km)

6

Malmöhusvägen

15

Malmöhus Slott

9

Lilla
Torg

36

Mariedalsvägen

Slotts-
trädgården

Slottsgatan

Grynbodgatan

Parkkanalen

MALMÖHUS

Kungsparken

Gustav
Adolfs
Torg

Torggatan

Akademibokhandeln

Slottsparken

Linneplatsen

King Oscars Väg

Regementsgatan

DAVIDSHALL

37

S:ta Förstadsgatan

35

48

Storgatan

17

Baners gatan

Davids
Halls
Torg

Davidshallsgatan

Fersensväg

51

50

Kasinogatan

Enlargement

19

0   100 m
0   0.05 miles

Rönngatan

Kärleksgatan

26

Östra
Rönneholmsvägen

Triangeln

Västra hamnkanalen

13

Norra Vallgatan

Hamngatan

Adelgatan

Göran Olsgatan

4

23

11

Master Johansgatan

1

12

8

Idrottsplats

Rådmansgatan

27

5

Själbodgatan

St Johannesgatan

Gråbrödersgatan

24

10

Carl Gustafs Väg

42

47

Stortorget

30

Lilla
Torg

Frans Suellsgatan

**Apoteket
Lejonet**

44

22

Kalendegatan

KRONBORG

3

Engelbrektsgatan

32

Baltzarsgatan

Pildammsparken

31

33

Grynbodgatan

Södergatan

Hamrelius

**GAMLA
STADEN**

Carl Gustafs Väg

25

Stora Nygatan

Malmborgsgatan

Pildammsvägen

Gustav
Adolfs Torg

Torggatan

Stadt
Hamburgsgatan

40

39

Lilla Nygatan

18

Pildammarna

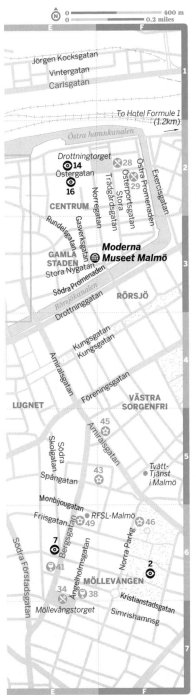

Ribersborgs Kallbadshus DAY SPA

(www.ribersborgskallbadhus.se; admission Skr55; ⊙9am-8pm Mon-Fri, to 9pm Wed, to 6pm Sat & Sun May-Aug, 10am-7pm Mon-Fri, to 8pm Wed, 9am-4pm Sat & Sun Sep-Apr) Ribersborg is a fetching sandy beach backed by parkland, about 2km west of the town centre. Off the beach, at the end of a 200m-long pier, is the adorable, wooden Ribersborgs Kallbadshus, an open-air naturist saltwater pool, with separate sections for men and women, and a wood-fired sauna dating from 1898. There is also a pleasant cafe.

City Boats Malmö BOATING

(www.cityboats.se; Amiralsbron, Södra Promenaden; per 30/60min Skr80/130; ⊙daily May-Aug, weekends Apr & Sep) To scoot round Malmö's canals in a pedal boat, head to City Boats Malmö, just east of Gustav Adolfs Torg.

Stapelbädden Skatepark SKATEBOARDING PARK

(www.stapelbaddsparken.se; Stapelbäddsgatan 1, 10am-3pm Mon-Fri summer) Swing by this intense urban jungle near the Turning Torso, at the northwest harbour redevelopment, to gasp at skaters – local and international – sliding, flying and occasionally tumbling from dizzying heights. Check out www.bryggeriet.org for more details on the city's vibrant skateboarding scene.

☞ Tours

Rundan BOAT

(www.stromma.se; adult/6-11yr Skr120/60) To experience Malmö by water, visit Rundan, opposite Centralstationen. Fifty-minute boat tours of the canals run regularly from May to September (10.30am to 9pm late June to late August, less frequently at other times), weather depending. It also rents bicycles (Skr150/day).

Medieval Cog Sail BOAT

(☑33 08 06; bokning@foteviken.se; Sat May-Aug) During the summer you can enjoy a one-hour sailing adventure on a replica of a 14th-century trading vessel or cog. Trips on the large cog cost Skr150 for adults and Skr75 for children.

Sightseeing Bus Tours BUS

(www.stromma.se; adult/6-11yr Skr190/95, free with Malmökortet) The 1½-hour sightseeing bus tours are great for getting your bearings. Tours run at 10am, 11.30am and 1.30pm daily (from early June to late August), with reduced services in May and September. A 2½-hour tour (adult/six to 16 years

Malmö

Top Sights
- Apoteket Lejonet ... D3
- Malmöhus Slott ... B3
- Moderna Museet Malmö ... E3

Sights
- Aquarium ... (see 9)
- 1 County Governor's Residence ... B5
- 2 Folkets Park ... F6
- 3 Form/Design Center ... A6
- 4 Galleri PingPong ... D5
- Hedmanska Gården ... (see 3)
- 5 Kockska Huset ... A5
- 6 Kommendanthuset ... B3
- 7 Malmö Chokladfabrik ... E6
- 8 Malmö Konsthall ... D5
- Malmö Kontsmuseum ... (see 9)
- 9 Malmö Museer ... B3
- 10 Rådhuset ... B5
- 11 Rosenvingeskahuset ... A5
- 12 Sankt Petri Kyrka ... B5
- 13 Sightseeing Bus Tours Departure ... A5
- 14 St Gertrud Quarter ... E2
- Stadsmuseum ... (see 9)
- 15 Teknikens och Sjöfartens Hus ... A3
- 16 Thottska Huset ... E2

Activities, Courses & Tours
- 17 Aq-va-kul ... C4
- 18 City Boats Malmö ... C7
- 19 Rundan ... B5
- 20 Stapelbädden Skatepark ... B1

Sleeping
- 21 Comfort Hotel Malmö ... E1
- 22 Hotel Baltzar ... B6
- 23 Hotel Duxiana ... A5
- 24 Mäster Johan Hotel ... A6
- 25 Scandic Hotel St Jörgen ... B7
- 26 STF Vandrarhem Malmö City ... C5

Eating
- Årstiderna ... (see 5)
- 27 Bastard Restaurant ... A5
- 28 Dolce Sicilia ... F2
- 29 Falafel No. 1 ... F2
- Fiskehoddorna ... (see 15)
- Izakaya Koi ... (see 30)
- 30 Johan P ... A6
- 31 Lemongrass ... A6
- 32 Lilla Kafferosteriet ... B6
- 33 Mästerlivs Supermarket ... A7
- 34 Möllevångstorget produce market ... E6
- 35 Mrs. Brown ... D4
- 36 Slottsträgården Kafé ... B3
- 37 Solde ... D4

Drinking
- Mello Yello ... (see 42)
- 38 Metro ... E6
- Moosehead ... (see 42)
- 39 Pickwick Pub ... B7
- 40 Systembolaget ... B7
- 41 Tempo Bar & Kök ... E6
- 42 Victors ... A6

Entertainment
- 43 Babel ... F5
- 44 Biograf Spegeln ... B6
- 45 Club Wonk ... F5
- 46 Debaser ... F6
- 47 Étage ... B6
- 48 Filmstaden Malmö ... D4
- Inkonst ... (see 7)
- 49 Kulturbolaget ... E6

Shopping
- 50 Chique ... D4
- Formargruppen ... (see 30)
- 51 Tjallamalla ... D4

Skr260/130) also includes a boat trip along Malmö's canals, running daily from 11.30am and 1.30pm, with weekend-only services in May and September. Pick up your ticket at the tourist office and the staff will show you where to catch the bus on Norra Vallgatan.

Malmö Bike Tours BICYCLE
(☎0708-46 25 40; www.malmobiketours.se; 2hr tour Skr250, rental day/week Skr149/650) Starting from Stortorget, Malmö Bike Tours runs two-hour and 3½-hour cycling trips around the city, covering major landmarks and lesser-known neighbourhoods. It also rents bicycles if you'd rather tour on your own. Book online, by phone or through the tourist office.

Malmö by Foot WALKING
(www.malmobyfoot.com; 1¼hr tour Skr80; ⏲Jul & Aug) A guided walk covering the history of Malmö from the Middle Ages to today. Tours go twice a day (11am and 12.45pm) from

Sankt Petri Kyrka. Book tickets through the tourist office.

✪ Festivals & Events

Malmö Festival
MUSIC

(www.malmofestivalen.se) Malmö's premier annual event – with 1.5 million visitors – is the week-long Malmö Festival in mid-August. The mostly free events include theatre, dance, live music, fireworks and sizzling food stalls.

Regnbågsfestivalen
CULTURAL

The week-long Regnbågsfestivalen (Rainbow Festival) is Malmö's queer celebration, held in late September and packed with exhibitions, films, parties and a pride parade. Contact RFSL-Malmö (✆611 99 62; malmo@rfsl.se; Monbijougatan 15), Malmö's gay and lesbian centre, for details.

🛏 Sleeping

The tourist office has a free online hotel booking service: follow the website's links (www.malmotown.com).

TOP CHOICE Mäster Johan Hotel
BOUTIQUE HOTEL €€

(✆664 64 00; www.masterjohan.se; Mäster Johansgatan 13; s/d incl breakfast Skr1290/1490; P@) Just off Lilla Torg is one of Malmö's finest slumber spots, with spacious, elegantly understated rooms featuring beautiful oak floors and snowy white fabrics. Bathrooms flaunt Paloma Picasso–designed tiles, there's a sauna and gym, and the immaculate breakfast buffet is served in a glass-roofed courtyard.

Hotel Duxiana
HOTEL €€

(✆607 70 00; www.malmo.hotelduxiana.com; Mäster Johansgatan 1; s/d/junior ste incl breakfast Skr890/1390/2190; @) Close to Centralstationen, ubersleek Hotel Duxiana is one for the style crew. In a palate of white, black and gunmetal grey, design features include Bruno Mattheson sofas and the same heavenly beds supplied to the world's first seven-star hotel in Dubai. Single rooms are small but comfy, while the decadent junior suites feature a claw-foot bathtub facing the bed. Breakfast is similarly chic.

STF Vandrarhem Malmö City
HOSTEL €

(✆611 62 20; malmo.city@stfturist.se; Rönngatan 1; dm/s from Skr220/450; @) Don't be put off by the exterior, this is a sparkling hostel right in the middle of the city with a lovely airy kitchen for cooking and an outdoor patio.

Staff are friendly and helpful and there is a good ice-cream shop across the street.

Comfort Hotel Malmö
HOTEL €€

(✆33 04 40; co.malmo@choice.se; Carlsgatan 10C; s/d incl breakfast from Skr590/880; P@) This convenient hotel – a stone's throw from both the train and ferry – has friendly staff and clean, modern rooms with all the amenities of a ship-shape business hotel, as well as a liberal breakfast.

Vandrarhemmet Villa Hilleröd
HOSTEL €

(✆26 56 26; www.villahillerod.se; Ängdalavägen 38; d from Skr520; @) This laid-back hostel sits in a delightful yellow house in the city's west. A nice garden and house plants keep things homely. If you need to cancel your reservation, do so before 6pm on the expected day of arrival or you'll be charged for the night. Take bus 1 or 3 from the city centre to get there.

Hotel Baltzar
HOTEL €€

(✆665 57 00; www.baltzarhotel.se; Södergatan 20; s/d economy 590/855, superior 950/1050; @) Though a bit worn around the edges, this pleasant hotel is smack in the heart of town (though remarkably quiet) in an imposing listed building. Economy rooms are functionalist, while the superior ones are spacious with elegant curtains, armchairs and antique furniture.

Scandic Hotel St Jörgen
HOTEL €€

(✆693 46 00; stjorgen@scandichotels.com; Stora Nygatan 35; s/d Skr750/850; P@) A sleek, minimalist foyer contrasts with more classically styled rooms at this friendly, upmarket chain. Most rooms have bathtub/shower combos and many look out onto Gustav Adolfs Torg. There are a few windowless 'cabin' rooms and it's a good idea to book online for the best rates.

Malmö Camping & Feriecenter
CAMPGROUND €

(✆15 51 65; www.firstcamp.se; Strandgatan 101; sites Skr320, 2-bed cabins Skr700) By the beach, this campsite has a great view of the Öresund bridge. It's about 5km southwest of the centre of town: take bus 4 from Gustav Adolfs Torg (Skr16).

Hotel Formule 1
MOTEL €

(✆93 05 80; www.hotelformule1.com; Lundavägen 28; r from Skr499) Bargain-basement Formule 1 is 1.5km east of Stortorget, with smallish, functional rooms sleeping up to three people for a flat rate.

MALMÖ & THE SOUTH MALMÖ

City Room
ACCOMMODATION SERVICES €

(☑795 94; www.cityroom.se; s/d Skr395/495) Private rooms or apartments from about Skr395 per person are available through City Room. The agency has no office address but the phone is staffed on weekdays from 9am to noon. Otherwise, contact the tourist office.

✖ Eating

Malmö isn't short on dining experiences, whether it's vegan grub chowed down in a grungy left-wing hang-out or designer supping on contemporary Nordic flavours. For sheer atmosphere, head to the restaurant-bars on Lilla Torg. Top-notch foodie hot spots dot the city and are your best bet for revamped Scanian classics.

TOP
CHOICE **Mrs. Brown**
SWEDISH €€€

(☑97 22 50; www.mrsbrown.nu; Storgatan 26; mains Skr185-255; ⊙Mon-Sat) Demure little Mrs. Brown is the kind of neighbourhood place you dream will open up near where you live. The open kitchen churns out modern Scandinavian home cooking using local and organic ingredients that will have you tipping your plate to spoon up the very last dribbles of sauce. Service is attentive, but not overbearing, and the dining room is decorated in a minimalist fashion that is both comforting and modish.

Salt & Brygga
ORGANIC €€€

(☑611 59 40; www.saltobrygga.se; Sundspromenaden 7, Västra Hamnen; mains Skr189-295; ⊙closed Sun & end Dec–mid-Jan) With an enviable view overlooking the Öresund bridge, this stylish, contemporary slow-food restaurant presents updated Swedish cuisine with a clear conscience. Everything is organic (including the staff's uniforms), waste is turned into biogas, and the interior is allergy-free. Flavours are clean and strictly seasonal.

Slottsträgården Kafé
CAFE €

(☑30 40 34; www.slottstradgardenskafe.se; Grynbodgatan 9; sandwiches from Skr51; ⊙11am-5pm Apr-Sep) There is no better way to enjoy summertime Malmö than to settle down under a white umbrella at this quaint cafe, tucked in the middle of the Slottsträgården. You'll be able to smell fennel and herbs while enjoying a sweet square of rhubarb crumble or a generous sandwich.

Dolce Sicilia
ICE CREAM €

(☑611 31 10; www.dolcesicilia.se; Drottningtorget 6; gelato from Skr27; ⊙noon-5pm Mon, 11am-7pm Tue-Sun) Head to Dolce Sicilia, run by certified Sicilians, for fresh, organic Italian-style gelato with flavours ranging from chilli chocolate to liquorice or forest berry. There's another location near the Turning Torso, at Västra Varvsgatan 37.

Bastard Restaurant
EUROPEAN €€€

(☑12 13 18; www.bastardrestaurant.se; Mäster Johansgatan 11; mains Skr195-225; ⊙5pm-midnight Tue-Thu, to 2am Fri & Sat) This hipster restaurant is about as close as you'll get to a gastropub in Sweden. Meals here are both hearty and distinctive, ranging from gourmet meat platters to blackened grilled chicken for two or pizza with snails. The bar is also a popular choice with locals.

Lemongrass
EUROPEAN €€

(☑30 69 79; www.lemongrass.se; Grynbodgatan 9; mains Skr158-258; ⊙6pm-late Mon-Sat) Slick Lemongrass is a nice change of pace from classic Scandinavian or European fair. The menu includes Thai classics like crispy beef, as well as a few Swedish-inspired surprises like spicy Longan deer.

Johan P
SEAFOOD €€€

(☑97 18 18; www.johanp.nu; Landbygatan 5; mains Skr175-495) With its white and black tiled floor, crisp tablecloths and bistro chairs Johan P could be on the French Riviera. There are lovely bisques, *moules meunière* (mussels cooked in wine) and chilled shellfish platters, all made with ingredients so fresh you'll be glad you're in Sweden, not France.

Årstiderna i Kockska Huset
SWEDISH €€€

(☑23 09 10; www.arstiderna.se; Frans Suellsgatan 3; mains Skr235-325; ⊙ 11.30am-midnight Mon-Fri, 5pm-midnight Sat) This top-notch restaurant serves meals in the vaults beneath Kockska Huset. Food is upscale Swedish, the atmosphere classic with crisp white table cloths and service quietly professional.

Izakaya Koi
ASIAN €€

(☑757 00; www.koi.se; Lilla Torg 5; mains Skr109-249; ⊙6pm-late Mon-Sat) On heaving Lilla Torget, Koi attracts crowds with excellent cocktails, sushi and other Asian-inspired nibbles. You'll find Malmö's trendsetters in the upstairs lounge, mingling on the dance floor or perched on white leather banquettes looking gorgeous well into the early hours.

Lilla Kafferosteriet
CAFE €

(📞48 20 00; www.lillakafferosteriet.se; Baltzarsgatan 24; sandwiches from Skr35; ⊗8am-7pm Mon-Fri, 10am-5pm Sat, 11am-5pm Sun) Canvas bags brimming with beans and a substantial coffee roaster act as decoration at this serious about-coffee cafe. Staff brew up an excellent cup of course and make the most of what is a lovely old building. There is a nice patio as well and tasty nibbles.

Falafel No. 1
FALAFEL €

(📞84 41 22; www.falafel-n1.se; Österportsgatan 2; from Skr35) Malmö residents are so fond of falafel that it even features in songs by local band Timbuktu. Orient House Falafel No. 1 is a long-standing favourite, or check out the website Everything About Falafel (www.alltomfalafel.se, in Swedish) for details on other venues.

Mästerlivs
SUPERMARKET €

(Engelbrektsgatan 15; ⊗9am-9pm) Self-caterers should head here.

Fiskehoddorna
SELF CATERING

(📞0768-56 93 61; Malmöhusvägen; ⊗6.30am-1pm Tue-Sat) Next door to the Teknikens och Sjöfartens Hus is a row of former fishermen's huts selling fresh fish.

The best produce market is on Möllevångstorget, from Monday to Saturday.

🍷 Drinking

Bars in Malmö generally stay open until around 1am, although some bars close later on Friday and Saturday evenings.

The heaving bars around Möllevångstorget tend to pull a more student, indie crowd.

The bars on Lilla Torg are great spots, with affable service, alfresco summer seating (you may have to wait for a table), tasty meals and everything from Chilean whites to outrageous cocktails.

Victors
BAR

(www.victors.se; Lilla Torg) Glam cocktails on Lilla Torg.

MOVING ON?

For tips, recommendations and reviews, head to shop.lonelyplanet.com to purchase a downloadable PDF of the Copenhagen chapter from Lonely Planet's *Denmark* guide.

Moosehead
BAR

(www.moosehead.se; Lilla Torg) A slightly more down-to-earth neighbour.

Mello Yello
BAR

(www.melloyello.se; Lilla Torg) Another Lilla Torg option with nice nibbles.

Pickwick Pub
PUB

(www.pickwickpub.se; Stadt Hamburgsgatan 12) Friendly, traditional pub.

Tempo Bar & Kök
LOUNGE

(www.tempobarokok.se; Södra Skolegatan 30) Trendy neighbourhood lounge for the student, indie crowd.

Metro
LOUNGE

(www.metropamollan.se; Ängelholmsgatan 14) Equally hip. Serves great grub.

Systembolaget
LIQUOR STORE

(Malmborgsgatan 6) Sells beers, wines and spirits.

☆ Entertainment

Pick up local newspaper *Sydsvenskan* on a Friday, when it contains the listings mag *Dygnet Runt* (which covers Lund as well as Malmö). Also, scan the weekly street press *Nöjesguiden*. They're both in Swedish but the club and film information is decipherable. Alternatively, take the regular train to Copenhagen for a huge array of options.

Nightclubs

Clubs generally stay open until around 1am, and to 3am, 4am or 5am on Friday and Saturday. The minimum age requirements (20 to 25) vary from venue to venue and from night to night, so bring ID. Entry usually costs between Skr100 and Skr200.

Debaser
DANCE

(📞23 98 80; www.debaser.se, in Swedish; Norra Parkgatan 2; ⊗7pm-3am) Stockholm's music club heavyweight has opened shop in Malmö, with live gigs and club nights spanning anything from indie, pop and hip-hop to soul, electronica and rock. There's a buzzing outdoor bar-lounge overlooking Folkets Park and decent grub until 10pm for a pre-party feed.

Kulturbolaget
LIVE MUSIC

(📞30 20 11; www.kulturbolaget.se; Bergsgatan 18) The White Stripes, The Strokes and Morrissey have all performed here but even if there's no one playing, 'KB' has a kicking bar and nightclub (usually Friday and Saturday).

Babel
LIVE MUSIC

(57 98 96; www.babelmalmo.se, in Swedish; Spångatan 38) This concert-club hybrid features regular soul, techno, pop and jazz gigs, with club nights on the weekend. The emphasis here is on high-quality variety, which can range from the dulcet tones of Sweden's Lisa Ekdahl to the thundering beats of DJ Theo Parrish.

Inkonst
LIVE MUSIC

(30 65 97; www.inkonst.com; Bergsgatan 29; 11pm-3am) This multifunction cultural hang-out serves up some brilliant club nights, pumping out anything from underground UK grime and garage to hip hop and rhythm and blues. Guest DJs have included the likes of Wiley and Ghetto. It also presents theatre and dance performances.

Étage
DANCE

(23 20 60; www.etagegruppen.se; Stortorget 6; 11pm-4am Mon & Thu, to 5am Fri & Sat) Central and mainstream, Étage boasts five bars, glammed-up party crowds and two crowded dance floors (one playing retro, the other the latest house tunes). It's enormous and loud so keep an eye on your friends or risk spending the evening trying to find them.

Club Wonk
GAY

(www.wonk.se; Amiralsgatan 23; before/after midnight Skr50/100; 11.30pm-5am Sat) Malmö's best bet for queer clubbers, Wonk works up the crowd with three bars, two dance floors and a karaoke lounge.

Cinemas

Malmö's numerous cinemas include the following:

Biograf Spegeln
CINEMA

(Stortorget 29) Alternative selections.

Filmstaden Malmö
CINEMA

(Storgatan 22) Hollywood releases.

Shopping

The current hot spot for up-and-coming designers and vintage threads is the streets around Davidshallstorg, south of Gamla Staden.

Tjallamalla
CLOTHING

(www.tjallamalla.co; Davidshallsgatan 15) Stockholm's legendary purveyor of new and emerging designers now feeds local trendsetters on cult labels like Whyszeck, Fröken Söt and Burfitt.

Chique
VINTAGE

(Kärleksgatan 3) In a district famed for vintage stores, this is one of the best. Its candy-store interior heaves with impeccable retro gems, from '70s Christian Dior handbags to dazzling '80s knits and studly cowboy boots.

Formargruppen
HANDICRAFTS

(www.formargruppen.se; Engelbrektsgatan 8) Representing a dynamic collective of Swedish artists, artisans and designers, this central shop-gallery stocks striking wares, from ceramics and pottery to jewellery and textiles.

ℹ Information

Emergency

Akutklinik (33 10 00, information service 1177; entrance 36, Södra Förstadsgatan 101) Emergency ward at the general hospital.
Police station (114 14; Porslinsgatan 6)

Internet Access

Malmö Stadsbibliotek (Regements gatan; 10am-7pm Mon-Thu, 10am-6pm Fri, 11am-3pm Sat) Free internet access at the library.
Sidewalk Express (Centralstationen; per hr Skr19)

Medical Services

You can call the dentist and doctor on duty on 1177.
Apotek Gripen (0771 45 04 50; Bergsgatan 48; 8am-10pm) After-hours pharmacy.

Money

Banks and ATMs are found on Södergatan.
Forex (Centralstationen; 7am-9pm) Money exchange, with another branch opposite Centralstationen on Skeppsbron, one on Gustav Adolfs Torg and another at Davidshallsgatan 27.
X-Change (Hamngatan 1; 8.30am-7pm Mon-Fri, 9am-4pm Sat) Money exchange.

Post

You can buy stamps and post letters from numerous shops and kiosks.

Tourist Information

Skånegården (34 12 00; www.malmotown .com; Skånegårdsvägen 5; 9am-5pm Mon-Fri, 10am-2.30pm Sat & Sun) On the E20, 800m from the Öresund bridge tollgate.
Tourist office (34 12 00; www.malmotown. com; Skeppsbron 2; 9am-7pm Mon-Fri, 10am-4pm Sat & Sun) Across from the Centralstationen; has free online hotel-booking service.
Tourism in Skåne (675 30 01; www.skane .com) Regional website with lots of information, tips, maps and booking service.

ℹ Getting There & Around

To/From the Airport

Flygbuss (www.flygbussarna.se) runs from Centralstationen to Sturup airport (adult/youth Skr99/79 one way) roughly every 40 minutes on weekdays, with six services on Saturday and seven on Sunday; a taxi shouldn't cost more than Skr400.

Air

Sturup airport (www.swedavia.se) is 33km southeast of Malmö. **SAS** (www.sas.se) has up to eight nonstop flights to Stockholm-Arlanda daily. **Malmö Aviation** (www.malmoaviation .se) flies as many as 11 times daily to Stockholm Bromma airport (from Skr390, one hour and five minutes).

Trains run directly from Malmö to Copenhagen's main airport (Skr105, 35 minutes, every 20 minutes), which has a much wider flight selection.

Bus

LOCAL & REGIONAL

Skånetrafiken (www.skanetrafiken.se) operates Skåne's efficient local bus and train networks (the latter known as Pågatågen).

Its buses operates in zones, with a single journey ranging from Skr19 within the city of Malmö to a maximum of Skr96 within the county. Local trains are your best bet for travel to/from the major towns in Skåne; buses are a good option for towns and out-of-the-way areas not on the train lines.

The customer desks in Centralstationen, Gustav Adolfs Torg and Värnhemstorget (at the east end of Kungsgatan) offer bus information and tickets, which cannot be bought onboard. Coop supermarkets and Pressbyrån newspaper kiosks also sell tickets. The main bus hubs are Centralplan (in front of Centralstationen), Gustav Adolfs Torg, Värnhemstorget and Triangeln. Malmökortet includes free city bus travel.

Most long-distance regional buses leave from the bus station on Spårvägsgatan, while a few go from the section of Norra Vallgatan in front of Centralplan. Bus 146 is a useful service to the ferries departing from Trelleborg (Skr54, 40 minutes); this service runs once or twice an hour. Bus 100 to Falsterbo (Skr54, one hour) is equally useful.

LONG-DISTANCE

There are two bus terminals with daily departures to Swedish and European destinations. **Travelshop** (Malmö Buss & Resecenter; www. travelshop.se; Skeppsbron 10), north of the train station, by the harbour, services (and sells tickets for) several companies, including **Swebus Express** (www.swebusexpress.com), which runs two to four times daily direct to Stockholm (Skr469 to Skr559, 8½ hours), four times to Jönköping (Skr209, 4½ hours) and up to 10 times daily to Göteborg (from Skr159, three to four hours); five continue to Oslo (Skr359, eight hours).

GoByBus (www.gobybus.se, in Swedish) has five buses on the Copenhagen–Malmö–Göteborg–Oslo route per day.

The second long-distance bus terminal, **Öresundsterminalen** (www.oresundsterminalen. se; Terminalgatan 10) is reached via bus 35 from Centralstationen towards Flansbjer (Skr19, 30 minutes). From here **Svenska Buss** (www. svenskabuss.se) runs a service to Stockholm (Skr340, 11 hours) via Karlskrona, six times weekly.

Eurolines also runs services from here to several European destinations; see p350 for details.

Trains are your best option for journeys to Copenhagen and beyond.

Car & Motorcycle

The E6 motorway runs north–south through Malmö's eastern and southern suburbs and its way from Göteborg to Trelleborg. The E65 motorway runs east to Ystad, the E22 runs northeast to Lund and Kristianstad, and the E20 heads west across the Öresund bridge (p186) to Copenhagen and north (with the E6) to Göteborg.

Several of the larger car-hire companies, such as **Avis** (☑airport 50 05 15; www.avisworld.com; Stormgatan 6, 778 30) and **Hertz** (☑33 07 70; www.hertz-europe.com; Jörgen Kocksgatan 1B) are represented at Sturup airport and directly opposite Centralstationen.

Parking in the city is expensive: typical charges start at Skr10 per hour or Skr110 per day (24 hours). Most hotels also charge for parking. Parking in municipal spaces (*gatukontoret*; ask the tourist office which symbol to look for) is free with Malmökortet.

Malmö's taxis are notorious for ripping people off – avoid them or at least agree on the fare with the driver before hopping in. The tourist office recommends **Taxi Skåne** (☑33 03 30) and **Taxi 97** (☑97 97 97).

Train

Pågatågen (local trains) operated by **Skånetrafiken** (www.skanetrafiken.se) run regularly to Helsingborg (Skr96, one hour), Landskrona (Skr78, 40 minutes), Lund (Skr42, 15 minutes), Simrishamn (Skr96, 1½ hours), Ystad (Skr78, 50 minutes) and other towns in Skåne. Bicycles are half-fare, but are not allowed during peak times except from mid-June to mid-August. The platform is at the end of Centralstationen and you buy tickets from the machine. International rail passes are accepted.

MALMÖ & THE SOUTH MALMÖ

The integrated Öresundregionen transport system operates trains from Helsingborg via Malmö and Copenhagen to Helsingør. The Malmö to Copenhagen Kastrup airport or Copenhagen central station trips take 20 and 35 minutes, respectively (both journeys Skr105); trains leave every 20 minutes.

X2000 (Skr303, 2½ hours) and regional (Skr211, 3¼ hours) trains run several times daily to/from Göteborg. X2000 (Skr674 to Skr1189, 4½ hours, hourly) and Intercity (Skr782, 6½ hours, infrequently) trains run between Stockholm and Malmö.

There are baggage lockers at Centralstationen for Skr30 to Skr50 per 24 hours.

Lund

📞046 / POP 105,300

Centred on a striking cathedral (complete with a giant in the crypt and a magical clock), learned Lund is a soulful blend of leafy parks, medieval abodes and coffee-sipping bookworms. The city buzzes with students during the school year and remains busy through the summer when visitors meander the cobblestone streets and enjoy the dense selection of top-notch museums.

Lund is Sweden's second-oldest town, founded by the Danes around 1000 and once the seat of the largest archbishopric in Europe. It's also the birthplace of the ink-jet printer!

⊙ Sights

Numerous galleries and small, special-interest museums and archives are dotted around town, many attached to university departments – enquire at the tourist office.

Domkyrkan   CHURCH

(Kyrkogatan; ⊙8am-6pm Mon-Fri, 9.30am-5pm Sat, 9.30am-6pm Sun) Lund's twin-towered Romanesque cathedral, Domkyrkan, is magnificent. Try to pop in at noon or 3pm (1pm and 3pm on Sunday and holidays) when the marvellous astronomical clock strikes up *In Dulci Jubilo* and the wooden figures at the top whirr into action. Within the crypt, you'll find Finn, the mythological giant who helped construct the cathedral, and a 16th-century well carved with comical scenes.

Kulturen   MUSEUM

(www.kulturen.com; Tegnerplatsen; adult/child/student/senior May-Aug Skr120/free/60/80, Sep-Apr Skr90/free/45/60; ⊙10am-5pm May-Aug, noon-4pm Tue-Sun Sep-Apr) Kulturen, opened in 1892, is a huge open-air museum filling two whole blocks. Its 30-odd buildings include everything from the meanest birch-bark hovel to grand 17th-century houses.

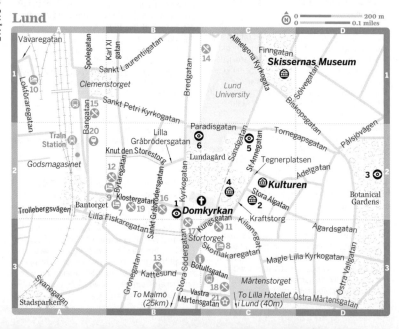

Permanent displays encompass Lund in the Middle Ages, vintage toys, ceramics, silver and glass (among many others); ask about guided tours in English. The popular outdoor cafe flanks several **rune stones**.

Skissernas Museum   ARTS CENTRE
(Sketch Museum; www.skissernasmuseum.se; Finngatan 2; adult/under 18yr Skr50/free; ⊙noon-5pm Tue-Sun, to 9pm Wed) The wonderful Skissernas Museum has the world's largest collection of sketches and designs for public artworks, from both Swedish and foreign artists, including Henri Matisse, Fernand Léger and Diego Rivera.

Historiska Museet   MUSEUM
(www.luhm.lu.se; Kraftstorg; adult/under 18yr Skr30/free; ⊙11am-4pm Tue-Fri, noon-4pm Sun)

Behind the cathedral, Historiska Museet has a large collection of pre-Viking Age finds, including a 7000-year-old skeleton. It's joined with **Domkyrkomuseet**, which explores the history of the church in the area; the rooms filled with countless statues of the crucified Christ are supremely creepy.

Drottens Arkeologiska Museum   MUSEUM
(www.kulturen.com; Kattesund 6A; admission free; ⊙9am-6pm Mon-Thu, 10am-6pm Fri & Sat) Subterranean Drottens Arkeologiska Museum contains the foundations of an 11th-century church, as well as a grisly collection of skeletons that build a picture of the Middle Ages through their diseases and amputations. Entrance is through the Gattostretto (p198) restaurant.

Botanical Gardens   GARDENS
(www.botaniskatradgarden.se; Östra Vallgatan 20; admission free; ⊙6am-9.30pm mid-May–mid-Sep, to 8pm mid-Sep–mid-May) The 8-hectare Botanical Gardens, east of the town centre, feature around 7000 species. Also on site are tropical **greenhouses** (admission free; ⊙noon-3pm).

University Building   UNIVERSITY
(cnr Kyrkogatan & Paradisgatan) The main university building, topped by four sphinxes representing the original faculties, is worth a peek.

Apoteket Svanen   HISTORIC BUILDING
(Kyrkogatan 5) Check out the recently restored pharmacy, close to the tourist office.

Hökeriet   HISTORIC BUILDING
(cnr St Annegatan & Tomegapsgatan; ⊙noon-4pm Sat & Sun) Across the park, Hökeriet is a vintage general store.

🛏 Sleeping

The tourist office can arrange a private room from Skr300 per person plus a Skr50 booking fee.

Lilla Hotellet i Lund   B&B €€
(☎32 88 88; www.lillahotellet.com; Bankgatan 7; s/d Skr850/1050; ⊙mid-Aug–mid-Jul; P@) Partly housed in an old shoe factory, this homely spot peddles cosy rooms (think patchwork quilts and DVD players), as well as a sunny courtyard and guest lounge.

Hotell Oskar   B&B €€
(☎18 80 85; www.hotelloskar.com; Bytaregatan 3; s/d Skr995/1195; @⊞) Tucked away in a petit, 19th-century townhouse, this central hotel has smashing rooms filled with sleek Scandi

design. It's also well equipped, with DVD players, kettles and stereos, as well as a back garden. Next-door **Ebbas Skafferi** (☑13 41 56; Bytaregatan 5; snacks from Skr39; lunch Skr75-135) is a nice cafe with a laid-back courtyard, green plants and flowers.

Grand Hotel
HOTEL €€€

(☑280 61 00; www.grandilund.se; Bantorget 1; s/d Skr1275/1775; @) Lund's most luxurious establishment is the Grand, which opened in 1899 and is resplendent with gilt and chandeliers. Rooms are smallish, but decorated in grand style with heavy wooden beds, Persian carpets and cherub wallpaper. Extras include a sauna and upmarket dining at Gambrinus (p198).

Hotel Ahlström
HOTEL €

(☑211 01 74; www.hotellahlstrom.se; Skomakaregatan 3; s/d with shared bathroom Skr670/850, d with bathroom Skr1100, all incl breakfast) Lund's oldest hotel is friendly and affordable, and on a quiet, central street. Rooms have parquet floors, cool white walls and washbasins (most bathrooms are shared). Breakfast is brought to your door.

STF Vandrarhem Lund Tåget
HOSTEL €

(☑14 28 20; info@hihostellund.se; Vävaregatan 22; dm Skr200) To find this quirky hostel, based in old railway carriages, look for a bridge over the tracks at the north end of the station. You'll see the hostel on your right as you come across. The triple bunks and tiny rooms are OK if you're cosying up with loved ones, but a little claustrophobic with strangers. Have a few Skr1 coins handy for the hot-water vending machines in the showers.

✗ Eating & Drinking

TOP
CHOICE **St Jakobs Stenugnsbageri** BAKERY €

(☑13 70 60; www.stjakobs.se; Klostergatan 9; baked goods Skr15-50; ☺9am-6pm Mon-Fri, 9am-5pm Sat, 11am-5pm Sun) Mouthwatering is the only way to describe the selection of stone-baked breads, knotted cardamom rolls, melt-in-your-mouth coconut lemon towers and crisp sugar cookies overflowing from the countertops and baking trays at St Jakobs. During the summer you're likely to see an enormous bowl of strawberries at the centre of it all, served with fresh cream of course.

Klostergatans Vin & Delikatess
WINE BAR €€

(☑14 14 83; www.klostergatan.se; Klostergatan 3; lunch Skr85-175, dinner mains Skr125-285) A French-style wine bar and delicatessen,

ideal for a quick bite or for a longer meal complete with crisp white tablecloths and a glass of the house wine. The menu definitely has a Gallic influence, using local ingredients. Its adjacent sister bakery Patisseriet has lovely cakes, coffees and sandwiches.

Piccolo
ICE CREAM €

(☑12 63 00; Kyrkogatan 2) Proper Italian gelati between the Domkyrkan and Stortorget.

Govindas
VEGETARIAN €

(☑12 04 13; Bredgatan 28; lunch Skr70; ☺lunch Mon-Sat) In a quiet, leafy cobbled courtyard, vegetarian Govindas is a hit with kronorconscious students and anyone craving a spicy curry and cool raita.

Gattostretto
ITALIAN €€

(☑32 07 77; www.gattostretto.se; Kattesund 6A; salads Skr75; mains Skr129-229 ☺9am-6pm Mon-Sat) Located over medieval ruins and co-run by an affable Roman chef, this breezy cafe-restaurant serves a tasty slice of *dolce vita*. Guzzle down proper Italian espresso and a slice of *torta rustica*, or long for Rome over hearty *ragù* or tri-coloured bruschetta.

Gambrinus
EUROPEAN €€€

(☑280 61 00; Bantorget 1; daily lunch special Skr125, dinner mains Skr235-295, Lund menu Skr395) The star turn at the Grand Hotel's gourmet nosh spot is the Lund menu, featuring creative interpretations of regional classics using seasonal local produce. While the speciality is sweetbreads, there's a vegetarian menu for herbivorous guests.

Saluhallen
SELF-CATERING €

(Mårtenstorget; ☺Mon-Sat) A mouthwatering market hall, it peddles reasonably priced grub, from fresh fish and piping-hot pasta to Thai, kebabs and croissants.

Café Ariman
CAFE €

(☑13 12 63; www.ariman.se; Kungsgatan 2B; snacks around Skr40; ☺11am-midnight Mon, 11am-1am Tue-Thu, 11am-3am Fri & Sat, 3-11pm Sun, closed Sun in summer) Head to this hip, grungy hang-out for cathedral views, strong coffee and fine cafe fare such as ciabatta, salads and burritos. It's popular with left-wing students: think nose-rings, dreads and leisurely chess games. From September to May, DJs hit the decks on Friday and Saturday nights.

ICA
SUPERMARKET

(Bangatan; ☺8am-10pm) Self-caterers should head here, opposite the train station.

Systembolaget   LIQUOR STORE

(Bangatan 10) For alcohol, Systembolaget is near the supermarket.

☆ Entertainment

Pick up the brochure *i Lund* from the tourist office for the entertainment run-down.

SF Bio Filmstaden   CINEMA

(Västra Mårtensgatan 12) Mainstream flicks.

❶ Information

Banks, ATMs and other services line the main street (Stora Södergatan, changing to Kyrkogatan).

Read about the **university** (www.lu.se) online, and check out www.lund.se for information about the town.

Forex Bangatan (Bangatan 8; ⊙8am-7pm Mon-Fri, to 4pm Sat); Västra Mårtensgatan (Västra Mårtensgatan 6; ⊙9am-7pm Mon-Fri, 10am-3pm Sat) Two central money-exchange offices.

Library (Sankt Petri Kyrkogatan 6; ⊙10am-8pm Mon-Thu, to 7pm Fri, to 4pm Sat, 1-5pm Sun) Free internet access.

Press Stop (Klostergatan 8; ⊙10am-6pm Mon-Fri, to 1pm Sat) Good choice of foreign magazines and newspapers.

Sidewalk Express (www.sidewalkexpress.se; per hr Skr19) Sidewalk Express internet terminals are found inside the 7-Eleven shop on Lilla Fiskaregatan.

Tourist office (☑35 50 40; www.lund.se; Botulfsgatan 1A; ⊙10am-6pm Mon-Fri, to 2pm Sat) At the southern end of Stortorget.

❶ Getting There & Away

Flygbuss (www.flygbussarna.se) runs regularly to Malmö's Sturup airport (Skr99); see p195.

Long-distance buses leave from outside the train station. Most buses to/from Malmö (except buses to Trelleborg and Falsterbo) run via Lund. See p195 for details.

It's 15 minutes from Lund to Malmö by train, with frequent Pågatågen departures (Skr39). Some trains continue to Copenhagen (Skr125, one hour). Other direct services run from Malmö to Kristianstad and Karlskrona via Lund. All long-distance trains from Stockholm or Göteborg to Malmö stop in Lund.

❶ Getting Around

Skånetrafiken (☑0771-77 77 77) local town buses cost Skr15 per ride; the terminal is on Botulfsplatsen, west of Mårtenstorget. For bike hire, head to **Godsmagasinet** (☑35 57 42; Bangatan; per day/week Skr20/130; ⊙6.30am-9.30pm Mon-Fri), a bicycle lock-up in the northernmost train-station building. Phone **Taxi Skåne** (☑33 03 30) for a taxi.

Falsterbo Peninsula

☑040

This laid-back peninsula 30km south of Malmö lures sun lovers with its sandy beaches and ornithologists with its impressive posse of feathered creatures. Eclectic extras include the Foteviken Viking Reserve and the offbeat amber museum.

❶ Information

Tourist office (☑42 54 54; turisten@vellinge. se; Videholms Allé 1A; ⊙10am-6pm Mon-Fri, to 2pm Sat & Sun mid-Jun–mid-Aug, 10am-noon & 1-4pm Mon-Thu, to 3pm Fri mid-Aug–mid-Jun) The area's major tourist office is in the same building as the Höllviken library just off Falsterbovägen. The town of Höllviken has banks and supermarkets.

BÄRNSTENSMUSEUM

Trapped in sticky resin 40 million years ago, insects fight, mate and feed in pieces of amber at the **Bärnstensmuseum** (Amber Museum; www.brost.se; Södra Mariavägen 4; adult/child Skr20/10; ⊙10am-6pm mid-Jul–mid-Aug, 11am-5pm mid-May–mid-Jul & mid-Aug–Sep, 11am-3pm Sat & Sun rest of year). It's small but interesting; museum staff acted as advisors to the makers of *Jurassic Park*.

The museum is near Höllviken's southern edge, just off the coast road towards Trelleborg.

FOTEVIKEN VIKING RESERVE

If you mourn the passing of big hairy men in longboats, find solace at one of Sweden's most absorbing attractions, about 700m north of Höllviken. **Foteviken Viking Reserve** (www.fotevikensmuseum.se; adult/6-15yr/family Skr80/30/200, cash only; ⊙10am-4pm Jun-Aug, 10am-4pm Tue-Fri May & start–mid-Sep) is an evocative 'living' reconstruction of a late–Viking Age village.

Around 22 authentic reconstructions of houses with reed or turf roofs have been built on the coast, near the site of the Battle of Foteviken (1134). These belong to various tradespeople, like the town's *jarl* (commander of the armed forces), juror and scribe; and the chieftain, whose home has wooden floorboards, fleeces and a Battle of Foteviken tapestry. There's even a shield-lined great hall (the Thinghöll), a lethally powerful war catapult and nifty Viking-made handicrafts to buy.

MALMÖ & THE SOUTH FALSTERBO PENINSULA

Amazingly, the reserve's residents live as the Vikings did, eschewing most modern conveniences and adhering to old traditions, laws and religions – even after the last tourist has left.

Viking Week is usually held in late June, and culminates in a Viking market, complete with agile warriors in training.

FALSTERBO & SKANÖR

Little Falsterbo Museum (☑47 22 42; www.kulturbron.com/falsterbomuseum.htm; Sjögatan; adult/child Skr20/10; ☺10am-7pm mid-Jun–Aug), at the southern tip of the peninsula, is a pleasing jumble: a small natural history centre, old shops and smithies, WWII mines and the remains of a 13th-century boat.

Falsterbo's long, white-sand beach is popular with locals and Malmö leisure-seekers. The hook-shaped island of Måkläppen is a nature reserve, off limits to the public from March to October. Residents include seals and over 50 species of birds, including little terns, Kentish plovers (rare in Sweden) and avocets; in the autumn, between one and three million migrating birds rest their wings here. Near the museum is Falsterbo Fågelstation (☑47 06 88; www.falsterbofagelstation.se; Sjögatan; 1hr guided tours per person Skr40, minimum Skr400 for groups of less than 10; ☺Apr, May & Aug-Oct, advanced booking required), a bird observatory studying these feathery visitors. Tours take place at the Falsterbo lighthouse.

The superfriendly Ljungens Camping (☑47 11 32; ftc@telia.com; Strandbadsvägen; sites Skr160-380; ☺Apr-Sep) is a couple of kilometres from Falsterbo. Its amenities include minigolf. For a more dressed-up option try Skanörs Gästgifvaregård (☑47 56 90; www.skanorsgastis.se; Mellangatan 13; s & d Skr1495) which couples 10 lovely double rooms with a stellar restaurant.

Da Aldo (☑47 40 26; www.aldo.se; Mellangatan 47; gelato from Skr28, piadina Skr59; ☺8.30am-10pm summer, 11am-6pm Wed-Sun rest of year), on the main street of Skanör, an easy 1.5km north of Falsterbo, is an outstanding cafe where Calabrian expat Aldo makes sublime gelato using strictly Italian ingredients and no added egg, cream or butter. Lunch options, from frittata and salads to *piadine* (Italian flat-bread sandwiches) and stuffed aubergine, are well priced and equally authentic. As for the coffee...*buonissimo!*

Skanörs Fiskrögeri (☑47 40 50; www.rogeriet.se; Skanörs Hamn; mains Skr218-393; ☺lunch & dinner Jun-Aug, dinner Thu & Fri, lunch & dinner Sat & Sun Apr-May & Sep) is a must for seafood lovers, as its harbourside location and white smokehouse chimneys attest. The fish soup is exquisite and there's a gourmet seafood deli that's perfect for putting together a beachside picnic.

Bus 100 (Skr54, 55 minutes, every 30 minutes Monday to Saturday, every 30 to 60 minutes Sunday) runs from Malmö to Falsterbo and Skanör.

Trelleborg

☑0410 / POP 41,000

Trelleborg is the main gateway between Sweden and Germany, with frequent ferry services. It's not really on the tourist trail: if you're entering Sweden from here, consider heading on for Malmö or Ystad.

◉ Sights

Trelleborgen   HISTORIC SITE

(☑73 30 21; admission free; ☺10am-5pm Jul & Aug, 1-5pm Mon-Thu rest of year) Trelleborgen is a 9th-century Viking ring fortress, discovered in 1988 off Bryggaregatan (just west of the town centre). It's built to the same pattern as Danish fortresses of the same era, showing the centralised power of Harald Bluetooth at work. A quarter of the palisaded fort and a wooden gateway have been re-created, as has a Viking farmhouse and a medieval house built within the walls. An on-site

---

DON'T MISS

APPLES, CIDER, CALVADOS?

A wander through the lovingly tended visitor's orchard at Kiviks Musteri (p207) will leave you parched and dying for a crunchy, just-tinged-with-pink apple. Quench your thirst at the *musteri* shop or better yet, splash out on an evening cider-to-calvados tasting (Skr395). Over two hours, you'll get to sip four- and 12-year old calvados (apple brandy), as well as the orchard's delicious hard cider, and there are plenty of snacks chosen to complement what you're drinking. Tastings take place on Fridays throughout the year and must be booked ahead.

visitors centre (✏adult/under 15yr Skr30/free) showcases finds from the archaeological digs, including Viking jewellery, grooming implements and a c 10th-century skull illustrating the ancient trend of teeth filing.

Trelleborgs Museum   MUSEUM
(✏73 30 50; museum@trelleborg.se; Östergatan 58; adult/under 20yr incl admission to Axel Ebbe Konsthall Skr30/free; ⊙noon-4pm Tue-Sun) Just east of the town centre, Trelleborgs Museum covers a wide range of themes, including a 7000-year-old settlement discovered nearby.

Axel Ebbe Konsthall   MUSEUM
(Hesekillegatan 1; adult/under 20yr Skr30/free, incl admission to Trelleborgs Museum; ⊙1-4pm Tue-Sun summer) By the town park, Axel Ebbe Konsthall features nude sculptures by Scanian Axel Ebbe (1868–1941). For a preview, check out the fountain Sjöormen, literally 'the sea monster', in Storatorget.

🍽 Sleeping & Eating
The tourist office can book private rooms from Skr300.

Hotel Duxiana
Dannegården   HISTORIC HOTEL €€€
(✏481 80; www.dannegarden.se; Strandgatan 32; s/d incl breakfast Skr890/1090, discounted to Skr700/952; ℗@) Trelleborg's most beautiful slumber spot is this old sea captain's villa. Run with quiet confidence by the Duxiana hotel chain, rooms here are discreetly luxurious, breakfast generous and staff pleasant. Extras include a reputable restaurant and gorgeous gardens.

Hotell Horizont   HOTEL €
(✏71 32 39; www.horizont.nu; Hamngatan 9; s/d Skr590/790; ℗❀@) Crash here for clean, modern rooms, some with harbour views. There is a reasonable restaurant, bar and cafe on the top-floor restaurant.

Dalabadets Camping   CAMPGROUND €
(✏149 05; www.dalabadetscamping.se; Dalabadets Strandväg 2; sites Skr220, 4-bed cabins from Skr500; ⊙Apr-Sep) This is the nearest campsite, over 3km to the east. It's a well-equipped place between Rd 9 and the beach.

Night Stop   MOTEL €
(✏410 70; www.hotelnightstop.com; Östergatan 59; s/d Skr250/350; ℗) Simple and functional with shared bathrooms, Night Stop has the cheapest beds in town. Open 24 hours, it's about 500m from the ferry (turn right along Hamngatan after disembarking), diagonally opposite the museum. Breakfast is an additional Skr50.

Café i Vattentornet   CAFE €
(✏73 30 70; Stortorget; sandwiches from Skr25; ⊙Mon-Sat) On the ground floor of the splendid 58m-high water tower (1912), Café i Vattentornet sells sandwiches, cakes and other yummy snacks, with fabulous outdoor tables in the summer.

Restaurang & Pizzeria Istanbul   TURKISH €
(✏44 44 44; Algatan 30; mains Skr60-220) This bustling place has a huge menu of pasta, pizza, salad and kebabs, plus pricier local fish and meat dishes.

ℹ Information
Banks and ATMs line Algatan.
Forex (CB Friisgatan 3; ⊙8am-8pm Mon-Fri, 8am-2pm Sat, 11am-3pm Sun) Money exchange.
Library (Astrid Lindgrens Allé 1; ⊙10am-7pm Mon-Fri, 10am-6pm Sat, 11am-2pm) Free internet access.
Tourist office (✏73 33 20; www.trelleborg.se/turism; Kontinentgatan 2; ⊙9am-6pm Mon-Fri, 10am-6pm Sat, 10am-5pm Sun Jun-Aug, 9am-5pm Mon-Fri Sep-May) Across from the ferry terminal.

ℹ Getting There & Away
Bus 146 runs roughly every half-hour between Malmö (Skr54, 45 minutes) and Trelleborg's bus station, some 500m inland from the ferry terminals. Bus 165 runs frequently Monday to Friday (five services Saturday and four services Sunday) from Lund (Skr66, one hour and five minutes). See p205 for bus travel from Ystad.

For details of international trains from Malmö to Berlin via Trelleborg, see p350.

Scandlines (www.scandlines.se) ferries connect Trelleborg to Sassnitz (twice daily each way) and Rostock (two or three daily). **TT-Line** (www.ttline.com) ferries shuttle between Trelleborg and Travemünde three to four times daily, and between Trelleborg and Rostock up to three times daily. Buy tickets inside the ferry building. See p352 for details.

Smygehuk
✏0410
Thanks to the power of geography – it's Sweden's most southerly point (latitude 55° 20' 3") – diminutive Smygehuk has become something of a tourist magnet, despite its modest attractions.

MALMÖ & THE SOUTH SMYGEHUK

To the east of the harbour, a summer tourist office (☑240 53; www.smygehuk.com; ⊙10am-7pm Jul, to 6pm Jun & Aug) and cafe sit inside **Köpmansmagasinet**, a renovated 19th-century warehouse with local exhibitions of fantastic handicrafts and art (for sale). Nearby, a huge 19th-century **lime kiln** recalls the bygone lime industry; it smoked its last in 1954.

West of the harbour, scramble to the top of the now-defunct **lighthouse** (17m), dating from 1883, and visit the tiny maritime museum inside **Captain Brinck's Cabin** (donation appreciated; ⊙summer). Opening hours are erratic; the lighthouse is managed by the hostel warden, and she opens it if/when she feels like it. A soothing **coastal path** features prolific bird life.

STF Vandrarhem Smygehuk (☑245 83, 70 70 14; www.smygehukhostel.com; s/d Skr300/480; ⊙mid-May–mid-Sep; ℗) is a comfortable, spotless and well-equipped hostel in the old lighthouse-keeper's residence, next to the lighthouse (see p169). Book ahead outside the high season.

Smyge Fisk Rökeri (www.smygerokeri.se; Skepparevägen 3; sandwiches from Skr45) packs people into its tiny shop like sardines. The smoke house's salmon baguettes and crayfish cakes on brown bread are worth the crush.

The Trelleborg to Ystad bus service (see p205) stops in Smygehuk.

Ystad

☑0411 / POP 28,000

Half-timbered houses, rambling cobbled streets and the haunting sound of a nightwatchman's horn give this medieval market town an intoxicating lure. Fans of writer Henning Mankell know it as the setting for his best-selling Inspector Wallander crime thrillers, while fans of drums and uniforms head in for the spectacular three-day **Military Tattoo** (www.ystadtattoo.se) in August.

Ystad was Sweden's window to Europe from the 17th to the mid-19th century, with new ideas and inventions – including cars, banks and hotels – arriving here first. Now a terminal for ferries to Bornholm and Poland, the port's transitory feel doesn't spread to the rest of Ystad: settle in for a few days and let the place work its magic.

◎ Sights

Half-timbered houses are scattered liberally round town, especially on Stora Östergatan.

Most date from the latter half of the 18th century, although the facade of beautiful **Änglahuset** on Stora Norregatan originates from around 1630.

Sankta Maria Kyrka
CHURCH

(Stortorget; ⊙10am-6pm Jun-Aug, to 4pm Sep-May, tours at 12.15pm & 2.30pm summer) Don't miss the Sankta Maria Kyrka. Ever since 1250, a night watchman has blown his horn through the little window in the church clock tower (every 15 minutes from 9.15pm to 3am). The watchman was traditionally beheaded if he dozed off! Among the highlights are a 17th-century baroque pulpit, along with a line of pews near the entrance for women who had recently given birth and hadn't yet been churched. **Latinskolan**, next to Sankta Maria Kyrka, is a late-15th-century brick building and the oldest preserved school in Scandinavia.

Klostret i Ystad
MUSEUM

(☑57 72 86; www.klostret.ystad.se, in Swedish; St Petri Kyrkoplan; adult/under 16yr Skr30/free, combined ticket with Ystads Konstmuseum Skr50; ⊙10am-5pm Mon-Fri, noon-4pm Sat & Sun Jul-mid-Aug, noon-5pm Tue-Fri, noon-4pm Sat & Sun mid-Aug–Jun) Klostret i Ystad, in the Middle Ages Franciscan monastery of Gråbrödraklostret, features local textiles and silverware. The monastery includes the 13th-century deconsecrated Sankt Petri Kyrkan (now used for art exhibitions), which has around 80 gravestones from the 14th to 18th centuries. Included in the same ticket is the **Ystads Konstmuseum** (www.konstmuseet. ystad.se, in Swedish; St Knuts Torg; adult/under 16yr Skr30/free, combined ticket with Klostret i Ystad Skr50; ⊙10am-5pm Mon-Fri, noon-4pm Sat & Sun Jul–mid-Aug, noon-5pm Tue-Fri, noon-4pm Sat & Sun mid-Aug–Jun). In the same building as the tourist office, its savvy collection of southern Swedish and Danish art includes work by the great Per Kirkeby.

Charlotte Berlins Museum
HOUSE

(☑188 66; Dammgatan 23; adult/under 16yr Skr20/ free; ⊙noon-5pm Mon-Fri, to 4pm Sat & Sun Jun-Aug, tours hourly from 11am) For fetching interiors, pop into Charlotte Berlins Museum, which is a late-19th-century middle-class abode.

🛏 Sleeping

Travellers with their own wheels can select from the B&B and cabin options along the scenic coastal roads on either side of Ystad. The tourist office can arrange B&B accom-

Ystad

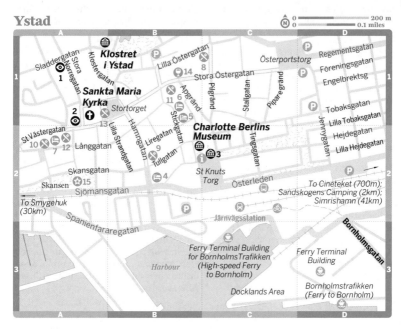

N ⌂ 0 ———————— 200 m
0 ———————— 0.1 miles

modation for around Skr600 to Skr800 per double room.

TOP CHOICE Mormor Anita's Place B&B €€

(☎070-686 53 76; www.mormoranitasplace.se; Stickgatan 13; d incl breakfast from Skr900) This tranquil B&B is located in a pale yellow 16th-century house, just around the corner from the tourist office. There are just three rooms, each fitted out with tasteful antiques, plush towels and period artwork. Fresh-baked bread at breakfast, friendly owners and a garden overflowing with roses make it worth planning ahead for.

Hotell Klara B&B €€

(☎0702-945 255; www.ystadhotell.se; Stickgatan 17; s/d Skr795/895; @) If you can't get into Anita's, Hotell Klara down the street is another excellent option. The half-timbered building contrasts sharply with the 12 modern and crisply renovated apartment rooms. Some have kitchenettes and there are laundry facilities.

Sekelgården Hotel HOTEL €€

(☎739 00; www.sekelgarden.se; Långgatan 18; s/d Skr895/995; P @) A romantic family-run hotel in a superb half-timbered house (1793), the rooms here take their inspiration from

Ystad

◉ Top Sights

◉ Sights

▣ Sleeping

✖ Eating

◉ Drinking

◉ Entertainment

historical styles or people. There's also a sauna and pretty courtyard.

Hotell Continental
HOTEL €€

(☑137 00; www.hotelcontinental-ystad.se; Hamngatan 13; s/d incl breakfast Skr1490/1690; P@) On the site of the old customs house, the Continental is reputedly Sweden's oldest hotel, having opened in 1829. Loaded with old-world charm (think grand chandeliered foyer and marble staircase), its rooms are less luxe, although all are clean with modern bathrooms and comfy beds.

Sandskogens Camping
CAMPGROUND €

(☑192 70; www.sandskogenscamping.se; sites Skr220, 4-person cabins Skr550; ☺May-Sep) This superfriendly (and superbusy) wooded site is 2km east of Ystad on Rd 9 to Simrishamn, across the road from the beach and STF hostel. Bus 572 drives past from town.

✖ Eating & Drinking

Most budget eating places are on Stora Östergatan, the main pedestrian street.

Book Café Host Morten
CAFE €

(☑134 03; Gåsegränd; ☺11am-3.30pm Tue-Sat) Plunge into that Henning Mankell novel at this adorable cafe, complete with book-crammed living room, 18th-century courtyard, and a delicious array of focaccias, pastries and coffee.

Store Thor
EUROPEAN €€

(☑185 10; www.storethor.se; Stortorget; lunch from Skr95, mains Skr98-275) Described as one of Ystad's best restaurants by Kurt Wallander in the movie *Täckmanteln,* Store Thor occupies the arched cellar of the old town hall (1572). Nibble on tapas, tuck into succulent grilled meats or enjoy the cognac raw-spiced salmon with dill-stewed potatoes. The square-side terrace is a hit with trendy summertime night owls

Bröderna M
PIZZERIA €€

(☑191 99; www.brodernam.se; Hamngatan 11; mains Skr175-199, pizzas from Skr58) Relaxed and contemporary, Bröderna M serves up Ystad's best pizza, ranging from classic margheritas to posh thin-crusted pies topped with prosciutto, rocket and pecorino. Main dishes are solid bistro fare: steak with red wine sauce or fish soup.

Bryggeriet
PUB €€

(☑699 99; www.restaurangbryggeriet.nu; Långgatan 20; mains Skr125-210) Unique Bryggeriet is a relaxed meat-leaning restaurant-pub in

---

INSPECTOR WALLANDER'S YSTAD

Fans of crime thrillers most likely know the name of Henning Mankell (1948–), author of the best-selling Inspector Wallander series. The books are set in the small, seemingly peaceful town of Ystad. The gloomy inspector paces its medieval streets, solving gruesome murders through his meticulous police work...but at a cost to his personal life, which is slowly and painfully disintegrating. The first book is *Faceless Killers,* but it's generally agreed that Mankell really hit his stride in number four, *The Man Who Smiled.* Impressively, Mankell's nail-biting stories have been translated into 41 languages.

Between 2005 and 2006, 13 Wallander films were shot in and around Ystad, starring Krister Henriksson in the lead role. The first, an adaptation of *Before the Frost,* is followed by 12 independent stories by Mankell. In 2008 a further 13 Wallander films were shot here, alongside a BBC-commissioned TV series starring Kenneth Branagh as Wallander. At time of writing, Branagh was said to be returning to film as many as six follow-up episodes.

Interactive film centre **Cineteket** (☑0411-57 70 57; www.ystad.se/cineteket; Elis Nilssons väg 8; adult/child Skr50/20; ☺10am-4pm Mon-Thu, Sat & Sun mid-Jun–Aug, times vary rest of year) runs guided tours at 2pm on Wednesday, Saturday and Sunday (adult/6 to 12 years Skr150/75) of the adjoining Ystad Studios, where sets include forensic detective Leif Nyberg's laboratory and the inspector's own apartment.

The Ystad tourist office provides a free map with featured locations in town. There's even an iPhone app, especially handy if you want directions to sites further afield. For a quirkier excursion around Wallander's Ystad, the volunteer fire brigade runs 45-minute tours starting at Stortorget on a veteran fire engine at 1pm and 4.45pm from late June to mid-August. Contact the tourist office for details, and book a few days in advance.

These days, Mankell spends much of his time in Maputo, Mozambique, where he juggles writing, running a theatre company and his AIDS education work. His wife, Eva Bergman, is the daughter of the late film director Ingmar Bergman.

an old brewery. The courtyard is an excellent spot to linger over a well-cooked meal and Ystad Färsköl, a beer brewed on the premises.

Maltes Mackor
SANDWICHES €

(☑101 30; Stora Östergatan 12; ☺Mon-Sat) Busy, with a great range of sandwiches and rolls.

Saluhallen
SELF-CATERING €

(Stora Västergatan; ☺8am-8pm) Located behind the church, handy for groceries.

Systembolaget
LIQUOR STORE

(Stora Östergatan 13) For alcohol.

☆ Entertainment

Ystads Teater
THEATER

(☑57 77 98; Sjömansgatan 13; tickets around Skr300) The extraordinary Ystads Teater has remained virtually unchanged since opening in 1894 and its repertoire spans operas, musicals, tango and big-band gigs. Guided tours (usually in Swedish) of the building take place daily from late June to August. Contact the tourist office for details.

❶ Information

Banks, and other services line Hamngatan.

Forex (Catterminalen, Hamntorget 2; ☺8am-8.30pm Mon-Fri, 9am-3pm Sat, 11am-3pm Sun) Money exchange.

Library (Surbrunnsvägen 12; ☺11am-7pm Mon-Thu, 11am-5pm Fri, 10am-2pm Sat) Free internet access.

Tourist office (☑57 76 81; www.ystad.se; St Knuts Torg; ☺9am-7pm Mon-Fri, 10am-6pm Sat & Sun mid-Jun–mid-Aug, 9am-5pm Mon-Fri rest of year) Just opposite the train station; it also offers free internet access.

❶ Getting There & Away

Boat

Unity Line (www.unityline.se) and **Polferries** (www.polferries.se) operate daily crossings between Ystad and Swinoujscie. Ystad's ferry terminal is within walking distance of the train station (drivers follow a more circuitous route).

Bornholmstrafikken (www.bornholmstrafikken.dk) runs frequent ferries and catamarans between Ystad and Rønne, on the Danish island of Bornholm: see p351. Catamarans operate from a terminal directly behind the train station.

Bus

Buses depart from outside Ystad train station. Bus 190 runs from Ystad to Trelleborg (Skr66, one hour) via Smygehuk 14 times daily on weekdays, six times on Saturday and twice on Sunday. The direct bus to Simrishamn (Skr48, one hour) via Löderup runs every 30 minutes in the summer.

SkåneExpressen bus 6 runs to Lund (Skr84, 1¼ hours, hourly weekdays, infrequently on weekends) and bus 4 runs three to nine times daily to Kristianstad (Skr60, 1¾ hours). Local train is the only way to get to Malmö.

Train

Pågatågen trains run roughly every hour (fewer on weekends) from Malmö (Skr78, 50 minutes). Other local trains run daily to Simrishamn (Skr42, 40 minutes).

❶ Getting Around

There are a handful of local bus services; all depart from outside the tourist office (St Knuts Torg). Try **Taxi Ystad** (☑720 00) for a taxi or **Roslins Cykel** (www.roslinscykel.se; Norra Zinkgatan 2; per day/week Skr65/325; ☺Mon-Fri 9.30am-6pm, to 3pm Sat year-round, 11am-3pm Sun Apr-Aug) for bike hire, located about 3km northeast of the city centre.

Around Ystad

LÖDERUPS STRANDBAD
☑0411

With its long, white-sand beaches, the Baltic resort of Löderups Strandbad, 4km east of Ales Stenar, is perfect for lounging, although it can get busy during the school holidays.

Dag Hammarskjölds Backåkra (Löderup; adult/under 15yr Skr30/free; ☺noon-5pm Tue-Sun end Jun–mid-Aug), about 1km east of Löderups Strandbad, was a summer house acquired by the secretary-general of the UN in 1957. Hammarskjöld was killed in a mysterious plane crash in Zambia four years later; many of his unusual belongings and souvenirs were moved to this peaceful place to form a memorial museum. The old farmhouse is set in a **nature reserve** of sand dunes, heath and wildflower meadows.

On the edge of the Hagestad Nature Reserve, **Löderups Strandbads Camping** (☑52 63 11; www.loderupsstrandbadscamping.se; sites Skr200, cabins from Skr500; ☺mid-Apr–Sep) is a pleasant spot in a pine forest next to the beach.

The family hotel **Löderups Strandbad Hotell** (☑52 62 60; www.loderupsstrandbad.com; s/d Skr740/940; Ⓟⓐ☒) is a popular summer spot, complete with sauna, heated outdoor pool and restaurant. It also rent cabins, most with sea views (rented by the week only in high season; Skr7900).

WORTH A TRIP

ALES STENAR

Ales Stenar has all the mystery of England's Stonehenge, with none of the commercial greed. It's Sweden's largest stone ship setting and an intriguing sight. The 67m-long oval of stones, shaped like a boat, was probably constructed around AD 600 for reasons unknown. Limited excavations at the site have revealed no body; it's possible that this wasn't a grave but a ritual site, with built-in solar calendar (the 'stem' and 'stern' stones point towards the midsummer sunset and midwinter sunrise).

The enigmatic ship is in the middle of a raised field, with an uncannily low and level 360-degree horizon. There is parking to the right off the main road or at the Kåseberga harbour, though the harbour area can get crowded and chaotic in the summer. In the summer, a tiny tourist office at the roadside parking lot gives out information and runs tours up to three times daily. From either place, the setting is a 1km walk.

Free to visit and always open, Ales Stenar lies 19km east of Ystad at Kåseberga. It's badly served by public transport. Bus 392 from Ystad runs daily in summer; at other times, take bus 570 from Ystad to Valleberga *kyrka* (church) and then walk 5km south to Kåseberga.

Near Strandbad, beside the main road, the helpful **STF Vandrarhem Backåkra** (☑52 60 80; www.backakra.se; dm Skr230; ☺mid-Jun–mid-Aug; P@) has simple but cheery rooms, a great garden and it's within walking distance of the beach. Book ahead in summer.

See p205 for bus details from Ystad.

Österlen

☑0414 / POP 19,400

Softly lit Österlen is an alluring area of waving wheat fields, tiny fishing villages and glorious apple orchards. Everything moves at a slow, seductive speed: cycling is the best way of fitting in with the tempo.

SIMRISHAMN

Summer holidaymakers mill around Simrishamn harbour, idly licking ice creams or waiting for the ferry to the Danish island of Bornholm.

◉ Sights & Activities

The quaint pastel-hued houses on **Lilla Norregatan** are worth a look, as is nearby **Sankt Nikolai Kyrka**. Engine-heads shouldn't miss **Österlens Motor & Teknikmuseum** (www.osterlensmotormuseum.se, in Swedish; Fabriksgatan 10; adult/7-14yr Skr100/60; ☺11am-5pm daily Jul & Aug, 11am-5pm Sat & Sun Apr-Jun & Sep-Oct), with its booty of classic cars, bikes and buggies.

The region is great for cycling and there are a variety of routes to choose from ranging from a 66km spin covering major food highlights to the 136km-long Österlen Trail.

The Simrishamn tourist office has free biking maps or get in touch with **Österlenguiderna** (☑70 518 33 29; www.osterlenguiderna.se), which rents bikes and runs organised tours.

🛏 Sleeping & Eating

Maritim Krog & Hotell　　　HOTEL €€
(☑41 13 60; www.maritim.nu; Hamngatan 31; s/d from Skr1050/1450; P@) The old blue building by the harbour is a wonderful boutique hotel with stylish decor and sea views. It's also home to a fantastic restaurant (mains Skr170 to SKr295) specialising in fish dishes.

STF Vandrarhem Simrishamn　　HOSTEL €
(☑105 40; www.simrishamnsvandrarhem.se; Christian Barnekowsgatan 10C; s/d Skr400/550; ☺Apr-mid-Nov; P@) Pick up a map before setting off – this place is well hidden, near the town hospital. It's worth seeking out, however, offering spotless, colourful, homely lodgings with bathroom and TV in every room. Outside summer, bookings are essential in summer.

Tobisviks Camping　　　CAMPGROUND €
(☑41 27 78; www.fritidosterlen.se; sites/cabins from Skr250/600; ☒) By the beach 2km north of the town centre, this serviceable site neighbours a swimming pool.

Evelinas Kök　　　EUROPEAN €€
(☑44 80 70; www.evelinaskok.se; Storgatan 3; mains Skr165-265; ☺noon-10pm Jul & Aug, shorter hours Sep-Jun) At the harbour end of Storgatan, Evelinas is in a pleasant peachy pink building with blue umbrellas protecting customers seated on the patio and cosy can-

dlelight indoors. The menu varies to take in the season's best, with dishes ranging from a classic hamburger on foccacia to baked flounder.

ⓘ Information

Banks and other services line Storgatan.

Tourist office (☑81 98 00; Varvsgatan 2; ☺9am-7pm Mon-Fri, 10am-6pm Sat & Sun Jul & Aug, 9am-5pm Mon-Fri rest of year) Has information on the whole of Österlen.

ⓘ Getting There & Around

BornholmExpress (www.bornholmexpress.dk; adult/6-14yr return Skr340/170) runs a ferry service between Simrishamn and Allinge (on the Danish island of Bornholm) from mid-June through to August.

SkåneExpressen bus 3 runs roughly every hour on weekdays (less frequently on weekends) from Simrishamn train station to Kristianstad (Skr48, 1¼ hours) via Kivik (not stopping at the Stenshuvud National Park access road). Simrishamn to Kivik is Skr19, 24 minutes. Bus 5 to Lund (Skr78, 1½ hours) runs up to 12 times on weekdays (and up to five times on weekends). There's a direct bus to Ystad via Löderup (Skr48, one hour) three to 13 times daily.

Local trains run up to 12 times daily from Simrishamn to Ystad (Skr39, 40 minutes), with connections from Ystad to Malmö and Lund.

For bike hire, try **Hotell Turistgården** (Storgatan 21; Skr100 first day, subsequent days Skr70/day; ☺Mon-Sat) or ask at the Simrishamn tourist office. Call **Taxi Österlen** (☑177 77) for a taxi.

GLIMMINGEHUS & SKILLINGE

The striking, five-storey **Glimmingehus** (Glimminge castle; ☑186 20; adult/under 19yr Skr60/free; ☺10am-6pm Jun–mid-Aug, 11am-4pm mid-Apr–May & mid-Aug–Sep, noon-4pm Sat & Sun Oct & early Apr), about 5km inland, has scarcely been tinkered with since its construction in the early 1500s, making it one of the best-preserved medieval castles around. Features include an all-encompassing moat and 11 resident ghosts! Guided tours in English at 3pm daily in July and August (at 3pm on weekends in June, September and October). In summer there's a stellar cafe and a program of medieval events and activities: contact the castle for details.

Sjöbacka Gård (☑301 66; info@sjobacka. nu; s/d from Skr600/795) is in the countryside west of Skillinge, the closest settlement to the castle. The B&B occupies a supercosy Scanian farmhouse complete with fireplace, antiques, heaving bookshelves and a gorgeous cobblestone courtyard to read in. Skillinge is a reasonably active fishing vil-

lage with a couple of restaurants and a fish smokehouse.

Bus 322 (Skr48, 50 minutes) runs up to four times daily between Skillinge and Ystad from mid-June to mid-August only.

KIVIK

Rosy apples and burial cists make for strange bedfellows in sleepy, soothing Kivik (north of Simrishamn).

Believed to be a site of ancient human sacrifice, **Kiviksgraven** (Kungagraven; adult/ under 16yr Skr20/free; ☺10am-6pm mid-May– Aug) is Sweden's largest Bronze Age grave, dating from around 1000 BC. It's an extraordinary shieldlike cairn, about 75m in diameter, which once contained a burial cist and eight engraved slabs. What you see inside are replicas; the tomb was looted in the 18th century. The on-site cafe hires informative audioguides (Skr15).

Nearby, **Kiviks Musteri** (www.kiviks.se, in Swedish; ☺Mar-Dec) is an apple orchard open to the public. There you can visit **Äpplets Hus** (adult/under 12yr Skr50/free; ☺10am-5pm late Mar-Nov), a museum devoted to the myths, history, cultivation and artistry of apples. Buy apple juice, cider and apple brandy from the well-stocked shop or try sampling some at an evening tasting (see p200). Kiviks Musteri is a few (signposted) kilometres out of town.

Kivik Strand Logi & Café (☑711 95; www. kivikstrand.se; Tittutvägen; d hostel/hotel from Skr880/980; ☺Apr-Oct; **P**), down by the beach in a meticulously restored 19th-century schoolhouse, is an immaculate hostel-B&B combo that's more chic boutique than backpacker bolt-hole. Pinewood floors, blue pinstripe wallpaper and sailboat models give this place a real fresh, summer seaside feel. The communal kitchen is seriously slick, and the obscenely cute cafe serves exceptional espresso. Book ahead.

In Kivik, **STF Vandrarhem Hanöbris** (☑700 50; www.hanobris.se; Eliselundsvägen 6; s/d Skr450/550; ☺Apr-Oct) offers clean rooms in a 19th-century dancehall given an unfortunate modernist makeover.

For bus information see p207.

STENSHUVUD NATIONAL PARK

Just 3km south of Kivik, this enchanting **national park** (www.stenshuvud.se) features lush woodland, marshes, sandy beaches and a high headland. Among its more unusual residents are orchids, dormice and tree frogs. Several superb walks in the area include the hike up to a 6th-century ruined hill fort. The long-distance path Skåneleden (www.skaneleden.org) also runs through the park, along the coast; the best section is from Vik to Kivik (two or three hours).

The Naturum (visitor centre; ☑708 82; ⊘11am-4pm mid-Aug–Sep, 11am-4pm Tue-Sun Feb–mid-Aug & Oct-Nov, closed Dec & Jan) is 2.5km from the main road. Rangers lead regular 1½-hour guided tours of the park (adult/child Skr25/10) covering everything from bird life to swamps. Call ahead to arrange an English-language tour.

Pretty Kaffestugan Annorlunda (☑704 75; www.kaffestuganannorlunda.se; ⊘early Apr-Aug), on the road to the Naturum, serves meals and snacks daily.

Kristianstad

☑044 / POP 77,250

Scruffy undertones aside, Kristianstad (kri-shan-sta) is worth a wander for its exquisite cathedral, quirky street sculptures and sprinkling of handsome 18th- and 19th-century buildings (among the 1970s dross).

Known as the most Danish town in Sweden, its construction was ordered by the Danish king Christian IV in 1614. Its rectangular street network still follows the first town plan, although the original walls and bastions have long gone. Both a major transport hub and gateway to Skåne's southern coast, it's also the region's administrative and political centre.

◉ Sights & Activities

For a walking tour round 23 of the town's stately buildings (including the Renaissance-style town hall and the restored rampart Bastionen Konungen), pick up the free English brochure *Kristianstad at Your Own Pace* from the tourist office.

Trefaldighetskyrkan
CHURCH

(Västra Storgatan 6; ⊘8am-4pm) One of the finest Renaissance churches in Scandinavia, Trefaldighetskyrkan was completed in 1628 when Skåne was still under Danish control. The light-filled interior still has many of its original fittings, including wonderfully carved oak pews and an ornate marble and alabaster pulpit.

Tivoliparken
PARK

Riverside Tivoliparken is great for a summertime evening stroll or a waffle or two at the much-loved cafe.

FREE Regionmuseet & Konsthall
MUSEUM

(☑13 52 45; www.regionmuseet.se; Stora Torg; ⊘11am-5pm Jun-Aug, noon-5pm Tue-Sun Sep-May) Originally intended as a palace, the building ended up being used as an arsenal. It now houses local history exhibits and art, handicrafts and silverware displays. The Café Miro (☑13 60 97; sandwiches & snacks Skr25-75) here serves great organic lunches, with herbs and flowers picked from the owner's garden.

FREE Filmmuseet
MUSEUM

(☑13 57 29; Östra Storgatan 53; ⊘1-6pm Mon-Fri Jul–mid-Aug, noon-5pm Sun Jan-Jun) Swedish film-making began in Kristianstad, so it's appropriate that Filmmuseet, Sweden's only film museum, is based here.

Naturens Bästa
BOAT TOUR

(www.flodbaten.se; ⊘May–mid-Aug & end Aug–mid-Sep) Naturens Bästa runs two-hour boat trips (adult/child/family Skr120/80/320) from Tivoliparken into Kristianstad's unique wetland area three times daily between May and early September. During the second half of August, you can still take tours, but they run from Åhus instead: contact the company or the tourist office to check departures and book tickets.

★ Festivals & Events

Kristianstadsdagarna
CULTURAL

(www.kristianstadsdagarna.nu, in Swedish) Held annually in July, Kristianstadsdagarna is a week-long festival with music, dance, exhibitions and foodie events, mostly held in Tivoliparken.

⊨ Sleeping

Budget accommodation is limited in town.

Bäckaskogs Slott
HISTORIC HOTEL €€

(☑530 20; www.backaskogslott.se; Barumsvägen 255, Kiaby; cottage s/d Skr450/700, castle Skr1180/1600, all incl breakfast; P@) This dreamy castle sits between two lakes 15km northeast of Kristianstad. Built as a monastery in the mid-13th century, it's a stunning spot, with different tiers of accommodation available in various wings and outhouses, and a well-priced restaurant. Bus 558 (Skr19, 20 minutes) from Kristianstad Resecentrum to Arkelstorp stops near the castle.

Best Western Hotel Anno 1937
HOTEL €€

(☑12 61 50; www.hotelanno.se; Västra Storgatan 17; s/d Skr795/995; @) A rustic beam here, a

Kristianstad

Kristianstad

◎ Sights
1 Bastionen Konungen	A1
2 Filmmuseet	B2
3 Regionmuseet & Konsthall	B2
4 Trefaldighetskyrkan	A2

◎ Activities, Courses & Tours
5 Naturens Bästa	A3

◎ Sleeping
6 Best Western Hotel Anno 1937	A1
7 First Hotel Christian IV	A2

◎ Eating
8 Kippers Källare	A1
9 Nya Café Fenix	B3
Supermarket	(see 10)

◎ Drinking
10 Systembolaget	B2

Spanish-style tapas take up much of the menu, but there are more substantial dishes like suckling pig or burgers.

There's a supermarket and Systembolaget inside the Domus shopping centre on Östra Boulevarden.

❶ Information

Lilla Torg has banks and ATMs.

Library (Föreningsgatan 4; ⊙10am-7pm Mon-Thu, Fri 10am-6pm, Sat 11am-3pm year-round, 11am-3pm Sun Sep-Apr) Free internet access.

Tourist office (☑13 53 35; www.kristianstad. se/turism; Stora Torg; ⊙10am-7pm Mon-Fri, to 3pm Sat, to 2pm Sun mid-Jun–mid-Aug, 10am-5pm Mon-Fri, to 2pm Sat rest of year)

❶ Getting There & Around

Skyways (☑0771-95 95 00) flies direct most days to Stockholm (from Skr500, one hour) from Kristianstad's **airport** (☑23 88 50), about 20km south of town. **Airport buses** (☑24 24 24; Skr120) depart from the Resecentrum 50 minutes before flight departure times.

Buses depart from the Resecentrum on Östra Boulevarden. Frequent SkåneExpressen buses include: bus 1 to Malmö (Skr96, 1½ hours), bus 2 to Lund (Skr84, 1½ hours), bus 3 to Simrishamn (Skr48, 1¼ hours) and bus 4 to Ystad (Skr60, 1½ hours); the latter two services run infrequently on weekends. **Svenska Buss** (www.svenska-buss.se) runs to Karlskrona (Skr110, 1¾ hours), Kalmar (Skr280, three hours and 25 minutes)

17th-century wall there: history pops up all over the place at this friendly hotel. Opposite the cathedral, its pale-toned rooms are a bit dull, but there are up-to-date touches like flat-screen TVs, a sauna and wi-fi.

First Hotel Christian IV   HOTEL €€
(☑20 38 50; www.firsthotels.com; Västra Boulevarden 15; s/d Skr798/998; ❷@) With parquet floors and stucco ceilings, Hotel Christian IV is certainly grand, if a little worn around the edges. The beautiful turn-of-the-century building was once a bank and one of the vaults now contains a wine cellar.

🍴 Eating & Drinking

Nya Café Fenix   CAFE €
(☑20 90 80; www.cafefenix.se; Östra Storgatan 69; sandwiches Skr50-70; ⊙9am-6pm Mon-Fri, 10am-4pm Sat) A hit with local hipsters, this sleek new cafe is best for its epic sandwiches and scrumptious pastries, cakes and muffins. Grab a pavement table, slip on some shades, and eye up the passing talent.

Kippers Källare   MEDITERRANEAN €€
(☑10 62 00; www.kippers.se; Östra Storgatan 9; mains Skr145-265; ⊙Tue-Sat) Listed in the *White Guide* (Sweden's foodie bible) and sporting a 17th-century arched cellar, this is the most atmospheric restaurant in town.

and Stockholm (Skr360, nine hours and 40 minutes).

Call **Avis** (☎10 30 20; Östra Storgatan 10) for car hire.

The train station is across town from the Resecentrum. Trains run daily to Lund (Skr96, one hour) and Malmö (Skr96, 1¼ hours); many services continue on to Copenhagen (Skr195, two hours). Regular trains also run to Helsingborg (Skr90, 1½ hours). Öresundstågen trains run every hour or two to Malmö (with connections at Hässleholm for Stockholm).

Call **TaxiKurir Kristianstad** (☎21 52 70) for a taxi.

Åhus

☎044 / POP 8980

The small coastal town of Åhus (about 18km southeast of Kristianstad) is a popular summer spot thanks to its long sandy **beach**. The area is also known for its **eels**: the Eel Coast runs south from Åhus, and this delicacy is served up boiled, fried, smoked, grilled or cooked on a bed of straw at restaurants and at autumn Eel Feasts throughout the region.

Åhus is home to the **Absolut Vodka distillery** (Köpmannagatan 29), where half a million bottles are produced daily. Free tours of the place run six times daily on weekdays from late June to the end of August. Tickets are available from the company's reception one hour before the tour begins. There is no prebooking and only 19 people are allowed on a single tour.

Naturens Bästa (p208) also runs its two-hour **boat trips** (adult/child/family Skr90/70/250) from Åhus from late June to the second half of August. Contact **Landskapet** (www.landskapet.se) or **Naturens Bästarun** (www.flodbaten.se) for details.

Very close to the harbour is **STF Vandrarhem Åhus** (☎24 85 35; www.cigarrkungenshus. se; Stavgatan 3; hostel dm/s/d Skr250/350/450, B&B per person from Skr295; ☺Mar-Nov; P@), an agreeable youth hostel and B&B based in a 19th-century cigar factory.

The harbour has several good dining options.

The **tourist office** (☎13 47 77; Järnvägsgatan 7; ☺10am-7pm Mon-Fri, 9am-5pm Sat, 10am-2pm Sun mid-Jun–Aug, 10am-5pm Mon-Fri mid-Apr–Sep) is well stocked and helpful with banks, supermarket, etc nearby.

Bus 551 runs several times an hour (roughly hourly on weekends) between Kristianstad and Åhus (Skr27, 21 minutes);

get off at the Glashyttan stop for the tourist office.

Helsingborg

☎042 / POP 129,000

At its heart, Helsingborg is a sparkly showcase of rejuvenated waterfront, metro-glam restaurants, lively cobbled streets and lofty castle ruins. With Denmark looking on from a mere 4km across the Öresund, its flouncy, turreted buildings feel like a brazen statement. It's hardly surprising: Helsingborg's strategic position on the sound saw it battled over and battered down with tedious regularity during the many Swedish-Danish wars. In 1709 the Danes invaded Skåne, but were finally defeated the following year in a battle just outside Helsingborg. One wonders what those armies would make of the over 14 million annual passengers who now traverse the sound with seasoned nonchalance.

⦿ Sights

TOWN CENTRE

Small and specialist museums (about the fire brigade, medical history, sport, schools and military defence) dot the town: contact the tourist office for details.

Kärnan   TOWER

(☎10 59 91; adult/7-18yr Skr40/20) Dramatic steps and archways lead up from Stortorget to the square tower Kärnan (34m), all that remains of the medieval castle. The castle became Swedish property during the 17th-century Danish-Swedish War, and was mostly demolished once the fighting stopped. The tower was restored from dereliction in 1894, and the view is regal indeed, though the top was closed at time of writing so check at the tourist office for updated visiting hours.

Dunkers Kulturhus   ARTS CENTRE

(www.dunkerskulturhus.se; Kungsgatan 11; exhibitions adult/under 18yr Skr70/free; ☺11am-6pm Mon-Fri, to 8pm Wed, to 5pm Sat & Sun, closed Mon Sep-Jun) Just north of the transport terminals, the crisp and white Dunkers Kulturhus houses the main tourist office, an interesting town museum and temporary art exhibitions (admission includes entry to both), plus a concert hall, urbane cafe, and design-savvy gift shop. The building's creator, Danish architect Kim Utzon, is the son of Sydney Opera House architect Jørn Utzon.

From here, saunter along **Norra Hamnen** (North Harbour), where sleek apartments,

Helsingborg

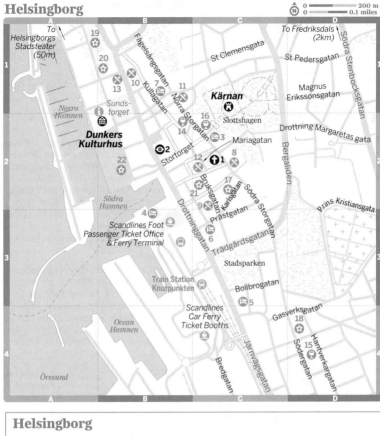

Helsingborg

◉ Top Sights

Dunkers Kulturhus	B2
Kärnan	C1

◉ Sights

1	Mariakyrkan	C2
2	Rådhuset	B2

⬢ Sleeping

3	Best Western Hotel Helsingborg	C2
4	Elite Hotel Marina Plaza	B3
5	Helsingborgs Vandrarhem	C3
	Hotel Maria	(see 12)
6	Hotell Linnéa	C3
7	Hotell Viking	B1

⊗ Eating

8	Bistro G	C2
9	Ebbas Fik	C2
10	ICA	B1
11	Koppi	B1
12	Olsons Skafferi	C2
13	Signe Bergqvuist-Kafferepet	B1

⬤ Drinking

	Helsing	(see 3)
14	Madame Mustache	B2
15	Systembolaget	D4
16	Utposten	C2

⬡ Entertainment

17	Biograf Röda Kvarn	C2
18	Filmstaden	D4
19	Helsingborgs Stadsteater	A1
20	Konserthus	B1
21	Tempel	C2
22	Tivoli	B2

restaurants and bars meet docked yachts and preened locals in one rather successful harbour-redevelopment project.

Mariakyrkan
CHURCH
(Mariatorget; ⊘8am-6pm Mon-Fri, 9am-6pm Sat & Sun) In the old town, the 15th-century Gothic brick Mariakyrkan has a magnificent interior, including a triptych dating from 1450 and an ornate Renaissance pulpit.

Rådhuset
HISTORIC BUILDING
(town hall; Stortorget) The mighty Rådhuset was completed in 1897 in neo-Gothic style and contains stained-glass scenes illustrating Helsingborg's history.

FREDRIKSDAL & SOFIERO
Just 2km northeast of the centre, the Fredriksdal area is well worth a visit. Take bus 1 or 7 to the Zoégas bus stop.

Fredriksdals Friluftsmuseum
MUSEUM
(www.fredriksdal.se; adult/under 18yr May-Sep Skr80/free, free other times; ⊘10am-6pm May-Aug, 11am-5pm Apr & Sep, 11am-4pm Oct-Mar) One of Sweden's best open-air museums, Fredriksdals Friluftsmuseum is based around an 18th-century manor house, with a street of old houses, a children's farm, a graphics museum and blissfully leafy grounds. Local wildflowers grace the beautiful botanic gardens, and there's a wonderful summer program of activities and performances in the French baroque open-air theatre. The museum entrance, located just off Hävertgatan, is an easy 250m walk south of the Zoégas bus stop on Ängelsholmsvägen.

Sofiero
GARDENS
(www.sofiero.se; Sofierovägen; adult/under 18yr Skr80/free; ⊘park 10am-6pm, palace & orangery 11am-6pm) About 5km north of the town centre, Sofiero is an impressive former royal summer residence and park with wonderful rhododendrons (best seen in full bloom in May and June) and top-notch summer concerts. Bus 219 runs out there.

Tropikariet
ZOO
(www.tropikariet.com, in Swedish; Hävertgatan 21; adult/3-12yr Skr90/45; ⊘11am-5pm Tue-Sun) Tropikariet is a semi-zoo, with reptile house, aquarium and exotic furry critters housed in faux natural habitats. It's just opposite the entrance to Fredriksdals museum.

🛏 Sleeping

TOP CHOICE **Hotel Maria**
HOTEL €€
(☑24 99 40; www.hotelmaria.se; Mariagatan 8A; s/d from Skr800/950; P @) Tucked away behind Olsons Skafferi (p213), Hotel Maria is utterly inspired, with each room flaunting a different historical style. Themes include National Romantic, art deco and '70s disco. Beds are divinely comfy, the staff friendly and there's a tapas bar downstairs.

Best Western Hotel Helsingborg
HOTEL €€
(☑37 18 00; www.hotelhelsingborg.se; Stortorget 20; s/d Skr900/1250; P @) In an elegant, early-20th-century building at the foot of the stairs to the Kärnan tower, Hotel Helsingborg boasts distinct, boutique-style rooms, a spa and a popular restaurant. Try for a room on the southwest corner for a grand view down the Stortorget and across to Denmark.

Hotell Viking
HOTEL €€
(☑14 44 20; www.hotellviking.se; Fågelsångsgatan 1; s/d from Skr800/970; P @) Trendy and urbane, this hipster hotel sets the tone from the get-go with velvet cushions, modern bookshelves and brass candlesticks decorating the lobby. Rooms are similarly chic and recently renovated. The most luxurious has a jacuzzi.

Hotell Linnéa
HOTEL €€
(☑37 24 00; www.hotell-linnea.se; Prästgatan 4; s/d incl breakfast Skr795/1395; P) Linnéa is central and affordable. Rooms are clean, if somewhat dull, and there is a decent Danish breakfast.

Elite Hotel Marina Plaza
HOTEL €€
(☑19 21 00; info.marinaplaza@elite.se; Kungstorget 6; s Skr880-1062; P @) Modern and luxurious, this hotel is conveniently located right by the harbour (the more expensive rooms have sea views). It's a big place with a number of restaurants and bars, and a sauna and gym.

Helsingborgs Vandrarhem
HOSTEL €
(☑14 58 50; www.cityvandrarhemmet.com; Järnvägsgatan 39; s/d Skr425/520) Despite a rather anonymous vibe, Helsingborg's only central hostel offers clean, comfortable rooms about 200m from Knutpunkten. Reception opens from 9am to noon and 3pm to 5pm.

Råå Vallar Camping
CAMPGROUND €
(☑18 26 00; raavallar@nordiccamping.se; Kustgatan; sites/cabins Skr190/450; 🚇) About 5km south of the city centre, by Öresund, this is a huge, well-equipped campsite, with a shop,

cafe and sandy beach. Take bus 1 from the town hall.

Eating

Helsingborg boasts an appetising selection of restaurants and cafes, although a fair few close on Sundays.

TOP CHOICE Olsons Skafferi
ITALIAN €€

(☏14 07 80; www.olsonsskafferi.se; Mariagatan 6; lunch Skr75-125, dinner mains Skr225-239; ⊘lunch & dinner Mon-Sat) Olsons is a super little spot, with alfresco seating on the pedestrian square right in front of Mariakyrkan. It doubles as an Italian deli and cafe, with rustic good looks, spangly chandeliers and pasta that would make Bologna proud. Be sure to finish things off in proper Italian fashion with Vino Santo and *cantuccini* (almond biscotti).

Signe Bergqvuist-Kafferepet
BAKERY €

(☏21 02 41; Dröttninggatan 17; cakes from Skr25; ⊘Mon-Sun) Helsingborg's oldest *konditori* (baker and confectioner), opened in 1889, puts years of baking experience to work churning out gorgeous loaves of bread, cookies and cakes. Enjoy a cardamom bun and excellent coffee in the high-ceilinged dining room, complete with chandeliers and a marble-topped espresso bar.

Bistro G
MEDITERANNEAN €€

(☏24 28 70; www.gastro.nu; Södra Storgatan 10; tapas Skr65-139; ⊘Wed-Sat 6pm-midnight) The little brother of Helsingborg award-winner Gastro, this trendy tapas bar serves Spanish dishes with a Swedish twist. Test the combination yourself with an order of herring with smoked almond potatoes side-by-side with sizzling *gambas* (prawns) or classic roasted Padron peppers.

Ebbas Fik
DINER €

(☏28 14 40; www.ebbasfik.se; Bruksgatan 20; cakes from Skr25, sandwiches Skr30-95; ⊘9am-6pm Mon-Fri, to 4pm Sat) It's still 1955 at this kitsch-tastic cafe, complete with jukebox, retro petrol pump and hamburgers made to Elvis' recipe. The extensive cafe menu also includes sandwiches, baked potatoes, milkshakes and American-style pie.

Pålsjö Krog
EUROPEAN €€

(☏14 97 30; www.palsjokrog.com; Drottninggatan 151; mains Skr189-249; ⊘from 11.30am Mon-Fri, from 1pm Sat & Sun) Near Villa Thalassa, 3km north of the city centre in the Pålsjö area, this is a great old seaside inn revamped into an elegant nosh spot. There's a fabulous veranda and outdoor seating, plus tasty, bistro-style dishes like fish soup or pepper steak.

Koppi
CAFE €

(☏13 30 33; www.koppi.se; Norra Storgatan 16; sandwiches/salads Skr60/70; ⊘Mon-Sat) This hip cafe-microroastery is your best bet for top-notch coffee. The savvy young owners sell their own roasted beans, alongside scrumptious edibles like fresh salads and gourmet ciabatta.

ICA
SUPERMARKET €

(Drottninggatan 48) The best centrally located supermarket.

For quick snacks, try the Knutpunkten complex on the seafront.

Drinking

There are several good pubs and bars around town. There's a Systembolaget on Södergatan.

Madame Mustache
BAR

(www.madamemoustache.se; Norra Storgatan 9) Comfortable bar and restaurant in a historic building; there's a pleasant outdoor courtyard.

Utposten
PUB

(Stortorget 17) Down-to-earth pub at the foot of the stairs to the Kärnan.

Helsing
COCKTAIL BAR

(Södra Storgatan 1) Chic bar with extensive selection of cocktails and ideal people-watching location

☆ Entertainment

Helsingborgs Stadsteater
THEATER

(☏10 68 10; Karl Johans gata 1) Helsingborgs Stadsteater has regular drama performances. Information and tickets are available from the tourist office.

Konserthus
CLASSICAL MUSIC

(☏10 42 70; Drottning-gatan 19) Regularly plays host to Helsingborg's Symphony Orchestra. Information and tickets are available from the tourist office.

Tivoli
DANCE

(☏18 71 71; www.thetivoli.nu; Kungsgatan 1) An enduring nightclub with a younger crowd and occasional live music.

Tempel LIVE MUSIC
(☎32 70 20; www.tempel.dj; Bruksgatan 2; ⊙from 10pm Thu-Sat) Live music and decent club nights on Fridays and Saturdays.

Biograf Röda Kvarn CINEMA
(www.biorodakvarn.se; Karlsgatan 7) Helsingborg's oldest cinema. It shows mostly independent films, but closes from mid-June to mid-August.

Filmstaden CINEMA
(Södergatan 19) For mainstream efforts.

ⓘ Information

The Knutpunkten complex on the seafront has currency-exchange facilities and ATMs, as well as left-luggage lockers. For banks, head to Stortorget.

Forex (www.forex.se; Level 1 Knutpunkten, Kungstorget 8; ⊙7am-9pm daily) Foreign exchange office.

Library (Stadsbibliotek; Stadsparken; ⊙9am-7pm Mon-Fri, 11am-4pm Sat) Free internet access (bring ID).

Tourist office (☎10 43 50; Kungsgatan 11; ⊙10am-6pm Mon-Fri, to 8pm Thu, to 5pm Sat & Sun) Well-stocked and conveniently located in Dunkers Kulturhus.

ⓘ Getting There & Away

The main transport hub is the waterfront Knutpunkten complex.

Boat

Knutpunkten is the terminal for the frequent **Scandlines** (www.scandlines.se) car ferry to Helsingør (one way with 6m car Skr390, no bookings without a vehicle).

Bus

The bus terminal is at ground level in Knutpunkten. Regional Skånetrafiken buses dominate (see respective destinations for details), but long-distance services are offered by **Swebus Express** (www.swebuse.se) and **GoByBus** (www.gobybus.se, in Swedish).

Both companies run north to Göteborg, continuing on to Oslo, and south to Malmö. They also operate services northeast to Stockholm via Jönköping and Norrköping. Fares to Stockholm cost around Skr545 (7½ hours), to Göteborg Skr125 (three hours) and to Oslo Skr321 (seven hours).

Train

Underground platforms in Knutpunkten serve SJ, Pågatågen and Öresundståg trains, which depart daily for Stockholm (Skr666, five to seven hours), Göteborg (Skr268, 2½ to three hours) and nearby towns including Lund (Skr79, 25 minutes), Malmö (Skr97, 40 miutes), Kris-

tianstad (Skr90, one hour and 20 minutes) and Halmstad (Skr105, one hour), as well as Copenhagen (Denmark) and Oslo (Norway).

ⓘ Getting Around

Bike hire (per day/week Skr120/650) is available at Travelshop, located at the bus station at Knutpunkten. Town buses cost Skr17 and run from Rådhuset (town hall). Contact **Avis** (☎15 70 80; www.avisworld.com; Angelholmsvagen 36) for car hire, and **Taxi Helsingborg** (☎18 02 00) for cabs.

Kulla Peninsula
☑042

A seductive brew of golden light, artisan studios and sleepy fishing villages, Skåne's northwest coast is a perfect place to spend a few soothing days.

ⓘ Getting There & Away

Bus 220 runs at least hourly from Helsingborg to Höganäs (Skr42, 40 minutes). From there, bus 222 runs every hour or two to Mölle (Skr27, 20 minutes), while bus 223 runs to Arild (Skr27, 20 minutes).

HÖGANÄS

Gateway to the Kulla Peninsula, the coal-mining town of Höganäs (21km north of Helsingborg) harbours a few cultural gems that are worth stopping for.

Pick up the free guide to Höganäs' impressive posse of public art, liberally sprinkled around town, at the tourist office. Two of the most entertaining works are a family of pigs on Storgatan and a levitating dog on Köpmansgatan.

More art beckons at Höganäs Museum & Konsthall (www.hoganasmuseum.se, in Swedish; Polhemsgatan 1; adult/under 18yr Skr50/free; ⊙1-5pm Tue-Sun Feb-late Dec), the highlight of which is a brilliant collection of witty, exquisitely humane sculptures from home-grown artist Åke Holm.

Höganäs Saltglaserat (☎33 10 20, 32 76 55; www.hoganassaltglaserat.se, in Swedish; Bruksgatan 36; ⊙10am-6pm Mon-Fri, 11am-4pm Sat & Sun Jun-Aug, 10am-4pm Fri, 11am-3pm Sat & Sun rest of year) is a famous pottery factory established in 1835. Its trademark brown salt-glazed pottery is a veritable national icon and its famous Höganäskrus (little jug) is mentioned in the opening line of August Strindberg's novel Natives of Hemsö.

Seven kilometres further north on Rd 111, Krapperups Slott (www.krapperup.se; Krapperups Kyrkovägen 13; admission free; ⊙garden year-round; ⊙cafe 11am-5pm daily mid-Jun–mid-Aug, 11am-5pm Sat & Sun rest of year, closed Jan) is one of Sweden's oldest estates and home to an exquisite garden. The manor's exterior is inlaid with giant white stars representing the coat of arms of the Gyllenstierna family, who lived here for centuries. One-hour tours of the building (Skr100; Easter to late June and mid-September to mid-October) can be booked by emailing info@krapperup.se. The grounds also house an art gallery and local museum, a cafe and a gift shop. The converted stables play host to the annual **Musik i Kullabygden** (☑tickets 0771-70 70 70; www.musikikullabygd.se, in Swedish), a week-long music festival in July spanning folk, jazz, classical and opera. Bus 222 from Höganäs stops at the estate.

Höganäs' small **tourist office** (☑33 77 74; www.hoganas.se; Centralgatan 20; ⊙9am-6pm Mon-Fri, 10am-2pm Sat & Sun mid-Jun-Aug, 9am-4.30pm Mon-Fri, mid-late Aug, 10am-4pm Mon-Fri late Aug-Sep & Apr–mid-Jun) is a good source of information on the entire Kullabygden area.

MÖLLE & SURROUNDS

The steep, picket-fence-pretty village of Mölle is the area's main tourist centre. It also enjoys a scandalous past. In the 19th century it was one of the first seaside resorts to encourage mixed bathing, much to the horror of the country...and to the delight of racy Berliners, who flocked here on a direct rail link from the German capital.

These days, people head in to enjoy **Kullaberg Nature Reserve** (http://k.inventit.dk; road toll Skr40), which occupies the tip of the Kulla Peninsula and houses Scandinavia's brightest lighthouse, **Kullens fyr** (☑34 70 56; adult/6-12yr Skr20/10; ⊙11am-4pm daily Feb-Nov), the light of which can be seen from 50km away.

The reserve offers a dramatic spectacle of plunging cliffs, windswept vegetation and incredible sunsets, and a number of **hiking trails** crisscross the area, leading to ancient caves, tide pools and secluded swimming spots.

Looking like a cubby house gone mad, the driftwood sculpture **Nimis** and its younger concrete sibling **Arx** stand on a beach on the peninsula's northern side. Created without permission by eccentric artist Lars Vilks, their existence has sparked several court cases between Vilks and the County Council, not to mention the odd fire and chainsaw attack. In 1996 the crafty Vilks founded micro-nation **Ladonia** (www.ladonia.net) at the site, effectively turning his works into protected 'national monuments'.

The reserve is a veritable wonderland for active types and its website is a good place to get an idea of available activities. Stop in at the **Naturum** (⊙11am-6pm daily Jun-Aug, 11am-4pm Sun-Thu, 11am-5pm Fri & Sat Feb-May, 11am-4pm Sep-Nov) for information on the area's flora, fauna and geology or try a **guided walking tour** (☑34 70 56). Whatever you do, don't leave without visiting the lighthouse.

The diving here is reputedly the best in Sweden and the helpful crew at **Kullen Dyk** (www.kullendyk.nu, in Swedish), 2km southeast of Mölle next door to First Camp Möllehässle, can get you flippered and submerged. You can also go on a one-hour **caving expedition** (www.kullabergsguiderna.se; adult/6-12yr Skr150/50; ⊙1pm & 3pm daily Jul–mid-Aug, less frequently rest of year) with experienced guides starting from the Naturum. Other options include abseiling (Skr200) down the primordial cliffs, porpoise safaris (by boat/from land Skr280/80) or you can try your luck at fishing (adult/under 12 years Skr450/250).

A novel way of exploring the area is on an **Icelandic horse**, one of the world's gentlest, smooth-gated equine breeds.

Five kilometres east of Mölle, the fishing village of **Arild** lays on the charm with its petite pastel houses, teeny-tiny harbour and supporting cast of roses, hollyhocks, butterflies and coastal nature reserves.

ⓘ KULLABERG ON HORSEBACK

One great way to experience the broad fields, woodlands and coastal scenery of the Kullaberg Peninsula is on horseback. There are a few different farms to choose from, running trips ranging from a few hours to several days. **Kullabergs Islandshäster** (☑33 52 44; www.kullabergsislandshastar.com) does 1½- and 2½-hour trips (Skr500/650) or there's a four-hour lunch expedition to Mölle (Skr990). **Hippo Tours** (☑88 04 66; www.hippotours.se) focuses on luxury weekend getaways (Skr3500), including a night at the historic boutique Hotel Rusthållargården in the picture-perfect fishing village of Arild. Both farms use smooth-gaited Icelandic horses.

Accommodation in the area generally isn't cheap and fills up fast.

Arild's oldest hotel, **Hotel Rusthållargården** (☑34 65 30; www.rusthallargarden. com; Utsikten 1; d incl breakfast from Skr1800; **P@☎**) has been managed by the same family since 1904 and is housed in a charming white and blue-trimmed farm building that dates back to 1675. Rooms in the main building are comfortable and quaint – think flowered wallpaper and wooden floors – and half have sea views. There is a swimming pool and excellent, mostly organic, breakfast.

Strand Hotell (☑34 61 00; www.strand-arild. se; Stora Vägen 42; d incl breakfast from Skr1170; **P@**), a civilised option in picture-perfect Arild, oozes old-world appeal. Four of the elegant rooms in the old building boast balconies with sea views, while the modern annexe features long, thin rooms with terraces and sea views for all. There's a fine in-house restaurant here, too.

Exuding faded grandeur, the **Grand Hotel Mölle** (☑36 22 30; www.grand-molle.se; Bökebollsvägen 11; s/d from Skr1100/1200; **P@**) sits regally above Mölle. Rooms are an agreeable blend of modern Scandi style and nautical undertones. For an especially posh experience, go for a room in the main building with a sea view, balcony and jacuzzi (double Skr3590). There's also an in-house gourmet restaurant.

The friendly **First Camp Möllehässle** (☑34 73 84; www.firstcamp.se/molle; powered sites from Skr275, 4-person cabin from Skr590) is a good bet. It's 2km southeast of Mölle.

Keep a sharp eye out for the sign marking the turn for **Flickorna Lundgren** (☑34 60 44; www.fl-lundgren.se; coffee & cookies Skr80; ⏰10am-6pm Jun-Aug, to 8pm mid-Jul–mid-Aug), a justifiably famous cafe in a gorgeous garden setting. Grab a large plate of pastries, your copper kettle and lose yourself in a cloud of flowers. It's wildly popular, so be prepared for crowds during the peak months of July and August.

Ellens Café i Ransvik (☑34 76 66; www. ransvik.se; sandwiches Skr55-85; ⏰11am-5pm daily Jul-Aug, 11am-5pm Fri-Mon Apr-Jun & Sep) is a long-standing favourite, overlooking a popular bathing spot about 1km beyond the Kullaberg toll booth. Munch happily on sandwiches, salads and the scrumptious carrot cake, before taking a dip from the rocks.

Just up from the harbour in Mölle, **Mölle Krukmakeri & Café** (☑34 79 91; Mölle Hamnallé 9; sandwiches from Skr75; ⏰10am-6pm Wed-Sun mid-Jun–late Aug, Sat & Sun late Aug–mid-Jun)

is a cosy cafe and ceramics gallery. Stock up on sleek, contemporary bowls, saucers or mugs before enjoying a cup of well-brewed coffee in the cafe's pleasant glass conservatory.

BLEKINGE

With its long coastline and safe harbours, Blekinge's past and present are faithfully fastened to the sea. Sweden and Denmark once squabbled over the area, a trump card in power games over the Baltic. The region's own prized possession is the Unesco-lauded naval town of Karlskrona, famed for its baroque design. The region's second-largest town, Karlshamn, was the exit point for thousands of 19th-century emigrants bound for America. Beyond the urban is a low-key landscape of fish-filled rivers and lakes, brooding forests and a stunning archipelago fit for lazy island-hopping.

Karlskrona

☑0455 / POP 62,340

If you like your Swedes in uniform, you'll appreciate Karlskrona. Marine cadets pepper the streets of what has always been an A-league naval base. In 1998 the entire town was added to the Unesco World Heritage list for its impressive collection of 17th- and 18th-century naval architecture.

It was the failed Danish invasion of Skåne in 1679 that sparked Karlskrona's conception, when King Karl XI decided that a southern naval base was needed for better control over the Baltic Sea. Almost immediately, it became Sweden's third-biggest city. Much of the town is still a military base, so to see certain sights you'll need to book a tour at the tourist office and have ID at the ready.

◎ Sights & Activities

Fortifications   HISTORIC BUILDING

Karlskrona's star is the extraordinary offshore **Kungsholms Fort**, with its curious circular harbour, built in 1680 to defend the town. Two-hour, guided **boat tours** (adult/12-18yr Skr210/50; ⏰10am mid-Jun–Aug) to the fort depart from Fisktorget, the tourist office or the Marinmuseum. Tickets must be pre-booked through the tourist office (bring ID). Another option is the boat operated by **Affärsverken** (www.affarsverken.se), which runs from Fisktorget and circles the fort in July,

Karlskrona

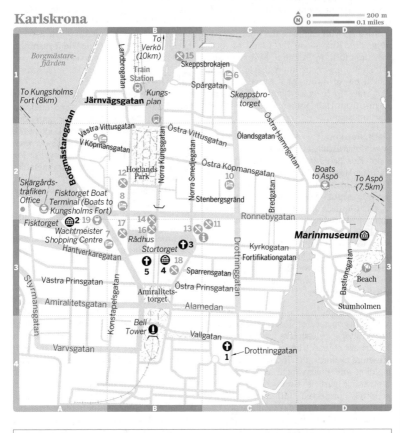

Karlskrona

◎ Top Sights

Marinmuseum D3

◎ Sights

1 Amiralitetskyrkan C4	
2 Blekinge Museum A3	
3 Fredrikskyrkan B3	
4 Museum Leonardo da Vinci	
Ideale B3	
Old Rosenbom .... (see 1)	
5 Trefaldighetskyrkan B3	

⬚ Sleeping

6 Clarion Collection Hotel	
Carlscrona C1	
7 First Hotel Ja B3	
8 Hotell Aston B2	

9 Hotell Conrad A2
10 STF Vandrarhem Trossö
Karlskrona C2

⊗ Eating

11 Restaurang Michelangelo C3	
12 Café Tre G B2	
13 Glassiärens Glassbar B3	
ICA .... (see 19)	
14 Lennarths Konditori B3	
15 Lisa's Sjökrog B1	
16 Nivå B3	
17 Nye Skafferiet B3	
18 Två Rum & Kök B3	

◎ Drinking

19 Systembolaget A3

June and August (adult/child Skr80/40); inform the tourist office of your visit in advance if you choose this second option.

Bristling with cannons, the tower **Drottningskärs Kastell** on the island of Aspö was described by Admiral Nelson of the British Royal Navy as 'impregnable'. You can visit it on an **Äspoleden**, a free car ferry that runs up to twice hourly in July and August from Handelshamnen, north of the Marinmuseum.

Marinmuseum MUSEUM
(www.marinmuseum.se; Stumholmen; adult/under 19yr Skr90/free; ⊙10am-6pm Jun-Aug, 11am-4pm May & Sep, 10am-4pm Tue-Sun Oct-Apr) The striking Marinmuseum is the national naval museum. Dive in for reconstructions of a battle deck in wartime, a hall full of fantastic figureheads, piles of model boats, and even some of the real thing – such as a minesweeper, the HMS *Västervik* and Sweden's royal sloop. There is also a pleasant **restaurant** (lunch Skr90) with a generous buffet lunch and waterside decking for a satisfying recharge.

Blekinge Museum MUSEUM
(www.blekingemuseum.se; Fisktorget; adult/under 19yr Skr50/free; ⊙10am-6pm Jun-Aug, noon-5pm Tue-Sun rest of year) The evocative Blekinge Museum explores the local fishing, boatbuilding and quarrying trades. The most captivating part is Grevagården, an impressively preserved 18th-century abode crammed with thousands of vintage objects, from fans and fashion to bizarre wax models of syphilis-plagued faces. Topping it off is a petite baroque garden and a pleasant cafe.

Museum Leonardo da Vinci Ideale MUSEUM
(www.kulenoviccollection.se; Stortorget 5; ⊙10am-6pm Mon-Sat, 11am-6pm Sun) Located in a castle of a building on the main square, this museum showcases the Kulenovic private collection of original art. There is also a great cafe, which hosts live music in the summer.

Stortorget SQUARE
Karlskrona's monumental square, Stortorget, was planned to rival Europe's best. Alas, the funds ran out, resulting in a somewhat odd mix of grand architectural gestures and humble stand-ins. Dominating the square are the courthouse, along with the baroque church **Fredrikskyrkan** (⊙11am-4pm Mon-Fri, 9.30am-2pm Sat) and **Trefaldighetskyrkan** (Trinity Church; ⊙11am-4pm Mon-Fri, 9.30am-2pm Sat), inspired by Rome's Pantheon.

Amiralitetskyrkan CHURCH
(Vallgatan 11) Sweden's oldest wooden church is the stocky Amiralitetskyrkan, with a gorgeous pastel interior that's worth a peek. Outside, the wooden statue **Old Rosenbom** raises his hat to charitable visitors.

☞ Tours

Pick a sunny summer afternoon for a tour around Karlskrona's **archipelago**, made up of almost 1000 islands. A three-hour tour costs Skr140/70 per adult/child. Contact the **Skärgårdstrafiken office** (☎783 00; www.affarsverken.se, in Swedish) at Fisktorget or log onto the Affärsverken website for timetables and information.

Enquire at the tourist office about two-hour **guided tours** around the old naval shipyard at Lindholmen or of the museums. Another option is to pick up the free *Object 560* brochure, which maps out a walking tour of architectural and historical highlights in town.

🛏 Sleeping

Hotell Aston HOTEL €€
(☎194 70; www.hotellaston.se; Landbrogatan 1; s/d incl breakfast Skr695/895; ℙ@) Third-floor Hotell Aston and its sister **Hotell Conrad** (☎36 32 00; Västra Köpmansgatan 12) are both smart central options. Aston has spacious rooms, with simple, modern furnishings. Conrad is flashier, and takes up three buildings, with decorations based on the era of the building: '70s, '80s and 'culture' from the late 1700s. Both serve an excellent breakfast; with luck you'll get waffles or scones.

First Hotel Ja HOTEL €€
(☎555 60; www.firsthotels.se; Borgmästaregatan 13; s/d incl breakfast Skr775/965; ℙ@) Karlskrona's top slumber spot boasts slick, hip, recently renovated rooms in white and charcoal hues, with blissful beds and flat-screen TVs. Hotel perks include a sauna, bar-restaurant and a full-blown breakfast buffet served in a pleasant atrium. Book online for the best rates.

Clarion Collection Hotel Carlscrona HOTEL €€
(☎36 15 00; www.hotelcarlscrona.se; Skeppsbrokajen; s/d incl breakfast & evening buffet Skr970/1070; ℙ@) Handy for the train station, this chain hotel combines original rustic beams and slinky furniture in the bar, and navy blues, greys and handsome wooden furnishings in its stately rooms.

ISLAND GETAWAY

STF Turiststation Tjärö (☑600 63; www.tjaro.com; dm from Skr400; ☺May-late Sep; @) lies on an idyllic island nature reserve, off the coast of Blekinge between Karlshamn and Karlskrona, with walking trails and peaceful beaches. The hostel – located in a cluster of prettily painted red farmhouse buildings – is highly recommended; breakfast is available and there's a cafe and fully licensed restaurant, plus boat and canoe hire. For Skr200 you can even try a floating sauna. Boats run from the little harbour town of Järnavik up to 10 times daily (adult/three to 12 years Skr100/40) – it's a good idea to call the hostel to confirm sailing times.

STF Vandrarhem Trossö Karlskrona HOSTEL € (☑100 20; www.karlskronavandrarhem.se; Drottninggatan 39; dm/s/d from Skr200/320/410) Modern, clean and friendly, this hostel has a laundry, TV room and backyard for kids to play in; parking on the opposite side of the street is free.

Dragsö Camping CAMPGROUND € (☑153 54; www.dragso.nu; Dragsövägen; sites/d/2-bed cabins from Skr225/450/500; ☺Apr–mid-Sep) This large, good-looking campsite, 2.5km northwest of town, is situated on a scenic bay. Facilities include boat and bicycle hire, plus a Karlskrona-themed minigolf course. Bus 7 stops about 1km short of the campground.

✖ Eating & Drinking

The ICA supermarket and Systembolaget are in the Wachtmeister shopping centre.

Nya Skafferiet DELI € (☑171 78; www.nyaskafferiet.se; Rådhusgatan 9; ☺Mon-Sat) Worldly Mediterranean cafe right behind the *rådhus*. The well-stocked deli offers a bounty of cheeses, *charcuterie,* breads and excellent coffee.

Lisa's Sjökrog SEAFOOD €€ (☑61 83 83; www.lisassjokrog.com; Skeppsbrokajen, Gästhamnen; mains Kkr155-295) Given its location on a floating pier in the middle of the guest marina, it's not surprising that locals flock here for seafood.

Glassiärens Glassbar ICE CREAM € (☑170 05; Stortorget 4; ☺May-Sep) The queues at this legendary ice-cream peddler are matched by the mammoth serves. Piled high in a heavenly waffle cone, the two-flavour option (Skr34) is a virtual meal.

Lennarths Konditori BAKERY € (☑31 03 32; Norra Kungsgatan 3; ☺Mon-Sat) Old-school bakery with a fantastic tubular retro ceiling and calorific treats; try the delectable *munk* (think doughnut meets apple strudel). **Café Tre G** (☑31 03 33; Landbrogatan 9), a good lunch stop, is run by the same owners.

Restaurang Michelangelo ITALIAN €€ (☑121 95; www.restaurangmichelangelo.se; Ronnebygatan 29; lunch Kkr79, dinner mains Skr169-225) Offers solid Italian fair – gnocchi humming with garlic or classic saltimbocca – in a flamboyantly frescoed dining room.

Två Rum & Kök EUROPEAN €€€ (☑104 22; 2rok.se; Södra Smedjegatan 3; fondue minimum 2 people Skr279, mains Skr200-298; ☺Mon-Sat) Another great choice for dinner is this gourmet den, best known for its magnificent fondue, with flavours ranging from French to BBQ.

Nivå STEAKHOUSE €€ (☑103 71; www.niva.nu; Norra Kungsgatan 1; light meals Skr45-140, grill Skr139-455; ☺Mon-Sat) Just off Stortorget, this steakhouse has a variety of light, well-priced dishes (nachos, burgers, salads), as well as heartier meals from the grill. It's also a popular evening bar; its doors stay open until at least 1am.

ⓘ Information

ATMs are in the Wachtmeister shopping centre on Borgmästeregatan.
Library (Stortorget 15-17; ☺10am-7pm Mon-Fri, to 1pm Sat) Free internet access.
Tourist office (☑30 34 90; www.visitkarlskrona. se; Stortorget 2; ☺9am-7pm Jun-Aug, 9am-5pm Mon-Fri, 10am-2pm Sat Sep-May, 9am-5pm Mon-Fri, noon-5pm Wed, 10am-2pm Sat rest of year) Internet access and super helpful staff.

ⓘ Getting There & Around

Ronneby airport (☑0457-255 90) is 33km west of Karlskrona; the Flygbuss leaves from Stortorget (adult/child Skr85/42.50). SAS flies to Stockholm-Arlanda daily, and Blekingeflyg (www. blekingeflyg.se) flies to Stockholm Bromma (from Skr633, 50 minutes) between one and four times daily.

Stena Line (www.stenaline.se) ferries to Gdynia (Poland) depart from Verkö, 10km east of Karlskrona (take bus 6).

The bus and train stations are just north of central Karlskrona. **Blekingetrafiken** (www.blekingetrafiken.se) runs public transport in the Blekinge region.

Svenska Buss runs daily from Malmö to Stockholm, calling at Kristianstad (Skr110, 2¼ hours) and Karlskrona (Skr110, 3½ hours). Swebus Express service 835 runs from Malmö to Kalmar, calling at Kristianstad (from Skr430, one hour and 25 minutes), Karlshamn (from Skr430, 2¼ hours) and Karlskrona (from Skr430, three hours).

Kustbussen runs eight times daily on weekdays, twice daily on weekends, each way between Karlskrona and Kalmar (from Skr80, one hour and 35 minutes), and between Karlshamn and Kalmar (from Skr80, 2½ hours).

Direct trains run at least 13 times daily to Karlshamn (Skr70, one hour) and Kristianstad (Skr122, two hours), at least seven times daily to Emmaboda (Skr57, 40 minutes), and 10 times to Lund (Skr192, two hours and 40 minutes) and Malmö (Skr192, three hours). Trains also run at least a couple of times to Göteborg (Skr360, five hours). Change at Emmaboda for Kalmar.

For a taxi, call **Zon Taxi** (☎230 50).

Karlshamn

☎0454 / POP 31,000

You'd never guess that quiet Karslhamn, with its quaint cobbled streets, old wooden houses and art-nouveau architecture, was once so wicked. Alcoholic drinks, tobacco, snuff and playing cards were produced in great quantities here, and it was a major 19th-century smugglers' den. It was also the port from where many Swedes left for America. One of the biggest free festivals, the **Baltic Festival** (Östersjöfestivalen; www.ostersjofestivalen.se) sees a quarter of a million people roll in for bands and a carnival parade in July.

◉ Sights

Utvandrar-monumentet MONUMENT
This poignant monument, in a park by the harbour, commemorates all America-bound emigrants. Its figures are characters from Vilhelm Moberg's classic *The Emigrants:* Karl Oscar, looking forward to the new country, and Kristina, looking back towards her beloved Duvemåla. Nearby, peer through the windows of a 300-year-old **fishing cottage**.

Karlshamns Kulturkvarter MUSEUM
(☎148 68; Vinkelgatan 8; admission Skr20; ☉1-5pm Tue-Sun summer, noon-4pm Mon-Fri rest of year) The 'culture quarter' museum has interesting information about Karlhamn's history of producing tobacco and *punsch* (strong alcoholic punch), as well as a replica of the city's liquor factory, complete with barrels, bottles and machinery. Beautiful 18th-century

houses include manor and merchant house **Skottsbergska Gården** (admission Skr10) and **Holländarhuset** (Dutchman's house).

🛏 Sleeping & Eating

First Hotel Carlshamn HOTEL €€
(☎890 00; carlshamn@firsthotels.se; Varvsgatan 1; s/d Skr899/999; ℗@) Rooms are spotlessly clean and comfortable, if stuck in the 1980s. The best offer harbour views. Other positives include a jacuzzi, sauna and restaurant.

STF Vandrarhem Karlshamn HOSTEL €
(☎140 40; stfturistkhamn@hotmail.com; Surbrunnsvägen 1C; dm Skr210; ℗) On the eastern side of the town grid, near the train station, this hostel offers good rooms, all with private bathrooms. Kids will love the nearby playground, created by children.

TOP
CHOICE **Fiskstugan** SEAFOOD €€
(☎190 35; www.delikatessrokeri.se; Vägga Fiskhamn; sandwiches Skr54-79, meals Skr82-219; ☉lunch & dinner mid-Apr–early Sep) A 25-minute stroll southeast of the centre, this unpretentious seafood restaurant sits on a pretty little harbour. Choose your nosh at the deli-style counter and settle down under a crisp white umbrella to enjoy the perfect maritime view while your food is cooked. Ask at the tourist office for directions.

Gourmet Grön ORGANIC €€
(☎164 40; Östra Piren, Biblioteksgatan 6; lunch buffet Skr95; ☉11.30am-3pm Mon-Fri; 🍴) This waterside award-winner serves wonderful buffets with a strong emphasis on vegetarian food. You can nibble on a ciabatta, tapas-style goodies or inventive spreads with Mediterranean influences.

Köpmannagården PIZZERIA €
(☎317 87; www.kopmannagarden.se; Drottninggatan 88; pizzas Skr69-95; ☉closed Tue) A good pit-stop, with a rustic summer courtyard, in the *kulturkvarter*.

❶ Information

Most services line Drottninggatan.
Tourist office (☎812 03; www.karlshamn. se; Pirgatan 2; ☉10am-7pm Mon-Fri) On Östra kajen. Can help with information and bookings.

❶ Getting There & Away

The bus and train stations are in the northeastern part of town. For information, see p219.

DFDS Seaways (www.dfdsseaways.se) sails once a day between Karlshamn and Klaipėda in Lithuania (one way from Skr500, 14 hours).

MALMÖ & THE SOUTH BLEKINGE

The Southeast & Gotland

Best Places to Eat

- » Bakfickan (p259)
- » Gröna Stugan (p241)
- » Saltmagasinet (p247)
- » Krakas Krog (p261)
- » Café Berget (p229)

Best Places to Stay

- » STF Stora Karlsö (p260)
- » Kosta Boda Art Hotel (p243)
- » Hotell Västanå Slott (p235)
- » Strand Hotell (p225)
- » Slottshotellet (p241)

Why Go?

Southeast Sweden is a treasure trove of stoic castles, storybook towns and magical islands.

Carved by the epic Göta Canal, Östergötland is home to lovable, lakeside Vadstena: St Birgitta's terrestrial stomping ground and home to a hulking Renaissance castle.

Further south, Småland sparkles with its ethereal forests, preserved pastel towns and show-off Kalmar castle. Snoop through Astrid Lindgren's childhood home in Vimmerby, pig out on peppermint rock in sweet-smelling Gränna or blow glass in the world-renowned Glasriket (Kingdom of Crystal).

Offshore Öland has a beguiling mix of dazzling beaches, windswept fields, windmills, ring forts and Iron Age burial sites. Not surprisingly, much of the island sits on the Unesco World Heritage list.

Yet the real ace of spades is the island of Gotland. One of Sweden's historical heavyweights, it's a mesmerising spectacle of rune-stone-scattered landscapes, hauntingly beautiful medieval churches and the walled, Hanseatic town of Visby (another Unesco favourite).

When to Go

Visby

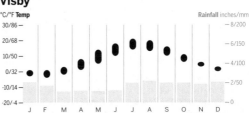

Jun–Aug Visitors drawn by warm summer days, Hultsfred Festival and Gotland's medieval week.

May & Sep Weather less predictable, but often just as nice. Easier to find places to stay.

Dec Christmas markets abound across Småland.

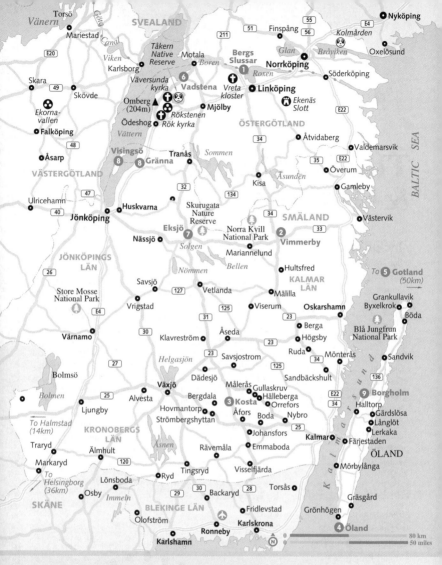

The Southeast & Gotland Highlights

1 Observe savvy captains navigating the lock-laced **Göta Canal** (p235) at **Bergs Slussar** (p229)

2 Visit Astrid Lindgren's childhood home at **Astrid Lindgrens Näs** (p248) or go Pippi-mad at **Astrid Lindgrens Värld** (p248) in Vimmerby

3 Browse for glass or blow your own in **Kosta** (p243) at the heart of the Glasriket

4 Watch the sun set from the haunting, southernmost point of **Öland** (p249)

5 Prowl the medieval walls, hunt for truffles or succumb to a culinary adventure on the cultured island of **Gotland** (p253)

6 Follow in pilgrims' footsteps during a visit to St Birgitta's church in **Vadstena** (p230)

7 Snap photos in the preserved wooden town of **Eksjö** (p236)

8 Burn off **Gränna** (p234) peppermint rock on a bike ride through the woods on peaceful **Visingsö** (p234)

9 Smell the roses in the royal gardens of **Solliden Palace** (p250) on Öland

ÖSTERGÖTLAND

Östergötland harbours gems on both sides of the Göta Canal, which threads diagonally across the region. Along its banks, the region's main towns are mostly 19th-century industrial heartlands, laced with some impressive postindustrial conversions. The region's west, bordered by the mighty lake Vättern, is a treat of flat, lush countryside steeped in ancient history. This is where you'll find Sweden's rune-stone superstar and the unmissable medieval town of Vadstena.

Norrköping

011 / POP 126,680

The envy of industrial has-beens all across Europe, Norrköping has cleverly regenerated its defunct mills and canals into a posse of cultural and gastronomic hang-outs fringing waterfalls and locks. Retro trams rattle down streets lined with eclectic architecture, while some 30km to the northeast, the animal park at Kolmården swaps urban regeneration for majestic Siberian tigers.

Norrköping's industrial identity began in the 17th century, but took off in the late 19th century when textile mills and factories sprang up alongside the swift-flowing Motala ström. Seventy percent of Sweden's textiles were once made here, the last mill shutting shop in the 1970s.

◉ Sights & Activities

Industrilandskapet   HISTORIC SITE

Industrilandskapet, Norrköping's star turn, is the impeccably preserved industrial area near the river. Pedestrian walkways and bridges lead past magnificent former factory buildings and around the ingenious system of locks and canals. The most thunderous waterfall is **Kungsfallet**, near the islet Laxholmen.

Within the area are several interesting museums, all with free admission. The innovative **Arbetets Museum** (www.arbetets museum.se; Laxholmen; ⊙11am-5pm, to 8pm Tue) documents working life. The seven-sided building, completed in 1917 and dubbed the 'flatiron', is a work of art in itself.

At the time of writing, the **Holmens Museum** was undergoing renovations; exhibits cover the history of Louis de Geer's paper factory, which was founded in the early 17th century.

KVARTERET KNÄPPINGSBORG

Some of Norrköping's best restaurants, cafes and shops are all tucked into this cleverly modernised block of warehouses and factory buildings at **Kvarteret Knäppingsborg** (www.knappingsborg.se). It's hard to go wrong here.

For seafood, try **Fiskmagasinet** (Skolgatan 1; lunches Skr90, mains Skr135-310; ⊙lunch & dinner Mon-Sat). Housed in a converted 19th-century *snus* (snuff) factory, urbane Fiskmagasinet combines an intimate bar with a casually chic dining room serving modern seafood dishes; think seafood platters or grilled scampi.

Mimmi's Visthus (www.mimmis visthus.se), around the corner, is an organic deli with delicious wraps, frittatas and salads. **Bagarstugan** (Skolgatan 1A; sandwiches Skr40-49, salads Skr59-65; ⊙7.30am-8pm Mon-Wed, to 10pm Sat) is a stylish bakery-bistro with two shops (the second branch is on Knäppingsborgsgatan); both peddle freshly baked cookies, cinnamon buns, muffins and scones, as well as salubrious salads and sandwiches.

Over the bridge, **Stadsmuseum** (15 26 20; Holmbrogränd; ⊙10am-5pm Tue, Wed & Fri, 11am-8pm Thu, noon-5pm Sat & Sun) delves into the town's industrial past, complete with still-functioning machinery, a great cafe and dynamic temporary exhibitions.

Louis de Geer Konserthus   ARCHITECTURE
(www.louisdegeer.com; Dalsgatan 15) A modern addition to the riverside scenery is the extraordinary 1300-seat Louis de Geer Konserthus, located in a former paper mill. Still containing the original balconies, it's a superb setting for orchestral, jazz and pop concerts.

FREE **Konstmuseum**   MUSEUM
(www.norrkoping.se/konstmuseet; Kristinaplatsen; ⊙noon-4pm Tue & Thu-Sun, to 8pm Wed Jun-Aug, 11am-5pm Wed & Fri-Sun, to 8pm Tue & Thu Sep-May) Over near Vasaparken, Konstmuseum is Norrköping's impressive art museum. Its collection boasts important early-20th-century works, including modernist and cubist gems, as well as one of Sweden's largest collections of graphic art.

Norrköping

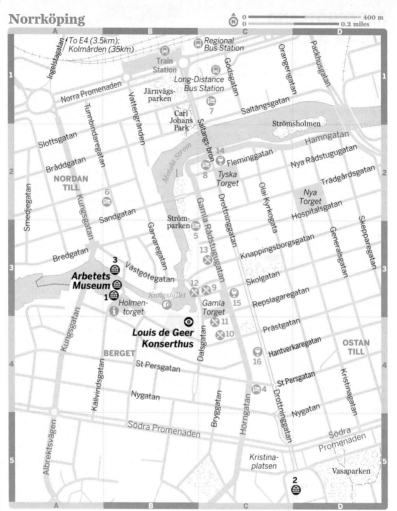

Bronze Age rock carvings
ARCHAEOLOGICAL SITE

Two kilometres west of the city centre, near the river, await fine examples of Bronze Age rock carvings, with an adjacent museum, **Hällristningsmuseet** (www.ffin.se, in Swedish; Himmelstalund; admission free; ⏰5.30-6.30pm Tue, 11am-3pm Sat & Sun May-Aug). Guided tours of the carvings must be booked in advance. The site is a 30-minute walk along the river.

Vintage Tram 1
TOUR

From July to mid-August, vintage tram 1 operates a short, guided tour through central Norrköping. Tours in English can be booked through the **tourist office** (www.upplev.norrkoping.se). It leaves from Söder Tull at 6pm and 6.30pm on Tuesdays and Thursdays (adults/four to 12 years Skr40/20). The tourist office runs one-hour **walking tours** of the industrial area in summer (Skr100).

Kolmården
ZOO

(www.kolmarden.com; adult/3-12yr Skr379/289; ⏰10am-7pm daily Jul–mid-Aug, to 5pm daily Apr-Jun & mid-Aug–end Aug, to 5pm Sat & Sun Sep-Oct) This zoo is Scandinavia's largest, with some 750 residents from all climates and conti-

Norrköping

nents. There is a safari park, marine world and tiger world. Entry into the **Djurparken** includes a dolphin show, and the park's biggest investment to date, a gondola over the safari park that began operating in 2011, is well worth a spin.

A separate **Tropicarium** (www.tropicarium. se; adult/4-15yr Skr100/60; ⊙10am-8pm daily Jul-mid–Aug, 10am-6pm Mon-Fri, to 7pm Sat & Sun May-Jun, shorter hours rest of year) opposite the entrance titillates with its motley crew of spiders, sharks, alligators and snakes.

You'll need a whole day to fully appreciate the zoo. Kolmården lies 35km north of Norrköping, on the north shore of Bråviken. Take regular bus 432 or 433 from Norrköping (Skr60, 40 minutes).

🛏 Sleeping

[TOP CHOICE] **Strand Hotell**   BOUTIQUE HOTEL €€
(📞16 99 00; www.hotellstrand.se; Drottninggattan 2; s/d Skr995/1295; @) A real gem in the heart of town, Hotell Strand takes up the 2nd floor of a gorgeous 1890 building overlooking the

Motala river and Drottninggattan. Operating as a hotel since the 1930s, Strand was restored with care in 2009; furniture and fabrics make the most of the building's existing features, such as cut-glass chandeliers and big bay windows.

Hotel Centric   HOTEL €
(📞12 90 30; www.centrichotel.se; Gamla Rådstugugatan 18-20; s/d Skr550/915; P @) Conveniently located near the Industrilandskapet, Hotel Centric is Norrköping's oldest hotel. Rooms are spacious, furniture solid and staff welcoming.

Scandic Hotel Norrköping City   HOTEL €€
(📞495 52 00; norrkopingcity@scandic-hotels.com; Slottsgatan 99; s/d Skr700/1310; P @) Near the train station, the Scandic City makes up for its dowdy foyer with crisp, modern rooms featuring retro-cool wallpaper and flat-screen TVs. erks include a sauna and jacuzzi.

STF Vandrarhem Turistgården   HOSTEL €
(📞10 11 60; www.turistgarden.se; Ingelstagatan 31; dm/s/d per person from Skr260/360/265; P @) A pleasing little hostel about 800m north of the train station.

STF Vandrarhem Abborreberg   HOSTEL €€
(📞0733 85 44 00; www.abborreberg.se; s/d Skr300/500; ⊙Apr–mid-Oct; P) Stunningly situated in a coastal pine wood 5km east of town, this sterling hostel offers accommodation in huts scattered through the surrounding park. The associated ice-cream parlour is a hit with gluttons. Take bus 116 to Lindö (Skr20).

🍴 Eating & Drinking

Jolla Choklad & Dessert   DESSERTS €
(www.jolla.se; Prästgatan 3; ⊙closed Sun) Head to this chocolate shop-cafe for exquisite homemade gelato and truffles, as well as espresso that could make an Italian barista weep.

Pappa Grappa Bar & Trattorian   ITALIAN €€
(www.pappagrappa.se; Gamla Rådstugugatan 26-28; mains Skr165-295; ⊙6pm-late Mon-Sat, pizzeria also open Sun) Gobble up a brilliant wood-fired pizza or slip into the vaulted restaurant for scrumptious antipasto.

Källaren Bacchus   EUROPEAN €€
(Gamla Torget 4; lunches Skr75, mains Skr125-285) A perennially popular restaurant-pub with a great summer garden courtyard and snug vaulted cellar. Steak is a speciality, while tasty fish dishes may include fried pikeperch with chilli-lime butter and potato pastry.

Pub Wasa PUB
(Gamla Rådstugugatan; ⏰6pm-3am Tue-Sat)
Favourite postwork drinking spot.

Kvarterskrogen Asken BAR
(www.krogasken.se; Kvarteret Knäppingsborg)
Polished bar with nice outdoor seating.

Bishop's Arms PUB
(Tyska Torget 2) Located at the Grand Hotel,
this is a good English-style pub with a great
river view.

The blocks between Drottninggatan and
Olai Kyrkogata contain shopping centres
that are packed with chain stores and supermarkets, as well as a **Systembolaget** (Drottninggatan 50B).

ℹ Information

Banks and ATMs line Drottninggatan.
Forex (www.forex.se; Drottninggatan 46;
⏰9am-7pm Mon-Fri, to 3pm Sat) Money
exchange.
Library (Stadsbiblioteket; Södra Promenaden
105; ⏰8am-7pm Mon-Thu, to 6pm Fri, 11am-
4pm Sat) Free internet access.
Tourist office (☏15 50 00; www.upplev.
norrkopping.se; Källvindsgatan 1; ⏰10am-6pm
daily Jul–mid-Aug, shorter hours rest of year)
Free internet access.

ℹ Getting There & Away

Sweden's third-largest airport, **Stockholm
Skavsta** (www.skavsta.se), is 60km away. To get
there take the train to Nyköping, then catch a
local bus. **Norrköping Airport** (www.norrkoping

flygplats.se) has direct flights from Copenhagen,
Munich and Helsinki.

The regional bus station is next to the train
station, and long-distance buses leave from
a terminal across the road. **Swebus Express**
(www.swebusexpress.com) has very frequent
services to Stockholm (Skr139, 2¼ hours) and
Jönköping (Skr199, 2½ hours), and several
services daily to Göteborg (Skr299, five hours)
and Kalmar (Skr259, four hours). **Svenska Buss**
(www.svenskabuss.se) runs similar, though less
frequent, routes.

Norrköping is on the main north–south railway
line, and **Sveriges Järnväg** (SJ; www.sj.se)
trains depart every one to two hours for Stockholm (Skr210 to Skr558, 1½ hours) and Malmö
(Skr320 to Skr1077, 3¼ hours). Trains run
roughly every hour north to Nyköping (Skr78 to
Skr87, one hour) and every 20 minutes south to
Linköping (Skr73, 25 minutes).

ℹ Getting Around

The minimum fare on Norrköping's urban transport is Skr20. Trams cover the city and are the
quickest option for short hops, especially along
Drottninggatan from the train station.

Taxis can be booked with **Norrköpings Taxi**
(☏30 00 00).

Linköping

🗺 013 / POP 145,000

Most famous for its mighty medieval
cathedral, Linköping fancies itself as
Norrköping's more upmarket rival. Its most
infamous claim to fame is the 'bloodbath
of Linköping'. Following the Battle of

THE SWEET STENCH OF SUCCESS

Take some slaughterhouse innards, add a splash of alcohol, mix them together with
human waste and heat the lot to 70°C. Pour the slush into an anaerobic digester, allow
30 days of decomposition and presto: ecofriendly biogas. This cleaner, greener energy
source is increasingly powering everything from Sweden's buses, trucks and cars to the
world's first biogas train, running between Linköping and Västervik. Carbon neutral and
renewable, its other benefit is that it's locally produced.

One of the largest producers of biogas is SvenskBiogas: its Linköping plant turns
a whopping 46,000 tonnes of waste each year into fossil-free fuel. The good news for
both SvenskBiogas and the environment is that the biogas market is booming. Green
cars made up over 40% of new car registrations in 2010 and government incentives are
expected to boost figures further. Enlightened local councils make 'switching to green' a
tempting option: ecofriendly cars are exempt from road tolls in Stockholm and enjoy free
parking in many large Swedish cities.

In small-town Växjö, where biogas is produced at the local sewage works, local politi-
cians decided back in the 1990s to make the town fossil-fuel free by 2030. Other targets
include slashing per capita carbon-dioxide emissions by 55% by 2015 and getting inhabitants to buy 45% of their foodstuffs from local or ecological producers within the same
time frame. Over half of Växjö's total energy already comes from renewable sources.

Linköping

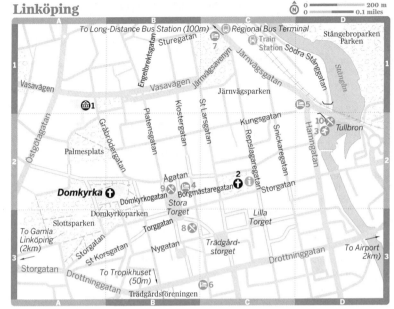

Stångebro (1598), many of King Sigismund's defeated Catholic army were executed here, leaving Duke Karl and his Protestant forces in full control of Sweden.

While quite the modern, industrial city today (manufacturer Saab is the major employer), pockets of its past survive in its churches, castle, museums and the picture-perfect streets around Hunnebergsgatan and Storgatan.

◉ Sights & Activities

Gamla Linköping & Valla Fritidsområde
HISTORIC SITE

The town's best attractions lie just outside the centre. **Gamla Linköping** (www.gamla linkoping.info; admission free), 2km west of the city, is one of the biggest living-museum villages in Sweden. It's a gorgeous combo of cobbled streets, picket-fenced gardens and around 90 19th-century houses. There are about a dozen themed museums (all free, with various opening times), artisan shops and a small chocolate factory. Take bus 12 or 19 (Skr20).

Just 300m through the forest is Valla Fritidsområde, a recreation area with domestic animals, a children's playground, minigolf, small museums and vintage abodes.

Domkyrka
CHURCH

(⊙9am-6pm) Made from blocks of hand-carved limestone, the enormous Domkyrka was the country's largest and most expensive church in the Middle Ages. Its foundations were laid around 1250 and its 107m spire and vast interior still impress. Inside sits a vivid 16th-century triptych by Dutchman Marten van Heemskerck. There are organ concerts on Thursdays in the summer.

Slotts- & Domkyrkomuseum   MUSEUM

(www.lsdm.se; adult/under 7yr/senior & student Skr50/free/40; ⊙noon-4pm Tue-Sun) The struggle between church and state is explored in the nearby castle's Slotts- & Domkyrkomuseum, where the bolshie King Gustav Vasa and the last Catholic bishop, Hans Brask, made friends, ate, drank and fell out again. Archaeological finds include two mummified black rats from the bishop's privy.

Östergötlands Länsmuseum   MUSEUM

(www.ostergotlandsmuseum.se; Vasavägen; adult/under 25yr Skr50/free; ⊙11am-4pm Tue-Sun) Just north of the Domkyrka, Östergötlands Länsmuseum has a decent European art collection (Cranach's painting of Eden, *Original Sin,* is wonderful, with a smiling Eve twiddling her toes), and Swedish art dating from the Middle Ages.

Sankt Lars Kyrka   CHURCH

(Storgatan; ⊙11am-4pm Mon-Sun) The concrete floor of Sankt Lars Kyrka was built in 1802 above the previous medieval church crypt. There are tours of the crypt on Tuesdays at 3pm, where fascinating finds include 11th-century gravestones, a teen skeleton (complete with fatal blow to the skull) and fragments of the medieval church's painted roof tiles.

Flygvapenmuseum   MUSEUM

(www.flygvapenmuseum.se; Carl Cederströms gata 2; adult/under 19yr Skr50/free; ⊙11am-5pm daily, to 8pm Wed Jun-Aug, 11am-5pm Tue-Sun, to 8pm Wed Sep-May) Approximately 7km west of the centre is Flygvapenmuseum, with exhibits on air-force history and 60 aircraft fit for a *Top Gun* remake. To get there, take bus 13.

Ekenäs Slott   CASTLE

(www.ekenasslott.se; tours adult/10-15yr Skr60/25; ⊙guided tours on the hour 1-3pm Tue-Sun Jul, Sat & Sun Jun & Aug) Built between 1630 and 1644, this is one of the best-preserved Renaissance castles in Sweden. Features include three spectacular towers, a moat, and furnishings from the 17th to 19th centuries. It's located 20km east of Linköping; you'll need your own transport to get there.

Kinda Canal   BOAT TOUR

While upstaged by the Göta Canal, Linköping boasts its own canal system, the 90km Kinda Canal. Opened in 1871, it has

15 locks, including Sweden's deepest. Cruises include evening sailings, musical outings and wine-tasting trips. For a simple day excursion, from late June to early August the **M/S Kind** (www.kindakanal.se; adult/6-15yr Skr330/165) leaves Tullbron dock at 10am on Tuesday, Thursday and Saturday, and travels to Rimforsa (return by bus or train included).

🛏 Sleeping

Park Hotel   HOTEL €€

(☎12 90 05; www.fawltytowers.se; Järnvägsgatan 6; s/d Skr795/990; P@) Disturbingly billed as Sweden's 'Fawlty Towers', this hotel resembles that madhouse in appearance only (yes, there's an elk head at reception). A smart family-run establishment close to the train station, it's peppered with chandeliers, oil paintings and clean, parquet-floored rooms, though rooms are crisply modern. There is afternoon tea (Skr 160) and a hearty breakfast buffet served in the hotel's pleasant dining room.

Hotell du Nord   HOTEL €€

(☎12 98 95; www.hotelldunord.se; Repslagaregatan 5; s/d from Skr760/950; P) Across from the Järnvägsparken, Hotell du Nord is pleasantly leafy and quiet. The main 19th-century building looks something like a doll's house, staff are friendly and the rooms light and pleasant (those in the aesthetically challenged rear building are freshly renovated and larger). There's a patio for outdoor summer breakfasts.

Linköping STF Vandrarhem
& Hotell   HOSTEL €

(☎35 90 00; www.lvh.se; Klostergatan 52A; s/d incl breakfast Skr595/650; @) This swish central hostel has hotel-style accommodation too, mostly with kitchenettes. All rooms have private bathrooms and TVs. Book ahead.

Best Western Hotel Linköping   HOTEL €€

(☎79 27 52; www.hotellinkoping.se; Hantverkaregatan 1; s/d incl breakfast Skr795/995; P@) Right off the Storatorget, this hotel is within a few minutes' walk of the city's main sights, restaurants and shopping. Rooms are modern and staff helpful. Breakfast is generous and there is an Italian cafe.

Hotell Östergyllen   HOTEL €

(☎10 20 75; www.hotellostergyllen.se; Hamngatan 2B; s/d incl breakfast from Skr495/690) Despite the forlorn ambience (think lino floors and anonymous corridors), this budget hotel

BERGS SLUSSAR

Bergs Slussar, 12km northwest of Linköping, is one of the most scenic sections of the Göta Canal: there are seven locks with a height gain of 19m – very impressive in canal terms! The nearby ruin **Vreta kloster**, Sweden's oldest monastery, was founded by Benedictine monks in 1120. While it's worth a look, the adjacent 13th-century **abbey church** is admittedly more interesting.

There's a small **tourist office** (☉9.30am-5pm in summer) in the same building as the beautifully located **STF Vandrarhem** (☎013-603 30; bergsslussar@sverige.nu; dm Skr245; ☉May-Aug) near the locks, with a cafe, minigolf and bike hire. You'll find a couple of cafes and restaurants out this way, including **Kanalkrogen** (meals Skr220-245), with a great range of meals and lockside view.

Buses 521 and 522 run regularly from Linköping.

---

offers cheap, comfy-enough rooms and decent breakfast not far from the train station.

Glyttinge Camping　　　CAMPGROUND €
(☎17 49 28; www.nordiccamping.se; Berggårdsvägen 6; sites from Skr190; ☉year-round) This huge campsite, with minigolf and cycle hire, lies 4km west of the city centre.

✖ Eating & Drinking

Most places to eat (and drink) are found around the main square or nearby streets, especially along buzzing Ågatan.

TOP CHOICE **Café Berget**　　　BAKERY €
(www.cafeberget.com; Klostergatan 38; cakes & pies from Skr35; ☉10am-6pm Mon-Fri, to 4pm Sat) Up a narrow set of stone stairs you'll find a sunny terrace, resplendent with flowers and ivy, which serves as the doorstep to this glorious little bolt-hole bakery. Café Berget serves up the most classic of Swedish baked goodies – vanilla cream hearts and blueberry tartlets – as well as coffee, tea and sandwiches, in lovingly restored rooms in this 1905 building.

Tropikhuset　　　CAFE €
(www.tropikhuset.nu; Trägårdsföreningen; sandwiches from Skr 79; ☉9am-6pm Mon-Fri, 10am-5pm Sat, 11am-5pm Sun) Grab a slice of cake and park yourself under a palm tree inside this cafe's pyramid greenhouse or enjoy the outdoor tables overlooking the Trägårdsföreningen. It's just south of the centre.

Stångs Magasin　　　SWEDISH €€€
(www.stangsmagasin.se; Södra Stånggatan 1; mains Skr135-495; ☉5pm-midnight Mon-Wed, to 1am Thu-Sat Jul & Aug, shorter hours in winter) In a 200-year-old warehouse down near the Kinda Canal docks, this elegant award-winner fuses classic Swedish cuisine with

continental influences – think stuffed trout with beet aioli, and veal entrecôte topped with sun-dried tomatoes.

Charken　　　AMERICAN €€
(http://charkenrb.alltomnet.com; Stora Torget 7; mains Skr145-175; ☉lunch 11.30am-2pm, dinner 5-10pm) Located right on the main square, Charken is a great for a cool beer and people-watching. Food is bistro style, solid and unpretentious. You'll find a good hamburger here or finger food such as garlic bread and peel-and-eat shrimp.

❶ Information

There are banks and other services around Stora Torget.

Library (Stadsbiblioteket; Östgötagatan 5; ☉10am-7pm Mon-Thu, to 6pm Fri, 11am-3pm Sat May-Aug, 8am-8pm Mon-Thu, to 6pm Fri, 11am-4pm Sat & Sun Sep-Apr) Free internet access (bring ID) and an excellent cafe.

Tourist office (☎90 00 70; www.visitlinkoping. se; Storgatan 15; ☉9am-1.20pm & 2.30-6pm Mon-Fri, 11am-3pm Sat & Sun) Right across from Sankt Lars Kyrka.

❶ Getting There & Away

The **airport** (☎18 10 30) is only 2km east of town. **Skyways** (www.skyways.se) flies direct to Stockholm-Arlanda on weekdays. **KLM** (www. klm.com) flies daily to Amsterdam. There's no airport bus, but taxi company **Taxibil** (☎14 60 00) charges around Skr150 for the ride.

Regional and local buses, run by **Östgöta Trafiken** (www.ostgotatrafiken.se), leave from the terminal next to the train station; route maps and timetables are available at the information office.

Journeys cost from Skr20; the 24-hour *dygnskort* (travel card; adult/under 26 years Skr140/110) is valid on all buses and local trains within the region. Tickets can be purchased at Pressbyrån outlets or at the train station.

Up to five express buses per day go to Vadstena (Skr110, one hour); otherwise change at Motala.

Long-distance buses depart from a terminal 500m northwest of the train station. Swebus Express runs 10 to 12 times daily to Jönköping (Skr159, 1½ hours) and seven to eight times daily to Göteborg (Skr269, four hours), and north to Norrköping (Skr69, 45 minutes) and Stockholm (Skr189, three hours).

Linköping is on the main north–south railway line. Regional and express trains run to Stockholm roughly every hour; express trains go to Malmö. Frequent regional trains run north to Norrköping (Skr78, 25 minutes). Kustpilen SJ trains run every few hours to Norrköping, Nyköping and Kalmar.

❶ Getting Around

Most city buses depart from Centralstationen. If you're looking to rent a bike to travel along the canal, get in touch with **Cykelaventyr** (www.cykelaventyr.se; per day Skr150), with locations in Borensberg (on the canal 10km north of Bergs Slussar) or Motala (15km north of Vadstena). For a taxi, ring **Taxibil** (📞14 60 00; www.taxibil.se).

Vadstena

📞0143 / POP 7540

On Vättern lake, Vadstena is a legacy of both church and state power, and today St Birgitta's abbey and Gustav Vasa's castle compete with each other for admiration. The atmosphere in the old town (between Storgatan and the abbey), with its wonderful cobbled lanes, evocative street names and wooden buildings, makes it an especially satisfying place to end a day of touring along the Göta Canal.

◉ Sights

Both the old courthouse **rådhus** (road house), on the town square, and **Rödtornet** (Sånggatan) are late-medieval constructions.

Vadstena Slott CASTLE

(📞62 16 00; www.vadstenadirect.se; Slottsvägen; adult/7-15yr Skr90/60; ⏰11am-6pm daily Jul–mid-Aug, to 4pm Jun & mid–late Aug, noon-3pm mid-May & early Sep) Overlooking the lake, the mighty Renaissance castle Vadstena Slott was the family project of the early Vasa kings. The lower floors contain a small historical display. The furnished upper floors are more interesting, but only open during guided tours (in English mid-May to mid-September; call ahead for times); it's worth going on one if only to visit the chapel, with its incredible 17-second echo!

Sancta Birgitta Klostermuseet MUSEUM

(www.sanctabirgitta.com; Lasarettsgatan; adult/8-18yr Sk60/30; ⏰10.30am-5pm daily Jul–early Aug, 11am-4pm Jun & rest of Aug, 11am-4pm Sat & Sun May, Sep & Oct) The Sancta Birgitta Klostermuseet is in Bjälboättens Palats (a royal residence that became a convent in 1384), and tells the story of St Birgitta's roller-coaster life and those of all her saint-and-sinner children. Artefacts include the coffin that she was brought back from Rome in.

Klosterkyrkan CHURCH

(abbey church; admission free; ⏰9am-8pm daily Jul, to 7pm Jun & Aug, to 5pm May & Sep) 'Of plain construction, humble and strong', Klosterkyrkan was built in response to one of St Birgitta's visions. After the church's consecration in 1430, Vadstena became *the* top pilgrimage site in Sweden. Step inside for medieval sculptures and carved floor slabs.

🛏 Sleeping

Chain hotels don't get a look-in here – pretty and personal is the rule. Book accommodation well in advance.

Vadstena Klosterhotel HOTEL €€

(📞315 30; www.klosterhotel.se; s/d from Skr1350/1650; 🅿@) History and luxury merge at this wonderfully atmospheric hotel

---

ALL HAIL HULTSFRED

Like a Glastonbury with spruce, the annual **Hultsfredsfestivalen** (Hultsfred Festival; www.hultsfredsfestivalen.se, ticket sales at www.eventim.se; 3-day pass from Skr1150) is one of Sweden's music-fest heavyweights, boasting five stages and acts spanning rock, pop and indie. Past line-ups have included the Prodigy, Morrissey and Swedish band the Hives. It's held over three or four days in mid-June, in small-town Hultsfred, around 20km south of Vimmerby. Most ticket types include access to the festival's camping area (check website for updates on one-, two- and three-day passes). Trains connect Hultsfred to Linköping (and major cities beyond). For further information, check the festival website.

in St Birgitta's old convent. The bathrooms are a wee bit dated, but the medieval-style rooms are great, with chandeliers and high wooden beds. Most boast lake views. The hotel also has simpler rooms with shared bathrooms and showers in a nearby cottage (single/double Skr690/890).

Pensionat Solgården
B&B €

(☑143 50; www.pensionatsolgarden.se; Strågatan 3; s/d from Skr540/790; ☺May–Sep) Set in an utterly adorable wooden villa, this family-run hotel boasts lovingly decorated rooms; some have private bathrooms and all have an art/artist connection. They're all *very* different – check the photos on the website to choose your favourite.

27ans Nattlogi
B&B €

(☑134 47; www.27ansnattlogi.se; Storgatan 27; s/d incl breakfast from Skr550/750; P) Wooden floors give a homely vibe to the six rooms (some with views of Klosterkyrkan). More-expensive rooms have private bathrooms.

STF Vandrarhem Vadstena
HOSTEL €

(☑765 60; Skän ningegatan 20; dm Skr250; P) A short walk from the town centre sits this big hostel, with affable staff, sunny dorms and a large underground kitchen decorated with cheery Dala horses. Book ahead from late August to early June.

Vadstena Camping
CAMPGROUND €

(☑127 30; sites Skr230, r & cabins from Skr350; ☺May–mid-Sep; ☒) A quality campsite near the lake, 2km north of town, it has family-friendly amenities including a beach with shallow waters, minigolf, boules, a sauna, a water slide, a kiosk, a cafe and a pub.

✕ Eating & Drinking

Hamnpaviljongen
SANDWICHES €

(snacks & sandwiches Skr45-75) In the park facing the castle is this alfresco cafe with decent sandwiches, light meals and a refreshing verdant vibe.

Restaurant Munkklostret
EUROPEAN €€€

(lunches Skr125, dinners Skr169-305; ☺noon-11pm daily Jun-Aug, from 6pm daily rest of year) The Klosterhotel's ravishing restaurant is the best nosh spot in town. Seasonal, succulent steak, lamb, game and fish dishes are flavoured with herbs from the monastery garden, and served in the monks' old dorms.

Rådhuskällaren
PUB €€

(www.radhuskallaren.com; Rådhustorget; mains Skr134-199) Under the old courthouse, this affable 15th-century cellar restaurant dishes out simple but filling burger, pasta and fish meals. Its outdoor area is a favourite afternoon drinking spot in summer.

CoopKonsum
SUPERMARKET

(Rådhustorget; ☺to 11pm) A central supermarket.

Systembolaget
LIQUOR STORE

(Hovsgatan 4) Nearby CoopKonsum.

❶ Information

You'll find banks and other services east of the castle, on Storgatan and around Stora Torget.

Tourist office (☑315 70; www.vadstena.com; ☺10am-2pm Mon-Sat May & Sep, to 6pm Mon-Sat, to 4pm Sun Jun & Aug, 10am-7pm Jul, to 2pm Mon-Fri rest of year) Located in the Rödtornet (Sånggatan). A great place to get details about town walks, boat tours and festivals.

❶ Getting There & Around

See Linköping (p229) for regional transport information. Only buses run to Vadstena – take bus 610 to Motala (for trains to Örebro), or bus 661 to Mjölby (for trains to Linköping and Stockholm). **Swebus Express** (www.swebusexpress.com) runs daily to/from Stockholm (Skr299, 4¼ hours). **Blåklints Buss** (www.blaklintsbuss.se, in Swedish) runs one to three services daily from the Viking Line Terminal in Stockholm to Vadstena (Skr220).

Cykelaventyr (www.cykelaventyr.se) in Borensberg (on the canal 10km north of Berg Slusser) or Motala (15km north of Vadstena) has bikes for rent (Skr150 per day).

Around Vadstena

RÖK

Sweden's most famous rune stone, the 9th-century **Rökstenen**, is near the church at Rök (just off the E4 on the road to Heda and Alvastra). It's a monumental memorial stone raised to commemorate a dead son, and features the longest runic inscription in the world. It's an ancient, intricate verse so cryptic that scholars constantly scrap over its interpretation. The outdoor exhibition and stone are always open.

Buses are virtually nonexistent, though the scenic flatlands around Vättern make for perfect cycling.

VÄVERSUNDA

The Romanesque 12th-century limestone **Väversunda kyrka**, situated 15km southwest of Vadstena, is a bizarre-looking church, and contains restored 13th-century wall paintings. The adjacent **Tåkern Nature Reserve** pulls in a diverse cast of birds; there's a birdwatcher's tower near the church.

Again, buses are hopeless; pedalling is your best option.

SMÅLAND

The region of Småland is one of dense forests, glinting lakes and bare marshlands. Historically it served as a buffer zone between the Swedes and Danes; the eastern and southern coasts in particular witnessed territorial tussles. Today it's better known for the Glasriket (Kingdom of Glass), a sparsely populated area in the central southeast dotted with crystal workshops. Småland is broken up into *län* (smaller counties): Jönköpings in the northwest, Kronobergs in the southwest and Kalmar in the east.

Jönköping & Huskvarna

♪ 036 / POP 123,710

Whenever you hear the scratching of matches on sandpaper, spare a thought for Jönköping – birthplace of the safety match. You can visit the restored production area here to learn more about this vital, but undervalued, necessity.

Fairy-tale illustrator John Bauer was inspired by the deep-green forests around Jönköping, and the town museum shows off his superb otherworldly drawings of trolls, knights and princesses. Other famous exports include ABBA's Agnetha Fältskog, and indie band The Cardigans.

From Jönköping, at Vättern's south end, an urban strip stretches 7km eastward, sucking in Huskvarna, which is famous for its sewing machines, chainsaws and motorbikes.

⊙ Sights & Activities

JÖNKÖPING

Tändsticksmuseet   MUSEUM
(www.matchmuseum.se; Tändsticksgränd 27; adult/ under 19yr Skr40/free, Nov-Dec free; ⊙10am-5pm Mon-Fri, to 3pm Sat & Sun Jun-Aug, 11am-3pm Tue-Sun Sep-May) Apparently 'the only match museum in the world', Tändsticksmuseet, in an old match factory, deals with this practical Swedish invention. It's quite an eye-opener: the industry was initially based on cheap child labour, workers frequently suffered

from repulsive 'phossy jaw', and it was common knowledge that phosphorus matches were good for 'speeding up inheritance and inducing abortions'.

Radio Museum   MUSEUM
(www.radiomuseum.home.se; Tändsticksgränd 16; admission Skr20; ⊙10am-5pm Mon-Fri, to 1pm Sat, 11am-3pm Sun Jun–mid-Aug, closed Sun & Mon mid-Aug–May) Near the Tändsticksmuseet, the Radio Museum boasts over 1000 radio sets and related memorabilia.

Jönköpings Länsmuseum   MUSEUM
(www.jkpglm.se; Dag Hammarskjölds Plats 2; adult/ under 18yr Skr40/free, Oct-Apr free; ⊙11am-5pm Mon, Tue & Thu-Sun, to 8pm Wed Jul & Aug, closed Mon Sep-Jun) At the time of writing, the Jönköpings Länsmuseum was undergoing renovations. Exhibits cover local history and contemporary culture, but the real reason for coming here is to see the haunting fantasy works of artist John Bauer (1882–1918).

Cruises   BOAT TOUR
(www.rederiabkind.se) From May to October, you can choose various cruises on Vättern, aboard the M/S *Nya Skärgården*. There's an evening buffet trip (Skr435), complete with local delicacies, while several other trips combine dinner and live music, costing around Skr445. The boat departs from Hamnpiren; bookings can be made at the tourist office or directly.

HUSKVARNA

From Jönköping, take bus 1 to Huskvarna (Skr20), 7km away.

Husqvarna Fabriksmuseum   MUSEUM
(www.husqvarnamuseum.se; Hakarpsvägen 1; adult/12-18yr/senior Skr50/20/40; ⊙10am-5pm Mon-Fri, noon-4pm Sat & Sun May-Sep, 10am-3pm Mon-Fri, noon-4pm Sat & Sun Oct-Apr) Square-jawed men going hunting while their wives snuggle up to their sewing machines: the Husqvarna Fabriksmuseum conjures up a vivid 1950s world. The factory began as an arms manufacturer, before diverting into motorbikes, chainsaws, cooking ranges and microwave ovens. The atmospheric museum charts the company's rise.

✪ Festivals & Events

For powerful drama, catch Huskvarna's **Fallens Dag** (Waterfall Day) on the last Saturday in August. When darkness falls the floodgates open and a torrential illuminated

Jönköping

waterfall is released; contact the tourist office for details.

🛏 Sleeping

JÖNKÖPING

Elite Stora Hotellet
HOTEL €€

(☎10 00 00; www.elite.se; Hotellplan; s/d Skr850/950; P@) The Elite is Jönköping's harbourside show-stopper. Rooms are chic, with either Carl Larsson–inspired undertones or a more contemporary combo of black-and-white photographs and natural hues. There's a sauna, pool table and slinky restaurant, as well as a banqueting hall fit for royalty.

City Hotel
HOTEL €€

(☎71 92 80; www.cityhotel.se; Västra Storgatan 25; s/d from Skr645/895; @) Dowdy, tired halls give way to rooms that are bright, clean and modern – think flat-screen TVs, giant photos of Jönköping, and oak-toned functionalist furniture – at this midrange, family-run hotel.

Grand Hotel
HOTEL €€

(☎71 96 00; www.grandhotel-jonkoping.se; Hovrättstorget; s/d Skr690/890; @) In a stately early-20th-century building, this homely central choice offers budget, standard and superior rooms. All are clean and comfy, many are spacious, and several look out over the square.

SweCamp Villa Björkhagen
CAMPGROUND €

(☎12 28 63; www.villabjorkhagen.se; Friggagatan 31; sites/r/cabins Skr220/395/795) About 3km east of town, this large lakeside campsite

Jönköping

◎ Sights
1 Jönköpings Länsmuseum	D2
2 Radio Museum	A1
3 Tändsticksmuseet	A1

🛏 Sleeping
4 City Hotel	A1
5 Elite Stora Hotellet	C1
6 Grand Hotel	D2

⊗ Eating
7 Hamnpiren Restaurants	C1
8 Mäster Gudmunds Källare	A1

offers various accommodation options, plus playgrounds and a water park for kids.

HUSKVARNA

STF Vandrarhem Huskvarna
HOSTEL €

(☎14 88 70; www.hhv.se; Odengatan 10; s/d per person Skr395/250; @) Standards are high at this sizeable year-round hostel. All rooms are sparkling and have TVs; breakfast is an additional Skr65.

🍴 Eating

For bobbing boats and tasty seafood, head straight for Jönköping's Hamnpiren (the harbour pier), where you'll find a row of restaurants with good lunch specials (around Skr75) and merry dinner crowds. For cheaper alternatives, try inside the Juneporten transport and shopping complex.

Pescadores
SEAFOOD €€

(www.pescadores.se; Svavelsticksgränd 23; mains Skr99-269; ⊙4-11.30pm Wed-Sat, shorter hours Sat

& Sun) A family-run fish restaurant located in one of the quirky brick buildings that once belonged to the match-making empire. The father and son owners were previously commercial crayfishermen, so they know their stuff. The menu features all the classics, from fish and chips, to gravlax and mussel soup. It's just west of the centre.

Mäster Gudmunds Källare   EUROPEAN €€
(www.mastergudmund.se; Kapellgatan 2; lunches Skr75, mains Skr149-219; ⊘11.30am-2pm & 6-10pm Mon-Fri, noon-10pm Sat, to 5pm Sun, closed Sun in summer) This much-loved restaurant sits in a 17th-century cellar, with beautiful vaulted ceilings and good-value lunches. Evening mains are mainly meaty and fishy local dishes, with a few nods to French fare.

ℹ Information

You'll find banks along Östra Storgatan.
Library (Dag Hammarskjölds plats 1; ⊘9am-7pm Mon-Fri, 11am-3pm Sat & Sun) Has internet access and a cafe. Adjacent to the Länsmuseum.
Tourist office (☑10 50 50; www.destina tionjonkoping.se, www.visit-smaland.com; ⊘9.30am-7pm Mon-Fri, to 3pm Sat & Sun mid-Jun–mid-Aug, 9.30am-6pm Mon-Fri, to 2pm Sat & Sun mid-Aug–mid-Sep & early Jun, 9.30am-6pm Mon-Fri, to 2pm Sat rest of year) In the Juneporten complex at the train station.

ℹ Getting There & Around

Jönköping airport (☑31 11 00) is located about 8km southwest of the town centre. **Skyways** (www.skyways.se) has daily flights to/from Stockholm Arlanda, and **SAS** (www.flysas.com) operates six flights weekly to/from Copenhagen. Bus 18 serves the airport, or else a taxi costs around Skr200.

Most local buses leave from opposite Juneporten on Västra Storgatan. Local transport is run by **Jönköpings Länstrafik** (www.jlt.se, in Swedish; Juneporten; ⊘7.30am-6pm Mon-Fri); there's an office with information, tickets and passes in Juneporten.

The long-distance bus station is next to the train station. There are at least eight daily **Swebus Express** (www.swebusexpress.com) services to Göteborg (Skr119, two hours) and Stockholm (Skr309, 4½ hours); at least three to Helsingborg (Skr269, three hours) and Malmö (Skr279, 4½ hours); and two to Karlstad (Skr269, four hours). **Bus4You** (www.bus4you. se, in Swedish) runs its Stockholm–Göteborg route via Jönköping several times daily. **Svenska Buss** (www.svenskabuss.se) also operates a

daily service each way between Göteborg and Stockholm.

Jönköping is on a regional train line; you'll need to change trains in either Nässjö or Falköping to get to or from larger towns. Train tickets can be purchased through **Tågkompani-et** (www.tagkompaniet.se, in Swedish).
Taxi Jönköping (☑34 40 00; www.taxijonkop ing.se) is the local taxi company.

Gränna & Visingsö
☑0390

All that's missing from Gränna are Oompa-Loompas. The scent of sugar hangs over the village, and shops overflow with the village's trademark red-and-white peppermint rock (*polkagris*). It's a bit touristy, but the steep streets, lakeside location and excellent polar exhibition redeem the place.

Across the water and 6km west is peaceful Visingsö. Connected by frequent ferries and home to Sweden's largest oak forest, it's a great place to cycle and relax.

◉ Sights & Activities

GRÄNNA

Gränna Museum:
Andréexpedition Polarcenter   MUSEUM
(adult/child/senior Skr50/20/30; ⊘10am-6pm daily mid-May–Aug, to 4pm Sep–mid-May) In the same building as the tourist office, Gränna Museum: Andréexpedition Polarcenter describes the disastrous attempt of Salomon August Andrée to reach the North Pole by balloon in 1897. It's riveting stuff, particularly the poignant remnants of the expedition: cracked leather boots, monogrammed handkerchiefs, lucky amulets, and mustard paper to ward off those polar winds.

Several sweet-makers have kitchens where you can watch the town's trademark sweets being made. One is **Grenna Polkagriskokeri** (www.polkagris.com; Brahegatan 39), directly opposite the tourist office, which uses an authentic 19th-century recipe. You can also catch crispbread in the making at **Gränna Knäcke** (www.grannaknacke.se; Brahegatan 43).

Don't be put off by Andrée's ballooning tragedy; for Skr1995 per person you can take a one-hour scenic **hot-air balloon trip** (www.flyg-ballong.nu) over the area.

VISINGSÖ

Visingsö has a 17th-century **church**, **castle** and **aromatic herb garden**. An extensive

THE GÖTA CANAL

Not only is the Göta Canal Sweden's greatest civil-engineering feat, idling along it on a boat or cycling the towpaths is one of the best ways to soak up Gotland's gorgeous countryside.

The canal connects the North Sea with the Baltic Sea, and links the great lakes Vättern and Vänern. Its total length is 190km, although only around 87km is human-made – the rest is rivers and lakes. It was built between 1802 and 1832 by a burly team of some 60,000 soldiers, and provided a hugely valuable transport and trade link between Sweden's east and west coasts.

The canal has two sections: the eastern section from Mem (southeast of Norrköping) to Motala (north of Vadstena on Vättern); and the western section from Karlsborg (on Vättern) to Sjötorp (on the shores of Vänern). The system is then linked to the sea by the Trollhätte Canal, in Västergötland. Along these stretches of the canal are towpaths, used in earlier times by horses and oxen pulling barges. Nowadays they're the domain of walkers and cyclists, with the occasional canalside youth hostel breaking the journey.

Boat trips are obviously a favourite way to experience the canal. You can go on a four- or six-day cruise of its entire length, travelling from Stockholm to Göteborg (or vice versa) and stopping to enjoy the wayside attractions; see p352 for more information. Shorter, cheaper boat trips along sections of the canal are also available – any tourist office in the area should be able to give you the low-down. Staff can also fill you in on the range of canoeing, cycling or even horse-riding possibilities along certain parts.

A good website for ideas and inspiration is www.gotakanal.se.

network of footpaths and bicycle trails leads through tranquil woods.

The beautiful lakes of Bunn and Ören, and their dark forests, inspired local artist John Bauer to paint his trolls and magical pools (you can see his work at Jönköpings Länsmuseum, p232). From June to mid-August, you can take a **boat tour** (www.trolska.se; adult/under 12yr Skr160/80; ☑tours 12.30pm Sat & Sun Jun, daily Jul–mid-Aug) to the lakes, departing from Bunnströms badplats, 2.5km from Gränna.

🛏 Sleeping & Eating

GRÄNNA

The tourist office arranges private rooms from Skr140 to Skr250 per person per night (plus Skr100 booking fee). For a choice of food in a great waterside setting, head down to the harbour (1.5km) where restaurants peddle everything from Greek, French and Italian fare to Swedish dishes (most places are open in summer only).

TOP CHOICE **Hotell Västanå Slott** HOTEL €€
(☑107 00; www.vastanaslott.se; d from Skr1490; ☑May-Dec; P) This stately manor house, about 6km south of town, is perfect for regal relaxation. Count Per Brahe owned it in the 17th century, although today it's decorated according to its 18th-century past, with chandeliers, brooding oil paintings and

suits of armour. Some rooms even have copper bathtubs. Woods around the castle are ideal for hikers and there is a golf course next door.

Hotel Amalias Hus BOUTIQUE HOTEL €€€
(☑413 23; www.amaliashus.se; s/d from Skr1350/1690; P@) Once owed by Amalia Eriksson, the creator of Granna's famous peppermint rock, this hotel boasts quaint rooms, done up with antique furniture, old-fashioned wallpaper and lace drapes, that make the most of the building's 18th-century quirks. You can even stay in what was once Amalia's kitchen!

Gyllene Uttern HOTEL €€
(☑108 00; www.gylleneuttern.se; s/d from Skr940/1255; P@) South of town is imposing Gyllene Uttern, an elegant hotel off the E4. Rooms are simple but masterful, views across the lake excellent and there are good-value packages including a 'Romantic' weekend option.

Strandterrassens Vandrarhem HOSTEL €
(☑418 40; www.strandterrassen.se; Hamnen; dm Skr250; P) Right beside **Grännastrandens Camping** (www.grannacamping.se; sites from Skr180, ☑Apr–mid-Oct), this hostel offers simple, bright, clean rooms in long wooden cabins, as well as a cafe.

THE SOUTHEAST & GOTLAND GRÄNNA & VISINGSÖ

Fiket   BAKERY €

(Brahegatan 57) The pick of Gränna's eateries is this time-warp bakery-cafe, complete with retro jukebox, chequered floor and record-clad walls. Tackle tasty grilled baguettes, quiches, salads and drool-worthy pastries, either indoors or on the breezy balcony.

VISINGSÖ

STF Vandrarhem Visingsö   HOSTEL €

(☑401 91; www.visingso-vandrarhem.se; dm/s/d per person Skr190/250/200, breakfast Skr75; ⊙May-Oct) This hostel, located in three buildings, with a separate kitchen-shower block, lies in an oak wood around 3km from the ferry pier.

Visingsö Värdshus   EUROPEAN €€

(☑404 96; www.vardshusetvisingso.se; mains Skr85-175; ⊙May-Aug) Expect simple meals such as grilled chicken, salads, burgers and baked potatoes at this rustic place in the woods. The speciality is fish from Vättern. It also runs a B&B (double Skr450 per person).

🍽 **Restaurant Solbacken**   ORGANIC €€

(www.restaurang-solbacken.se; mains Skr90-220; ⊙May-Aug) Local fish also find themselves on the menu at this lively restaurant, pub and pizzeria at Visingsö harbour. The fish is smoked at the owners' own farm and the kitchen is certified by Sweden's organic and sustainability label Krav.

❶ Information

Brahegatan, the main street of Gränna, has a bank and an ATM.

Gränna tourist office (☑036-10 38 60; www.grm.se; Grenna Kulturgård, Brahegatan 38; ⊙10am-6pm daily mid-May–Aug, to 4pm Sep–mid-May) In the same building as the library and Gränna Museum.

Library (Grenna Kulturgård, Brahegatan 38; ⊙10am-7pm Mon-Thu, to 1pm Fri) Free internet (bring ID). Upstairs from the Gränna tourist office.

Visingsö tourist office (☑036-10 38 89; www.visingso.net; ⊙10am-5pm daily May-Aug, to 7pm late Jun–mid-Aug, 11am-6pm Mon, 8am-2pm Tue-Fri Sep-Apr) At the harbour. Offers bicycle hire (per three hours/day Skr50/80).

❶ Getting There & Around

Local bus 101 runs hourly from Jönköping to Gränna (Skr65, one hour). Bus 120 runs several times Monday to Friday from Gränna to the mainline train station in Tranås (Skr65, one hour). Daily Swebus Express destinations include Göteborg, Jönköping, Linköping, Norrköping and Stockholm. Swebus Express services stop 3km outside Gränna. Catch bus 121 into town or walk (30 minutes).

The Gränna–Visingsö **ferry** (☑410 25) runs half-hourly in summer (less frequently the rest of the year). Return tickets for foot passengers are Skr50 per adult, and Skr25 for those aged between six and 15 years; a bicycle is Skr30 and a car with up to five passengers is Skr230.

Eksjö

☑0381 / POP 16,440

Eskjö is one of the most exquisitely preserved wooden towns in Sweden. The area south of Stora Torget was razed to the ground in a blaze in 1856, paving the way for beautiful neoclassical buildings. To the north of the square, buildings date back to the 17th century. Both sides will have you swooning over the jumble of candy-coloured houses and flower-filled courtyards.

⊙ Sights

Fornminnesgårdens Museum   MUSEUM

(Arendt Byggmästares gatan 22; admission Skr10; ⊙11am-5pm Mon-Sat mid-Jun–mid-Aug) Stroll through the town's delightful streets and yards, especially those north of Stora Torget. Check out the buildings at Fornminnesgårdens Museum; some were built in the 1620s. Exhibits chart the history of the area from the Stone Age to modern times.

Eksjö Museum   MUSEUM

(Österlånggatan 31; admission Skr50; ⊙11am-6pm Mon-Fri, 11am-3pm Sat & Sun Jul & Aug, 1-5pm Tue-Fri, to 3pm Sat & Sun Sep-Jun) Award-winning Eksjö Museum tells the town's story from the 15th century onward. The top floor is devoted to local Albert Engström (1869–1940), renowned for his burlesque, satirical cartoons. Eksjö was once known as the 'Hussar Town', and the region's long-standing military connections are also explored at the museum. The town hosts a **tattoo** (www.eksjotattoo.se) in early August, complete with plenty of military pomp and circumstance.

Aschanska Gården   HISTORIC BUILDING

(Norra Storgatan 18) Aschanska Gården is an evocative 19th-century bourgeois house with guided tours at 1pm and 4pm daily July and August (Skr 50), as well as Christmas tours in December (Skr 60).

Skurugata Nature Reserve
NATURE RESERVE

The Skurugata Nature Reserve, 13km north-east of Eksjö, is based around a peculiar 800m-long fissure in the rocks. Its sides tower to 56m, yet in places the fissure is only 7m wide. In times past, the ravine was believed to harbour trolls and thieves. The nearby hill of Skuruhatt (337m) offers impressive forest views. You'll need your own transport to get here.

Höglandsleden
HIKING, CYCLING

Try some berry picking or just enjoy woodland tranquillity on the well-maintained Höglandsleden (highland trail), which passes through the reserve; ask the tourist office for details of this walking trail and of the Höglandstrampen cycle route (laminated cycle cards cost Skr30).

🛏 Sleeping

TOP CHOICE Hotell Vaxblekaregården
B&B €€

(✆140 40; www.vaxblekaregarden.com; Arendt Byggmästares gata 8; s/d Skr750/1095; @) Set in a converted 17th-century wax-bleaching workshop, this boutique number features stylish, pared-back rooms with wooden floorboards, Carl Larsson–inspired wallpaper and wrought-iron bedheads. The lounge-laced backyard hosts barbecues and live-music gigs on Saturday evenings from mid-June to mid-August.

SSTF Vandrarhem Eksjö
HOSTEL €

(✆361 70; vandrarhem@eksjo.se; Österlånggatan 31; dm/s/d per person Skr210/310/245) In the heart of the old town, this hostel was named Sweden's greenest vandrarhem (hostel) in 2010. It is based in a supremely quaint wooden building, with a gallery running round the upper floor. Reception is at the tourist office.

Eksjö Camping
CAMPGROUND €

(✆395 00; www.eksjocamping.se; sites Skr150, 2-/4-bed cabins from Skr300/450) This friendly nook by picturesque Husnäsen, about a kilometre east of town, has a restaurant and cafe, plus minigolf and good swimming. There's also a hostel (dorm beds Skr300).

🍴 Eating & Drinking

Lennarts Konditori
BAKERY €

(Stora Torget) With an outdoor terrace and views of dramatic Stora Torget, the place to go for cakes, crêpes and quiche is this old-school konditori (bakery-cafe).

Keskin's
GREEK €

(Norra Storgatan 57; pizzas Skr69-85, à la carte dishes Skr75-195) Known for its Greek specialities, as well as hearty pastas and thin-crust pizza.

Lilla Caféet
CAFE €

(Norra Storgatan 24) Lovely cakes and coffee at this quaint little shop on Storgatan.

Hemköp
SUPERMARKET

(Österlånggatan) Located centrally.

Systembolaget
LIQUOR STORE

(Södra Storgatan 4) Also central.

ℹ Information

The tourist office (✆361 70; www.visiteksjo.se; Norra Storgatan 29; ⊙8am-8pm daily Jul–mid-Aug, 10am-6pm Mon-Fri, 10am-2pm Sat rest of year) can arrange English-language guided town tours or audio guides for Skr45 or Skr40, respectively, from Monday to Saturday from late June to early August. The hire of bicycles (Skr60/225 per day/week) and two-person tandems (Skr90/250) is also available.

ℹ Getting There & Around

The bus and train stations are in the southern part of town. The tiny länståg (regional train) runs up to seven times daily to/from Jönköping. Local buses run to Nässjö (Skr35, hourly to 6pm, then less frequently Monday to Friday, three to four at weekends). Swebus Express runs one bus daily from Jönköping to Eksjö.

Växjö
✆0470 / POP 82,000

A venerable old market town, Växjö (vak-choo, with the 'ch' sound pronounced as in the Scottish 'loch'), in Kronobergs län, is an important stop for Americans seeking their Swedish roots. In mid-August, Karl Oscar Days (www.karloskardagarna.se) commemorates the mass 19th-century emigration from the area, and the Swedish-American of the year is chosen. The town's glass museum, packed with gorgeous works of art and plenty of history, is another highlight.

⊙ Sights & Activities

Smålands Museum
MUSEUM

(www.smalandsmuseum.se; Södra Järnvägsgatan 2; adult/under 19yr/student Skr50/free/20; ⊙10am-5pm Mon-Fri, 11am-5pm Sat & Sun Jun-Aug, closed Mon Sep-May) This museum has a truly stunning exhibition about Sweden's 500-year-old glass industry, with objects spanning medieval goblets to cutting-edge contemporary

Växjö

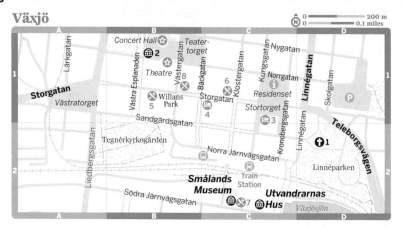

sculptures. It even houses a *Guinness World Records* collection of Swedish cheese-dish covers – 71 in total. There's a great cafe and the ticket price covers adjacent Utvandrarnas Hus.

Utvandrarnas Hus
MUSEUM

(Emigrant House; www.utvandrarnashus.se; Vilhelm Mobergs gata 4; adult/under 19yr/student Skr50/free/20; ⏰10am-5pm Mon-Fri, 11am-5pm Sat & Sun Jun-Aug, closed Mon Sep-May) Utvandrarnas Hus boasts engrossing displays on the emigration of over one million Swedes to America (1850–1930). It also includes a replica of Vilhelm Moberg's office and original manuscripts of his famous emigration novels. The centre also houses an excellent research

facility (open 10am to 4pm, Wednesday to Friday only, reservations required) for those tracing their Swedish ancestors (see p318).

FREE Växjö Konsthall
MUSEUM

(Västra Esplanaden 10; ⏰noon-6pm Tue-Fri, to 4pm Sat & Sun) Opposite the library, Växjö Konsthall showcases contemporary work by local and national artists; expect anything from minimalist ceramics to mixed-media installations.

Domkyrkan
CHURCH

(Cathedral; Linnégatan; ⏰9am-5pm) Looking like an ode to Pippi Longstocking, the bizarre Domkyrkan has been struck by lightning and repeatedly ravaged by fire – the latest renovation was in 1995. Waiting inside is a fine 15th-century altar and a whimsical contemporary sculpture by Erik Höglund. Don't miss the Viking rune stone in the eastern wall.

Kronobergs Slott
CASTLE

(⏰11am-7pm, to 9pm Fri & Sat; adult/under 19 yr Skr25/free) In 1542 Småland rebel Nils Dacke spent Christmas in Kronobergs Slott, now a ruin. The 14th-century castle is on a small island (reached by footbridge) in Helgasjön, about 8km north of the town. **Boat trips** (www.ryttmastaregarden.se; adult/6-12yr Skr150/75; ⏰Wed, Sat & Sun Jun–early Sep) on S/S *Thor*, Sweden's oldest steamship, built in 1887, leave from below the ruins. Take bus 1B from town.

Enquire at the tourist office about guided summer **walking tours** (⏰5.30pm Tue & Thu; Skr50) of town.

Sleeping

Elite Stadshotellet
HOTEL €€
(☎134 00; info@vaxjo.elite.se; Kungsgatan 6; s/d Skr850/1190; P@) Right on the Stortorget and beautifully renovated, this hotel couples crisply modern rooms with the glamour of a look-at-me 19th-century building. Single rooms aren't particularly roomy but all are smart and comfortable, and there's a slinky glassed-in restaurant-bar for urbane sipping and supping.

First Hotel Cardinal
HOTEL €€
(☎72 28 00; cc.cardinal@choice.se; Bäckgatan 10; s/d Skr790/990; P@) A jump up in quality, the central Cardinal offers simple, stylish rooms with Persian rugs and the odd antique touch. There's also a small fitness centre, a bar and a restaurant serving modern Nordic nosh.

Växjö Vandrarhem
HOSTEL €
(☎630 70; www.vaxjovandrarhem.nu; Evedalsvägen; s/d per person Skr380/250; P@) Located at the lakeside recreation area of Evedal, 6km north of the centre, this former spa hotel dates from the late 18th century. All rooms have washbasins, and there's a big kitchen, a laundry and a wonderful lounge in the attic. It's well loved, so book early.

Nearby Evedals Camping (www.evedalscamping.com; sites Skr225) is another pleasant option.

Eating & Drinking

TOP CHOICE PM & Vänner
EUROPEAN €€€
(www.pmrestauranger.se; Storgatan 24; mains Skr195-295; ☉closed Sun) A stylish bistro complete with black-and-white tiled floors and wicker chairs, PM & Vänner serves up new-school Swedish flavours with global twists. Local produce sparkles in dishes ranging from grilled cod with summer chanterelles to Småland veal. It also runs mouth-watering bakery Bröd & Sovel (Storgatan 12), down the street, and popular nightclub Loft & Terrassen (Västergatan 10).

Askelyckan
BAKERY €
(Storgatan 25) This traditional corner bakery-cafe is a top lunch spot, with sandwiches, baguettes, great pastries and a large shady courtyard.

Kult
CAFE €
(meals around Skr70) Smålands Museum's in-house cafe serves brilliant hot and cold gourmet sandwiches, pies, salads, soup, spuds and cakes. In summer, nibble blissfully in the cute courtyard.

Information

Pedestrianised Storgatan has banks and other services.

Library (Västra Esplanaden 7; ☉8am-7pm Mon-Thu, to 6pm Fri, 10am-3pm Sat May-Aug, 8am-8pm Mon-Thu, to 6pm Fri, 10am-4pm Sat, noon-4pm Sun rest of year) Free internet access.

Tourist office (☎73 32 80; www.turism.vaxjo.se; Residenset, Stortorget; ☉9.30am-6pm Mon-Fri, 10am-2pm Sat Jun-Aug, 9.30am-4.30pm Mon-Fri rest of year) On the main square.

Getting There & Away

Småland Airport (www.smalandairport.se) is 9km northwest of Växjö. **SAS** (www.flysas.com) has direct flights to Stockholm-Arlanda; **Fly Smaland** (www.flysmaland.com) to Stockholm, Berlin and Visby; and **Ryanair** (www.ryanair.com) to Düsseldorf Weeze. An airport bus (Flygbussen) connects with flights (Skr20); otherwise, take a **taxi** (☎135 00; from Skr220).

Länstrafiken Kronoberg (www.lanstrafikenkron.se) runs the regional bus network, with daily buses to Halmstad, Jönköping and Kosta. Long-distance buses depart beside the train station. **Svenska Buss** (www.svenskabuss.se) runs one or two services daily to Eksjö (Skr210, 1½ hours), Linköping (Skr280, 3¼ hours) and Stockholm (Skr370, 6½ hours).

Växjö is served by SJ trains running roughly hourly between Alvesta (on the main north–south line; Skr41 to Skr72, 15 minutes) and Kalmar (Skr121, 1¼ hours). A few trains run daily directly to Karlskrona (Skr118, 1½ hours), Malmö (Skr231, two hours) and Göteborg (Skr267, 3¼ hours).

Kalmar
☎0480 / POP 62,815

Not only is Kalmar dashing, it claims one of Sweden's most spectacular castles, with an interior even more perfect than its turreted outside. Other local assets include Sweden's largest gold hoard, from the 17th-century ship *Kronan* and the storybook cobbled streets of Gamla Stan (Old Town) to the west of Slottshotellet.

The Kalmar Union of 1397, when the crowns of Sweden, Denmark and Norway became one, was agreed to at the castle.

Kalmar

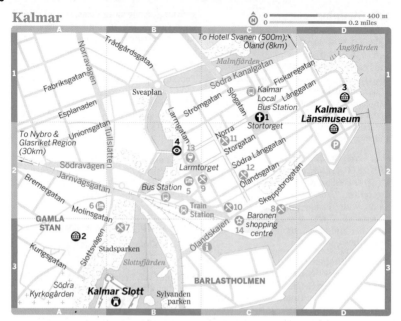

☉ Sights

Kalmar Slott
CASTLE

(www.kalmarslott.kalmar.se; adult/3-17yr/18-26yr Skr90/60/65; ☉10am-6pm daily Jul-mid-Aug, to 5pm end Aug, to 4pm May, Jun & Sep, shorter hours rest of year) Fairy-tale turrets, a drawbridge, a foul dungeon and secret passages...yes, Kalmar Slott has everything that a proper castle should. This powerful Renaissance building was once the most important in Sweden, and it's fortified accordingly. It also boasts one of the best-preserved interiors from the period.

King Erik's chamber is a real scene-stealer. Erik's rivalry with his brother Johan caused him to install a secret passage in the loo! There's also a superb suspended ceiling in the **Golden Hall**; eye-boggling wall-to-wall and floor-to-ceiling marquetry in the **Chequered Hall**; an elaborate **bed**, stolen as war booty then carefully vandalised so that no Danish ghosts could haunt it; and a delightful **chapel**, one of Sweden's Most Wanted for weddings.

For more information, join one of the **guided tours** (in English at 11.30am, 1.30pm & 2.30pm Jun–mid-Aug, 11.30am only mid-Aug–early Oct), included in the admission price. There are also children's activities here in summer.

Kalmar Länsmuseum
MUSEUM

(www.kalmarlansmuseum.se; Skeppsbrogatan 51; adult/under 18yr Skr80/60; ☉10am-5pm daily Jul-Aug, 10am-4pm Mon-Fri, 11am-4pm Sat & Sun Jun, Sep-Dec) The highlight of this fine museum, in an old steam mill by the harbour, are finds from the 17th-century flagship *Kronan*. The ship exploded and sank just before a battle in 1676, with the loss of almost 800 men. It was rediscovered in 1980, and over 30,000 wonderfully preserved items have been excavated so far, including a spectacular gold hoard, clothing and musical instruments.

Kalmar Sjöfartsmuseum
MUSEUM

(Södra Långgatan 81; adult/7-12yr Skr30/10; ☉11am-4pm daily mid-Jun–mid-Sep) Aft and slightly to port of the Kalmar Länsmuseum, Kalmar Sjöfartsmuseum houses an eccentric maritime collection, with bottled ships, foghorns and things made out of knots and armadillos.

Domkyrkan
CHURCH

(Cathedral; Stortorget; ☉8am-3.30pm Mon-Fri, to 6.30pm Wed, 9am-4pm Sat & Sun) Home to a spectacular pulpit, the baroque Domkyrkan was designed by Tessin, King Karl X Gustav's favourite architect. For the low-down, plug into one of the audiophones by the main door.

Kalmar

Krusenstiernska Gården GARDENS
(Stora Dammgatan 11; ⊙11am-6pm Mon-Fri, noon-5pm Sat & Sun Jun-Aug, closed Sat Jul, 11am-5pm Mon-Fri, noon-5pm May, 11am-4pm Mon-Fri Sep) Krusenstiernska Gården is a stuck-in-time 19th-century middle-class home, around 500m from the castle's entrance. **Tours** (adult/6-12yr Skr25/7) of the house are on the hour, but entry to the beautiful gardens and cafe is free.

Kalmar Konstmuseum MUSEUM
(www.kalmarkonstmuseum.se; Stadsparken; adult/under 20yr/senior Skr50/free/40; ⊙noon-5pm Tue & Thu-Sun, to 7pm Wed) The striking Kalmar Konstmuseum, in the park near the castle, dishes out brilliant temporary exhibitions featuring local and global art-scene 'It' kids.

Västerport GATE
Built in 1658, the craggy Västerport was the original point of entry into the city.

🛏 Sleeping

⎮TOP⎮ **Slottshotellet** HOTEL €€
(☑882 60; www.slottshotellet.se; Slottsvägen 7; s/d incl breakfast Skr695/1295; ℗@) Kalmar's top pick is this wonderfully romantic, cosy hotel, based in four buildings in a gorgeous green setting near the castle. Most rooms have antique furnishings and some even feature vintage Swedish tile stoves. Staff are wonderful, there's an on-site summer restaurant and delicious breakfast.

Frimurarehotellet HOTEL €€
(☑152 30; www.frimurarehotellet.com; Larmtorget 2; s/d Skr1290/1490; @) In the heart of the action, this hotel makes the most of a lovely 19th-century building, complete with polished wooden floors and a plant-filled lounge with complimentary tea, coffee and biscuits. Rooms are spacious if dully furnished and there is one cheaper room (Skr1250) with a hallway shower.

Hotell Svanen HOTEL €
(☑255 60; www.hotellsvanen.se; Rappegatan 1; dm Skr195, s/d from Skr385/490; ℗@) This 'low-price hotel' is an excellent choice, with simple, pleasing rooms with cable TV and private toilets. The SVIF hostel (see p341) is part of the hotel, sharing the all-day reception, kitchen, drinks machines and sauna. Svanen is on the island of Ängö, about 1km north of town; walk or take bus 402.

Stensö Camping CAMPGROUND €
(☑888 03; www.stensocamping.se; Stensövägen; sites/cabins Skr170/500; ⊙Apr-Oct; @) There are family-friendly facilities galore at this campsite, 3km southwest of town, including swimming; boat, canoe and bicycle rental; a restaurant; and minigolf. Buses 401 and 411 stop around 600m away.

✖ Eating & Drinking

Kalmar has plenty of good food and a variety of scenes to choose from, whether you want showy sailboats, a clear view of the castle or to people-watch on Larmtorget.

⎮TOP⎮ **Gröna Stugan** EUROPEAN €€
(www.gronastuganikalmar.se, in Swedish; Larmgatan 1; mains Skr165-290; ⊙5pm-11pm Mon-Sat, to 9pm Sun) Located in an unassuming, mint-green building complete with round windows reminiscent of a ship, this gem of a restaurant serves up dishes that are gorgeous on the plate and even better to eat. Leave space for dessert; the blueberry pancakes with raspberry panna cotta and syrup may have you begging the chef for the recipe.

Kullzenska Caféet CAFE €
(1st fl, Kaggensgatan 26; snacks from Skr30) Original tile stoves and antique furniture dot the eight genteel rooms of this appealing cafe.

THE SOUTHEAST & GOTLAND SMÅLAND

Located in a lovely building dating back to 1771, it's an especially comfortable place to settle down with a cup of coffee and slice of fruit crumble.

Calmar Hamnkrog
SEAFOOD €€

(www.calmarhamnkrog.se; Skeppsbrogatan 30; mains Skr149-285) With the main dining area jutting out over the water and sailboats within spitting distance, harbourside Hamnkrog is a pleasantly marine place to settle down for a meal. Its prodigious seafood dishes match the setting.

Restaurang Källaren Kronan
EUROPEAN €€

(www.kallarenkronan.com; Ölandsgatan 7; mains Skr135-275; ☻closed Mon) Six cellars have been transformed into a high-calibre experience, with meals served under a cosy vaulted ceiling. There's even a 1660s menu, with mains like salmon poached in wine with crayfish and root vegetables. Otherwise, the menu is replete with Swedish classics like meatballs and gravlax.

Ernesto in Totale
ITALIAN €€

(www.ernestokalmar.se; Södra Långgatan 5; mains Skr148-298; ☻lunch Sat & Sun, dinner Mon-Sun) Run by a real-deal Neapolitan, this Italian cafe, restaurant and bar attracts scores of people with its baristi, extensive menu (including Neapolitan-style pizzas) and well-mixed drinks.

Byttan
FRENCH €€

(www.byttan.nu; Stadsparken; Sunday brunch Skr119, mains Skr149-285) In the park by the castle, sassy resto-bar Byttan combines a chichi terrace with velour lounges and a crackling fire inside. The bistro-style menu ranges from grilled meats to salads, with a competent cocktail list to sex things up. There's live music in summer.

Krögers
PUB €€

(www.krogers.se; Larmtorget 7; mains Skr139-159) Enjoying an enviable location on a fountain-studded square, this restaurant has a great patio that is ideal for people-watching and enjoying summer concerts on Larmtorget. The menu is solid, pub-style fair that ranges from hamburgers to salmon fillet or the region's popular *toast skagen* with shrimp mayonnaise.

☆ Entertainment

Biostaden
CINEMA

(☑122 44) The Biostaden cinema is in the Baronen shopping centre on Skeppsbrogatan.

ℹ Information

You'll find banks and other services on Storgatan.

Library (Tullslätten 4; ☻9am-7pm Mon-Wed, from 10am Thu, 9am-6pm Fri, to 3pm Sat, closed Sun) Offers free internet access. Bring ID.

Tourist office (☑41 77 00; www.kalmar.com; Ölandskajen 9; ☻9am-9pm Mon-Fri, 10am-5pm Sat & Sun late Jun–mid-Aug, to 7pm Mon-Fri & to 4pm Sat rest of Jun & Aug, shorter hours rest of year) Handy for information on the region.

ℹ Getting There & Around

The **airport** (www.kalmarairport.se) is located 6km west of town. **SAS** (www.flysas.com) flies several times daily to Stockholm-Arlanda, while **Kalmarflyg** (www.kalmarflyg.se, in Swedish) flies to Stockholm Bromma and Prag. The Flygbuss airport bus (Skr40) provides connections to central Kalmar. A taxi to/from the airport costs about Skr150.

For bicycle hire, contact **Baltic Skeppsfournering** (☑106 00; www.balticskeppsfournering. se; Ölandskajen; per day/week Skr120/500; ☻Mon-Sat), directly across the street from the tourist office.

All regional and long-distance buses depart from the train station; local town buses have their own station on Östra Sjögatan. Regional buses are run by **Kalmar Länstrafik** (www. klt.se, in Swedish), and these include buses to Öland.

Roughly three **Swebus Express** (www. swebusexpress.com) services daily run north to Västervik (Skr189, two hours), Norrköping (Skr279, four hours) and Stockholm (Skr309, 6½ hours); and one to three services daily run south to Karlskrona (Skr59, 1¼ hours), Karlshamn (Skr99, two hours), Kristianstad (Skr159, three hours), Lund (Skr229, four hours) and Malmö (Skr219, 4½ hours).

Svenska Buss (www.svenskabuss.se) has four services per week on the same route; journey times and prices are similar. **Silverlinjen** (www. silverlinjen.se, in Swedish) runs one to three daily direct buses from Öland to Stockholm (Skr300), calling at Kalmar; reservations are essential.

SJ trains run every hour or two between Kalmar and Alvesta (Skr155 to Skr240, 1¼ hours), where you can connect with the main Stockholm–Malmö line and with trains to Göteborg. Trains run to Linköping up to nine times daily (Skr227, three hours), also with connections to Stockholm.

Taxi Kalmar (☑44 44 44) can help you get around town.

Glasriket

With its hypnotic glass-blowing workshops, the **'Kingdom of Crystal'** (www.glasriket.se) is Sweden's third-biggest drawcard after Stockholm and Göteborg. There are at least 11 glass factories (look for *glasbruk* signs), most with long histories: Kosta, for example, was founded in 1742. The region is also immensely popular with Americans tracing their ancestors, many of whom emigrated from this area at the end of the 19th century.

The glassworks have similar opening hours, usually 10am to 6pm Monday to Friday, 10am to 4pm Saturday and noon to 4pm Sunday. Expert glass designers produce some extraordinary avant-garde pieces, often with a good dollop of Swedish wit involved. Factory outlets have substantial discounts on seconds (around 30% to 40% off), and larger places can arrange shipping to your home country.

There's a Glasriket Pass (Skr95), allowing free admission into 'hot shops' and museums, and discounts on purchases and *hyttsill* parties; it's a good deal if you want to try glass-blowing, *hyttsill* and buy some pieces, but if you're just browsing, skip it.

Most of Glasriket is in Kalmar *län*, with some in Kronobergs *län;* all parts are covered in this section.

❶ Getting There & Around

Apart from the main routes, bus services around the area are practically nonexistent. The easiest way to explore is with your own transport (beware of elk). Bicycle tours on the unsurfaced country roads are excellent; there are plenty of hostels, and you can camp almost anywhere except near the military area on the Kosta–Orrefors road.

Kalmar Länstrafik's bus 139 runs from mid-June to mid-August only and calls at a few of the glass factories. The service operates four times per day on weekdays, once on Saturday, and runs from Nybro to Orrefors and Målerås. Year-round bus services connect Nybro and Orrefors (up to nine weekdays), and Kosta is served by regular bus 218 from Växjö (two or three daily).

Buses and trains run from Emmaboda to Nybro and Kalmar (roughly hourly); trains also run to Karlskrona, Växjö and Alvesta, from where there are direct services to Göteborg and Stockholm.

KOSTA
☑ 0478

Kosta is where Glasriket started in 1742. Today the **Kosta Boda** (www.kostaboda.com) complex pulls in coachloads of visitors, who raid the vast discount outlets. It's touristy, but the Kosta Boda Art Hotel, exhibition gallery and great cafes make it a good base for exploration. There are plenty of glass-blowing demos in the old factory quarters, and a **tourist office** (☑507 05; ☺9.30am-5.30pm Mon-Fri, 10am-5pm Sat, 11am-5pm Sun).

For a close encounter with a beautiful bandy-legged elk, head for **Grönåsens Älgpark** (www.moosepark.net; admission Skr50; ☺10am-6pm daily Apr–mid-Sep, to 5pm mid-Sep–Oct), Sweden's biggest elk park, located 3km west of town towards Orrefors. You can admire these gentle creatures on a 1.3km walk in the forested enclosure (Skr40). Ironically, you can also buy elk sausages to roast on the outdoor barbecue or purchase an elk-skin baseball cap. And, talking of horror, don't miss the display in the building behind the shop: you'll drive 50% slower after you've seen the crumpled metal and lolling tongue...

Kosta Boda Art Hotel (☑348 30; www.kostabodaarthotel.se; Stora vägen 75; s/d

---

HYTTSILL PARTIES

Glassworks were once more than just a workplace – they were a community hub and an after-hours gathering spot for workers, hunters and vagrants. They were the place to go to keep warm on long winter evenings, tell stories, make music and enjoy the company of others. Naturally, good grub and drink were a vital part of these gatherings – strong aquavit (a potent, vodka-like spirit) was shared and food was cooked using the furnaces and cooling ovens. Today visitors to Glasriket can partake in *hyttsill* parties, schmoozing at long tables and munching on trad-style dishes such as salted herring, smoked sausage and the regional speciality *ostkaka* (cheesecake).

Parties cost Skr295 to Skr960 (under 10s are free), and include beer, soft drinks and coffee (aquavit costs extra). They're held almost daily from June to August at the larger glassworks of Kosta, Målerås and Pukeberg. Contact the regional tourist offices, the glassworks themselves or book online (www.glasriket.se).

DON'T MISS

A CULTURAL BLOW-OUT

Feel inspired by Glasriket's top designers? If so, have a go at **glass-blowing** (Skr195; ☺mid-Jun–mid-Aug). Several hotshots – Orrefors, Kosta, Pukeberg and Johansfors – allow you to blow, shape and 'open out' the treacly molten glass yourself. It's great fun and careful guidance ensures you'll end up with a vase or bowl to enjoy for years to come. Your masterpiece has to cool for two hours before you can take it away.

Skr1100/1750; P@), made with 100 tonnes of glass, is worth a detour in and of itself. In-house assets include a designer glass bar and stunning pool, and each of the 102 rooms features glasswork and textiles by Kosta Boda artists. Even if you don't stay the night, drop in for the mouth-watering buffet lunch at the **Linnéa Art Restaurant** (Skr245). For the best prices check the hotel's website for package deals.

On the edge of Kosta village, the friendly **Kosta Bad & Camping** (☏505 17; www.glasriketkosta.se; sites/cabins Skr155/450; ☺Apr-Oct; ☏) includes a sauna, kids' pool and a shop.

Inside the factory's outlet store, the **Kosta Boda Art Café** serves tasty quiches and grilled sandwiches for around Skr55.

NYBRO
☏0481 / POP 19,640

Quiet Nybro has two lovely glassworks and was once a centre for hand-blown light bulbs (!).

Of the two glassworks, 130-year-old **Pukeberg** (www.pukeberg.se; Pukebergarnas väg), just southeast of the centre, is perhaps more interesting for its quaint setting. **Nybro** (www.nybro-glasbruk.se; Herkulesgatan) is smaller and laced with quirky items (think Elvis Presley glass platters).

There's a homestead museum, **Madesjö Hembygdsgård** (☺1-5pm daily mid-May–mid-Sep), about 2.5km west of town. Housed inside the 200m-long *kyrkstallarna* (former church stables), it contains an admirable collection, with cannonballs, clothing, coffins, carpenters tools, a classroom and a fantastic (ice-)cycle – and they're just the things beginning with 'C'.

Joelskogens Camping (☏450 86; www.laget.se/nybroifcamping; Grönvägen 51; sites/cabins Skr150/350; ☺May–mid-Sep) Campers should head for this little lakeside campsite just out of the centre, with basic facilities (a kitchen, laundry and shop) and a small beach.

The local STF hostel, **Nybro Lågprishotell & Vandrarhem** (☏109 32; www.nybrovandrarhem.se; Vasagatan 22; s/d Skr395/550; P), near Pukeberg, is clean and comfortable, though a little run-down. More-expensive 'hotel' rooms (Skr490/790) have cable TV, nonbunk beds and private showers and toilets. You can also rent bicycles.

The town's **tourist office** (www.nybro.se, in Swedish; Engshyttegatan 6; ☺7am-5pm Mon-Fri, 9am-2pm Sat, noon-6pm Sun mid-Jun–Aug, closed Sat rest of year) is at the train station. SJ trains between Alvesta and Kalmar stop here every hour or two. Regional bus 131 runs to/from Kalmar.

ORREFORS
☏0481

Established in 1898, **Orrefors** (www.orrefors.se; ☺year-round) is arguably the most famous of Sweden's glassworks. The huge site is home to a factory with glass-blowing demonstrations, plus a large shop and a shipping service. The ubersleek museum-gallery showcases a range of stunning glassworks spanning 1910 to the present day, as well as housing a stylish bar-cum-cafe **Kristallbaren** (sandwiches Skr60).

There is also an excellent hostel, **Vandrarhem Orrefors** (☏300 20; www.orreforsvandrarhem.se; Silversparregatan 14; s/d Skr350/420), conveniently located near the factory, which is a good choice for staying in the area if you want to avoid the bustle of Kosta. It boasts quaint red houses surrounding a grassy garden, and the peaceful rooms have proper beds. Breakfast is available on request (Skr50).

Opposite the hostel is the **Orrefors Bed & Breakfast** (☏301 30; www.bnb.nu; Silversparregatan 17; s/d Skr520/590; ☺Jun-Aug), which has simple yet comfortable rooms with shared facilities.

In the factory grounds, **Orrefors Värdshus** (meals around Skr95; ☺11.30am-4pm) is an inn that serves good lunches.

OTHER GLASSWORKS
☏0481

Don't miss the glassworks at Gullaskruv, about 6km northwest of Orrefors. Here, Uruguayan-born artist **Carlos R Pebaqué** (www.carlosartglass.com) creates extraordinary vases in his one glass oven.

The large and popular **Mats Jonasson factory** (www.matsjonasson.com), 8km further northwest in Målerås, features work by the famous glass-blower who is especially well known for his skilled glass-painting. The original glassworks was founded in 1890. There's also a restaurant for a postshopping refuel.

Increasingly attracting attention are glass-blowers Bertil Vallien at **Åfors** (☑342 74; Galleri Åfors) and Jan-Erik Ritzman and Sven-Åke Carlsson at **Transjö Hytta** (www.transjohytta.se).

A kilometre or so southeast of Gullaskruv, **Hälleberga Bed & Breakfast** (☑320 21; www.halleberga.se, in Swedish; Hälleberga 108; s/d incl breakfast Skr350/650; **P**), a youth hostel-turned-B&B, boasts a tranquil rustic setting. Rooms all have washbasins, and linen is included in the price.

Handy for the Mats Jonasson glassworks, **Malerås Vandrarhem** (☑311 75; http://maleras.eu; Lindvägen 5, Målerås; s/d per person Skr220/200; **P**), an SVIF hostel, is another cheap, simple option.

Oskarshamn

☑0491 / POP 26.300

Oskarshamn is useful for its regular boat connections with Gotland, with a few sights to help kill time.

Sights

Döderhultarmuseet   MUSEUM
(adult/child/senior Skr50/free/35; ☺9am-6pm Mon-Fri, 10am-4pm Sat & Sun Jun-Aug, 9am-4.30pm Mon-Fri, 10am-2pm Sat rest of year) Upstairs in Kulturhuset, Döderhultarmuseet features around 200 works by home-grown artist Axel Petersson 'Döderhultarn' (1868–1925), who captured local characters and occasions in vigorous and funny woodcarvings. Also upstairs, with the same opening hours, **Sjöfartsmuséet** showcases local maritime exhibits. One admission price covers entry to both museums.

Blå Jungfrun National Park   NATURE RESERVE
Blå Jungfrun (Blue Maiden), a 1km-long granite island, is known as the 'Witches' Mountain' because, according to tradition, this is where they gather every Easter to meet the devil. The island is a nature reserve with fantastic scenery, gnarled trees, blue

hares and bird life, and the curious stone maze **Trojeborg**.

Between mid-June and August a local launch, **M/S Solkust** (www.solkustturer.se; adult/7-15yr Skr250/125), departs up to five times weekly (usually *not* Monday and Tuesday) from Brädholmskajen, the quay at the head of the harbour in Oskarshamn, allowing passengers 3½ hours to explore the island. Book online or contact the tourist office.

Sleeping & Eating

There's no outstanding eateries, but there are a couple of pleasant ones.

Vandrarhemmet Oscar   HOSTEL **€**
(☑158 00; www.forumoskarshamn.com; Södra Långgatan 15-17; hostel dm/s/d Skr180/305/410, hotel s/d Skr650/800; **P @**) This shiny hotel-hostel hybrid – located opposite the bus station and around the corner from the tourist office – is a convenient budget option. Rooms have TV, fans and bathrooms – only the kitchen for self-caterers gives it away as a hostel.

Orchidea Kulturcafe   CAFE **€**
(www.orchideakulturcafe.se; Kungsgatan 6; snacks from Skr45) One of Oskarshamn's better cafes, Orchidea serves up great coffee, cakes and sandwiches in a pleasantly airy, whitewashed room with views out onto Kungsgatan.

Steakhouse Oscar   STEAKHOUSE **€€**
(Lilla Torget; mains Skr99-269) This place serves steaks and Swedish fare, with a couple of vegetarian options.

Information

There are ATM machines at the Flanaden shopping centre.
Tourist office (☑881 88; www.oskarshamn.se; Hantverksgatan 18; ☺9am-6pm Mon-Fri, 10am-3pm Sat & Sun) Located in Kulturhuset, along with the library, which has free internet access.

Getting There & Away

Oskarshamn Airport (www.oskarshamnairport.se) is 12km north of town and **Skyways** (www.skyways.se) flies direct to Stockholm-Arlanda three times daily Monday to Friday.

Boats to Visby depart from the Gotland Ferry Terminal near the now-disused train station, daily in winter and twice daily in summer. The M/S *Solsund* **ferry** (www.olandsfarjan.se; adult/child Skr150/100) to Byxelkrok, Öland, departs twice daily in summer from the ferry terminal off Skeppsbron; see p250 for more information.

Long-distance bus services stop at the very central bus station. Regional bus services run up to six times daily from Oskarshamn to Kalmar (Skr76, 1½ hours) and Västervik (Skr68, one hour).

Swebus Express has four daily buses between Stockholm and Kalmar, calling in at Oskarshamn. The closest train station is in Berga, 25km west of town. Here, regional trains run from Linköping and Nässjö. Local buses connect Berga and Oskarshamn.

Västervik

📞 0490 / POP 36,460

Västervik is a bustling, picturesque coastal summer resort, with cute cobbled streets, buzzing nightlife, sandy beaches just east of town, and 5000 islands on the doorstep. Harried by the Danes in its early years, it bloomed into a major shipbuilding centre between the 17th and 19th centuries. Famous sons include former tennis player Stefan Edberg and ABBA's Björn Ulvaeus. Björn often returns in mid-July for **VisFestivalen** (www.visfestivalen.se), Västervik's famous folksong festival.

◎ Sights & Activities

Old Buildings HISTORIC BUILDING

Ask the tourist office for its town-walking brochure, which leads you round the best of Västervik's beautiful old buildings. **St Petri Kyrka** (Östra Kyrkogatan 67) is a dramatic mass of spires and buttresses, while the older, calmer **St Gertruds Kyrkan** (Västra Kyrkogatan) dates from 1433 and has taken lightning strikes and riots in its stride.

Nearby, **Aspagården** (Västra Kyrkogatan 9), dating from the 17th century, is the oldest wooden house in town. Other abodes from the 1740s can be seen at picture-perfect **Båtmansstugorna** (Båtmansgatan) – former ferrymen's cottages.

Västerviks Museum MUSEUM

(www.vasterviksmuseum.se; Kulbacken; adult/under 18yr Skr40/free; ◎11am-4pm Mon-Fri, 1-4pm Sat & Sun Jun-Aug, closed Sat rest of year) Displays at this museum, just north of the tourist office, cover the town's history. You'll also find **Unos Torn**, an 18m-high lookout tower with archipelago views, here.

Live in Nature ROCK CLIMBING, HORSEBACK RIDING

(www.liveinnature.se; Kallernäs gård) Live in Nature organises rock-climbing and horse-riding trips on Icelandic ponies out of a farm south of Västervik.

M/S Loftahammar BOAT TOUR

(adult/child Skr180/90) Archipelago tours depart from Skeppsbron daily from mid-June to the end of August. Contact the tourist office for information and tickets, or buy tickets directly at the Skärgårdsterminalen pier kiosk (www.skargardstrafik.se, in Swedish).

For a full day of touring on the archipelago, bikes can be rented on the island of Hasselö and from Handelsboa at **Hasselö Sand** (www.hasselo.com; adult/child Skr75/50). A **taxiboat** (📞910 19; www.solido.se) runs Monday, Wednesday and Friday out to both Hasselö and Sladö in the summer.

🛏 Sleeping

The town bursts at the seams in summer, so book your accommodation ahead.

Västerviks Stadshotell HOTEL €€

(📞820 00; www.stadshotellet.nu; Storgatan 3; s/d Skr950/1035; 🅿@) Right in the middle of things, Stadshotell flaunts modern, comfortable rooms, a sauna, jacuzzi and gym, and private parking.

Akrells i Båtmansgränd HISTORIC HOTEL €

(📞317 67, 194 03; Strömsgatan 42; cottages per person Skr400) While they're a little rundown, there is something to be said for spending a night in one of these 18th-century fishermen's cottages, located in the atmospheric old part of town. Most sleep four and have their own kitchen, though bathrooms are shared.

Lysingsbadets HOSTEL €

(📞25 8000; www.lysingsbadet.se; low-/high-season sites Skr200/325, hostel beds per person Skr135/170, cabins from Skr195/405; 🅿🏊) This huge, five-star 'holiday village' by the sea (2.5km southeast of town) features a restaurant, golf, a swimming pool, beaches, and boat, bicycle and kayak hire, as well as extra activities like pony trekking. The hostel opens June to August, but cabins and hotel rooms are available year-round.

✕ Eating & Drinking

Västervik's fast-food speciality is French fries, mashed potato and shrimp salad (Skr25); look out for it at stands along the waterside.

Waterside Fiskaretorget is a hive of activity, studded with several restaurant-bars that have popular summer terraces.

The Systembolaget is on Kvarngatan.

Västervik

lamps and the odd elk head crank up the eccentricity.

ℹ Information

At the time of writing, the **tourist office** (☎25 40 40; www.vastervik.com; Strömsholmen; ⊙9am-7pm Mon-Fri, 10am-5pm Sat & Sun Jul–mid-Aug, 10am-6pm Mon-Fri, 10am-3pm Sat & Sun Jun & late Aug, shorter hours rest of year) had premises in the town hall on Stortorget. It's due to return to its normal location, a striking old art-nouveau bathhouse, on an islet linked by road to the town centre.

Library (Spötorget; ⊙ 10am-7pm Mon-Thur, to 5pm Fri, to 2pm Sat, closed Sat in summer) Free internet access.

ℹ Getting There & Away

Long-distance buses stop outside the train station, at the eastern edge of the town centre. Trains run between Västervik and Linköping up to 10 times daily (Skr136, 1¾ hours). Daily bus services run roughly every hour to 90 minutes to Vimmerby (Skr60, one hour), and every two hours to Oskarshamn (Skr68, one hour) and Kalmar (Skr92, 2¾ hours).

Svenska Buss runs to Stockholm, Kalmar, Karlskrona and Malmö four times per week. Swebus Express runs a Västervik–Vimmerby–Eksjö–Jönköping–Göteborg route.

TOP CHOICE Saltmagasinet   ORGANIC €€€
(www.saltmagasinet.se; Kulbaken; mains Skr250-345; ⊙lunch 11.30am-3pm, dinner from 5pm Mon-Sat) Located on the same hill as the Unos Torn, Saltmagasinet boasts great views and was named the city's best restaurant for four years running in the *White Guide,* Sweden's food bible. It's also among the top 10 best places in Sweden to enjoy organic and fair-trade cuisine. Smoked fish, beet soup, lamb; everything is beautifully presented and prepared. It also runs a brilliant bakery, located in the same building as the restaurant.

Restaurang Smugglaren   EUROPEAN €€€
(www.smugglaren.se; Smugglaregränd 1; mains Skr250-345; ⊙from 6pm Mon-Sat) In a cosy wooden building tucked down an alley off Strandvägen, Smugglaren dresses up Swedish classics such as beef with lingonberries or salmon tournedos. Model ships, paraffin

Vimmerby

☎0492 / POP 15,600

Vimmerby is the birthplace of Astrid Lindgren, and home to one of Sweden's favourite drawcards – a theme park based on the Pippi Longstocking books. Almost everything in town revolves around the strongest girl in the world – there's little escape!

Sights & Activities

Astrid Lindgrens Värld   AMUSEMENT PARK
(www.alv.se; adult/3-12yr/family Jun-Aug Skr335/225/1065, rest of year Skr150/10/415; ☺10am-6pm daily Jun-Aug, to 5pm Sat & Sun Sep, full hours on website) Young children and Pippi Longstocking aficionados shouldn't miss Astrid Lindgrens Värld, on the northern edge of town. Actresses dressed as Pippi (complete with gravity-defying pigtails) sing and dance their way around the 100 buildings and settings from the books. Prices drop outside peak season, as there are fewer activities and theatre performances. Cars are charged a cheeky Skr30. The theme park is a 15-minute walk from central Vimmerby.

There's a reasonably priced restaurant, a fast-food joint and coffee shops in the park. Dedicated fans can crash at the on-site camping ground.

Astrid Lindgrens Näs   CULTURAL BUILDING
(☑ 76 94 00; www.astridlindgrensnas.se; Prästgården 24; adult/6-14yr Skr80/50; ☺10am-8pm daily early Aug, to 6pm Jun, Jul & mid-Aug–Sep, to 4pm May, 11am-3pm Wed-Sat rest of year) Nearby you'll find Astrid Lindgrens Näs, a fascinating cultural centre set on the farm on which Lindgren grew up. There's a permanent exhibition about the writer's life – 'I write to still the child in myself' – and temporary exhibitions inspired by Lindgren's stories and legacy. The true highlight, however, is the 30-minute guided tour (adult/child Skr95/50; ☺daily in summer, by appointment only rest of year) of Lindgren's childhood home, which she faithfully restored in the 1960s. Guides bring the place to life with entertaining anecdotes, which you can ponder over a decent coffee and a book at the centre's mod-chic cafe and gift shop. Call for tour times.

When you've reached ginger-plait overload, wander down Storgatan for a fix of quaint 18th- and 19th-century wooden abodes.

Museet Näktergalen   MUSEUM
(Sevedegatan 43; adult/child Skr20/10; ☺noon-5pm Mon-Fri, 11am-2pm Sat mid-Jun–mid-Aug, noon-4pm Wed-Fri, 11am-2pm Sat mid-Aug–Sep) Another option is Museet Näktergalen, a petite 18th-century house with traditionally painted walls and ceilings.

Sleeping & Eating

There's lots of accommodation in town, much of it offering theme-park packages; ask the tourist office for details.

Vimmerby Stadshotell   HOTEL €€
(☑121 00; www.vimmerbystadshotell.se; Stora Torget 9; s/d Skr1195/1395; P @) You can't miss this dashing pink building on the town square. Rooms aren't as grand as the exterior implies, but they're comfortable, with cable TV and minibars. Staff are friendly and the in-house restaurant serves some of the better food in town and has a nice view out over the square.

Vimmerby Vandrarhem   HOSTEL €
(☑100 20; www.vimmerbyvandrarhem.nu; Järnvägsallén 2; r from Skr470; P @) This cheerful hostel, based in a fine wooden building, is right near the train station. There are more-expensive doubles available, with proper (nonbunk) beds, plus a garden that has a barbecue.

Camping Ground   CAMPGROUND €
(☑798 11; sites/4-bed cabins from Skr360/1745; ☺mid-May–Aug) For those who are visiting the theme park, these sites and cabins are conveniently located on the premises.

Konditori Brödstugan   BAKERY €
(Storgatan 42; meals around Skr65) One very busy lunch spot is this bakery-cafe, with a wide choice of quiches, salads, baked potatoes and hot dishes.

Information

Facing Stora Torget is Vimmerby's helpful **tourist office** (☑310 10; www.vimmerbyturistbyra.se; Rådhuset 1, Stångågatan 29; ☺9am-8pm daily late Jun–mid-Aug, to 6pm Mon-Fri, to 2pm Sat & Sun late Jun & end Aug, shorter hours rest of year).

Getting There & Away

All bus and train services depart from the Resecentrum, downhill past the church from Stora Torget. Swebus Express runs to Eksjö, Jönköping and Göteborg, and in the other direction to Västervik (Skr70, 1¼ hours). Svenska Buss operates daily between Stockholm, Linköping and Vimmerby.

South of Vimmerby, bus services continue on to either Oskarshamn, Åseda, or Kalmar and Nybro.

Trains run several times daily south to Kalmar and north to Linköping.

ÖLAND

📞 0485 / POP 25,000

Like a deranged vision of Don Quixote, Öland is *covered* in old wooden windmills. Symbols of power and wealth in the mid-18th century, they were a must-have for every aspiring man about town and the death knell for many of Öland's oak forests. Today 400 or so remain, many lovingly restored by local windmill associations.

At 137km long and 16km wide, the island is Sweden's smallest province. Once a regal hunting ground, it's now a hugely popular summer destination for Swedes – the royal family still has a summer pad here. The island gets around two million visitors annually, mostly in July. Around 90% of them flock to the golden shores fringing the northern half of the island to bask and bathe. Behind the beaches, fairy-tale forests make for soulful wanders.

Öland

South of Färjestaden, the entire island is a Unesco World Heritage Site, lauded for its unique agricultural landscape, in continuous use from the Stone Age to today, and peppered with runic stones and ancient burial cairns.

There are surprisingly few hotels, but you can stay in innumerable private rooms (booked through the tourist offices), more than 25 campsites and at least a dozen hostels (book ahead). Camping between Midsummer and mid-August can cost up to Skr300 per site.

Locals like to think of the island as Sweden's Provence and food-linked walking tours and farmers markets abound. **Ölands Skördefest** (www.skordefest.nu), the island's three-day harvest festival in late September, is Sweden's biggest.

ℹ️ Information

The bridge from Kalmar lands you on the island just north of Färjestaden, where there's a well-stocked **tourist office** (☑89 00 00; www.olandsturist.se; ☺9am-7pm Mon-Fri, to 6pm Sat, to 5pm Sun Jul–mid-Aug, 9am-6pm Mon-Fri, to 5pm Sat, to 3pm Sun May & Jun, shorter hours rest of year, closed late Dec–early Jan) at the Träffpunkt Öland centre. Staff can book island accommodation (for a Skr195 booking fee), as well as organise themed packages, including cycling, spa and gourmet getaways. Model monks and ring forts illustrate the island's history in the Historium inside the tourist office, and there's a Naturum (in Swedish) for wildlife-spotters.

There's a smaller tourist office in Borgholm.

ℹ️ Getting There & Around

Bicycle

There are no bicycle lanes on the bridge between Öland and Kalmar, so cyclists should exercise caution! Bicycles aren't allowed on the bridge in summer – instead there's free Cykelbuss or Cykelfärje services to get you across (roughly hourly; enquire at the tourist office in Kalmar). If you fancy pedalling your way across Öland, check www.cyklapaoland.se for cycling routes and other handy information. **Bikeisland** (www.bikeisland.se) offers cycling packages and also food-linked walking tours.

The following shops hire out bicycles in summer for around Skr100 per day, or about Skr400 a week:

Byxelkroks Cykeluthyrning (☑070-579 61 00; Hamnkontoret, Byxelkrok)

Färjestadens Cykelaffär (☑300 74; www.cykelaffaren.se; Storgatan 67, Färjestaden)

Hallbergs Hojjar (☑109 40; Köpmangatan 19, Borgholm)

Boat

From mid-June to mid-August, **M/S Solsund** (www.olandsfarjan.se) sails twice daily from Byxelkrok (northwest Öland) and Oskarshamn (on the mainland 60km north of Kalmar). One-way tickets are Skr150/100 per adult/seven to 16 years. A car and up to five passengers costs Skr600, and a bicycle is free.

Bus

Silverlinjen (www.silverlinjen.se, in Swedish) runs one to two daily direct buses from Öland to Stockholm (adult/child Skr300/200 if booked online, 6½ hours), calling at Kalmar; reservations are essential.

Buses connect all the main towns on the island from Kalmar, and run every hour or two to Borgholm (Skr52, one hour) and Mörbylånga (Skr36, one hour). A few buses per day run to Byxelkrok and Grankullavik (both Skr92, around 2¼ hours), in the far north of the island, including bus 106. Services to the south are poor, with some improvement May to August.

Borgholm & Around

Öland's 'capital' and busiest town, Borgholm seeps a vaguely tacky air with its discount shops and summer hordes of teens on the pull. The most dramatic (and satisfying) sight is the enormous ruined castle on its outskirts. Be prepared for a bit of a traffic jam through town if you're visiting during the peak summer months.

⊙ Sights

Borgholms Slott CASTLE
(www.borgholmsslott.se; adult/12-17yr Skr70/40; ☺10am-6pm daily May-Aug, to 4pm Apr & Sep) Northern Europe's largest ruined castle, Borgholms Slott, looms just south of town. This epic limestone structure was burnt and abandoned early in the 18th century, after life as a dyeworks. There's a great museum inside and a nature reserve nearby, as well as summer concerts and children's activities.

Solliden Palace GARDENS
(www.sollidensslott.se; adult/7-17yr Skr75/45; ☺11am-6pm daily mid-May–mid-Sep, last entry 5pm) Sweden's most famous 'summer house', Solliden Palace, 2.5km south of the town centre, is still used by the Swedish royals. Its exceptional gardens are open to the public and are well worth a wander. The idyllic cafe

at the palace entrance is ideal for a post-garden break.

VIDA Museum & Konsthall   MUSEUM

(www.vidamuseum.com; adult/under 15yr Skr50/free; ☉10am-6pm daily Jul–early Aug, to 5pm May, Jun & early Aug-Sep, to 5pm Sat & Sun only Apr & Oct-Nov) VIDA Museum & Konsthall is a strikingly modern museum and art gallery in Halltorp, about 9km south of Borgholm. Its finest halls are devoted to two of Sweden's top glass designers.

Gärdslösa kyrka   CHURCH

(☉11am-5pm daily mid-May–mid-Sep) On the east coast, about 13km southeast of Borgholm, is Gärdslösa kyrka, the best-preserved medieval church (1138) on Öland, with reasonably intact wall and ceiling paintings.

🛏 Sleeping

The tourist office can help you find rooms around town.

Hotell Borgholm   HOTEL €€

(☏770 60; www.hotellborgholm.com; Trädgårds-gatan 15; s/d Skr1335/1535; ✱@) Cool grey hues, bold feature walls, pine wood floors and smart functionalist furniture make for stylish slumber at this urbane hotel. Rooms are spacious, with those on the top floor (Skr1885) being especially chic. Owner Karin Fransson is one of Sweden's top chefs, so a table at the restaurant here is best booked ahead (tasting menu Skr995).

Ebbas Vandrarhem
& Trädgårdscafé   HOSTEL €

(☏103 73; www.ebbas.se; Storgatan 12; s/d per person Skr350/260; ☉May-Sep) Right in the thick of things, Ebbas cafe has a small STF hostel above it. Five of the cosy lemon-yellow rooms overlook the gorgeous rose-laced garden, and four the bustling pedestrianised main street. There's a kitchen for self-caterers...or just pop downstairs for decent hot and cold grub (lunch Skr99), served until 9pm in summer (earlier at other times). Book ahead in summer.

Villa Sol   B&B €

(☏56 25 52; www.villasol.nu; Slottsgatan 30; s/d without bathroom from Skr450/800) Villa Sol has a super garden and small but thoughtfully decorated rooms, each with its own colour scheme. Prices exclude breakfast, but there is a guest kitchen. Rooms with private bathrooms cost around Skr150 extra.

Kapelludden Camping
& Stugor   CAMPGROUND €

(☏56 07 70; Sandgatan 27; www.kapelludden.se; sites from Skr365, 6-bed cabins Skr1250, weekly rental only in high season; @✉) Just near the tourist office, this beachside campsite is the handiest. It's a huge place (some 450 sites) and has five-star, family-oriented facilities, so expect it to be a bit rowdy in summer.

🍴 Eating & Drinking

Robinson Crusoe   EUROPEAN €€

(www.robinsoncrusoe.se; Hamnvägen; lunch Skr98, mains Skr158-268) Down by the harbour, Robinson Crusoe is ideal for getting away from the crowded summer chaos of Borgholm. The menu ranges from Öland flounder to rack of lamb. There is live music in summer.

Nya Conditoriet   BAKERY €

(Storgatan 28) This busy old-fashioned bakery-cafe serves yummy sandwiches and pastries.

ℹ Information

Tourist office (☏890 00; Storgatan 1; ☉9am-6pm Mon-Fri, to 5pm Sat, 10am-4pm Sun Jul, 9am-6pm Mon-Fri, 10am-4pm Sat late May–Jun, shorter hours rest of year) Located at the marina end of Storgatan.

Northern Öland

At Sandvik on the west coast, about 30km north of Borgholm, Sandvikskvarn (www.sandvikskvarn.se; mill entry adult/child Skr20/free; ☉noon-8pm daily May-Sep, to 10pm mid-Jun–mid-Aug) is a Dutch-style windmill built in 1856 and one of the largest in the world. In summer you can climb its seven storeys for good views across to the mainland. The rustic restaurant serves the local speciality, lufsa (baked pork and potato; Skr69), and there's an adjacent pizzeria (pizzas from Skr75) and minigolf.

Atmospheric Källa kyrka, at a little harbour about 36km northeast of Borgholm, off Rd 136, is a fine example of Öland's medieval fortified churches. The broken rune stone inside shows the Christian cross growing from the pagan tree of life.

Grankullavik, in the far north, has sandy beaches and summer crowds; Lyckesand is one of the island's best beaches and the strangely twisted trees and ancient barrows at the nearby Trollskogen (Trolls' Forest) nature reserve are well worth a visit. On the far north's western edge is the beautiful **Neptuni åkrar** nature reserve, famed for its spread of blue viper's bugoss flowers in early summer.

Neptuni Camping (☎284 95; www.neptunicamping.se; Småskogsvägen; sites Skr185, cabins from Skr400), a wild and grassy place, is handy for people jumping off the ferry in Byxelkrok, and has good amenities.

Kaffestugan (www.kaffestuganiboda.se; Böda; sandwiches Skr45-50, salads Skr60-80; ☺7am-6pm daily Jun-Aug, 8am-5pm Fri-Sun May-Sep), just north of the town church on the main road in tiny Böda, is a clued-up cafe that roasts its own fair-trade coffee and bakes everything from luscious berry tarts and vanilla-cream hearts to organic breads and cardamom rolls.

Lammet & Grisen (www.lammet.nu; Löttorp; ☺from 4.30pm) is pleasantly located out in the countryside 5km west of Löttorp. It's best known for its all-you-can-eat evenings (adult Skr329), with whole spit-roasted lamb and pork on the menu, plus live entertainment. The restaurant is particularly family friendly.

Central Öland

Fortresses, a zoo and a charming farm village are central Öland's star attractions. The largest settlement is Färjestaden (Ferry Town), where you'll find banks, services and a Systembolaget. The town lost its purpose in life after the bridge was built, although an effort has been made to rejuvenate the old jetty.

Ölands Djurpark (www.olandsdjurpark.com; admission Skr300; ☺10am-5pm daily mid-May–mid-Aug, 11am-4pm Apr–mid-May & mid-Aug–Oct) is a zoo, amusement park and water park favoured by families, just north of the bridge near the tourist office. Kids under 1m tall get in free.

The largest Iron Age ring fort in Sweden, **Gråborg** was built as the Roman Empire was crumbling. Its impressively monumental walls measure 640m around, even though much of the stonework was plundered for later housing. After falling into disuse, the fort sprang back to life around 1200, when the adjacent **St Knut's chapel** (now a ruin) was built. The Gråborg complex is about 8km east of Färjestaden, just off the Norra Möckleby road; you need your own transport to get there.

The vast **Ismantorp fortress**, with the remains of 88 houses and nine mysterious gates, is deep in the woods, about 20km northeast of Ölands Djurpark. Drive north to Rälla and take a right on Högsrumsvägen; keep following this road (it turns into Vedbygatan) for about 10km to reach the fortress. It's an undisturbed fortress ruin, illustrating how the village's tiny huts were encircled by the outer wall; Eketorp is an imaginative reconstruction of similar remains. The area, just south of the Ekerum–Långlöt road, can be visited at any time.

A 17km **hiking trail** leads from Gråborg to Ismantorp fortress.

The best open-air museum on Öland is **Himmelsberga** (www.himmelsbergamuseum.com; adult/5-15yr Skr60/20; ☺10am-5.30pm daily Jun–mid-Aug, 11am-5pm mid-end Aug, 11am-5pm Sat & Sun Sep), a farm village on the east coast at Långlöt. Its quaint cottages are fully furnished. There's hay in the mangers and slippers by the door; it's so convincing you'd swear the inhabitants just popped out for a minute. Extras include a petite cafe and quaint handicrafts shop.

STF Vandrarhem Ölands Skogsby (☎383 95; www.vandrarhskogsby.se; s/d per person Skr220/190; ☺mid-Apr–Sep; **P**) is a charming, low-fuss STF hostel based in a flowery old wooden house, 3km southeast of Färjestaden. It claims to be Sweden's oldest (opened in 1934) and is still managed by descendants of the original owner. The Färjestaden–Mörbylånga bus 103 (Skr25) runs past at least five times daily.

There are a few good eateries at the old jetty in Färjestaden, including **På Kaj4** (www.kaj4.se; Hamnplan 4; mains Skr139-225; ☺11.30am-midnight daily Jun-Aug, shorter hours rest of year), which serves down-to-earth food such as burgers and grilled chicken salad. Best of all, there's a large sunny terrace with appetising views over Kalmarsund.

Southern Öland

The southern half of the island has made it onto Unesco's World Heritage list. Its treeless, limestone landscape is hauntingly beautiful and littered with the relics of human settlement and conflict. Besides linear villages, Iron Age fortresses and tombs, this area is also a natural haven for plants and wildlife.

⊙ Sights & Activities

Stora Alvaret   NATURE RESERVE
Birds, insects and flowers populate the striking limestone plain of Stora Alvaret. Birdwatching is best in May and June, which is also when the Alvar's rock roses and rare orchids burst into bloom. The plain occupies most of the inland area of southern Öland, and can be crossed by road from Mörbylånga or Degerhamn.

Mysinge & Gettlinge   HISTORIC SITE
The ancient grave fields of Mysinge and Gettlinge, stretching for kilometres on the ridge alongside the main Mörbylånga–Degerhamn road, include burial sites and standing stones from the Stone Age to the late Iron Age. The biggest single monument is the Bronze Age tomb **Mysinge hög**, 4km east of Mörbylånga, from where there are views of almost the whole World Heritage Site.

Eketorp   ARCHAEOLOGICAL SITE
(☎66 20 00; www.eketorp.se, in Swedish; adult/6-14yr Skr110/60; ☉11am-5pm daily May-Jun & mid–end Aug, 10.30am-6pm Jul–mid-Aug) If you can't picture how the ring forts looked in their prime, take a trip to Eketorp. The site has been partly reconstructed to show what the fortified villages, which went in and out of use over the centuries, were like in medieval times. Children will love the scampering pigs, and the fort is particularly fun when there are re-enactment days – phone for details. Excavations at the site have revealed over 26,000 artefacts, including three tonnes of human bones; some of the finds are on display at the little **museum** inside. There's a free daily **tour** in English from late June to the end of August (11.15am, 1.15pm and 2.15pm). The fort is 6km northeast of Grönhögen; there are several buses (summer only) from Mörbylånga.

Gräsgårds Fiskehamn   HARBOUR
On the east coast, about 5km north of Eketorp, Gräsgårds Fiskehamn is a delightful little fishing harbour. A little further north, there's an 11th-century rune stone at **Seby**, and in **Segerstad** there are standing stones, stone circles and over 200 graves.

Öland's Southernmost Point   LANDMARK
Öland's southernmost point is a stark, striking spectacle of epic sky, sea and rock-strewn pastures. A nature reserve, almost surrounded by sea, it's justifiably popular with bird-watchers. There's a free **Naturum** (www.ottenby.se; ☉10am-6pm daily Jul–mid-Aug, 11am-5pm May, Jun & mid-Aug–Sep, 11am-4pm Apr, Oct & Nov, 11am-4pm Fri-Sun Mar), a great cafe-restaurant and, at 42m, Scandinavia's tallest lighthouse, **Långe Jan** (adult/7-15yr Skr30/10) to climb.

⊨ Sleeping & Eating

You'll find supermarkets in Mörbylånga.

Gammalsbygårdens Gästgiveri   B&B €€
(☎66 30 51; www.gammalsbygarden.se; s/d Skr700/900; ☉closed Christmas-Easter; P@) This country farmhouse sits on the hauntingly beautiful southeast coast, 5km north of Eketorp. The picture-perfect lounge is complemented by cheerful rooms with whitewashed walls and cosy floor heating. A couple have private balconies. The restaurant serves fish, venison, lamb and heavenly deserts. Booking ahead is essential.

Mörby Vandrarhem & Lågprishotell   HOSTEL €
(☎493 93; www.morbyhotell.se; Bruksgatan; hostel s/d Skr350/550, hotel s/d Skr650/850; ☉May-Aug; P@⊛) In the small village of Mörbylånga, this place has a mixture of hostel- and hotel-style accommodation. The big, anonymous building is a bit hospital-like, but there's a pool and plenty of space, with a park and beaches nearby, as well as bikes for hire.

Kajutan Hotell & Vandrarhem   HOTEL €
(☎408 10; www.hotellkajutan.se; hostel d Skr500, hotel s/d Skr890/1090) Kajutan is down by Mörbylånga harbour. Rooms are clean, if a bit dark and airless. There's a busy bar-restaurant for handy munching (mains Skr13 to 185); summer lunches, served in a sunny courtyard, are a particular hit.

GOTLAND

☎0498
Gorgeous Gotland has much to brag about: a Unesco-lauded capital, truffle-sprinkled woods, A-list dining hot spots, talented artisans and more hours of sunshine than anywhere else in Sweden. It's also one of the country's richest historical regions, with around 100 medieval churches and countless prehistoric sites, from stone ship settings and burial mounds to hilltop fortress remains. Information boards indicate sites along roadsides.

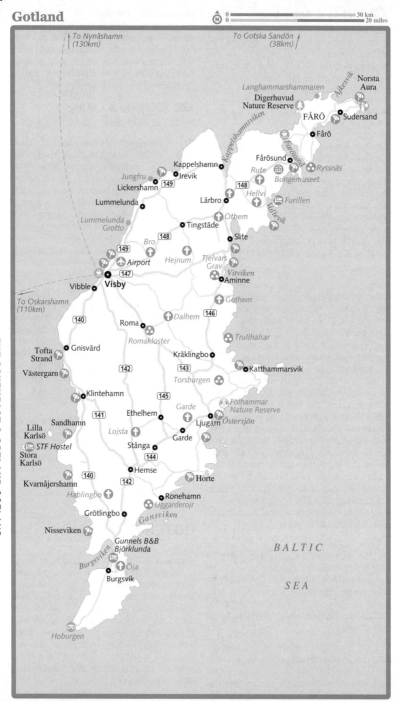

The island lies nearly halfway between Sweden and Latvia, in the middle of the Baltic Sea, roughly equidistant from the mainland ports of Nynäshamn and Oskarshamn. Just off its northeast tip lies the island of Fårö, most famous as the home of Sweden's directing great, the late Ingmar Bergman (see p262). The island national park of Gotska Sandön lies 38km further north, while the petite islets of Stora Karlsö and Lilla Karlsö sit just off the western coast.

Information on the island abounds; both www.gotland.net and www.guteinfo.com are good places to start.

Getting There & Away

Air

There are regular **Skyways** (www.skyways.se) flights between Visby and Stockholm's Arlanda and Bromma airports (up to three times a day for each airport). Flights between Stockholm and Visby generally cost from Skr492; click on the 'Low fare calendar' link on the website to check for the best prices.

The cheaper local airline is **Gotlands Flyg** (www.gotlandsflyg.se), with regular flights between Visby and Stockholm Bromma (one to eight times daily). Prices start at Skr338 one way; book early for discounts, and enquire about stand-by fares (adult/one to 25 years Skr608/408). Popular summer-only routes include Göteborg, Hamburg, Oslo and Helsingfors (Helsinki).

The island's **airport** (☎26 31 00) is 4km northeast of Visby. Catch a taxi into/from town (around Skr150) or there is an airport bus during summer.

Boat

Year-round car ferries between Visby and both Nynäshamn and Oskarshamn are operated by **Destination Gotland** (www.destinationgotland.se). There are departures from Nynäshamn one to six times daily (about three hours). From Oskarshamn, there are one or two daily departures in either direction (three to four hours).

Regular one-way adult tickets for the ferry start at Skr230, but from mid-June to mid-August there is a far more complicated fare system; some overnight, evening and early-morning sailings in the middle of the week have cheaper fares.

Transporting a bicycle costs Skr50; a car usually starts at Skr345, although, again, in the peak summer season a tiered price system operates. Booking a nonrefundable ticket, three weeks in advance, will save you money. If you're thinking of taking a car on the ferry between mid-June and mid-August, reserve a place well in advance.

Getting Around

There are over 1200km of roads in Gotland, typically running from village to village through picture-perfect landscapes. Cycling on the quiet roads is heavenly, and bikes can be hired from a number of places in Visby. The forested belt south and east of Visby is useful if you bring a tent and want to take advantage of the liberal camping laws.

Many travel agents and bike-rental places on the island also rent out camping equipment. In Visby, hire bikes from Skr85 per 24 hours at **Gotlands Cykeluthyrning** (☎21 41 33), behind the tourist office on the harbour. It also rents tents (Skr100/500 per day/week), or for Skr280 per day (Skr1400 per week) you can hire the 'camping package': two bikes (or one tandem bike), a tent, a camping stove and two sleeping mats. **Gotlands Resor** (☎20 12 60; www.gotlandsresor.se; Färjeleden 3) offers similar packages.

Kollektiv Trafiken (☎21 41 12) runs buses via most villages to all corners of the island. The most useful routes, which have connections up to seven times daily, operate between Visby and Burgsvik in the far south, Visby and Fårösund in the north (also with bus connections on Fårö), and Visby and Klintehamn. A one-way ticket will not cost you more than Skr68 (although if you take a bike on board it will cost an additional Skr40), but enthusiasts will find a monthly ticket good value at Skr675.

A few companies and service stations offer car hire. **Avis** (☎21 98 10; www.avisworld.com; Donners Plats 2) in central Visby or **Europcar** (☎21 50 10; www.europcar.com; Visby flygplats) at the airport offer rentals starting from Skr654.

Visby

POP 22,240

The port town of Visby is medieval eye candy and enough in itself to warrant a trip to Gotland. Inside its thick city walls await twisting cobbled streets, fairy-tale wooden cottages, evocative ruins and steep hills with impromptu Baltic views. The city wall, with its 40-plus towers and the spectacular church ruins within, attest to the town's former Hanseatic glories.

A Unesco World Heritage Site, Visby swarms with holidaymakers in summer, and from mid-June to mid-August cars are banned in the old town. For many, the highlight of the season is the costumes, performances, crafts, markets and re-enactments of **Medeltidsveckan** (Medieval Week; www.medeltidsveckan.com), held during the first or second week of August. Finding

Visby

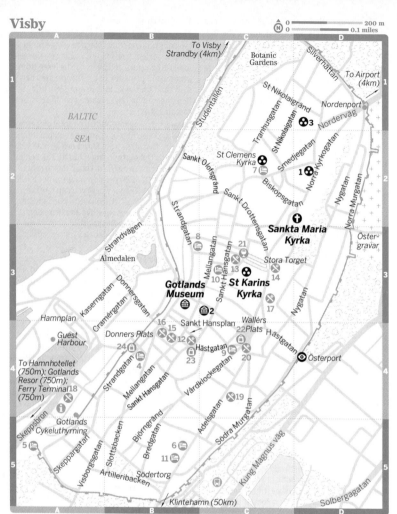

accommodation during this time is almost impossible unless you've booked ahead.

☉ Sights & Activities

The town is a noble sight, with its 13th-century wall of 40 towers – savour it for a few hours while walking around the perimeter (3.5km). Also take time to stroll around the Botanic Gardens and the narrow roads and scandalously cute lanes just south of the gardens. Pick up a copy of the booklet *Visby on Your Own* (Skr40, available at the tourist office), which will guide you around

the town and give you interesting snippets of local history.

In summer the tourist office also organises guided walking tours of the town (adult/child Skr110/65), with English-language walks up to four times a week.

Medieval Churches CHURCH
St Karins Kyrka on Stora Torget is one of the most stunning of Visby's medieval churches (there are 10 within the city's walls). The church has a beautiful Gothic interior and was founded by Franciscans in 1233. The church was extended in the early

Visby

14th century, but the monastery was closed by the Reformation and the church fell into disrepair. Other ruins include **St Nicolai Kyrka**, built in 1230 by Dominican monks. The monastery was burned down when Lübeckers attacked Visby in 1525. The **Helge And Kyrka** ruin is the only stone-built octagonal church in Sweden, built in 1200, possibly by the Bishop of Riga; the roof collapsed after a fire in 1611.

Sankta Maria kyrka CHURCH

(Cathedral of St Maria; www.visbydf.se; ⊙9am-9pm daily Jul-Aug, to 5pm rest of year) The ruins contrast with the stoic Sankta Maria kykra. Built in the late 12th and early 13th centuries and heavily touched up over the centuries, its whimsical towers are topped by baroque cupolas. Soak up the beautiful stained-glass windows, carved floor slabs and the ornate carved reredos. Alongside several of the ruins, the cathedral is used for intimate **music concerts** in summer. Check the tourist office website for details.

Gotlands Museum MUSEUM

(www.gotlandsmuseum.se; Strandgatan 14; adult/under 20yr/senior Skr100/free/80; ⊙10am-6pm daily, closed for Midsummer) Gotlands Museum is one of the mightiest regional museums in Sweden. While highlights include amazing 8th-century pre-Viking picture stones, human skeletons from chambered tombs and medieval wooden sculptures, the star turn is the legendary Spillings horde. At 70kg it's

the world's largest booty of preserved silver treasure. Included in the ticket price is entry to the nearby **Konstmuseum** (Sankt Hansgatan 21; adult/under 20yr/senior Skr50/free/40; ⊙noon-4pm Tue-Sun, closed for Midsummer), which has a small permanent collection that primarily focuses on Gotland-inspired 19th- and 20th-century art. More exciting are the temporary exhibitions, which often showcase contemporary local artists.

⨳ Sleeping

Hotell S:t Clemens B&B €€

(☑21 90 00; www.clemenshotell.se; Smedjegatan 3; s/d Skr1050/1365; @) Located at the northeastern corner of the botanical garden, this family-run hotel is just a stone's throw away from the vine-covered ruins of the ghostly St Clemens kyrka. It takes up five historical buildings and has two gardens ideal for enjoying a cup of coffee in the morning sunshine.

Visby Logi & Vandrarhem HOSTEL €€

(☑52 20 55; www.visbylogi.se; Hästgatan 14 & Sankt Hansgatan 31; s/d from Skr950) Petite hostel located in two historic houses – one from the 16th century, one from the 17th – on Sankt Hansgatan and Hästgatan. Rooms are simple, decorated in white and greys, and there is a rustic courtyard at Hästgatan.

Clarion Hotel Wisby LUXURY HOTEL €€€

(☑25 75 00; cl.wisby@choice.se; Strandgatan 6; s/d Skr1770/2170; @) Top of the heap in Visby

THE ISLAND OF CHURCHES

Gotland boasts the highest concentration of medieval churches in northern Europe. A God-pleasing 92 inhabit villages outside Visby; more than 70 still harbour medieval frescoes and a few also contain extremely rare medieval stained glass. Visby alone has a dozen church ruins and a fairy-tale cathedral.

A church was built in most villages between the early 12th century and the mid-14th century, Gotland's golden age of trading. After 1350, war and struggle saw the money run out and the tradition end. Ironically, it was the lack of funds that helped keep the island in an ecclesiastical time warp; the old churches weren't demolished, and new ones weren't constructed until 1960. Each church is still in use, and the posse of medieval villages still exist as entities.

Most churches are open 9am to 6pm daily from mid-May to late August. Some churches have the old key in the door even before 15 May, or sometimes the key is hidden above the door. *The Churches in the Diocese of Visby* is a particularly useful English-language brochure, available free from tourist offices or online at www.gotland.info.

is the luxurious, landmark Wisby. Medieval vaulted ceilings and look-at-me candelabra contrast with funky contemporary furnishings. The gorgeous pool (complete with medieval pillar) occupies a converted merchant warehouse.

Hotel Villa Borgen   HOTEL €€
(☑20 33 00; www.gtsab.se; Adelsgatan 11; s/d Skr1050/1195; @) This place has satisfying rooms set around a pretty, quiet courtyard, and an intimate breakfast room with French doors and stained glass for that boutique feeling. The same owners also run Wisby Jernvägshotellet (☑20 33 00; www.gtsab.se; Adelsgatan 8; 2-/4-bed room from Skr495/595; ⏱year-round), a small, comfortable and spotless hostel next door.

Fängelse Vandrarhem   HOSTEL €
(☑20 60 50; www.visbyfangelse.se; Skeppsbron 1; dm from Skr290, s/d per person Skr370/580) As hard to get into as it once was to get out of, this hostel offers beds year-round in the small converted cells of an old prison. It's in a handy location, between the ferry dock and the harbour restaurants, and there's a cute terrace bar in summer. Reserve well in advance and always call ahead before arriving, to ensure someone can let you in. Sheets cost an extra Skr80.

Värdshuset Lindgården   HOTEL €€
(☑21 87 00; www.lindgarden.com; Strandgatan 26; s/d Skr1250/1450; @) This is a sound central option, with rooms set facing a soothing garden beside a popular restaurant. Dine outdoors and listen to music in the romantic courtyard in summer.

Visby Strandby   CAMPGROUND €
(☑20 33 00; www.gtsab.se; Rd 149, Snäck; sites from Skr110, 4- to 6-bed cabins from Skr995; @⛱; ⏱May-Sep) This recommended campsite lies 4km north of Visby and within walking distance of a small but popular sandy beach. Facilities include a small shop, a restaurant, a swimming pool and minigolf, with wi-fi available in the cabins. A bus service connects the site to Visby. You must have a Scandinavian Camping Card (Skr130) to check in; they can be bought at reception.

Hamnhotellet   HOTEL €€
(☑20 12 50; www.visbyhamnhotell.se; Färjeleden 3; s/d incl breakfast Skr1400/1500; P@) Close to the ferry terminal, Hamnhotellet offers clean, comfortable rooms and a decent buffet breakfast. Opt for the cheaper annexe rooms (about Skr300 less), which are perfectly adequate with private bathroom and TV.

Gotlands Resor   ACCOMMODATION SERVICES €€
(☑20 12 60; www.gotlandsresor.se; Färjeleden 3) This travel agency, in Hamnhotellet, books stylish, fully equipped cottages (from Skr995 per night) in eastern and northern Gotland. Bookings for summer should be made six months ahead. The agency also organises bike hire and rents camping equipment.

✕ Eating & Drinking

There are more restaurants per capita in Visby than in any other Swedish city. Most are clustered around the old-town squares, on Adelsgatan or at the harbour. Wherever you choose, do not pass up a chance to try *saffranspankaka* (a saffron pancake with berries and cream), the island's speciality. You'll find it at many cafes in Visby and around the island, usually for around Skr60.

Other hang-outs around the harbour are a hit on warm summer days and evenings, including the cheap stalls selling ice cream, sandwiches and pizza inside Saluhall 1.

TOP CHOICE **Bakfickan** SEAFOOD €€
(www.bakfickan-visby.nu; Stora Torget 1; mains Skr137-359; ⊙lunch & dinner) White tiled walls, merrily strung lights and boisterous crowds define this foodie-loved bolt hole, where enlightened seafood gems might include *toast skagen* (shrimps, dill and mayonnaise), pickled herrings on Gotland bread or Bakfickan's fish soup. It's the best of Gotland, on a plate.

50 Kvadrat EUROPEAN €€€
(www.50kvadrat.se; S:t Hansplan; mains Skr220-395) Award-winning within eight months of opening, the appropriately named 50 Kvadrat (in reference to the petite, 49-setting dining room) cooperates with local farms and butchers to specialise in nose-to-tail eating. Emphasis is on beef, but there are lovely seafood and vegetarian options as well.

Visby Crêperie & Logi CREPERIE €
(www.creperielogi.se; crêpes Skr39-149, ⊙11am-11pm daily May-Aug, 11am-2pm & 4-11pm Tue-Sun Sep-Apr) Cheapish, cheerful and a hit with arty types, this lovable corner bolt hole serves scrumptious crêpes, from a moreish lamb, chèvre, honey, rocket and almond combo to a wicked chocolate composition sexed up with white chocolate chunks and ice cream.

Café Amelia CAFE €
(Hästgatan 3; sandwiches Skr55-79; ⊙9am-6pm daily Jun-Aug) This hip cafe puts the emphasis on fresh food, from crisp salads to sinfully good carrot cake. There's also a chic vintage boutique if you feel like trying on 1960s summer frocks and funky hats while waiting for your coffee.

G:a Masters PUB €€
(www.gamlamasters.com, in Swedish; meals Skr175-295; ⊙6pm-2am in summer) Upscale Swedish pub food, from club sandwiches to meatballs, is G:a Masters' speciality. On a corner right

off the main square, the restaurant's terrace is ideal for people-watching.

Bolaget FRENCH €€
(www.gamlabolaget.se; Stora Torget 16; mains Skr179-229; ⊙to 2am, closed Mon in winter) Take a defunct Systembolaget shop, chip the 'System' off the signage, and reinvent the space as a buzzing, bistro-inspired hot spot. Staff are amiable and the summertime square-side bar seating is perfect for a cool break.

Skafferiet CAFE €
(www.skafferietvisby.se; Adelsgatan 38; sandwiches from Skr75; ⊙closed Sun) This casual lunch spot with wooden floors and cosy atmosphere offers salubrious sandwiches and lip-smacking cakes and pastries.

Donners Brunn EUROPEAN €€€
(www.donnersbrunn.se; Donners Plats; mains Skr260-325) A long-standing favourite for a luxury feed, Donners Brunn's menu blends Swedish and global flavours. The alfresco summer bar is a fine spot for a peaceful beer or well-shaken cocktail overlooking Donners Plats.

Gutekällaren BEER HALL
(www.gutekallaren.com; Stora Torget) A restaurant-bar with seemingly infinite levels of seating, from cellars to balconies, also home to nightclubs loved by summer crowds.

🛍 Shopping

Gotländsk Konst & Form ARTS & CRAFTS
(Wallérs plats 5) Cool local art and handicrafts are the focus at this artisans' cooperative, with stock ranging from textiles and threads to ceramics, pottery, jewellery, glassware and painting.

Kvinnfolki HANDICRAFTS
(www.kvinnfolki.se; Donners Plats 2) This is another great place for idiosyncratic local handicrafts, whether it's funky bags with a folk twist, ceramic colanders or downright quirky mugs.

Kränku DRINK
(Sankt Hansplan 4) Tea fiends head here for local blends, which make for soothing, civilised souvenirs.

ℹ Information

Bank (Adelsgatan) With ATM.

ICA supermarket (Stora Torget) Sells stamps, as does the tourist office.

Library (Cramergatan; ☉10am-7pm Mon-Fri, 11am-3pm Sat & Sun) Free internet access (Skr20 mid-June to mid-August).

Tourist Information Centre (☑20 17 00; www.gotland.info; Skeppsbron 4-6; ☉ 9am-6pm Mon-Fri, 10am-4pm Sat & Sun mid-end Aug, shorter hours rest of year) The tourist office is at the harbour.

Around Visby

There's not much but forest and farmland until you're at least 10km from Visby. If you're heading northeast, visit the remarkable Bro church, which has several 5th-century picture stones in the south wall of the oratory, beautiful sculptures and interior lime paintings.

Heading southeast on Rd 143, on your way to Ljugarn, pull over to check out the 12th-century Cistercian monastery ruin Romakloster (admission free, guided tour per group Skr800; ☉10am-6pm daily May-Sep, shorter hours rest of year), a kilometre from the main road. Summer theatre performances here start at Skr250 (tickets from Visby tourist office or book online at www.romateatern.se). The 18th-century manor house is also impressive.

Dalhem, 6km northeast of the Cistercian monastery, has a large church with some 14th-century stained glass (the oldest in Gotland) and magnificent (albeit restored) wall and ceiling paintings; take note of the scales of good and evil. There's also a historic steam railway (www.gotlandstaget.se; adult/4-12yr Skr50/30; ☉11.15am-3.45pm Wed, Thu & Sat Jul–early Aug, Sun only Jun & rest of Aug) and museum in Dalhem.

The town of Klintehamn has a good range of services. From here, you can catch a passenger-only boat to the island nature reserve Stora Karlsö (www.storakarlso.se) one to three times daily from May to early September (adult/six to 15 years return Skr295/145, 30 minutes). Remote as it is, the island is home to extensive bird life, including thousands of guillemots and razorbills, and well worth the time it takes to get there. You can visit the island as a day trip (with 4½ hours ashore) or stay overnight.

STF Stora Karlsö (☑24 04 50; www.storakarlso.se; s/d Skr 450/900; ☉May-Aug), Stora Karlsö's simple STF hostel, is a really special choice if you want to get away from it all. Visitors can opt to stay in a modern beach house, in the old lighthouse itself or in the lighthouse-keeper's former living quarters (p169), where linen and room service are included in the price. There's also a nature exhibit, restaurant and cafe on the island. Book ahead.

Pensionat Warfsholm (☑24 00 10; www.warfsholm.se; sites Skr100, s/d from Skr490/690), in Klintehamn, is a hotel-hostel combo sporting a beautiful waterside location and restaurant. Beds in the more expensive rooms have lovely lace coverlets and antique lamps.

Eastern Gotland

Ancient monuments include the Bronze Age ship setting, Tjelvars grav, 1.5km west of Rd 146 (level with Visby), and its surrounding landscape of standing stones. Gothem church is one of the most impressive in Gotland; the nave is decorated with friezes dating from 1300. Torsburgen, 9km north of Ljugarn, is a partly walled hill fort (the largest in Scandinavia) measuring 5km around its irregular perimeter.

Ljugarn is a small seaside resort, and there are impressive *raukar* (column) formations at Folhammar Nature Reserve, 2km north. Southwest of Ljugarn and the village of Alskog, the impressive Garde church has four extraordinary medieval lich gates and an upside-down medieval key in the door; the original 12th-century roof is still visible.

Around 20km north of Ljugarn, in the tiny hamlet of Kräklingbo, Leonettes Konst & Keramik (☑533 40; www.leonette.com; Hajdeby, Kräklingbo) is home to Californian expat Dan Leonette and his highly regarded, idiosyncratic ceramics and art, created using techniques like raku and sawdust firing. In summer you can watch the master fire his wares (call ahead for times).

Truffle-hunting safaris (www.gotlandstryffel.se) in the area are a unique way for foodies to discover more about this delicacy and local produce in general. Check the websites for package prices, which include a five-star dinner (featuring truffles, of course) and an accommodation option.

🛏 Sleeping & Eating

There's a Konsum supermarket in Ljugarn, and some fine dining options in the area.

🏡 **TF hostel Ljugarn** HOSTEL €
(☑49 31 84; ljugarn@gotlandsturist.se; dm from Skr200; ☉mid-May–Aug) This place has a fine

OLOFSSON & BÄCKMAN: GOTLAND TRUFFLE HUNTERS

Truffle harvesters Ragnar Olofsson and Camilla Bäckman are Gotland natives.

What sparked your passion for truffles? We got interested in truffles in 2001, when we read an article about an Uppsala researcher studying Gotland truffles. Most locals had no idea what they were picking up at the time, even though the island was covered in them. Farmers were skeptical of the idea at first, but then a journalist wrote about it and as the media interest grew, so did the public's curiosity. In 2007 between 100kg and 200kg of truffles were harvested, with a value of Skr5 per gram (or Skr5000 per kilogram). Much to the dismay of the French, our Burgundy truffles are exactly the same as theirs.

Where can you eat them? We're now supplying some of Sweden's top restaurants, and we even sell to hot dining spots in Reykjavik and Helsinki.

When is truffle season? Gotland is no longer just a summer destination, with growing numbers heading over for the truffle-harvesting season in October and November.

How can you hunt yourself? We offer truffle safari packages, which include a truffle hunt with Lizzie and Java (our fluffy, truffle-sniffing Lagotto Romagnolo dogs). As you can see, we've come a long way since the days when locals thought we were harvesting chocolate.

spot at the eastern end of the Ljugarn village (down by the water).

TOP CHOICE **Krakas Krog** SCANDINAVIAN €€€
(www.krakas.se, in Swedish; Kräklings 223, Katthammarsvik; mains Skr270-315; ⏰4-10pm Wed-Sun early Jun–Sep) The owners of Krakas Krog make a point of sourcing their ingredients from Gotland's fields, woods and sea, including frogs' legs direct from the garden. Meals are served on the porch and in the petite dining room of a building that once served as a bank. The menu is replete with local delicacies: eggs with morels and beets, turkey in truffle broth or Baltic Sea turbot with sage butter.

Smakrike Krog & Logi SCANDINAVIAN €€€
(www.smakrike.se; Claudelins väg 1, Ljugarn; mains Skr245-345; ⏰5-11pm daily Jun-Aug, to 9pm Fri & Sat only Sep-Dec & Mar-May; P @) Meals at Smakrike Krog capture the essence of a true Swedish summer. The restaurant's menu follows the seasons and the affable owners also operate a stylish bed and breakfast upstairs (singles/doubles Skr1100/1650).

Bruna Dörren PIZZERIA €
(www.brunadorren.nu; Strandvägen 5, Ljugarn; pizzas Skr60-95, mains Skr95-189) A casual restaurant and pizzeria, with a spacious outdoor courtyard and beachside location.

Northern Gotland & Fårö

It's hard to imagine a better way to absorb the area than by cycling up to Fårö and following the bike trails around the beautiful, windswept little island. There's an information centre (⏰22 40 22; www.faroframtid.se; ⏰10am-5pm daily Jul & Aug, 10am-5pm Fri-Sun May–mid-Jun & Sep) with internet access in Fårö town.

The grotto (www.lummelundagrottan.se; adult/child Skr130/70; ⏰May-Sep) south of Lummelunda is the island's largest.

The temperature here is a cool 8°C, so rug up. The impressive *raukar* formations at nearby Lickershamn are up to 12m high; look out for Jungfru (signposted), with its haunting legend.

Step back in time at the Bungemuseet (www.bungemuseet.se; adult/under 16yr Skr100/free; ⏰11am-6pm daily Jul–mid-Aug, 10am-5pm Jun & mid–end Aug, 11am-4pm early Sep), an open-air museum with 17th- to 19th-century houses, picture stones dating from AD 800 and a historic playground. It's near the northeastern tip, about 1km south of where the ferry connects to Fårö. Across the road is a cute cafe with superlative saffron pancakes.

The frequent ferry to Fårö is free for cars, passengers and cyclists. This island, once home to Ingmar Bergman, has magnificent *raukar* formations; watch the sunset at Langhammarshammaren if you can. At the island's eastern tip, the rocks by Fårö lighthouse are laced with fossils. British troops who fought in the Crimean war are buried at **Ryssnäs** in the extreme south; obey signs posted along roads here, as this area is still used for military exercises.

🛏 Sleeping & Eating

Lickershamns Semesterby　　CAMPGROUND €
(☑27 24 30; www.lickershamns-semesterby.se; sites/cabins Skr590/730, week-long rental only during high season) Low-key campsite near the sea and within easy walking distance to Lickershamn's sleepy harbour and pleasant restaurant.

STF Lärbro　　HOSTEL €
(☑22 50 33; dm from Skr200; ⊗reception 8-11am & 5-10pm) A good hostel on Rd 148 between Visby and Fårösund; opens mid-May to August. It has a gym for hostel guests (Skr100).

Lummelunda Hostel　　HOSTEL €
(☑27 30 43; www.lummelundavandrarhem.se; cabins from Skr650; ⊗May-Sep) There's a beachside hostel with basic cabins in Lummelunda, as well as a pleasant cafe near the harbour.

Lickershamnskrogen　　SWEDISH €€
(☑27 24 25; www.lickershamnskrogen.se; mains Skr159-295) Near the Jungfru trailhead at Lickershamn, this place serves both local and Med-style dishes and tapas, and there's a hut selling smoked fish.

Gotska Sandön National Park

Isolated **Gotska Sandön**, with an area of 37 sq km, is an unusual island with lighthouses at its three corners, 30km of beaches, sand dunes, pine forest and a church. There's a fantastic network of trails right around the island.

There is a **hostel** (☑24 04 50; info@resestugan.se; s/d Skr300/800; ⊗mid-May–early Sep); facilities are basic, so bring all supplies with you.

Boats (☑24 04 50; ⊗mid-May–early Sep) run from Fårösund and Nynäshamn three to four times weekly when operating (Skr895/1095 return from Fårösund/Nynäshamn).

Southern Gotland

As you head south, stop off at **Lojsta** to see the deepest lakes in Gotland, the remains of an early medieval fortress and a fine church.

BERGMAN WEEK

The wild, mysterious landscape of Fårö is not easily forgotten, as anyone who has visited can testify. The tiny island just off the northern tip of Gotland particularly haunted Ingmar Bergman (1918–2007), the legendary Swedish director, who first visited Fårö in 1960 while scouting locations for *Through a Glass Darkly*. Bergman ended up living and working on the island for 40 years, shooting seven films on the island, and is now buried there.

Since 2004 Fårö has been home to **Bergman Week** (www.bergmanveckan.se), a six-day celebration of Bergman's life and work. The event consists of a film series, guest speakers (recently including fellow filmmaker Jan Troell), master classes and tours of film locations around the island. Renovations of the vacant Fårö school building to house a new **Bergman Centre** (www.bergmancenter.se) began in 2010; once complete, the centre will host exhibits, lectures, workshops and screenings, as well as a cafe and library. The current centre (open noon to 6pm in summer) can set you up with your very own Bergman guide (Skr1875 for two hours), or try a Bergman bus safari (tours from 3pm to 5pm or 3pm to 9pm Skr295/495).

Jannike Åhlund, one of the people behind Bergman Week who knew Bergman, described the director as curious, with a quick intellect and a great sense of humour, as well as childish, vengeful and a lover of gossip. Her two favourite Bergman films? *Autumn Sonata* and *Wild Strawberries*.

To get the most of Fårö, Åhlund recommends: walking along the wild and magnificent Norsta Aura beach; renting a bike and pedalling the 7km-long *rauker* (column formation) road to enjoy the huge rock formations up close; eating lunch at the **Crêperie Tati** (Friggars; snacks from Skr35); checking out the '50s memorabilia at **Kutens Bensin** (Broskogs; www.kuten.se) or listening to a rockabilly concert on a summery Friday or Saturday night; and riding on **Icelandic horses** (☑70 690 0432, 22 14 44; fia@faroislandshastar.se).

Hemse is a commercial centre, with good services (such as supermarkets, banks and a bakery). About 10km south, the Hablingbo church boasts three lavishly carved doorways, a votive ship, carved floor slabs and rune stones. The red-brick STF Vandrarhem Hablingbo (☑48 71 61; www.gutevin.se, in Swedish; Hablingo; dm Skr280; ☺May-Sep; @) is next to Gute Vingård – a good restaurant and commercial vineyard.

Maria's Hästeri (www.mariashasteri.se), 9km south in Grötlingbo (another 10km south from Hablingbo) is a friendly stable that organises horse-riding tours lasting from a couple hours to a full day complete with lunch. In Björklunda, 10km further south, Gunnels B&B Björklunda (☑49 71 90; www.gunnelsbjorklunda.se; hostel dm/s Skr200/250, B&B s/d Skr600/800; ⓟ) vaguely recalls a Greek villa with its whitewashed buildings and blue trim. Furnishings and decorations are somewhat dated, but rooms are clean and comfy. Some have private kitchenettes.

The small town of Burgsvik is another convenient commercial centre further south. Just north of town, the Öja church dates from 1232 and has Gotland's highest church tower (67m). It has a magnificent cross, and the wall and ceiling paintings are remarkably detailed. Look for the inscribed stone slabs under the covered shelter just outside the churchyard.

Seven kilometres south of Burgsvik, in the old Vamlingbo prästgård (vicarage) on Rd 142, Museum Lars Jonsson (☑20 26 91; www.larsjonsson.se; adult/under 18yr Skr40/free; ☺11am-5pm daily May–mid-Sep, call ahead to check hours rest of year) showcases delicate paintings and watercolours by local artist Lars Jonsson, famed for his depictions of Gotland's bird life and coastal landscapes. There's also a cinnamon-scented cafe, Naturum and soothing garden.

On the eastern coast near Ronehamn, Uggarderojr is a huge, late–Bronze Age cairn with nearby traces of settlement. The cairn, probably a navigation marker, is now a long way inland due to postglacial uplift.

Östersund &
the Bothnian Coast

Why Go?

The north of Sweden seems to have it all. There are endless pristine forests where the odds of encountering elk, reindeer and bear are high and the hiking is splendid. There are jagged mountains that provide Sweden's best skiing in winter, and host the best mountain biking in summer, along with every other mountain sport you can imagine. On the other hand, you are never too far from the bright lights of civilisation: you can go monster-spotting in Östersund (yes, you read that correctly!), party with locals in the student towns of Gävle, Umeå and Luleå, or just enjoy the laid-back rhythm of life in the pretty coastal towns, rich in historical sights and medieval churches. Slow down even further by lingering in the tiny fishing villages and sampling the fresh catch, or strike out for Höga Kusten's remote islands and wonder why the Swedes invented *surströmming* (fermented herring).

When to Go
Sundsvall

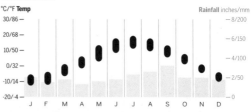

Mar–Apr Still plenty of snow, but the weather is warming up.

Jul (last week) Rock out at the three-day Storsjöyran festival in Östersund.

Aug (last week) Fill your belly with crayfish on Höga Kusten's islands.

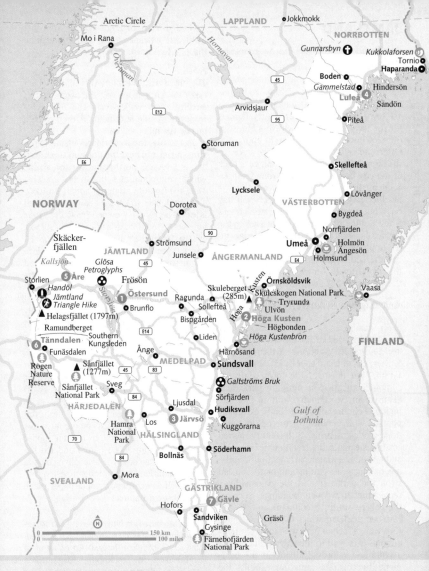

Östersund & the Bothnian Coast Highlights

1 Check out **Östersund** (p266), home of the Storsjöodjuret – the Lake Monster

2 Travel along **Höga Kusten** (p280), northern Sweden's most beautiful coastline

3 Meet northern Sweden's wild beasts in **Järvzoo** (p277)

4 Visit Sweden's largest church town, **Luleå** (p286)

5 Go wild in Sweden's outdoor adventure central, **Åre** (p269)

6 Go hiking in the pristine wilderness of **Tänndalen** (p271)

7 Visit **Sveriges Järnvägsmuseet** (p273), in Gävle Sweden's best railway museum

JÄMTLAND

Östersund

📞063 / POP 58,000

Sitting on the shore of the enormous Storsjön (Great Lake), Östersund is the largest town in the area, particularly famous for the local answer to Loch Ness Monster: Storsjöodjuret. The best way to appreciate Östersund is to take the footbridge across to the adjacent island of Frösön and gaze back at the city in profile, ideally around sunset. Seen in that light, this fun-loving town is hard to resist. Dedicated sightseers will stay busy, but what Östersund really encourages is relaxation: in summer, people flock to the terrace bars and cafes at the water's edge (often hopping in for a quick dip) or idly wander the pedestrianised shopping streets in the stroll-friendly centre, stopping here and there for a beer or an ice cream.

◎ Sights & Activities

TOP CHOICE Jamtli   MUSEUM
(www.jamtli.com; adult/child mid-Jun–Aug Skr110/free, Sep–mid-Jun Skr60/free; ⊙11am-5pm daily Jun-Aug, closed Mon Sep-May; 🖫) Don't miss Jamtli, 1km north of the town centre. It combines an open-air museum park (à la Skansen in Stockholm) with a first-rate regional culture museum, both extremely popular with families. In the outdoor section, guides wearing 19th-century period costumes explain the traditions of the area and encourage visitor participation in milking, baking, grass cutting and more. You can stroll the paths around the painstakingly reconstructed wooden buildings, such as the bakery, smithy, woodman's cottage and 18th-century farm, which is still run as such. Kids can get acquainted with different farm animals, run wild in the playground or ride a children's railway. Indoors, in the basement, the regional museum exhibits the Överhogdal Tapestry, a Christian Viking relic from around AD 1100 that features animals, people, ships and buildings (including churches). It's one of the oldest of its kind in Europe and may even predate the famous Bayeux tapestry. If you're interested in monster-spotting, check out the display devoted to the creature, Storsjöodjuret; those with a taste for the macabre will appreciate the pickled monster embryo.

Guided tours in English leave from just inside the entrance at 2pm daily mid-June through to August.

Frösön   ISLAND
The nicest way to explore this island, which takes its name from Frö, the pagan god of fertility, is to walk across the footbridge from the middle of Östersund, then catch a bus up the hill.

Just across the footbridge, outside Landstingshuset and near the Konsum supermarket, is Sweden's northernmost rune stone, which commemorates the arrival of 'East Man', the first Christian missionary, in 1050.

A good place to keep the kids entertained is the 42-acre, family-owned Frösö Zoo (www.frosozoo.se; adult/child/family Skr180/90/500; ⊙10am-4pm mid-late Jun & Aug, to 6pm Jul; 🖫), which specialises in exotic animals. Five kilometres west of the centre of Östersund is the restored, late-12th-century Frösöns kyrka (⊙8am-8pm summer), with its distinctive separate bell tower, built on a sacrificial site to the ancient gods *(æsir)* and incredibly popular for midsummer weddings. Catch buses 5 and 3, respectively.

Moose Garden   FARM
(📞070-363 6061; www.moosegarden.com; Orviken 145; adult/child Skr100/40; ⊙tours 11am, 1 & 3pm late Jun–mid-Aug; 🖫) If you've heard of Sweden's 300,000 elks but have yet to see one 'king of the forest' in the flesh, you can drive southwest to this moose farm just outside Östersund, home to 18 tame moose which are happy to be petted and fed bananas. The moose farm also offers on-site accommodation and unique moose products, such as ecofriendly toilet paper made from moose droppings.

FREE Färgfabriken Norr   ART GALLERY
(www.fargfabriken.se/norr; Byggnad 33, Infanterigatan 30; ⊙noon-4pm Thu-Sun) An offshoot of Färgfabriken in Stockholm, Färgfabriken Norr is a huge new art space across the E14 motorway from Jamtli. It's a cavernous room with an ambitious curatorial scope; the initial exhibition included work by some 80 artists, including David Lynch and JG Thirlwell, representing pretty much all forms, from painting, sculpture and video to installations using broken glass, body hair and lightning, but at the time of writing, it had just passed to new management.

Östersund

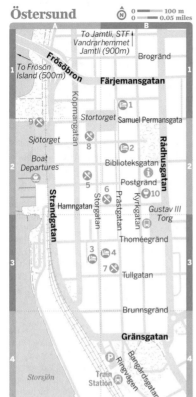

Östersund

🛌 Sleeping
1 Clarion Grand Östersund................... B1
2 Hotel Emma...B2
3 Hotel Jämteborg....................................A3
4 Pensionat Svea B3

🍴 Eating
5 Brunkullans Krog A2
6 Captain Cook..B2
7 Lilla Siam..B3
8 Törners Konditori A2
9 Törners Konditori (Summer)..............A2

🍷 Drinking
10 Solo..B2

★☆ Festivals & Events

Storsjöyran   MUSIC
(Great Lake Festival; www.storsjoyran.se) A gigantic, raucous annual three-day music festival, Storsjöyran is held in the town centre in late July/early August and features a range of local and international artists, from The Ark to Blondie. Some 55,000 people attend, so note that beds are scarce and expensive around then.

🛏 Sleeping

Book in advance during Storjöyran Festival, as budget accommodation in particular fills up quickly.

Badhusparken   BEACH
Just north of the harbour, by the footbridge leading over to Fröson island, is the town's most popular stop for sunbathing and a brisk swim. In winter you can swim in the specially cut hole in the ice further south along the waterfront before making a dash to the nearby mobile sauna and hot tub (Skr95; 4-7pm Tue & Thu mid-Feb–mid-Apr).

S/S Thomée   CRUISE
(adult/child Skr80/40, Lake Storsjön tour Skr100/45; ⊗tours Tue-Sun Jun-early Sep) For those who want to try their luck at spotting the lake monster, the old S/S *Thomée* steamship runs a variety of cruises, including themed tours, dinner tours and trips to the small castle-capped island of Verkön (Skr130/45). Book through the tourist office (☑14 40 01; www.ostersund.se/thomee); the complicated schedule's posted on a sign by the boat at the harbour.

🔝 Hotel Emma   HOTEL €€
(☑51 78 40; www.hotelemma.com; Prästgatan 31; s/d from Skr940/1090, discounted to Skr695/850; ℙ🐾) Emma couldn't be better located: it's on the main pedestrian shopping street, right above a whisky bar. The individually decorated rooms are nestled into crooked hallways on two floors, with homey touches like squishy armchairs and imposing ceramic stoves; some rooms have French doors facing the courtyard and buttery wood floors. Parking costs Skr60 per overnight stay.

Hotel Jämteborg   HOTEL €€
(☑51 01 01; www.jamteborg.se; Storgatan 54; hostel dm Skr230, d Skr480; ℙ) This friendly place offers hostel beds, B&B or hotel rooms in several centrally located buildings. The hotel section has cheerful rooms in bright colours that defy Sweden's 'earth tones only' rule; all hotel rooms include private bathrooms and breakfast. Run by the same owners, Pensionat Svea across the street has further options.

GLÖSA PETROGLYPHS

Glösa, 40km northwest of Östersund and by the Alsensjön lake, has some of Sweden's finest **Stone Age petroglyphs**. The carvings, on rock slabs beside a stream, feature large numbers of elk and date from 5000 BC. There's also an excellent reconstruction of a **Stone Age hut** and replicas of skis, snowshoes, a sledge and an elk-skin boat.

Nearby are some displays about elk hunting using traps (prohibited since 1864) and more modern methods. There are roughly 13,000 *fångstgropar* (pit traps) in Jämtland, set in lines across migration routes; a short walk through the woods (follow the sign saying *Fornminne*) will take you to four of them.

Take bus 156 to Nälden or bus 154 to Ånge and change to either to bus 532 or 533 (Skr83, 60 to 90 minutes, three daily), then follow the sign from the public road (a 500m walk).

Clarion Grand Östersund   HOTEL €€€

(☑55 60 00; www.clarionostersund.se; Prästgatan 16; d/ste from Skr1370/2370; 🅿🌊) Östersund's most luxurious option, popular with the business set, offers plush rooms, a superb restaurant featuring excellent northern Swedish and international cuisine and extras such as pool and sauna.

STF Vandrarhemmet Jamtli   HOSTEL €

(☑12 20 60; www.jamtli.com; Museiplan; dm/s/d from Skr175/245/300; 🅿) Popular hostel inside the gates of Jamtli museum park inside a low, barnlike wooden building. There are two- to five-bed dorms, and facilities are all top-notch.

🍴 Eating & Drinking

Törners Konditori   CAFE €

(www.tornerskonditori.se; Badhusparken; meals from Skr65; ⊙breakfast, lunch & dinner Mon-Fri, breakfast & lunch Sat, lunch Sun; 🍴) This cute cafe at the water's edge serves coffee, cakes and ice cream in a summery park setting. It's only open in summer, but there's another **branch** (Storgatan 24) that's open all year, which has tasty daily lunch specials ranging from goulash to chicken curry, as well as great sandwiches and salads.

Brunkullans Krog   SWEDISH €€

(www.brunkullanskrog.se Postgränd 5; meals from Skr250; ⊙lunch Mon, lunch & dinner Tue-Fri, dinner Sat) Pub with a wonderfully atmospheric, candlelit 19th-century wooden interior. The menu features Swedish classics and upscale versions of basic bar food, like a decadent bacon-cheeseburger or a quesadilla made with crème fraiche. The weekday lunchtime specials are excellent value (Skr95).

Captain Cook   PUB €

(www.captaincook.se; Hamngatan 9; meals from Skr170; ⊙lunch & dinner daily) Particularly on weekends, you'll find locals and travellers packing this joint which combines three great ingredients: Aussie pub grub (try the Aussie burger), live blues and rock and over 16 beers on tap, including Belgian. Rattle your dags and get down here early to grab a table.

Lilla Siam   THAI €

(www.lillasiam.com; Prästgatan 54A; meals from Skr190; ⊙lunch & dinner Mon-Fri, dinner only Sat & Sun; 🍴) Affordable, authentic Thai restaurant with a good lunch buffet and a classy dinner menu full of Thai staples, including plenty of vegetarian dishes.

TOP CHOICE Solo   COCKTAIL BAR

(www.solobar.se; Kyrkagatan 45; ⊙dinner Wed-Sun) Run by local celebrity chef 'Stoffe' Anderson, chic Solo describes itself as a 'concept' rather than just a restobar. See if you agree after sampling its 55 cocktails and the food, which vacillates between such crowd pleasers as the Deluxe Waffle and the steak, beautifully presented and executed.

ℹ Information

The **tourist office** (☑14 40 01; www.visitoster sund.se, www.jamtland.info; Rådhusgatan 44; ⊙9am-5pm Mon-Fri, 10am-3pm Sat & Sun) is opposite the town hall.

ℹ Getting There & Around

AIR The **airport** (☑19 30 00) serving both Östersund and Åre is on Frösön island, 11km west of the town centre. The airport bus leaves regularly from the bus terminal (adult/child Skr70/20). SAS flies to Stockholm (nine daily);

Nextjet serves Luleå and Umeå (two daily). During the ski season, the airport receives charter flights from London Heathrow, Manchester, Amsterdam and Copenhagen.

BUS Daily bus 45 runs north from Östersund to Gällivare and south to Mora, stopping in all major towns along the way. There are one or two daily departures for Åre with bus 155, while bus 63 heads east to Umeå twice daily.

TRAIN In summer the daily 7.15am Inlandsbanan train heads north to Gällivare (Skr962, 14½ hours) via Arvidsjaur (Skr610, 8¾ hours) and Jokkmokk (Skr833, 12½ hours). Inlandsbanan also runs south to Mora (Skr 414, five hours, one daily at 7.10am). SJ departures from Östersund include two or three trains daily to Stockholm via Uppsala, a daily train to Göteborg and three trains heading west to Storlien via Åre.

Åre

📞 0647 / POP 9700

Beautifully situated in a mountain valley by the shores of lake Åresjön, Åre is Sweden's most popular skiing resort (www.skistar.com/are): 30,000 people invade the village during the November to mid-May skiing season. Given the sheer number of outdoor adventures available to fresh-air fiends, it's a wonder that Åre hasn't yet become backpacker central. Skiing and snowboarding competitions take place in winter, while in July Åre hosts the **Åre Bike Festival** and the hardcore **Åre Extreme Challenge**, with spa treatments available to those worn out by all the sporty stuff. You may well spot reindeer around Åre: the Åre valley is a reindeer herding ground for three Sami villages who own around 15,000 reindeer between them.

◉ Sights & Activities

Kabinbana CABLE CAR

(☉10am-4pm daily late Jun-late Sep; adult/child Skr120/95) Taking you almost to the top of Mt Åreskutan, the only gondola in Scandinavia is worth taking for the awesome views alone. It departs from behind Åre's main square and goes up to a viewing platform (1274m) complete with Åre's most expensive (and picturesque) cafe.

TOP CHOICE **Åre Bike Park** MOUNTAIN BIKING

(www.arebikepark.com) In summer the slopes of Mt Åreskutan become an enormous playground dedicated to mountain biking – the Åre Bike Park. There are more than 30 trails spanning over 40km of track, ranging from beginner to extreme (the trails are graded using the same system as ski slopes). The Kabinbanan cable car, the Bergbanan funicular, and the VM6:an and Hummelliften chairlifts are fitted with bike racks to help you up the mountain. You can rent bikes and safety equipment at **Åre Bikes** (📞073 84; www.aremtb.se).

Hiking HIKING

Popular short hikes include the 30-minute scramble to the top of Mt Åreskutan from the Kabinbana viewing platform and the two-hour hike down to the village from the same spot. The tourist office stocks booklets and maps detailing multiple hikes in the area. The area west of Åre is popular among fell walkers, and there's a network of STF wilderness huts and lodges here for enthusiasts, especially around Sylarna, one of Sweden's finest mountains for trekking and climbing. (The huts don't take reservations,

---

STORSJÖODJURET – THE LAKE MONSTER

Just imagine…you're sitting by lake Storsjön at dusk when you notice a dark shadow rise out of the water. Could it be just ripples in the wake of a passing boat? Perhaps a couple of elk swimming? How can you be sure? Or could it be the head of Storsjöodjuret – the Lake Monster that dwells somewhere in the dark waters of the 91m deep lake Storsjön. Sightings of the **Storsjöodjuret** (www.storsjoodjuret.com) – the only such monster of its kind in Sweden – were made as early as 1635, when the description of a strange animal with a black serpentine body and catlike head first appeared in a folk tale. The Frösö Runestone does in fact depict a serpentlike creature and the Lake Monster has had such a grip on the public imagination that in 1894 a hunt for it was organised by a special committee put together by King Oscar II. However, the Norwegian whalers specially hired for the job came back empty-handed; it seems that the Storsjöodjuret did not go for the dead pig used as bait. Every summer there are claims of new sightings, and the monster was granted protected status as an 'endangered species' in 1986, only for that status to be revoked in 2005.

INLANDSBANAN

The Inlandsbanan route is covered by a combination of *rälsbuss* (railcar) and steam train, but only from late June (just after Midsummer) to mid-August. Travel on the line is slow as the average speed is 50km/h, so Inlandsbanan is now more of a tourist attraction than an efficient means of transport. It rolls through northern Sweden, stopping in places of interest and particularly picturesque spots, the journey accompanied by the commentary of guides.

For the history of the Inlandsbanan, visit the Inlandsbanan Museum (p294).

but you're guaranteed a spot to sleep, even if it's the floor.)

Mt Åreskutan
SKIING

The Mt Åreskutan (1420m) ski area boasts 45 ski lifts, 100 pistes and 1000 vertical metres of skiable slopes, including a 6.5km downhill run. The skiing conditions are best from February, when daylight hours increase.

Åre Äventyrbutik
SNOW SPORTS

(☑512 20; www.areaventyr.se; per person Skr2500) Provides snow-related thrills like off-piste skiing and heli-skiing. Also offers trial courses (from Skr550) and day courses (from Skr1495) in kiteboarding (snowboarding with a kite), kitewing (skiing or snowboarding with a sail) and snowfering (windsurfing on snow or ice).

Camp Åre
SNOWMOBILE

(☑525 25; www.campare.se) There are over 1130km of snowmobile trails around Åre and guided snowmobile safaris (from Skr500 for two hours) are arranged via Camp Åre, which also arranges driving on ice.

Åre Sleddog Adventures
SLEDDING

(☑303 81; www.aresleddog.se) If you prefer to race across the frozen wastes without a motor, this outfit offers anything from two-hour tours (Skr800) to five-day expeditions with camping (from Skr9990).

Summer activities on offer include mountainboarding – think snowboarding with wheels – with Åre Mountainboard (☑0707-60 74 70; www.aremountainboard.se); rock climbing, caving and canoeing with ATI Mountain Experience (☑352 53; www.mountainexperience .se); zorbing – rolling around in a giant padded bubble – with Zåreb (☑0707-60 74 70; www.zareb.se); hillcarting – like gocarting, but down, down, down! – with Åre Hillcart (☑0707-60 74 70; www.arehillcart.se); paragliding and hang-gliding with Skysport (☑511

86; www.skysport.se); and white-water rafting, ranging from gentle Class II to challenging Class IV+ with Nature's Best operator JoPe Fors & Fjäll (☑314 65; www.jope.se). Whew!

🛏️ Sleeping & Eating

Accommodation fills up quickly in winter, so plan well ahead.

⭐TOP CHOICE STF Vandrarhem Åre
HOSTEL €

(☑301 38; www.brattlandsgarden.se; dm Skr175, s/d from Skr300/400; P🐾) This hostel is a lovely spot on an old farmstead up a hill, run by a warm, helpful family happy to advise you about the surrounding area and arrange Icelandic pony rides. Rooms are tucked into red wooden buildings and there's a huge living room-dining area and a large, well-equipped kitchen. The place is 6km east of Åre, in Brattland; a daily bus connects it to town, although service is spotty. No wi-fi.

Fjällgården
HOTEL €€

(☑145 00; www.fjallgarden.se; s/d from Skr645/1190; P) Up on the hillside, this is as much an activity centre as a hotel. It offers fishing, mountain biking, golf, horse riding, paddling and a chance to try the zipline, which lets you fly across the valley on a tiny string. Rooms are large, plush and full of light, and decorated in faux-rustic, après-ski style.

⭐TOP CHOICE Åre Bageri
BAKERY €

(www.arebageri.se; Årevägen 55; meals from Skr110; ☺breakfast & lunch) A sprawling organic cafe and stone-oven bakery with a comfy, shabby-chic atmosphere, this place lends itself to lingering. In addition to great coffee, pastries and huge sandwiches, it does an enormous all-you-can-eat breakfast spread for Skr79 (7am to 10.30am).

Broken
AMERICAN €

(www.broken-are.com; meals from Skr200; ☺lunch & dinner) Just off the main square, this American-style diner dishes up what every hungry biker secretly craves: Philly cheese steak, mega fajitas, ribs and jumbo hamburgers, followed by banana splits and washed down with frozen margaritas.

Twins STEAKHOUSE €
(www.twinsare.se; meals from Skr165; ☺lunch Mon & Tue, lunch & dinner Wed-Sat) Spacious lodge-like restaurant grilling up Argentinian steak. The weekday lunch menu includes daily Swedish specials such meatballs with lingonberry sauce.

ⓘ Information

Åre's **tourist office** (☑177 20; www.visitare.se, www.are360.com; ☺10am-6pm Mon-Fri, to 3pm Sat & Sun) is combined with the public library above the train station and has free internet access.

ⓘ Getting There & Away

BUS Bus 155 runs east to Östersund (Skr128, 1½ hours, one or two daily). Bus 157 runs west to Duved (Skr23, 15 minutes, up to 14 daily) and bus 571 connects Duved to Storlien (Skr81, 50 minutes, three daily).

TRAIN Åre has east-bound departures for Östersund (Skr118, 1¼ hours, three daily) and overnight trains to Stockholm (Skr645, 11 hours, one daily). West-bound services run to Trondheim, Norway (Skr250, 2½hr, two daily) via Storlien (Skr66, 45 minutes, three daily).

Storlien & Around

☑0647

If Åre is the winter party town, Storlien, a microvillage near the Norwegian border, is its smaller, quieter counterpart (the Swedish king himself has a winter chalet here).

Besides the skiing (day pass Skr280), there is excellent hiking in the area, particularly the multiday hike south to Tänndalen. There are some gentler, shorter hikes around the village, where you can go cloudberry-picking and mushrooming.

Storvallens Fjällgården (☑700 50; www.storvallensfjallgard.se; dm Skr200, s/d from Skr335/800), 600m off the E14 about 4.5km east of Storlien, in Storvalen, provides top-quality accommodation in simple dorm rooms and rooms with warm, wood-panelled common areas, a good restaurant (there's also a guest kitchen), sauna and good hiking advice. It's also the starting point for the Southern Kungsleden. The upmarket **Restaurant Flamman** (Vintergatan 48; meals Skr250-350; ☺lunch & dinner daily in summer, Fri-Sun rest of year) offers imaginative dishes using local cheeses, meats and berries.

The **tourist office** (☑704 00; www.storlianturistbyra.se; ☺9-11.30am & 4.30-7pm mid-Jun–Aug), near the train station, has plentiful information on hiking in the area.

From Storlien, trains run east to Åre (Skr66, 45 minutes, three daily) and west to Trondheim, Norway (Skr220, 1¾ hours, two daily).

HÄRJEDALEN

Funäsdalen & Tänndalen

☑0684 / POP 2800

Funäsdalen is a small, narrow mountain village arranged along a single road – because that's the only place flat enough to be accessible when the area is buried in snow for half the year. Dominated by the impressive peak Funäsdalsberget, the village and surrounding area are popular with hikers, skiers and other outdoor sports enthusiasts – understandably, as the landscape is vast and varied. Beyond Funäsdalen, Route 84 leads uphill to diminutive Tänndalen, an even better destination for hikers.

◉ Sights & Activities

Härjedalens Fjällmuseum MUSEUM
(www.fjallmuseet.se; Rörovägen 30; adult/child Skr100/free; ☺10am-6pm late Jun-late Sep; ⌖) Härjedalens Fjällmuseum has displays covering the South Sami, who still herd their reindeer in from the nearby Mittådalen and Brändåsen villages, and settlement of this area by local farmers and miners. There's a fun play area for kids which includes a secret tunnel, and the adjacent Fornminnesparken open-air section features 19th-century buildings from this area.

TOP CHOICE Hiking HIKING
The most extensive hiking routes begin from Tänndalen – the starting point for the Southern Kungsleden, which runs all the way to Storlien. Twenty kilometres from Tänndalen, the trail passes along the ski slopes of Ramundberget before the steep terrain takes you up to Sweden's southernmost glacier on Helagsfjället (1797m), the highest peak in the area. Then you have two choices: either to tackle the challenging 50km stretch through what it arguably

Sweden's most beautiful mountain country, via the STF-run *fjällstation* at Sylarna and Blåhammaren, finishing up at the Storvalen youth hostel near Storlien (p271), or else you can make your way down to Ljungdalen (18km; www.ljungdalen.com), where you can catch bus 613 to Östersund.

An easier 76km trail runs south between Tänndalen and Grövelsjön in Dalarna, passing alongside Lake Rogen, part of Rogen Nature Reserve. With its scattering of lakes among pine-covered ridges, the reserve is a favourite destination for kayaking and canoeing among foreign visitors. It is also home to Sweden's only herd of musk oxen; if you come across them, keep your distance as they are ferocious when stampeding and can easily outrun you; they run faster uphill than downhill. Naturum (☑242 00; ⊙9am-8pm mid-Jun–Aug) has an information centre on the Rogen Nature Reserve 15km south of Funäsdalen at Tännäs Fiskecentrum. Much of the trail rambles through ancient pine forest, though there's a relatively steep section near Tänndalen that requires you to ascend Rödfjället (1243m). Three STF-run mountain huts – at Skedbro (21km), Rogen (17km) and Storrödtjärn (16km from Rogen and 22km to Grövelsjön) – provide accommodation along the way.

Skiing

For skiing, head to Ramundberget (20km north of Funäsdalen) and Tänndalen (12km west), which offer both downhill and nordic sections. Between them, they comprise 24 ski lifts and 75 runs, and the 300km of cross-country trails constitute the longest ski system in the world.

🛏 Sleeping & Eating

⟨TOP CHOICE⟩ STF Tänndalen/Skarvruets Fjällhotel
HOTEL €

(☑221 11; www.skarvruet.com; dm Skr185-200, s/d Skr230/380; 🅿) This great mountain hotel and hostel on a steep hillside in Tänndalen certainly looks the part: stuffed stags' heads and log fire in the cosy lounge-cum-bar and adorable Home Sweet Home rugs in the most homey rooms imaginable. The well-equipped hostel is located inside several red cottages with awesome views of the mountains across the valley. Hikes and nordic ski tracks start from the parking lot. Take bus 623 from Funäsdalen.

Hotel Funäsdalen
HOTEL €€

(☑214 30; www.hotell-funasdalen.se; dm summer/winter Skr225/325, B&B s/d Skr685/845, hotel s/d from Skr845/1090; 🅿☒) This is the go-to accommodation in Funäsdalen: a large, modern hotel with cosy dorms and attractive hotel rooms in two levels of fanciness. It's open all year and has a good restaurant (the daily lunch draws in lots of locals), a jacuzzi and pool.

🏠TF mountain huts
HOSTEL €

(dm Skr330; ⊙early Jul–mid-Sep & mid-Feb–mid-Apr) The STF-run mountain huts at Skedbro, Rogen and Storrödtjärn cannot be booked in advance and operate on a first come, first served basis. Each has around 20 beds and fully equipped kitchen; pay the warden on arrival.

STF Sylarna
LODGE €

(☑0647-722 00; www.sylarna.com; sites/dm/s/d Skr90/150/400/700; ⊙late Feb-Apr & late Jun-late Sep; ☒) Attractive mountain lodge with sauna, provisions shop and equipment rental. Dorms are for guests who don't mind sleeping with 19 other people.

STF Blåhammaren
LODGE €€

(☑0647-722 00; www.stfblahammaren.com; dm/d Skr275/900; ⊙late Feb-April & late Jun-late Sep; ☒) Sweden's highest mountain lodge (1080m) with awesome views from the sauna. Excellent base for hiking, biking and skiing.

ℹ Information

The tourist office (☑155 80;www.funasdalen. se; Rörosvägen 30; ⊙9am-6pm Mon-Fri, 10am-6pm Sat & Sun mid-Jun–Sep), inside the Fjällmuseum, has plenty of info on the attractions in the surrounding area and can advise on and arrange fishing, canoeing, biking and rock-climbing in summer and snow-mobile safaris, skiing and dogsledding in winter.

ℹ Getting There & Around

Härjedalingen (www.harjedalingen.se, in Swedish) runs buses between Stockholm and Funäsdalen (Skr370, nine hours), via Gävle and Järvsö, several days a week. From Funäsdalen, local bus 623 runs to Tänndalen (Skr25, 10 minutes, one to three daily except Sunday); in winter there are ski buses also. Bus 613 runs between Ljungdalen and Åsarna (Skr160, two hours, one daily except Saturday) where you can transfer to bus 164 to Östersund or else catch the Inlandsbanan. Bus 164 runs from Funäsdalen via Åsarna to Östersund (Skr210, 3½ hours, one or two daily).

THE BOTHNIAN COAST

Gävle

📍 026 / POP 92,000

Infamous among certain naughty young-sters because its name (pronounced *Yerv-luh*) sounds a lot like a Swedish curse word, Gävle, about 175km north of Stockholm along the E4 motorway, is a lively univer-sity town that's been a prosperous industrial centre since the late 19th century, when it exported local timber and iron. Founded in 1446, Gävle is officially Norrland's oldest town, but not much of its original incarna-tion remains due to a devastating fire in 1869.

◎ Sights & Activities

TOP CHOICE Länsmuseum Gävleborg   MUSEUM
(www.lansmuseetgavleborg.se; Södra Strandgatan 20; admission free; ⊙10am-4pm Tue, Thu & Fri, 10am-8pm Wed, noon-4pm Sat & Sun) The coun-ty museum, Länsmuseum Gävleborg, has beautifully designed exhibitions on regional culture through the ages, from prehistory to the 'golden era' (mid-19th century) to mod-ern times, with re-created sitting rooms and shopfronts, the life stories of key figures in Gävle's history, and multimedia augmenta-tion. Gävle's porcelain factory played a huge role in local industrial development, and you can see some of its finer specimens here. The excellent **Rettig Art Gallery** occupies the top two floors and showcases one of the most important collections of Swedish art, from neoclassicism to super-realism and postmodernism, with a special section dedi-cated to the Gothenburg Colourists.

TOP CHOICE Sveriges Järnvägsmuseet   MUSEUM
(www.jarnvagsmuseum.se; Rälsgatan 1; adult/child Skr50/free; ⊙10am-5pm Jun-Aug; 🚼) One of the best museums of its kind, the national rail museum, inside Gävle's former engine shed, traces the history of the railway in Sweden through a series of colourful displays and quirky facts. It's a great favourite with fami-lies, and apart from numerous old locomo-tives and carriages that you can clamber inside (including the 1859 hunting coach belonging to King Karl XV), the ample col-lections of miniature train models on dis-play and an X2000 simulator (Skr5), which allows you to 'drive' Sweden's fastest train, there are toy railways for the little ones to play with and even a small outdoor railway for them to ride. To get here, walk to the southern end of Muréngatan, and then fol-low the cycle path to the museum.

Mackmyra Svensk Whisky & Whiskyby   DISTILLERY
(www.mackmyra.se; Kungsbäcksvägen; ⊙10am-5pm Sat, tours Jun-Aug) For grown-ups, there's whisky-tasting at Mackmyra Svensk Whisky, established in 1999 as the first Scandinavian malt-whisky distillery. It's set in a historic *bruk* (works) about 10km west of Gävle. Mackmyra Journey tours (Skr450) must be booked in advance via the website; they depart from the Clarion Wynn Hotel. Mack-myra now has the additional Whiskyby dis-tillery and lookout tower just west of Gävle, off E4; a visit is included in the tour, though Whiskyby can be visited separately (open 10am to 5pm).

Gamla Gefle   MUSEUM
A fire in 1869 wiped out most of the col-ourful old wooden buildings that formed the town's core. Today the little cluster that

---

THE GÄVLE GOAT

Gävle's most famous resident is a 13-metre tall straw Gävle Goat – a giant version of the traditional Yule Goat. It's been making an appearance at Slottstorget in early December since 1966 and every year attempts are made to burn it down. Bets are made locally and internationally as to whether the goat will go down before Christmas or before New Year's Eve. Since this seasonal vandalism really, erm, gets their goat, city authorities have at-tempted to prevent the goat's untimely demise by treating it with flame-retardant chemi-cals and monitoring it with security cameras. This has not deterred would-be vandals: in 1976, parties unknown drove a car into it and in 2005, the cameras captured the image of two arsonists dressed as Santa and a gingerbread man shooting a flaming arrow at it. The only time the goat was burned down 'legally' was during the shooting of the Swedish film *Black Jack* in 1990, when the director paid the hefty Skr100,000 fine (the cost of building the goat) for the privilege.

Gävle

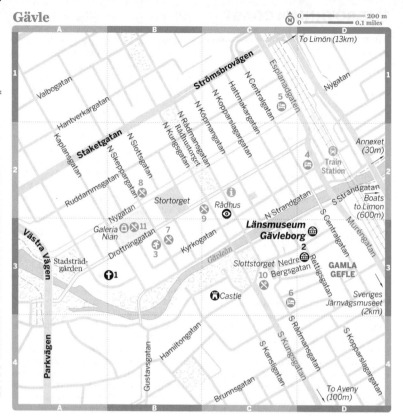

Gävle

survived the fire is preserved in the rickety jumble that is Gamla Gefle, just south of the city centre. It's fun to wander through and surprisingly easy to get lost in, considering its tiny size. One of the houses is now **Joe Hillgården** (www.joehill.se; Nedre Bergsgatan 28; admission free; ☺noon-6pm Jul–mid-Aug), a museum marking the birthplace of the US labour-union organiser. Hill was wrongly convicted of a murder and executed in Utah in 1915. Some of his folk songs form part of the memorial here.

Furuvik   AMUSEMENT PARK
(www.furuvik.se; adult/child Skr195/165; ☺31 May-Aug; ⊞) There's been a circus on the site of Furuvik for aeons. This entertainment zone, which now incorporates roller coasters, an Aqua Jungle pool area with water slides and zoo about 12km southeast of Gävle, aims to provide a little of everything; you can act like a monkey on the amusement rides and then see the real thing at the ape enclosure.

It's also the site for the Scandinavian Country Music Fair and other festivities. Take the Furuvik-bound bus from bus stop D (late June to early August).

Limön
ISLAND

From late May to late August daily **boat tours** (adult/child each way Skr40/25, up to 3 daily) run from Södra Skeppsbron to the island of Limön, part of the surrounding archipelago and very popular with sun worshippers. The island has a **nature trail**, and several forested walking paths, **mass grave** and **memorial** to the sailors of a ship that was lost here in the early 1800s.

Heliga Trefaldighets kyrka
CHURCH

At the western end of Drottninggatan, the oldest of the churches in Gävle has an 11th-century **rune stone** inside, as well as incredible woodcrafter decoration – the work of German craftsman Ewardt Friis.

🛏 Sleeping

Järnvägshotellet & Annexet
HOTEL €€

(☑12 09 90; www.jarnvagshotellet.nu; s/d incl breakfast Skr525/695, Annexet s/d Skr735/975; 🅿🛜) Just across a public square from the train station, this small family-run hotel in a historic building has 18 individually decorated rooms with TVs. The separate Annexet at Norra Skeppbron has just eight modern en-suite rooms. Call ahead to get the building code. Student discounts available.

STF Vandrarhem Gamla Gefle
HOSTEL €

(☑62 17 45; stf.vandrarhem@telia.com; Södra Rådmansgatan 1; dm/s/d Skr185/360/480; ⊙mid-Jan–early Dec) Set in one of Gamla Gefle's old-style wooden buildings around a flowering courtyard, this quiet hostel is popular with local travellers of all ages. There are cosy nooks and crannies and a good guest kitchen. Breakfast buffet costs Skr70.

Scandic-CH
HOTEL €€€

(☑495 84 00; www.scandic-hotels.se; Nygatan 45; s/d from Skr1450/1670, discounted to Skr1050/1350; 🅿❋🛜) Near the train station is this business-friendly hotel, which overcomes chaininess with cheery staff and small perks like bicycles for guests to borrow. Rooms are typical Scandinavian style: Ikea-style furniture and bedding, flat-screen TVs and eco-conscious wall art.

Aveny
HOTEL €€

(☑615 590; www.aveny.nu; Södra Kunsgatan 31; s/d Skr695/950; 🅿) Family-run budget hotel south of the river with brightly decorated rooms and a homey feel.

🍴 Eating

⬛ TOP CHOICE Church Street Saloon
TEX-MEX €€

(Kyrkogatan 11; meals from Skr180; ⊙dinner Mon-Fri, lunch & dinner Sat) Locals stampede this Wild West–themed saloon, encrusted with cowboy kitsch, looking to rustle up some Tex-Mex. The steaks, enchiladas, ribs, buffalo wings and Macho Nachos arrive on plates the size of serving platters, so come hungry. On Friday and Saturday nights after 10pm, the bar wenches hitch up their skirts and dance the can-can on the bar.

Helt Enkelt Bar & Kök
SWEDISH €€

(www.heltenkelt.org; Norra Kungsgatan 3; meals from Skr175; ⊙dinner Mon-Fri & Sun, lunch & dinner Sat ☑🎵) All Scandinavian chic and clean flavours, Helt Enkelt overflows with locals who come for the likes of potato pancakes with lingonberries, grilled Arctic char, lamb

---

WORTH A TRIP

FÄRNEBOFJÄRDEN NATIONAL PARK

About half water, Färnebofjärden occupies 260 sq km south of Gysinge, an ironworks town south of Gävle. It's bisected by the river Dalälven and has excellent fishing and enough sandy beaches to please those nature lovers who prefer the type of wildlife typically seen on Swedish beaches in the summer. But primarily the park is known as a birdwatcher's paradise, with ospreys, sea eagles, seven types of woodpecker, Ural owls and capercaillie.

Get information and maps at the **Naturum visitor centre** (☑0291-47 10 40; Gysinge Bruk; admission free; ⊙10am-5pm Apr-Sep, 11am-4pm Wed, Sat & Sun Oct-Dec), which also has a small exhibition about the local wildlife and ecology. There are five rustic cabins in the park (no electricity or water), two of which are open year-round, which can be booked through Naturum.

There's no public transport to the park.

SKIN ART

If you want a permanent souvenir of your visit to Gävle, **Fallen Angel** (☑614 148; www.fallenangeltattoo.com; Norra Skeppergatan 3) will be happy to oblige. The proprietress is the first tattoo artist in Scandinavia to practise electrodermography, which is typically used to remove tattoos, but is now used as a decorating tool in its own right. Instead of introducing pigment to your skin, it removes it, so you're left with a smooth pale scar in the shape of your choice!

burger with truffle sauce and other modern takes on Swedish dishes. There are several vegetarian options also, such as asparagus risotto, and the kids get their own set menu (Skr50).

Coffee Lounge
INTERNATIONAL €

(www.coffee-lounge.se; Nygatan 21; meals from Skr100; ☺closes at 6pm Sat, 5pm Sun; ☑) This bright, trendy cafe on the main drag is a great place to people-watch and it does so much more besides the signature latte art coffees: filled bagels, generous salads made with bulgur wheat and quinoa and daily pasta specials abound for as little as Skr70.

Lam's Terrass
THAI €

(Slottstorget 3; meals from Skr150; ☺lunch & dinner; ☑) Thai joint serving spicy dishes either inside at stylish restaurant booths or on its namesake terrace on Gävle's ultimate cruising street.

Naked Juice Bar
SANDWICHES €

(Galeria Nian; meals from Skr59; ☺11am-7pm) Toasted, filled focaccia, meaty and veggie fajita wraps, and fresh soups and mega fruit smoothies.

❶ Information

The **tourist office** (☑177 117; www.gavle.se, www.gastrikland.com; Stadshuset, Drottninggatan 22; ☺8am-6pm Mon-Fri, 10am-5pm Sat, noon-4pm Sun mid-Jun–late Aug) has brochures aplenty on the city and surrounding area.

❶ Getting There & Away

BUS Long-distance bus services leave from behind the train station. For Ybuss departures, take a 'Busstaxi' (Skr50, paid when you book your ticket) from the train station to Gävlebro. **Ybuss** (www.ybuss.se) runs daily to Sundsvall (Skr225, three to 3½ hours, three to seven daily), Umeå (Skr375, 6½ to 7½ hours, three to five daily) and Östersund (Skr350, 5½ to 6¼ hours, once daily except Saturday). **SGS Bussen** (www.sgsbussen.nu) runs to Stockholm (Skr130, two hours, five to six daily).

TRAINS From Gävle, there are numerous daily services to Stockholm (Skr162, 2½ to 4½ hours) via Uppsala (Skr116, one hour), 11 departures to Sundsvall (Skr106, two to 2½ hours), and one or two trains to Kiruna (Skr724, 15 hours) via Luleå (Skr521, 12½ hours), and three to Östersund (Skr205, 2½ to 4½ hours).

Hudiksvall & Around

☑0650 / POP 14,850

Having survived no less than 10 major fires and a major Russian onslaught in 1721 that left only the church intact, it's a wonder that Hudiksvall is still standing! What was once a prosperous trading and shipping centre (earning it the nickname 'Glada Hudik' or 'Happy Hudik') is now an attractive little town with a cute harbour surrounded by red wooden fishermen's storehouses (*Möljen*), where the locals like to linger. The most exciting time to visit is in early July, during the 10-day cultural Musik vid Dellen festival (www.musikviddellen.se), held in the countryside around Hudik, which includes folk music and other spectacles.

◎ Sights & Activities

TOP CHOICE / **Hälsinglands Museum**
MUSEUM

(Storgatan 31; admission free; ☺noon-4pm Mon, 10am-4pm Tue-Fri, noon-4pm Sat) The Hälsinglands Museum covers local history, culture and art, including a re-created cottage interior with traditional painted furniture and costumes from the region. Highlights are the eerily illuminated medieval church art, including a particularly striking Madonna, carved by local artist Haaken Gulleson, and the Malsta rune stone from around AD 1000, engraved with the Helsinge runic script (unfortunately, the museum doesn't have an English translation). Upstairs is reserved for an early cubism exhibition by Swedish artists John Sten and Dick Beer.

Jacobs Kyrka
CHURCH

Just southwest of the centre, the unusually ornate Jakobs kyrka dates from 1672. Its exterior is still pockmarked from the 18th-century Russian cannonball onslaught, though if you think that the citizens of Glada Hudik haven't had a good clean out since then, the cannonball by the steps to the pulpit is, in fact, a replica.

Fiskarstan
HISTORICAL BUILDING

Beyond Möljen, along Hamngatan, is the grander Fiskarstan (Fishermen's Town), consisting of partially preserved, elegantly wood-panelled merchants' yards and winter dwellings of local fishermen, dating back to the early 19th century.

🛏 Sleeping & Eating

Malnbadens Camping & STF Hudiksvall
HOSTEL €

(📞132 60; www.malnbadenscamping.com; sites from Skr140, dm/s/d Skr210/340/420; 🅿) Four kilometres east of the centre of Hudiksvall, this is a large, popular lakeside caravan park (with campsites) that's also home to the pleasant STF hostel, inside red wooden cottages, open year-round, with canoes for rent and a decent lakeside restaurant. Bus 5 runs out here in summer, but weekend times are inconvenient, so its best to have your own wheels.

First Hotell Statt
HOTEL €€

(📞150 60; www.firsthotels.se; Storgatan 36; s/d from Skr1175/1900; 🅿❄🔁) This upmarket 19th-century hotel, where the timber barons earned the town its nickname with their carousing, has a nautical theme and comfortable though not overly memorable rooms. Attached are a restaurant and the town's only nightclub, which is apparently the place to be on weekends.

Möljens
TOP CHOICE
SWEDISH €

(Möljen; ☺lunch) Sometimes, perfection lies in sheer simplicity. Follow the crowds to this takeaway counter at the end of the row of red wooden buildings and perch on the steps by the water to devour your flavoursome, freshly fried herring sampler (three kinds for Skr25) or a *strömmingrulle* (fried herring in a wrap; Skr55).

Radjos Restaurang
STEAKHOUSE €€

(www.radjos.se; Åhlenshusét; meals from Skr160; ☺lunch & dinner) Elegant surroundings and meat and more meat on the menu – from meatballs and pork tenderloin with chanterelle sauce to the grand steak (Skr275). This is a good place to try the region's specialities, such as the baked goat's cheese with honey or the famous Västerbotten cheese.

Hot Chilli
ASIAN €

(www.hotchilli.se; Hamngatan 5, meals from Skr 120; 🥢) Bustling, informal joint specialising in tasty satay skewers and Chinese and Thai dishes, including good vegetarian options. The lunch specials are a steal at Skr79.

ℹ Information

You'll find banks and other services on Storgatan and Drottninggatan.

The **tourist office** (📞191 00; www.hudiksvall. se/turism; www.halsingland.com; Storgatan 33; ☺10am-4pm Mon-Fri) has internet access and information on the area, much of it in Swedish only, though the bilingual staff are very helpful.

ℹ Getting There & Away

BUS The bus station is next to the main train station, by the harbour. Ybuss travels to Gävle (Skr125, 1½ hours to two hours 20 minutes, two to five daily), Östersund (Skr280, 3¾ hours, one daily except Saturday), Stockholm via Uppsala (Skr260, 3¾ to 4½ hours, two to five daily) and

---

WORTH A TRIP

JÄRVSÖ: INTO THE WILD

Järvsö's biggest attraction is **Järvzoo** (📞0651-403 06; http://jarvzoo.se; adult/child/under 5yr Skr175/95/free; ☺10am-5pm Jun-Aug; 🚼), an animal park devoted to northern Swedish wildlife. A 3km boardwalk leads you past the spacious enclosures housing large mammals such as elk, reindeer, musk oxen and roe deer. The adjacent **Rovdjurcentret** is home to predators which include brown bears, wolves, wolverines, lynx, honey buzzards and snowy owls, who seem contented in relatively natural environments. If you want to wake up with the wolves, you can stay over in three comfortable, en suite 'Wolf Panorama' rooms (single/double Skr1450/1900, including breakfast and entry fee).

Trains run north from Järvsö to Östersund, and south to Gävle and Stockholm.

Umeå (Skr305, 5½ to six hours, one to four daily).

TRAIN SJ trains run to Sundsvall (Skr85 to Skr145, 50 minutes, six to 12 daily), Gävle (Skr112 to Skr152, one hour 20 minutes, nine to 12 daily), Söderhamn (Skr64 to Skr145, 30 minutes, nine to 12 daily) and Stockholm (Skr264 to Skr364, 2½ to three hours, seven to 10 daily).

Sundsvall

🕿060 / POP 50,000

When Sundsvall burned to the ground in 1888 after a spark from the Selånger steamboat set the town brewery alight, civic leaders made a decision to have the old wooden houses rebuilt in stone, separated by wide avenues. This immediately set Sundsvall apart from the other towns along the Bothnian coast, making them look like poor provincial cousins by comparison. Unfortunately, this move forced poorer residents (including the workers who rebuilt Sundsvall) to the city's outskirts while wealth and power collected in the centre.

👁 Sights & Activities

TOP CHOICE Kulturmagasinet MUSEUM
(Sjögatan; admission free) Down near the harbour, Kulturmagasinet is a magnificent restoration of some old warehouses and now contains the library and **Sundsvall Museum** (⏱10am-7pm Mon-Thu, to 6pm Fri, 11am-4pm Sat & Sun), which has engaging exhibits of the history of Sundsvall, natural history and geology. There's a permanent art exhibition upstairs featuring 20th-century Swedish artists and the superb temporary exhibitions have recently included Edward C Curtis' early-20th-century photography of Native Americans.

Norra Stadsberget LANDMARK
One of the most popular activities is the hike up to the 19th-century viewing tower on the Norra Stadsberget hill (150m), from which you get sweeping views of the city, squeezed into a space between the sea and surrounding hills. To get here, take Skolhusallén across the river and follow the signs for the youth hostel, or else take Norra Berget–bound bus 70 (four to five daily) from platform K.

Södra Stadsberget LANDMARK
The southern hill, Södra Stadsberget (250m), has an extensive plateau that is good for hiking, with trails up to 12km long. Buses 70 and 71, respectively, run to the two hills from platform K (four to five daily) in summer.

Alnö Gamla Kyrka CHURCH
The large island just east of Sundsvall, Alnö, has the magnificent **Alnö Gamla Kyrka** (⏱noon-6pm mid-Jun–mid-Aug), 2km north of the bridge (at Vi). The old church, below the road, is a mixture of 12th- and 15th-century styles. Whitewashing damaged the lower parts of the wall paintings in the 18th century, but the upper wall and ceiling paintings are nearly perfect. The painting was probably done by one of Albertus Pictor's pupils. Even better is the late-11th-century carved wooden **font** in the new church across the road; the upper part combines Christian and Viking symbolism, while the lower part shows beasts that embody evil. Catch bus 1 to Vi from platform C (two hourly), then take a Plus bus to the churches (every one or two hours).

🛏 Sleeping

Lilla Hotellet HOTEL €€
(🕿61 35 87; www.lilla-hotellet.se; Rådhusgatan 15; s/d Skr650/850; 🅿) In a stone building designated a historical monument (since it was built the year after the great fire), this small family-run hotel has a great location and a friendly vibe. The eight spacious rooms with high ceilings have interesting architectural details, such as ceramic tile stoves.

Elite Hotel Knaust HOTEL €€€
(🕿608 00 00; www.elite.se; Storgatan 13; d incl breakfast from Skr1350; 🅿) In a striking 19th-century building on Sundsvall's main pedestrian drag, this opulent hotel is full

---

HORNSDALET ARCHIPELAGO

The Hornsdalet Archipelago to the east of Hudiksvall is one of the most attractive in Sweden – all deserted beaches, forested islets and tiny fishing villages with weathered wooden houses and traditional coastal smokeries. Attractive **Kuggörarna**, about 30km east of Hudiksvall, is an excellent example of just such a village. The coast is also a good place to witness the raised beaches caused by postglacial uplift (still going on) and forests that are growing in boulder fields.

HERE BE DRAGONS

In a bid to fight fire with fire, the residents of Sundsvall adopted the dragon as the town's symbol the last time the town burned to the ground. (And, just to make sure, stone became the building material of choice.) As with Gävle's goats, you will find brightly painted dragons – a favourite with local children – all over the city centre. Each is annually sponsored by a company who pay a local artist to decorate it, and the town's favourite dragon wins a prize.

of old-world charm. Besides the beautiful lobby, the rooms are decorated in classical style and have high ceilings. The breakfast buffet is excellent, though wi-fi is not free.

STF Vandrarhem Sundsvall　HOSTEL €
(☑61 21 19; www.gaffelbyn.se; Gaffelbyvägen; dm Skr150, s/d from Skr225/350; ℗⚏) The STF hostel is above the town on Norra Stadsberget, and has both older rooms and more expensive modern rooms with private bathroom. There's a BBQ area in summer as well as a large playground for kids. The 20-minute walk to the hostel from the city centre is pleasant, but take bus 70 (summer only) from the train and bus stations if you've got heavy bags.

Sleep In　　　　　　, HOSTEL €
(☑070-555 32 50; www.sleepin.se; Trädgårdsgatan 43; r per person Skr300; ℗) Cubelike, windowless but well-ventilated twin rooms, each bed with own TV, reading light and wardrobe. Get your key at the Thai restaurant next door and be careful not to leave it in your room, or else you'll get locked out.

✗ Eating

The largest selection of restaurants is along Storgatan.

TOP
CHOICE **Tant Anci & Fröcken Sara**　CAFE €
(www.tantancifrokensara.com; Bankgatan 15; meals from Skr95; ⊙breakfast, lunch & dinner Mon-Fri, 5pm Sat & Sun; ☑) Humongous bowls of soup or salad are the speciality at this adorable organic cafe, where you can also get hearty sandwiches, giant bowls of pasta and pastries. There are only a few tables, but you can grab the food to go.

Invito Ristorante Italiano　ITALIAN €€€
(☑15 39 00; www.invitobar.se; Strogatan 6-8; meals from Skr400; ⊙lunch & dinner) The service at this fine dining establishment is as polished as the decor, and the chef successfully blends Italian cuisine with local seasonal ingredients, so you'll be looking at gnocchi with reindeer and juniper sauce, grilled venison and cloudberry tiramisu. The four-course tasting menu (Skr650) is well worth the splurge and the sommelier can help you choose from an extensive wine list. The weekday lunch specials are only Skr90.

Chaow-Praya River　　　　THAI €
(www.thaisundsvall.se; Trädgårdsgatan 43; meals from Skr130; ⊙lunch & dinner; ☑) With its dark polished wood interior, and plants everywhere, this Thai place convincingly conjures the feel of the tropics both through its food and interior. The dishes are vibrant and spicy and the weekday lunch buffet is excellent value.

❶ Information

Tourist office (☑61 04 50; www.sundsvallturism.com, www.upplev mittsverige.nu; Stora Torget; ⊙10am-6pm Mon-Fri, also 10am-4pm Sat Jul & Aug) Has information on activities, including summer boat tours.

❶ Getting There & Away

AIR **Midlanda Airport** (☑19 76 00) is 22km north of Sundsvall; buses run from the bus station three to eight times daily (Skr90) to connect with weekday SAS and City Airline flights to Göteborg, Luleå and Stockholm.

BUS Buses depart from the Sundsvall bus station, near Kulturmagasinet. Ybuss runs daily to Östersund (Skr200, 2½ hours, one to two daily except Saturday), Gävle (Skr225, three to 3½ hours, four to five daily) and Stockholm (Skr285, five to six hours, four to eight daily). Länstrafiken Västerbotten buses 10 and 100 run to Umeå (Skr310, 3½ to five hours; up to 11 daily) and other coastal towns.

TRAIN Trains run west to Östersund and south to Söderhamn, Gävle and Stockholm. The station is just east of the town centre on Landsvagsalen, which is a continuation of Köpmangatan.

Härnösand

☑0611 / POP 25,280

Once a pre-Viking trading post on the island of Härnön, Härnösand was burned to the ground three times in the 1700s: once when drunken churchgoers set the place on fire by accident, once by schoolboy pranksters, and once when Russian Cossacks flattened the town in 1721, destroying all but three buildings. Härnösand's square is lined with attractive 18th-century buildings, and its pretty harbour fills up with yachts in July when Härnösand celebrates its maritime heritage. Länsmuseet Västernorrland (www.murberget.se; Murberget; admission free; ☺11am-6pm Tue-Sun) is an excellent regional museum with permanent exhibitions that include furniture, historic photographs and Sami handicrafts. The adjacent open-air museum, Friluftsmuseet Murberget, is the second largest of its kind in Sweden and features over 80 buildings, including a 19th-century shop, traditional farmhouses, smithy, church and school in the style typical of this part of Norrland. The museums are a 30-minute walk from the centre; or else take bus 2 or 52 from Nybrogatan near the Rådhuset.

Directly across the street from the cathedral in a restored building that dates from 1844, STF Mitti Härnösand (☑243 00; www.mittiharnosand.com; Franzengatan 14 & Köpmangatan 7; dm/s/d Skr150/250/350, s/d/tr Skr300/450/600; ☺reception 8-10am & 3-5pm; ⓟ) has excellent facilities and is in a handy location. Even more centrally located is the second building on Köpmangatan, which features bright en-suite rooms and a guest kitchen.

One of the best restaurants in town, Ruom Thai (Storgatan 34; meals from Skr140; ☺lunch & dinner) really delivers when it comes to fiery, aromatic red and green curries and assorted noodle dishes.

The tourist office (☑881 40; www.harnosand.se; Stora Torget 2; ☺9am-6pm Mon-Fri, 10am-3pm Sat & Sun Jun-Aug) is located on the main square and sells guides to the Höga Kusten.

Bus 100 runs to Sundsvall (Skr85, 45 minutes, five to seven daily) and Umeå (Skr263, 2¾ to four hours, seven daily). Ybuss runs daily to Gävle (Skr265, 3½ to 4½ hours, four to six daily) and Stockholm (Skr325, 5½ to 6½ hours, four to six daily).

Höga Kusten

☑0613

Cross the Höga Kustenbron, the spectacular suspension bridge over the Ångerman river – Norrland's answer to the Golden Gate Bridge, one of the longest in the world (1867m) – and you find yourself amid some of the most dramatic scenery on the Swedish coastline. The secret to the Höga Kusten's (High Coast's) spectacular beauty is elevation; nowhere else on the coast do you find such a mountainous landscape, with sheer rocky cliffs – the highest in Sweden – plunging straight down to the sea, as well as lakes, fjords and dozens of tranquil islands, covered in dense pine forest. The region was recently recognised as a geographically unique area and listed as a Unesco World Heritage Site in 2000.

The combined processes of glacial retreat and land rising from the sea (which continues today at a rate of 8mm per year) are responsible for this stunning scenery. Höga Kusten stretches from north of Härnösand to Örnsköldsvik, and it's a wonderful area for scenic drives along the narrow twisty roads. Either town makes a handy base for exploration, though even more rewarding is a stay on the Högbonden, Ulvön and Trysunda islands.

These can be reached by a combination of buses and boats (summer only), though due to the scarcity of public transport, it's much easier to explore the area with your own set of wheels. That's unless, of course, you wish to walk the Höga Kusten Leden, a 129km hiking trail stretching from Höga Kustenbron to Örnsköldsvik (see p282).

ⓘ Information

The regional tourist office (☑504 80; www.hogakusten.com, www.bestofhighcoast.com; ☺10am-6pm Jun-Aug), located inside Hotell Höga Kusten, just north of Höga Kustenbron suspension bridge, can help you with information on exploring the region. It's open year round and has a detailed map of the scenic byways, boat timetables and guidebooks on the Höga Kusten Trail.

Naturum Höga Kusten (☑70 02 00, www.naturumhogakusten.se; ☺9am-7pm late Jun–mid-Aug, shorter hours mid-Aug–Oct) is located off the E4 north of the village of Docksta, at the foot of the steep Mt Skuleberget (285m). Apart from stocking practical info on the Höga Kusten, local hiking routes and rock-climbing routes (grades 2 to 3), it stages lectures and events and offers guided tours of the Skuleskogen National Park.

HÖGBONDEN

A tiny island in the southern part of Höga Kusten, Högbonden is only 15 minutes by boat from the villages of Bönhamn and Barsta. It's famous for its 100-year-old lighthouse – the island's only building – atop the highest point of the island's rocky plateau that soars above the tree line. The island is bisected by a narrow gorge, and its hills and cliffs lend themselves to exploration. Although you can pay a quick visit to the island along with hordes of summer day trippers, it's best to stay overnight at the **Vandrarhem Högbonden** (☑230 05, 420 49; www.hogbonden.se; dm Skr300-350; ☺May-Oct) inside the lighthouse, a cosy place with two- and four-bed rooms, a library, guest kitchen and summer cafe that will be your only source of sustenance unless you bring your own food. There are no TVs or internet here; the main attractions here are sunset-watching or diving off the jetty (signposted *bastu*) and relaxing in the wood-burning sauna by the sea. Book well in advance.

ULVÖN

☑0660

The largest island in the Höga Kusten archipelago, Ulvön is famous for its regatta (14 to 18 July) and for the production of *surströmming;* it's possible to purchase the noxious (or delightful, depending on your outlook) stuff in the shops at Ulvöhamn, the island's one-street village. A picturesque fishermen's settlement with traditional red-and-white wooden houses, it's worth a visit for the tiny 17th-century **chapel** decorated inside with colourful murals, and very popular with summer day trippers. A cycle path leads you to the preserved 17th-century fishing village of **Sandviken** at the north part of the island. If you wish to linger overnight, the plush **Ulvö Skarrgårdshotell** (☑22 40 09; www. ulvohotell.se; d Skr2048-2390) is conveniently located by the quay; its superb restaurant has a seasonal menu featuring local ingredients. A cheaper spot is the **hostel** (☑522-291 84; www.ulvon.se; s/d/tr Skr445/580/860; ☺Apr-Sep); walk uphill, beyond the chapel.

The tiny **tourist office** (☑22 40 93; www. ulvon.com;☺noon-3pm late Jun–mid-Aug), near the quay, has bikes for rent.

TRYSUNDA

A small island with a namesake village consisting of cute fishermen's houses clustered around a little U-shaped bay, Trysunda has an attractive **wooden chapel**, dating back to 1655 – the oldest along the Bothnian Coast. There are also some great secluded spots for bathing, reachable by the walking paths that run through the woods; just pick your own flat rock by the water or else head to the sandy cove at Björnviken, on the east side of the island. You can walk around the whole of Trysunda in an hour or two, but overnight stays are available at **Trysunda Gästhamn** (☑430 38; www.trysunda.com, in Swedish; Skr250 per person), a guesthouse consisting of two cabins with beds and guest kitchens. You can order breakfast and lunch here, or else purchase some smoked fish at the village shop, which also stocks free maps of the island.

❶ Getting There & Around

BUS You can reach most departure points for boats by public transport. Buses are infrequent on weekends. Länstrafiken Västerbotten buses 10 and 100 (at least six daily) run between Härnösand and Örnsköldsvik, stopping at

---

SURSTRÖMMING – A DEADLY DELIGHT

The fishing villages of southern Norrland – particularly those along the Höga Kusten – are known for a local delicacy that'll make the majority of your Swedish friends grimace with disgust, though aficionados consider it to be the ultimate treat. The tradition of eating fermented herring goes back to the 16th century in Ulvön. Today, *surströmming* is made by placing herring in tins filled with light brine; the small amount of salt used leads to the fermentation process which, in turn, produces noxious gases that blow the tins up into football shapes during the four- to 10-week process. These gases contain toxins high enough to make this delicacy ineligible for sale in the EU for health reasons and the 'aroma' produced when the tins are opened makes most people run for cover; restaurants won't open them on their premises because you can never get rid of the smell. *Surströmming* is traditionally consumed in early autumn, accompanied by chopped onion and small, sweet, almond-shaped potatoes, washed down with beer or akvavit. If you're lucky (or unlucky!), you might chance upon last year's tins in shops along the Höga Kusten.

DON'T MISS

THE HIGH COAST TRAIL

The Höga Kusten Leden (High Coast Trail) is 129km long and runs the entire length of the Höga Kusten, starting at the northern end of the Höga Kustenbron and finishing at the summit of Varvsberget, the hill overlooking Örnsköldsvik. The trail is divided into 13 sections, each between 15km and 24km in length, with accommodation at the end of each section consisting mostly of rustic cabins. Buses running along the E4 stop at either end of the trail, as well as by the Lappuden, Ullånger, Skoved, Skule Naturum and Köpmanholmen villages along the way, close to the different sections of the trail. The trail is well signposted but it's best to pick up a detailed booklet and map at either the Härnösand or Örnsköldsvik tourist office.

Parts of the trail involve an easy ramble, whereas other sections will challenge you with steep uneven ground. Take food and plenty of drinking water with you.

The trail takes in some of the most beautiful coastal scenery in Sweden, from rocky coastline and sandy coves to lush countryside, dense evergreen forest and deep ravines, including Slåtterdalskrevan, a 200m-deep canyon in Skuleskogen National Park, through which part of the trail passes. The 26-sq-km park, which lies between Docksta and Köpmanholmen, is a Unesco World Heritage Site due to its wealth of fauna and flora: the park is home to the lynx, roe deer, mink and other shy animals, as well as all four of Sweden's game birds: the black grouse, willow grouse, capercaillie and hazel hen.

A recommended detour from the trail is north of Docksta, towards Norrgällsta (1.4km), where you can either hike up Mt Skuleberget or take a cable car (Skr90; ☉10am-5pm Jun-Aug) to the top to appreciate the all-encompassing view. The Skuleberget cave is another popular attraction – it was once a hideout for bandits. Other worthwhile diversions include Dalsjöfallet (1.5km from the main trail), a waterfall that lies halfway between Skuleberget and Gyltberget mountains, and lake Balestjärn, with its crystal-clear waters, in the middle of the small peninsula to the north of Köpmanholmen.

Ullånger, Docksta and Bjästa. From Örnsköldsvik, bus 421 runs to Köpmanholmen via Bjästa (Skr 51, 40 minutes, up to 11 daily). The villages of Bönhamn and Barsta are not reachable by public transport.

BOAT M/S Ronja ferry (☎105 50; www.hkship.se; adult/child return Skr150/50) to Högbonden departs Barsta from early May to mid-June and from mid-August to early October (noon Friday to Sunday), and leaves both Barsta and Bönhamn from mid-June to mid-August four times daily.

M/S Kusttrafik ferry (☎105 50; www.hkship.se; adult/child Skr195/70) to Ulvön leaves Ullånger for Ulvöhamn via Docksta daily at 9.30am, returning from Ulvöhamn at 3pm between June and August.

MF Ulvön ferry (☎070-651 92 65; www.ornskoldsvikshamn.se; ☉mid-Jun–mid-Aug) to Ulvöhamn and Trysunda leaves Köpmanholmen for Ulvöhamn (adult/child Skr150/90 return, 1½ hours, four daily) and separately for Trysunda (adult/child Skr120/80, 30 minutes, twice daily). From late May to mid-June and mid-August to mid-September, there are reduced services, calling at Ulvöhamn twice daily and at Trysunda once or twice daily. From January to late May and mid-September to

December, both destinations are served daily; check website for times.

Örnsköldsvik

☎0660 / POP 28,617

Famous within Sweden for producing the handsome ice-hockey star Peter 'Foppa' Forsberg, Örnsköldsvik is a good base for exploring the Höga Kusten.

The Örnsköldsviks Museum & Konsthall (www.museumkonsthall.se; Läroverksgatan 1; adult/child Skr25/free, special exhibits Skr150/100; ☉11am-8pm Tue, to 4pm Wed-Sat) covers 9000 years of local history and includes a section on the Sami. Upstairs you'll find the works on Bror Marklund, one of Sweden's most important 20th-century sculptors.

Another sculptor, Hans Hedberg (1917–2007), was born just south of Örnsköldsvik, and you can see some of his work – including his signature huge sculptures of fruit and eggs – at the Hans Hedberg Museum (Arken; admission free, guided tours Skr20; ☉8am-5pm Mon-Fri) in the shiny modern building by the harbour.

About 5km south of the centre is **Gene Fornby** (adult/child Skr70/40; ☉noon-5pm Jul-mid-Aug), a reconstruction of a 6th-century Iron Age farm, complete with actors in period costume taking part in a wide range of activities, from baking to iron working.

In town, you can stay at the landmark **First Hotel Statt** (☑26 55 90; www.firstho tels.se; Lasarettsgatan 2; s/d from Skr1239/1420, discounted to Skr790/990; P✿🐾), with great views of the bay, a terrace bar and a weekend nightclub. The international menu at **Café UH** (www.cafeuh.se; Lasarettsgatan 9; meals from Skr90; ☉breakfast, lunch & dinner) includes BBQ ribs, lasagne and tabouleh.

The **tourist office** (☑881 00; www.orn skoldsvik.se/turism; Strandgatan 24; ☉10am-5pm Mon-Fri, to 3pm Sat), inside Paradisbadet, sells guides to the Höga Kusten.

Bus 100 runs south to Sundsvall (Skr188, two to three hours, five to six daily) and north to Umeå (Skr137, 1½ to two hours, seven daily).

Umeå

☑090 / POP 114,075

With the vibrant feel of a college town (it has around 30,000 students), Umeå is a welcome outpost of urbanity in the barren north. It's one of the fastest-growing towns in Sweden and an agreeable place in which to hang out, wind down or stock up for an outdoor adventure.

Umeå is also widely considered the most 'metal' town in Sweden, thanks to its thriving metal and straight-edge music scene. Legendary hardcore band Refused started here, and an annual music festival, **House of Metal** (www.houseofmetal.se), takes place at Folkets Hus in early February – the darkest time of the year, of course.

👁 Sights & Activities

TOP CHOICE **Gammlia** MUSEUM

(www.vsb.se; admission free; ☉10am-5pm mid-Jun-mid-Aug; 🚻) The centrepiece of this cluster of museums is the excellent **Västerbottens Museum**, which traces the history of the province from prehistoric times to Umeå today, with well-presented exhibitions including photographs of the Sami and an absolutely enormous skis-through-the ages collection which includes the world's oldest ski (5200 years old). Next door is **Bildmuséet**, the riveting modern-art museum, which features temporary exhibitions of

thought-provoking works. These are surrounded by the large **Friluftsmuséet**, an open-air historic village where staff wear period clothes and demonstrate traditional homestead life. Paths, teeming with strolling families, meander past the **Fiske och Sjöfartsmuseum**, with its nautically themed displays, and the bakery, where you can watch demonstrations on how to make *tunnbröd*, the thin unleavened bread typical of northern Sweden. Horse-drawn carriage rides are available – a big hit with the little ones! It takes around 20 minutes to walk to Gammlia, or else you can take buses 2 or 7.

Älgens Hus FARM

(Västernyliden 23; adult/child Skr120/60; ☉noon-6pm Tue-Sun mid-Jun–late Aug; 🚻) This elk farm, 70km west of Umeå along Route 92, near Bjurholm, is your chance to meet the (tame) King of the Forest face to face. There are also teepees and cabins if you wish to bunk with the hooved ones overnight, a museum dedicated to all things elk, and even a small dairy where the ultrarare elk cheese is produced. At Skr3000 per kg, this is the most expensive cheese you'll ever taste, so savour it! Don't forget to pick up bananas beforehand, as elks love them.

Holmön ISLAND

Holmön, known as the sunniest place in Sweden, is a 15km-long offshore island with a **boat museum** (adult/child Skr20/free; ☉mid-Jun–mid-Aug) and a collection of traditional craft, plus a good quayside restaurant and swimming beaches. In July there's a rowboat race to Finland, which is only 36km away. **Ferries** (www.holmon.com) depart two to three times daily from Norrfjärden (check the website for timetables), 26km northeast of Umeå; take bus 118 (Skr50). If the sea freezes in winter, you can take a snowmobile or hydrocopter across the ice.

🛏 Sleeping

STF Vandrarhem Umeå HOSTEL €

(☑77 16 50; www.umeavandrarhem.com; Västra Esplanaden 10; dm/s/d from Skr160/260/410; P) This busy and efficient youth hostel, one of the few in the region that's actually occupied by youth, has rooms that vary in quality: try to nab a space in one of the newer rooms with beds, as opposed to the rather basic dorms with bunk beds. It's in a great location: a residential neighbourhood at the edge of the town centre, though we believe that it's a wee bit cheeky to charge the price

Umeå

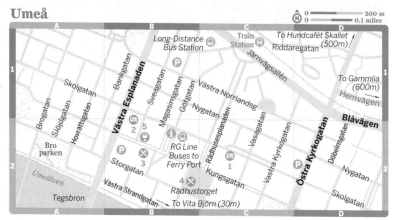

Umeå

🛏 Sleeping
1 Comfort Hotel Winn..............................C2
2 STF Vandrarhem Umeå B2

✖ Eating
3 Allstar B2
4 Rex Bar Och Grill.................................B2

🍷 Drinking
5 Schmäck B2

of a single if you're the only traveller in the dorm.

Hotel Pilen   HOTEL €€
(☎14 14 60; www.hotellpilen.se; Pilgatan 5; s/d Skr775/975; P🛏) This small boutique hotel has comfortable, unfussy, freshly refurbished rooms and is located in a quiet area some 600m from the town centre and close to the river. There's a recommended restaurant attached and a new wing with a pool and a sauna has just been added.

Comfort Hotel Winn   HOTEL €€
(☎10 07 30; www.resdags.se; Skolgatan 64; s/d incl breakfast. Skr1280/1480; P) Under new management, the former Royal Umeå has kept the spacious, clean-lined, Scandi-chic rooms and the fancy sauna. Hotel guests can work off the calories they picked up at the on-site Restaurant Victor, which features international dishes, at the convenient on-site gym. There's also a generous buffet breakfast included in the tariff.

✖ Eating & Drinking

TOP CHOICE **Rex Bar och Grill**   SWEDISH €€€
(☎090 70 60 50; www.rexbar.com; Rådhustorget; meals from Skr400; ☺breakfast, lunch & dinner) This popular establishment has northern Swedish cuisine meeting French brasserie in a convincing explosion of flavour. Choose from the likes of reindeer steak or *cote de boeuf,* preceded by oysters and followed by cloudberries and ice cream, or stop by for the awesome weekend brunch, which includes pancakes and bacon, American-style (Skr155). Dinner reservations on the weekend are recommended.

Vita Björn   SWEDISH €
(www.vitabjorn.se; Kajen 12; meals from Skr99; ☺lunch May-Sep; ✔) Perch yourself on the sunny deck of this boat-cum-restaurant and choose from a casual international menu of caesar salad, veggie burgers, baked salmon and pork tenderloin, or else go for the Swedish star – the fresh grilled herring.

Hundcafét Skallet   CAFE €
(www.skallet.se; Östra Kyrkogatan 64; meals from Skr75; ☺Sun-Fri; ✔🛏) Order from a menu of foccacias, cakes and pies (including the tasty mozzarella-and-pesto pie) while your dog chooses from a dog burger or a dog biscuit. Barking mad!

Allstar   AMERICAN €
(www.allstarbar.se; Kungsgatan 50A; meals from Skr120; ☺dinner Mon-Thu, lunch & dinner Fri-Sun) Extremely popular American-style sports bar serving Junk Food Deluxe: nachos, quesadillas, chicken wings and all that jazz.

Schmäck   CAFE €

(www.schmack.se; Kungsgatan 49; coffees from Skr18; ☺Mon-Sat; ☑) At this funky, laid-back coffee shop-chocolaterie, you can sample the latest chocolate decadence, sip fair-trade coffee and browse the little design boutique adjoining the cafe.

❶ Information

Tourist office (☑16 16 16; www.visitumea.se; Renmarkstorget 15; ☺9am-7pm Mon-Fri, 10am-4pm Sat, noon-4pm Sun Jun–mid-Aug) Located on a central square.

❶ Getting There & Around

AIR The **airport** (☑71 61 00) is 4km south of the city centre. SAS and Malmö Aviation each fly to Stockholm up to seven times daily. There are also direct flights to Luleå, Göteborg and Kiruna, and Air Baltic flights connect Umeå with Riga, Latvia.

BOAT **RG Line** (www.rgline.com) operates ferries between Umeå and Vaasa (Finland) once or twice daily (Sunday to Friday). A bus to the port leaves from near the tourist office an hour before RG Line's departures.

BUS The long-distance bus station is directly opposite the train station. Ybuss runs services south to Gävle (Skr375, 6½ to 7½ hours, three to five daily) and Stockholm (Skr430, nine to 9½ hours, three to six daily), stopping at all the coastal towns.

Buses 20 and 100 run up the coast to Haparanda (Skr356, 6¾ to 7¾ hours, four to six daily) via Luleå (Skr310, four to 4¾ hours) and Skellefteå (Skr169, two to 2½ hours). Bus 63 runs twice daily to Östersund (Skr339, 5¾ to six hours).

Local buses leave from Vasaplan on Skolgatan. The **Flygbuss** (☑16 22 50) leaves the airport for the city centre 10 minutes after every flight from Stockholm (Skr40, 20 minutes).

TRAIN Two overnight SJ trains leave daily for Stockholm (Skr813, 10 hours), while the northbound trains to Luleå (Skr265, 4½ to 5½ hours, two daily) stop in Boden, from where there are connections to Kiruna (Skr565, 5½ to 6½ hours, two daily) and Narvik, Norway(Skr674, ten to 10½ hours, two daily).

Skellefteå

☑0910 / POP 32,425

Constructed in 1845, Skellefteå is dominated by the impressive **Bonnstan**, a *kyrkstad* (church town) consisting of 392 weathered log cabins, built for the faithful coming from afar who needed a place to park their horse and rest their weary heads; many of them are still used as summer houses by locals. The owners are forbidden by law to renovate the houses due to their protected status.

Bonnstan's centrepiece is the striking white neoclassical **Skellefteå Landsförsamling Kyrka** (☺10am-4pm Mon-Fri), dating from 1800 in its current incarnation, but inside is the 13th-century **Virgin of Skellefteå**, carved out of walnut – the rarest of the church's medieval sculptures. Nearby, there's a footbridge to the small island of **Kyrkholmen**, featuring a tiny summer cafe specialising in coffee and waffles. Down the hill from the church is **Lejonströmsbron**, Sweden's longest wooden bridge, built during the year 1737 and the site of a skirmish between the Swedes and the Russians in 1741. The riverside Nordanå park is home to the cultural and historical collections of the **Skellefteå Museum** (www.skellefteamuseum.se; admission free; ☺10am-7pm Tue-Thu, noon-6pm Fri-Sun) and the thought-provoking modern-art exhibitions of **Museum Anna Nordlander** (http://man.skelleftea.org, in Swedish; ☺10am-7pm Tue-Thu, noon-6pm Fri-Sun).

WORTH A TRIP

BODEN

Built to protect Sweden against marauding Russians, the military town of Boden, 36km northwest of Luleå, is surrounded by no less than five forts and has a no-longer-top-secret nuclear bunker carved deep into the rock. The grandest of forts, **Rödbergsfortet** (www.rodbergsfortet.com; tours adult/child Skr100/75; ☺tours 11am-3pm late Jun-early Aug), had 15,000 serving there during WWII. Stay close to your guide lest you be lost in its vast corridors forever. At the hands-on **Försvarsmuseum** (Military Defence Museum; www.forsvarsmuseum.se; Granatvägen 2; adult/child Skr60/40; ☺11am-4pm Mon-Sun; ☑), where you can hop inside a tank and 'fly' a helicopter, it's not clear who'll enjoy the experience more, you or your child.

Behind the church, **Stiftsgården** (☏72 57 00; www.stiftsgarden.se; Brännvägen 25; dm Skr240, s/d from Skr290/480, hotel s/d from Skr890/1090; ℗) has cute whitewashed hotel rooms and simpler dorms in the STF hostel annex. In the centre, **Café Lilla Mari** (Nygatan 33; ⊙11am-6pm), in a secluded little courtyard, offers sandwiches from Skr45, hot lunches from Skr70 and an array of desserts.

The **tourist office** (☏73 60 20; www.skelleftea.se; Trädgårdsgatan 7; ⊙10am-6pm Mon-Fri, 10am-3pm Sat, noon-3pm Sun late Jun-early Aug) is on the corner of the pedestrianised Nygatan and the central square.

Buses 20 and 100 depart for Haparanda (Skr284, 4½ to 5½ hours, five daily), Luleå (Skr158, 2½ hours, five to eight daily) and Umeå (Skr269, 2¼ hours, six daily).

Luleå

☏0920 / POP 45,050

Luleå is the capital of Norrbotten, chartered in 1621, though it didn't become a boom town until the late 19th century when the Malmbanan railway was built to transport iron ore from the Bothnian Coast to Narvik, Norway. The town centre moved to its present location from Gammelstad in 1649 because of the falling sea level (8mm per year), due to postglacial uplift of the land. A university town and an important high-tech centre, Luleå is a pedestrian-friendly town with several parks and a sparkling bay with a marina.

☉ Sights

TOP
CHOICE **Gammelstad**   CHURCH TOWN

(Old Town; www.lulea.se/gammelstad; admission free; ⊙24hr) If you just can't get enough of those little red Swedish cottages with the white trim and lace curtains, head for the mother lode: the Unesco World Heritage–listed Gammelstad. The largest church town in Sweden was the medieval centre of northern Sweden; the 1492-built stone **Nederluleå church** (⊙8am-6pm Jun–mid-Aug) has a reredos worthy of a cathedral and a wonderfully opulent pulpit. Four hundred and twenty-four wooden houses

---

DON'T MISS

LULEÅ ARCHIPELAGO

This extensive offshore **archipelago** (www.lulea.se/english) contains some 1700 large and small islands, most of them uninhabited and therefore perfect for anything your wild imagination might dictate: skinny-dipping, berry picking, camping wild...we can go on! The larger islands, decorated with classic red-and-white Swedish summer cottages, are accessible by boat from Luleå in summer; for the rest you'll need your own transport. Facilities are limited, so most visitors come as picnicking day-trippers.

Sandön, the largest permanently inhabited island and the easiest to access from Luleå, features an attractive beach in **Klubbviken bay** and a walking path running across pine moors.

The distinguishing feature of **Junkön** is a 16th-century windmill; fishermen catch herring and whitefish here in summer.

Besides the numerous bird species that nest on **Rödkallen**, the southernmost large island, it's famous for the 1872 lighthouse that was 'retired' a hundred years later and turned into a historical monument.

Kluntarna is the all-in-one island, with holiday cottages and all the different bits of scenery you'll find on the other islands – pine forest, seabird colonies and fishing villages.

Småskär is a rocky, semiwild place that's home to a bird sanctuary and a few secluded cottages for rent.

If you love bleak beauty, you'll adore **Brändöskär**, lashed by the wind and the waves in the outermost archipelago.

Hindersön, populated since the 1500s by a motley crew of fishermen, farmers and seal catchers, is the only island that is still being farmed.

Regular boats depart from Södra Hammen from late June to early August; check timetables at the tourist office. Most islands are served by the daily M/S *Kungsholm*, with additional services to Klubbviken with M/S *Stella Marina;* to get to Rödkallen, catch the M/S *Favourite*. Fares are Skr50 to Klubbviken, Skr400 to Rödkallen and Skr100 to all the other islands.

Luleå

(where the pioneers stayed overnight on their weekend pilgrimages) and six church stables remain. Some of the buildings are open to the public and the alleyways are lovely to walk around.

Guided tours (Skr30) leave from the Gammelstad **tourist office** (☑45 70 10; worldheritage.gammelstad@lulea.se; ⊙9am-6pm mid-Jun–mid-Aug) hourly between 10am and 4pm from mid-June to mid-August.

Adjoining the church village is an open-air museum, **Hägnan** (www.lulea.se/hagnan; admission free; ⊙11am-5pm Jun–mid-Aug; 🚼), a re-creation of a 19th-century village, staffed by guides and actors in period costume, which houses an 'olde tyme' candy store and where you can have a go at baking bread or assisting the blacksmith.

Bus 9 runs hourly from Luleå; disembark at the Kyrkbyn stop.

FREE **Norrbottens Museum** MUSEUM
(www.norrbottensmuseum.nu; Storgatan 2; ⊙10am-4pm Mon-Fri, noon-4pm Sat & Sun Jun-Aug; 🚼) Apart from its extensive displays on the history of Norrbotten, Norrbottens Museum is worth a visit just for the Sami section, with its interesting collection of photos, tools, and dioramas depicting traditional reindeer-herding Sami life, as well as a nomad tent for kids. The little ones will love the re-created 19th-century playrooms.

Teknikens Hus MUSEUM
(www.teknikenshus.se; adult/under 4yr Skr60/free; ⊙10am-4pm daily mid-Jun–Aug; 🚼) Curious minds of all ages will love the gigantic,

Luleå

⊙ Sights
1 Norrbottens Museum...........................A2

🛏 Sleeping
2 Aveny...C1
3 Citysleep...B1
4 Elite Luleå...B1

⊗ Eating
5 Baan Thai...C1
6 Cook's Krog.......................................B1
7 Roasters..C1

⊖ Drinking
Bishop's Arms................................(see 4)
8 Bistro Bar Brygga.............................B1

educational playground that is Teknikens Hus, within the university campus 4km north of town. The museum has hands-on exhibitions about everything from hot-air balloons and rocket launching to the aurora borealis, plus there's a planetarium. Take bus 4 or 5 to Universitetsentrén.

🛏 Sleeping

SVIF Vandrarhem Kronan HOSTEL €
(☑43 40 50; www.vandrarhemmetkronan.se; Kronan H7; dm/s/d Skr175/270/390; 🅿) About 3km from the centre, this hostel, which is open year-round and also popular with locals, is the best budget option in the area. It features spotless shared facilities and a guest kitchen, and is set in a forested location. To get here, take any bus heading toward Kronanområdet.

Elite Luleå
HOTEL €€

(📞27 40 00; www.lulea.elite.se; Storgatan 15; s/d from Skr892/1147, discounted to Skr450/800; 🅿❄) Luleå's most sumptuous hotel, the grand Elite is more than a hundred years old, with classically decorated and beautifully refurbished rooms. All bathrooms are decked out in Italian marble and the plusher suites come with whirlpool tubs as well. Weekend prices are particularly affordable.

Aveny
HOTEL €€

(📞221 820; www.hotellaveny.com; Hermelinsgatan 10; s/d incl breakfast Skr790/970; 🅿❄) This homey hotel has individually designed rooms, decorated in soft pastel shades, and true to its name, corridors decorated to look like avenues and shopping streets. There's a sauna to chill out in and an extensive breakfast buffet.

Citysleep
HOSTEL €

(📞420 002; www.citysleep.se; Kyrkogatan 16; dm per person Skr250) Central hostel consisting of two twin rooms and a quad, complete with fully equipped kitchen and shared facilities. Book online to get your door codes, since there's no reception.

✕ Eating & Drinking

TOP CHOICE Cook's Krog
SWEDISH €€€

(📞201 025; www.cookskrog.se; Storgatan 17; meals Skr85-250; ❂dinner Mon-Sat) Carnivores rejoice, for this restaurant, inside the Quality Hotel, is Luelå's top spot for steak, reindeer and other Norrbotten specialities. Treat yourself to the five-course menu (Skr695) which includes whitefish, grilled reindeer steak and cloudberries with ice cream. Reservations recommended on weekends.

Baan Thai
THAI €€

(Kungsgatan 22; meals Skr160-280; ❂lunch & dinner) All dark wood and gold Buddha statues, this authentic Thai restaurant on the main drag is perpetually filled with locals. Dishes such as the *chu chi pla* (deep fried fish curry) are particularly good but ask the staff to spice it up if you want the true Thai fire.

Roasters
CAFE €

(Storgatan 43; meals Skr90-145; ❂10.30am-8pm) With a prime location for people-watching, especially in pleasant weather when outdoor tables open in the middle of the street, this superpopular cafe serves coffee, salads, sandwiches and a varied lunch menu and segues into an after-work drinks hang-out as the day progresses.

Bishop's Arms
PUB

(Elite Lulea, Storgatan 15) Yes, this pseudo-English pub may be a chain, but it's also one of Luleå's most popular watering holes. Whisky lovers can sample over 200 kinds.

Bistro Bar Brygga
PUB

(Norra Hamn) In summer this party boat in the harbour, affectionately known as 'BBB' is the place to, erm, B. Think floating disco with good pub food.

ℹ Information

The **tourist office** (📞45 70 00; www.visitlulea.se; Skeppsbrogatan 17; ❂10am-7pm Mon-Fri, 10am-4pm Sat & Sun) is inside Kulturens Hus.

ℹ Getting There & Around

AIR The **airport** (📞24 49 00) is 9km southwest of the town centre. SAS, Direktflyg, NextJet and City Airline fly regularly to Stockholm, Sundsvall, Umeå and Pajala. Take the **airport bus** (📞122

KUKKOLAFORSEN

Fifteen kilometres north of Haparanda along Rte 99, you reach the scenic spot where the Torneälv river is covered with the white crests of the **Kukkolaforsen rapids**. In summer locals hunt for whitefish using medieval dip nets from the rickety-looking jetties; the last weekend of July, **Sikfestival** (whitefish festival) is dedicated to grilling the catch on open fires. There's an excellent tourist village here, which includes a **camping ground and cabins** (📞310 00; www.kukkolaforsen.se; sites Skr200, 3-bed cabins from Skr650; 🅿), plus a restaurant, smokery and four types of sauna. Take bus 53.

Further along Route 99, 35km north of Haparanda is **Hulkoffgården** (📞320 15; www.hulkoff.se; s/d Skr600/1000; 🅿), a luxurious B&B in a yellow farmhouse. Its restaurant is the best in the area, with imaginatively executed northern Swedish specialities made from organic, locally sourced ingredients; order in advance.

00) from outside the Comfort Hotel on Storgatan (adult/child/under 25yr Skr50/25/38).

BUSES Buses 20 and 100 run north to Haparanda (Skr155, 2½ to 3½ hours) and south to Umeå (Skr295, four to five hours), stopping at all the coastal towns. Bus 44 connects Luleå with Lappland destinations such as Gällivare (Skr271, 3½ to 4½ hours) and Jokkmokk (Skr207, three hours) at least twice daily.

TRAIN There are two overnight trains to Stockholm (Skr521, 14 hours) via Gävle (same price, 12 hours) and Uppsala (same price, 13 hours), while two daily trains connect Luleå with Narvik, Norway (Skr422, 6½ to seven hours) via Kiruna (Skr166, 3½ to four hours) and Abisko (Skr408, five to 5½ hours).

Haparanda

📞0922 / POP 10,200

Haparanda was founded in 1821 across the river to compensate the loss of Finnish Tornio, an important trading centre, to Russia in 1809. When both Sweden and Finland joined the EU, the two towns declared themselves a single Eurocity. Still, you may think that Sweden pulled the short straw: Tornio has the art galleries and the vibrant nightlife, whereas what does Haparanda have? An enormous Ikea.

Haparanda's other two distinguishing features are the Haparanda kyrka on Östra Kyrkogatan, built in 1963 and subsequently awarded the prize for Sweden's ugliest church, and the grand red-brick railway station, dating back to 1918. There are plans to eventually resume services between Luleå and Torneo via Haparanda.

With its supercentral location on the main square and modern rooms with bright, bold furnishings, Svefi Hotel & Vandrarhem (📞688 02; www.svefi.net; Torget 3; hostel s/d Skr275/500, s/d Skr450/650; P) attracts the budget-conscious international clientele. At the south end of town, Cape East (📞80 07 90; www.capeeast.se; Sundholmen; d/ste from Skr999/2900; P🏊) caters to the opposite end of the spectrum, with an ultraluxurious spa boasting the world's largest sauna and a gourmet restaurant serving the likes of reindeer steak and Arctic char.

Haparanda's main tourist office (📞120 10; www.haparandatornio.com; Green Line; ⏰9am-7pm Mon-Fri, 10am-6pm Sat & Sun Jun-early Aug) is shared with Tornio on the 'green line'.

Tapanis Buss (📞129 55; www.tapanis. se) runs express coaches from Stockholm to Haparanda two to three times a week (Skr700, 9¼ hours). Buses 20 and 100 run south along the coast to Luleå (Skr155, 2½ hours) and Umeå (Skr356, 6¾ to 7¾ hours) via all major coastal towns, and the daily (except Saturday) bus 53 connects Haparanda to Kiruna (Skr345, six hours) via Pajala (Skr216, 2½ to three hours).

ÖSTERSUND & THE BOTHNIAN COAST HAPARANDA

Lappland & the Far North

Includes »

Best Places to Eat

» Icehotel Restaurant (p305)
» Café Gasskas (p298)
» Sånninggården (p294)
» Camp Ripan Restaurang (p304)
» Kraja (p296)

Best Places to Stay

» Icehotel (p306)
» Båtsuoj Sami Camp (p296)
» Hotel Arctic Eden (p303)
» Tärnaby Lapland B&B (p293)
» Abisko Fjällturer (p307)

Why Go?

Lappland is Europe's last true wilderness. With a grand mountain range, endless forest and countless pristine lakes as your playground, it's your chance to be a true explorer. Its great swathes of virgin land are dotted with reindeer – this is Sami country still, and your chance to delve into the reindeer herders' centuries-old way of life.

Travelling in the far north of Sweden can draw you into an unusual rhythm. The long, lonely stretches between towns are epic, and often completely deserted apart from the ever-present reindeer. Extreme natural phenomena are at their strongest here – in summer you'll be travelling under the perpetual light of the midnight sun, in winter under the haunting colours of the northern lights. During the colder months Lappland is a different country: a white wilderness traversed by huskies and snowmobiles and punctuated with colourful Sami winter markets.

When to Go

Kiruna

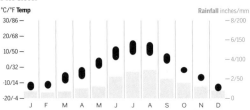

Jan Snow sculpting, ice-skating competitions and dogsled races at the Kiruna Snow Festival.

Feb Shop til you drop at Lappland's biggest winter market in Jokkmokk.

Aug Hit the trails in the national parks during the dependably warmest and driest month.

Strömsund

🎵 0670 / POP 3516

North of Östersund (p266) along the E45, Strömsund is the first town of any size – in this case, a two-street affair sitting amid some extensive waterways popular with kayakers. The **tourist office** (✆164 00; www. stromsund.se; Storgatan 6; ☺10am-6pm Mon-Fri, to 3pm Sat late Jun–mid-Aug) provides informa-

tion on the Vildmarksvägen (Route 342). If you wish to break your journey here, **Grand Hotel** (✆611 00; www.hotelnordica.se; Bredgårdsgatan 6; s/d Skr550/800; 🅿) has spacious, modern rooms inside an early 20th-century building and serves a good weekday buffet lunch.

Bus 45 passes by daily on the Gällivare–Jokkmokk–Arvidsjaur–Sorsele–Storuman–Östersund route.

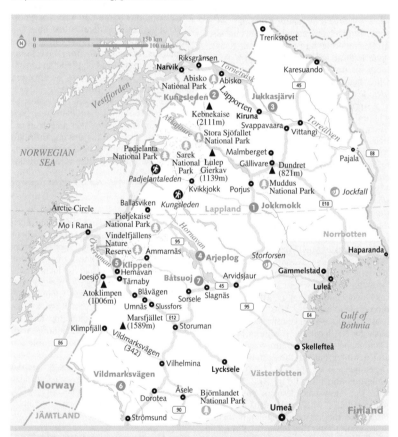

Lappland & the Far North Highlights

❶ Check out Sami crafts, reindeer races and revelry at the **Jokkmokk Winter Market** (p298)

❷ Hike **Kungsleden** (p308), Sweden's longest hiking trail

❸ Reside inside the **Icehotel** (p304), Lappland's

spectacular ice dwelling, in Jukkasjärvi

❹ View the largest collection of Sami silver creations at the Silvermuseet in **Arjeplog** (p296)

❺ Sample Northern Sweden's culinary delicacies

at **Sånninggården** in **Klippen** (p294)

❻ Drive **Vildmarksvägen** (p291), Lappland's most beautiful road

❼ Experience the Sami way of life at **Båtsuoj Sami Camp** (p296)

Vildmarksvägen

Strömsund marks the beginning of one of the most spectacular drives in Sweden. Vildmarksvägen (Route 342), also known as the Wilderness Road, stretches for around 500km, first running northwest towards the mountains before skirting the Norwegian border and then winding its way back to the E45. The first section runs through dense evergreen forest, punctuated by numerous lakes – perfect for skinny dipping, since you're unlikely to encounter anyone else. The surrounding forest is also home to Sweden's highest bear population, so if you're lucky (or unlucky) you may well spot one. Other big mammals that can be found here include elk, lynx, wolverine and fox.

A worthwhile detour is just left of Bågede, where a rocky track leads towards the impressive 43m Hällsingsåfallet, a waterfall that tumbles into an 800m-long canyon. Near the Norwegian border, across the bridge from Route 345, is Gäddede, the only village of any real size. At the Gäddede tourist office (☑0627-105 00; www.froskviken. se) you can arrange spelunking tours into the Korallgrotan (Coral Cave) – Sweden's longest cave near Stora Blåsjon, a lake 50km north of Gäddede.

By Gäddede, you'll pass a sign for the Mountain Moose Moosepark (☑0672-211 20; ⊙11am-4pm early Jun–late Aug; adult/under 7yr Skr100/free; ☑) where you can stop for cake and children can pet the two tame moose. Just past the lake, a small road leads to Ankarede, a centuries-old meeting place for the local Sami, who gather at its 1898 chapel for Midsummer celebrations and a winter market the first weekend of December.

Beyond the lake, Route 345 climbs up onto the enormous, desolate Stekkenjokk plateau, dotted with stone cairns and reminiscent of the Peruvian highlands, before descending to the tiny village of Klimpfjäll (this stretch of road is closed October through early June). A turn-off 13km east leads to the late-18th-century Sami church village at Fatmomakke (www.fatmomakke. se), where you find traditional Sami *kåtor* (wooden dwellings) and log cabins. Silver shamanistic Sami jewellery was found here in 1981.

Twenty kilometres further east, you reach Saxnäs, a small village set in a scenic spot between lakes, and considered a paradise for fishing folk. The small STF Hostel Kultsjögården (☑0940-700 44; www.kultsjogarden. se; dm/s/d Skr160/240/350) has comfortable rooms above a restaurant-pub (the only place in the area to eat outside of peak season), plus a few small cabins. The staff can plan fishing excursions, and advise you about hiking and cycling in the area. Nearby is the plusher Saxnäsgården (☑0940-377 00; www.saxnas.se; s/d Skr850/1100, hostel s/d Skr400/450), a large wooden lodge complex with swish hotel rooms and more basic hostel accommodation. There's a luxurious spa with indoor pool and the staff can organise all manner of activities, from heli-skiing, snowmobile safaris and dogsledding in winter, to guided hikes, boat trips, angling and tours of Fatmomakke in summer.

The road ends 3km north of the nearest village of Vilhelmina – another great base for fishing in the nearby lakes and rivers.

Allow at least day for driving the Vildmarksvägen and fill up on petrol beforehand; the only petrol station is in Gäddede.

Storuman

☑0951 / POP 6595

Though it sounds like a villain from *Lord of the Rings*, Storuman is more about harnessing hydroelectric power than spreading chaos and darkness over the Shire. This one-street town sits along the 2000km-long Blåvägen (Blue Highway; www.blavagen. com) that runs from Norway's Atlantic coast all the way to the shores of Russia's Lake Onega. Storuman's distinguishing features include the old railway hotel building with a wonderfully ornate wooden interior, presently housing the library.

The cheerful yellow Hotell Luspen (☑333 80; www.hotelluspen.se; hostel s/d from Skr330/450, hotel s/d incl breakfast Skr660/770) by the train station offers en suite hotel rooms and dorms; breakfast (Skr45) available.

The tourist office (☑141 11; www.storuman. se; Järnvägsgatan 13; ⊙9am-5pm Mon-Fri, 10am-2pm Sat Jun-Aug) inside Hotell Luspen can advise you of good fishing spots in the surrounding area.

Bus 45 runs daily on the Gällivare-Jokkmokk–Arvidsjaur–Sorsele–Storuman–Östersund route. Buses also run west to Tärnaby and east to Umeå, while the twice-weekly Lapplandspilen (☑0940-150 40; www.lapplandspilen.se) buses run from

Hemavan to Stockholm, via Storuman (Skr750). In summer, Inlandsbanan trains stop here.

Tärnaby & Hemavan

📞 0954

Tärnaby, an elongated one-street village that sits on the shores of Gäutan lake, and Hemavan, its smaller counterpart 18km north, are both popular centres offering access to all manner of outdoor adventures. From superb hiking and skiing to checking out Sami villages and traditional holy sights, exploring caves and paddling canoes to driving around and admiring the view – it just depends on your interests, and the moods of the weather gods.

◉ Sights & Activities

TOP CHOICE **Atoklimpen** LANDMARK

(📞 information 0954-104 50) For anyone interested in Sami culture, it's worth going out of your way to visit Atoklimpen (1006m), a monolithic, bare mountain 35km west of Tärnaby that has been regarded as holy and the object of worship since the nomadic society's early days. Evidence, dating back to the 15th century, of sacrifices, camping and reindeer herding are scattered across the area; a 3km trail leads up to the top. Near the car park (off Rd 1116) is a peat hut and small cottage. A Sami couple built the hut in 1920 and the cottage in 1925, at a time when the government forbade the Sami to build permanent structures; the ensuing debate over the cottage helped to change the law in 1928.

Laxfjället HIKING

A good way to start your visit is to hike to the top of Laxfjället (820m) for perspective-shifting views of the surrounding lakes and mountain ranges. There are five trails (all of which are described in the brochure provided by the tourist office), the steepest and most direct being the Yellow Trail that runs underneath the ski lift.

Laisaleden Trail HIKING

For a longer hike, try the Laisaleden trail, which starts out along Drottningsleden (Queen's Trail). To catch the trail, follow signs to a turn-off 15km north of the Tärnaby tourist office along the main road; there's a

parking lot with signposts to the trail at the top of the hill.

Hemavan HIKING, MUSEUM

Hemavan is the southern entry to Kungsleden (p308) which passes through the Vindelfjällen Nature Reserve. Up the hill is **Naturum** (📞 380 23; www.vindelfjallen.se; ⏰ 9am-4.30pm Mon-Fri May–mid-Jun, 9am-6pm daily mid-Jun–Aug), where there's an exhibit on the local flora and fauna. Staff can provide information about trekking and day hikes in the area.

Hemavan Bike Park MOUNTAIN BIKING

(www.bikepark.nu) In warm weather, ski slopes become mountain biking routes. A chairlift 2km north of central Hemavan is adapted to carry bikes so that you can perform a hair-raising descent from the top and there's a specially designed network of trails that make up the Hemavan Bike Park that will challenge any serious biker.

Ski Areas SKIING

Many of Sweden's champion skiers hail from this area, most notably Ingemar Sten-mark, who was the recipient of an Olympic gold medal twice. It's a given that cross-country skiing is popular in the area, but both Tärnaby and Hemavan also offer decent downhill skiing (day ski pass Skr300), Tärnaby having a more extensive ski area. If you are interested in heli-skiing, snow mobile safaris and other winter activities, pay a visit to the tourist office, which can be arrange such activities.

🛏 Sleeping & Eating

TOP CHOICE **Tärnaby Lapland B&B** B&B €€

(📞 107 00; www.tarnabylapland.com; Blåvägen 18; dm Skr220, s/d from Skr500/700; 🅿 @) The funnest place to stay in town. It's run by Matt and Lindy, a thoroughly entertaining Australian-Swedish couple who go out of their way to make sure you enjoy the area. Spotless rooms with water views hold comfortable dorm or double beds. There's a guest kitchen, lounge area, sauna, high-tech showers and free use of bicycles and canoes. A separate building houses a warm, wood-lined cafe-pub and tiny bookshop; the cafe serves lunch in summer months.

STF Hostel Hemavan HOSTEL €

(📞 0954-300 02; www.svenskaturistforeninggen. se/hemavan; dm Skr175, s/d from Skr330/450; 🅿 ✳ ❄) A sprawling complex of a hostel, it's

DON'T MISS

SÅNNINGGÅRDEN

At the tiny village of Klippen, about 6km north of Hemavan, the cheery dining room inside the barnlike **Sånninggården** (☑0954-330 00; www.sanninggarden.com; ☺lunch & dinner) has chequered tablecloths and a stuffed ptarmigan on the metal chandelier, giving the place a deceptively rustic feel. This is where Sweden's gourmets come to feast on such local delicacies as reindeer steak, Arctic char fillet with Västerbotten cheese, and pheasant fillet with chanterelle pie. There are vegetarian options for those uncomfortable with consuming the local wildlife, and the magnificent desserts – such as cloudberries with ice cream – will please even the most jaded of palates.

perpetually busy with hikers. The separate blocks are each equipped with a kitchen, and there is internet in the main building as well as a cafeteria and lively bar upstairs. Swimming pool available for guest use.

**STF Vandrarhem Tärnaby/
Åkerlundska gården**   HOSTEL
(☑104 20; dm Skr195-220, s/d from Skr350/470; ☺Jan-May & mid-Jun–mid-Sep; ℗) Newly renovated hostel with awesome views across the valley and modern facilities. The on-site restaurant is famous for its vast breakfast buffet (around Skr75).

ℹ Information

Tourist office (☑104 50; www.hemavantarnaby.se; ☺8.30am-7pm Mon-Fri, 10am-6pm Sat & Sun mid-Jun–mid-Aug, 9am-5pm Mon-Fri rest of year) On the Blåvägen (Blue Hwy) that runs through the village. Buy maps, fishing licences and snow-scooter licences here, as well as arrange tours and activities.

ℹ Getting There & Away

Länstrafiken bus 45 runs to Mora (5½ hours, two to four daily). Buses 31, 35, 319 and 320 run west to Hemavan (Skr41, 30 minutes, two to five daily), while bus 63 runs northeast to Umeå (six hours, two to four daily).

Sorsele & Ammarnäs

☑0952 / POP 1300

Railway enthusiasts should pull up at Sorsele for the entertaining **Inlandsbanemuseet** (adult/child Skr20/free; ☺9am-5pm Mon-Fri) at the train station, covering the history of the railway. The adjoining **tourist office** (☑140 90; www.sorsele.se) can arrange activities such as fly-fishing; the two nearby rivers are particularly good for trout and grayling, while nearby lakes are the place to fish for Arctic char.

From Sorsele, Route 363 leads to tiny Ammarnäs, nestled in a bowl by the Ammarfjället mountains and used by Sami herders for centuries. Even now, a third of the population makes their living from reindeer husbandry. Ammarnäs is a great destination for hikers, who can tackle the wildest part of the Kungsleden (p308) from here or else embark on easier day hikes, such as the 8km jaunt to the top of Mt Kaissats (984m) that runs from the Stora Tjulträsk at the western end of the village.

The only accommodation in the village is **Ammarnäsgården** (☑0952-600 03; www.ammarnasturism.com; dm Skr185, s/d Skr495/790; ℗☒), a modern hotel with adjoining youth hostel in a superbly picturesque location. There is a sauna and pool in the basement, and the hotel's restaurant serves a mix of northern Swedish and international dishes (two-course dinner Skr185).

The **tourist office** (☑600 00; www.ammarnas.nu; ☺9am-5pm mid-Jun–mid-Sep) on the main road can help organise Icelandic-pony rides in summer and dogsledding and snowmobiling in winter.

Sorsele is served daily by bus 45 along the Gällivare–Östersund route, while bus 341 runs from Sorsele to Ammarnäs (Skr115, 1¼-1¾ hours, one to three daily).

Arvidsjaur

☑0960 / POP 6599

If you're coming from another town along the E45, Arvidsjaur, with its busy main street, will seem like a bustling metropolis. Established several centuries ago as a Sami marketplace and meeting spot, Arvidsjaur is home to two-dozen Sami families who still make a living from reindeer herding.

Between December and April dozens of test drivers from different car companies descend on the town to stage their own version of Top Gear – putting fast machines through their paces on the frozen lakes.

◉ Sights & Activities

Arvidsjaur really comes into its own in winter. Apart from the usual ice fishing, cross-country skiing and snow-shoe walking, visitors can take part in more high-octane pursuits: there are over 600km of snowmobile tracks around Arvidsjaur, with two- and four-hour tours offered by **Super Safari** (☑104 57; from Skr950); you can test your extreme motoring skills on the 1.8km ice track with **Arctic Car Experience** (☑137 20; www.arctic-car.de; Östra Kyrkogatan 18; 2hr Skr2550); and dogsled tours in a nearby nature reserve are available with **Nymånen** (☑070-625 3042; www.nymanen.com), one of the largest Siberian husky kennels in Lappland and certified Nature's Best.

FREE Lappstaden   CHURCH TOWN
(tours Skr50; ⊙10am-7pm, tours 6pm Jun-Aug) The first church was built in Arvidsjaur in 1607, and church attendance laws enacted (thanks to the zealous priests and enforced by the monarchy) imposed a certain amount of pew time upon the nomadic Sami, so to make their church visits more manageable they built small cottages (*gåhties*) for overnighting. Some 80 of these are preserved now in Lappstaden, just across Storgatan from the modern church. The buildings are square with pyramid-shaped roofs, typical of the Forest Sami, and are still in use. During the last weekend in August, Lappstaden is home to **Storstämning**, an annual feast, party and Sami association meeting.

Steam Train   TRAIN
(☑104 56; adult/child Skr200/free, Inlandsbanan travellers Skr150) From mid-July to mid-August, an immensely popular 1930s steam train makes return evening trips to Slagnäs on Friday and Saturday, departing at 5.45pm and returning around 10pm. It stops along the way at Storavan beach for a barbecue and swim.

Lapland Rafting Cafe   RAFTING
(☑070-253 05 83; www.laplandraftingcafe.se; from Skr750; ⊙late Jun–late Aug) Offers white-water rafting trips on the nearby Piteälven, ranging from an hour-long gentle float to Class IV-V rapids for experienced rafters.

🛏 Sleeping & Eating

Lapland Lodge   B&B €€
(☑137 20, 0768-47 57 17; www.laplandlodge.eu; Östra Kyrkogatan 18; s/d Skr650/850, f Skr950-1050; [P][@]) Next to the church, this friendly B&B offers a range of room configurations in a pretty yellow house with contemporary comforts (spa bathtubs, flatscreen TVs, free wi-fi) amid antique style (decorated with old wooden skis, antlers and snowshoes). An outdoor Jacuzzi and sauna are available, and snowmobile tours run in winter.

Silver Cross 45   HOSTEL €
(☑070-644 2862; www.silvercross45.se; Villavägen 56; dm Skr125, s/d Skr250/400; [P][@][🏠]) Doubling as a gallery for glass creations, this family-friendly hostel has cosy wood-panelled rooms and shared facilities. Price includes bed linen – a budget range anomaly.

Hotell Laponia   HOTEL €
(☑555 00; www.hotell-laponia.se; Storgatan 45; s/d Skr690/820) A large, modern hotel over-run with test drivers in winter, this is also one of the nicer places to eat in town – the restaurant-bar serving a very good weekday buffet (Skr79) as well as northern Swedish specialities à la carte.

Hans På Hörnet   CAFE €
(Storgatan 21; salads from Skr55; ⊙10am-5pm Mon-Sat) A very local spot, serving inexpensive lunches: salads, sandwiches and pies.

❶ Information

Tourist office (☑175 00; www.polcirkeln.nu; Östra Skolgatan 18C; ⊙9.30am-6pm Mon-Fri, noon-4.30 Sat & Sun Jun-Aug) Just off Storga-tan, the town's main road.

❶ Getting There & Around

AIR Arvidsjaur Airport (☑0960-173 80; www.ajr.nu), 11km east of the centre, has frequent connections to Stockholm-Arlanda (two hours, two daily Monday to Friday, one daily Saturday and Sunday) with **Nextjet** (www.nextjet.se). During the winter season it's served by two to three flights weekly from Frankfurt, Hannover, München and Stuttgart.

BUS The bus station is at Västlundavägen, in the town centre behind the large Konsum super-market. Popular bus routes include bus 45 south to Östersund (Skr419, 7¼ hours, two daily) and north to Gällivare (Skr271, 3¾ hours, one daily) via Jokkmokk (Skr188, 2¼ hours), as well as daily bus 200 to Bodö, Norway (Skr360, seven hours) via Arjeplog (Skr113, one to 1¼ hours) – also served by bus 10.

TRAIN Arvidsjaur is connected by daily Inlandsbanan trains in summer to Östersund (Skr610, 8¾ hours), Gällivare (Skr352, five hours and 50 minutes) and Jokkmokk (Skr223, three hours).

Arjeplog

☑0961 / POP 2200

Eighty-five kilometres northwest of Arvidsjaur, the one-street Sami town of Arejplog (Árjepluovve, in Sami) sits on the Silvervägen (Silver Rd) surrounded by prime fishing country of 8700 lakes (each local has their favourite). In winter, the opportunity to test-drive cars on the frozen lakes attracts the hardiest of visitors – temperatures have been known to drop below –50°C.

Arjeplog's star attraction is its excellent Silvermuseet (Silver Museum; www.silvermuseet.arjeplog.se; Torget; adult/child Skr60/free; ⊙10am-noon & 1-6pm Mon-Fri, 10am-2pm Sat). Housed in what used to be a nomad school, it traces the history of the town and its main industries – silver-mining and logging – through colourful, well-presented displays. The nature display focuses on native plants and their traditional uses by the Sami, but the tour de force is the vast collection of Sami silver objects – the most extensive of its kind – including belt buckles, ornate spoons and goblets, and collars that would traditionally have been passed down from mother to daughter. Linger in the basement cinema to catch the engaging slideshow and voiceover describing life in Arjeplog.

The most central place to stay is the budget Hotel Lyktan (☑612 10; www.hotel

lyktan.com; Violvägen 2; s/d Skr325/435; P), with clean, basic twin rooms, enormous guest kitchen and lounge in the cavernous basement. The rooms above the kitchen get seriously warm.

There's one exception to the lacklustre eating scene: the restaurant at Kraja (☑315 00; www.kraja.se), a catch-all hotel and campsite on its own little peninsula just west of town, combines lake views with great local cuisine; try the elk burger or the steamed Arctic char.

The helpful tourist office (☑145 20; www.polcirkeln.nu; Silvermuseet; ⊙ 10am-noon & 1-6pm Mon-Fri, 10am-2pm Sat) has plenty of info on the surrounding area.

ℹ Getting There & Away

East-bound buses 26 and 200 run to Arvidsjaur (Skr113, 1¼ hours, two to four daily) and Skellefteå (Skr240, 3¼ hours, one to three daily). West-bound bus 200 (Silverexpressen) runs to Bodö in Norway (Skr420, 5½ to 6¼ hours, one daily except Saturday) via Jäkkvikk (Skr91, one hour, one to two daily except Saturday).

Jokkmokk

☑0971 / POP 5192

The capital of Sami culture, and the biggest handicraft centre in Lappland, Jokkmokk (Dálvvaddis, in Sami) has not only the definitive Sami museum but is also the site of a huge annual winter market gathering. Just north of the Arctic Circle, it's the only town in Sweden which has a further education college that teaches reindeer husbandry, craft-making and ecology using the Sami language. Jokkmokk is the jumping-

BÅTSUOJ SAMI CAMP

If you wish to experience the life of the Forest Sami, look no further than Båtsuoj (☑0960-651 026, www.batsuoj.se). Tom and Lotta Svensson are two of the few reindeer herders who practise their traditional livelihood full-time. Well, almost. They also offer visitors an introduction to their way of life.

You can stop by for a couple of hours (Skr200), watch reindeer get rounded up using lassoes, learn about traditional Sami dwellings and anti-bear storage huts, and sip coffee cooked over an open fire while sitting inside a *lavvu* (tent). To delve deeper, linger overnight (Skr950) – learn about the shaman religion from your hosts, eat reindeer grilled over a wood fire, go fishing and sleep on reindeer skins inside a *kota* (typical Forest Sami log hut) at night. In winter, walks with reindeer (Skr100) and afternoon visits to the camp are available on Sunday only; book ahead.

To get here, take the road running immediately south from Arjeplog, or else take the E45 west of Arvidsjaur for around 50km. The Sami camp is near the village of Gasa, 17km north of the village of Slagnäs.

LOCAL KNOWLEDGE

TOM SVENSSON: SAMI REINDEER HERDER

How long have you been a reindeer herder? All my life, ever since I left school.

Is it possible to survive by reindeer-herding alone? It's difficult. A family needs to own at least 1000 reindeer to make a living from full-time herding. In summer, we lose 50 to 60% of our calves to predators: bears, lynx, wolverines, even wolves sometimes – though wolves are not allowed up here, they are captured and brought back to the south of Sweden. Many herders have to do other things: tourism, hunting...

Do you hope that your children will carry on herding reindeer, like yourself? My children help out already; you need the whole family to do it. It's hard physical work, so you don't get many female reindeer herders. But I am hoping that my son will continue my work.

How has reindeer herding changed in recent times? In the old days, we would have had to round up reindeer on foot, with dogs. We still use dogs (I have three working dogs), but now we use modern technology to help with the spring migration and rounding up the herds – snowmobiles, GPS tracking, even helicopters. We don't stand still.

off point for visiting the four national parks which are part of the **Laponia World Heritage Area** (p297) and it makes a great base for all manner of outdoor adventures year-round.

◉ Sights & Activities

TOP CHOICE **Ájtte Museum** MUSEUM

(www.ajtte.com, in Swedish; Kyrkogatan 3; adult/child Skr60/free; ◔9am-6pm daily mid-Jun–mid-Aug, 10am-4pm Mon-Fri, to 2pm Sat rest of year) This illuminating museum is Sweden's most thorough introduction to Sami culture. Follow the 'spokes' radiating from the central chamber, each dealing with a different theme – from traditional costume, silverware and 400-year-old magical painted shamans' drums, to replicas of sacrificial sites and a diagram explaining the uses and significance of various reindeer entrails. One section details the widespread practice of harnessing the rivers in Lappland for hydroelectric power and the consequences this has had for the Sami people and their territory, and there is a large fauna exhibit featuring some impressive stuffed mammals and birds of prey. The beautifully showcased collection of traditional silver jewellery features collars, now making a comeback among the Sami after a long absence.

TOP CHOICE **Sami Duodji** GALLERY

(www.sameslodjstiftelsen.se, in Swedish; Porjusvägen 4; ◔10am-5pm Mon-Fri) If you can't make it to the Winter Market, this gallery and crafts centre is your one-stop shop for diverse, authentic Sami handicraft year-round.

Lappkyrkan CHURCH

(Storgatan; ◔9am-4pm) The octagonal red wooden church is worth a visit; it's from 1976 but was built in the style of its 1753 predecessor. The colour scheme is inspired by Sami clothing; in winter, the space between the timbers used to hold coffins awaiting the spring thaw, which allowed for graves to be dug.

Jokkmokks Fjällträdgård GARDENS

(adult/child Skr30/free, free with Ájtté Museum ticket; ◔Mon-Fri 11am-5pm, Sat & Sun noon-5pm) This botanical garden by the lake introduces local flora, such as glacier crowfoot, moorking and mountain avens, as well as plants traditionally used by the Sami for medicinal purposes. A marked path around the lake features information boards about local wildlife.

☞ Tours

Arctic Husky Adventures DOGSLEDDING

(✆070-519-8591; www.arctichuskyadventures.com) A specialist in dogsled trips. From hour-long introductions (Skr750) to seven-day expeditions (Skr16,500); guests with disabilities welcome.

🛏 Sleeping & Eating

Accommodation must be booked well in advance for the Winter Market weekend.

Hotel Jokkmokk HOTEL €€

(✆777 00; www.hoteljokkmokk.se; Solgatan 45; s/d from Skr860/1025; ℗) Overlooking picturesque Lake Talvatis, Jokkmokk's nicest hotel has thoroughly modern, cosy

DON'T MISS

JOKKMOKK WINTER MARKET

Winter travellers should by no account miss the annual Winter Market (www.jokkmokks marknad.se), held the first Thursday through Saturday in February – it's the most exciting (and coldest!) time to be here, with temperatures as low as -40°C. The market is the oldest and biggest of its kind, attracting some 30,000 people annually – going strong since 1605 when King Karl XI decreed that markets should be set up in Lappland to increase taxes, spread Christianity and exert greater control over the nomadic Sami. It's the biggest sales opportunity of the year for Sami traders who come to make contacts and see old friends, while the visitors can splurge on the widest array of Sami *duodji* (handicraft) in the country.

The Winter Market is preceded by the opening of the smaller Historical Market and several days of folk music, plays, parades, local cinematography, photography exhibitions, food tasting sessions and talks on different aspects of Sami life – all of which merge seamlessly into the Winter Market. Highlights include the merry chaos of reindeer races on the frozen Lake Talvatissjön behind Hotel Jokkmokk, with unruly reindeer veering off the track and scattering the spectators.

rooms, a superb sauna in the basement and another by the lake (for that refreshing hole-in-the-ice dip in winter). The large restaurant, shaped like a Sami *kåta* (hut), appropriately serves the likes of elk fillet and smoked reindeer with juniper berry sauce.

STF Vandrarhem Åsgård   HOSTEL €
(☑559 77; www.jokkmokkhostel.com; Åsgatan 20; dm Skr130-185, s/d Skr310/410; ☉reception 8-10am & 5-8pm; P@) This family-run STF hostel has a lovely setting among green lawns and trees, right near the tourist office. It's a comfortable place with numerous bunk beds, kitchen, TV lounge, basement sauna (Skr20 per person) and internet access.

TOP CHOICE Café Gasskas   NORTHERN SWEDISH €€€
(Porjusvägen 7; meals Skr220-440) This friendly coffee-shop-turned-gourmet-spot offers such local delights as reindeer steak, Arctic char ravioli, elk burger, and white chocolate soup with angelica (a plant widely used by the Sami). It's also an excellent place to catch Sami folk music some evenings.

Restaurant Ájtte   SAMI €€
(Ájtte Museum; meals Skr150-200, buffet Skr160; ☉noon-4pm) This fine Sami restaurant makes it possible to enhance what you've learned about the local wildlife by sampling some of them – from *suovas* (smoked and salted reindeer meat) to grouse with local berries. The weekday lunchtime buffet serves home-style Swedish dishes.

❶ Information

Tourist office (☑222 50; www.turism. jokkmokk.se; Stortorget 4; ☉9am-7pm Mon-Fri, 10am-6pm Sat & Sun mid-Jun–Aug) Stocks detailed brochures on activities and tours in the area; has internet access.

❶ Getting There & Away

BUS Buses arrive and leave from the bus station on Klockarvägen. Bus 94 only runs in summer. Daily bus 45 connects Jokkmokk with Östersund (Skr483, 9¾ hours) via Arvidsjaur (Skr188, 2¼ hours) in the south and Gällivare (Skr124 1¼ to 1¾ hours) in the north, while bus 44 runs northeast to Luleå (Skr207, 2¾ hours, one or two daily).

TRAIN In the summer only, daily Inlandsbanan trains head south to Östersund (Skr833, 12½ hours) via Arvidsjaur (Skr129, three hours) at 8.43am, and north to Gällivare (Skr129, two hours) at 7.38pm.

Around Jokkmokk

PADJELANTA NATIONAL PARK

The largest national park in Sweden, Padjelanta covers 1984 sq km. The park gets its name from the Sami name Badjelánnda, meaning 'higher land', and appropriately consists of a vast plateau surrounding two huge lakes: Vastenjávvre and Virihávvre (allegedly Sweden's most beautiful lake).

The popular 139km Padjelantaleden (Padjelanta Trail) can be hiked in eight to 14 days (use Fjällkartan BD10 and Fjällkartan BD7). The hilly terrain isn't exceptionally challenging: boardwalks cover the boggy sections, and all rivers are bridged. The southern section, from Kvikkjokk to Staloluokta (four or five days), is the most popular. At the northern end (by lake Akkajaure), you can start at either of the STF huts, Vaisaluokta or Áhkká (the latter is easier). There are huts at regular intervals along the trail; STF runs the Såmmarlappa, Tarrekaise and Njunjes huts at the southern end of the trail, and the hostel at Kvikkjokk, while the rest are maintained by Sami villages under the name Badjelánnda Laponia Turism (BLT). You can buy provisions at Staloluokta, Såmmarlappa, Tarrekaise and Kvikkjokk.

To reach the northern end of the trail, take bus 93 from Gällivare to Ritsem (3½ hours, twice daily, mid-June to mid-September) and connect with the STF ferry (once or twice daily, late June to mid-September) to Vaisaluokta and Änonjálmme, 1.5km north of the Áhkká STF hut. For details of boats from the end of Padjelantaleden to Kvikkjokk (up to three daily, July to mid-September), call ☎0971-210 12.

Lapplandsflyg (☎0971-210 40; www.lapplandsflyg.se) has two helicopter flights daily between Kvikkjokk and Staloluokta between late June and early September (adult/child Skr950/670). Flights continue on to Ritsem between mid-July and mid-August (adult/child Skr1700/1200).

KVIKKJOKK

Tiny Kvikkjokk (Huhttán in Sami), around 100km west of Jokkmokk, is on the Kungsleden (p308) and the Padjelantaleden, and is an ideal jumping-off point for Sarek National Park.

Several fantastic day-walks start from the village, including climbs to the mountain Snjerak (809m; three hours return) and a steeper ascent of Prinskullen (749m; three hours return). Follow signs to a car park at the top of the hill to find the trail; if you instead continue straight ahead until the road ends, you'll find another car park and the STF Kvikkjokk Fjällstation (☎0971-210 22; www.svenskaturistforeninggen.se/kvikkjokk; dm Skr275, s/d Skr575/775; ☉late Jan–mid-Nov & mid-Dec–late Dec), a picturesque mountain station on the banks of a roaring river and your only accommodation option. There's a small shop selling provisions and a restaurant serving Swedish standards, as well as fully equipped guest kitchens. The staff have plenty of information on hiking trails and hiking conditions.

Bus 47 runs from Kvikkjokk to Jokkmokk (Skr155, two hours, one daily).

SAREK & STORA SJÖFALLET NATIONAL PARKS

Experienced and well-kitted trekkers will meet their match in Sarek National Park. Named after Sarektjåhkkå (2098m) and full of sharp peaks and huge glaciers, the park is particularly rich in wildlife such as bear, wolverine and lynx. Trekking here is certainly not for novices – hikers must be prepared for very rugged conditions. There are no tourist facilities within the park, major trails are often washed out or in poor repair, there are rivers to cross, and the extremes of terrain are exacerbated by volatile weather conditions.

Bordering Sarek to the north is the mountainous and thickly forested Stora Sjöfallet National Park (www.storasjofallet.com), dominated by Áhkká (2105m), known as the 'Queen of Lappland' and crowned with ten glaciers. The Kungsleden (p308) dips briefly into the southeastern corner of Sarek and passes through Stora Sjöfallet. At the eastern end of the park you can cross the Stora Lulevatten lake on the STF ferry to STF Saltoluokta Fjällstation (☎0973-410 10; www.svenskaturistforeninggen.se/saltoluokta; dm/d Skr295/990; ☉Mar-Apr & mid-Jun–mid-Sep), a hostel consisting of a main timber building and five satellite guesthouses with an Arctic colour scheme, an equipment shop and a wood-fired sauna. The on-site restaurant serves excellent northern Swedish dishes, and there are numerous guided adventures available, including kayaking, fishing and a hike up Lulep Gierkav (1139m) for great views of the two parks.

Bus 93 runs from Gällivare to Ritsem, at the western end of Stora Sjöfallet, stopping at Kebnats and Vakkotavare (mid-June to mid-September).

PORJUS

On the E45 between Jokkmokk and Gällivare, the little town of Porjus is worth pulling over for the Northern Lights Centre (☎070-242 2812; www.arctic-color.com; Stationshuset, Strömgatan 45; ☉6-9pm Mon-Sat, 1-9pm Sun mid-Jun–mid-Aug) inside the old railway station building – home to the work of English photographer Patricia Cowern, who specialises in photographing the aurora borealis.

If you're feeling peckish, you can pick up reindeer, elk and fish, smoked Sami-style, at Björn Thunborg Viltaffar AB (www.thunborgviltaffar.se; Strömgatan 32), the local gourmet institution.

Bus 45 stops in Porjus on the way to and from Jokkmokk and Gällivare.

Gällivare

📞 0970 / POP 16,225

Gällivare (Váhtjer, in Sami), the last stop on the Inlandsbanan, and its northern twin, Malmberget, are surrounded by forest and dwarfed by the bald Dundret hill. The town has a strong Sami presence and, after Kiruna, Malmberget (Ore Mountain) is the second-largest iron-ore mine in Sweden. Like Kiruna, the area's sustaining industry is simultaneously threatening the town with collapse, so buildings are gradually being shifted to sturdier ground.

The strong Sami presence in Gällivare is reflected in its monuments. The bronze statue in the park next to the church, by local sculptor Berto Marklund, is called *Tre seitar* (seite being a Sami god of nature); it symbolises the pre-Christian Sami religion. Just off Lasarettsgatan, on the way from the church to the train station, there is a granite statue of the *Thinking Sami Man*. The granite came from Dundret hill and the inscription reads: 'Mine was the land in the past. Care for my people in the future.'

◉ Sights & Activities

Dundret   NATURE RESERVE

Dundret (823m) is a nature reserve with excellent views of the town, Malmberget and the Aitik copper mine, and a favourite spot for viewing the midnight sun; the tourist office organises transfers (Skr 200; 11pm early June to mid-July, 10pm mid- to late July). In summer, the **Fjallstugan cafe** (◷6pm–1am) at the top serves coffee and waffles . In winter there are four Nordic courses and 10 ski runs of varying difficulty, and the mountaintop resort rents out gear. If you have your own car, it's a rather hair-raising drive to the top.

The Mines   MINE

In Malmberget there are two colossal mines with separate guided tours run by the tourist office between mid-June and early August. Descend into the bowels of the earth to marvel at the immense, noisy trucks (five times the height of a human!) labouring in the darkness of the underground **LKAB iron-ore mine tour** (admisssion Skr330; ◷tours daily 9.30am). The **Aitik open-pit copper mine** (admission Skr330; ◷tours 2.30pm Mon, Wed, Fri & Sat) is Sweden's largest, producing 18 million tonnes of copper ore per year. The view of the pit from the top of the hairpin bends is particularly impressive.

Gruvmuseet   MUSEUM

(Puoitakvägen; adult/child Skr50/free; ◷10.30am–1pm & 2-5pm Mon-Fri mid-Jun–early Aug; guided tours in English available) If you like mines, you will simply love this mining museum, covering every aspect of the gruelling work over a 250-year span.

FREE Gällivare Museum   MUSEUM

(Storgatan 16; ◷11am-3.30pm Mon-Fri, noon-2pm Sat mid-Jun–Aug) The Gällivare Museum has exhibitions on the navvies (railway workers), Sami culture and early settlers, plus a collection of local artefacts and the famous Mosquito Museum (relocated from a nearby bog).

Nyakyrkan   CHURCH

(Lasarettsgatan 10; ◷8am-5pm Mon-Fri, 10am-4pm Sat & Sun Jun-Aug) The attractive, white 'new' Sami church, from 1882. Its shape, reminiscent of a traditional Sami dwelling, is particularly picturesque in winter when surrounded by snow.

VISIT SÁPMI

Started in 2010, **Visit Sápmi** (www.visitsapmi.com) is a Gällivare-based initiative owned by the **Swedish Sami Association** (www.sapmi.se) that aims to become the first port of call for any visitor to Sweden with an interest in Sami life, be it staying with reindeer herders, attending a *yoik* (traditional singing session) session or purchasing *duodji* (certified handicrafts) from the best craftsmen. With an emphasis on sustainable ecotourism, Visit Sápmi aims to have contact with every Sami entrepreneur in Sweden, assisting them with establishing themselves, and awarding the Sápmi Experience quality label to operators who meet their criteria regarding sustainable practices.

At the moment, Visit Sápmi is focusing on establishing links with the Sami communities Sweden, though in time it plans to expand its operations to Norway, Finland and Russia, enabling visitors to fully explore all of Sápmi.

Ettöreskyrkan   CHURCH
(⊘8am-5pm Mon-Fri, 10am-4pm Sat & Sun Jun-Aug) The diminutive old church near the train station is also worth a look, nicknamed the 'one-öre church' because that's the amount each household had to contribute to get it built back in 1755.

🛏 Sleeping & Eating

Gällivare Camping   CAMPGROUND €
(☑100 10; www.gellivarecamping.com; Kvarkbacksvägen 2; sites Skr160, dm/s Skr200/250, 2-/4-bed cabins from Skr550/750; 🐾) This year-round campsite shares a lovely riverside spot with the *hembygdsområde*, an old homestead. Cabins are set up more like apartments, with excellent, modern facilities. Campers and hostel guests have use of wi-fi and sauna, and reception can arrange snowmobile and dogsledding tours in winter.

Grand Hotel Lapland   HOTEL €€
(☑77 22 90; www.grandhotellapland.com; Lasarettsgatan 1; s/d Skr850/1077) This modern hotel opposite the train station is particularly popular with the business set and high-end Inlandsbanan travellers; rooms are comfortable and airy. The ground level **Vassara Pub** (⊘lunch & dinner), which has covered outdoor seating for summer, serves sumptuous local specialities such as reindeer Arctic char and cloudberry tiramisu, as well the less expensive burgers and fries.

Stay In   HOSTEL €
(☑070 216 6965; Lasaretsgatan 3; s/d Skr300/600) At this rambling complex next to the Grand Hotel Lapland, self-caterers share the several fully-equipped kitchens and TV lounges with local hospital staff. Alongside neat doubles, there's even a table-tennis table and a downstairs canteen serving Swedish standards. Reserve in advance to gain access to building.

Nittaya Thai   THAI
(Storgatan 21B; meals Skr130-200; ⊘lunch & dinner Tue-Sun, lunch only Mon) Authentic Thai cuisine in attractive surroundings. The changing weekday lunch buffet is a bargain and the red curries stand out.

🛈 Information

Tourist office (☑166 60; www.gellivarelapland.se; Storgatan 16; ⊘9am-7pm Mon-Fri, 9am-3pm Sat & Sun late Jun–mid-Aug) Can organise tours of the mines, and the midnight sun tour.

🛈 Getting There & Away

BUS Regional buses depart from the train station. En route to Ritsem (Skr295, 3½ hours, one daily), bus 93 stops at Kebnats and Vakkotavare along the Kungsleden in Stora Sjöfallet National Park (mid-June to mid-September only). Bus 1 to Malmberget departs from directly opposite the Gällivare church.

Daily bus 45 runs to Östersund (Skr483, 11 hours) via Jokkmokk (also covered by bus 44, Skr124, 1¼ hours to 1¾ hours, five daily) and Arvidsjaur (Skr271, 3¾ hours), while bus 10 serves Luleå (Skr271, 3½ hours to 4½ hours, two or three daily) via Kiruna (Skr155, 1½ hours to two hours).

TRAIN The summer Inlandsbanan runs south to Östersund (Skr960, 13 hours, one daily at 6.50am) via Jokkmokk (Skr129, 2 hours) and Arvidsjaur (Skr352, 6 hours). Other departures include the twice-daily westbound train to Narvik (Skr293, 4½ hours) via Kiruna (Skr97, one to 1½ hours) and Abisko (Skr187, 2½ hours), and the eastbound train to Luleå (Skr148, 2½ to three hours, three daily).

Muddus National Park

Covered in primeval forest, the 500-sq-km Muddus National Park lies around 20km north of Jokkmokk along the E45, accessed from its southern end, via the village of Skaite (turn off at Liggadammen). The gently undulating terrain is ideal for novice hikers, and there are huts at regular intervals along the two trail loops, 24km and 44km long respectively, both of which start and end at Skaite and take in the attractive Muddus Falls. The park is rich in fauna and home to the whooper swan, lynx, elk and bears.

Kiruna

☑0980 / POP 23,407

The citizens of Kiruna (Giron, in Sami) live up to their nickname – the 'No-Problem People' – by remaining unperturbed at the news that their city is on the verge of collapsing into an enormous mine pit. Plans are to move the railway, the E10 highway and about 450 homes a couple of miles northwest by 2013, with the rest of the town centre to follow gradually. Kiruna has an industrial vibe to it, with the earth around it scarred by mine works and strewn with slag heaps, but its proximity to the Kungsleden (p308), Kebnekaise (p305) and the Icehotel (p306) makes it the most visited destination in the north.

◉ Sights & Activities

TOP CHOICE **LKAB Iron-Ore Mine** MINE

Kiruna owes its existence to the world's largest iron-ore deposit, 4km into the ground. The government-run mining company LKAB originally mined via open pits, but switched in the 1960s to tunnelling underground; the action now happens 914m below the surface. A visit to the depths of the LKAB iron-ore mine consists of being bussed to the InfoMine – a closed-off section of a mine tunnel, where you can hear mind-blowing stats and view jaw-droppingly large mining equipment, such as the mills used to crush ore. Tours leave daily from the tourist office between June and August (adult/student/child Skr295/195/50); check times for English tours.

Even if you don't descend into the underworld, hiking up **Luossavaara hill**, northwest of the centre, allows you to appreciate the sheer size of the mines from above.

Kiruna kyrka CHURCH

(Gruvvägen; ⊙10am-9pm summer) Kiruna kyrka, built to look like a huge Sami *kåta* (hut), is particularly pretty against a snowy backdrop (it was voted Sweden's most beautiful building in 2001).

FREE **Stadshus** BUILDING

(Town Hall; Hjalmar Lundbohmsvägen; ⊙9am-6pm) Another landmark (and a recipient of Sweden's most beautiful public building prize back in 1964), is the Stadshus, which houses a modest art collection and an odd display of Sami handicrafts.

Esrange SPACE CENTRE

(www.sscspace.com) Some 45km northeast of Kiruna is the space base Esrange, a facility where scientists research outer space and climate change as well as atmospheric phenomena like the northern lights. In 2014, Virgin Galactic is due to commence with its commercial passenger space flights from here. For those interested in just what exactly people do in space, detailed four-hour **tours** (☑668 00; adult/student/child Skr595/545/298) of the facility depart from the tourist office at 1pm; summer only, book in advance.

☞ Tours

TOP CHOICE **Nutti Sami Siida** REINDEER SLEDDING

(☑213 29; www.nutti.se) One of Nature's Best (an endorsement given to tour operators who have certain eco-credentials), this specialist in sustainable Sami ecotourism arranges visits to the Ráidu Sami camp to meet reindeer herders (Skr1490), reindeer sled excursions (from Skr1950) and their tour de force – an eight-day reindeer sleigh trip through the tundra to the Norwegian border, staying in Sami tents and wilderness huts (Skr31,500).

Active Lapland DOGSLEDDING

(☑076-104 5508; www.activelapland.com; Solbacksvägen 22) This experienced operator offers anything from two-hour dogsled rides (Skr1050) and rides under the northern lights, to airport pick-ups by dog sleigh (Skr5200).

THE MIDNIGHT SUN

Northern Sweden's most spectacular attractions are its natural phenomena. In summer, beyond the Arctic Circle, the sun does not leave the sky for weeks on end. You can see the midnight sun just south of the Arctic Circle as well (Arvidsjaur is the southernmost point in Sweden where this happens) due to the refraction of sunlight in the atmosphere. The midnight sun can be seen on the following dates in the following places:

TOWN	MIDNIGHT SUN
Arvidsjaur, Haparanda	20/21 Jun
Arjeplog	12/13 Jun to 28/29 Jul
Jokkmokk	8/9 Jun to 2/3 Jul
Gällivare	4/5 Jun to 6/7 Jul
Kiruna	28/29 May to 11/12 Jul
Karesuando	26/27 May to 15/16 Jul
Treriksröset	22/23 May to 17/18 Jul

Kiruna

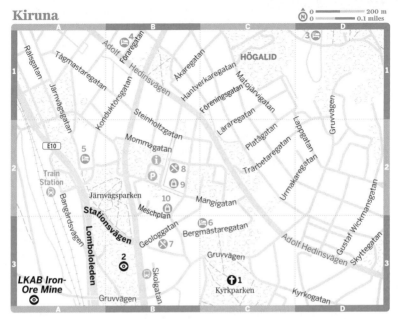

Lapland Tourist & Service SNOWMOBILE
(☏070-549 6547; www.lapland-tourist-service.
se) It's all about the snowmobile – from
day trips (Skr1450) to three-day wilderness adventures combined with ice fishing
(Skr10,850).

✹ Festivals & Events

Kiruna Snow Festival SNOW-SCULPTING
Held during the last week of January, the
Kiruna Snow Festival is based around a
snow-sculpting competition. The tradition
began in 1985 as a space-themed snow-
sculpture contest to celebrate the launching of a rocket (*Viking*) from nearby space
base Esrange (p302), and now draws artists
from all over to carve ever more elaborate
and beautiful shapes out of the snow. It also
features reindeer-sled racing, with Sami
traditions also emphasised.

🛏 Sleeping

Hotel Arctic Eden HOTEL €€€
(☏611 86; www.hotelarcticeden.se; Föraregatan
18; s/d Skr990/1600; 🅿🏊) What do Sami art,
Thai food and swimming pools have in common? Nothing, except that they all come together at Kiruna's most luxurious lodgings.
The hotel's rooms are an effortless blend of
Sami decor and modern technology, there's
a plush spa (featuring Swedish massage, of
course) and indoor pool, and the friendly
staff can book all manner of outdoor adventures. There are two restaurants on the
premises, serving fine northern Swedish and
Thai cuisines respectively.

LAPPLAND & THE FAR NORTH

Camp Ripan
CAMPGROUND €€

(☑630 00; www.ripan.se; Campingvägen 5; sites Skr150, hotel s/d from Skr1400/1735, cabins from Skr1195; P⊠) This large and well-equipped campsite, with swimming pool, has hotel-standard chalets and stylish rooms with Sami-inspired art – in addition to its caravan and tent sites. Numerous guided excursions on offer.

STF Vandrarhem & Hotell City
HOTEL €€

(☑hostel 171 95, hotel 666 55; www.kirunavan drarhem.se, www.hotellcity.se; Bergmästaregatan 7; dm/s/d from Skr200/440/500, hotel s/d incl breakfast Skr750/800; P) This catch-all hotel-and-hostel combo has a gleaming red-and-white colour scheme in its modern hotel rooms and cosy dorms. Hostel guests who want to use the sauna will have to pay extra. Breakfast is not included in the hostel tariff but can be added on to the bill.

Hotel Vinterpalatset
HOTEL €€

(☑677 70; www.vinterpalatset.se; Järnvägsgatan 18; s/d incl breakfast from Skr820/1050; P@) Pretty, spacious B&B rooms inside a dark-brown wooden building near the train station. The decadent breakfast includes cured salmon and roast game.

Eating & Drinking

TOP CHOICE Camp Ripan

Restaurang
NORTHERN SWEDISH €€

(Campingvägen; lunch buffet Skr99, meals Skr145-595; ☺breakfast, lunch & dinner; ☑). Located at the camping ground (of all places), the unusually expansive lunch buffet that's heavy on the veggies is very good value, but the real

---

WORTH A TRIP

VITTANGI MOOSE FARM

Elk are pretty remarkable: they can run up to 65km/h, they can jump up to 2.5m into the air, they can swim, they can even dive and eat water plants growing on the bottoms of lakes. To admire these magnificent creatures up close, stop by the **Vittangi Moose Farm** (☑070-247 6906; www.moosefarm. se; adult/child Skr120/60; ⊞), home to 11 elk, most of them tame. The visit includes a short video presentation on local wildlife.

It's located in Vittangi, halfway between Kiruna and Karesuando; follow the signs for Älgpark.

---

draw is the Sami-inspired à la carte menu featuring local seasonal produce. Go for the three-/five-/seven-course taster menus to sample smoked reindeer with lingonberries, moose ragout, ptarmigan, and sponge cake with cloudberries.

Thai Kitchen
THAI €

(Vänortsgatan 8; meals Skr75-115; ☑) Don't let the plastic tablecloths fool you – this informal joint cooks up excellent Thai dishes, though if you want the authentic spice levels, ask them to kick it up a notch. The sour and spicy glass noodles are superb.

Café Safari
CAFE €

(Geologgatan 4; meals Skr45-75; ☑) This is the nicest cafe in town – a long skinny room with good coffee, outstanding cakes (try the pecan pie) plus light meals such as sandwiches, quiche and baked potatoes. The sunny terrace is perpetually crowded in warm weather.

Shopping

Ateljé Nord
HANDICRAFT

(www.ateljenord.com; Lars Janssonsgatan 23; ☺noon-6pm Mon-Fri, 10am-2pm Sat) Shop run by a handicraft collective; a good place to meet the artisans who specialise in different types of Sami craft.

Máttárahkká
HANDICRAFT

(www.mattarahkka.se; ☺10am-6pm Mon-Fri, to 5pm Sat in summer, shorter hours rest of year) Five kilometres outside Kiruna, this well-established craft shop features Sami art and a wide selection of handicrafts, including knives, reindeer antler jewellery, leatherwork and colourful wool-and-reindeer-skin gloves. There's a sauna and hot tub on the roof. To get here, drive on the E10 towards Narvik; turn right shortly after a viaduct.

Information

Tourist office (☑188 80; www.kirunalap land.se; Folkets Hus, Lars Janssonsgatan 17; ☺8.30am-9pm Mon-Fri, to 6pm Sat & Sun Jun-Aug, 10am-3pm Mon-Sat Sep-May) Located on the main square; has internet access and can book various tours.

Getting There & Around

AIR Kiruna Airport (☑680 00), 7km east of the town, has flights with SAS to Stockholm (two to three daily), to Umeå (one daily, weekdays only) and to London Heathrow (one to two daily, winter only). The airport bus (☑156 90) runs between the tourist office and airport during peak season.

LAPONIA WORLD HERITAGE AREA

The vast Laponia stretches for 9400 sq km, comprising the mountains, forests and marshlands of Padjelanta, Sarek, Stora Sjöfallet and Muddus national parks. Unusually for a World Heritage Area, it's recognised both for its cultural wealth and natural wealth. Established in 1996, Laponia encompasses ancient reindeer grazing grounds of both the Mountain and Forest Sami, whose seven settlements and herds of around 50,000 reindeer are located here. The Sami still lead relatively traditional lives, following the reindeer during their seasonal migrations. The Mountain Sami winter in the forests, where there is lichen for their herds, and move into the mountains in summer, while their Forest counterparts follow their herds through the forests year-round.

BUS Daily bus 91 runs to Narvik, Norway (Skr255, 2½ hours) via Abisko (Skr155, 1¼ hours) and Riksgränsen (Skr155, two hours) at 1.50pm. Other departures include bus 501 to Jukkasjärvi (Skr35, 25 minutes, two to eight daily), buses 10 and 52 to Gällivare (Skr155, 1½ hours, two or three daily), and the daily (except Saturday) bus 53 to Haparanda (Skr345, 5¼ to six hours) via Pajala.

TRAIN There is a daily overnight train to Stockholm (Skr724, 16¾ hours) via Uppsala (Skr724, 15¾ hours) at 5.35pm. Other destinations include Narvik, Norway (Skr207, 2½- to ¼ hours, three daily) via Abisko (Skr107, one to 1½ hours) and Riksgränsen (Skr91, three hours), Luleå (Skr166, 3½ to four hours, three daily) and Gällivare (Skr60, 1¼ hours, three daily).

Nikkaluokta & Kebnekaise

Tiny Nikkaluokta, 66km west of Kiruna, is one of the entrance points to the Kungsleden (p308). It's also the base for those wishing to hike or climb Sweden's highest mountain, Kebnekaise (2106m); the views of the surrounding peaks and glaciers are incredible on a clear day.

In July and August, the marked trail up the southern flank is usually snow-free and no technical equipment is required to reach the southern top. Getting to the northern top (2097m) from the southern top involves an airy traverse of a knife-edge ice ridge with a rope, an ice axe and crampons. The trip involves 1900m of ascent and descent. Allow 12 hours to reach the southern top, and an extra 1½ hours if you want to include the northern top.

The best maps to use are the Calazo 1:100,000 *Kebnekaisefjällen* or the very detailed 1:20,000 *Fjällkartan Kebnekaise*. Guided hikes and ice climbing can be arranged at **STF Kebnekaise Fjälstation** (☏0980-550 00; www.svenskaturistforeningen.se/kebnekaise; dm Skr450, d/q from Skr1450/1900;

☉late Feb–early May & mid-Jun–late Sep), a large, attractive mountain lodge nestled at the foot of Mt Kebnekaise. A popular entry point to the Kungsleden, it has equipment rental and gear shop, sauna and an excellent restaurant serving three daily meals (three-course dinner Skr360).

Twice-daily bus 92 runs between Kiruna and Nikkaluokta (Skr114, one hour), a 19km hike away.

Jukkasjärvi

☑0980 / POP 519

The Icehotel has firmly put this one-street village on the world map.

Jukkasjärvi is also home to **Jukkasjärvi kyrka** (Marnadsvägen; ☉9am-8pm summer), the oldest church in Lappland (1608). The brightly-painted altarpiece by Uppsala artist Bror Hjorth, cut out in teak, depicts scenes with the revivalist preacher Lars Levi Laestadius. In the centre of the birch organ above the entrance hangs a shaman's drum, merging the Sami sun symbol with the Christian cross. The organ itself has three sounds: birdsong, drum, and reindeer hooves.

Near the church is **Nutti Sámi Siida** (☏213 29; www.nutti.se; Marknadsvägen 84; adult/student/child Skr100/80/50; ☉10am-6pm Jun-Aug, tours 10.30am, 2pm, 4.30pm), a reindeer yard that you can tour with a Sami guide to learn about reindeer farming and Sami culture. Here you can book tours (p302), pick up excellent Sami *duodji* (certified handicrafts) and arrange a stay at the nearby **Reindeer Lodge** (2-person cabins Skr600) – four cosy rustic cabins in the woods, with a wood-heated sauna and fully equipped kitchen.

At **Restaurang Hembygdsgården** (meals Skr80-100; ☉11am-5pm) by the river, you can fill up on jacket potatoes, Norbotten cheese-

ICEHOTEL

From a humble start in 1989 as a small igloo, originally built by Yngve Bergqvist to house an art gallery, the **Icehotel** (☑668 00; www.icehotel.com; Marnadsvägen 63; s/d from Skr2700/3800, ste Skr7000, cabins from Skr2100; ℗) at Jukkasjärvi, 18km east of Kiruna, has since grown into an international phenomenon.

The Icehotel building comprises an entrance hall and a main walkway lined with ice sculptures and lit with electric lights, with smaller corridors branching off towards the 67 suites. The beds are made of compact snow and covered with reindeer skins, and you are provided with sleeping bags used by the Swedish army for Arctic survival training, guaranteed to keep you warm despite the -5°C temperature inside the rooms (and in winter that's nothing – outside the hotel it can be as low as -30°C).

There are heated bathrooms near the reception, and you leave your valuables and most of your possessions in lockers so that they don't freeze. It's a good idea to stuff your clothes into the bottom of your sleeping bag, otherwise they'll resemble a washboard. Come morning, guests are revived with a hot drink and a spell in the sauna. Guest spend just one night in the Icehotel itself (it's an experience, not a comfortable night's sleep) so the hotel provides warm accommodation as well: 30 satellite Aurora Houses – bungalows, decorated in contemporary Scandinavian style, with skylights for viewing the northern lights – scattered around the frozen monolith.

The best place to eat for miles around is the **Icehotel Restaurant** (☑668 84; meals Skr300-600; ☺lunch & dinner; ☑); besides the novelty of plates and bowls made from Torne river ice in winter, beautifully-presented dishes include grilled Arctic char, reindeer steak and cloudberry mousse.

This custom-built 'igloo' also has an **Ice Church**, popular for weddings (giving new meaning to the expression 'cold feet') and the **Absolut Icebar**, where you drink from ice glasses while admiring the ice sculptures (warm clothing provided).

For the first time, in June 2011, a smaller version of the Icehotel opened inside a giant freezer warehouse, containing an Icebar, three rooms, and an ice-sculpting workshop for guests – so visitors can have the winter experience in summer.

Winter adventures include snowmobile safaris, skiing, ice-fishing, dogsledding, Sami culture tours, and northern lights safaris, while summer activities comprise hiking, rafting, canoeing, fishing and Ranger all-terrain buggy tours.

Nonguests can visit the Icehotel during winter (until 6pm); in summer there are guided tours for those interested in the construction of the hotel.

and-honey sandwiches and Swedish standards such as meatballs.

Bus 501 runs between Kiruna and Jukkasjärvi (Skr35, 25 minutes, two to eight daily).

Abisko

☑0980

Easy access to spectacular scenery makes Abisko (Ábeskovvu, in Sami) one of the highlights of any trip to Lappland. The 75-sq-km **Abisko National Park** spreads out from the southern shore of scenic lake Torneträsk. It's framed by the striking profile of Lapporten, a 'gate' formed by neighbouring hills that serves as the legendary gate to Lappland. This is also the driest part of Sweden, and consequently has a relatively long hiking season.

Abisko has two train stops – Östra station puts you in the centre of the tiny, tiny village, while Abisko Turiststation is across the highway from the STF lodge.

◉ Sights & Activities

Hiking is the big draw here – trails are varied in both distance and terrain, and while most people come here to tackle part (or all) of the 450km-long Kungsleden (p308), there are plenty of shorter rambles.

Excellent day hikes include the 8km hike to the Kårsa Rapids, over the Ábeskoeatnu river and then along the left fork of the signposted Kårsavagge (Gorsavággi, in Sami) trail through birch and pine forest, and the great 14km, four-hour return hike along Paddus nature trail, past an STF reconstruction of a traditional Sami camp, leading to Báddosdievvá, a former Sami sacrificial site with awesome views of Lapporten and lake Törnetrask.

Longer hikes include the overnight trip to the Gorsajökeln glacier, staying overnight at the STF hut at heart of the Kårsavagge (Gorsavággi) valley, west of Abisko (15km each way), and the 39km-long Rallarvägen (Navvy Road) to Riksgränsen, running parallel to the railway line and used by railway construction workers in the early 20th century. A good side venture from Rallarvägen is the 10km return trip to the enormous boulders and impressive rock formations of Kärkevagge (Gearggevággi) valley from Låktatjåkka (short train/bus ride from Abisko) with Trollsjön (Rissájáurre) the 'Sulphur Lake' at the end of the valley, its clear blue waters named after the colour of burning sulphur.

For hikes in this area, employ the map *Fjällkartan BD6* or *Calazo Kungsleden* (Skr120), both available at the STF lodge and Naturum.

Aurora Sky Station   LOOKOUT

(www.auroraskystation.com; one-way/return from Skr125/155; ☺9.30am-4pm, also 10pm-1am Tue, Thu & Sat mid-Jun–mid-Jul) Across the highway from the STF Turiststation, a chair lift takes you up the neighbouring Mt Nuolja (1169m), where those without vertigo can enjoy epic views from the deck of the **Panorama Café** (☺9.30am-4pm), part of the Aurora Sky Station. In summer this is a prime spot from which to see the midnight sun; in winter, to view the northern lights. You can come up on a guided tour (Skr590), enjoy a three-course dinner with an incredible view

---

AURORA BOREALIS

The otherworldly lights of the aurora borealis, named after the Roman goddess of dawn and the Greek name for the north wind, have captivated the imagination of the people of the north and travellers alike for centuries. A truly awe-inspiring sight, the the celestial spectacle of the streaks in the sky – from yellowish-green to violet, white and red – are caused by the collision of energy-charged sun particles with atoms in the Earth's magnetic field and are visible in the north of Sweden between October and March.

(Skr1490) or even stay overnight (Skr2950, dinner included).

🛏 Sleeping & Eating

TOP CHOICE **Abisko Fjällturer**   HOSTEL €

(☑401 03; www.abisko.net; dm/d Skr200/250; P☺) This backpacker's delight has comfortable doubles and dorms with wide bunks, sharing two guest kitchens and a wonderful wooden sauna. Brothers Tomas and Andreas keep a large team of sled dogs; day-packages in winter include accommodation, two or four hours' driving your own dog sled, sauna, snowshoes and skis (with two/four hours dogsledding Skr1000/1500). In summer, your hosts can organise caving, hiking and fishing tours. To find the place, cross the railway tracks 150m east of Abisko Östra station.

STF Abisko Turiststation & Abisko Mountain Lodge   HOSTEL €

(☑402 00; www.abisko.nu; dm Skr210, hotel s/d from Skr790/1390, hostel dm Skr 250, s/d from Skr530/740; ☺8am-9pm 22 Dec-3 Jan, 15 Feb-4 May, 6 Jun-21 Sep; P☺) This huge place overlooking Torneträsk lake has 300 beds in dorms, cabins and private rooms, and is constantly bustling with hikers. Guest kitchens, a basement sauna, excellent facilities and knowledgeable, friendly staff ensure the hostel's popularity, so book in advance. There's a small supply shop and expensive trekking equipment rentals, as well as an excellent restaurant where you can treat yourself to pre-hike organic breakfast (Skr100) and post-hike sumptuous three-course dinner (Srk330). Guided day treks (from Skr590), caving (Skr390), fishing (Skr490) and Sami Camp exhibition tours (Skr120) available.

ℹ Information

The **Naturum** (☑401 77; www.naturumabisko. se; ☺9am-6pm Tue-Sat early Jun–Sep, Feb-Apr) office next to STF Abisko Turiststation & Abisko Mountain Station has detailed maps and extensive information on the Kungsleden, and the helpful staff are happy to answer questions and make suggestions based on the amount of time you have.

ℹ Getting There & Away

Buses and trains stop at Abisko Östra (main village) and Abisko Turiststation – the start of the Kungsleden, five minutes apart. Bus 91 runs east to Kiruna (Skr155, 1¼ hours, one daily) and west to Narvik (Skr160, 1½ hours, one daily) via Riksgränsen (Skr65, 40 minutes).

Trains run to Kiruna (Skr107, 1-1½ hours, three daily) and to Narvik (Skr67, two hours, three daily) via Riksgränsen (Skr41, 45 minutes, three daily).

Kungsleden

Kungsleden (King's Trail) is Sweden's most important hiking and skiing route, running for 450km from Abisko to Hemavan. The route is split into five mostly easy or moderate sections, with **STF mountain huts** (dm Skr360, sites Skr80; ☉mid-Feb–early May & late Jun–mid-Sep), each manned by a custodian, spaced out along the route 10 to 20km from one another (first come, first served). Eleven of the 16 huts sell provisions, and full kitchen facilities are provided, but you'll need your own sleeping bag and there's no electricity. The fifth section, between Kvikkjokk and Ammarnäs, in not covered by STF, so you must stay in private accommodation in villages, or camp wild.

The most popular section is the one from Abisko to Nikkaluokta; Sweden's highest mountain, Kebnekaise (2106m), is a glorious extra (p305). During the summer you are likely to meet the local Sami herding their reindeer all along the Kungsleden, as it's part of the Laponia World Heritage Area (p297).

ABISKO TO KEBNEKAISE

From Abisko it's 86km to Kebnekaise Fjällstation (around five days of hiking), and 105km to Nikkaluokta if you're leaving the trail at Kebnekaise (around seven days). The best maps to use are the detailed (1:100,000) *Fjällkartan BD6* or Calazo (www.calazo.se) *Kungsleden*. Fjällkartan cover a slightly wider area around the Kungsleden and are

one-sided, whereas Calazo are doublesided and water-resistant.

This section of Kungsleden runs through the dense vegetation of Abisko National Park, mostly following the valley, with wooden boardwalks over the boggy sections and bridges over streams. The highest point along the trail is the Tjäkta Pass (1150m), with great views over the Tjäktavagge Valley.

There are five STF huts along the trail: Abiskojaure (in a lovely lakeside setting), Alesjaure (with a sauna and a great view from the mountain ridge), Tjäktja (before Tjäktja Pass), Sälka (a good base for a day's hiking in the surrounding area) and Singi. The STF has mountain lodges at Abisko (p307) and Kebnekaise (p305).

KEBNEKAISE TO SALTOLUOKTA

This section is 52km (or about three to four days) from Kebnekaise Fjällstation and 38km from Singi to Saltoluokta. The best maps to use are *Fjällkartan BD8* or Calazo *Kebnekaisefjällen*.

In summer, you can shorten the extra 19km hike from Nikkaluokta to Kebnekaise Fjällstation by 5km by catching a boat across Ladjojaure lake. South of Singi, 14km from Kebnekaise, this quieter section of the trail runs through scenery less dramatic than around Kebnekaise. You may have to row yourself 1km across lake Teusajaure (there's an STF boat service in peak season) and then cross the bare plateau before descending to Vakkotavare through beech forest. There's excellent fishing at the Kaitumjaure and Teusajaure lakes and the views of Sarek National Park on the approach to Vakkotavare are nothing short of fabulous.

Everyone takes the bus along the road from Vakkotavare to the quay at Kebnats (Skr110), where there's an STF ferry across the Langas lake to Saltoluokta Fjällstation

WORTH A TRIP

RIKSGRÄNSEN

A tiny ski-resort town tucked just inside the border with Norway, Riksgränsen is the only place in Sweden where you can ski into Norway and back on the Midsummer weekend at midnight. Dominating the hillside, **Riksgränsen** (☏400 80; www.riksgransen.nu; s/d from Skr1350/2000; ☉mid-Feb–Midsummer; P☒) is a large resort that's hugely popular with skiers in the winter season; its luxurious spa centre, complete with outdoor hot tubs overlooking Vassijaure lake, is an awesome spot to unwind, après-ski. Rental of downhill ski gear costs from Skr350 per day, and day lift-passes start at around Skr400. Rooms in the comfy little annex, Meteorologen, are available year-round and are homier and cheaper.

Trains stop in Riksgränsen on the way from Kiruna to Narvik, as does bus 91.

(Skr40). STF has mountain lodges at Keb-nekaise and Saltoluokta, and four huts en route, at Singi, Kaitumjaure, Teusajaure and Vakkotavare.

SALTOLUOKTA TO KVIKKJOKK

This section is 73km, or around four days of hiking; the best maps to use are *Fjällkartan BD10* or Calazo *Sarek & Padjelanta*. From Saltoluokta, it's a long and relatively steep climb to Sitojaure (six hours), where you cross a lake using the boat service run by the hut's caretaker, followed by a boggy stretch with wooden walkways over the worst sections. At Aktse, on the shores of Laitaure Lake, you are rewarded with expansive views of the bare mountainous terrain, before you cross the lake using the row-boats provided.

Aktse is an excellent base for side trips into Sarek National Park, while Pårte is a favourite spot for fishing in nearby streams. To reach Kvikkjokk you must pass through pine forest, with a good chance of spotting wild game.

TF has lodges at Saltoluokta and Kvikkjokk (p299), and huts at Sitojaure, Aktse and Pårte en route.

KVIKKJOKK TO AMMARNÄS

This is the wildest and most difficult section of the park, recommended for experienced hikers only. It stretches for 157km, or about eight to 10 days of hiking; the best maps to use are *Fjällkartan BD14* (north) and BD16 (south) or else Calazo *Kvikkjokk-Ammarnäs*. You must bring your own tent, as accommodation is very spread out.

First, you take the boat across Saggat lake from Kvikkjokk before walking to Tsiellejåkk, from where it's 55km to the next hut at Vuonatjviken. Then cross Riebnesjaure lake and another one from Hornavan to the village of Jäkkvikk, from where the trail runs through Pieljekaise National Park. From Jakkvikk it's only 8km until the next hut, followed by another stop at the village of Adolfström, then cross Iraft lake before making for the cabins at Sjnjultje. Here the trail forks: either take the direct 34km route to Ammarnäs, or take a 24km detour to Rävfallet with an additional 20km to Ammarnäs.

You'll find private accommodation at Tsielejåkk, Vuonatjviken, Jäkkvikk, Pieljekaise, Adolfström, Sjnjultje, Rävfallet and Ammarnäs.

AMMARNÄS TO HEMAVAN

This section is 78km, or around four days' worth; the best maps to use are *Fjällkartan AC2* or Calazo *Ammarnäs-Hemavan*. Most of the southern section of Kungsleden runs through Vindelfjällens Nature Reserve. This trail is the easiest of the five sections, mostly consisting of a gentle ramble through beech forest and wetlands, and over low hills. There's a long steep climb (8km) through beech forest between Ammarnäs and Aigert, but at the top you are rewarded with an impressive waterfall. From Aigert, you can do a detour up Stor Aigert (1100m) for great surrounding views. It's possible to bypass Aigert altogether by taking a boat across the marsh towards Serve, the next hut.

To reach Syter, you cross the wetlands known as the Tärnasjö Archipelago using the network of bridges, stopping at the hut by Tärnasjö Lake for a spell in the sauna (it's also possible to catch a boat across the lake to shorten your hike). The hike up to Syter peak (1768m) from Syter hut is greatly recommended and the view on the way down from Viterskalet to Hemavan, taking in Norway's Okstindarnas glaciers, is particularly spectacular.

The STF has hostels at Ammarnäs (p294) and Hemavan (p293), and five huts en route at Aigert, Serve, Tärnaskö, Syter and Viterskalet, all of which sell provisions.

ⓘ Getting There & Away

Frequent trains stop at Abisko en route from Kiruna to Narvik, Norway. Inlandsbanan stops at Jokkmokk in summer.

The bus routes to other starting points along the Kungsleden are: Kiruna to Nikkaluokta on bus 92 (Skr114; one hour, two daily); Gällivare to Ritsem via Kebnats and Vakkotavare on bus 93 (Skr295, 3½ hours, one daily); Jokkmokk to Kvikkjokk on buses 47 and 94 (Skr155, two to 2½ hours, two to three daily); Arjeplog to Jäkkvik on buses 104 and 200 (Skr91, one hour, one or two daily except Saturday); Sorsele to Ammarnäs on bus 341 (Skr112, 1¼ to 1¾ hours, one to three daily); and Umeå via Tärnaby to Hemavan on buses 31 and 319 from Tärnaby (Skr257, six hours, one or two daily).

Karesuando

🔊 0981 / POP 350

Karesuando (Gárasavvon, in Sami), across the bridge from the Finnish town of Kaaresuvanto, is the northernmost church village in Sweden, and it feels that way: utterly remote and exquisitely lonely. Still, scratch under the surface of this one-elk town – a Sami reindeer herder community – and you'll find some good reasons for having travelled this far north. The area revels in the romance of extremes: the midnight sun shines here from late May to mid-July, but in winter the temperature hits -50°C. Karesuando's frontier feel is reflected in the four languages spoken by the locals (sometimes all at once): Swedish, Finnish, Sami and Norwegian.

Karesuando boasts Sweden's northernmost church (☉24hr), built in 1816; the wooden altar sculpture represents local revivalist preacher Lars Levi Laestadius, his disciple Johan Raatamaa and the Sami girl Maria. Nearby is the Vita Huset (guided tours Skr30; ☉8am-4pm Mon-Fri), a folk museum with evocative photos depicting Finn civilians fleeing the retreating German forces in 1944. A short walk west of the tourist office is the Laestadius Pörte, the log cabin (☉24hr) which was home to Lars Levi Laestadius and his family between 1826 and 1849.

Sámiid Viessu, inside the old Viktoriahemmet – a building donated by Queen Victoria in 1922 as a hospital and shelter for the Sami – is now the headquarters of the Sami union, as well as a Sami art and handicraft exhibition and museum.

The choices for resting your weary head are Karesunado Vandrarhem (☑200 00; dm/s Skr150/300), a riverside hostel with a well-equipped kitchen but a poorly ventilated interior (choose between fresh air or becoming a mosquito buffet), or Hotel

KAAREVAARA VIEWPOINT

For all-encompassing views of the endless tundra surrounding the village, head east out of Karesuando along Route 99 for a few minutes, then take the right turn marked Kaarevaara past a small lake and up the hill.

Karesuando (☑200 00; s/d Skr650/700), opposite and under the same management as the hostel, with Sami-inspired decor and the village's only restaurant.

The tourist office (☑202 05; www.karesu ando.se; ☉8am-4pm Mon-Fri), next to the bridge to Finland, has information on the region, as well as Norway and Finland, and internet access.

Bus 50 runs once daily between Karesuando and Kiruna via Vittangi (Skr207, 2½ to three hours).

Pajala

☑0978 / POP 2200

Pajala, made famous in the hugely popular Swedish novel and film *Popular Music*, has a tiny town centre, a nice riverside pathway, and is a place with deeply-rooted Torne Valley culture, where the locals speak Tornedalsfinska (Torne Valley Finnish), and Swedish takes second place.

Pajala Fair (one week in July), attended by over 40,000 people each year, is the place

TRERIKSRÖSET – WHERE THREE LANDS MEET

Treriksröset, the spot marking the meeting point of Sweden, Norway and Russia (today's Finland), lies 100km northwest of Karesuando.

If driving, cross the bridge from Karesuando to the Finnish Kaaresuvanto, and then take the E8 route northwest to Kilpisjärvi (110km). Alternatively, take the daily bus departing Kaaresuvanto (1¾ hours, €19, one daily at 2.35pm) and then hike the 11km woodland trail from the north side of the village to the small Lake Goldjärvi where a yellow concrete 'bell' marks the spot.

To shorten your hike to just 3km each way, hop aboard the M/S Malla (☑358 (0)16 537783), which sails from Kilpisjärvi to Koltaluokta (45 minutes, €20 return, 10am, 2pm, 6pm late June to early August), an old Sami residence. The boat waits at Koltaluokta for two hours.

Since the daily bus from Kilpisjärvi to Kaaresuvanto departs at 1.40pm, you have no choice but to stay overnight; Lapland Hotel Kilpis is quite basic but has a decent restaurant.

Check up-to-date bus timetables at www.matkahuolto.fi and bring mosquito repellent for the hike. And don't forget that Finland is one hour ahead of Sweden.

to pick up some excellent handmade Sami knives, reindeer-skin bags, smoked fish and more.

The **tourist office** (☑100 15; www.pajala. se; ☺8am-4pm Mon-Fri) is near the bus station, overlooked by a giant wooden model of a great grey owl – the symbol of the town. Nearby is one of the world's largest circular sundials, there being 18 to 25 minutes' difference between solar time and a normal watch. Towards the river is **Laestadius pörtet** (www.laestadiusfriends.se; Laestadiusvägen 36; Skr65 ☺10am-6pm mid-Jun–mid-Aug), home of Lars Levi Laestadius from 1849 until his death 12 years later, containing many personal objects and an exhibition dedicated to his life and work.

Twenty-five kilometres west of Pajala, family-run **Forest Hotel** (☑203 80; www. foresthotel.se; Niemenrova 43, Tärendö; s/d Skr890/1190, s/d with shared facilities Skr400/690; 3-night winter packages per person Skr8490; P@) attracts international travellers with its multiday winter packages, which include snowmobile tours, dogsledding and reindeer sleigh rides. The hot tub and 'nature's own' spa are superb, and the restaurant draws on Torneland and Sami influences, serving up Finnish bread, barbecued reindeer and capercallie (a type of local game bird). In Pajala itself, **Snickarbacken Lägenhetshotell**

ROMP WEEK

It's not quite what you think! The notorious **Romp Week** (Römppäviiko), a cultural fair complete with live music and food stalls held during the last week of September in Pajala, recalls the debauchery of 1987, when women from around Europe came and celebrate the village's 400th anniversary and some stayed on to marry the local lumberjacks.

(☑100 70; www.snickarbacken.se; Kirunavägen; d Skr490, 2-/4-/8-person apt Skr690/790/890) offers impeccable apartment-style suites, as well as double rooms and a good weekday dinner buffet.

❶ Getting There & Away

AIR The new **Pajala-Ylläs Airport** (☑510 10, http://start.pajala.se) currently has two departures to Luleå on weekdays.

BUS Bus 55 serves Luleå (Skr245, three to 3½ hours, one to two daily). Bus 53 runs east to Haparanda (Skr216, 2½ to three hours, one to three daily) and west to Kiruna (Skr216, 2¾ to three hours, one to two daily except Saturday); change in Vittangi for Karesuando (Skr245, 3½ hours, one daily).

Understand Sweden

population per sq km

STOCKHOLM MALMÖ GÖTEBORG

≈ 1155 people

Sweden Today

Change in the Weather

The past few years have been strange ones for Sweden, as changes in the economy and political mood have led people to question long-held assumptions. For decades the country has been viewed by left-leaning types as an almost utopian model of a socialist state, a successful experiment that gave hope to progressives everywhere. But recently that perception has been shifting.

The Social Democrats, who've held a majority of the government (and therefore shaped national policy) for most of the past 80 years, have begun to lose their influence. The first big blow came in 2006: partly as a result of the general sense that Sweden had been relying too heavily on unemployment benefits and had become a nation of 'bystanders', the long-entrenched party lost its leadership position in the Swedish Parliament. The newly formed centre-right Alliance Party (made up of four centre-right parties – the Moderate Party, the Liberal Party, the Christian Democrats and the Centre Party) won the election, with Prime Minister Fredrik Reinfeldt campaigning on a 'work first' platform.

The most recent election, in September 2010, saw the Social Democrats' worst results since 1921: they won just over 30% of the seats in Parliament. The Alliance Party, which Reinfeldt is largely credited with putting together, won 173 of the 349 seats, meaning Reinfeldt continues as prime minister.

This gradual political shift hasn't come out of nowhere. Some trace it back to 1986 and the infamous murder of Prime Minister Olof Palme (1927–86), who was assassinated as he walked home from the cinema. The murder and bungled police inquiry shook ordinary Swedes' confidence in their country, institutions and leaders. Afterwards, the

» Population: 9.09 million

» GDP: $354.7 billion

» GDP per capita: $39,100

» Annual inflation: 1.3% (2010)

» Unemployment: 8.4%

Top Films

The Seventh Seal (1957) Ingmar Bergman pits man against Death in a cosmic chess game.
Songs from the Second Floor (2000) Roy Andersson's bleak meditation on modern humanity.

Top Books

The Girl with the Dragon Tattoo (2009) Stieg Larsson's Millennium Trilogy has been a global phenomenon.
Faceless Killers (1997) Henning Mankell's detective series, with Kurt Wallander, starts here.

Greeting People

In Sweden the catch-all greeting is 'hej'. For someone you know well, say 'tjena' (sheh-na). In Felli Sami, the most common of the Sami languages, the greeting is 'buorre beaiv', to which you reply 'ipmel atti'.

belief systems
(% of population)

87 Lutheran

13 Other

if Sweden were 100 people

89 would be Swedish
3 would be Finn & Sami (Lapp)
1 would be Iranian
6 would be Other

fortunes of the Social Democrats took a turn for the worse as various scandals came to light.

This was followed by a world recession in 1992, during which the country's budgetary problems culminated in frenzied speculation against the Swedish krona. In November of that year the central bank (Sveriges Riksbank) was forced to abandon fixed exchange rates and let the krona float freely. The currency immediately devalued by 20%, interest rates shot up by a world-record-breaking 500% and unemployment flew to 14%; the government fought back with tax hikes, punishing cuts to the welfare budget and the scrapping of previously relaxed immigration rules.

With both the economy and national confidence severely shaken, Swedes narrowly voted in favour of joining the European Union (EU), effective from 1 January 1995. (Sweden drew the line at adopting the common currency, however, and retains its use of the krona.)

The country's willingness to make hard choices (such as selling off public assets) and a strict fiscal policy may be one reason it has emerged from the 2008 economic crisis in better financial shape than most. Sweden entered the recession with a budget surplus. Which isn't to say it wasn't hit hard: in late 2008, thanks to a drop in demand for exports caused by the global recession, Sweden's GDP fell nearly 5%. But by 2010 the economy had started growing again, and growth was expected to continue. At the time of writing, economic conditions were looking up, and unemployment was gradually dropping.

» Mobile telephones: 11.426 million (2009)

» Internet users: 8.398 million

» Internet domain: .se

People & Immigration

Sweden's population is relatively small given the size of the country – with around nine million people spread over the third-largest country in Western Europe, it has one of the lowest population densities on the

Dos & Don'ts

» Be prepared to take off your shoes inside the front door when visiting a Swedish home.

» On formal occasions, wait for the host to welcome you to the table before eating or drinking and don't clink glasses (it's considered vulgar).

Myths

In spite of popular belief, Sweden is not a nation of Bjorn Borgs and Anita Ekbergs. The country's self-image is changing gradually. As hip-hop artist Timbuktu (himself the Swedish-born son of a mixed-race American couple) once told the *Washington Post*, 'Sweden still has a very clear picture of what a Swede is. That no longer exists – the blond, blue-eyed physical traits. That's changing. But it still exists in the minds of some people'.

continent. Most Swedes live in the large cities of Stockholm, Göteborg, Malmö and Uppsala. Conversely, the interior of Norrland is sparsely populated.

About 30,000 Finnish speakers form a substantial minority in the northeast, near Torneälven.

Sweden first opened its borders to mass immigration during WWII. At the time it was a closed society, and new arrivals were initially expected to assimilate and 'become Swedish'. In 1975 Parliament adopted a new set of policies that emphasised the freedom to preserve and celebrate traditional native cultures.

In 2007, the small town of Södertälje, 30km south of Stockholm, welcomed 1268 Iraqi refugees – more than what was accepted that year by the US and Canada combined.

» Highest point: Kebnekaise (2106m)

» People per physician: 380

» Adult literacy: roughly 100%

» Price of petrol: Skr14.28 per litre

Tip of the Tongue

Other than immigration, always a hot topic, what are Swedes talking about these days? Jobs are a major topic – finding them, keeping them, being paid sufficiently for them. Though unemployment overall is shrinking, it's still unusually high among young people. At the time of research, Swedes are talking about local versions of the American anticapitalism protests on Wall Street, which had spread to Stockholm, and a recent EU study that showed that Sweden has twice as many incidents of rape reported than the UK. Swedes are also talking about the work of Swedish poet Tomas Tranströmer, who won the 2011 Nobel Prize in Literature.

Other topics of conversations you'll commonly overhear while travelling in Sweden include organic food and sustainable cuisine; the outrageous weather (true at any time of year); and coffee.

Immigration

» Swedish residents born abroad: 14.1%

» Immigrants to Sweden (2009): 102,280

» Main immigrant groups: Finns, Iraqis, ex-Yugoslavia nationals, Somalis, Iranians, Norwegians, Danes, Turks, Poles

Child Care

In Sweden child care is guaranteed for all children aged two to six years. Parents receive 480 days of paid leave at 80% of a government-determined salary cap between the child's birth and eighth birthday. Parents decide how to divide it, but 60 days are reserved for the father. This helps explain the matter-of-fact way in which Swedish men and women share child-rearing duties. Travellers frequently remark upon the large number of men they see pushing baby strollers around.

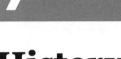

History

It is difficult to reconcile the images of neutral modern-day Sweden with that of a country that spent much of its existence at war with its neighbours, yet it is precisely that bloody history that has shaped it into its present peace-loving entity.

Imagine Sweden's history as a play in three acts. Act I: a clatter of hooves, and reindeer tentatively set foot on stage, closely pursued by fur-clad hunter-gatherers – the predecessors of the Sami. Other minor characters venture into the land of the midnight sun and the Arctic night: the curious Greek explorers and the Roman traders. Then in a flash of steel and fearsome yells, the Vikings charge on stage to raid and plunder.

Act II: the action is split between the court and the battlefield, and the plot, full of intrigue, is worthy of Shakespeare himself. Royal dynasties follow one another in rapid succession; nobles conspire against the king; there's fratricide by poisoned pea soup; an androgynous girl-king ascends the throne only to flee, dressed as a man; a king is assassinated at a masked ball and another during battle. Battles are fought on frozen lakes, at sea and in the mountains. Sweden's territory expands and then rapidly contracts.

Act III: Sweden's dreams of greatness lie in tatters following military defeats and the loss of its colonies. It is peacetime and population is growing. Railways are laid, mines are dug, trees are felled, cities grow. Sweden is largely untouched by the turmoil of the World Wars and focuses on improving the lives of its own citizens before turning its sights to the rest of the world. An international player and member of the UN, Sweden welcomes scores of refugees; the homogenous-looking cast quickly becomes a diverse one. And just when a happy ending is near, the final plot twist brings murder and tragedy.

Top Five World Heritage Sites in Sweden

» Hanseatic town of Visby

» Naval port of Karlskrona

» Gammelstad church village, Luleå

» Höga Kusten

» Laponia

TIMELINE	**c 10,000 BC**	**1800– 500 BC**	**500 BC**
	Ice sheets melt and hunter-gatherer tribes, the predecessors of the Sami, follow reindeer into a newly uncovered Sweden. The oldest human settlement is set up near Arjeplog.	*Hällristningar* (petroglyphs) illustrating Bronze Age beliefs appear in many parts of Sweden, such as Dalsland and Bohuslän. The sun, hunting scenes and ships are common themes.	The runic alphabet arrives, probably from the Germanic region. It is used to carve inscriptions onto monumental rune stones (there are around 3000 in Sweden) well into medieval times.

TRACING YOUR ANCESTORS

Around a million people emigrated from Sweden to the USA and Canada between 1850 and 1930. Many of their 12 million descendants are now returning to find their roots.

Luckily, detailed parish records of births, deaths and marriages have been kept since 1686 and there are *landsarkivet* (regional archives) around the country. The national archive is **Riksarkivet** (☎010-476 70 00; www.ra.se).

SVAR Forskarcentrum (☎010-476 7700; www.svar.ra.se) holds most records from the late 17th century until 1928. You can pay the staff here to research for you or look for yourself.

Utvandrarnas Hus (Emigrant House; p238) in Växjö is a very good museum dedicated to the mass departure. Attached is the **Swedish Emigrant Institute** (☎0470-201 20; www.utvandrarnashus.se), with an extensive research centre that you can use (Skr413 per search).

Also worth a look is *Tracing Your Swedish Ancestry,* by Nils William Olsson, a free do-it-yourself genealogical guide (40 pages). Get a copy by emailing your name and address to ancestry@swedennewyork.com, or download it from the New York Consulate-General of Sweden's website: www.swedenabroad.com (under Visit Sweden in the menu).

The First Arrivals

In the beginning, there was ice. In the grip of the last ice age Sweden was an inhospitable place, but perhaps less so than Siberia, where the first hunter-gathers originated around 10,000 years ago. As the ice retreated, tribes from central Europe migrated into the south of Sweden, and ancestors of the Sami people hunted wild reindeer into the northern regions.

As the climate improved between 1800 BC and 500 BC, Bronze Age cultures blossomed. Huge Bronze Age burial mounds, such as Kiviksgraven in Österlen, suggest that powerful chieftains had control over spiritual and temporal matters.

After 500 BC, the Iron Age brought about technological advances, demonstrated by archaeological finds of agricultural tools, graves and primitive furnaces, but as the climate worsened again, the downturn in agriculture coincided with the arrival of the Svea – powerful tribes who ended up settling much of Sweden. By AD 600, the Svea people of the Mälaren valley (just west of Stockholm) had gained supremacy, and their kingdom, Svea Rike, gave the country of Sweden its name: Sverige.

c 800

Birka, founded on Björkö (an island in Lake Mälaren lake), becomes a powerful Viking trading centre. Byzantine and Arab coins have been found here, confirming the existence of trade routes.

1008

Sweden's first Christian king, Olof Skötkonung, is baptised at St Sigfrid's Well in Husaby, but worship continues in Uppsala's pagan temple until at least 1090.

» Re-enactment of Viking battle

Vikings & Christians

Scandinavia's greatest impact on world history probably occurred during the Viking Age, when hardy pagan Norsemen set sail for other shores. The Swedish Vikings were more inclined towards trade than their Norwegian or Danish counterparts but their reputation as fearsome warriors was not unjustified. At home it was the height of paganism; Viking leaders claimed descent from Freyr, 'God of the World', and celebrations at Uppsala involved human sacrifices.

The Vikings sailed a new type of boat that was fast and highly manoeuvrable, but sturdy enough for ocean crossings. Initial hit-and-run raids along the European coast were followed by major military expeditions, settlement and trade. The well-travelled Vikings settled part of the Slavic heartland, giving it the name 'Rus' and ventured as far as Newfoundland, Constantinople (modern-day Istanbul) and Baghdad, setting up trade with the Byzantine Empire.

For many centuries, Sweden remained stubbornly pagan, with Christianity only taking hold when Sweden's first Christian king, Olof Skötkonung (c 968–1020) was baptised. By 1160, King Erik Jedvarsson (Sweden's patron saint, St Erik) had virtually destroyed the last remnants of paganism.

Rise of the Swedish State

By the 13th century, royal power disintegrated over succession squabbles between the Erik and Sverker families, with medieval statesman Birger Jarl (1210–66) rising to fill the gap.

His son, King Magnus Ladulås (1240–90) granted numerous privileges to the church and the nobility, including freedom from taxation. At the same time, he earned the nickname 'lock barn' for forbidding the aristocracy from living off the peasantry when moving from estate to estate.

After deposing his eldest son Birger (1280–1321) for fratricide, the nobility looked to Norway for their next ruler, choosing the infant grandson of King Haakon V of Norway. When Haakon died without leaving a male heir, the kingdoms of Norway and Sweden were united (1319).

The increasingly wealthy church began to show its might in the 13th and 14th centuries, commissioning monumental buildings such as the Domkyrka (Cathedral) in Linköping (founded 1250), and Scandinavia's largest Gothic cathedral in Uppsala (founded 1285).

However, in 1350 the rise of state and church endured a horrific setback when the Black Death swept through the country, carrying off around a third of the Swedish population.

The Vikings, by Magnus Magnusson, is an extremely readable history book, covering their achievements in Scandinavia (including Sweden), as well as their wild deeds around the world.

1160	1252	1350s	1434
King Erik Jedvarsson destroys the last remnants of paganism in Sweden. The pagan temple at Uppsala is replaced with a Christian church.	The city of Stockholm is founded by the king's statesman Birger Jarl, who effectively runs the country.	Following the Black Death, St Birgitta (1303–73) founds a nunnery and cathedral in Vadstena, which becomes Sweden's most important pilgrimage site.	High taxation imposed by the Kalmar Union to fund wars against the Hanseatic League make Erik of Pomerania deeply unpopular; the peasantry rise in the Engelbrekt revolt.

The Birth & Death of a Union

The Black Death created a shortage of candidates for the throne. In 1364, the nobles installed Albrecht of Mecklenburg as their ruler, but baulked at his attempts to wield his own power. Their revolt was aided by Danish regent Margareta and the Union of Kalmar (1397) united Denmark, Norway and Sweden under one crown.

Erik of Pomerania, Margareta's nephew, held that crown until 1439, his rule marred by a constant struggle against the Hanseatic League – a group of well-organised merchants who established walled trading towns in Germany and maintained a strong presence in the young city of Stockholm.

Out of the chaos following his deposition, Sten Sture the Elder (1440– 1503) eventually emerged as 'Guardian of Sweden' in 1470, going on to fight and defeat an army of unionist Danes at the Battle of Brunkenberg (1471) in Stockholm.

The word 'viking' is derived from *vik*, meaning bay or cove, and is probably a reference to vikings' anchorages during raids.

KRISTINA, QUEEN OF CONTROVERSY

Queen Kristina (1626–89) lived an eccentric and eventful life. Her father, Gustav II, very fond of his youngest and expecting great things from her, instructed that the girl be brought up as though she were a prince, then promptly went off and died in the Battle of Lützen, leaving his six-year-old successor and his country in the hands of the powerful Chancellor Oxenstierna.

Kristina received a boy's education, becoming fluent in six languages, skilled in the art of war, and took her oath as king, not queen, earning her the nickname 'Girl King'. Childish spats with Oxenstierna increased as she grew older; after being crowned queen in 1644, she delighted in testing her power, defying him even when he had the country's best interests at heart.

In 1649 Kristina made public her desire not to marry, and named her beloved cousin Karl X Gustav, who was besotted with her, her heir to the throne. Kristina's ever-erratic behaviour culminated in her abdication in 1654. She threw on men's clothing and rode through Denmark on horseback thus disguised; due to tense relations between the two countries, she couldn't have travelled safely as herself. Kristina finished up in Rome, where she did the unforgivable: converted to Catholicism – a scandalous act on the part of a daughter of the champion of Protestantism. She is the only woman to be buried in the basilica of St Peter's.

Kristina was immortalised in August Strindberg's 1901 play, her life chronicled in Veronica Buckley's biography *Christina, Queen of Sweden*, and fictionalised in the 1933 film, *Queen Christina*, starring Greta Garbo. A strong female character known for her bisexuality, in modern times she's become a lesbian icon, while her cross-dressing has made her a favourite of the transgender community.

1439–70	1520	1523	1523
Following the short-lived replacement of Erik of Pomerania, succession struggles begin again: two powerful Swedish families, the unionist Oxenstiernas and the nationalist Stures, fight for supremacy.	After granting a full amnesty to Sture's followers, Christian II goes back on his word: over 80 nobles and clergy are arrested, tried and butchered in the 'Stockholm Bloodbath'.	The Kalmar Union, which united Denmark, Sweden and Norway for over 130 years, is finally broken up.	Gustav becomes the first Vasa king after Sweden's withdrawal from the Kalmar Union: he marches into Stockholm and is crowned on 6 June, now the country's national day.

In a move of retaliation that sounded the Union's deathknell, Christian II of Denmark invaded Sweden and killed the regent Sten Sture the Younger (1493–1520), adding a massacre in Stockholm's Gamla Stan to his list of accomplishments.

The Vasa Dynasty

The brutal 'Stockholm Bloodbath' sparked off a major rebellion under the leadership of the young nobleman Gustav Ericsson Vasa (1496–1560). It was a revolution that almost never happened: having failed to raise enough support, Gustav was fleeing for the Norwegian border when two exhausted skiers caught him up to tell him that the people had changed their minds. This legendary ski journey is celebrated every year in the Vasaloppet race (p140) between Sälen and Mora.

Gustav I ruled from 1523 to 1560, leaving behind a powerful, central-ised nation state. He introduced the Reformation to Sweden (principally as a fundraising exercise) and passed the power on to his descendants though the 1544 parliament act that made the monarchy hereditary.

After Gustav Vasa's death in 1560, bitter rivalry broke out among his sons. His eldest child, Erik XIV (1533–77), held the throne for eight years in a state of not-unjustified paranoia. After committing a trio of injudicious murders at Uppsala Slott (p109), Erik was deposed by his half-brother Johan III (1537–92) and poisoned with pea soup at Örbyhus Slott (p115).

The last of the male Vasa rulers, 17-year old Gustav II Adolf (1594–1632) proved to be a military genius, recapturing southern parts of the country from Denmark and consolidating Sweden's control over the eastern Baltic. He was killed in battle on 6 November 1632, a day remembered for centuries in Sweden as a moment of national trauma. The blood-stained leather jacket he was wearing, and his stuffed horse Streif, can be seen in the Livrustkammaren in Stockholm.

Gustav II Adolf's daughter Kristina was still a child in 1632, and her regent continued her father's warlike policies. In 1654 Kristina abdicated in favour of her cousin Karl X Gustav, ending the Vasa dynasty.

Rise & Fall of the Swedish Empire

The zenith and collapse of the Swedish empire happened remarkably quickly. During Karl XI's reign, successful battles were waged against Denmark and Norway, the latter resulting in the seizure of Bohuslän, Härjedalen and Jämtland, and the empire reached its maximum size when Sweden established a short-lived American colony in what is now Delaware.

Inheritor of this huge and increasingly sophisticated country was 15-year old King Karl XII (1681–1718), an overenthusiastic military

At Kalmar Slott, you can see Erik XIV's bedroom, complete with a secret passage to escape from his brother Johan. Not that it helped him, mind.

1527	1563–70	1618–48	1628
Reformation parliament passes a law that transfers the property of the church to the state and places the church under the state's direct control (repealed in 2000).	During the Vasa brothers' reigns, there are wars against Lübeck and Poland, and the Danes try and fail to reassert sovereignty over Sweden in the Northern Seven Years War.	Devout Lutheran Gustav II intervenes in the Thirty Years War between Protestants and Catholics, invading Poland and defeating his cousin King Sigismund III, but dying in battle in 1632.	After a send-off full of pomp and ceremony, the royal warship *Vasa* sinks on her maiden voyage, having barely made it out of Stockholm's harbour.

adventurer who spent almost all of his reign at war. Karl XII cost Sweden its Latvian, Estonian and Polish territory, with the Swedish coast sustaining damaging attacks from Russia, and he died in mysterious circumstances in 1718.

The Age of Liberty

Despite the country's decline, intellectual enlightenment streaked ahead and 18th-century Sweden produced some celebrated writers, philosophers and scientists, including Anders Celsius, whose temperature scale bears his name; Carl Scheele, the discoverer of chlorine; and Carl von Linné (Linnaeus), the great botanist who developed theories about plant reproduction.

Although not history textbooks, Vilhelm Moberg's four novels about 19th-century Swedish emigration are based on real people, and bring this period to life. They're translated into English as *The Emigrants, Unto A Good Land, The Settlers* and *The Last Letter Home*.

Gustav III (1746–92) was a popular and sophisticated king who granted freedom of worship and was surprisingly successful in the maritime battle in the Gulf of Finland against Russia in 1790. Still, his costly foreign policy earned him enemies in the aristocracy and led to his assassination.

The rule of his son Gustav IV Adolf (1778–1837), forced to abdicate after getting drawn into the Napoleonic Wars and permanently losing Finland (one-third of Sweden's territory) to Russia, ended unrestricted royal power with the 1809 constitution.

Out of the blue, Napoleon's marshal Jean-Baptiste Bernadotte (1763–1844) was invited by a nobleman, Baron Mörner, to take the Swedish throne – which he did, along with the name Karl Johan. Judiciously changing sides, he led Sweden, allied with Britain, Prussia and Russia, against France and Denmark.

Emigration & Industrialisation

Industry arrived late in Sweden (during the second half of the 19th century), but when it did come it transformed the country from one of Western Europe's poorest to one of its richest.

Significant Swedish inventions, including dynamite (Alfred Nobel) and the safety match (patented by Johan Edvard Lundstrom), coupled with efficient steel-making and timber exports and a thriving textiles industry, added to a growing economy and the rise of the new middle class.

Coupled with discontent in the countryside and exacerbated by famine, industrialisation led to enormous social changes – from mass emigration to the rapid growth of labour and social movements such as unionisation.

Sweden (Not) at War

Sweden declared itself neutral in 1912, and remained so throughout the bloodshed of WWI. Swedish neutrality during WWII was ambiguous:

1658	1709	1789	1792
The last remaining parts of southern Sweden still in Danish hands are handed over at the Peace of Roskilde after Swedish troops successfully invade Denmark across the frozen Kattegatt.	After Russia, Poland and Denmark form an anti-Sweden alliance, the Swedish army is crushed by the Russians at Poltava in 1709 – a battle that ends Sweden's time as a superpower.	The coup d'etat mounted by Gustav III curtails parliamentary powers and reintroduces absolute rule.	At a masked ball in 1792, Gustav III is surrounded by conspirators and shot in the back of the head by Jacob Johan Anckarström, the captain of the king's regiment.

letting German troops march through to occupy Norway and selling iron ore to both warring sides certainly tarnished Sweden's image, leading to a crisis of conscience at home and international criticism.

On the other hand, Sweden was a haven for refugees from Finland, Norway, Denmark and the Baltic States; downed Allied aircrew who escaped the Gestapo; and many thousands of Jews who escaped persecution and death.

On his death, it was discovered that Frenchman Jean-Baptiste Bernadotte (king of Sweden for 26 years) had a tattoo that read 'Death to kings!'

Beyond the Wars

After WWII and throughout the 1950s and '60s, the Social Democrats continued with the creation of *folkhemmet* (the welfare state). The idea

MURDER MOST MYSTERIOUS

Sweden doesn't seem to have much luck when it comes to high-profile assassinations. King Karl XII (1681–1718) was mysteriously shot dead while inspecting his troops during a winter siege in Trondheim, Norway. While Norwegians take credit for the killing, the theory that Karl XII had been shot by one of his own men, disgruntled because the king's many military losses cost Sweden its rank as a great power, has persisted among historians ever since. Permission was sought to have the king's body exhumed from its resting place so that experts might establish the chemical composition of the bullet and solve this 18th-century whodunit once and for all. Sadly, permission was denied.

Less than a century later, in March 1792, King Gustav III was assassinated at a masked ball in the foyer of the Royal Opera House. The assassination – later the subject of a Verdi opera – was the result of a conspiracy hatched by nobles alarmed at the king's autocratic ways. His principal assailant, Jacob Johan Anckarström, was stripped of his lands and titles before being flogged as a common criminal, and when he was nearly dead he was decapitated.

This trend of unsolved high-profile deaths has continued to the present day. In 1986, Social Democrat Prime Minister Olof Palme (1927–86) was shot dead by a mystery man as he walked home from the cinema with his wife on a frigid February night. Questions remain unanswered and conspiracies abound, but no progress has been made with the case to date. The murder and bungled police inquiry shook ordinary Swedes' confidence in their country, institutions and leaders.

Another shocking, though less mysterious, political murder was of Foreign Minister Anna Lindh (1957–2003), again rocking Sweden to the core. She was stabbed while shopping in the ladies' department at the Nordiska Kompaniet department store in central Stockholm, unaccompanied by bodyguards. Her attacker, Miajailo Mijailovič, escaped, only to be caught later using DNA evidence and sentenced to life imprisonment. Far-right involvement was suspected – Lindh was a vocal supporter of the euro and an outspoken critic of both the war in Iraq and Italy's Silvio Berlusconi – but it appears that her attack was not politically motivated.

1814	1921	1953	1994
After Napoleon's defeat, Sweden forces Denmark to swap Norway for Swedish Pomerania. The Norwegians object, and Swedish troops occupy most of the country, the forced union lasting until 1905.	In the interwar period, a Social Democrat–Liberal coalition government takes control and introduces reforms, including an eight-hour working day and universal suffrage for adults aged over 23.	Dag Hammarskjöld is elected Secretary-General of the UN. Under his guidance, the UN resolves the 1956 Suez Crisis.	The ferry *Estonia* sinks during a storm on the Baltic Sea, killing 852 passengers, including 551 Swedes.

Blood on the Snow by Jan Bonderson explores the killing of Olof Palme with a reconstruction of the night of the murder along with details of the peculiar police conduct and the various conspiracy theories – in addition to suggesting an alternate theory.

of a socially conscious society with financial security for all began with the coalition of 1936 between the Social Democrats and the Farmers' Party and introduced unemployment benefits, child care, paid holidays and much more. The standard of living for ordinary Swedes rose rapidly and real poverty was virtually eradicated.

Sweden began to take an active (peaceful) role in world affairs in the second half of the 20th century, offering asylum to those fleeing from political oppression worldwide. Prime Minister Olof Palme (1927–86) was deeply involved in questions of democracy, disarmament and Third World issues when he was assassinated on the streets of Stockholm in 1986.

In the last 25 years, Sweden has become an affluent country with a strong economy and one of the most comprehensive welfare systems in the world. While nonaligned militarily, Sweden's troops have taken part in numerous NATO peacekeeping missions and the country's immigration policies have transformed a largely homogenous society into a multi-ethnic one.

1995

Sweden joins the European Union.

2001

Parliament votes 260 to 48 against abolishment of the monarchy, even though the monarch ceased to have any political power in 1974.

2009

Victoria, Crown Princess of Sweden, marries Daniel Westling, her personal trainer, thus becoming the first Swedish royal to marry a commoner.

ANDERS BLOMQVIST / LONELY PLANET IMAGES ©

» Drottningholms Slott

The Swedish Landscape

The Land

Geography

Physically, Sweden is long and thin – about the size of California, with a surface area of around 450,000 sq km. It's mostly forest (nearly 60% of the landscape) and is dotted with about 100,000 inland lakes. This includes Vänern, Western Europe's largest lake, at 5585 sq km. There's also 7000km of coastline, plus scads of islands – the Stockholm archipelago alone has around 24,000 of them. The largest and most notable islands are Gotland and Öland on the southeast coast.

From its position on the eastern side of the Scandinavian peninusla, Sweden borders Norway, Finland and Denmark – the latter a mere 4km to the southwest of Sweden and joined to it by a spectacular bridge and tunnel. The northernmost one-seventh of the country lies within the Arctic Circle.

> Sweden is a long, drawn-out 1574km from north to south, but averages only about 300km in width.

The mountains along the border with Norway are graced with alpine and Arctic flowers, including mountain avens (with large, white, eight-petalled flowers), long-stalked mountain sorrel (an unusual source of vitamin C), glacier crowfoot, alpine aster and various saxifrages. Orchids grow on Öland and Gotland. Up north are forests of Scots pine, Norway spruce and firs; the southern part of the country is now mostly farmland.

Geology

Between 500 and 370 million years ago, the European and North American continental plates collided, throwing up an impressive range of peaks called the Caledonian Mountains, which were as tall as today's Himalayas. Their worn-down stubs form the 800km-long Kjölen Mountains along the Norwegian border – among which is Kebnekaise (2106m), Sweden's highest mountain.

Parts of Skåne and the islands of Öland and Gotland consist of flat limestone and sandstone deposits, probably laid down in a shallow sea east of the Caledonian Mountains during the same period.

LÄN & LANDSKAP

The 25 historical regions called *landskap* are denominators for people's identity and a basis for regional tourist promotion, and are used throughout this book. The 21 counties *(län)* in Sweden form the basis of local government, and these county administrations are responsible for things like regional public transport *(länstrafik)* and regional museums *(länsmuseum)*.

HOW'S THE WEATHER?

Sweden has a mostly cool, temperate climate, but the southern quarter of the country is warmer than the rest. The average maximum temperature for July is 18°C in the south and around 14°C in the north. Long hot periods in summer aren't unusual, with temperatures soaring to over 30°C. Likewise, the west coast is warmer than the east, thanks to the warming waters of the Gulf Stream.

The harsh Lappland winter starts in October and ends in April, and temperatures can plummet as low as -50°C. Snow can accumulate to depths of several metres in the north, making for superb skiing, but snow depths in the south average only 20cm to 40cm. It usually rains in winter in the far south (Skåne).

Norway's mountain ranges act as a rain break, so yearly rainfall is moderate. Swedish summers are generally sunny with only occasional rainfall, but August can be wet.

Lake Siljan, in the central south, marks the site of Europe's largest meteoric impact: the 3km-wide fireball hurtled into Sweden 360 million years ago, obliterating all life and creating a 75km ring-shaped crater.

Wildlife

The lemming is the smallest but most important mammal in the Arctic regions – its numbers set the population limits for everything that preys on it.

Thanks to Sweden's geographical diversity, it has a great variety of European animals, birds and plants. And thanks to its relatively sparse population, there are several areas in the country where it's likely you'll see some of them in the wild. But if you have no luck, Grönklitt Björnpark has an endangered-animal breeding program with lions, tigers and bears in large, natural-looking enclosures.

Sweden's big carnivores – the bear, wolf, wolverine, lynx and golden eagle – are all protected species. Wolf hunting was banned in the 1970s, after the wolf population had been hunted nearly to extinction, but in 2010 the Swedish Parliament authorised a culling to bring the newly resurgent species' numbers back down to 210 wolves. (This drew protests as well as a stern letter from the European Commission's environmental commissioner requesting that Sweden stop the hunt.) Most of the country's wolf population is in Dalarna and Värmland.

The Swedish Environmental Protection Agency (www.naturvardsverket.se) has detailed information on Sweden's policies regarding endangered animals, as well as several articles about enjoying and protecting the landscape and its natural occupants.

The more solitary wolverine, a larger cousin of the weasel, inhabits high forests and alpine areas along the Norwegian border. There are an estimated 680 in Sweden, mostly in Norrbotten and Västerbotten.

Brown bears were persecuted for centuries, but recent conservation measures have seen numbers increase to about 3200. Bears mostly live in forests in the northern half of the country, but are spreading southward.

Swedish elk are slightly smaller than their closely related American relatives.

Another fascinating forest dweller is the lynx, which belongs to the panther family and is Europe's only large cat. Sweden's 1200 to 1500 lynx are notoriously difficult to spot because of their nocturnal habits.

Not all of Sweden's wild creatures are predatory, of course. The iconic elk (moose in the USA) is a gentle, knobby-kneed creature that grows up to 2m tall. Though they won't try to eat you, elk are a serious traffic hazard, particularly at night: they can dart out in front of your car at up to 50km/h.

Around 260,000 domesticated reindeer roam the northern areas under the watchful eyes of Sami herders. Like elk, reindeer can be a major traffic hazard.

Hikers encountering lemmings in the mountains may be surprised when these frantic little creatures become enraged and launch bold attacks. The mouselike lemmings are famous for their extraordinary reproductive capacity. Every 10 years or so the population explodes, resulting in denuded landscapes and thousands of dead lemmings in rivers and lakes and on roads.

Musk ox were reintroduced into Norway in the late 1940s, and herds have wandered into Sweden, notably in Härjedalen county. Angry adults have a habit of charging anything that annoys them.

Forests, lakes and rivers support beavers, otters, mink, badgers and pine martens. Weasels and stoats are endemic in all counties; northern varieties turn white in the winter and are trapped for their fur (ermine).

The fearsome-looking brown bear's favourite food is... blueberries!

Bird Life

Sweden is home to all kinds of bird life. Some of the best birdwatching sites are on Öland, including the nature reserve at its southernmost tip (p249), as well as Getterön Nature Reserve, Tåkern Nature Reserve, Hornborgasjön, between Skara and Falköping in Västergötland, and the national parks Färnebofjärden, Muddus and Abisko.

The golden eagle is one of Sweden's most endangered species. It's found in the mountains, and is easily identified by its immense wingspan.

Coastal species include common, little and Arctic terns, various gulls, oystercatchers, cormorants, guillemots and razorbills. Territorial Arctic skuas can be seen in a few places, notably the Stockholm archipelago and the coast north of Göteborg.

Look for goldcrests in coniferous forests. A few spectacular waxwings breed in Lappland, but in winter they arrive from Russia in large numbers and are found throughout Sweden. Grouse or capercaillie strut the forest floor, while ptarmigan and snow buntings hang out above the treeline along the Norwegian border.

Sweden has a wide range of wading and water birds, including the unusual and beautiful red-necked phalaropes, which only breed in the northern mountains. Other waders you're likely to encounter are majestic grey herons (southern Sweden), noisy bitterns (south-central Sweden), plovers (including dotterel, in the mountains) and turnstones.

For more details about birdwatching, contact Sveriges Ornitologiska Förening (Swedish Ornithological Society; ☎08-612 25 30; www.sofnet. org, in Swedish).

For proof we aren't making up these crazy bird names, read *Where to Watch Birds in Scandinavia* by Johann Stenlund.

Sea Life

Sprats and herring are economically important food sources. Among other marine species, haddock, sea trout, whiting, flounder and plaice are reasonably abundant, particularly in the salty waters of the Kattegatt and Skagerrak, but the cod is heading for extinction due to overfishing.

Indigenous crayfish were once netted or trapped in Sweden's lakes, but overfishing and disease have driven them to extinction.

Grey and common seals swim in Swedish waters, although overfishing has caused a serious decline in numbers. In 1988 and 2002, thousands of seals were wiped out by the phocine distemper virus (PDV) after pollution weakened their immune systems. Common dolphins may also be observed from time to time.

You can swim – and fish for trout and salmon – in the waters by Stockholm's city centre.

The North and, particularly, the Baltic Seas are suffering severe pollution, eutrophication and vast algae blooms, caused partly by nitrogen run-off from Swedish farms. As a result, herring, sprats and Baltic salmon contain much higher than average levels of cancer-causing dioxins; they're still being sold in Sweden at the time of writing, but with a health warning attached.

Overfishing of these waters is also a huge cause for concern, with cod and Norwegian lobster on the verge of extinction. Fishing quotas are

ARCTIC PHENOMENA

Aurora Borealis

There are few sights as mesmerising as an undulating aurora. Although these appear in many forms – pillars, streaks, wisps and haloes of vibrating light – they're most memorable when they take the form of pale curtains, apparently wafting on a gentle breeze. Most often, the Arctic aurora appears faint green, light yellow or rose-coloured, but in periods of extreme activity it can change to bright yellow or crimson.

The visible aurora borealis, also called northern lights *(norrsken)*, are caused by streams of charged particles from the sun and the solar winds, which are diverted by the earth's magnetic field towards the polar regions.

Because the field curves downward in a halo surrounding the magnetic poles, the charged particles are drawn earthward here. Their interaction with atoms in the upper atmosphere (about 160km above the surface) releases the energy that creates the visible aurora. During periods of high activity, a single auroral storm can produce a trillion watts of electricity with a current of one million amps.

The best time to catch the northern lights in Sweden is from October to March.

Midnight Sun & Polar Night

Because the earth is tilted on its axis, the polar regions are constantly facing the sun at their respective summer solstices, and are tilted away from it in winter. The Arctic and Antarctic Circles, at latitudes 66°32'N and 66°32'S respectively, are the southern and northern limits of constant daylight on the longest day of the year.

The northern one-seventh of Sweden lies north of the Arctic Circle, but even in central Sweden the summer sun is never far below the horizon. Between late May and mid-July, nowhere north of Stockholm experiences true darkness; in Umeå, for example, the first stars aren't visible until mid-July. Although many visitors initially find it difficult to sleep while the sun is shining brightly outside, most people get used to it.

Conversely, winters in the far north are dark and bitterly cold, with only a few hours of twilight to break the long polar nights. During this period, some people suffer from seasonal affective disorder (SAD), which occurs when they're deprived of the vitamin D provided by sunlight. Its effects may be minimised by taking supplements of vitamin D (as found in cod liver oil) or with special solar spectrum light bulbs.

determined by the EU as a whole, and there's been a constant struggle to achieve balance between sustainable fish stocks and consumer demand.

National Parks

Sweden was the first country in Europe to set up a national park (1909). There are now 29, along with around 2600 smaller nature reserves; together they cover about 9% of Sweden. The organisation Naturvårdsverket oversees and produces pamphlets about the parks in Swedish and English, along with the excellent book *Nationalparkerna i Sverige* (National Parks in Sweden).

Four of Sweden's large rivers (Kalixälven, Piteälven, Vindelälven and Torneälven) have been declared National Heritage Rivers in order to protect them from hydroelectric development.

The right of public access to the countryside *(allemansrätten)* includes national parks and nature reserves; see p41 for details.

Northern Sweden

Abisko Northern gateway to the Kungsleden hiking track.
Haparanda Skärgård Beaches, dunes and migrant bird life.
Muddus Ancient forests and muskeg bogs, superb birdwatching.
Padjelanta High moorland; great hiking.
Pieljekaise Moorlands, birch forests, flowering meadows and lakes.

Sarek Wild mountain ranges, glaciers, deep valleys; expert hiking.
Stora Sjöfallet Famous waterfall; hydroelectric development.
Vadvetjåkka Large river delta containing bogs, lakes, limestone caves.

Central Sweden

Ängsö Tiny island; meadows, deciduous forest, bird life, spring flowers.
Björnlandet Natural forest, cliffs and boulder fields.
Färnebofjärden Bird life, forests, rare lichens and mosses.
Fulufjället Contains Njupeskär, the country's highest waterfall at 93m.
Garphyttan 111-hectare park, fantastic springtime flowers.
Hamra Only 800m by 400m; virgin coniferous forest.
Kosterhavet The sea and shores surrounding the Koster Islands.
Sånfjället Natural mountain moorland with extensive views.
Skuleskogen Hilly coastal area, good hiking.
Tresticklan Natural coniferous forest, fine bird life.
Tyresta Stockholm's own national park.
Töfsingdalen Wild and remote; boulder fields, pine forest.

Four of the national parks in Lappland – Mud-dus, Padjelanta, Sarek and Stora Sjöfallet – are Unesco World Heritage Sites.

Southern Sweden

Blå Jungfrun Island with granite slabs, caves, labyrinth.
Dalby Söderskog Forest, wildlife.
Djurö Bird life and deer on an archipelago.
Gotska Sandön Sandy isle featuring dunes, dying pine forest.
Norra Kvill 114-hectare park; ancient coniferous forest.
Söderåsen Deep fissure valleys, lush forests; hiking and cycling.
Stenshuvud Coastal park; beaches, forest, moorland.
Store Mosse Bogs with sand dunes, bird life.
Tiveden Hills, forests, lakes, boulder fields, beaches.

Environmental Issues

Ecological consciousness in Sweden is very high and reflected in concern for native animals, clean water and renewable resources. Swedes are fervent believers in sorting and recycling household waste. Most plastic bottles and cans can be recycled – supermarket disposal machines give Skr0.50 to Skr1 per item.

Two organisations that set standards for labelling products as ecologically sound are the food-focused KRAV (www.krav.se), a member of the International Federation of Organic Agriculture Movements, and Swan (www.svanen.se), which has a wider scope and certifies entire hotels and hostels.

Linked to its environmental concerns is the challenge of protecting the cultural heritage of the Sami people. The harnessing of rivers for hydroelectric power can have massive (negative) impact on what has historically been Sami territory, whether by flooding reindeer feeding grounds or by diverting water and drying up river valleys. In general, the mining, forestry and space industries have wreaked havoc on Sami homelands. For more about the Sami, see p336.

True North: The Grand Landscapes of Sweden, by Per Wästberg and Tommy Hammarström, contains stunning images by some of Sweden's top nature photographers.

Environmental Organisations

Naturvårdsverket (Swedish Environmental Protection Agency; ☏08-698 10 00; www.naturvardsverket.se) Government-run central environmental authority, with an extensive and informative website.
Svenska Ekoturismföreningen (Swedish Society of Ecotourism; ☏063-12 12 44; www.ekoturism.org) Promotes environmentally friendly tourism.
Svenska Naturskyddsföreningen (Swedish Society for Nature Conservation; ☏08-702 65 00; www.snf.se/english.cfm) Excellent website on current environmental issues.

Design & Architecture

By Stuart Harrison
Stuart Harrison hosts *The Architects on RRR* radio show,
interviewing and talking about design and architecture from
around the world. He also designed and built a suite at the
Icehotel with artist Lucas Ihlein in 2005.

While it can be hard to separate modern Swedish design from the success of general Scandinavian design, it is the predominantly Swedish
embrace of modernity and craft that has fostered admiration around the
world for decades. A drive towards simplicity that appeared in the 19th
century saw the enthusiasm for Swedish design grow even more. This
small country has been a catalyst for a broader fascination with European popular modernism and the quintessentially Scandinavian approach.

The Swedish tradition of craft can be seen in all forms of design:
architecture, textiles, fashion, stonemasonry, carpentry and particularly
glass. In the southern province of Småland you'll find many of Sweden's
craft traditions, and glassmaking has been here for well over 100 years.
Home to well-known brands Orrefors and Kosta Boda, the cluster of glass-
blowing factories has consolidated over time. A high point of glass
design was in the 1960s, when traditional figurative forms were met
with abstracted patterning as young designers were given the chance to
compete with more-established figures.

> Contemporary
> design and
> architecture
> generally follow
> global trends, but
> the characteristi-
> cally Swedish
> interests of
> nature and craft
> are evident when
> cruising through
> blogs such as the
> snappy emmas
> designblogg
> (www.emmas.
> blogg.se).

History

Along with a scattering of Romanesque and Gothic imports from mainland Europe, Sweden's architecture has a classical sensibility, as seen in
the grand streets of Stockholm. The Renaissance was embraced at the
peak of Sweden's power in the 16th and 17th centuries, and set up the
nation's core historic architecture.

Magnificently ornate baroque architecture arrived (mainly from Italy)
during the 1640s while Queen Kristina held the throne. This is perhaps
best seen in the buildings at Kalmar, just outside Stockholm, a historical centre of power and where the first union of Denmark, Norway and
Sweden was formed in 1397. Kalmar's Domkyrkan (Cathedral), designed
in 1660, the adjacent Kalmar Rådhus (Town Hall) and Drottningholms
Slott (1662) were all designed by the court architect Nicodemus Tessin the
Elder. Tessin the Younger designed the vast 'new' Kungliga Slottet (Royal
Palace) in Stockholm after the original palace was gutted by fire in 1697.

Pre-Renaissance examples include the Romanesque Domkyrkan in
Lund, consecrated in 1145 and still dominating the city centre with its
two imposing square towers. Fine Gothic churches can be seen at the
Mariakyrkan in Sigtuna (completed in 1237) and Uppsala's Domkyrkan,

consecrated in 1435. The island of Gotland, however, is your best bet in Sweden for ecclesiastical Gothic architecture, with around 100 medieval churches scattering across the ancient landscape.

Modernity was, as elsewhere, born in the 19th century out of urban and social upheaval, the move to cities and industrialisation. From the harsh conditions of expanding Stockholm and Göteborg (Gothenburg) a social state emerged, the basis for modern Sweden.

The movements were sequential but overlapping. The transitional National Romanticism was an often decorative classical free-style with Arts and Crafts influences. Known locally as Jugendstil it has strong similarities to the more continental art nouveau. Following this period, abstracted and more international modernism took hold, and Stockholm's 1930 exhibition introduced modern design and the Swedish architects of the 20th century.

Key Architects

The transition to modernity through the early 20th century can be seen particularly in the world of Erik Gunnar Asplund (1885–1940), Sweden's most important architect. The best of Asplund's work is in the capital, such as Stockholm's Stadsbiblioteket (City Library; 1932) with its plutonic forms wrestling classical and modernist tendencies. A little further out of the centre at the graceful Skogskyrkogården (Woodland Cemetery) you'll find perhaps the greatest collection of work from the Swedish master, and many of the pavilions are collaborations with the less prolific Sigurd Lewerentz (1885–1975).

Asplund was typical of the Swedish approach. He travelled widely as a young designer, returning to his homeland to make an architecture both of its time and true to Swedish tradition. It contrasted with the more aggressive radical modernism of France and Germany, and set the tone for Finnish master Alvar Aalto.

Asplund and Lewerentz were profoundly influential on English-born architect Ralph Erskine (1914–2005), who formed a practice in Sweden in 1939. The adopted son of Swedish architecture embodied social ideas into a layered form of modernism, typical of the Nordic outlook. His Ortdrivaren housing project in the northern iron-ore-mining city of Kiruna dates from the early 1960s and has held up incredibly well.

Kiruna faces an uncertain future as land subsidence from the mine has given need to move the town, with all buildings to be demolished

Key Turn-of-the-Century Buildings in Stockholm

» Fredrik Lilljekvist's Royal Dramatic Theatre (1908)

» Ferdinand Boberg's Rosenbad (1902)

» Ragnar Östberg's Stockholm City Hall (1911)

DESIGN & ARCHITECTURE KEY ARCHITECTS

FROZEN ART & DESIGN

The Icehotel (p306), in the small village of Jukkasjärvi just outside of Kiruna, not only started the global trend of ice hotels and bars, it has become a focus for collaboration between artists and designers from Sweden and around the world. The Icehotel now boasts an open submission process for creatives around the world to come to Sweden to design and build a suite in the ephemeral hotel, which opens typically in late December and then melts entirely by the following April.

The hotel is made from both snow and ice, the superstructure built in a manner similar to rammed earth, with snow blown and compacted onto Gothic archlike steel forms that produce simple vaulted spaces. Artists then create suite interiors using a combination of malleable snow with ice, which is far more like stone in the way it is treated – a heavy material cut into smaller usable blocks using chainsaws and then chiselled and crafted into shape.

A wide range of artists come to the Icehotel, both local and international. Regulars include fourth-generation stonemason Mats Nilson and younger designer Jens Thoms Ivarsson. Theirs is a very Swedish practice, drawing on both crafted tradition and embracing contemporary design.

FLATPACK FURNITURE TAKES OVER THE WORLD

Ingvar Kamprad was 17 years old when he created Ikea in the city of Älmhult, in the craft-focused province of Småland – and he has gone on to become one of the world's richest men.

The Ikea name (a combination of Kamprad's initials and those of the farm and village where he grew up) was officially registered in 1943. Initially selling pens, watches and nylon stockings, furniture was added to the company's products four years later, gradually evolving into the Ikea-designed flatpack creations so familiar today.

There was almost an early end to the Ikea empire when the first Stockholm shop and all its stock burned down in 1970. But, besides his devotion to work and obsession with cost-cutting, Kamprad also seems to thrive on adversity – Ikea bounced back.

The influence of Ikea has been enormous – and like other global brands it has sought to bring simple, good design to the whole world, in an affordable way. Cheap and innovative designs were born out of Swedish modern design – the idea of the house as the starting point of good design, rather than the end.

The clean-cut company was rocked in 1994 by revelations that Kamprad once had links with a pro-Nazi party in Sweden (he later offered a public apology, and expressed much regret for this time of his life).

The famously frugal Kamprad has now taken a back seat, but ownership is still within the family – control over his empire now divvied up among his three children and divided into a series of complex charity and trust entities. Today Ikea has stores in 40 countries; branches first opened in Australia in 1975, Saudi Arabia in 1983, the US in 1985, Britain in 1987, China in 1998 and Russia in 2000.

except possibly the imposing Stadshus (Athur von Schmalensee; 1963) and the well-liked Kiruna kyrka (Gustaf Wickman; 1912), an early example of an attempted fusion between local Sami forms and the Gothic tradition, built in timber.

Design Hubs

One hot spot of design and innovation in recent times has been the post-industrial city of Malmö. The old docks northwest of Gamla Staden (Old Town) were converted into ecologically focused housing for the new century. Its landmark Turning Torso (2005) – a twisting residential tower designed by Catalan architect Santiago Calatrava – is an arresting sight dominating the skyline.

Close by is the Öresund bridge (Georg KS Rotne; 2000) connecting the two metropolitan areas of Malmö and Copenhagen, effectively joining them in one trans-country city. Malmö has become a commuter base for Danish residents in Copenhagen as result of this remarkable piece of infrastructure – after it reaches the end of the bridge section the road and rail lines literally disappear into the water, to become a tunnel until it emerges next to Copenhagen airport. It's quite a sight from the air, especially when seen next to Copenhagen's magnificent series of aero-generators that line its side of the Öresund strait.

Within Stockholm, contemporary design and culture found a robust home in 1974 in the excellent Kulturhuset, a large modernist pavilion holding a wide range of cultural activities. Designed by Peter Celsing, it's like a big set of drawers offering their wares onto the large plaza outside, Sergels Torg; the *torg* (town square) is the modern heart of Stockholm, and standing at its centre is Kristallvertikalaccent (Crystal Vertical Accent), a wonderful, luminescent monument to modernity and glassmaking traditions. Designed by sculptor Edvin Öhrström, it was the result of a 1962 competition. Sergels Torg itself has a distinctive triangular ground pattern, a modern backdrop for protests and markets, with the T-Centralen metro station underneath.

Stand-out architectural firms include the established Wingårdh, but emerging practices such as Elding Oscarson show a restrained international influence. Lund & Valentin in Göteborg (Gothenburg) have, since 1952, been a good index of architectural tastes, as seen in their postmodern Gothenburg Opera (1994).

Swedish Pop Culture

Sweden's literature and cinema favour a weighty, Gothic sense of drama blended with gallows humour and stark aesthetics – essentially the opposite of its best-known pop music, in other words.

Swedish Cinema

Sweden led the way in the silent-film era of the 1920s with such masterpieces as *Körkarlen* (The Phantom Carriage), adapted from a novel by Selma Lagerlöf and directed by Mauritz Stiller. In 1967 came Vilgot Sjöman's notorious *I Am Curious – Yellow,* a subtly hilarious socio-political film that got more attention outside Sweden for its X rating than its sharp commentary (and in-jokes about the king). Still, with a few such exceptions, one man has largely defined modern Swedish cinema to the world: Ingmar Bergman. With deeply contemplative films such as *The Seventh Seal, Through a Glass Darkly* and *Persona,* the beret-topped director explored human alienation, the absence of god, the meaning of life, the certainty of death and other light-hearted themes.

More recently, the towns of Trollhättan and Ystad have become film-making centres, the former drawing the likes of wunderkind director Lukas Moodysson, whose *Lilja 4-Ever, Show Me Love* and *Tillsammans* have all been both popular and critical hits. Lebanese-born Josef Fares *(Jalla! Jalla!, Kopps, Zozo, Leo)* is part of a new guard of second-generation immigrant directors. Alongside Iranian-born directors Reza Bagher *(Wings of Glass)* and Reza Parsa *(Before the Storm),* Fares has turned a spotlight on the immigrant experience in Sweden. His uncharacteristically dark 2007 feature, *Leo,* also marks Fares' on-screen debut.

Another Swedish award-winner is director Roy Andersson, once dubbed a 'slapstick Ingmar Bergman'. His film *Du levande* (You, the Living) scooped up three prizes (including best picture) at Sweden's prestigious Gulbagge Awards in 2008. Another huge success that year was Tomas Alfredson's odd, quiet teenage-vampire story, *Let the Right One In.*

But of course the big news recently in Swedish cinema is the film version of Stieg Larsson's runaway hit series of crime novels, starting with *The Girl with the Dragon Tattoo* (2009). Starring Michael Nyqvist and Noomi Rapace, the Swedish trilogy has already received an American remake, with Daniel Craig as journalist Mikael Blomkvist.

Swedish Literature

Historically, the best known of Sweden's artistic greats have been writers, chiefly the poet Carl Michael Bellman (1740–95), influential dramatist and author August Strindberg (1849–1912), and children's writer Astrid Lindgren (1907–2002).

JAZZ

Jazz is huge among Swedes; for a primer, look for records by Lars Gullson, Bernt Rosengren and Jan Johansson.

FEEL-BAD SWEDISH FILMS

The Swedish film industry is active and varied, but most people associate it with the godfather of gloom, Ingmar Bergman. Many filmmakers have followed in his grim footsteps:

» *Songs from the Second Floor* (Roy Andersson; 2000), a post-apocalyptic urban nightmare in surreal slow motion; it's not for everyone.

» *Lilya 4-Ever* (Lukas Moodysson; 2002), a grim tale of human trafficking.

» *Ondskan* (Evil; Mikael Håfström; 2003), violence at a boys' boarding school.

» *Zozo* (Josef Fares; 2005), a Lebanese orphan makes his way to Sweden alone, then has culture shock.

» *Darling* (Johan Kling; 2007), harsh economic realities bring together a shallow, privileged party girl and a sweet old man in an unlikely friendship.

» *Let the Right One In* (Tomas Alfredson; 2008), an excellent, stylish, restrained take on the horror-film genre that gets at what it's like to be a lonely preteen in a cold, hostile world.

During WWII some Swedish writers took a stand against the Nazis, including Eyvind Johnson (1900–76) with his *Krilon* trilogy, completed in 1943, and the famous poet and novelist Karin Boye (1900–41), whose novel *Kallocain* was published in 1940. Vilhelm Moberg (1898–1973), a representative of 20th-century proletarian literature and controversial social critic, won international acclaim with *Utvandrarna* (The Emigrants; 1949) and *Nybyggarna* (The Settlers; 1956).

Contemporary literary stars include playwright and novelist Per Olov Enquis (1934–), who achieved international acclaim with his novel *Livläkarens besök* (The Visit of the Royal Physician; 2003), in which King Christian VII's physician conspires with the queen to seize power.

Mikael Niemi's (1959–) novel *Populärmusik från Vittula* (Popular Music; 2003), a coming-of-age story of a wannabe rock star in Sweden's remote north, became an international cult hit, as well as a 2004 film directed by Iranian-born Swedish director Reza Bagher. Nonfiction meister Sven Lindqvist (1932–) is famous for his hard-hitting, sometimes controversial titles. His most famous offering is arguably *Utrota varenda jävel* (Exterminate All the Brutes; 1992), exploring the Holocaust-like devastation European colonists wrought on Africa. More recently, his book *Terra Nullius* (2005, translated into English in 2007) is a powerful, moving history of colonial Australia and the attempted destruction of Aboriginal culture.

Crime Fiction

The massive success of the Millennium Trilogy, by the late journalist Stieg Larsson (he was the second-best-selling author in the world for 2008), has brought new and well-deserved attention to Swedish crime fiction. *The Girl with the Dragon Tattoo* (originally titled Men who Hate Women; 2005) is the tip of the iceberg when it comes to this genre; Swedish crime writers have a long and robust history. A few places to start include Håkan Nesser, whose early novels *The Mind's Eye* (1993) and *Woman with Birthmark* (1996) have at last been translated into English; and Sweden's best-known crime fiction writer, Henning Mankell, whose novels are mostly set in Ystad and feature moody detective Kurt Wallander.

THE STORYBOOK WARRIOR

Long before the Spice Girls cashed in on girl power, a Vimmerby-born, Stockholm-based secretary was psyching up little girls with tales of the red-headed, pigtailed, strongest girl in the world. The secretary was Astrid Lindgren (1907–2002) and her fictional rebel the infamous Pippi Longstocking. In a postwar world of silenced children and rigid gender roles, Pippi was bold, subversive and deliciously empowering. She didn't care for beauty creams, she was financially independent and she could even outlift the strongest man in the world, Mighty Adolf.

The character herself first found life in 1941 when Lindgren's pneumonia-struck daughter, Karin, asked her mother for a story about 'Pippi Longstocking'. The curious name inspired Lindgren to spin a stream of tales about the original wild child, which became an instant hit with Karin and her friends.

While recovering from a sprained ankle in 1944, Lindgren finally put her tales to paper and sent them to a publisher. Rejected but undefeated, she sent a second story to another publisher and scooped second prize in a girls' story competition. The following year, a revamped Pippi manuscript grabbed top honours in another competition, while her story *Bill Bergson Master Detective* shared first prize in 1946.

This was just the beginning of a prolific, award-winning career that would include picture books, plays and songs translated into over 50 languages, as well as work in radio, TV and film.

Arguably, Lindgren's greatest legacy to Sweden has been her influence on the rights and protection of society's most vulnerable, from children and the poor to animals. In 1976 Swedish newspaper *Expressen* published an allegorical opinion piece she wrote on an unjust tax-system loophole that saw self-employed writers paying 102% tax on their earnings. Not only did it lead to an amendment in the taxation law, but it also influenced the fall of the Social Democrats, who had been in power for 44 years. In 1978 Lindgren used her acceptance speech for the Peace Prize of the German Book Trade to express her views on the issue of violence against children, rousing intense debate. The following year, Sweden became the world's first nation to ban the smacking of children.

Must-Reads

One of the best ways to get inside the collective mind of a country is to read its top authors. Some of the most popular works by Swedish authors include *The Long Ships* (1954) by Frans Gunnar Bengtsson, *The Wonderful Adventures of Nils* (1906–07) by Selma Lagerlöf, *The Emigrants* series (1949–59) by Wilhelm Moberg, *Marking* (1963–64) by Dag Hammarskjöld, *Röda Rummet* (1879) by August Strindberg, and *The Evil* (1981) by Jan Guillou.

Swedish Music

Any survey of Swedish pop music should probably start with ABBA, the iconic, dubiously outfitted winner of the 1974 Eurovision Song Contest (with 'Waterloo'). More-current Swedish successes are pop icon Robyn, indie melody-makers Peter Björn & John, and the exquisitely mellow José González, whose cover of the Knife's track 'Heartbeats' catapulted the Göteborg native to international stardom. Others include the Field, aka Alex Wilner, and Kristian Matsson, the singer-songwriter who goes by the Tallest Man on Earth.

ABBA is the fourth-best-selling music act in history, after Elvis, the Beatles and Michael Jackson – the group has sold over 375 million records worldwide.

Other home-grown stalwarts include the Hives, the Cardigans, Sahara Hotnights, the Shout Out Louds and Håkan Hellström, who is much lauded for his original renditions of classic Swedish melodies.

Swedish songwriters and producers are sought-after commodities: Denniz Pop and Max Martin have penned hits for pop divas such as Britney Spears and Jennifer Lopez, while Anders Bagge and Bloodshy & Avant (aka Christian Karlsson and Pontus Winnberg) co-created Madonna's 2005 album *Confessions on a Dance Floor*.

The Sami

Sápmi: the Land of the Sami

Europe's only indigenous people, the ancestors of the Sami migrated to the north of present-day Scandinavia, following the path of the retreating ice. They lived by hunting reindeer in the area spanning from Norway's Atlantic coast to the Kola Peninsula in Russia, collectively known as Sápmi. By the 17th century, the depletion of reindeer herds had transformed the hunting economy into a nomadic herding economy.

Until the 1700s, the Sami lived in *siida* – village units or communities, migrating for their livelihoods, but only within their own defined areas. Those areas were recognised and respected by the Swedish government until colonisation of Lappland began in earnest, and the Sami found their traditional rights and livelihoods threatened both by the settlers and by the establishment of borders between Sweden, Norway, Finland and Russia.

The Sami Information Centre in Östersund (www.samer.se) is a treasure trove of information on all aspects of Sami life – from history and present-day culture to politics and food.

Who is a Sami?

In Sweden today, the stereotype of the nomadic reindeer herder has been replaced with the multifaceted reality of modern Sami life. According to the Sámediggi (Sami Parliament) statutes, a Sami is a person who feels oneself to be Sami, who either knows the Sami language or who has had at least one parent or grandparent who spoke Sami as their mother tongue.

The Sami population of Sápmi numbers around 100,000, out of which around 45,000 live in Norway, 27,000 or so in Sweden, slightly less in Finland and some 2000 in Russia. These numbers are approximate, as a census has never taken place.

Famous people of Sami descent include Joni Mitchell and Renee Zellweger.

Sami Language

Particularly precise when it comes to describing natural phenomena, the landscape and reindeer, Sami is not a single language. There are, in fact, 10 Sami languages spoken across Sápmi, which belong to the Finno-Ugrian language group and are not related to any Scandinavian language.

YOIK

One of the cornerstones of Sami identity is the *yoik* (or *joik*), a form of self-expression that has traditionally provided a bond between the Sami and nature. The *yoik* is a rhythmic poem or song composed for a specific person, event or object to describe and remember their innate nature. The *yoiking* tradition was revived in the 1960s, and it's now performed in many different ways – including experimental *yoik* and hard *yoik*, pioneered by young artists.

Sweden officially recognises the Sami languages as minority languages and international law decrees that Sami children are entitled to mother-tongue education in Sami. In practice, however, it hasn't always proved possible to find Sami-speaking teachers, and some municipalities feel that it costs too much to provide education in Sami.

Sami Religion

Sami beliefs and mythology have traditionally revolved around nature, and Shamanism was widespread until the 17th century. The *noaidi*, or shamans, bridged the gap between the physical world and the spiritual world; when in a trance, it was thought that they could shape-shift and command natural phenomena.

In 1685 it was decided by the monarchy and the church that the Sami must be converted to Christianity. Idolatry trials were held, shaman drums burned and sacred sites desecrated. However, not all effects of Christianity were negative: Laestadianism helped to alleviate the poverty and misery of the Sami in 19th-century Lappland.

'A Lapp Must Remain a Lapp'

From the 1800s onward, Sweden's policies regarding the Sami were tinted with social Darwinist ideas, deeming the Sami to be an inferior race fit only for reindeer husbandry. The nomadic Sami were prevented from settling lest they become idle and neglect their reindeer. A separate schooling system was set up, with Sami children denied admission to regular public schools. Under the *Nomad Schools Act* of 1913, they were taught in their family's tent *(lávvu)* for three years by teachers who moved between Sami settlements in summer. After three more years of limited schooling in winter, they were considered sufficiently educated without becoming 'civilised'.

Despite demands that nomad schools should meet the same standards as regular Swedish schools, the situation did not improve until after WWII, when the Sami began to actively participate in the struggle for their rights, forming numerous associations and pressure groups.

Sami Government

The Sami in Sweden are represented by the Sámediggi (Sami Parliament), comprising 31 members. It oversees many aspects of Sami life, from representing reindeer-herding interests and promoting Sami culture and organisations to distributing funds from state financial support and appointing the board of directors for Sami schools. However, while it acts in an advisory capacity to the Swedish government, the Sámediggi does not have the power to make decisions regarding land use.

The Swedish Sami also take part in the Sámiraŧŧi, the unifying body for the Sami organisations across Sápmi and international Sami interests. Sámiraŧŧi is an active participant in the WCIP (World Council of Indigenous Peoples).

Sami Rights & Today's Challenges

The Sami claim the right to traditional livelihoods, land and water, citing *usufruct* (age-old usage) and the traditional property rights of the Sami *siidas* (villages or communities), which are not formally acknowledged by Sweden. The Swedish state is yet to ratify the International Labour Organisation's Convention 169, which would recognise the Sami as an aboriginal people with property rights, as opposed to just an ethnic minority.

Sami Duodji

Since time immemorial, Sami crafts have combined practicality with beauty. 'Soft craft', such as leatherwork and textiles, has traditionally

Only half of all Sami can actually read and speak Sami, and Sami from different language groups have trouble understanding one another. Of the 10 Sami languages, the most common is North Sami, spoken by around 17,000 of the 50,000 Sami speakers.

Traditional Sami clothing, or *gákti*, comes with its own varied and distinctive headgear and is one of the most distinct symbols of Sami identity. The Sami can tell at a glance which part of Sápmi another is from, or whether the wearer is unaccustomed to wearing Sami garments.

PEOPLE OF THE EIGHT SEASONS

For centuries, Sami life revolved around reindeer. Thus the Sami year traditionally has eight seasons, each tied to a period of reindeer herding:

Gidádálvve (Springwinter; early March to late April) Herds are moved from the forests to calving lands in the low mountains during the spring migration.

Gidá (Spring; late April to late May) Calves are born. Leaves and grass are added to the reindeers' diet.

Gidágiesse (Springsummer; end of May to Midsummer) Herds are moved to find more vegetation for calves and their mothers. Reindeer mostly rest and eat. Herders repair temporary homes.

Giesse (Summer; Midsummer to end of August) Reindeer move to higher ground to avoid biting insects. Herders round them up and move them into corrals for calf marking.

Tjaktjagiesse (Autumnsummer; end of August to mid-September) Reindeer build up fat for the winter. Some of the uncastrated males *(sarvss)* are slaughtered in specially designated corrals. Meat is salted, smoked and made into jerky.

Tjaktja (Autumn; mid-September to mid-October) Reindeer mating season. The reindeer stay mostly in the low mountains, where they feed on roots and lichen.

Tjaktjadálvve (Autumnwinter; mid-October to Christmas) Reindeer are divided into grazing groups *(sijdor)* and taken to winter grazing grounds in the forest. Surplus reindeer are slaughtered.

Dálvve (Winter; Christmas to the end of February) Herders frequently move the reindeer around the forests to make sure the reindeer get enough lichen to eat.

been a female domain, whereas men have predominantly pursued 'hard crafts', such as knife-making, woodwork or silverwork.

Traditional creations include wooden *guksi* (drinking cups) or other vessels, made by hollowing out a burl and often inlaid with reindeer bone; knives, with abundantly engraved handles made of reindeer antler and equally decorative bone sheaths; and silverwork – anything from exquisitely engraved spoons, belt buckles and brooches to earrings and pendants.

In the 1970s there was a revival of Sami handicraft; since then, genuine Sami handwork that uses traditional designs and materials has borne the Sámi Duodji trademark.

The red, blue, green and yellow of the Sámi flag, designed by Norway's Astrid Båhl in 1986, correspond to the colours of the traditional Sami costume, the *kolt*, while the red and blue halves of the circle represent the sun and the moon, respectively.

Who's Who of Sami Crafts

Reputable Sami craftspeople are scattered all around Lappland. Here are just a few:

Randi and Kristin Marainen (☎0981 320 12; www.marainenssilver.se; Vittangi) Silversmiths specialising in traditional Sami jewellery and custom-made modern designs.

Ellenor Walkeapää (☎0702-124 124; www.eallidesign.se; Västra strand 326, Porjus) Cotton and linen clothing with Sami designs.

Jesper Eriksson (☎0730-332 252; www.j-eriksson.com; Jokkmokk) Woodwork inlaid with engraved reindeer antler, knives.

Monica L Edmondson (☎070-375 7388; www.edmondson; Tärnaby) Award-winning glasswork and textiles.

Nils-Johan Labba (☎070-513 0094; http://nilsjohan.labba.se; Kengisgatan 14b, Kiruna) Woodwork, knives, leather and reindeer-bone jewellery, leather belts.

Monica Svonni (☎120 70; www.svonni.com; Klippgatan 11, Jokkmokk) Textile, leather and pewter creations as well as wood carvings.

Survival Guide

Directory A-Z

Accommodation

Accommodation in Sweden is generally of a high standard. We list room prices for the summer season, typically mid-June through August, unless otherwise stated; standard weekday prices during the rest of the year might be much higher.

» € less than Skr800
» €€ Skr800–1600
» €€€ more than Skr1600

Cabins & Chalets

Swedes are all for the outdoors, and cabins and chalets (stugor) are everywhere, either at campsites or scattered through the countryside. Most contain four beds, with two- and six-person cabins sometimes on offer, too. They're particularly good value for small groups and families, costing between Skr350 and Skr800 per night. In peak summer season, many are rented out by the week (generally for Skr1000 to Skr5000).

The cheapest cabins are simple, with bunk beds and little else (bathroom and kitchen facilities shared with campers or other cabin users). Chalets are generally fully equipped with their own kitchen, bathroom and even living room with TV. Bring your own linen and clean up yourself to save cleaning fees of around Skr500.

Pick up the catalogue Campsites & Cottages in Sweden from any tourist office, or check out www.stuga.nu.

Camping

Camping is wildly popular in Sweden, and there are hundreds of campsites all over the country. Most open between May and August only. The majority are busy family holiday spots with fantastic facilities, such as shops, restaurants, pools, playgrounds, canoe or bike rentals, minigolf, kitchens and laundry facilities. Most also have cabins or chalets.

Camping prices vary (according to season and facilities) from around Skr150 for a small site at a basic ground to Skr250 for a large site at a more luxurious campsite. Slightly cheaper rates may be available if you're a solo hiker or cyclist.

You must have a Camping Card Scandinavia to stay at most Swedish campsites. Apply for one in advance by writing to **Sveriges Camping & Stugföretagares Riksorganisation** (www. camping.se) or fill in the form on the website; otherwise pick up a temporary card at any Swedish campsite. One card covers the whole family (per year Skr140).

Primus and Sievert supply propane gas for camping stoves, and containers are available at petrol stations. T-sprit Röd (methylated spirit; denatured alcohol) for Trangia stoves can be bought at petrol stations, and Fotogen (paraffin; kerosene) is sold at paint shops such as Fargtema and Spektrum.

Hostels

Sweden has well over 450 hostels (vandrarhem), usually with excellent facilities. Outside major cities, hostels aren't backpacker hang-outs but are used as holiday accommodation by Swedish families, couples or retired people. Another quirk is the frequent absence of dormitories, meaning you often have to rent out a room rather than a bed; some hostels have singles and doubles with en suite bathrooms that are almost of hotel quality, for very reasonable rates. About half of hostels open year-round; many others open from May to September, some open

---

BOOK YOUR STAY ONLINE

For more accommodation reviews by Lonely Planet authors, check out hotels.lonelyplanet.com. You'll find independent reviews, as well as recommendations on the best places to stay. Best of all, you can book online.

only from mid-June to mid-August.

Be warned, Swedish hostels keep very short reception opening times (except in Stockholm and Göteborg): generally from 5pm to 7pm, and 8am to 10am. The secret is to prebook by telephone – reservations are recommended in any case, as good hostels fill up fast. If you're stuck arriving when the front desk is closed, you'll usually see a number posted where you can phone for instructions. (Hostel phone numbers are also listed in the free guidebooks published annually by STF and SVIF.)

Sleeping bags are usually allowed if you have a sheet and pillowcase; bring your own, or hire them (Skr50 to Skr65). Breakfast is sometimes available (Skr50 to Skr75). Before leaving, you must clean up after yourself; cleaning materials are provided. Most hostels are affiliated with STF or SVIF, but there are other unaffiliated hostels also with high standards of accommodation.

STF

About 320 hostels are affiliated with Svenska Turist-föreningen (STF; ☎08-463 21 00; www.svenskaturistfore ningen.se), part of Hostelling International (HI). STF produces a free detailed guide to its hostels, but the text is in Swedish only (the symbols and maps are easy to understand). Hostel details on its website are in English. All STF hostels have kitchens.

Holders of HI membership cards pay the same rates as STF members. Nonmembers can pay Skr50 extra (Skr100 at mountain lodges) or join up at hostels (adult/child Skr295/150 annually). In this book we quote prices at STF hostels for members. Children under 16 pay about half the adult price.

SVIF

Around 200 hostels belong to Sveriges Vandrarhem i Förening (SVIF; ☎0413-55 34 50; www.svif.se). No membership is required and rates are similar to those of STF hostels. Most SVIF hostels have kitchens, but you sometimes need your own utensils. Pick up the free guide at tourist offices or SVIF hostels.

Hotels

Private, family-owned hotels with individuality are few and far between: the big hotel chains (with comfortable but often rather bland rooms) tend to monopolise hotel accommodation options.

Sweden is unusual in that hotel prices tend to fall at weekends and in summer (except in touristy coastal towns), sometimes by as much as 40% or 50%. In this book, we've listed the standard summer rates, as that's when most people will be visiting, but be aware that prices may be nearly double at other times of year. Many hotel chains are now also offering a variety of low rates for online booking. Hotel prices include a breakfast buffet unless noted in individual reviews. Ask at tourist offices for the free booklet

Hotels in Sweden or visit www.hotelsinsweden.net.

Travellers on a budget should investigate the two cheapest hotel chains, both with flat rates for rooms. Formule 1 (www.hotelfor mule1.com; Skr520) has four hotels: Göteborg, Jönköping, Malmö and Stockholm; the small but functional rooms have shared facilities and can sleep up to three people. Ibis (www.ibishotel.com; Skr595-900) hotels offer simple rooms with private facilities. Breakfast is additional at both chains.

The following hotels are the most common midrange and top-end chains:

Best Western (www.best western.se)
Choice (www.choicehotels.se)
Countryside (www.countrysi dehotels.se)
Ditt Hotell (www.ditthotell. se)
Elite (www.elite.se)
First (www.firsthotels.com)
Radisson SAS (www.radis son.com)
Scandic (www.scandic-hotels. com)
Sweden Hotels (www. swedenhotels.se)

PRACTICALITIES

» Use the metric system for weights and measures.

» Watch out for *mil,* which Swedes may translate into English as 'mile' – a Swedish *mil* is actually 10km.

» Some shops quote prices followed by '/hg', which means per 100g.

» Use the PAL system for video recorders and players.

» Plug appliances into the round, continental-style two-pin sockets for (220V, 50Hz AC) power supply.

» Domestic newspapers (including the Göteborg and Stockholm dailies and evening tabloids) are in Swedish only. A good selection of English-language imports is sold at major transport terminals, Press Stop, Press-byrån and tobacconists – even in small towns.

» Try National Swedish Radio (variable stations around the country, see www.sr.se for a directory) for classical music and opera, pop and rock.

» National TV channels TV1 and TV2 broadcast mainly about local issues, in Swedish only. TV3, TV4 and TV5 have lots of shows and films in English.

Radisson SAS and Elite are the most luxurious. Scandic is known for being environmentally friendly. The top-end Countryside chain has the most characterful rooms, in castles, mansions, monasteries and spas.

Mountain Huts & Lodges

Most mountain huts (fjällstugor) and lodges (fjällstationer) in Sweden are owned by STF. There are about 45 huts and nine mountain lodges, usually spaced at 15km to 25km intervals, primarily in the Lappland region. Reception hours are quite long as staff members are always on site. Basic provisions are sold at many huts and all lodges, and many lodges have hiking equipment for hire.

STF huts have cooking and toilet facilities (none has a shower, but some offer saunas). Bring your own sleeping bag. Huts are staffed during March and April and also from late June to early September. You can't book a bed in advance, but no one is turned away (although in the peak of summer this may mean you sleep on a mattress on the floor). Charges for STF or HI members vary depending on the season, and range from Skr190 to Skr350 (children pay about Skr75), with the highest charges on northern Kungsleden. Nonmembers pay Skr100 extra. You can also pitch a tent in the mountains, but if you camp near STF huts you are requested to pay a service charge (members/nonmembers Skr60/80), which gives you access to any services the hut may offer (such as kitchen and bathroom facilities).

At the excellent STF mountain lodges, accommodation standards range from hostel (with cooking facilities) to hotel (with full- or half-board options), and overnight prices range from Skr200 to around Skr800. There are often guided

activities on offer for guests, plus they usually have a restaurant and shop.

Private Rooms, B&Bs & Farmhouses

Many tourist offices have lists of rooms in private houses, which is a great way of finding well-priced accommodation and getting to meet Swedish people. Singles/doubles average Skr350/450.

Along the motorways (primarily in the south), you may see 'Rum' or 'Rum & Frukost' signs, indicating informal accommodation (frukost means breakfast) from Skr300 to Skr400 per person. Kitchen facilities are often available, and those who bring their own sheets or sleeping bags may get a discount.

The organisation **Bo på Lantgård** (☑035-12 78 70; www.bopalantgard.org) publishes a free annual booklet on farmhouse accommodation (B&B and self-catering), available from any tourist office. B&B prices average Skr300 per person in a double room. Prices for self-caterers range from Skr300 to Skr850 per night, depending on the time of year, facilities and number of beds.

Business Hours

General opening hours are listed here, but there are variations (particularly in the largest cities, where opening hours may be longer). Hours are listed in individual reviews where they differ substantially from these.

Banks 9.30am to 3pm Mon-Fri; some city branches 9am to 5pm or 6pm.

Bars & pubs 11am or noon to 1am or 2am.

Department stores 10am to 7pm Monday to Saturday (sometimes later), noon to 4pm Sunday.

Government offices 9am to 5pm Monday to Friday.

Restaurants Open for lunch from 11.30am to 2pm, and dinner between 6pm and 10pm; often closed on Sunday and/or Monday.

Shops 9am to 6pm Monday to Friday, 9am to 1pm Saturday.

Supermarkets 8am or 9am to 7pm or 9pm.

Systembolaget 10am to 6pm Monday to Friday, 10am to 2pm (often until 5pm) Saturday, sometimes with extended hours on Thursday and Friday evenings.

Tourist offices Usually open daily Midsummer to mid-August, Monday to Friday only the rest of the year.

Customs Regulations

Duty-free goods can only be brought into Sweden from non-EU countries and Åland. Tobacco products and alcoholic drinks can only be brought into Sweden duty-free by those over 18 and 20, respectively.

Duty-free alcohol allowances for travellers from outside the EU are: 1L of spirits, 2L of fortified wine, 2L of wine and a quantity of beer that must be included within the Skr1700 limit. The tobacco allowance is 200 cigarettes, 50 cigars or 250g of smoking tobacco.

The limits on goods brought into Sweden with 'tax paid for personal use' from within the EU are more generous: 10L of spirits, 20L of fortified wine, 90L of wine (but no more than 60L of sparkling wine) and 110L of beer. The tobacco allowance is 800 cigarettes, 400 cheroots, 200 cigars or 1kg of tobacco.

Going through customs rarely involves any hassles, but rules on illegal drugs are strictly enforced; you may be searched on arrival, especially if you're travelling from Denmark. Live plants and animal products (meat, dairy etc) from outside the EU, and all animals, syringes and weapons must be declared to customs on arrival. For the latest regulations, contact **Swedish Customs** (☎0771-23 23 23; www.tullverket.se).

Discount Cards

City Summer Cards

Göteborg, Malmö, Stockholm and Uppsala have worthwhile tourist cards that get you into their major attractions and offer parking, travel on public transport and discounts at participating hotels, restaurants and shops; see the individual city in the destination chapters for details.

Hostel & Student Cards

A Hostelling International (HI) card means cheaper beds in STF hostels, mountain stations and cabins. You can join the STF at hostels and many tourist offices while in Sweden (membership adult/16 to 25 years/six to 15 years/family Skr295/150/30/450).

The most useful student card is the International **Student Identity Card** (ISIC; www.isic.org; per person $22), which offers discounts on many forms of transport (including some airlines, international ferries and local public transport) and on admission to museums, sights, theatres and cinemas.

Seniors

Seniors normally get discounts on entry to museums and other sights, and they can usually purchase discounted cinema and theatre tickets, air tickets and other transport fares. No special card is required to receive this discount, but show your passport if you are asked for proof of age (the minimum qualifying age is generally 60 or 65 years).

Electricity

230V/50Hz

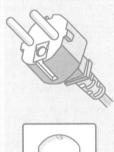

230V/50Hz

Embassies & Consulates

A list of Swedish diplomatic missions abroad (and links) is available at **Sweden Abroad** (www.swedenabroad.com). The diplomatic missions in the following table are in Stockholm, although some

neighbouring countries also have consulates in Göteborg, Malmö and Helsingborg.

Food

Eating listings are designated with one of three price categories. These price estimates do not include drinks.
» **€** less than Skr75
» **€€** Skr75–185
» **€€€** more than Skr185

Gay & Lesbian Travellers

Sweden is a famously liberal country and allows gay and lesbian couples to form registered partnerships and to adopt children. The national organisation for gay and lesbian rights is **Riksförbundet för Sexuellt Likaberättigande** (RFSL; ☎08-501 62 900; www.rfsl.se; Sveavägen 57-59). Gay bars and nightclubs in the big cities are mentioned in this book, but ask local RFSL societies or your home organisation for up-to-date information. The *Spartacus International Gay Guide*, published by Bruno Gmünder Verlag (Berlin), is an excellent international directory of gay entertainment venues, but it's best used in conjunction with more up-to-date listings in local papers; as elsewhere, gay venues in the region can change with the speed of summer.

Another good source of local information is the free monthly magazine *QX*. You can pick it up at many clubs, shops and restaurants in Stockholm, Göteborg, Malmö and Copenhagen (Denmark). The magazine's website (www.qx.se) has excellent information and recommendations in English.

One of the capital's biggest parties is the annual **Stockholm Pride** (www.stockholmpride.org), a five-day festival celebrating gay culture, held between late July and early August. The

EMBASSIES & CONSULATES IN SWEDEN

COUNTRY	TELEPHONE	WEBSITE	ADDRESS
Australia	☎08-613 29 00	www.sweden.embassy.gov.au	8th fl, Klarabergsviaducten 63
Canada	☎08-453 30 00	www.canadaemb.se	Klarabergsgatan 23
Denmark	☎08-406 75 00	www.ambstockholm.um.dk, in Danish	Jakobs Torg 1
Finland	☎08-676 67 00	www.finland.se/fi, in Finnish & Swedish	Gärdesgatan 9-11
France	☎08-459 53 00	www.ambafrance-se.org, in French & Swedish	Kommendörsgatan 13
Germany	☎08-670 15 00	www.stockholm.diplo.de, in German & Swedish	Skarpögatan 9
Ireland	☎08-545 040 40	www.embassyofireland.se	Hovslagargatan 5
Netherlands	☎08-556 933 00	www.netherlands-embassy.se	Götgatan 16A
Norway	☎08-665 63 40	www.norge.se	Skarpögatan 4
UK	☎08-671 30 00	www.britishembassy.se	Skarpögatan 6-8
USA	☎08-783 53 00	stockholm.usembassy.gov	Dag Hammarskjöldsväg 31

extensive program covers art, debate, health, literature, music, spirituality and sport.

Insurance

Depending on the type of policy you choose, insurance can cover you for everything from medical expenses and luggage loss to cancellations or delays in your travel arrangements.

In Sweden, EU citizens pay a fee for all medical treatment (including emergency admissions), but showing an EHIC (European Health Insurance Card) form will make matters much easier. Enquire about the EHIC well in advance at your social security office, travel agent or local post office. Travel insurance is still advisable, however, as it allows treatment flexibility and will also cover ambulance and repatriation costs.

If you do need health insurance, remember that some policies offer 'lower' and 'higher' medical-expense options, but the higher one is chiefly for countries that have extremely high medical costs, such as the USA. Everyone should be covered for the worst possible scenario, such as an accident requiring an ambulance, hospital treatment or an emergency flight home. You may prefer a policy that pays health-care providers directly, rather than you having to pay on the spot and claim later.

Worldwide travel insurance is available at www.lonelyplanet.com/travel_services. You can buy, extend and claim travel insurance online anytime – even if you're already on the road.

Internet Access

If you plan to carry your notebook or palmtop computer with you, remember that the power-supply voltage in Sweden may vary from what you have in your home country. To avoid frying your electronics, use a universal AC adaptor (many laptop adaptors already include this; check the label on your power cord) and a plug adaptor, which will enable you to plug in anywhere. For comprehensive advice on travelling with portable computers, visit the **World Wide Phone Guide** (www.kropla.com) website.

Most hotels have wireless LAN connections, and some even have laptops you can borrow. Nearly all public libraries offer free internet access, but often the half-hour or hour slots are fully booked for days in advance by locals, and facilities may occasionally be blocked. Many tourist offices offer a computer terminal for visitor use (sometimes free of charge).

Internet cafes are rarely found outside big cities because most Swedes have internet access at home. Where internet cafes do exist, they're full of teenage lads playing computer games. You will typically be charged around Skr1 per online minute, or Skr50 per hour. Wireless-internet access at coffee shops, train stations and hotels is on the increase, although in many cases you will have to pay a fee before you can use it.

Legal Matters

If arrested, you have the right to contact your country's embassy, which can usually provide you with a list of local lawyers. There is no provision for bail in Sweden. Sweden has some of the most Draconian drug laws in Western Europe, with fines and possible long prison sentences for possession and consumption.

Maps

Tourist offices, libraries and hotels usually stock free local town plans.

The best maps of Sweden are published and updated regularly by Kartförlaget, the sales branch of the national mapping agency, **Lantmäteriet** (☎026-63 30 00; www.lantmateriet.se); they can be bought at most tourist offices, bookshops and some youth hostels, service stations and general stores.

Motorists planning an extensive tour should get *Motormännens Sverige Vägatlas* produced by Kartförlaget (around Skr280 at most shops), with town plans and detailed coverage at 1:250,000 as far north as

Sundsvall, then 1:400,000 for the remainder.

The best tourist road maps are those of Kartförlaget's *Vägkartan* series, at a scale of 1:100,000 and available from larger bookshops. Also useful, especially for hikers, is the *Fjällkartan* mountain series (1:100,000, with 20m contour interval); these cost around Skr127 apiece and are available at larger bookshops, outdoor equipment stores and STF mountain stations.

To purchase maps before you arrive, try **Kartbutiken** (☎08-20 23 03; www.kartbutiken.se; Kungsgatan 74, Stockholm).

Money

Sweden uses the krona (plural kronor) as currency. One krona is divided into 100 öre. See p14 for typical costs and exchange rates.

Cash & ATMs

The simplest way to get money in Sweden is by accessing your account using an ATM card from your home bank. Bankomat ATMs are found adjacent to many banks and around busy public places such as shopping centres. They accept major credit cards as well as Plus and Cirrus cards. Note that many ATMs in Sweden will not accept PINs of more than four digits; if your PIN is longer than this, just enter the first four and you should be able to access your account. Be aware that some ATMs withdraw from your cheque account without giving you the option to choose a different account. ATMs in busy locations often have extremely long queues and can run out of money on Friday and Saturday night.

Credit Cards

Visa and MasterCard are widely accepted; American Express, Discover and Diners Club less so. Credit cards can be used to buy train tickets

but are not accepted on domestic ferries, apart from sailings to Gotland. Electronic debit or credit cards can be used in most shops.

If your card is lost or stolen in Sweden, report it to one of the following appropriate agencies:
American Express (☎336-393 1111)
Diners Club (☎08-14 68 78)
MasterCard (☎020-79 13 24)
Visa (☎020-79 56 75)

Moneychangers

Banks around the country exchange major foreign currencies.

Forex (☎0200-22 22 20; www.forex.se) is the biggest foreign money exchange company in Sweden, with good rates and branches in major airports, ferry terminals and town and city centres; these are noted where appropriate in the destination chapters.

Tipping

Hotels Optional; small tip (Skr10/day) for housekeeping is appreciated.

Restaurants & Bars Not expected, except at dinner (when 10% to 15% for good service is customary).

Taxis Optional; most people round up the bill to the nearest Skr10.

Travellers Cheques

Banks around the country accept international brands of travellers cheques. They may charge up to Skr60 per travellers cheque, so shop around and compare service fees and exchange rates before handing over your money.

Forex charges a service fee of Skr15 for each travellers cheque exchanged.

Photography

Camera supplies are readily available in all the large cities. Expert, a chain of electrical-goods shops, sells a wide range of photography gadgets.

It's particularly important to ask permission before taking photos of people in Sami areas, where you may meet resistance. Photography and taking videos are prohibited at many tourist sites, mainly to protect fragile artwork. Photographing military establishments is forbidden. Observe signs, and when in doubt, ask permission.

Technical challenges include the clear northern light and glare from water, ice and snow, which may require use of a UV filter (or skylight filter) and lens shade; and the cold – most cameras don't work below -20°C.

Lonely Planet's *Travel Photography*, by Richard I'Anson, contains some handy hints.

Post

Swedish postal service **Posten** (✆020-23 22 21; www. posten.se) has a network of around 3000 counter services in shops, petrol stations and supermarkets across the country. Look for the yellow post symbol on a pale-blue background, which indicates that postal facilities are offered.

Most Swedes now buy their stamps and post letters while going about their grocery shopping. If your postal requirements are more complicated (such as posting a heavy parcel), ask at the local tourist office. Package services are offered at certain office-supply stores.

Mailing letters and postcards weighing up to 20g within Sweden costs Skr5.50; it's Skr11 to elsewhere in Europe and beyond. Airmail will take a week to reach most parts of North America, perhaps a little longer to Australia and New Zealand. Packages weighing 2kg cost around Skr285 by airmail within Europe and Skr300 outside Europe.

Public Holidays

Midsummer brings life almost to a halt for three days: transport and other services are reduced, and most shops and smaller tourist offices close, as do some attractions. Some hotels close between Christmas and New Year, and it's not uncommon for restaurants in larger cities to close during late July and early August.

School holidays vary from school to school, but in general the kids will be at large for Sweden's one-week main sports holiday (February/March), the one-week Easter break, Christmas, and from June to August.

Many businesses close early the day before and all day after official public holidays.

Nyårsdag (New Year's Day) 1 January

Trettondedag Jul (Epiphany) 6 January

Långfredag, Påsk, Annandag Påsk (Good Friday, Easter Sunday & Monday) March/April

Första Maj (Labour Day) 1 May

Kristi Himmelsfärds dag (Ascension Day) May/June

Pingst, Annandag Pingst (Whit Sunday & Monday) Late May or early June

Midsommardag (Midsummer's Day) First Saturday after 21 June

Alla Helgons dag (All Saints' Day) Saturday, late October or early November

Juldag (Christmas Day) 25 December

Annandag Jul (Boxing Day) 26 December

Note also that Midsommarafton (Midsummer's Eve), Julafton (Christmas Eve; 24 December) and Nyårsafton (New Year's Eve; 31 December) are not official holidays, but are generally nonworking days for most of the population.

Telephone

Swedish phone numbers have area codes followed by a varying number of digits. Look for business numbers in the **Yellow Pages** (www. gulasidorna.se, in Swedish). The state-owned telephone company, Telia, also has phone books, which include green pages (for community services) and blue pages (for regional services, including health and medical care).

Public telephones are usually to be found at train stations or in the main town square. They accept phonecards or credit cards (although the latter are expensive). It's not possible to receive return international calls or make international collect calls on public phones.

For international calls dial ✆00, followed by the country code and then the local area code. Calls to Sweden from abroad require the country code ✆46 followed by the area code and telephone number (omitting the first zero in the area code).

Mobile phone codes start with ✆010, ✆070, ✆076, ✆073 and ✆0730. Toll-free codes include ✆020 and ✆0200 (but can't be called from public telephones or abroad!)

Directory assistance (✆118 119) International.

Directory assistance (✆118 118) Within Sweden.

Emergency services (✆112) Toll-free.

Mobile Phones

It's worth considering bringing your mobile phone from your home country and buying a Swedish SIM card, which gives you a Swedish mobile number. Vodafone, for example, sells a local SIM card for around Skr95, which you then need to load with at least Skr100 worth of credit. You can purchase top-ups at many stores, including petrol stations and Pressbyrån shops. Your mobile may be locked onto your local network in your home country, so ask your home network for advice before going abroad.

Phonecards

Telia phonecards (*telefonkort*) for public pay phones cost Skr50 and Skr120 (for 50 and 120 units, respectively) and can be bought from Telia phone shops and newsagents.

You can make international telephone calls with these phonecards, but they won't last long! For international calls, it's better to buy (from tobacconists) one of a wide range of phonecards, such as a Star phonecard, which give cheap rates for calls abroad. These are generally used in public phone boxes in conjunction with a Telia card: so you might have to put the Telia card into the phone, dial the telephone number shown on the back of your cheap international phonecard, then follow the instructions given. International collect calls cannot be made from pay phones.

Time

Sweden is one hour ahead of GMT/UTC and is in the same time zone as Norway and Denmark as well as most of Western Europe. When it's noon in Sweden, it's 11am in London, 1pm in Helsinki, 6am in New York and Toronto, 3am in Los Angeles, 9pm in Sydney and 11pm in Auckland. Sweden also has daylight-saving time: the clocks go forward an hour on the last Sunday in March and back an hour on the last Sunday in October.

Timetables and business hours are quoted using the 24-hour clock, and dates are often given by week number (1 to 52).

Toilets

Public toilets in parks, shopping malls, libraries, and bus or train stations are rarely free in Sweden; though some churches and most museums and tourist offices have free toilets. Except at larger train stations (where there's an attendant), pay toilets cost Skr5 to Skr10, usually payable by coin only. Recently the trend has been towards pay-by-SMS.

Tourist Information

Local Tourist Offices

Most towns in Sweden have centrally located tourist offices (*turistbyrå*) that provide free street plans and information on accommodation, attractions, activities and transport. Brochures for other areas in Sweden are often available. Ask for the handy booklet that lists addresses and phone numbers for most tourist offices in the country; the website of **Swedish Tourism Associated** (www.turism.se) also has this information. See the Information section in each destination chapter for contact details of regional tourist offices.

Most tourist offices are open long hours daily in summer; from mid-August to mid-June a few close down, while others have shorter opening hours – they may close by 4pm, and not open at all at weekends. Public libraries or large hotels are good alternative sources of information.

Tourist Offices Abroad

The official website for the **Swedish Travel and Tourism Council** (www.visit-sweden.com) contains loads of excellent information in many languages, and you can request to have brochures and information packs sent to you.

The following tourist offices can assist with enquiries and provide tourist promotional material by phone, email or post (most don't have a walk-in service). In countries without a designated tourist office, a good starting point for information is the nearest Swedish embassy.

France (☏01-70 70 84 58; servinfo@suede-tourisme.fr; Office Suédois du Tourisme et des Voyages, 11 rue Payenne, F-75003 Paris)

Germany (☏069-22 22 34 96; info@swetourism.de; Schweden-Werbung für Reisen und Touristik, Michaelisstrasse 22, DE-20459 Hamburg)

UK (☏020-7108 6168; info@swetourism.org.uk; Swedish Travel & Tourism Council, 5 Upper Montagu St, London W1H 2AG)

USA (☏212-885 9700; usa@visit-sweden.com; Swedish Travel & Tourism Council, PO Box 4649, Grand Central Station, New York NY 10163-4649)

Travellers with Disabilities

Sweden is one of the easiest countries to travel around in a wheelchair. People with disabilities will find transport services with adapted facilities, ranging from trains to taxis – contact the operator in advance for the best service.

Public toilets and some hotel rooms have facilities for disabled people; **Hotels in Sweden** (www.hotelsinsweden.net) indicates whether hotels have adapted rooms. Some street crossings have ramps for wheelchairs and audio signals for visually impaired people, and some grocery stores are wheelchair accessible.

For further information about Sweden, contact **De Handikappades Riksförbund** (☏08-685 80 00; www.dhr.se), the national association for the disabled.

Also, contact the travel officer at your national support organisation; they may be able to put you in touch with tour companies that specialise in travelling with disabilities.

Visas

Citizens of EU countries can enter Sweden with a passport or a national identification card (passports are recommended) and stay up to three months. Nationals of Nordic countries (Denmark, Norway, Finland and Iceland) can stay and work indefinitely, but nationals of other countries require residence permits (*uppehållstillstånd*) for stays of between three months and five years; there is no fee for this permit for EU citizens.

Non-EU passport holders from Australia, New Zealand, Canada and the US can enter and stay in Sweden without a visa for up to three months. Australian and New Zealand passport-holders aged between 18 and 30 can qualify for a one-year working-holiday visa.

Citizens of South Africa and many other African, Asian and some Eastern European countries require tourist visas for entry. These are only available in advance from Swedish embassies (allow two months); there's a nonrefundable application fee of €60 for most applicants. Visas last up to three months, and extensions aren't easily obtainable.

Non-EU citizens can also obtain residence permits, but these must be applied for before entering Sweden. An interview by consular officials at your nearest Swedish embassy is required – allow up to eight months for this process. Foreign students are granted residence permits if they can prove acceptance by a Swedish educational institution and are able to guarantee that they can support themselves financially.

Migrationsverket (☎011-15 60 00; www.migrationsverket.se) is the Swedish migration board and it handles all applications for visas and work or residency permits.

Work

Non-EU citizens require an offer of paid employment prior to their arrival in Sweden. They need to apply for a work permit (and residence permit for stays over three months), enclosing confirmation of the job offer, completed forms (available from Swedish diplomatic posts or over the internet), two passport photos and their passport. Processing takes six to eight weeks, and there's a nonrefundable application fee of Skr1000.

EU citizens only need to apply for a residence permit (free) within three months of arrival if they find work, then they can remain in Sweden for the duration of their employment (or up to five years).

Australians and New Zealanders aged 18 to 30 years can qualify for a one-year working holiday visa. Full application details are available online through **Migrationsverket** (www.migrationsverket.se).

Work permits are only granted if there's a shortage of Swedish workers (or citizens from EU countries) with certain in-demand skills; speaking Swedish may be essential for the job. Students enrolled in Sweden can take summer jobs, but these can be hard to find and such work isn't offered to travelling students.

Plenty of helpful information can be found online from the **Arbetsförmedlinga** (AMV; Swedish National Labour Market Administration; www.ams.se).

Transport

GETTING THERE & AWAY

Flights, tours and rail tickets can be booked online at lonelyplanet.com/bookings.

Entering the Country

Sweden's main airport is Stockholm-Arlanda. Entry is straightforward; most visitors simply need to fill out and hand over a brief customs form and show their passport at immigration. See p348 for visa information.

Air

Airports & Airlines

The main airport is Stockholm-Arlanda, which links Sweden with major European and North American cities. Göteborg Landvetter is Sweden's second-biggest international airport. Stockholm Skavsta (100km south of Stockholm, near Nyköping) and Göteborg City both serve budget airline Ryanair. For travelling between international airports and city centres, see the Getting Around sections in the relevant chapters. Scandinavian Airlines System (SAS) is the regional carrier.

Göteborg City
(www.goteborgcityairport.se)
Göteborg Landvetter
(www.swedavia.se)
Stockholm Arlanda
(www.arlanda.se)
Stockholm Skavsta
(www.skavsta-air.se)

The following airlines fly into Sweden:
Air France
(www.airfrance.com)
Blue1
(www.blue1.com)
British Airways
(www.britishairways.com)
Lufthansa
(www.lufthansa.com)
Ryanair
(www.ryanair.com)
SAS
(www.flysas.com)

Continental Europe

SAS offers numerous direct services between Stockholm and European capitals including Amsterdam, Brussels, Geneva, Moscow, Paris and Prague. Many services are routed via Copenhagen. Similar routes leave from Göteborg (Gothenburg).

Finnair has direct flights from Helsinki to Stockholm (around 15 daily) and Göteborg (up to four services daily).

Skyways has several flights daily from Copenhagen to Swedish regional centres such as Karlstad, Linköping, Norrköping and Örebro.

The budget airline Ryanair has frequent flights from Stockholm Skavsta to Barcelona, Brussels, Düsseldorf, Frankfurt, Hamburg, Milan, Paris, Riga and Rome.

UK & Ireland

Budget airline Ryanair flies from London Stansted to Stockholm Skavsta, Göteborg City and Malmö's Sturup airport; Glasgow Prestwick to Stockholm Skavsta and Göteborg City; London Luton to Västerås; and Shannon to Stockholm Skavsta.

Between London Heathrow and Stockholm-Arlanda, several commercial airlines have regular daily flights, including SAS, British Airways and bmi.

SAS flies at least four times daily from Stockholm-Arlanda to Manchester and Dublin via London or Copenhagen. SAS also flies daily between London Heathrow and Göteborg.

City Airline has two flights weekly from Göteborg Landvetter to Birmingham and Manchester.

USA

Icelandair has services from Baltimore-Washington, Boston, New York, Minneapolis and Orlando via Reykjavík to Stockholm. SAS's North American hub is New York City's Newark Airport, with direct daily flights to/from Stockholm.

Land

Border Crossings

Direct access to Sweden by land is possible from Norway, Finland and Denmark (via the Öresund toll bridge). Border-crossing formalities are nonexistent.

Train and bus journeys between Sweden and the continent go directly to ferries.

Eurolines (☑031-100240; www.eurolines.com) Has an office inside the bus terminals in Sweden's three largest cities: Stockholm, Göteborg and Malmö. Full schedules and fares are listed on the website.

GoByBus (☑0771-15 15 15; www.gobybus.se, in Swedish, Norwegian & Danish) Long-distance buses within Sweden and to Oslo, Norway, and Copenhagen, Denmark.

Sveriges Järnväg (SJ; ☑0771-75 75 99; www.sj.se) Train lines with services to Copenhagen.

Swebus Express (☑0200-21 82 18; www.swebusexpress. se) Long-distance buses within Sweden and to Oslo and Copenhagen.

Denmark

BUS

Eurolines runs buses between Stockholm and Copenhagen (Dkr285, nine hours, at least three per week), and between Göteborg and Copenhagen (Dkr205, 4½ hours, daily). Swebus Express and Go-ByBus both run regular buses on the same routes. All companies offer student, youth (under 26) and senior discounts.

CAR & MOTORCYCLE

You can drive from Copenhagen to Malmö across the Öresund bridge on the E20 motorway. Tolls are paid at Lernacken, on the Swedish side, in either Danish or Swedish currency (single crossing per car Skr375), or by credit or debit card.

TRAIN

Öresund trains operated by Skånetrafiken (www. skanetrafiken.se) run every 20 minutes from 6am to midnight (and once an hour thereafter) between Copenhagen and Malmö (one-way Skr105, 35 minutes) via the bridge. The trains usually stop at Copenhagen airport. From Copenhagen, change in Malmö for Stockholm trains.

Frequent services operate between Copenhagen and Göteborg (Skr330, four hours) and between Copenhagen, Kristianstad and Karlskrona.

Finland

BUS

Frequent bus services run from Haparanda to Tornio (Skr15, 10 minutes). **Tapanis Buss** (☑0922-129 55; www. tapanis.se, in Swedish) runs express coaches from Stockholm to Tornio via Haparanda twice a week (Skr570, 15 hours). **Länstrafiken i Norrbotten** (☑020 47 00 47; www.ltnbd.se) operates buses

as far as Karesuando, from where it's only a few minutes' walk across the bridge to Kaaresuvanto, Finland.

There are also regular regional services from Haparanda to Övertorneå (some continue to Pello, Pajala and Kiruna) – you can walk across the border at Övertorneå or Pello and pick up a Finnish bus to Muonio, with onward connections from there to Kaaresuvanto and Tromsø, Norway.

CAR & MOTORCYCLE

The main routes between Sweden and Finland are the E4 from Umeå to Kemi and Rd 45 from Gällivare to Kaaresuvanto; five other minor roads also cross the border.

Germany

BUS

Eurolines runs services from Göteborg to Berlin (Skr709, 17 hours, three weekly).

TRAIN

Hamburg is the central European gateway for Scandinavia, with direct trains daily to Copenhagen and a few on to Stockholm. Direct overnight trains run daily between Berlin and Malmö via the Trelleborg–Sassnitz ferry (www.berlin-night-express. com, couchette €89, nine hours).

Norway

BUS

GoByBus runs from Stockholm to Oslo (Skr425, 7½ hours, fives times daily) via

---

CLIMATE CHANGE & TRAVEL

Every form of transport that relies on carbon-based fuel generates CO_2, the main cause of human-induced climate change. Modern travel is dependent on aeroplanes, which might use less fuel per kilometre per person than most cars but travel much greater distances. The altitude at which aircraft emit gases (including CO_2) and particles also contributes to their climate change impact. Many websites offer 'carbon calculators' that allow people to estimate the carbon emissions generated by their journey and, for those who wish to do so, to offset the impact of the greenhouse gases emitted with contributions to portfolios of climate-friendly initiatives throughout the world. Lonely Planet offsets the carbon footprint of all staff and author travel.

Karlstad, and from Göteborg to Oslo (Skr265, four hours, seven daily). Swebus Express has the same routes with similar prices. In the north, buses run once daily from Umeå to Mo i Rana (eight hours) and from Skellefteå to Bodø (nine hours, daily except Saturday); for details, contact **Länstrafiken i Västerbotten** (☑0771-10 01 10; www.tabussen.nu) and **Länstrafiken i Norrbotten** (☑0771-10 01 10; www.ltnbd.se).

CAR & MOTORCYCLE
The main roads between Sweden and Norway are the E6 from Göteborg to Oslo, the E18 from Stockholm to Oslo, the E14 from Sundsvall to Trondheim, the E12 from Umeå to Mo i Rana, and the E10 from Kiruna to Bjerkvik.

TRAIN
Trains run daily between Stockholm and Oslo (Skr500 to Skr700, six to seven hours), and at night to Narvik (Skr810, about 20 hours). You can also travel from Helsingborg to Oslo (Skr750, seven hours), via Göteborg.

UK
BUS
Eurolines has regular routes to the UK from Sweden.

TRAIN
Connections from the UK go through the Channel Tunnel to Continental Europe. You usually have to book each section separately. From London, a 2nd-class single ticket (including couchette) costs around £250 to Stockholm. For reservations and tickets, contact **Deutsche Bahn UK** (www.bahn.co.uk).

Sea
Ferry connections are frequent. Most lines offer substantial discounts for seniors, students and children. Most prices quoted are for single journeys at peak times (weekend travel, overnight

crossings, mid-June to mid-August); other fares may be up to 30% lower.

Denmark
GÖTEBORG–FREDRIKSHAVN
Stena Line (☑031-704 00 00; www.stenaline.se) Three-hour crossing. Up to six ferries daily. Pedestrian/car and five passengers/bicycle Skr195/1535/375.

Stena Line (Express) Two-hour crossing. Up to three ferries daily. Pedestrian/car and five passengers/bicycle Skr300/1795/400.

HELSINGØR–HELSINGBORG
This is the quickest route and has frequent ferries (crossing time around 20 minutes).
HH-Ferries (☑042-19 80 00; www.hhferries.se) 24-hour service. Pedestrian/car and up to nine passengers Skr30/385.

Scandlines (☑042-18 63 00; www.scandlines.se) Similar service and prices to HH-Ferries.

VARBERG–GRENÅ
Stena Line (☑031-704 00 00; www.stenaline.se) Four-hour crossing. Three or four daily. Pedestrian/car and five passengers/bicycle Skr195/1535/285.

YSTAD–RØNNE
BornholmsTrafikken (☑0411-55 87 00; www.bornholmstrafikken.dk) Conventional and fast services (1½ hours, 80 minutes, two to nine times daily). Pedestrian/car and five passengers/bicycle from €24/141/26.

Eastern Europe
To/from Estonia, **Tallink** (☑08-666 6001; www.tallink.ee, in Estonian) runs the routes Stockholm–Tallinn and Kapellskär–Paldiski.
Scandlines (☑08-5206 02 90; www.scandlines.dk) operates Ventspils–Nynäshamn ferries around five times per week.

To/from Lithuania, **Lisco Line** (☑0454-33680; www.lisco.lt) operates daily between Karlshamn and Klaipėda.
To/from Poland, **Polferries** (☑040-121700; www.polferries.se) and **Unity Line** (☑0411-556900; www.unityline.pl) have daily Ystad–Swinoujscie crossings. Polferries also runs Nynäshamn–Gdańsk. **Stena Line** (☑031-704 0000; www.stenaline.se) sails Karlskrona–Gdynia.

Finland
Helsinki is called Helsingfors in Swedish, and Turku is Åbo.
Stockholm–Helsinki and Stockholm–Turku ferries run daily throughout the year via the Åland islands. These ferries have minimum age limits; check before you travel.

STOCKHOLM–ÅLAND ISLANDS (MARIEHAMN)
Prices quoted are for return trips, foot passengers only.
Ånedin-Linjen (☑08-456 22 00; www.anedinlinjen.se, in Swedish) Six hours, daily. Couchette Skr115, berth from Skr355.

Birka Cruises (☑08-702 72 00; www.birkacruises.com) A 22-hour round-trip. One or two daily. Berth from Skr480. Prices include supper and breakfast.

Eckerö Linjen (☑0175-258 00; www.eckerolinjen.fi) Runs to the Åland islands from Grisslehamn.

STOCKHOLM–HELSINKI
Silja Line (☑08-22 21 40; www.silja.com) Around 15 hours. Ticket and cabin berth from about €130.

Viking Line (☑08-452 40 00; www.vikingline.fi) Operates the same routes with slightly cheaper prices (from €100).

STOCKHOLM–TURKU
RG Line (☑090-18 52 00; www.rgline.com) Runs the routes Umeå–Vaasa and Sundsvall–Vaasa.

Silja Line (☑08-22 21 40; www.silja.com) Eleven hours. Deck place €11, cabins from

€45; prices are higher for evening trips. From September to early May, ferries also depart from Kapellskär (90km northeast of Stockholm); connecting buses operated by Silja Line are included in the full-price fare.

Viking Line (☑08-452 40 00; www.vikingline.fi) Operates the same routes with slightly cheaper prices. In high season it offers passage from both Stockholm and Kapellskär.

Germany
GÖTEBORG–KIEL

Stena Line (☑031-704 00 00; www.stenaline.se) Fourteen hours. One crossing nightly. Pedestrian/car and up to five passengers from Skr520/1390.

TRELLEBORG–ROSTOCK

Scandlines (☑042-18 61 00; www.scandlines.se) Six hours (night crossing 7½ hours). Two or three daily. Pedestrian/car and up to nine passengers/passenger with bicycle Skr210/1160/245.

TT-Line (☑0410-562 00; www.ttline.com) Operates the same as Scandlines, with similar prices.

TRELLEBORG–SASSNITZ

Scandlines (☑042-18 61 00; www.scandlines.se) A 3¾-hour trip. Two to five times daily. Pedestrian/car and up to nine passengers/passenger with bicycle Skr145/1050/210. A fuel surcharge of Skr50 to Skr80 may be added.

TRELLEBORG–TRAVEMÜNDE

TT-Line (☑0410-562 00; www.ttline.com) Seven hours. Two to five daily. Car and up to five passengers from Skr1350, Skr50 surcharge for bicycle. Berths are compulsory on night crossings.

Norway

There's a daily overnight **DFDS Seaways** (☑031-65 06 80; www.dfdsseaways.com)

ferry between Copenhagen and Oslo (from €120 per passenger), via Helsingborg. Passenger fares between Helsingborg and Oslo (14 hours) cost from Skr1100, and cars Skr475, but the journey can't be booked online; you'll need to call.

A **Color Line** (☑0526-620 00; www.colorline.com) ferry between Strömstad, Sweden, and Sandefjord, Norway, sails two to six times daily (2½ hours) year-round. Tickets cost from Nkr180 (rail passes get 50% discount).

GETTING AROUND

Public transport is heavily subsidised and well organised. It's divided into 24 regional networks (*länstrafik*), but with an overarching **Resplus** (www.samtrafiken. se) system, where one ticket is valid on trains and buses. Timetables are available online.

Air

Airlines in Sweden

Domestic airlines in Sweden tend to use **Stockholm-Arlanda** (☑08-797 60 00; www.lfv.se) as a hub, but there are 30-odd regional airports. Flying domestic is expensive on full-price tickets, but discounts are available on internet bookings, student and youth fares, off-peak travel, return tickets booked in advance or low-price tickets for accompanying family members and seniors.

The following is a selection of Sweden's internal flight operators and the destinations they cover.

Malmö Aviation (☑040-660 29 00; www.malmoaviation.se) Göteborg, Stockholm and Umeå.

SAS (☑0770-72 77 27; www.flysas.com) Arvidsjaur, Borlänge, Gällivare, Göteborg, Halmstad, Ängelholm-Helsingborg, Hemavan, Hultsfred, Jönköping, Ka-

lmar, Karlstad, Kiruna, Kramfors, Kristianstad, Linköping, Luleå, Lycksele, Malmö, Mora, Norrköping, Oskarshamn, Oskersund, Skellefteå, Stockholm, Storuman, Sundsvall, Sveg, Torsby, Trollhättan, Umeå, Vilhelmina, Visby, Västerås, Örebro and Örnsköldsvik.

Skyways (JZ; ☑0771 95 95 00; www.skyways.se) Arvidsjaur, Borlänge, Göteborg, Halmstad, Hemavan, Jönköping, Karlstad, Kramfors, Kristianstad, Linköping, Lycksele, Mora, Norrköping, Skellefteå, Stockholm, Storuman, Sundsvall, Trollhättan, Vilhelmina, Visby and Örebro.

Air Passes

Visitors who fly SAS to Sweden from North America or Asia can add on a Visit Scandinavia Air Pass, allowing one-way travel on direct flights between any two Scandinavian cities serviced by SAS and its partner airlines. A coupon for use within Sweden costs from US$51 (Stockholm–Kiruna is higher); international flights between Sweden, Denmark, Norway and Finland cost US$90. For the latest, call SAS or check www.flysas. com.

Bicycle

Cycling is an excellent way to see Sweden and is a very common mode of transport for Swedes. Most towns have separate lanes and traffic signals for cyclists. Helmets are compulsory for all cyclists under age 15.

Boat
Canal Boat

The canals provide cross-country routes linking the main lakes. The longest cruises, on the Göta Canal from Söderköping (south of Stockholm) to Göteborg, run from mid-May to mid-September, take at least four days and include the lakes between.

Rederiaktiebolaget Göta Kanal (☎031-15 83 11; www.gotacanal.se) operates three ships over the whole distance at fares from Skr9775 to Skr17,275 per person for a four-day cruise, including full board and guided excursions.

Ferry

An extensive boat network and the 16-day Båtluffarkortet (Boat Hiking Pass; Skr420) open up the attractive Stockholm archipelago (p99). Gotland is served by regular ferries (p255) from Nynäshamn and Oskarshamn, and the quaint fishing villages off the west coast can normally be reached by boat with a regional transport pass – enquire at the Göteborg tourist offices.

Bus

You can travel by bus in Sweden on any of the 24 good-value and extensive *länstrafik* networks (see respective destinations for contact details) or on national long-distance routes.

Express Buses

Swebus Express (☎0200 21 82 18; www.swebusexpress. se) has the largest network of express buses, but they only serve the southern half of the country (as far north as Mora in Dalarna). There's no need to reserve a seat on Swebus Express services. Generally, tickets for travel between Monday and Thursday are cheaper, or if they're purchased over the internet or more than 24 hours before departure; if you're a student or senior, it's worth asking about fare discounts.

Svenska Buss (☎0771-67 67 67; www.svenskabuss.se) and **GoByBus** (☎0771-15 15 15; www.gobybus.se) also connect many southern towns and cities with Stockholm; prices are often slightly cheaper

than Swebus Express, but services are less frequent.

North of Gävle, regular connections with Stockholm are provided by several smaller operators, including **Ybuss** (☎0771-33 44 44; www. ybuss.se, in Swedish), which has services to Sundsvall, Östersund and Umeå.

Regional Networks

The *länstrafik* bus networks are well integrated with the regional train system, with one ticket valid on any local or regional bus or train. Rules vary but transfers are usually free if they are within one to four hours. Fares on local buses and trains are often identical, though prices can vary wildly depending on when you travel and how far in advance you buy tickets.

Bus Passes

Good-value daily or weekly passes are usually available from local and regional transport offices, and many regions have 30-day passes for longer stays, or a special card for peak-season summer travel.

Car & Motorcycle

Sweden has good roads, and the excellent E-class motorways rarely have traffic jams.

Automobile Associations

The Swedish national motoring association is **Motormännens Riksförbund** (☎020-21 11 11; www.motormannen.se).

Bringing Your Own Vehicle

If you're bringing your own car, you'll need vehicle registration documents, unlimited third-party liability insurance and a valid driving licence. A right-hand-drive vehicle brought from the UK or Ireland should have deflectors fitted to the headlights to avoid dazzling oncoming traffic. You must carry a

reflective warning breakdown triangle.

Driving Licences

An international driving permit isn't necessary; your domestic licence will do.

Hire

To hire a car you have to be at least 20 (sometimes 25) years of age, with a recognised licence and a credit card.

International rental chains Avis, Hertz and Europcar have desks at Stockholm-Arlanda and Göteborg Landvetter airports, and offices in most major cities. The best car-hire rates are generally from larger petrol stations (like Statoil and OK-Q8) – look for signs saying *biluthyrning* or *hyrbilar* (both mean car hire).

Avis (☎0770-82 00 82; www. avisworld.com)
Europcar (☎020-78 11 80; www.europcar.com)
Hertz (☎0771 211 212; www. hertz-europe.com)
Mabi Hyrbilar (☎08-612 60 90; www.mabirent.se) National company with competitive rates.
OK-Q8 (☎020-85 08 50; www.okq8.se, in Swedish) Click on *hyrbilar* in the website menu to see car-hire pages.
Statoil (☎08-429 63 00; www.statoil.se/biluthyrning, in Swedish) Click on *uthyrningsstationer* to see branches with car hire, and on *priser* for prices.

Road Hazards

In the north, elk (moose, to Americans) and reindeer are serious road hazards; around 40 people die in collisions every year. Look out for the signs saying *viltstängsel upphör*, which mean that elk may cross the road, and for black plastic bags tied to roadside trees or poles, which mean Sami have reindeer herds grazing in the area. Report all incidents to police – failure to do so is an offence.

ROAD DISTANCES (KM)

	Gävle	Göteborg	Helsingborg	Jönköping	Kalmar	Karlstad	Kiruna	Linköping	Luleå	Malmö	Skellefteå	Stockholm	Sundsvall	Umeå	Uppsala	Örebro
Göteborg	520															
Helsingborg	690	220														
Jönköping	450	150	240													
Kalmar	560	350	290	215												
Karlstad	325	250	470	245	455											
Kiruna	1090	1645	1785	1540	1660	1420										
Linköping	365	280	365	130	235	230	1440									
Luleå	755	1300	1440	1210	1310	1080	342	1116								
Malmö	740	280	65	290	290	530	1835	415	1500							
Skellefteå	620	1185	1310	1075	1175	950	470	970	135	1360						
Stockholm	175	480	565	330	415	305	1265	205	930	620	795					
Sundsvall	215	765	890	670	770	540	875	575	540	955	405	390				
Umeå	485	1010	1140	935	1040	810	605	850	270	1230	135	660	270			
Uppsala	110	485	615	380	460	285	1195	250	860	665	725	70	320	590		
Örebro	235	285	450	200	350	115	1340	115	970	495	840	200	445	705	170	
Östersund	385	795	990	790	950	560	815	680	595	1075	470	560	185	370	490	590

In Göteborg and Norrköping, be aware of trams, which have priority; overtake on the right.

Road Rules

In Sweden, you drive on and give way to the right. Headlights (at least dipped) must be on at all times when driving. Seatbelts are compulsory, and children under seven years old should be in the appropriate harness or child seat.

The blood-alcohol limit in Sweden is 0.02% – having just one drink will put you over. The maximum speed on motorways (signposted in green and called E1, E4 etc) is 110km/h, highways 90km/h, narrow rural roads 70km/h and built-up areas 50km/h. The speed limit for cars towing caravans is 80km/h. Police using hand-held radar speed detectors have the power to impose on-the-spot fines of up to Skr1200.

Hitching

Travellers who decide to hitch should understand that they are taking a small but potentially serious risk; consider travelling in pairs and let someone know where you're planning to go. Hitching isn't popular in Sweden and very long waits are the norm. It's prohibited to hitch on motorways.

Local Transport

In Sweden, local transport is always linked with regional transport *(länstrafik)*. Regional passes are valid both in the city and on the rural routes. Town and city bus fares are around Skr20, but it usually works out cheaper to get a day card or other travel pass.

Swedish and Danish trains and buses around the Öresund area form an integrated transport system, so buying tickets to Copenhagen from any station in the region is as easy as buying tickets for Swedish journeys.

Tours

Recommended tours appear throughout this book, but the youth-hostel organisation STF is reliably good:
Svenska Turistföreningen (STF; Swedish Touring Association; ☑08-463 21 00; www.svenskaturistforenin gen.se) Events and tours mostly based on outdoor activities (eg kayaking and hiking).

Train

Sweden has an extensive and reliable railway network, and trains are certainly faster than buses. Many destinations in the northern half of the country, however, cannot be reached by train alone. The following are the two main train operators in the country:

Inlandsbanan (☎0771-53 53 53; www.inlandsbanan.se) One of the great rail journeys in Scandinavia is this slow and scenic 1300km route from Kristinehamn to Gällivare. Several southern sections have to be travelled by bus, but the all-train route starts at Mora. It takes seven hours from Mora to Öster-sund (Skr414) and 15 hours from Östersund to Gällivare (Skr962). A pass allows two weeks' unlimited travel for Skr1595.

Sveriges Järnväg (SJ; ☎0771-75 75 75; www.sj.se) National network covering most main lines, especially in the southern part of the country.

Tågkompaniet (☎0771-44 41 11; www.tagkompaniet.se, in Swedish) Operates excellent overnight trains from Göte-borg and Stockholm north to Boden, Kiruna, Luleå and Narvik, and the lines north of Härnösand.

Costs

Ticket prices vary tremendously depending on the type of train, class, time of day, and how far in advance you buy the ticket. Full-price 2nd-class tickets for longer journeys cost about twice as much as equivalent bus trips, but there are various discounts available, especially for book-ing a week or so in advance (*förköpsbiljet*), online, or at the last minute. Students, pensioners and people aged under 26 get a steep discount.

All SJ ticket prices drop from late June to mid-August. Most SJ trains don't allow bicycles to be taken onto trains (they have to be sent as freight), but some in southern Sweden do; check when you book your ticket.

Train Passes

The Sweden Rail Pass, Eurodomino tickets and international passes, such as Inter-Rail and Eurail, are accepted on SJ services and most regional trains.

The **Eurail Scandinavia Pass** (www.eurail.com) entitles you to unlimited rail travel in Denmark, Finland, Norway and Sweden; it is valid in 2nd class only and is available for four, five, six, eight or 10 days of travel within a two-month period (prices start at youth/adult US$235/315). The X2000 trains require all rail-pass holders to pay a supplement of Skr65. The pass also provides free travel on Scandlines' Helsingør to Helsingborg route, and 20% to 50% discounts on the following ship routes.

ROUTE	OPERATOR
Frederikshavn–Göteborg	Stena Line
Grenå–Varberg	Stena Line
Helsinki–Åland–Stockholm	Silja Line
Stockholm–Tallinn	Silja Line
Stockholm–Riga	Silja Line
Turku–Åland–Stockholm/Kappelskär	Silja Line
Turku/Helsinki–Stockholm	Viking Line

Some of the main rail routes across the country:

» Stockholm north to Uppsala–Gävle–Sundsvall–Östersund

» Stockholm west to Örebro–Karlstad–Oslo

» Stockholm west to Örebro–Göteborg

» Stockholm south to Norrköping–Kalmar

» Stockholm south to Norrköping–Malmö–Copenhagen

Language

As a member of the North Germanic or Scandinavian language family, Swedish has Danish and Norwegian as the closest relatives. It is the national language of Sweden, spoken by the majority of residents (around 8.5 million). In neighbouring Finland it shares official status with Finnish and is a mandatory subject in schools, but it's the first language for only about 300,000 people or 6% of Finland's population.

The standard language or *Rikssvenska* reek·*sven*·ska (lit: kingdom-Swedish) is based on the central dialects from the area around Stockholm. Some of the rural dialects that are spoken across the country are quite diverse – for example, *Skånska* skawn·ska, spoken in the southern province of Skåne, has flatter vowels (and sounds a lot more like Danish), whereas *Dalmål* daal·mawl, spoken in the central region of Dalarna, has a very up-and-down sound.

Most Swedish sounds are similar to their English counterparts. One exception is fh (a breathy sound pronounced with rounded lips, like saying 'f' and 'w' at the same time), but with a little practice, you'll soon get it right. Note also that ai is pronounced as in 'aisle', aw as in 'saw', air as in 'hair', eu as the 'u' in 'nurse', ew as the 'ee' in 'see' with rounded lips, and ey as the 'e' in 'bet' but longer. Just read our coloured pronunciation guides as if they were English and you'll be understood. The stressed syllables are indicated with italics.

BASICS

| Hello. | *Hej.* | hey |
| Goodbye. | *Adjö./Hej då.* | aa·*yeu*/hey daw |

Yes.	*Ja.*	yaa
No.	*Nej.*	ney
Please.	*Tack.*	tak
Thank you (very much).	*Tack (så mycket).*	tak (saw *mew*·ke)
You're welcome.	*Varsågod.*	var·sha·*gohd*
Excuse me.	*Ursäkta mig.*	oor·*shek*·ta mey
Sorry.	*Förlåt.*	feur·*lawt*

How are you?
Hur står det till?   hoor stawr de til

Fine, thanks. And you?
Bra, tack. Och dig?   braa tak o dey

What's your name?
Vad heter du?   vaad *hey*·ter doo

My name is ...
Jag heter ...   yaa *hey*·ter ...

Do you speak English?
Talar du engelska?   taa·lar doo *eng*·el·ska

I don't understand.
Jag förstår inte.   yaa feur·*shtawr* in·te

ACCOMMODATION

Where's a ...?	*Var finns det ...?*	var fins de ...
campsite	*en camping-plats*	eyn *kam*·ping·plats
guesthouse	*ett gästhus*	et *yest*·hoos
hotel	*ett hotell*	et hoh·*tel*
youth hostel	*ett vandrar-hem*	et *van*·drar·hem

WANT MORE?

For in-depth language information and handy phrases, check out Lonely Planet's *Scandinavian Phrasebook*. You'll find it at **shop.lonelyplanet.com**, or you can buy Lonely Planet's iPhone phrasebooks at the Apple App Store.

SAMI LANGUAGES

Sami languages are related to Finnish and other Finno-Ugric languages. Five of the nine main Sami languages are spoken in Sweden, with speakers of each varying in number from 500 to 5000.

Most Sami speakers can communicate in Swedish, but relatively few speak English. Knowing some Sami words and phrases will give you a chance to access the unique Sami culture.

Fell (Northern) Sami

The most common of the Sami languages, Fell Sami is considered the standard Sami variety. It's spoken in Sweden's far north around Karesuando and Jukkasjärvi.

Written Fell Sami includes several accented letters, but it still doesn't accurately represent the spoken language – even some Sami people find the written language difficult to learn. For example, *giitu* (thanks) is pronounced 'geech-too', but the strongly aspirated 'h' isn't written.

Hello.	*Buorre beaivi.*
Hello. (reply)	*Ipmel atti.*
Goodbye.	
(to person leaving)	*Mana dearvan.*
(to person staying)	*Báze dearvan.*
How are you?	*Mot manna?*
I'm fine.	*Buorre dat manna.*
Yes.	*De lea.*
No.	*Li.*
Thank you.	*Giitu.*
You're welcome.	*Leage buorre.*

1	*okta*
2	*guokte*
3	*golbma*
4	*njeallje*
5	*vihta*
6	*guhta*
7	*cieza*
8	*gávcci*
9	*ovcci*
10	*logi*

Do you have a ... room?	*Har ni ...?*	har nee ...
single	*ett enkeltrum*	et en·kelt·rum
double	*ett dubbeltrum*	et du·belt·rum

How much is it per ...?	*Hur mycket kostar det per ...?*	hoor mew·ket kos·tar de peyr ...
night	*natt*	nat
person	*person*	peyr·shohn

DIRECTIONS

Where's the ...?
Var ligger ...? var li·ger ...

What's the address?
Vilken adress är det? vil·ken a·dress air de

Can you show me (on the map)?
Kan du visa mig (på kartan)? kan doo vee·sa mey (paw kar·tan)

How far is it?
Hur långt är det? hoor lawngt air de

How do I get there?
Hur kommer man dit? hoor ko·mar man deet

Turn ...	*Sväng ...*	sveng ...
at the corner	*vid hörnet*	veed heur·net
at the traffic lights	*vid trafik-ljuset*	veed tra·feek·yoo·set
left	*till vänster*	til ven·ster
right	*till höger*	til heu·ger

It's ...	*Det är ...*	de air ...
behind ...	*bakom ...*	baa·kom ...
far away	*långt*	lawngt
in front of ...	*framför ...*	fram·feur ...
left	*till vänster*	til ven·ster
near (to ...)	*nära (på ...)*	nair·ra (paw ...)
next to ...	*bredvid ...*	breyd·veed ...
on the corner	*vid hörnet*	veed heur·net
opposite ...	*mitt emot ...*	mit ey·moht ...
right	*till höger*	til heu·ger
straight ahead	*rakt fram*	raakt fram

EATING & DRINKING

Waiter!
Vaktmästern! vakt·mes·tern

What would you recommend?
Vad skulle ni anbefalla? vaad sku·le nee an·be·fa·la

What's the local speciality?
Vad är den lokala specialiteten? vaad air deyn loh·kaa·la spe·si·a·li·tey·ten

Do you have vegetarian food?
Har ni vegetarisk mat?   har nee ve·ge·*taa*·risk maat

I'll have ...
Jag vill ha ...   yaa vil haa ...

Cheers!
Skål!   skawl

I'd like (the) ...	*Jag skulle vilja ha ...*	yaa *sku*·le *vil*·ya haa ...
bill	*räkningen*	*reyk*·ning·en
drink list	*drickslistan*	*driks*·lis·tan
menu	*menyn*	me·*newn*
that dish	*den maträtt*	deyn *maat*·ret

Could you prepare a meal without ...?	*Kan ni laga en maträtt utan ...?*	kan nee *laa*·ga eyn *maat*·ret *oo*·tan ...
butter	*smör*	smeur
eggs	*ägg*	eg
meat stock	*köttspad*	*sheut*·spaad

Key Words

bar	*bar*	bar
bottle	*flaska*	*flas*·ka
breakfast	*frukost*	*froo*·kost
cafe	*kafé*	ka·*fey*
children's menu	*barnmeny*	barn·me·*new*
cold	*kylig*	*shew*·lig
cup	*kopp*	kop
daily special	*dagens rätt*	*daa*·gens ret
dinner	*middag*	*mi*·daa
drink	*dricka*	*dri*·ka
food	*mat*	maat
fork	*gaffel*	*ga*·fel
glass	*glas*	glaas
hot	*varm*	varm
knife	*kniv*	kneev
lunch	*lunch*	lunsh
market	*torghandel*	*tory*·han·del
menu	*meny/ matsedel*	me·*new/ maat*·sey·del
plate	*tallrik*	*tal*·reek
restaurant	*restaurang*	res·taw·*rang*
snack	*mellanmål*	*me*·lan·mawl
spoon	*sked*	fheyd
teaspoon	*tesked*	*tey*·fheyd
with	*med*	me
without	*utan*	*oo*·taan

Signs

Signs	
Ingång	Entrance
Utgång	Exit
Öppet	Open
Stängt	Closed
Förbjudet	Prohibited
Toaletter	Toilets
Herrar	Men
Damer	Women

Meat & Fish

chicken	*kyckling*	shewk·*ling*
fish	*fisk*	fisk
herring	*sill*	sil
lobster	*hummer*	*hu*·mer
meat	*kött*	sheut
meatballs	*köttbullar*	*sheut*·bu·lar
salmon	*lax*	laks
tuna	*tonfisk*	*tohn*·fisk
venison	*rådjur*	*rawd*·yur

Fruit & Vegetables

blueberries	*blåbär*	*blaw*·bair
carrot	*morot*	*moh*·rot
fruit	*frukt*	frukt
mushrooms	*svamp*	svamp
potatoes	*potatis*	poh·*taa*·tis
raspberries	*hallon*	*haa*·lon
strawberries	*jordgubbar*	*yohrd*·gu·bar
vegetable	*grönsak*	*greun*·saak

Other

bread	*bröd*	breud
butter	*smör*	smeur
cake	*kaka*	*kaa*·ka
cheese	*ost*	ost
egg	*ägg*	eg
jam	*sylt*	sewlt
rice	*ris*	rees
soup	*soppa*	*so*·pa

Drinks

beer	*öl*	eul
coffee	*kaffe*	ka·fe

(orange) juice	(apelsin-) juice	(a·pel·seen·) djoos
milk	mjölk	myeulk
mineral water	mineral- vatten	mi·ne·raal· va·ten
red wine	rödvin	reud·veen
soft drink	läsk	lesk
sparkling wine	mousserande vin	moo·sey·ran·de veen
tea	te	tey
water	vatten	va·ten
white wine	vitt vin	vit veen

EMERGENCIES

Help!	Hjälp!	yelp
Go away!	Försvinn!	feur·shvin
Call ...!	Ring ...!	ring ...
a doctor	efter en doktor	ef·ter en dok·tor
the police	polisen	poh·lee·sen

It's an emergency!
Det är ett nödsituation! — de air et neud·si·too·a·fhohn

I'm lost.
Jag har gått vilse. — yaa har got vil·se

Numbers		
1	ett	et
2	två	tvaw
3	tre	trey
4	fyra	few·ra
5	fem	fem
6	sex	seks
7	sju	fhoo
8	åtta	o·ta
9	nio	nee·oh
10	tio	tee·oh
20	tjugo	shoo·go
30	trettio	tre·tee
40	fyrtio	fewr·tee
50	femtio	fem·tee
60	sextio	seks·tee
70	sjuttio	fhu·tee
80	åttio	o·tee
90	nittio	ni·tee
100	ett hundra	et hun·dra
1000	ett tusen	et too·sen

I'm sick.
Jag är sjuk. — yaa air fhook

It hurts here.
Det gör ont här. — de yeur ont hair

I'm allergic to (antibiotics).
Jag är allergisk mot (antibiotika). — yaa air a·leyr·gisk moht (an·tee·bee·oh·ti·ka)

Where are the toilets?
Var är toaletten? — var air toh·aa·le·ten

SHOPPING & SERVICES

Where's the ...?	Var ligger ...?	var li·ger ...
bank	banken	ban·ken
post office	posten	pos·ten
tourist office	turistinfor- mationen	too·rist·in·for- ma·fhoh·nen

Where's the local internet cafe?
Var finns det lokala Internet kaféet? — var fins de loh·kaa·la in·ter·net ka·fey·et

Where's the nearest public phone?
Var ligger närmaste publiktelefon? — var li·ger nair·ma·ste pub·leek·te·le·fohn

I'm looking for ...
Jag letar efter ... — yaa ley·tar ef·ter ...

Can I look at it?
Får jag se den? — fawr yaa se deyn

Do you have any others?
Har ni några andra? — har nee naw·ra an·dra

How much is it?
Hur mycket kostar det? — hoor mew·ke kos·tar de

That's too expensive.
Det är för dyrt. — de air feur dewrt

What's your lowest price?
Vad är dit lägste pris? — vaad air dit leyg·ste prees

There's a mistake in the bill.
Det är ett fel på räkningen. — de air et fel paw reyk·ning·en

TIME & DATES

What time is it?
Hur mycket är klockan? — hur mew·ke air klo·kan

It's (two) o'clock.
Klockan är (två). — klo·kan air (tvaw)

Half past (one).
Halv (två). (lit: half two) — halv (tvaw)

At what time ...?
Hur dags ...? — hur daks ...

At (10) o'clock.
Klockan (tio). — klo·kan (tee·oh)

in the morning	förmiddagen	feur·mi·daa·gen
in the afternoon	eftermiddagen	ef·ter·mi·daa·gen
yesterday	igår	ee·gawr
tomorrow	imorgon	ee·mor·ron

Monday	måndag	mawn·daa
Tuesday	tisdag	tees·taa
Wednesday	onsdag	ohns·daa
Thursday	torsdag	torsh·daa
Friday	fredag	frey·daa
Saturday	lördag	leur·daa
Sunday	söndag	seun·daa

January	januari	ya·nu·aa·ree
February	februari	fe·bru·aa·ree
March	mars	mars
April	april	a·preel
May	maj	mai
June	juni	yoo·nee
July	juli	yoo·lee
August	augusti	aw·gus·tee
September	september	sep·tem·ber
October	oktober	ok·toh·ber
November	november	noh·vem·ber
December	december	dey·sem·ber

TRANSPORT

Public Transport

Is this the ... to (Stockholm)?	Är den här ... till (Stockholm)?	air den hair ... til (stok·holm)
boat	båten	baw·ten
bus	bussen	bu·sen

Is this the ... to (Stockholm)?	Är det här ... till (Stockholm)?	air de hair ... til (stok·holm)
plane	planet	plaa·net
train	tåget	taw·get

What time's the ... bus?	När går ...?	nair gawr ...
first	första bussen	feursh·ta bu·sen
last	sista bussen	sis·ta bu·sen
next	nästa buss	nes·ta bus

One ... ticket (to Stockholm), please.	Jag skulle vilja ha en ... (till Stockholm).	yaa sku·le vil·ya haa eyn ... (til stok·holm)
one-way	enkelbiljett	en·kel·bil·yet
return	returbiljett	re·toor·bil·yet

At what time does it arrive/leave?
Hur dags anländer/ avgår den? hoor daks an·len·der/ aav·gawr deyn

How long will it be delayed?
Hur mycket är det försenat? hoor mew·ket air dey feur·shey·nat

What's the next station/stop?
Vilken är nästa station/hållplats? vil·ken air nes·ta sta·fhohn/hawl·plats

Does it stop at (Lund)?
Stannar den på (Lund)? sta·nar deyn paw (lund)

Please tell me when we get to (Linköping).
Kan du säga till när vi kommer till (Linköping)? kan doo say·ya til nair vee ko·mer til (lin·sheu·ping)

Please take me to (this address).
Kan du köra mig till (denna address)? kan doo sheu·ra mey til (dey·na a·dres)

Please stop here.
Kan du stanna här? kan doo sta·na hair

Driving & Cycling

I'd like to hire a ...	Jag vill hyra en ...	yaa vil hew·ra eyn ...
bicycle	cykel	sew·kel
car	bil	beel
motorbike	motor-cykel	moh·tor·sew·kel

air	luft	luft
oil	olja	ol·ya
park (car)	parkera	par·key·ra
petrol/gas	bensin	ben·seen
service station	bensin-station	ben·seen·sta·fhohn
tyres	däck	dek

Is this the road to (Göteborg)?
Går den här vägen till (Göteborg)? gawr den hair vey·gen til (yeu·te·bory)

I need a mechanic.
Jag behöver en mekaniker. yaa be·heu·ver eyn me·kaa·ni·ker

I've run out of petrol/gas.
Jag har ingen bensin kvar. yaa har ing·en ben·seen kvar

I have a flat tyre.
Jag har fått punktering. yaa har fawt punk·tey·ring

GLOSSARY

Note that the letters **å**, **ä** and **ö** fall at the end of the Swedish alphabet, and the letters **v** and **w** are often used interchangeably (you will see the small town of Vaxholm also referred to as Waxholm, and an inn can be known as a *värdshus* or *wärdshus*). In directories like telephone books they usually fall under one category (eg *wa* is listed before *vu*).

(m) indicates masculine gender, (f) feminine gender and (pl) plural

aktie bolaget (AB) – company

allemansrätt – literally 'every person's right'; a tradition allowing universal access to private property (with some restrictions), public land and wilderness areas

apotek – pharmacy

ateljé – gallery, studio

avgift – payment, fee (seen on parking signs)

bad – swimming pool, bathing place or bathroom

bakfickan – literally 'back pocket'; a low-profile eatery usually associated with a gourmet restaurant

bankautomat – cash machine, ATM

bastu – sauna

bensin – petrol, gas

berg – mountain

bibliotek – library

biljet – ticket

biljetautomat – ticket machines (eg for street parking)

biluthyrning – car hire

bio, biograf – cinema

björn – bear

brännvin – aquavit

bro – bridge

bruk – factory, mill, works

bryggeri – brewery

butik – shop

centrum – town centre

cykel – bicycle

dag – day

dal – valley

domkyrka – cathedral

drottning – queen

duodji – Sami handicraft

dygnet runt – around the clock

dygnskort – a daily transport pass, valid for 24 hours

ej – not

ej motorfordon – no motor vehicles

expedition – office

fabrik – factory

fest – party, festival

fika – coffee and cake

fiskkort – local permits

fjäll – mountain

fjällstation – mountain lodge

fjällstugor – mountain huts

flod – large river

flyg – aeroplane

flygbuss – airport bus

flygplats – airport

folkhemmet – welfare state

friluft – open-air

fyr – lighthouse

fäbod – summer livestock farm

fågel – bird

färja – ferry

fästning – fort, fortress

förbund – union, association

förening – organisation, association

förlag – company

galleri, galleria – shopping mall

gamla staden, gamla stan – 'old town', the historical part of a city or town

gammal, gamla – old

gatan – street (often abbreviated to 'g')

gatukontoret – municipal parking spaces

gatukök – literally 'street kitchen'; kiosk, stall or grill selling fast food

glögg – mulled wine

gott och enkelt – good and simple

gruva – mine

gräns – border

gákti – traditional Sami clothing

gåhties – cottages

gård – yard, farm, estate

gästhamn – guest harbour, where visiting yachts can berth

hamn – harbour

hembygdsgård – open-air museum, usually old farmhouse buildings

hemslöjd – handicraft

hjörtron – cloudberry

hotell – hotel

hus – house

husmanskost – homely Swedish fare; what you would expect cooked at home when you were a (Swedish) child

hyrbilar – car hire

hällristningar – rock carvings

i – in

idrottsplats – sports venue, stadium

joik – see *yoik*

järnvägsstation – train station

kaj – quay

kanot – canoe

karta – map

Kartförlaget – State Mapping Agency (sales division)

kloster – monastery

kombibiljett – combined ticket

konditori – baker and confectioner (often with an attached cafe)

konst – art

kontor – office

kort – card

krog – pub, restaurant (or both)
krona (kronor) – the Swedish currency unit
kulle – hill
kulturkvarter – culture quarter
kung – king
kust – coast
kyrka – church
kyrkogård – graveyard
kyrkstad – church town
kåta – Sami hut
källare – cellar, vault
kök – kitchen

landskap – province, landscape
lastmoped – motorised bike
lavin – avalanche
lavvu – tent
lilla – lesser, little
linbana – chairlift
län – county
länskort – county pass
länsmuseum – regional museum
länstrafiken – public transport network of a *län*
länståg – regional train

magasin – store (usually a department store), warehouse
magasinet – depot
Midsommardag – Midsummer's Day; first Saturday after 21 June (the main celebrations take place on Midsummer's Eve)
museet – museum
mynt – coins

natt – night
nattklubb – nightclub
naturreservat – nature reserve
naturum – visitor centre at national park or nature reserve
Naturvårdsverket – Swedish Environmental Protection Agency (National Parks Authority)

nedre – lower
norr – north
norrsken – northern lights (aurora borealis)
nyheter – news

och – and

palats – palace
pendeltåg – commuter train
pensionat – pension, guesthouse
P-hus – multistorey car park
polis – police
punsch – strong alcoholic punch
på – on, in

raukar – limestone formations
RFSL – Riksförbundet för Sexuellt Likaberättigande (national gay organisation)
riksdag – parliament
rum – room
rådhus – town hall
rälsbuss – railcar

SAS – Scandinavian Airlines Systems
Schlager – Catchy, camp, highly melodic pop tunes that are big on sentimentality, and commonly featured at the Eurovision Song Contest
siida – Sami village units or communities
sjukhus – hospital
sjö – lake, sea
skog – forest
skål – cheers
skärgård – archipelago
slöjd – handicraft
slott – castle, manor house
smörgås – sandwich
smörgåsbord – Swedish buffet
STF – Svenska Turistföreningen (Swedish Touring Association)
stolen – chair
stor, stora – big or large

stortorget – main square
strand – beach
stuga (stugor/na) – cabin (cabins)
stugby – chalet park; small village of cabins
surströmming – fermented herring
svensk – Swedish
Sverige – Sweden
SVIF – Sveriges Vandrarhem i Förening; hostelling association
Systembolaget – state-owned liquor store
söder – south

teater – theatre
telefonkort – telephone card
torg, torget – town square
torn – tower
trädgård – garden open to the public
tull – customs
tunnelbana, T-bana – underground railway, metro
turistbyrå – tourist office

vandrarhem – hostel
vecka – week
vik – bay, inlet
väg – road
värdshus – inn, restaurant
väst – west (abbreviated to 'v')
västra – western

wärdshus – inn

yoik – a type of traditional Sami singing (also referred to as *joik*)

älv – river

ö – island
öst – east (abbreviated to 'ö')
östra – eastern
övre – upper

behind the scenes

SEND US YOUR FEEDBACK

We love to hear from travellers – your comments keep us on our toes and help make our books better. Our well-travelled team reads every word on what you loved or loathed about this book. Although we cannot reply individually to postal submissions, we always guarantee that your feedback goes straight to the appropriate authors, in time for the next edition. Each person who sends us information is thanked in the next edition – the most useful submissions are rewarded with a selection of digital PDF chapters.

Visit **lonelyplanet.com/contact** to submit your updates and suggestions or to ask for help. Our award-winning website also features inspirational travel stories, news and discussions.

Note: We may edit, reproduce and incorporate your comments in Lonely Planet products such as guidebooks, websites and digital products, so let us know if you don't want your comments reproduced or your name acknowledged. For a copy of our privacy policy visit lonelyplanet.com/privacy.

OUR READERS

Many thanks to the travellers who used the last edition and wrote to us with helpful hints, useful advice and interesting anecdotes:

Beata Andorka, Patrik Aqvist, Kevin Campbell, Marco Di Pauli, Alessandra Furlan, Mikhail Grozovski, Ellen IJspeert, Kirk Johnson, Marie Lambert, Sophia Lambert, Jonathan May, Jeff Moritz, Hugo Nilsson, Bas and Annemarie Oosterkamp, Vic Sofras, Anders Thorsell, Jan Willem van Hofwegen, Guy Voets, Frank Wiesemann

AUTHOR THANKS

Becky Ohlsen

Thanks to my co-authors for all their help and hard work on the book; Mom for the excellent company and fresh perspective; Anno Superstar for the impromptu breakfast chat; Travis Gardner for the sweet mobile office; and friends Mike Russell, Jennifer Spratly, Margo DeBeir, Matthew Stearns, Mats Sjöberg and Gunnel Nordlund.

Anna Kaminski

Many thanks to my fellow authors, Becky and Kari, and our esteemed editors, Maryanne,

Glenn and Katie. I'm particularly grateful to Fredrik and Louise for the pre-trip advice; to Katja (Nutti Sami Siida), Tom and Lotta (Båtsuoj Sami Camp) and Lennart (Visit Sápmi) for the inspiration; and to Erik, Amelie and the Stormtrooper (Gävle), Ali, Hendrik and Marcus (Luleå), Johann (Kiruna), Akshey (Kungsleden), Katja (Östersund) and Papa Fahr Out (Stockholm) for the hospitality, advice and companionship on the road.

K Lundgren

Thanks to Ursula Elvegard, Mats Nordstrom, Ragnar Oloffson, Annika Axelsson, Jannike Ahlund, Nina Peri, Brian Murphy, Reidun Lundgren and Stig the Hållö ferryman.

ACKNOWLEDGMENTS

Climate map data adapted from Peel MC, Finlayson BL & McMahon TA (2007) 'Updated World Map of the Köppen-Geiger Climate Classification', *Hydrology and Earth System Sciences*, 11, 163344.

Cover photograph: Red timber house on Tjörn on the west coast of Sweden; DJS/Imagebroker. Many of the images in this guide are available for licensing from Lonely Planet Images: www.lonelyplanetimages.com.

This Book

This 5th edition of Lonely Planet's Sweden guidebook was researched and written by Becky Ohlsen, K Lundgren and Anna Kaminski. Stuart Harrison wrote the Design & Architecture chapter, and the History chapter was compiled with the assistance of Nicolas Kinloch. The previous edition was written by Becky Ohlsen and Cristian Bonetto.

This guidebook was commissioned in Lonely Planet's London office, and produced by the following:

Commissioning Editors Katie O'Connell, Glenn van der Knijff

Coordinating Editors Victoria Harrison, Asha Ioculari

Coordinating Cartographer Valeska Canas

Coordinating Layout Designer Sandra Helou

Managing Editors Barbara Delissen, Martine Power, Kirsten Rawlings

Managing Cartographer Alison Lyall

Managing Layout Designer Chris Girdler

Senior Editor Susan Paterson

Assisting Editors Holly Alexander, Emma Gilmour, Kim Hutchins, Karyn Noble, Charlotte Orr, Ross Taylor

Assisting Cartographers Jane Chapman, Mark Griffiths

Cover Research Jessica Boland

Internal Image Research Sabrina Dalbesio, Naomi Parker, Rebecca Skinner

Language Content Branislava Vladisavljevic

Thanks to Ryan Evans, Yvonne Kirk, Gerard Walker, Kathleen Munnelly, Maryanne Netto, Trent Paton

index

how to use this book

These symbols will help you find the listings you want:

- ◉ Sights
- 🐾 Beaches
- 🏃 Activities
- 🍃 Courses
- 👉 Tours
- 🎌 Festivals & Events
- 🛏 Sleeping
- ✖ Eating
- 🍷 Drinking
- ☆ Entertainment
- 🔒 Shopping
- ℹ Information/ Transport

Look out for these icons:

- **TOP** CHOICE — Our author's recommendation
- **FREE** — No payment required
- 🖉 — A green or sustainable option

Our authors have nominated these places as demonstrating a strong commitment to sustainability – for example by supporting local communities and producers, operating in an environmentally friendly way, or supporting conservation projects.

These symbols give you the vital information for each listing:

- ☏ Telephone Numbers
- ☺ Opening Hours
- Ⓟ Parking
- ⊝ Nonsmoking
- ✳ Air-Conditioning
- @ Internet Access
- ☎ Wi-Fi Access
- ☒ Swimming Pool
- ✒ Vegetarian Selection
- ⊕ English-Language Menu
- ♦ Family-Friendly
- ☃ Pet-Friendly
- ▣ Bus
- ⊞ Ferry
- Ⓜ Metro
- Ⓢ Subway
- ⑤ London Tube
- ▣ Tram
- ▣ Train

Reviews are organised by author preference.

Map Legend

Sights
- 🐾 Beach
- ⚭ Buddhist
- 🏰 Castle
- ✝ Christian
- ☬ Hindu
- ☪ Islamic
- ✡ Jewish
- ❶ Monument
- 🏛 Museum/Gallery
- ⊗ Ruin
- ⊛ Winery/Vineyard
- 🐾 Zoo
- ◉ Other Sight

Activities, Courses & Tours
- ⊝ Diving/Snorkelling
- ⊛ Canoeing/Kayaking
- ⊙ Skiing
- ⊛ Surfing
- ⊛ Swimming/Pool
- ⊛ Walking
- ⊛ Windsurfing
- ⊛ Other Activity/ Course/Tour

Sleeping
- ⊟ Sleeping
- ⊝ Camping

Eating
- ⊗ Eating

Drinking
- ⊙ Drinking
- ⊝ Cafe

Entertainment
- ⊛ Entertainment

Shopping
- ⊛ Shopping

Information
- ⊠ Post Office
- ⓘ Tourist Information

Transport
- ⊛ Airport
- ⊗ Border Crossing
- ⊛ Bus
- ⊷ Cable Car/ Funicular
- ⊛ Cycling
- ⊝ Ferry
- Ⓜ Metro
- ⊛ Monorail
- Ⓟ Parking
- Ⓢ S-Bahn
- ⊛ Taxi
- ⊕ Train/Railway
- ⊛ Tram
- ⊝ Tube Station
- ⓤ U-Bahn
- • Other Transport

Routes
- Tollway
- Freeway
- Primary
- Secondary
- Tertiary
- Lane
- Unsealed Road
- Plaza/Mall
- Steps
- ⌇⌇ Tunnel
- Pedestrian Overpass
- Walking Tour
- Walking Tour Detour
- Path

Boundaries
- International
- State/Province
- Disputed
- Regional/Suburb
- Marine Park
- Cliff
- Wall

Population
- ✪ Capital (National)
- ◉ Capital (State/Province)
- ● City/Large Town
- ● Town/Village

Geographic
- ⌂ Hut/Shelter
- ⊙ Lighthouse
- ⊙ Lookout
- ▲ Mountain/Volcano
- ⊙ Oasis
- ⊙ Park
-)(Pass
- ⊙ Picnic Area
- ⊙ Waterfall

Hydrography
- River/Creek
- Intermittent River
- Swamp/Mangrove
- Reef
- Canal
- Water
- Dry/Salt/ Intermittent Lake
- Glacier

Areas
- Beach/Desert
- + + + Cemetery (Christian)
- × × × Cemetery (Other)
- Park/Forest
- Sportsground
- Sight (Building)
- Top Sight (Building)

OUR STORY

A beat-up old car, a few dollars in the pocket and a sense of adventure. In 1972 that's all Tony and Maureen Wheeler needed for the trip of a lifetime – across Europe and Asia overland to Australia. It took several months, and at the end – broke but inspired – they sat at their kitchen table writing and stapling together their first travel guide, *Across Asia on the Cheap*. Within a week they'd sold 1500 copies. Lonely Planet was born.

Today, Lonely Planet has offices in Melbourne, London and Oakland, with more than 600 staff and writers. We share Tony's belief that 'a great guidebook should do three things: inform, educate and amuse'.

OUR WRITERS

Becky Ohlsen

Coordinating Author; Stockholm & Around; Uppsala & Central Sweden Becky visits Sweden about twice a year for work and family. Her mother grew up in Uppsala, and holiday trips to her grandmother in Stockholm are an annual tradition. Becky loves spending time in Stockholm, especially during the winter holidays, but her favourite parts of the country are out in the middle of nowhere, be it around Ales Stenar in the south or lost in the bleak expanses of Jämtland up north. Becky has written about Scandinavia for Lonely Planet since 2004. She has also covered the Pacific Northwest, and parts of midwestern USA and Great Britain.

Read more about Becky at:
lonelyplanet.com/members/BeckyOhlsen

Anna Kaminski

Östersund & the Bothnian Coast; Lappland & the Far North Anna has been dreaming of Scandinavia ever since she read Norse myths and legends as an impressionable five-year-old. A fan of the extreme north (and south), she has roamed the wilds of Siberia, Norway, Patagonia and Tierra del Fuego before venturing north of Stockholm. Anna feels lucky to write about northern Sweden, which has seen her barrelling down a deserted road under the midnight sun in a landscape reminiscent of her native Russia, dodging reindeer, and sampling delights such as reindeer, cloudberries and fermented herring!

K Lundgren

Göteborg & the Southwest; Malmö & the South; the Southeast & Gotland Born in Norway, K's great-great-grandfather sailed to the US on the *Wisconsin* in 1888 from southern Sweden, lending a personal twist to her research. K will always have a soft spot for the cardamom buns and copper kettles of Flickorna Lundgren on the Kulla Peninsula, as well as the area around Kalmar, and thinks that visiting a lighthouse is a must – chilly dips in the sea, birdwatching, sharing shrimp, bread and wine with complete strangers – the essence of a Swedish summer.

Contributing Author

Stuart Harrison is an architect and communicator. He is director of award-winning practice Harrison and White and teaches in design and architectural history. He broadcasts on radio stations 3RRR and ABC Australia, and has authored two books on innovative housing, including *Forty-Six Square Metres of Land Doesn't Normally Become a House*.

Published by Lonely Planet Publications Pty Ltd
ABN 36 005 607 983
5th edition – May 2012
ISBN 978 1 74179 726 8
© Lonely Planet 2012   Photographs © as indicated 2012
10 9 8 7 6 5 4 3 2
Printed in China

Although the authors and Lonely Planet have taken all reasonable care in preparing this book, we make no warranty about the accuracy or completeness of its content and, to the maximum extent permitted, disclaim all liability arising from its use.